THE STRATEGY
PATHFINDER

2ND EDITION

Further praise for *The Strategy Pathfinder*

"Do we really need another book on strategy? Well *The Strategy Pathfinder* is one with an attitude! Its effective use of an impressively broad range of micro-cases that cover the main concepts of business strategy gives students a succinct and very practical approach to the subject."

Peter Hagström, Stockholm School of Economics

"The unique micro-cases in this book will surely spark energetic discussion in the classroom. The diversity of international companies and strategic issues in the cases provides an unusually broad set of examples from which to draw."

Constance E. Helfat, Dartmouth College

"*The Strategy Pathfinder* represents a refreshing and engaging method for teaching strategy. The processes and cases, which define the book, provide excellent learning materials that bring a real-life experience to students."

Stuart Sanderson, Bradford University

"The concise presentation and critical reflection on strategy concepts and tools; the use of live cases; and the inclusion of rarely covered yet highly relevant topics, such as the role of power in strategic decision-making and the challenge of managing change, make *The Strategy Pathfinder* a welcome alternative to conventional strategy textbooks."

Stefan Manning, University of Massachusetts

THE STRATEGY
PATHFINDER

2ND EDITION

CORE CONCEPTS AND LIVE CASES

DUNCAN ANGWIN · STEPHEN CUMMINGS · CHRIS SMITH

WILEY

John Wiley & Sons, Inc.

This edition first published 2011
© 2011 Duncan Angwin, Stephen Cummings, Chris Smith

Registered office
John Wiley & Sons Ltd, The Atrium, Southern Gate, Chichester, West Sussex, PO19 8SQ,
United Kingdom

For details of our global editorial offices, for customer services and for information about
how to apply for permission to reuse the copyright material in this book please see our
website at www.wiley.com.
The right of the author to be identified as the author of this work has been asserted in
accordance with the Copyright, Designs and Patents Act 1988.

Reprinted May 2011

Wiley also publishes its books in a variety of electronic formats. Some content that appears
in print may not be available in electronic books.

Designations used by companies to distinguish their products are often claimed as
trademarks. All brand names and product names used in this book are trade names,
service marks, trademarks or registered trademarks of their respective owners. The
publisher is not associated with any product or vendor mentioned in this book. This
publication is designed to provide accurate and authoritative information in regard to the
subject matter covered. It is sold on the understanding that the publisher is not engaged
in rendering professional services. If professional advice or other expert assistance is
required, the services of a competent professional should be sought.

Library of Congress Cataloging-in-Publication Data

Angwin, Duncan, author.
The Strategy Pathfinder : Core Concepts and Live Cases / Duncan Angwin, Stephen
Cummings, Chris Smith. —2
p.   cm
Includes bibliographical references and index.
ISBN 978-0-470-68946-2 (pbk.)
1. Strategic planning.   2. Stragegic planning—Case studies.   I. Cummings, Stephen David,
1967-, author.   II. Smith, Chris, author.   III. Title.
HD30.28.A5315   2011
658.4'012—dc22
2010045351

A catalogue record for this book is available from the British Library.

ISBN 978-0-470-68946-2 (paperback), ISBN 978-1-119-99017-8 (ebk),
ISBN 978-1-119-99588-3 (ebk), ISBN 978-1-119-99589-0 (ebk)

.5pt Book Antique by MPS Limited, a Macmillan Company, Chennai, India
ted in Great Britain by TJ International Ltd, Padstow, Cornwall, UK

Contents

The Strategy Pathfinder Map

The Strategy Pathfinder is arranged into 11 chapters or pathways, preceded by a short introduction (or "instruction manual"). Each pathway focuses on a set of core concepts followed by seven "live cases" that readers can use to test their ability to use those concepts. A dashed line around a live case's title square indicates that it focuses on a not-for-profit (NFP) organization. Each pathway/chapter contains at least one NFP case, thereby creating an NFP track through *The Strategy Pathfinder* for those who wish to focus on this path. In addition, readers may choose to focus on a particular geographic area by consulting The Strategy Pathfinder World Map on page xi.

▶▶▶ **Introduction: Pathways to Strategy**

Strategy matters → What is strategy? → Why *The Strategy Pathfinder* is a different kind of strategy textbook → How *The Strategy Pathfinder* works

PART I: THE STRATEGIC ENVIRONMENT

1. Macro-Shocks

Open systems thinking → bounded rationality → Icarus paradox → scanning/monitoring/forecasting/assessing → scenario thinking → PEST/ESTEMPLE analysis → impact matrix → SWOT/TOWS analysis → strategic agility

| Steinway | French Army | Flora Holland | Nike | Rover | South Africa | China Airways |

2. Movers and Shakers

Corporate governance → chain of ownership → principles/agents → role of the CEO and directors → stakeholder analysis → using management consultants → government influences → power/interest matrix → lobbying

| Disney | Safeway | Carlton TV | Lafarge | Brasilia | NHS | MGMT |

3. Industry Dynamics

Margins → perfect and imperfect competition → industry life cycle → critical success factors → industry structure → the five forces of industry → the value net → complementors and cooperation

| Sportsware | Carrefour | McDonalds | DELL | Ranbaxy | BMX | RA Maroc I |

PART II: THE STRATEGIC ORGANIZATION

4. Corporate Strategy

The M-form organization → corporate strategy → forms of diversification → portfolio management → growth-share (or BCG) matrix → parenting advantage → sharing activities → transferring skills → centralization versus decentralization

| Z | GE | Golden Promise | easyGroup | Telco | Tata | RA Maroc II |

5. Strategic Positioning

Competitive advantage → positioning → cost advantage → differentiation advantage → focus advantage → generic strategy matrix → strategy clock → advantage categories → game theory → the value chain → strategic groups → resource-based view → CASIS and VIRO analysis

| Tesco | Tele2 Russia | Mother's Preference | Taytos | IBB | World Cities | InBev |

6. Corporate Identity

National culture and context → the Porter diamond → organization culture → McKinsey's 7-S framework → the cultural web → corporate identity, image and personality → authenticity → vision, mission and values

| Pokemon | Pharmacia | Mojo/MDA | John Smith's | Hyundai | NZ Police | BBC & C5 |

7. Organic Strategy

The relational organization → social systems → knowledge societies and learning organizations → signature stories → communities of practice → social capital → networks → resources and dynamic capabilities → emergence, process and practice → the balanced scorecard

F1 | The Band | WaMu | Prudential | Deutsche Bank | AAS | Dalai Lama

PART III: STRATEGIC ADVANCES

8. Crossing Borders

Internationalization and globalization → theories of absolute and comparative advantage → expansion strategies → M&A strategies → divestment and retrenchment → eclectic theory → country clusters → leveraging national advantage → international business structures

Kodak | Korean Air | Vodafone/ Mannesman | Coca-cola/ Toyota | Banque de Sud | Red Cross/ Crescent | HSBC

9. Guiding Change

Increasing pace of change → 8-steps of change → different levels of change → evolutionary versus revolutionary change → different change needs → styles of managing change → instigators of change → resistance to change → leadership and strategic change

Pringle | Reliant | Baraka | Churches | Oakland A's | elBulli | Little Chef

PART IV: STRATEGIC FUTURES

10. Sustain Ability

The firm and the wider environment → sustainable development and sustainability → environmental integrity → corporate economic prosperity → corporate social equity → the triple bottom line → reputation → business ethics → greenwashing versus the good corporate citizen

McDonalds | Monsanto | Marcos | Handi Ghandi | Il Ngwesi | Air New Zealand | Royal Mail

11. Maverick Strategies

Beyond "best practice" → Blue Ocean strategy → S-curves → worst, good, promising and next practices → diversity → urgency → entrepreneurial + financial flair → design thinking → stratography → 6 degrees of strategic innovation

| Apple/Ford | IRL | Synear | Venture Capital | Egg | Danone | CCCP |

Additional Material: Integrative cases, Chapter and Case Authors, Notes, Using Strategy Pathfinder for Assessments and Exams, References, Glossary, Index ►►►

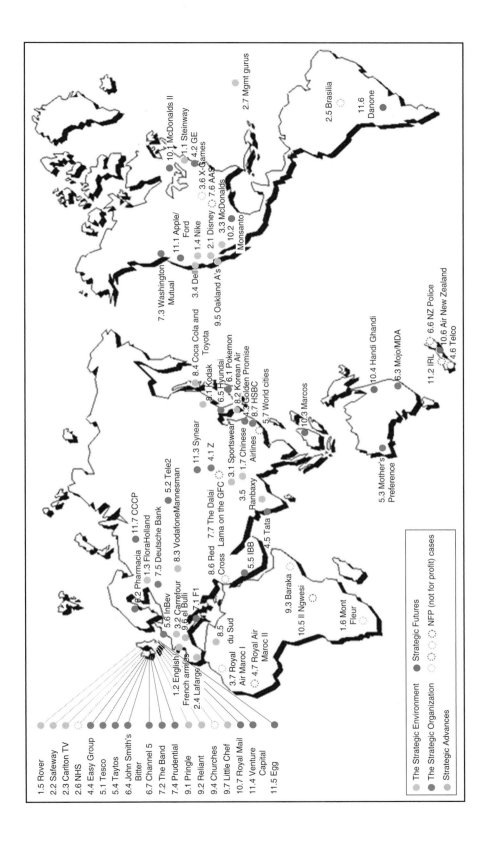

Pathways to Strategy

Strategy Matters. . .

Strategy matters in business:

Steve Jobs's brilliant **strategy** *[for the Apple iPod business] was to marry the hardware device with the web service with the desktop. And that kind of* **strategy** *is very difficult to copy (which makes it even more* **strategic***).*

"A Gallant attempt at making IT interesting. . ."

Silicon Valley Watcher, Tom Foremski, August 18, 2005

Strategy makes a difference in politics (and anyone involved in business knows that politics matters in business too). Good strategy helped Barrack Obama to become President of the United States. Here's one journalist's distillation of Obama's keys to his strategic and political success in the 2008 campaign:

1. **Define your character.** *When you create a consistent character that embodies your deepest principles people perceive you as "whole" and trustworthy. We align with leaders who are aligned with themselves. According to Joel Benenson, the primary pollster for the Obama campaign, Obama's image was more clearly defined than McCain's. . . As a result people perceived Obama as a truth teller...*

2. **Create a strong, positive and consistent message.** *Barack Obama had one elegant philosophical approach that was simple to assimilate and understand. "Voters are looking for the remedy not the replica." His strategy was to position his opponent, John McCain, as the replica and himself the remedy. . . Distilling your message into one clear sentence has deep resonance.*

3. **Communicate casually via video.** *David Plouffe, one of Barack Obama's campaign managers, created home-made-looking online videos discussing strategies to keep supporters and organizers excited, engaged, and involved. . . These videos are similar to the ones friends might send to each other to stay connected on Facebook, YouTube or MySpace.*

"Barack Obama's Campaign **Strategy**"

Examiner.com, Susan Harrow, December 2, 2008

Strategy also matters in the media and in public relations (which also plays a big role in business and politics these days):

It has long been the norm for Project Runway to film collections by the last three designers standing plus one decoy to avoid the seemingly inevitable leaks and spoilers -- a challenge more daunting than ever now that everyone in the Fashion Week audience has some kind of instant communications device in hand throughout. But those of us who were invited. . . to attend last week's fashion show hit the jackpot, unexpectedly treated to a record ten collections on the runway – that would be collections by the final three (whoever they may be), the traditional decoy finalist and six additional possible contenders, all of them still in play on the show. . . Adding so many extra collections was a brilliant **strategy***, seeing as it is seemingly impossible for the media to keep secrets in the new digital world. . .*

"Inside the Season Finale of Lifetime's Project Runway"

HuffingtonPost.com, Ed Martin, February 17, 2010

And strategy shapes results in football too (and many have compared the media, politics, and business to a game).

I've looked at the Dutch **strategy** *– it is invariably a strong middle field with a consistent 4-5-1* **strategy***. Spain regularly plays 4-4-2, more aggressive than the Dutch style. Spain is incredibly good on defense and on making things happen on the attack, just enough to take home a win. Holland also has an incredibly strong defense – does it have the brilliance of 2010 Spain on the attack? Ah, this will be a thinking person's World Cup Final, that's for sure!*

Tribe.net, Timborg, July 7, 2010

It is easy to recognize that strategy plays an important role in success and failure in human endeavor, but it can be more difficult to define what strategy actually is.

What is Strategy?

Strategy has been defined by many different cultures and people. Alfred Chandler, writing in 1962, outlined what many regard as the "classical" definition: "*. . .the determination of the long-run goals and objectives of an enterprise, and the adoption of courses of action and the allocation of resources necessary for carrying out these goals.*"

However, while this definition coincided with what most regard as the beginning of the subject we call strategic management, other cultures had developed similar definitions related to military practice. The word *strategy* was developed to name a new military and political leadership position developed in the city of Athens in the 6th century BC, as a combination of the words *stratos*, which meant "army" (or more correctly an army spread out over the ground), and *agein*, meaning "to lead." In another continent at about the same time the military philosopher Sun Tzu defined strategy as "*. . . the great work of the organization. In situations of life or death, it is the Tao of survival or extinction.*"

In the 1980s writers built upon these traditions refining our views of what strategy was about. The Japanese–American scholar Kenichi Ohmae described strategy as "*. . . the plan enabling a company to gain, as efficiently as possible, a sustainable edge* *over its competitors."* While the world's most highly regarded management guru, Peter Drucker, suggested that a strategy was *". . . a firm's **theory** about how to gain competitive advantages"* over its competition.

By the end of the 1980s, new types of strategy scholar, more schooled in human and organizational behavior than warfare or industrial economics, were challenging the idea that strategy was about great ideas, long-term plans, and rational theories. They believed that instead of focusing on what strategy *is* it would be more realistic and useful to examine *how* strategy develops. And they believed that strategy happened as collections of small activities, some rational some not, that created trajectories followed by organizations. Henry Mintzberg thus claimed that strategy was *". . . a pattern of behavior that emerges over time,"* and then embarked on a series of debates with Igor Ansoff about whether strategy was about rational design from the top of an organization (Ansoff) or patterns that emerged from the bottom (Mintzberg). In keeping with Mintzberg's view, proponents of the increasingly influential "resource-based view of the firm," such as Jay Barney (see Chapter 5), defined strategy as *". . . a pattern of resource allocation that enables firms to maintain or improve their performance."*

By focusing on the patterns and processes that led to strategy, rather than the content of what a strategy is, writers like Mintzberg and Barney discovered that rather than one unifying definition, there were in fact many schools of thought about where strategy came from. In a book called *Strategy Safari*, Mintzberg and his co-authors outlined 13 different strategy schools. No one perspective should be seen as superior, argued Mintzberg; they are just different views of the same object, and the view taken by an organization should depend on the nature of that organization: for some larger, more established, organizations strategy would probably come from design and planning; for smaller or more dynamic organizations, culture or the values of an entrepreneurial founder would be a more important shaper of strategy.

Henry Mintzberg's Strategy Process Schools

The **Design School** – strategy is the result of senior managers using conscious rational analysis to design a fit between organizational strengths and weaknesses and environmental opportunities and threats.

The **Planning School** – reflects the design school view, but strategy here is decomposable into distinct steps and supporting frameworks like the Value Chain or the 5 Forces of Industry.

The **Positioning School** – views strategy as selection from generic options or frameworks (e.g., the Generic Strategy Matrix) based on the formalized analysis of the specific industry and market situation.

The **Environmental School** – focuses on the environment's influence in steering firms toward strategic options. Senior managers are seen here to have far less agency and control over strategic decisions.

The **Cognitive School** – concerned with understanding the mental processes or psychology of the strategist that lead to particular strategic decisions.

The **Learning School** – views the strategy development process as emerging incrementally over time through trial, error, and learning from environmental shifts and questioning present assumptions.

The **Cultural School** – concentrates on the influence of pre-existing organizational and/or regional culture and common belief systems in promoting particular strategic choices.

The **Consensus School** – similar to the cultural school, but here consensus about a strategy emerges from the mutual adjustment of key stakeholders as they learn from each other over time.

The **Power School** – strategizing is influenced by politics and focuses on bargaining, persuasion, and confrontation between various interested parties and the power dynamics that exist between a firm and its strategic partners and other networks.

The **Entrepreneurial School** – represents a move away from precise designs or plans, toward looser notions such as "visions" and "perspectives," typically articulated by the CEO or Senior Management.

The **Process School** – the strategic role of senior managers as defining and controlling the processes by which strategy is developed are key determinates of strategies.

The **Configuration School** – organizations are coherent but time-varying clusters of resources, characteristics, and behaviours. Strategy involves defining a desired end state (configuration) and mapping a series of steps to get there. "Configuration" draws upon many of the other strategy schools.

Source: adapted from Mintzberg et al. 1998.

We were confronted with this plurality of definitions of strategy when compiling a book called *Images of Strategy*. There we took the view when seeking to introduce the subject that while we could not in any certainty say absolutely what a good strategy *was* or even where it should come from, we could, based on our experience, say what a good strategy *did*.

Borrowing liberally from a paper entitled "Substitutes for Strategy" by Karl Weick, we posited that a good strategy, be it a big plan or a pattern made up of lots of smaller activities, or the result of a brilliant entrepreneur, or designed by a committee, would both *orient* and *animate* an organization. It would, in other words, give focus, direction, and purpose to an organization (orientation), and encourage and move people to seek to achieve expectations for an organization or surpass and recreate these expectations (animation).

Weick had himself borrowed liberally from others in outlining what a strategy should do as opposed to what it is. In particular, he related the story we paraphrase below to indicate that focus and movement were strategically more important than an accurate master plan or a particular type of corporate culture.

A lieutenant of a detachment in the Alps sent a reconnaissance unit into the wilderness. It began to snow, and unexpectedly continued to snow for two days. The unit did not return. The lieutenant feared that he had dispatched the unit to death. But, on the third day they came back. How had they made their way? "Yes," they said: We thought ourselves doomed. We had no maps or other equipment with which to ascertain our position or a route out. But then one of us found a tattered map in a seldom used pocket. That calmed us down. The map did not seem to quite fit the terrain but eventually we found our bearings and after a few wrong turns eventually found our way. The lieutenant looked at the map. "This isn't a map of the Alps," he said. "It's a map of the Pyrenees."

In the above example, one organizing image or pathway helped to orient and animate a group, moving participants from dormant to strategic. In *Images of Strategy* we presented the view that being strategic or "strategized" is what happens when an organization is oriented and animated, and that a strategy could be achieved through many different images (depending on what it was that most helped to orient and animate an organization). If an organization has little of either, it has a long way to go strategically. If an organization is all orientation (lots of meetings and weighty analysis and detailed plans) but its people are uninspired, then it is underperforming strategically – as is an organization high on animation but without a collective sense of direction.

With the benefit of hindsight, however, we would add another definitional element of what a good strategy should do, and it is an assumption that underlies and thus unifies all of the definitions we have described here. Strategy is about orientation, and animation, and *integration*.

Even if a firm is in more than one business or has more than one brand or type of product (as most businesses do) it will be being strategic if these activities are effectively coordinated – i.e., if its integrated whole is greater than the sum of its parts. Whether such integration comes as a result of a plan or a particular culture or an entrepreneurial vision, or whether it comes from a pattern of activities over time or a rational decision from the top, does not matter. It is the outcome of these activities – in the form of greater integration – that makes such activities strategic.

More than encompassing myriad definitions of strategy, this view is in keeping with the very reasons why firms emerge. As authors like Coase and Williamson have been reminding us for nearly one hundred years, firms emerge because their integrative (i.e. strategic) efforts outperform a free market.

Figure 1 demonstrates our view of what becoming strategic is about. If an organization starts from a position of low orientation, animation, and integration, it will become more strategic as it follows pathways that help it to orient and animate its people, which should at the same time encourage greater integration of understanding and effort. Becoming more strategic, in this manner, is what this book, *The Strategy Pathfinder*, is about. Its purpose is to help you to help the organizations you work with (or may work with in the future) to achieve greater orientation, animation, and integration of effort.

As such, we have divided the essential threads and themes in the strategic literature (along with some of the very latest new thinking) into 11

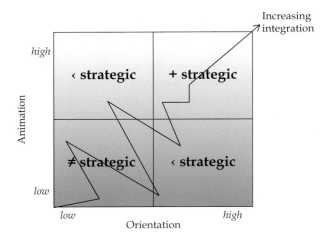

Figure 1 Being strategic is about becoming oriented, animated, and integrated

different pathways that can help organizations to become more strategic in this way. We have arranged these 11 pathways graphically in Figure 2 to aid your understanding of how the various parts of *The Strategy Pathfinder* fit together in this endeavor.

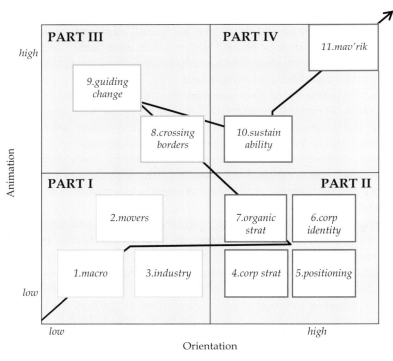

Figure 2 Eleven orienting, animating and integrating pathways toward becoming more strategic

In Part I, The Strategic Environment, we examine what we believe to be the foundations upon which any strategic understanding can be based. In Macro-Shocks we show how big and seemingly small shifts in the macro-environment can have substantial effect upon an organization's future. These shocks, or anticipation of them, will begin to orient and animate an organization's strategy. In Movers and Shakers we look at how particular players operating within the industrial and wider environments may have the power to shape, enable or disrupt a strategy and how such movers may best be worked with. And in Industry Dynamics we explore how the industry environment in which an organization operates creates a particular type of "playing field" which should be understood in order to make the most of strategic opportunities.

Having laid this foundation, Part II, The Strategic Organization, describes four pathways that can aid the development of a greater sense of orientation. The first, Corporate Strategy, looks at strategies for ensuring that a firm provides greater strategic value than the sum of it parts. Then, Strategic Positioning discusses approaches for effectively targeting a firm's products or services at the market. Whereas the first two chapters of Part II draw on what we might see as the more conventional or classical definitions of strategy as a rational, top-down, design process, the next two are focused more on developing a greater sense of strategic orientation through understanding how strategy can also emerge from human behavior patterns over time. Corporate Identity investigates the latest thinking with regard to how "softer" or more "human" aspects such as values, character, culture, and vision can shape an organization's strategic direction. In Organic Strategy we cover the newer schools of thought, which look at the practice of strategy as comprising a wide range of micro-activities which can accumulate into particular orientations over time, where an organization is seen as being similar to a social organization.

Having developed a clearer sense of orientation, Part III, Strategic Advantage, changes tack to look at how this orientation can spur animation to change and develop, to build upon this greater sense of direction. Crossing Borders considers how firms may expand (or contract) through acquisition, diversification, alliances, internationalization, or retrenchment. Guiding Change explores how strategic change involves the combination of revolutionary and evolutionary approaches to transformation.

The final part of *The Strategy Pathfinder,* Strategic Futures, considers two possibilities for the strategized (or oriented, animated, and integrated) organization: first, how might a strategy or strategic advantage be sustained while being mindful of the organizations relationship with the wider environment; second, how might innovation lead to the opening up of new strategic possibilities and environments. In Sustain Ability we focus upon two things that are often seen as separate: sustainable competitive advantage and the sustainability of resources, and notice how these things may increasingly be seen as integrated. In Maverick Strategies we explore the latest research and thinking with regard to creativity and innovative strategy development.

Why *The Strategy Pathfinder* is a Different Kind of Strategy Textbook

Strategy texts are often rather dry and sterile products that seem to view the reader as a consumer: "read this, then replicate it." We think that business today is too complex, too varied, and too interesting for this approach to work well. We wrote *The Strategy Pathfinder* to put strategy making into the hands of the reader, to make you (the student, the manager) a "producer" of orientation, animation, and integration, and to subsequently breathe life back into strategy. Hence, *The Strategy Pathfinder* represents a different way to learn about strategy. It is founded on six learning principles, based on our 60 years of experience working with executives, MBAs, and undergraduates across five continents.

1. Symbols, colours and space can provide a structure that aids learning

We've written elsewhere about the importance of graphical representations in communicating strategy (See Angwin, et al 2011). And, wherever possible we've attempted to use colour coding, graphical symbols, and space as memory aids for, and ways of involving the reader in, the concepts explored in this book. Consequently, we use:

- Different colour shades and tabs (light silver, dark silver, light gold and dark gold) to mark out the different parts and pathways so that they are clearly differentiated and easy to find.
- Colour-coded iPad-type forms as labels for the chapters and cases.

- Geographical symbols to depict what part of the world the companies in each live case or the issue they are facing originates from.

- And, if the organization is Not for Profit, and part of *The Strategy Pathfinder* NFP track, it is identified by dashed lines in the contents pages and by the letters NFP in the iPad screens at the head of the cases.

- Other textbooks list "key learnings," which is a good idea. But because learnings are more likely to be remembered if you generate and write them, *The Strategy Pathfinder* provides empty note tabs at the end of each chapter where you can write your "key learnings" from the chapter and perhaps draw lines between these where you see links. Subsequently, at the end of each chapter you will be able to generate your own "mind-map" to help you to revise the key aspects of each part of this book (we get you started with one pre-prepared elements at the end of Chapter 1, page 15) And, wherever possible we provide 'note-paper' at the end of the cases. Moreover, in our experience, writing notes and drawing on a book is an excellent way of learning it, so please don't limit your drawing to the tabs and note pages.

2. There are no different editions of this book for different geographical locations

Many strategy textbooks produce local editions where examples and cases that originate from that area are inserted in an attempt to make the material more relevant. However, today's strategists are just as likely to work for, or with, companies from another country as they are to work with companies from their own homeland. Furthermore, as national barriers diminish, all business has become international – your competitors/suppliers/customers could come from anywhere. Therefore, strategists need to be comfortable with problems from all parts of the globe and dealing with local concerns, globally. Hence our cases are from every corner of the world (see the case location map on page xi).

3. Less means more

Unlike conventional strategy texts *The Strategy Pathfinder* isn't a pile of theories and concepts 1400 pages long. By synthesizing and presenting essential pathways through the complexities of the strategy jungle, *The Pathfinder's* contents can comfortably all be covered in a course, or in a weekend, enabling you to build momentum and stay enthused. Our Pathfinder Compasses at the end of each chapter, and our extensive references and bibliography at the end of the book, will provide you with a number of routes should you wish to delve deeper down a particular strategy path.

4. Strategy cases should strike you like strategy problems in real-life, not like academic exercises

The Strategy Pathfinder isn't weighed down by enormous cases that throw in every detail but are difficult to relate to. It is built around "live cases" on real-life strategy issues faced by real organizations. In our experience, such cases are much more effective ways of animating discussion. They are both more engaging and more like the strategy situations that people encounter in reality than the traditional Harvard-style strategy cases. They are more real because, like life, they hit you with a problem, and then *you* have to form a case – using your wits to gather more information, forming opinions, and testing these against the opinions of others – before deciding upon recommendations about how best to proceed. Conventional cases tend to hand students the case on a plate: suggesting that all they need is contained in the same 20 pages of charts, tables, and text that are placed fully-formed before them and their peers. This is also why live cases are more engaging. They force you to think about past experiences, do more research, surf the Internet, and form your own opinions. In other words, they encourage you to take ownership. They make you a producer of strategic ideas and insights, rather than a consumer. Also, because *The Strategy Pathfinder's* live cases are brief, you can be interacting with them and debating them with others in a matter of minutes.

At the end of the first live case in every chapter (apart from the last one on Maverick Strategies, where the emphasis is completely on thinking originally) we provide you with some ideas as to how you might have gone about answering the questions posed. But after that, the answers are up to you to think through yourself, and debate your views, and the views of others, with colleagues, class-mates, or peers.

5. Strategy teaching should draw on the latest available technology

This open approach that sees students as producers of knowledge, as well as consumers of traditional frameworks and theories, encourages the use of the latest technology in the classroom or when reading the book at home. Because *The Strategy Pathfinder*'s cases do not contain the "whole story" (and because, we believe, the whole story in strategy is open to interpretation in any event), they require further "real-time" research and debate. Searching on the compa-nies or the issues that arise in the live cases using tools like Google, YouTube and Wikipedia, in combination with more conventional forms of library research and readings, can provide the basis for lively and organic debates about what you would do if you were advising the managers or other stakeholders in the cases.

Some strategy texts attempt to keep up with technology by providing more information: in extra compact discs or password-protected websites. But, in a world where the degree of information available on an organization or an issue cannot be contained, and where students and practitioners may be just as adept at searching for new information as a professor or strategy expert, this would seem to us to exacerbate a problem rather than solve it. What puts *The Strategy Pathfinder* at the cutting edge of technology, and why we use the term "live cases," is that they are "open-source" and ongoing. Readers are empowered to use the lat-est technology to uncover the latest information on which to base their arguments.

6. Strategic issues don't cease when the case study writer finishes writing the case

When using a management textbook to teach a class, a question that often crops up is "should we answer the questions as if we were at the point when the case ends, or how things are today?" We believe that the former approach is unreal-istic and confusing (how do we know what managers in a company might have known on the date the case was written?), and given the approach we have out-lined above, we believe it is unnecessary when using *The Strategy Pathfinder*. All of our cases should be viewed as living documents and hence can be done in real time. If you find in your investigations that one of the companies in a particular live case has failed or been acquired by another company, this is not a problem: such is life. Changes in circumstance are a further interesting development, and a strategic reality, that should inform your strategic analysis. You should ask: Why did the company fail? Why was it acquired? You should not try to imagine that you don't know these things.

How *The Strategy Pathfinder* Works

To illustrate how you can use this book, let's take a live case and look at how you might develop your knowledge of strategy through applying yourself to the issues that it raises. The case is about a fast-food operation called Cereality that is seeking to grow through franchising. We've taken it from an earlier edition of *The Strategy Pathfinder* where it appeared in the Strategic Positioning chapter. The question is: "will its strategic business model allow it to succeed?" The case is presented below.

Cereality

The idea, explains David Roth, co-founder of Cereality Cereal Bar and Café, "is to become the Starbucks of cereal." Cereality simply provides bowls of common branded cereals such as Cheerios, Lucky Charms, and Quaker Oats to which customers can add toppings and milk, but some commentators believe that Roth and co-founder Rick Bacher may actually be on to something.

The pair began testing a prototype store at the end of 2003 at Arizona State University (the store took just two months to turn a profit as students flocked to it), and by the end of 2004 new outlets had been opened in Philadelphia and Chicago with 15 more stores planned to open in 2005. Thinking further ahead, Roth and Bacher are currently also negotiating for space at train stations, arenas, airports, and hotels.

The founders claim they created Cereality "to celebrate the very personal nature of enjoying a good bowl of cereal, anywhere and at any time. It's a life-long staple, and yet nobody had ever figured out a way to make it work in fast food." At Cereality customers can get a 32-oz. bowl of branded cereal, or combine brands as they wish, and select from toppings like fruit, nuts, and candy and different kinds of milk for about $3. Or they can choose ready-made mixes selected by Cereality staff (called "Cereologists"). Cereality also does Smoothies made with cereal (Slurrealities™); and goods baked with cereals (Cereality Bars™ and Cereality Bites™). Bacher seems to be serious when he boasts that: "Cereality is so unique, it has a patent pending."

Customers are greeted by waiting staff wearing pyjamas in surroundings that are comfortably homely. "I wanted to create a totally cool experience where all of those (cereal) rituals and habits can be celebrated out of the home," explains Roth. In so doing, Cereality is hoping to cash in on the comfort and nostalgia that people attach to breakfast cereal. *USA Today* wrote that this: "latest fast-food concept is so absurdly simple, self-indulgent, and reflective on one's inner child that; well, how can it fail?"

Cereal makers, who have been trying to find an outlet for their products beyond the breakfast table for decades and have been battling the current trend toward "low-carbs" that has contributed to an 8% decline in cereal sales in the five years to 2004, have been keen to get behind Roth and Bacher's venture. Quaker has invested an undisclosed amount in Cereality, and General Mills and Kellogg have offered business advice. In return, the big cereal companies not only get another distribution channel, but valuable information as well. Cereality kiosks gather interesting data on who's buying what and what combinations of cereals and toppings are popular. The pilot store has already yielded some surprises, such as a strong yearning among collegians for *Cinnamon Toast Crunch*, and that Quaker's old-fashioned *Life* brand is the number one seller.

Roth claims to have been inspired by the cereal-loving characters on the TV show *Seinfeld:* the show which boldly claimed to be "about nothing" but was greatly loved and tremendously successful. There are some that might say that serving bowls of cereal commonly available in any supermarket is similarly a "nothing" strategy. But could Cereality become as successful as its role models *Starbucks* and *Seinfeld*?

Having read the case, it is clear that while it provides some clues as to how one might answer the question: "will its strategic business model allow it to succeed?"; more research would help. Given that this case relates to the Strategic Positioning chapter, one might look at the core concepts in that chapter and think through Cereality's strategy using a framework like the value chain (shown on page 144) and ask how its business model enables the reduction of costs while maintaining relatively high prices. This might reveal that the combination of taking the preparation of hot food out of the fast-food equation, while using branded cereals in a novel and experiential environment creates a large margin between cost and price, and what seems like a competitive advantage.

Further investigation on the internet might raise some doubts about whether this advantage is sustainable. A simple search on Cereality would reveal a YouTube clip from a television program called *The Big Idea* where host Donny Deutsch proclaims Cereality's simple approach as one of the cleverest strategies ever. . .

But there is also an article from *Time* magazine that points out that the company will find it difficult to protect itself from imitators, or indeed its big name suppliers and potential competitors like Starbucks, should their model become a success.

This might lead the reader to delve deeper, into Chapter 5, and use a framework like CASIS for thinking about whether a competitive advantage is sustainable. This framework suggests that a strategy should be Congruent with things that are seen as critical success factors in an industry; is not Appropriable by competitors or suppliers; cannot be easily Substituted for by customers, is Inimitable; and its development can be Supported by the organization.

While Cereality's strategy of reducing the cost of providing fast food is absolutely congruent with critical success factors in the fast-food industry, Cereality's "big idea" can easily be appropriated or imitated by competitors, new start-ups or suppliers looking to forward integrate, or substituted by customers (they could easily eat the same cereals at home). And, without a large number of franchisees queuing up to open Cereality stores, a

☑ Congruent
☒ Not Appropriable
☒ Not Substitutable
☒ Inimitable
☒ Supportable Organizationally

need to grow quickly and establish a well-known brand (as Starbucks did) cannot be supported organizationally.

And if the reader was doing this case after reading Chapters 1 through 5, their development of the Cereality live-case might be added to by thinking back through the strategy pathways covered in earlier chapters. For example:

- The macro-shocks issue of an organization trying to sell non-essentials at a high price in a recession (Chapter 1);
- the fact that the key movers & shakers, like Quaker, General Mills, and Starbucks, could squeeze Cereality if they wished to (Chapter 2);
- that protecting a strategy from new entrants or forward integrating suppliers is a key to sustaining high margins in an industry (Chapter 3).

This is but one approach to one live-case, but it illustrates the learning possibilities when the reader is seen as more than just a consumer of historical conventions, as is often the case with other strategy texts. Strategy should not be a static subject. It is dynamic and contestable. Many more strategy concepts and live cases from around the world follow in *The Strategy Pathfinder*'s 11 chapters, waiting to be read, explored, debated, and updated.

About the Authors

Duncan Angwin is Professor of Strategy at Oxford Brookes University, UK. His expertise is in Mergers and Acquisitions and Strategic Practice. He sits on the Advisory Board of the M&A research centre, Cass Business School, is senior judge for the Management Consultancy Association's awards and Chair of the Practice of Strategy awards panel, Strategic Management Society conference.

Stephen Cummings is Professor of Strategy at Victoria Management School, Victoria University of Wellington, New Zealand. His other books include *Recreating Strategy, Images of Strategy and Creative Strategy: Reconnecting Business and Innovation.*

Chris Smith is a Senior Lecturer in Strategy at the University of Adelaide Business School in South Australia. A former senior executive in Australian and UK companies he now writes and teaches about strategy as enacted in various contexts.

WE WOULD LIKE TO THANK OUR COURSE PARTICIPANTS AT THE FOLLOWING UNIVERSITIES WHO HAVE HELPED TO DEVELOP, CRITIQUE AND TEST THE LIVE-CASES AND PATHWAYS IN THIS BOOK:

UNIVERSITY OF WARWICK, UK
VICTORIA UNIVERSITY OF WELLINGTON, NEW ZEALAND
ADELAIDE UNIVERSITY, AUSTRALIA
SAID SCHOOL OF BUSINESS, OXFORD UNIVERSITY, UK
UNIVERSITY OF GEORGETOWN, USA
VLERICK BUSINESS SCHOOL, BELGIUM
ECOLE NATIONALE PONTS DE CHAUSSEES, PARIS, FRANCE
ECOLE HASSANIA, CASABLANCA, MOROCCO
CHINESE UNIVERSITY OF HONG KONG, CHINA
MELBOURNE BUSINESS SCHOOL, AUSTRALIA
HEC, PARIS FRANCE
OXFORD BROOKES UNIVERSITY, UK
DANUBE UNIVERSITY KREMS, AUSTRIA

Part I The Strategic Environment

Does the flap of a butterfly's wings in Brazil set
off a tornado in Texas?

Edward Lorenz and Philip Merilees

If it be now, 'tis not to come; if it be not to come,
it will be now; if it be not now, yet it will come: the
readiness is all.

William Shakespeare's Hamlet

1
Macro-Shocks

Who would have thought an unknown volcano on an island in the middle of the North Atlantic Ocean, with an unpronounceable name (Eyjafjallajökull), would have caused such trouble to so many people and businesses around the world? Like hundreds of thousands of other hapless travelers, two of the authors of this book were stranded in France and Singapore respectively, as airports closed and airlines hastily cancelled flights in response to air regulators deeming the airspace over northern Europe to be unsafe for flying. Apparently traveling through a volcanic dust plume results in the production of glass shards inside a jet engine – not recommended for man or machine. The immediate effect of grounding fleets of aircraft was chaos on the ground as passengers struggled to find alternative methods of transport. Some, such as the well-known comedian John Cleese, went to great lengths and considerable expense to overcome the obstacle – he was reported to have spent $5,000 on obtaining a taxi from Oslo, Norway, to Belgium to catch a Eurostar train traveling through the channel tunnel to reach his home in London. Thousands of other travelers were less lucky as Eurostar's capacity to absorb the surge in demand was exhausted quickly. Less reported, but equally important, were thousands of supply chains of goods, from foodstuffs to industrial components, which ground to a halt, causing huge disruption to business and consumers. The estimated cost to European Carriers was estimated by the International Air Transport Association at $200 m. Although the volcanic and atmospheric conditions have since changed, it was the action of the airlines, such as British Airways (which estimates losses from the incident at around $80 m), which pushed regulators to reopen the airspace, as they argued vociferously that existing regulations were far too tight. Within a few days, flights were largely back to normal although it is worth noting that volcanologists on Iceland are deeply concerned that a much larger volcano next to Eyjafjallajökull may have been triggered into erupting very soon.

One reason for the intensity of the shock and the unpreparedness of so many businesses was that this specific event, a volcanic eruption with widespread effects in northern Europe, seemed so unlikely. Icelandic volcanoes do not have a history of disrupting continental air traffic. Other events in the world were absorbing top management attention. Shocks projected on the basis of past experience, such as flu epidemics, and terrorism, have been occupying the minds of strategists as they think through possible future scenarios and contingency plans. Nevertheless, the Eyjafjallajökull event was major, catastrophic, and unanticipated with shock waves resounding around the world, impacting on people, businesses, organizations, and governments across multiple geographic regions, with differing intensities at different times.

Volcanic eruption is one extreme example of what is called a **macro-shock**: a major event in the broad context within which business is embedded, and over which business can exert little, if any, control. While sudden unexpected major contextual changes grab attention as they excite major reactions from a wide range of stakeholders (witness the media frenzy surrounding the BP oil leak in the Gulf of Mexico in 2010), macro-contextual change may also be more gradual in nature. For instance, the growing problems posed by climate change, aging populations and declining fossil fuel reserves are major challenges forcing businesses to adjust or perish.

Consequently, the primary pathway toward better strategy development may be the realization that organizations and their strategies do not operate in a vacuum. They are **open systems** that take resources and information *from* the environment and transform them into products and services that are fed back *into* the environment. This open systems perspective emphasizes the interconnectedness of the firm and multiple levels of the environment. For instance, Canada's top mutual funds, Chile's copper mines, and Europe's steel companies are all outperforming expectations because of events on the other side of the world, namely the recent surge in China's economy. Some of these key forces in the business environment are illustrated in Figure 1.1.

Organizations are subject to a wide range of shocks from such forces. Institutional pressures from regulators, stock markets, governments (explored in Chapter 2, Movers and Shakers) can directly affect how industries and businesses operate; industry-level shocks and the actions of competitors, suppliers, customers (discussed in Chapter 3, Industry Dynamics and Chapter 5, Strategic Positioning), together with shocks internal to the business (see Chapter 9, Guiding Change), can all have major consequences for an organization. However this chapter focuses on the broad macro-environment beyond these levels, where firms have little direct influence. From this **deterministic** perspective, organizations are constantly buffeted on the seas of change, and the key is to anticipate and to adjust to these macro-pressures in order to survive.

Beyond Bounded Thinking: Anticipating the Consequences of Macro-Pressures

The volcanic eruption disaster had a differential impact on organizations and industries. For some the effect was direct and specific. The airline industry suffered immediate close down, loss of revenue, and reputational damage. The impact also had a direct effect on other industries, such as the demand for short-break holidays which experienced a significant slump because of fears over the

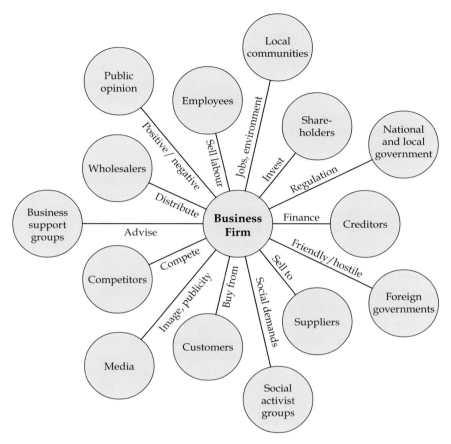

Figure 1.1 Some of the many interactions between businesses and their environment (Source: Davis and Frederick, 1984)

safety of flying. For other industries the effect was indirect, emphasizing the connectedness point made earlier. Support industries, such as catering and insurance, were hit and businesses depending upon airfreight for high-value low-weight items were seriously disrupted. For instance, manufacturing companies operating on a just-in-time basis were struggling as critical components could not be obtained. Macro-shocks may also have a delayed impact. Pressures for change in the way airline companies operate in hazardous air conditions is causing many businesses to re-evaluate the need for face-to-face business meetings – investing in virtual meeting room technology instead. In some instances the duration of the effect(s) can be short lived; airlines such as Air France were quickly back to operating at full capacity, while for other businesses the effects still linger – the insurance industry is still dealing with claims, and effects on air quality and micro climatic changes may yet have health consequences.

Moreover, macro-shocks may not always be negative in their impact upon businesses. Innovation may be encouraged as alternative technologies suddenly have a window of opportunity (perhaps aircraft engine design may alter as a consequence), institutions may revisit prevailing rules and regulations in order to safeguard businesses and customers in the future and some businesses may benefit directly from the shock – ironically Icelandic tourism has experienced a boom, with visitors keen to see an exploding volcano.

Macro-shocks often reverberate for some time, triggering other after-shocks either in a literal sense (the neighboring volcano is still expected to erupt with far greater negative consequences) or metaphorically – the huge cost to airlines of this episode is resulting in different flying patterns and investments in alternative engine technologies. This seismic characterization of a macro-shock as an earthquake, sending a major disruptive pulse or pulses into the environment, lends itself to structural analysis of consequences. The pulses, or ripples, tend to follow a predictable entropic pattern, allowing their consequences for the environment, to be anticipated by a skillful strategist. On the other hand, where macro-shocks occur in a social system, such as 9/11, the decay effects may be different to an earthquake, and indeed may escalate, which would make the prediction of consequences altogether more complex.

In any event, macro-shocks do need to be interpreted with care as they can be ignored or distorted to serve 'blinkered' corporate purposes. Emerging shocks, such as the credit crunch of 2008/9, could have been anticipated and used as an opportunity to carry out deep restructuring changes far earlier than was actually necessary. In this instance, business should not be viewed as an entirely passive recipient of change. Less bounded thinking and more forthright anticipation of environmental concerns could have lessened the effect of this Global Financial Crisis.

It is fairly safe to say that most businesses did not anticipate or plan for Eyjafjallajökull's eruption, even though there is evidence that Icelandic geologists were aware that something of this sort might occur. Why should it be so difficult for businesses to predict an event like this, which may harm their business? Businesses may be limited in the way in which they perceive the world and potential threats. This cognitive limitation, or **boundedness,** may mean that they just do not perceive potential threats as they focus too narrowly on their activities. In addition, as our opening quotation about butterflies and tornados suggests, major events may have their origins in rather obscure and minor happenings. The Icelandic volcano is far away from major flight paths and so is obscure in those terms – and geological time is notoriously hard to reconcile with social conceptions of time. However, in conjunction with unusual meteorological conditions, the effect of the eruption was magnified substantially to disrupt global air traffic.

Edward Lorenz, in trying to predict weather patterns at MIT during the 1960s, is widely credited with recognizing that very small differences in initial conditions are rapidly amplified by evolution into complex patterns. By rounding the numbers in his calculations, from six to three places, widely divergent trajectories arose rapidly in his predictions from reality. Such observed complexity has led to the term "chaos" being applied, implying that prediction of the future is impossible. Ian Stewart in his book *Does God Play Dice?*[1] takes a more optimistic view, observing that chaos and order, rather than being polar opposites, are in fact intertwined so that irregular behavior is governed by a deterministic system. Such systems are not truly random and so, for small parts of the complexity, some order can be determined.

Fortunately not all macro-shocks fall into the category of being very difficult to predict. For instance, it is widely known that world oil resources are depleting rapidly and will cease to be a major energy source later in this century. This will be a huge shock to the way businesses operate and will require fundamental shifts in organization's strategy. However, businesses are aware of this coming change and Honda and Toyota are already committing vast resources to R&D to produce alternative ways to power cars, such as the use of hydrogen cells, dual fuel engines, lithium-ion batteries. The interconnectedness of these firms, as shown in Figure 1.1, could result in major changes throughout the entire value chain, from supplier relationships to customer perceptions of what makes a good car. In this instance, some firms are clearly anticipating a macro-shock and are adjusting to compensate for a new reality.

Detecting Movements in the Macro Environment

Some automobile manufacturers do not appear to be taking any substantial measures in anticipation of an impending oil crisis. This may in part be explained by individual firms' propensity for perceiving macro-shocks. As we shall see later in the book, firms can be so bounded in their perceptions, often when they are at the peak of their success, that they fail to perceive, or through arrogance choose to ignore, changes and trends that do not fit their conception of how the world will be. Danny Miller has likened this situation to the Icarus Paradox, where the Greek boy, learning how to fly successfully with wings of feathers and wax made by his doting father, flew too close to the sun with disastrous consequences. Firms that have successful strategies but which fail to adjust to a changing macro-context can suffer terrible damage and may even be doomed. One remembers IBM, once the most creditworthy institution on the planet, being brought to its knees by a major *technological* change – the rise of the desktop PC – which destroyed a large proportion of the mainframe business. In the UK, Marks & Spencer was the greatest retailer in the nation's history and yet failed to perceive, or at least to acknowledge, changing *social* tastes and fashions in the high street. Profits crashed, its share price plummeted, swathes of senior executives "left," and the firm was subjected to a takeover bid.

Other firms have invested significant resources in attempting to understand how the macro-environment may change. Royal Dutch/Shell is famous for its development of scenario planning techniques, and benefited from being able to anticipate the effects of the 1973 oil crisis by selling off its excess oil supplies before the worldwide glut in 1981. This raises the question: How should firms view the macro-environment?

> The environment is not a very mysterious concept. It means the surroundings of an organization; the climate in which the organization functions. The concept becomes challenging when we try to move from simple description of the environment to analysis of its properties.[2]

Ginter and Duncan's article, quoted above, provides a good example of R.J. Reynolds' activities in detecting the implications of the US Surgeon General's report on the harmful effects of smoking. Firms should engage continually in four activities, the first letters of which form the acronym SMFA:

1. **Scanning** for warning signs, macro-changes, and trends that will affect the firm.
2. **Monitoring** for specific trends and patterns.
3. **Forecasting** to develop projections of anticipated outcomes of those trends.
4. **Assessing** to determine timing and effects of macro-changes on the firm.

Analyzing Macro-Environmental Drivers

Which areas of the macro-environment should be scanned, monitored, forecasted, and assessed? For the purposes of strategic analysis, and under what might be termed the outside-in analytical framework, the complexity of interaction of an organization with its external environment may be decomposed into macro-influences, meso-influences (firms, consumers, suppliers influencing the industry), and micro-influences (firms competing in the same industry as the focal firm). **Competitive strategy** embraces the micro and meso levels and is the bridge between the company and the environment in which it operates. The degree of influence of a large focal company is greatest at the center of Figure 1.2 – where decisions are made about the firm's strategies, resource

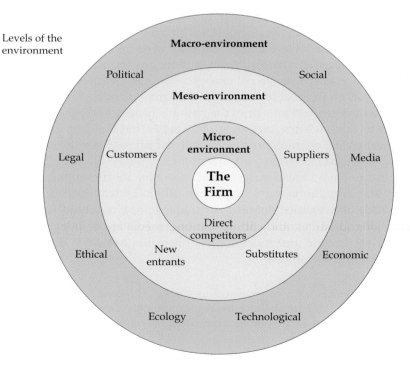

Figure 1.2 Conceptual decomposition of the business and its environment to structure strategic analysis

policies, and **configuration** – and then declines outward across successive boundaries. (The strength of this influence, or bargaining power, will vary by firm, as discussed in Chapter 5, Strategic Positioning.)

Adopting this outside-in approach is useful to avoid myopia, or seeing the world in the firm's own image. A common conceptual tool for embracing the macro-environment is the **PEST analysis**, which stands for Political, Economic, Social, and Technological issues. The value of the technique is in identifying drivers for change in the broad context that could affect the firm's industry and the firm itself. PEST is a *process* technique as it makes explicit how forces in the macro-environment will change over time, rather than offering a snap-shot view – a criticism often directed at many other strategy frameworks. PEST's other advantage is as a handy acronym that helps strategists to avoid *partial* coverage of a large macro-territory. Indeed it has been remarked that the worst failing of a strategist is not to see the whole picture, or the "elephant issue!" There can be a natural tendency for analysis to be skewed toward economic and financial issues, perhaps because they are more tractable (data may be more readily available and there are convenient tools and techniques available for their analysis) and there are significant institutional pressures to engage in this legitimating language. PEST and its derivatives (outlined below) offer an important protection against this bias. Good sources of data for its components can be found on the websites of the Economist Intelligence Unit (www.eiu.com), the World Bank (www.worldbank.org), and Business Environment Risk Intelligence (www.beri.com).

Since PEST was developed, other important macro-categories have emerged to reflect today's more varied business environment. We have coined **ESTEMPLE**, which is illustrated in Figure 1.3, to incorporate these new categories.

ESTEMPLE adds ecological, ethical, legal and media factors to our appreciation of the macro-context, reflecting a groundswell in current concerns regarding: the sustainability of the ecological environment and the role of the firm in its management/consumption (see Chapter 10, Sustain Ability); the need to address different ethical standards across borders, triggered by stakeholder actions (such as government intervention and investor sell-offs), altering codes of practice, and influenced business decisions (see, respectively, Chapters 7, 8, and 10, Organic Strategy, Crossing Borders, and Sustain Ability); the growing body of research that shows that the media are an independent force in influencing and shaping social opinion. For instance, national media are important in generating national solidarity and shaping perceptions of threat[3] when, for example, foreign firms launch hostile takeover bids. Through dramatizing risk to the loss of national resources, jobs, identities, and culture, national media are defining the nation and mobilizing response.[4] The importance of the media is evident when markets are moved and corporate policies and actions influenced contrary to the dictates of rational economics.

Organizing for the Future

Clearly all these issues are present continuously in the macro-context, but the important question for the strategist is which ones will be relevant, how might these change over time, and which of these factors, or collection of factors, will

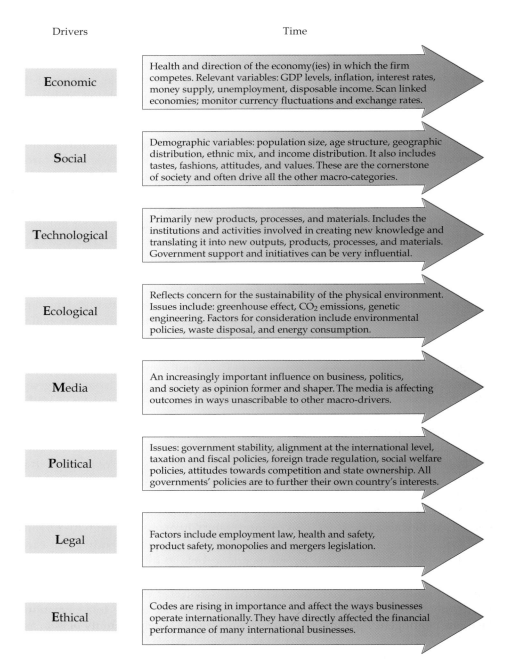

Drivers | Time

Economic — Health and direction of the economy(ies) in which the firm competes. Relevant variables: GDP levels, inflation, interest rates, money supply, unemployment, disposable income. Scan linked economies; monitor currency fluctuations and exchange rates.

Social — Demographic variables: population size, age structure, geographic distribution, ethnic mix, and income distribution. It also includes tastes, fashions, attitudes, and values. These are the cornerstone of society and often drive all the other macro-categories.

Technological — Primarily new products, processes, and materials. Includes the institutions and activities involved in creating new knowledge and translating it into new outputs, products, processes, and materials. Government support and initiatives can be very influential.

Ecological — Reflects concern for the sustainability of the physical environment. Issues include: greenhouse effect, CO_2 emissions, genetic engineering. Factors for consideration include environmental policies, waste disposal, and energy consumption.

Media — An increasingly important influence on business, politics, and society as opinion former and shaper. The media is affecting outcomes in ways unascribable to other macro-drivers.

Political — Issues: government stability, alignment at the international level, taxation and fiscal policies, foreign trade regulation, social welfare policies, attitudes towards competition and state ownership. All governments' policies are to further their own country's interests.

Legal — Factors include employment law, health and safety, product safety, monopolies and mergers legislation.

Ethical — Codes are rising in importance and affect the ways businesses operate internationally. They have directly affected the financial performance of many international businesses.

Figure 1.3 Conceptual decomposition of the macro-environment using ESTEMPLE

drive change in the business context? The extent to which the strategist can make sense of all this data will be influenced by the turbulence of the context. This will determine the extent to which future environmental configuration(s) can be predicted and hence the ability of firms to anticipate effectively.

As shown in Figure 1.4, the turbulence of the environment can be conceived in three dimensions[5] of:

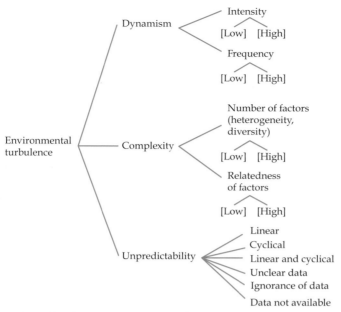

Figure 1.4 Dimensions of environmental turbulence (Source: Adapted from Volberda, 1998)

1. dynamism (intensity and frequency of change);
2. complexity (number, relatedness and diversity of factors);
3. unpredictability (cyclicality of change and clarity of data).

Clearly where an environment is highly dynamic, very complex, and unpredictable, attempting to anticipate and plan for specific macro-change is largely a waste of time and resources. In these situations of considerable ambiguity, firms have to explore their contexts, scan for weak signals, and indeed try to be active in creating the future. However, where sense can begin to be made of the environment, with patterns detected or several potential futures identified, firms can begin to anticipate and plan for the future. A technique for dealing with an alternate future, or a range of futures,[6] is **scenario thinking**. This is the construction of detailed plausible alternative views about the future based on groupings of key environmental drivers. Scenarios should *not be predictive* but consider plausible futures that allow managers to explore a set of possibilities and increase their perceptiveness of the key forces at work in the environment. This can be used to facilitate contingency planning and/or to work against the possibility of bounded thinking and the Icarus Paradox. For Royal Dutch/Shell, scenario development had two goals: (1) a protective goal to enable the firm to anticipate and understand the risks involved in doing its business, and (2) an entrepreneurial goal to discover new strategic options. In creating "macrocosms" Royal Dutch/Shell used scenarios as a fundamental aid to changing mental models of future opportunities and risk.[7]

If the environment is more predictable in nature, or clear enough, then forecasting through extrapolation can allow a more precisely configured view of the future and more tightly specified planning. Here we may use an **impact matrix** (see Figure 1.5) to quantify the probability of an external shock happening and

Environmental drivers	Impact	Probability	Potential Impact	
Economic • Favourable –5% increase in energy consumption • Oil demand increased 7% and expected to continue to rise	5	100%	5.0	Opportunity?
Social • Negative impact but small scale	–2	10%	–0.2	
Technological • Very important – anticipating correctly can be decisive	4	10%	0.4	
Ecological • Trends to reducing consumption of 'dirty products – have to adopt new technologies	–3	40%	–1.2	Threat?
Media • Increasingly important. Attacked socially, environmentally	–2	20%	–0.4	
Political • Stable domestic regime and domestic policies has positive impact – can invest • Unstable Middle East inflates oil prices – a benefit	4	50%	2.0	Watch closely
Legal • Gap between laws and implementation: impact is slight	–1	30%	–0.3	
Ethical • Corruption and lack of transparency intensifies competition	–2	30%	–0.6	Threat?

Figure 1.5 Impact matrix for Oil Refining Company
Key:
IMPACT assessed here between +5 and −5
Probability assessed here as likelihood of effect out of 100% over next 5 years
Note:
This is a summary matrix of previous matrices which examined sub drivers within each of the ESTEMPLE categories. Note that categories may have widely differing numbers of drivers, may vary in their importance relative to each other and in some instances there may be categories with no relevant factors in the time frame under review.

the extent to which it is likely to impact upon firm performance. Where environments are largely static, firms can plan for the future with confidence and rely on precedents to guide their decisions.[8]

In "Strategy under Uncertainty," published in *The Harvard Business Review* in 1997, Hugh Courtney, Jane Kirkland, and Patrick Viguerie show which strategy tools might be appropriate for different levels of environmental uncertainty (see Table 1.1).

Of course, the techniques and tools described are not ends in themselves. They are planning tools to improve the quality of executive decision-making. Some techniques, such as single-point forecasting, lend themselves easily to integration with central planning. However, managers are apt to be confused with the multi-point forecasting of scenarios, complaining that three or four forecasts are less helpful than one. This is to misunderstand the purpose of scenarios: full-blown strategies should not be developed for each scenario and then each tested against the other by some financial means such as Discounted Cash Flow (DCF) to see which scenario is the best (even if a management team were willing to do this). The temptation should also be resisted of assigning probabilities to scenarios as

Table 1.1 Appropriate strategy tools

	Clear enough future	Alternate futures	A range of futures	True ambiguity
What can be known	A single forecast precise enough for determining strategy	A few discrete outcomes that define the future	A range of possible outcomes but no natural scenarios	No basis to forecast the future
Analytic tools	Traditional strategy tool kit	Decision analysis; Option valuation models; Game theory; Scenario planning	Latent demand research; Technology forecasting; Scenario planning	Analogies and pattern recognition; Nonlinear dynamic models

Adapted from Courtney, Kirkland, and Viguerie (1997)

this is more the preserve of forecasting and would negate the exercise. The aim is to develop a strategy within the framework of alternative futures provided by the scenarios. The strategy can then be tested against the scenarios for its resilience and management can be forewarned of possible vulnerabilities.[9] Ian Wilson, in his article "From Scenario Thinking to Strategic Action" published in *Technological Forecasting and Social Change*, highlights how scenarios can be used to strengthen strategy formation and suggests four levels of sophistication from sensitivity/risk assessment for a specific strategic decision to the development of a strategy resilient to a wide range of business conditions. A fuller treatment of scenario development is contained in Van der Heijden's classic work, *Scenarios: The Art of Strategic Conversation*.

Strategic Agility: Flexing With the Environment

As the world becomes increasingly interconnected, the ability of organizations to be agile and steer a path between rigidity and flexibility becomes a strategic imperative. Rigidity is often promoted by the drive for efficiencies in complex operations in stable environments, whereas flexibility and the ability to respond 'willy-nilly' to change can be a difficult characteristic for small entrepreneurial firms to shake off. Real problems can occur where macro-forces demand change and yet the firm is structurally rigid and therefore resistant to alteration.[10] These structural rigidities impede change and may result in 'strategic drift', where the organization begins to fall badly out of alignment with the changing business context.[11]

The most heavily used technique to assess this matching of the firm to its environment, to avoid drift, is a **SWOT analysis**, in which a firm's *internal* strengths and weaknesses are explicitly matched against *external* opportunities and threats. In revealing mismatches between the firm and its environment, strategic options can be generated to enhance the **fit*ness*** of the firm.

It is critical to remember that SWOT is not just about generating lists of factors, as the analysis only has value if there is an explicit comparison, or fitting, of strengths against opportunities and threats and weaknesses against opportunities and threats. While many students and practitioners may well use SWOT as a starting place for their analysis, the technique has many weaknesses used in this way, not least the issue of how strengths and weaknesses are actually determined. For instance, what are the strengths identified relative to? In our experience, one way of avoiding long lists of strengths or weaknesses that don't relate to the external competitive environment is to reverse SWOT into a TOWS analysis, whereby environmental threats and opportunities are examined *before* summarizing organizational strengths and weaknesses. As you might expect in this chapter's deterministic view of strategy (and this is contrary to other viewpoints expressed in later chapters), here the outside-in perspective is encouraged. In any event, SWOT/TOWS is best used as the culmination of some other, more focused, analysis. So it may be useful to perform an ESTEMPLE analysis first and then plot out an impact matrix as a way of determining macro-environmental threats and opportunities. These can then be related to an organization's fitness through comparison with internal strengths and weaknesses. Furthermore, SWOT/TOWS analysis can summarize insights on different layers of the external environment in addition to macro-environmental concerns, and so can include influences from the meso-industry and competitive environment, which we shall cover in later chapters.

Underlying much of the discussion so far about the firm changing in response to its anticipation of macro-shocks, is the notion of fit, or fit*ness*, of strategy. Much of the writing on the strategy of the organization is the extent to which the firm "fits" with the context (cf. strategic gap analysis), or whether its "fit" will improve or deteriorate over time – a more dynamic view. This external consonance is important on the basis that misalignment will lead to firm underperformance. For organizational ecologists, firms cannot change easily because of structural rigidities and organizational routines (of which more later). Some large companies, however, can and do exhibit strategic agility. Nokia of Finland, for instance, started life as a timber company, moved into white goods manufacturing, and latterly has been hugely successful in mobile phones. However, such change is difficult, often requiring substantial alterations in **competencies**. Lou Gerstner is regarded as a brilliant strategist for having taught "the elephant" (a.k.a IBM) to dance after its near fatal "Icarus" fall. To some extent, the strategic issue for managers is whether the gradual change of a company – or "logical incrementalism"[12] – is fast enough to accommodate step changes in the environment or macro-shocks. And, "punctuated equilibrium" events like Eyjafjallajökull may always force radical and comprehensive change in the company or its demise.[13]

One of the most influential business books of the last decade is *Competing for the Future* by Gary Hamel and C.K. Prahalad. They argue that too many companies focus on competing in the present and do not devote enough time to creating the future. They argue that firms need to go beyond the static analysis of fitting their environment and instead should *stretch* and *leverage* their resources to redefine both the company and its context. For them, the key is not to anticipate the future but to create it. This suggests a philosophical shift from a more deterministic viewpoint, in which the macro-environment determines the success or failure of organizations, to an individualist, or *voluntarist* view where managers make a difference and can influence and shape the future context. For Gary Hamel: "The company that is evolving slowly is already on its way to extinction."[14] His solution is that revolution must be met with revolution. This discontinuous renewal perspective echoes Michael Hammer's "Reengineering Work: Don't Automate, Obliterate," which advocates that managers should take bold steps and dare to accept high risk. It is an all-or-nothing proposition with an uncertain result.

In contrast, Masaaki Imai's famous book, *Kaizen: The Key to Japan's Competitive Success*, argues that continuous improvement best explains the competitive strength of so many of Japan's companies. This view stresses the importance of evolution and continuous learning. For Imai, Western companies have an unhealthy obsession with one-shot solutions and revolutionary change. In our view, today's strategists must be agile enough to recognize the virtues of both extremes. They should assess the particular organizations they advise in their macro-contexts, and create hybrid approaches that attempt to anticipate, analyze, and influence the future, be aware and adaptive in the present to take advantage of opportunities as they emerge, and seek to be consistent in maintaining and building strengths that enable organizational fitness in a changing environment. While rare "Black Swan" events – the happening of the completely unexpected – will always occur, this concept, popularized by Nassim Taleb, does not mean that the future is therefore completely unknowable and always negative. Foresight and agile configurations allow organizations to adjust and adapt to the unexpected and exploit positive potentials – not all businesses have fared badly from Eyjafjallajökull – and the explicit consideration of macro-drivers and strategic positioning can really work to an organization's advantage. Like the flap of a butterfly's wings mentioned at the head of this chapter, we may never know what a particular macro-shock, from the largest eruption to smallest environmental ripple, might lead to: but for strategists 'the readiness is all'.

At the end of each chapter (before the live cases), we provide a collection of sticky note shapes for you to outline what you believe to be the key learnings from the chapter and the relationships between these. In this, the first chapter, we've got you started by providing some suggestions, but in the following chapters these note pages will be left blank for you to fill in."

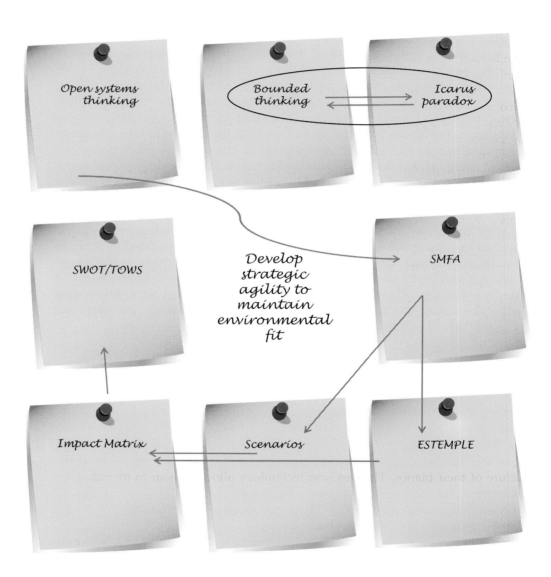

1-1 Broadwoods and Steinway:
Canoes versus Ironclads

In 1843, Broadwoods, England, was the greatest instrument manufacturer in the world. Admired for its association with the great composers, such as Ludwig van Beethoven, it had a highly skilled workforce and a reputation for producing the finest of pianos. But by 2000, Broadwoods was just a shell company, outsourcing all piano production to Asia and licensing piano tuners for instrument maintenance. What had gone wrong for this world-class firm?

In 1851 there was a census, which showed that Broadwoods was one of just 12 factories in London, employing over 300 people. These craftsmen fashioned and adjusted by hand all the 3,800 pieces that went into making a Broadwoods piano. The instrument consisted of a wooden frame strengthened by sophisticated wooden braces and some metal tension bars. This allowed the piano frame to take up to 16 tons of force from its strings, of which there was one per note. The firm produced around 2,500 pianos per year, which was 15% of England's total piano production. Broadwoods' own output was 2.5 times greater than its nearest rival.

1851 also saw the Great Exhibition being held at Crystal Palace, London, where manufacturers from all over the world displayed their finest wares and competitions were held to judge which were superior. England exhibited 66 pianos, France, with producers such as Pleyel, showed 45 pianos, and Germany displayed 26 pianos. The English efforts were rewarded with 12 medals, the French with nine and the Germans with eight. Unfortunately the records documenting the number of gold medals are missing but, in numeric terms, the English pianos appear dominant.

At this time, two German brothers, Steinway, were attempting to introduce radical ideas on piano manufacture into Germany. However, the highly conservative and restrictive German guild system made it impossible for them to operate. They therefore decided to leave for America where they discovered a more sympathetic context and two innovations that were to revolutionize piano manufacture. To plow up vast areas of newly discovered land for agricultural purposes, the Americans had become highly skilled in casting plowshares from iron. In addition, to remove the local Indian inhabitants, and to survive in the Wild West, it was necessary to develop a sophisticated handgun, the key feature of which, from the Steinways' perspective, was a highly reliable, accurate, and sensitive trigger mechanism. The Steinways adopted both of these innovations in the manufacture of their pianos. The cast iron technology allowed them to manufacture cast frames, and the handgun trigger arrangements allowed them to produce a highly sensitive and accurate key and hammer mechanism – a good example of a weapon being turned into an art product!

The advantage of the Steinways' "American system," as it became called, was that the cast iron frame could tolerate up to 30 tons of force from its strings. This allowed the use of much heavier strings, which could generate a far more powerful and richer tone as well as more compact pianos. This was particularly important for upright pianos, which, until this time, had really been grand pianos on their side. The new hammer mechanism gave greater sensitivity to the pianist and its precise vertical movement greatly reduced the clatter of key mechanisms associated with pianos of that era. Overall these innovations also allowed cost savings of some 30%.

The next big piano exhibition was again in London in 1862. Although the jury was accustomed to pre-Steinway sounds, two gold medals were awarded to Steinway pianos, one gold medal to a copy of a Steinway, and one to a Broadwoods as a *souvenir des travaux passes*. Nevertheless, the leading industry paper at the time, the *London Musical Standard*, wrote: "We [meaning the English piano industry] have no reason to dread competition in the manufacture of music instruments."

In 1873 the tables were completely turned on the English at the next big exhibition, which was staged in Vienna. England exhibited 12 instruments, France 34, and Germany 129. The Steinways' American system was now adopted by all successful European firms and its dominance was epitomized in an advertisement at the time "as a MODERN IRONCLAD WARSHIP to a CANOE." In 1878 at another exhibition there was a modest square piano, which was barely noticed. It came from Japan and its makers were Yamaha.

A reasonable indicator of Broadwoods' performance in overseas markets can be seen in Australian import figures for English pianos from 1862 to 1902, among which Broadwoods was the most prominent manufacturer. In 1862, Australia imported 100 pianos from England and just five from Germany. By 1886, imports from each country were running at similar levels of 230 per year. However, by 1902 over 500 pianos were being imported from Germany alone, compared with just 35 from England.

At this time, the managers of Broadwoods were described as "sleepers" not "thrusters," and "gentlemen" rather than "players." When one director died in 1881, he left a huge fortune of £424,000 and his obituary declared: "He took no share in the active portion of the business but was, however, an enthusiastic yachtsman." A new board member, appointed in 1890, was educated at Cambridge University and Eton College. He was a keen farmer, oarsman, and swimmer – "few could equal him at plunging." He traveled extensively, "shot his tiger," but apparently visited no piano factories.

1. *Using an ESTEMPLE analysis, identify the macro-environmental drivers for change in the piano industry.*
2. *Construct an impact matrix to show how these changes affected Broadwoods.*
3. *Add another column to this matrix and show how these changes affected Steinway.*

◀◀◀ Ironclads versus canoes: Some ideas toward a "model answer". . .

The ironclad versus canoes case shows the calamitous decline of the once world-beating firm of Broadwoods. As such it resonates with other major collapses in corporate history, such as the fall of IBM, Marks & Spencer, and Rover Cars. The way in which the ironclad victory case can be analyzed is transferable to these other disasters.

1. Using an ESTEMPLE analysis, identify the macro-environmental drivers for change in the piano industry

In assessing Broadwoods' evolution over time, we detect a slow but sustained drift away from its previously strong environmental fit. An **ESTEMPLE** analysis shows substantial changes in the macro-environment. Changes in **technology** in the agriculture and military industries began to be adopted in the piano industry, radically altering the way in which the piano was constructed. It was now possible to produce pianos with enhanced abilities at lower cost. The **social** context was also propitious. The Steinways found American society to be far more tolerant of their ideas than the German craft system. Their "American system," with its greater volume and richer tone, suited music being composed at the time, which relied increasingly on the rich sonorities of the instrument in complex harmonies and its percussive sounds. It is instructive that this new type of "romantic" music, pioneered by Beethoven some 50 years earlier, had now moved beyond the abilities of contemporary instruments, which he regarded as inadequate and lacking in powerful tone. Customers were also becoming more demanding, wanting more product for their money. Interestingly one might argue that the **media** in the case are more backward- than forward-looking, and worked toward preserving the status quo and the maintenance of Broadwoods' reputation. It is possible that in this time of a weakening British Empire, there was some patriotism behind these sentiments. **Politically** and **economically**, the decline of the Empire at the turn of the century might be seen as a contributory factor in the decline in Broadwoods' export sales.

Against this shifting macro-context, Broadwoods had barely changed its structure, competitive model, or product. Indeed, it was very late in introducing a cast iron frame, as well as over-stringing, long after it had become commonplace in the industry. Broadwoods hardly invested in R&D and relied heavily on its superior craft skills. Its management was passive rather than active, more interested in external unrelated activities, and not sensitive to a changing context. In this sense Broadwoods displays sustained **strategic drift**.

Broadwoods' problem was that its original competitive advantage – a wide range of products with a highly skilled labor content – had become a **core rigidity**. The new manufacturing methods and procedures introduced by the Steinways struck at the very heart of the Broadwoods' model and undermined the value of their cherished assets. To move toward the Steinway system would have necessitated the removal of large amounts of skilled labor and the reduction in importance of many who remained in the company. The use of a SWOT analysis would make explicit the growing gap between the demands of a changing macro-environment, identified in the ESTEMPLE, and the unchanging nature of the capabilities and resources deployed by Broadwoods. This inertia can be explained by routinized behavior and a disinterested management team perhaps lulled into a false sense of security by their previous successes – an Icarus Paradox.

2 & 3. Construct an impact matrix to show how these changes affected Broadwoods; and a further column about its main competitor, Steinway.

An impact matrix can draw upon ESTEMPLE categories in order to identify major changes which are likely to affect an industry. These are ordered vertically and the probability and severity of changes are estimated along the horizontal axis (see Figure 1.5 for an example). The matrix can be adapted in many ways in order to increase its level of sophistication, so for instance there could be explicit recognition of the estimated timing of anticipated changes. In the case in hand the emphasis is upon comparing two companies in the same industry. A simple **impact matrix** (see Figure 1-1.1) shows the ways in which Broadwoods and Steinway were affected by macro-shocks.

Another useful way of conceiving of Broadwoods' situation is in a model of industry evolution (see Figure 1-1.2). Here we can see that Broadwoods stalled in a game of diminishing returns over product evolution, whereas Steinway had pushed forward into improving the manufacturing process, which was being copied by competitors.

Key macro-influences	Broadwoods	Steinway
Economic trends Growing demand as markets opening up and pianos increasingly seen as inspirational item	High labor costs and inefficient production —	Beginnings of automation + +
Social trends Convergence of customer requirements	Many diverse products —	Central product planning + +
Technology trends Innovations in – iron frame – heavier strings – superior key action	Low investment in R&D —	High investment in R&D and willingness to experiment + +
Media European establishment norms – UK music press favored Broadwoods – Establishment used to "Broadwoods sound"	Technicians well respected Links with great composers + +	Up-starts —
Political – Decay of the British Empire	Contracting British controlled markets —	Opportunity + +

Figure 1-1.1 Comparative Impact matrix

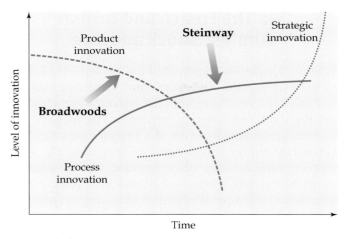

Figure 1-1.2 Industry evolution

►►►

1-2 The French and British Armies: Shock and awe

The French mounted knight had dominated the battlefields of Europe for centuries. His heavy armour, powerful weapons, and maneuverability made him virtually invincible and capable of wrecking the organization of opponents, ripping holes in enemy lines and intimidating advances. His military power was echoed in the economic and political power of a French elite knightly class that had developed an elaborate code of chivalry and military conduct.

In 1346, however, King Edward III of England was conducting a successful campaign through Normandy where he had met little resistance. In moving his 8,000 men northward to link up with Flemish allies, he was suddenly confronted by a far larger French army at Crécy.

Edward arranged his forces around a hilltop from which he could observe the lay of the land. With his rear protected by forest and high ground, the enemy would try a frontal attack across open fields. To repulse the assault, Edward placed his yeoman archers to the fore. The English had learnt just how effective archers' bows could be from bitter experiences in their border conflicts with the Welsh and Scottish. The English had begun to put this learning to good use by diverting a good portion of their increased wealth garnered from subduing their Celtic neighbors toward the development of technology such as the longbow. To encourage competence in the bow, competitions had been introduced around the English counties along with edicts making archery a compulsory activity. Subsequently, Edward's longbow archers had an effective range of 300 yards, were able to hit a human target at 100 yards, and could penetrate three inches of oak. With a direct hit, even armour would not deflect their arrows.

French lines were fronted with Genoese crossbowmen. Crossbow bolts could pierce the heaviest armour and these mercenaries could fire at a rate of two bolts a minute. However, despite the deadly nature of this weapon, the French nobility bitterly resented the ability of such "peasantry." Indeed, in keeping with these beliefs, the French Catholic Church forbade the use of this "lowly" weapon by Christians against Christians. It therefore tended to be marginalized and under-utilized in battle by the ruling classes.

Behind the crossbowmen stood the armoured French knights on heavy war-horses supported by footmen. However, at Crécy, the narrow road to the battle-field was heavily congested. Supply carts and necessary equipment could not get through to serve the lines ahead.

The Genoese were the first to fire, but their volley fell short. Before they could reload and advance, the English let loose barrage after barrage of arrows. The Genoese, normally protected by large wooden shields, were vulnerable as most of their shields were still in the supply carts. Hundreds were killed, defenceless against the hail of arrows.

A wave of French knights then charged over the Genoese ramparts, aiming to crash through the English line and break their formation. But they too were engulfed in lethal English arrows. Although the rounded surfaces on the French armour deflected the deadly tips, flat surfaces, chain mail, and open helmets did not, and the horses, being much less well protected, fell with their riders. Once grounded, the French knights were virtually defenceless against the English foot-men who slaughtered them with axes and daggers.

The French made repeated assaults, but by the end of the day it was said that 16,000 Frenchmen had perished to England's 300. The scale of the defeat was such that nearly every noble family in France was affected directly.

The new technology of the massed English archers had changed the landscape of war. However, the French responded to this blow to their pride and chivalry by investing further in armour. Chain mail was replaced by armour plate and warhorses also had armour plate covering vital areas. The plates became thicker and helmets had visors added. While their operational elements were reinforced, France's strategic approach to warfare remained unchanged.

Almost 70 years later, in October 1415, Henry V led the English on another campaign in France. After capturing Harfleur and proceeding toward Calais, dwindling supplies, poor weather, and casualties weakened Henry's army. Large numbers of French knights began to converge on Henry's position, detect-ing the weakening condition of their foe. At Agincourt the French army was four times the size of the English force and now blocked their path. Henry was forced to fight.

The French were supremely confident of defeating the English through their superior numbers, the weakened condition of the English, and the superb qual-ity of their knights. Their commander, who was not of noble birth, intended to send foot soldiers into battle first and then carry out a flanking maneuver with the knights to destroy the English archers. However, Henry assembled his army on plow land made muddy by recent rain and placed his archers in the narrowest part of the battlefield, where sharpened stakes were set in the ground with bow-men and men at arms arranged among them to enable them to crouch, "hedge-hog-like," upon an assault by the French. This maneuver prevented the French from outflanking the English archers, as they had thick forest on either side which forced the French to make a frontal assault across muddy fields.

To intimidate the English archers, the French promised to cut both of their bow fingers off to prevent them from ever drawing a bow again. The English archers now taunted the French by waving those two fingers in the air. This show of defiance so enraged the French knights, vastly superior in number, that they charged across the muddy field without their commander's approval. Hail after hail of English arrows followed and, as before, knights and horses were cut down. The huge numbers of knights also meant that those behind continued to press forward, preventing those in front from maneuvering, crushing those that had fallen, and impaling others on the English stakes: "so great was the undisciplined violence and pressure [of the second French line] that the living fell on top of the dead." In this carnage the English men at arms then came for-ward to finish off the floundering French knights. The French losses were again immense, with an estimated 6,000 dead in the first 90 minutes of battle. In total the English lost just 150 men.

Despite these huge defeats, French nobles continued to patronize the armour-ers of Europe for a further 130 years. The incremental changes to armour only made the knights slightly less vulnerable to arrows, while making them slower, less maneuverable, and thus easier targets. Indeed, the French investment in armour continued well beyond the point when firearms made it totally obsolete.

1. *Why did the French lose at Crécy?; Why did they lose again at Agincourt?*
2. *How did the French approach to battle change over this time period?*
3. *Use a SWOT or TOWS analysis to summarize why the English defeated the French in these two battles.*

Case Notes:

1-3 FloraHolland: Flower power

You're about to land at Amsterdam's Schiphol airport. As you survey the flat Dutch landscape below, your eye catches sight of what seems like row upon row of low-lying buildings, covering an area of what must be the equivalent of 100 football fields. If you have ever experienced this sight and wondered what was housed in those buildings, it is the Aalsmeer Flower Auction of FloraHolland, the world's third largest building in terms of floor space. Buy a bunch of flowers anywhere in the world, be it San Francisco, London, Singapore, or Tokyo, and it is likely that they passed through this site only a day or two before. In just a few short years FloraHolland has cornered the world's flower auction market. It has done so by matching technological developments, the social and geographical advantages of its location, and an acute sense of what its buyers want: to provide not only an efficient service, but also one that adds value to both growers and buyers alike. How does it work?

First, blooms from across Europe are sent to Aalsmeer to be auctioned. There, they are graded for quality, perfume, color, etc. and are placed in lots onto carts, somewhat similar to the golf carts that are familiar on many US or Japanese golf courses. The carts are guided into the auction rooms before hundreds of buyers sitting in a tiered horseshoe-shaped "theater." A console is positioned immediately in front of each buyer which he or she activates to make a bid. On the wall in front of the buyers, and behind each lot as it is driven out on to the floor, is a giant clock that is used to "count down" the price of each lot. (Remember that in a Dutch auction – we are in the Netherlands, after all – the price starts at a high point and is counted down.) The first bidder to push their "buying button" purchases the lot – a very efficient decision-making process.

Once the bid has been made, the carts are automatically dispatched to the buyer's loading bay and, while the auction continues, invoices are automatically prepared. In this way, once the auction is over, the buyers can settle their accounts and return to their loading bay to find all of their purchases already loaded for transport. Speed of transaction is of the essence, of course, since the blooms have a very short shelf life. And the Dutch auction system – including the IT employed by FloraHolland – is particularly effective in this regard.

But there is more to the Aalsmeer service than efficiency. Information is provided to all growers and buyers, and it is this additional information that sets FloraHolland's level of service apart from its competition. For example, the growers that supply Aalsmeer are fed information on demand trends to enable them to bring on their blooms faster or slower to meet demand and get the best price. In turn, buyers can rely on getting what they want, when they want it. Moreover, buyers have come to rely on the FloraHolland's provision of information on varying demand the world over, and their expertise in grading the blooms has become something of a quality guarantee.

Thus, FloraHolland not only provides an efficient auction service, it also provides added value services to its customers in the form of information – and this is enabled by the IT systems it has employed. While the IT systems can be readily and easily copied by the competition, the expertise and goodwill FloraHolland has accrued over the years means that it has been able to sustain its advantage.

This enabled it to be a prime-mover as more and more of the auctioning process has been automated. The level of trust that has been build up has made an increasing number of buyers comfortable about purchasing remotely on-line, based on virtual images of the stock lots through FloraHolland's i-KOA (Internet Kopen Op Afstand) system. By 2010 45% of all purchases were bought remotely through i-KOA, further enabling Aalsmeer to increase its throughput without increasing the physical size of its facilities to accommodate more buyers.

Moreover, innovations promoted by the Internet and other technological advances in the macro-environment have now been fed back to the auction room floor. FloraHolland's development of "Image Auctioning" means that flowers and plants will no longer need to be driven out on to the bidding floor. Instead an image of the lot will be projected from the storeroom to a giant screen on the bidding floor. This both reduces costs by further speeding up the logistics of delivery, and improves flower quality by keeping the flowers in the conditioned environment of the stockroom.

1. What macro environmental factors has FloraHolland taken advantage of?
2. What scenarios should FloraHolland consider in thinking about its future strategy?
3. Use a SWOT or TOWS analysis to summarize why FloraHolland has been successful.

Case Notes:

1-4 Nike: Local actions, global effects?

Nike was founded in 1964 when Phil Knight put an MBA project he'd written into practice with Bill Bowerman, his former track coach at the University of Oregon. At a time when established companies were manufacturing sports shoes in high-wage economies, Knight's project had shown that decreasing transport costs would mean that higher margins could be gained by sourcing shoes from countries with low labor costs. Nike began by importing shoes from Japan. However, one morning Bowerman was standing in his kitchen and had an idea. He made an outsole by pouring a rubber compound into a waffle iron. The waffle trainer was born and Nike became a design company rather than just an importer.

Initially, Nike outsourced almost all of its production to plants in Japan. However, in the early 1970s, as costs there began to rise, it was switched to Taiwan and Korea. By 1982, only Nike's headquarters and design facility (or "campus" as it is called) were located in the USA. In 1999, Nike employed 13,000 people in the USA, while its 350 subcontractors employed nearly 500,000 in plants in China, Vietnam, and Indonesia.

Knight and Bowerman's personalities fired Nike's purpose: a love of athletics, an appreciation of the views of real athletes, and a relentless appetite for competition and striving for *number 1*. "Every time I tour people around [the Nike 'campus']," explains Geoff Hollister, who ran track with Knight at college, "I show them a picture of Phil Knight running behind Jim Grelle. Grelle was a champion and Knight never caught him – but he never stopped pursuing."

Knight's passion for athletic excellence attracted young and confident employees with a similar outlook. According to Nelson Farris, another of Knight's former track teammates: "We like employees who aren't afraid to tee it up." The campus culture was subsequently pervaded with an "athletistocracy" that placed athletic achievement through innovative design above everything else. An article in *The Sunday Times* recently claimed that the words "I work for Nike" seem to have the same appeal as "I work for NASA" did 30 years ago. Those on the Nike campus developed a particular pride in their work. Once part of the fraternity, they are famously devotional. Many have tattoos of Nike's trademark "swoosh" on their bodies.

Nike's values are powerfully expressed in their marketing. The swoosh – which ranks alongside McDonald's golden arches and Coca-Cola's red and white logo as being recognized by 97% of Americans – speaks of a no-nonsense emphasis on speed and performance. The Nike tag-line "Just Do It" (born in 1988 when an advertising executive told Nike staff that: "You Nike guys, you just do it") is the second most recognizable slogan in the USA after the Marlboro Man.

In the words of one commentator, this devotion and recognition enabled Nike to "instill its products with a kind of holy superiority." And this "holiness" and the continued growth that ensued saw Nike go from strength to strength. Its share price rose 3,686% in the period from 1980 to 1997. Nike overtook Reebok to become market leader in sports shoes in 1988. In the three years to 1996 Nike more than doubled sales, moving from a 32% share of the market in 1994 to 45% in 1996. In the three years to 1997, the group tripled in size, with worldwide sales up to $9 billion and profits to $800 million.

After achieving number one status in sports footwear Nike pursued an increasing number of new initiatives. In 1992, Knight claimed that he wanted Nike to be not just the world's best athletic shoemaker but "the world's best sports and fitness company." In an interview in the *Harvard Business Review* that same year, Knight described a further transformation in Nike. "For years we thought of ourselves as a production-oriented company, meaning we put all our emphasis on designing and manufacturing the product. But we understand now that the most important thing we do is market the product. We've come around to saying that Nike is a marketing-oriented company." The new emphasis on marketing saw Nike seek to exploit and ram home the rebel image, with "Just Do It" supported with slogans like "You don't win second you lose first."

Nike moved into further pastures – including "redefining retailing" – with the launch of Nike Town stores (described as being "more like theme parks than shops"), and becoming more fashion conscious in its product design. The initial response, from journalists, at publications like *Vogue* at least, was positive. Moreover, Nike set out to "redefine and expand the world of sports entertainment" with a joint venture with a Hollywood talent agency. The aim here was to package up events in which Nike endorsers like Charles Barkley and Michael Jordan were involved and then sell this on to sponsors and media companies. Nike's director of advertising outlined the potential: "Forget the business Nike's in at the moment. This is going to boom across the map, and massive amounts of money can be made." By 1996, Nike was increasingly slapping its swoosh on everything from sunglasses to footballs to batting gloves and hockey sticks, with Nike's VP of corporate communications proclaiming that "We are not a shoe company." Phil Knight's stated objective for Nike in 1996's annual report was the "'Swooshification' of the world."

However, 1997 saw a decline in Nike's fortunes. Analysts predicted that Nike's share of the world athletic market would drop from 47% in 1997 to 40%; correspondingly, profits had fallen by 69% at the end of 1997. The share price, which stood at $72 at the beginning of 1994, hit $30 in August 1998. Standard & Poor's subsequently downgraded its outlook on Nike from "stable" to "negative." The normally gung-ho Knight admitted to *Advertising Age* in 1998 that: "Everything we have tried over the past six months simply has not worked." What happened?

In the ever-fickle fashion stakes, even Nike's own people admitted that "we're just not cool any more." Marketing guru Peter York claims that "Nike [knows that they are] not what matters at the moment," and that this recognition has led to there being: ". . . an air of desperation about them now. They're doing too many special runs and limited editions, trying too hard to keep their cool. They've had brilliant brand marketing, but their brand stretches are unproven."

Even more problematic, however, were the protest groups and media investigations focusing on alleged abuses at Nike's foreign factories. The allegations made included employing children sold to the factories by brokers; poor air quality caused by petroleum-based solvents leading to breathing problems in some factories; paying well under the minimum wage; and the lack of sick pay and compensation, even for industrial injuries. Internet sites with names like www.boycottnike and www.nike-sucks fueled the anti-Nike feeling that these allegations generated.

While Nike was actually doing little that was different from other sports-wear companies, Medea Benjamin, director of *Global Watch,* admitted that Nike was targeted because it was "the biggest and it sets the trends. I wish we had the resources to look at Reebok, Adidas, and Converse, but we don't." Indeed, it was not just that Nike had become the biggest; it had also become the loudest. As Thomas Bivins, Professor of Public Relations at the University of Oregon, argued: "When a company goes out of its way to create an image [like Nike's], it is going to be a big target."

Nike responded as if they were mounting a legal defense. They sought to distance themselves from the factories, claiming that what their contractors did was none of their business. After this failed to wash, Nike's PR spokesperson declared that: "In a country where the population is increasing by 2.5 million a year, with 40% unemployment, it is better to work in a shoe factory than not have a job." But the public response just got worse.

In January 1997, Andrew Young, former US ambassador to the UN, visited Nike plants in Vietnam, Indonesia, and China and declared that they were "as clean and modern" as any in the USA. However, the big news story turned out to be the discovery that Nike paid for his trip and that he was shepherded by Nike people and only introduced to appropriately briefed staff. In Britain, the magazine *The Big Issue* begged readers to boycott Nike. Even Nike's move into soccer was subjected to negative scrutiny. After Brazil's defeat by France in the 1998 World Cup, many believed that Nike had bullied Brazil's coach into playing another Nike endorser, Ronaldo, even though he was obviously unfit. Newspaper articles drew links between Nike and Nike endorser Mike Tyson and declared "Nike is one bad dude."

Phil Knight originally refused to comment on the protests, then denied all charges of slave labor, then branded his accusers "activists." However, 1998 marked what The *Financial Times* called "a stunning reversal." Knight came out and personally responded to the criticisms. He explained that: "Basically, our culture, and our style, is to be a rebel, and we sort of enjoy doing that." However, he conceded that "Now that we've reached a certain size, there's a fine line between being a rebel and being a bully, and yeah, we have to walk that line." In May of 1998, Knight unveiled a plan to improve the conditions of 350,000 Nike workers in Asia. Nike would sever ties with contractors because of "unacceptable working conditions"; increase wages by up to 40% for individuals in entry-level foot-wear manufacturing jobs; improve air quality by switching to water-based rather than petroleum-based adhesives; and increase its minimum working age to 18. And it set up www.nikeworker.com, where people could find information about Nike's production practices. The *Transnational Resource and Action Center,* one of Nike's most vocal critics, subsequently stated that relations with Nike were greatly improved, while the third annual "Protest Nike day" scheduled for the end of 1998 failed to draw any protesters.

However, Nike did not stop there. In 1998 Knight explained that Nike would undergo a total "holistic reorganization." Nike spokespeople admitted that the company had made poor decisions in every area. Tom Clarke, Nike's Chief Operating Officer, confessed "We'd gotten stale on design." Nelson Farris, a Nike employee for 25 years, admitted that "I've been to Chinese-run factories and though we improved upon that, it obviously wasn't good enough. Now we're looking at how we run our company. Are we making the right product? Is our service, our advertising, good enough? Are we good enough people?" The bad publicity had certainly had an impact on the mood of Nike's employees. Farris continued, "It has demoralized a lot of people. We haven't been as on top of things as we'd perhaps have liked. We've got to learn to do business much better." Suddenly, the company whose strength of purpose meant that it seldom stopped to question anything was pondering everything.

One result of this pondering was an attempt to soften Nike's image by watering down "Just Do It" to the new catchphrase "I Can" in the USA in 1998. "At a time when cynicism in sports is at an all-time high, 'I Can' is an effort to return to a focus on the positive," said Bob Wood, Nike's marketing VP. The *Financial Times* announced that with the "unveiling of the new softer 'I Can' slogan to replace 'Just Do It', Nike may be about to take a [huge] step." However, some industry watchers were not so convinced and many customers seemed confused by the change of tack and what Nike now stood for.

Postscript:

Late in 2009, a driving accident involving Tiger Woods (who had more than any other figure become the face of Nike in the 00s, and had been given his own Nike sub-brand Tiger Woods Golf – TWG) led to revelations of Woods' serial adultery which shattered Woods' previously stellar public image. These revelations forced the player to take a break from the game and seek counseling.

Other companies that had sponsored and utilized Woods' image in their advertising, such as consulting firm Accenture and telecoms giant AT&T, dropped him quickly after the allegations of infidelity surfaced. But Nike stood by Woods.

Nike brand president Charlie Denson told AFP in an interview. "Time will ultimately tell what his image ends up being," he said. "'One thing that we do know is that he is still just as good a golfer as he was a year ago. In relationship to that, the way we continue to drive our golf business, he's one of our major contributors and we would expect him to be in the future as well."

---

1. *How do you account for Nike's tremendous success up until the mid-90s?*
2. *Using ESTEMPLE, explain why Nike suffered a severe decline in 1997.*
3. *Do you think the decision not to dump Tiger Woods shows that Nike did not learn from their environmental shocks of the late 1990s, or that it shows they did learn from their later overreaction to those shocks?*

1-5 Rover: Slipping or skidding?

In the 1950s, the Rover Car Company was a highly successful small firm operating in a niche. After World War II, demand had been increasing steadily as disposable incomes and social expectations had risen. It was a time of post-war patriotism, and Rover's conservatively styled cars, built in Britain, had wide appeal. Many cars were also exported.

Rover P4 saloons were conservatively styled and appealed to the professional classes, such as doctors and solicitors. The cars had sumptuous interiors with handmade leather seats and polished wood fascia. The company also led the way in technological developments, such as with the creation of a gas turbine car. Design innovations added to the firm's reputation for quality, with its new models being perceived as cutting edge. The Rover 2000, launched in the 1960s, was a radical new design and a huge hit with customers.

While the car market continued to grow during the 1960s, Rover found itself unable to meet demand, quoting waiting times of up to 3 years. At the same time there was a considerable rise in car imports from the continent so that, by the 1970s, one in seven cars sold in Britain was a continental car. The firm recognized the need for greater scale economies and invested in machinery to improve efficiency and reduce the need for, and costs of, skilled labor. To operate these machines, large numbers of unskilled workers were hired.

While technology was being widely adopted by major car manufacturers, at Rover, skilled workers argued that the machines didn't really replace them. For instance, although a highly sophisticated and very expensive computer-controlled paint shop was installed, skilled workers argued that they were still needed to deal with parts of the paintwork not covered adequately by the automated process. Workers were also paid for each task they undertook. Every time a new machine was installed, wages had to be renegotiated.

At this time, trade union power in Rover, and across the UK, was very high. The unions in Rover were very militant and there was real suspicion that this militancy was encouraged by communists attempting to destabilize the capitalist system. The number of strikes reached epidemic proportions with as many as 100 per year. The strikes also seemed to be called over the most inconsequential of issues.

Top management recognized that Rover's profits were not rising as quickly as the cost of developing new cars. The rising costs of new technology were a growing burden and R&D was increasingly expensive. Despite the introduction of greater automation, frequent strikes meant the company was still producing far too few cars. At this time the view became established that Rover was too small to compete world wide. The Government therefore backed a series of mergers between many of Britain's car companies to form British Leyland (BL).

In 1973, oil prices surged upwards causing a slump in demand for new vehicles. This forced BL into the red. The Government took the view that the UK car industry, predominantly BL, had to be preserved. In 1975, the Government took a stake in its ownership and poured £1.4 bn into the company. The most modern car factory in Europe was built to produce 3,000 cars per week, but only managed 1,500 because of outdated working practices. At this time BL was losing £1 m per day. At the same time, cars imported from Japan were finding ready buyers in the UK market, where reliability was valued.

To stem the bleeding, Sir Michael Edwardes was appointed to turn BL around. His recommendation was to reduce the size of the company and to get rid of the union activists, Red Robbo (the factory union leader) in particular. Although he knew this would meet with fierce union resistance, Sir Michael believed that the workers were fed up with incessant strikes. He decided to go around the unions and ballot the workers directly about the need for mass redundancies. Although close, Sir Michael won. Red Robbo departed, mass redundancies took place, and union power was reduced substantially. However, despite the cuts, BL still had insufficient funds to invest to produce cars of a similar quality to the Japanese imports.

To address Rover's main weaknesses of poor mass production, poor technology, and a lack of capital for investment, an alliance was formed with Honda. From Honda's perspective, Rover offered good distribution and a design competence for the UK and European markets. The first joint product was the Rover 800, which turned out to be the most successful car since the 1960s. It had Rover styling but contained Honda engines and gearboxes. At the same time, however, there were mass resignations of Rover's engineers who felt that they were now being overlooked. Rover's engineering center was subsequently put up for sale.

Now that BL had regained profitability, the UK Government tried to sell the company but there were no offers from other car companies. Eventually British Aerospace bought the firm, although it was widely suspected that this was a political deal and not one focused on developing BL for the future. Shortly afterwards, Rover was purchased by BMW who invested huge sums in new product development and the introduction of German practices. Honda immediately withdrew from the alliance and viewed the sale as a breach of trust.

While BMW poured in billions into creating new car designs to complement its own range, such as the Land Rover Defender, a new Mini, and new 45 and 75 models, it encountered huge problems at the massive manufacturing facility at Longbridge. Despite sending in hundreds of BMW engineers from Germany, the problems remained. There were also intractable difficulties in dealing with the myriad suppliers who resisted change. BMW's losses were so significant that the parent company was being harmed by "the English Patient" and made strategically vulnerable to takeover. There were rumors that Ford was even in talks with BMW's owners. Facing sustained losses of £500 m per year, BMW sold Rover to a management buyout team, although they kept the Mini and 4x4 production lines.

1. *Why was Rover successful in the 1950s?*
2. *What macro-environmental factors drove change in the car industry post-1950s and why did Rover decline?*
3. *In what ways was the alliance with Honda beneficial to both companies? And why did BMW buy Rover?*

1-6 South Africa: The Mont Fleur Scenarios

In the early 1990s, South Africa was beginning to prepare a transition from a repressive, apartheid regime to a democratic nation. There was a great deal of anxiety, fear and trepidation about what the future would hold. Financial markets were jittery; and all of the communities of what would come to be called the "rainbow nation" were nervous. Nobody could know how the future would unfold; the only certainty was that things would be very different.

Things in South Africa today are nowhere near perfect, but things have turned out better than most people expected. A little known component in the transition was the Mont Fleur Scenarios.

In 1991 a team of 22 people of all races and a range of professions (from economists, to community leaders, to social workers) began to meet at Mont Fleur near Stellenbosch. They were brought together under the tutelage of Adam Kahane. Kahane was a part of the team at Royal Dutch Shell who had first developed the concept of "Scenario Planning". The Mont Fleur group's purpose was to develop possible scenarios relating to the governance of South Africa's future.

Thirty possible stories about the course of events that might take place over the next decade (to 2002) were elicited, distilled and then refined down into four possible scenarios or pathways for the future flight of South Africa: Ostrich, Lame Duck, Icarus, and Flight of the Flamingo. Their story-lines are outlined below.

- **Ostrich:** This was a story of a government with its proverbial head stuck in the sand, not wanting or able to face up to the past and the present reality and responsibilities.
- **Lame Duck:** This was a government like a bird with a broken wing, who, after a long ponderous transition, can't get off the ground and becomes incapacitated.
- **Icarus:** Like the mythical Greek youth who had been given wings of wax with which he could fly, the government here embarks on a massive spending spree to meet all the backlogs and needs of the past, flies too close to the sun and crashes and burns because its quick fix policies are not sustainable.
- **Flight of the Flamingo:** Just as flamingos take some time to get ready for take-off, making sure that the group is in good order before launch, in this scenario economic growth would be slow yet steady – and thus sustainable. And just as flamingos take off and fly together, going from a gangly awkward gathering to graceful airborne flock, a smooth flight would only result after much forethought, organization, and making sure that all systems and communities were ready to go.

The report written on this scenario thinking exercise (and the four scenarios themselves) has come to have a great deal of influence among South Africa's political, social and economic leaders. And many have linked a range of post-Apartheid achievements, from South Africa's relative financial success, generally smooth political transition, and ability to attract and run major sporting events, such as Rugby and Soccer World Cups, to the forethought that went into the Mont Fleur Scenarios and their subsequent dissemination.

1. *Why do you think the development of these four scenarios was a useful process for those concerned with developing a strategy for South Africa's future?*
2. *Why is it important to involve a broad range of people in a scenario thinking process like this?*
3. *When might scenario thinking be of use to strategists or managers?*

Case Notes:

1-7 China Airlines: Expo, Olympics, SARS, and the Government

For every World Cup football tournament, Expo, or Olympics that can generate millions of new passengers for an airline industry, there is a SARS outbreak or an act of terrorism that can bring it to its knees. These macro-shocks provide massive opportunities as well as threats to companies that have freedom to anticipate and respond.

The domestic airline industry in China had previously been purely reactive to changes in its environment, largely because of the dominating effect of Government influence through CAAC (Civil Aviation Authority of China) regulations. However, huge changes were taking place in Government policy as well as across the country as a whole, with rapid deregulation and increasing engagement with the forces of globalization. Senior executives in the industry realized that if the trend toward deregulation continued, they would need to move from being purely reactive toward anticipating macro-shocks and being prepared to deal with these uncertainties. With China looking forward to hosting the Olympics in 2008 and World Expo in 2020, senior airline executives felt they should appraise their positions in the light of what the future might bring.

In 2001 CAAC controlled three large airlines based in Beijing, Shanghai, and Guangzhou. The eastern part of China is the most prosperous part of the country and accounts for the majority of domestic air routes. These three airlines control 80% of the total market. There are also some 30 registered commercial airlines, some based in the major eastern urban centers and assisted by provincial government aid but the majority are located further inland in new economic zones, providing connections to the coastal areas. The airlines are massively in debt, with estimates around RMB 112bn and the gearing of individual businesses being around 80%. Recently two of the three CAAC airlines were listed and the third is set to follow. The Government remains the main shareholder, with 51%, but it is hoped greater foreign involvement will bring increased efficiency and greater fiscal responsibility. It is the perception of competitors that the CAAC hopes its three airlines will drive out or absorb local competition, although this is contrary to the spirit of deregulation and a reduction in Government influence. Earlier attempts at deregulation, by allowing price competition, caused significant damage to the CAAC-controlled companies. Today's competitors are restricted to competing on price within a 40% range of the CAAC's published fare, although under-table discounts are known, and also by **differentiation** through flying to secondary cities.

By 2001, China's airline industry was carrying 60 million passengers and was sixth in the world by volume. It continues to grow at twice the global rate and will become the global leader by 2020.

In 2002, Hu Jin Tao was appointed Chairman and is widely expected to continue to build on the economic foundation laid by former leaders Deng and Jiang. The stated focus is to maintain the prosperity of the east while developing growth of the inland western provinces. This will be achieved by encouraging foreign investments to flow into central and western regions across a wider range of sectors than before, particularly the service sector. This seems to be in recognition that the costs of manufacturing in the eastern area are now higher than in countries such as Indonesia. The last two decades have seen substantial inflows of FDI and, by 2000, 1,330 regions were designated open to FDI. Most investments, however, have been in the eastern region, with Beijing receiving $1.97 bn, Shanghai $2.83 bn, and Guangdong $1.65 bn. By comparison Xinjian, a territory one-sixth the size of the nation, received just $21.6 m.

The Government is pushing the "Go West" policy to curb the migration of poor rural workers to the east. Large-scale infrastructure developments, such as the Xinjian natural gas pipeline, will help create many jobs. At the moment, most of China's more than one billion population is just above the poverty line and air travel is an unobtainable luxury. There is also significant social uncertainty, which has led to a series of bombings in the last decade. There were eight bombings in Tibet and in northern China 108 were killed in 2001. However, the Government is reducing air fares on selected routes to increase the number of travelers. Already central and provincial governments are drafting economic incentives to accelerate investments inland, and these include the creation of tourist hotspots. Tourism is recognized as a rapid stimulant to economies and central government has allocated RMB 861 m toward this end. However, success is dependent upon an adequate and suitable infrastructure. With large distances to be covered, rail is too slow and suitable roads too expensive to build. Under CAAC guidelines and WTO agreements, foreign enterprises are being encouraged to invest in airport construction, airport management, and other supporting industries. This help is needed if the target of 150 new airports all over China, to establish regional hubs, is to be realized. The "Go West" initiative could have far-reaching implications for an airline industry largely based on point-to-point services of the coastal area.

China hosted the Olympics in Beijing in 2008 and the Expo in Shanghai in 2010. The massive publicity surrounding these events has attracted substantial foreign business and tourists will further stimulate the eastern region. However, relationships with Taiwan are a continuing cause for concern since the pro-independence Democratic Progressive Party came to power in 2000. Although its rhetoric has softened somewhat since then, there is no trend in its actions.

Today there are over one million Taiwanese business people in Shanghai and Shenzhen and more would move if Taiwan, fearing a brain-drain, had not imposed restrictions on some segments of its economy. During 2003, Taiwanese planes have been allowed to land in Shanghai via Hong Kong for the first time in 50 years and there are talks that Chinese airlines may get a similar favor. Direct cross-strait flights could be major business for airlines serving the main eastern cities. However, if political tensions develop, a war would have disastrous regional and international consequences for both countries.

China's GDP has been growing steadily over the last decade and, with it, people's disposable income. The number of domestic traveler visits has increased from 659 million (1998) to 1.61 billion (2007). However, growth is not homogeneous. Despite huge investment in the western regions the gap between eastern urban inhabitants and the western rural population continues to widen in terms of population density and income. The most prosperous cities, and largest markets for air travel, are Shanghai, Guangzhou, and Beijing, where residents earn an average of 56% more than the national average. The growth of the cities has been fueled by the real estate market but there is now talk of the kind of property bubble that dragged down Japan's economy. Restrictions on foreign purchases have been lifted and there has been soaring demand for urban property over the last three years.

A further major international issue is the increasing pressure for China to float its currency in the world market. At the moment, a low RMB makes China's products artificially cheap and competitive. The current recession has brought this issue to a head as the US economy struggles to revive itself. In 2009, China's exports to the USA were worth $296.4bn but it imported just $69.6bn. This disparity could lead to a trade war.

Having identified key macro-forces which could exert a powerful effect on the airline industry, senior airline executives wondered what to do next in constructing the future.

1. What are the environmental drivers for change in the Chinese airline industry?
2. Construct three future scenarios about the future of the Chinese airline industry and outline the implications of each for: (a) the three main firms and (b) the regional competitors.
3. In what ways might the scenarios challenge the prevailing mental models of Chinese airlines?

Case Notes:

[eBay] have got to get their act together and decide what they are – they cannot be black-marketeers of tickets.

Harvey Goldsmith, Live 8 promoter for Bob Geldof

Anything to do with the Lions tour bought over the Internet [from TradeMe] runs a grave risk of being a scam or tickets that have been procured illegally and must be shut down.

Steve Tew, Deputy Chief Executive, New Zealand Rugby Union

In 2005 Bob Geldof, an aging former rock star and concert promoter, and his Live 8 organization spoke out against eBay selling on Live 8 tickets for people who had successfully taken part in a ticket ballot and then sought to make a quick profit. eBay acted as quickly and as best it could to close down the practice. Just two months earlier, the New Zealand Rugby Union criticized TradeMe, a local eBay equivalent, for reselling rugby tickets on behalf of people who also successfully took part in a ticket ballot and were also seeking to make a quick profit. TradeMe did little to stop the practice. Why is it that, in certain contexts, some can shake and move a company's strategy with a few choice words while in other contexts similar words have a negligible effect?

This chapter examines who the influential movers and shakers are. More specifically:

1. Who runs the company and for whom is the company run?
2. What are the constraints on the Chief Executive's power?
3. Who are the movers and shakers that influence a firm's strategy?
4. How can different stakeholder interests be managed?

Who Runs the Company and For Whom is the Company Run?

In March 2005, Bernie Ebbers, CEO of the telecoms giant WorldCom, was convicted of nine criminal counts for an $11 bn (£5.7 bn) accounting fraud that led to the largest bankruptcy in US history (*Financial Times*, March 19, 2005). Further high-profile trials of top executives – Jeffrey Skilling and Kenneth Lay (Enron), Dennis Kozlowski (Tyco), and Richard Scrushy (HealthSouth) – also took place for alleged corporate wrongdoing. Even the most fêted of US CEOs, the legendary Jack Welch, came under scrutiny, accused of excessive expenses, with a Manhattan apartment, limousine services, security guards, corporate jet, and the best seats at sporting and artistic events, to name but a few. These incidents show an increasing concern for understanding and appraising the role and responsibilities of such "Imperial Chief Executives." To assess the actions of these top executives, fundamental questions concerning the relationship between top management and stakeholders need to be addressed.

In an Anglo-American context, conventional wisdom is that the company should be run for its owners, the shareholders, as ultimate beneficiaries. However, as the opening examples show, there is suspicion that Imperial Chief Executives run their firms more for themselves than for shareholders. How has this come about?

Apart from owner-managed firms and small businesses, shareholders do not have the expertise to run the firms in which they have ownership and so require a professional executive to manage the business for them. This means that ownership of the business is separated from control of wealth and results in a principal–agent relationship.[1] The Chief Executive is an agent for the principal (shareholders) and is responsible for maximizing the value of the principal's investment.

The quality of the principal–agent relationship depends on the agent receiving sufficient incentive to work diligently in the principal's best interests. For this reason, Chief Executives are highly incentivized through salary and benefits to maximize company performance. In this light, perhaps the benefits attributed to Jack Welch earlier are justifiable as being a small price to pay for winning the services of an outstanding Chief Executive?

Particularly noteworthy in incentivizing top executives is the granting of large numbers of shares and the use of share options to align their interests with those of shareholders. The logic is that if top executives stand to benefit personally and substantially by being able to exercise their options, then they will work to improve the share price to enable this to take place, and, in so doing, benefit shareholders. Of course, this method is not without problems – beneficiaries of these options may be incentivized to maximize short-term profits at the expense of the long-term future of the business.[2]

Where a problem can occur is when agents have the opportunity to benefit at the expense of shareholders. For instance, while some consumption of benefits by Chief Executives is likely to be beneficial to the firm, as it may assist in attracting and retaining good managers, excessive consumption can destroy shareholder value. Former Tyco CEO, Kozlowski, was accused of this by the Securities and Exchange Commission for failing to disclose multimillion-dollar low-interest loans (US SEC, 2002). This divergence of interests is known as an **agency problem**.[3] Evidence can be seen in the enthusiasm for Chief Executives to grow their firms. It is well known that their personal reward and prestige is positively related to the size of their firm and so they have an incentive to increase it beyond the optimal level. When Chief Executives have access to cash flow in excess of that needed to fund all available projects of the firm with positive net present value, the potential for overinvestment is particularly serious. This excess cash should be paid out to investors[4] but is likely to be reinvested at rates well below the corporate cost of capital, particularly in diversifying acquisitions. It is to avoid the worst excesses of the agency problem that various constraints exist on CEO power.

What are the Constraints on CEO power?

The recent surge in court cases against high-profile Chief Executives makes the issue of controls on top management, or corporate governance, a very topical issue. **Corporate governance** focuses on who the firm should serve, the distribution of power and relationships among different stakeholders, and the selection and conduct of senior management. It recognizes that the Chief Executive is embedded in a hierarchy of power relationships, consisting of many different groups each with claims and influence upon the firm. The most immediate influence on the Chief Executive is through the chain of ownership.

In small private companies, the owners may be a small number of family members who may or may not have a role in the running of the business itself. While the number of shareholders may be small, the tensions and struggles between family members over the direction of the business can be extraordinary and involve issues far removed from just the maximization of shareholder value. For larger public firms, ownership is far more complex. Just by looking at the share register, one may well find the number of direct share-owners running into thousands of individuals dispersed around the globe. For the majority of these owners, their shares will represent only a fraction of the total issued share capital and so their individual ability to influence the firm will be very low. Individuals may also buy into the firm indirectly (through investment funds, for example) and may not even be aware of the companies in which they have a stake. The same applies for funds placed with pension funds under the management of trustees.

In most share registers of public companies the largest shareholders will be institutions rather than private shareholders. The investment managers of pension funds as well as investment trusts therefore have substantial influence over the firm's management. However other institutions, such as insurance companies, also build sizable stakes. Investment banks, for instance, may have substantial holdings in their own right and in countries such as Germany and Japan, commercial banks are major holders of equity in leading companies.[5] In these countries cross-shareholding is common, unlike the Anglo-American system, and this leads to illiquidity in dealing. It has been argued that this structural difference affects the extent to which shareholders push for shorter or longer term results.

Often, substantial owners of shares may be other companies, either as a pure investment or as competitors keeping informed of a rival's activities and using share ownership as a hedging strategy. It is worth noting that all of these shareholders have their own agendas and time frames. For instance, in the short term, a firm may well have a significant portion of its shares controlled by arbitrageurs whereas pension funds may be committed for the longer term.

One type of ownership is that of the non-equity principal. These are generally banks, which, through the provision of loans and other forms of finance, such as bonds, have ownership rights over the firm's assets. Generally speaking, these non-equity principals become influential when there may be material changes to the nature of the firm, in its ownership, such as when a firm is subject to a takeover bid, or in its financing, when the firm may be trying to raise funds. Debt holders become very significant in influencing CEOs and top management when the firm is in poor financial health. Indeed, there can come a point where the value of the equity is virtually nil and debt holders control the firm and wield the power rather than holders of equity.

The parties described above can be thought of as a chain of principal–agent relationships, with the Chief Executive being the agent of the Board of Directors, which in turn is the agent of institutional managers and long-term investors, who are agents for trustees, who are agents for the ultimate principal, the beneficiaries (see Figure 2.1).

Between each of these links, information is passed to safeguard the interests of the principal. In the Anglo-American system, the law states that certain information needs to be disclosed to all shareholders. This is done by sending out annual report and accounts together with notification of any material changes to the firm. However, the richness of information obtained, over and above this legally specified minimum, is broadly proportional to the size of the shareholding and the resources available for making this collection. For instance, pension fund managers are likely to meet personally with top management, attend all meetings scheduled by the firm, and speak fairly regularly on the telephone. Individual shareholders, however, may just receive annual report and accounts if

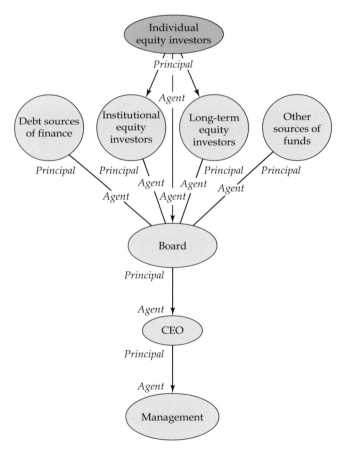

Figure 2.1 Principal–agent chain

direct shareholders, and, if holding shares through an investment fund, may not even receive this information, but a performance report for the fund as a whole.

Mechanisms internal to the firm, to align the Chief Executive's interests with those of the owners, are financial incentive schemes. The logic is that if the shareholders become rich, then so should the Chief Executive. These schemes may include increasing share ownership and compensation arrangements based on accounts, markets, and contingencies (such as long-term incentive plans, LTIPs). While they reward Chief Executive focus on improving selected performance measures, these techniques can be counterproductive. For instance, if a Chief Executive's remuneration is tied to firm profitability, actions may be taken to boost that profitability by starving the firm of investment for future growth. Other internal mechanisms include improving internal controls and monitoring, through (1) the performance and pay review process and (2) corporate governance (The Cadbury Report 2003). Corporate governance generally insists on the separation of Chairman and Chief Executive roles to avoid undue concentration of executive power (see Disney vs. Disney in Case 2-1). The Chairman is primarily responsible for managing external relations while the Chief Executive is responsible for day-to-day operations and relationships within the company. All Executive Directors report to the Chief Executive (but not non-executive Directors).

Outside of the firm, ownership influence can be achieved by large minority shareholders and activist investors. They have an incentive to collect information and monitor management. A prominent mover and shaker in the UK is Tony Bolton, previously a highly successful manager of US fund-managed Fidelity Group. Nicknamed "the quiet assassin," he has been very active as an influential institutional investor, bringing about the removal of a number of Chief Executives (see live Case 2-3 on Carlton).

Poorly performing top executives may also be subject to a hostile takeover as a disciplinary force. The bid for Disney by Comcast was interpreted widely as a criticism of the way that Michael Eisner, Disney's Chairman and CEO, managed the company (see live Case 2-1). For Harvard Professor Michael Jensen, hostile bids are evidence of a market for corporate control, where executives compete for the ownership of the firm to manage its resources effectively. Where a bundle of resources, or a firm, is managed badly, better performing managers will act to replace them through a hostile takeover. This threat of takeover, which is prevalent in the US and UK systems, may be seen as a primary external means of ensuring good managerial performance.

Who Are the Other Movers and Shakers that Influence Firm Strategy?

Apart from the movers and shakers of institutional shareholders and senior managers, there are many other stakeholders who do not have direct ownership or management rights over the firm, but depend on the organization to fulfill their own goals and are thus motivated and able to influence the organization's strategy. A range of these stakeholders are depicted as the "roots" nourishing the organizational "tree" in Figure 2.2. It is increasingly the case that if the organization's

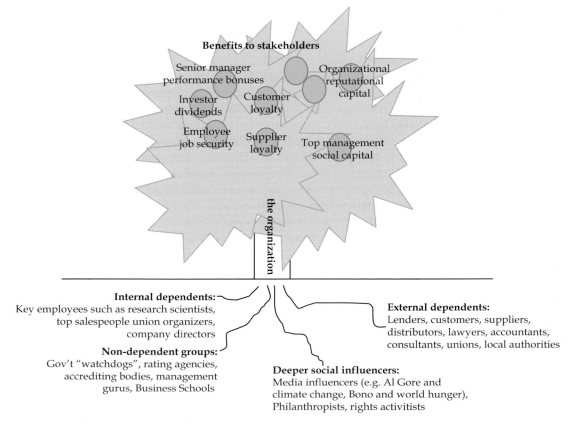

Figure 2.2 A stakeholder root system

owners wish to enjoy the fruits of the organization, their managers must be sure to tend to the roots that sustain or can damage the organization's resources. If key stakeholders withdraw their support they can cause the organization to wither.

As the figure shows, non-shareholding stakeholders can be divided into four stakeholder groups: external dependent; internal dependent; non-dependent; and other, more difficult to categorize, social influencers who may shape opinions in spheres deeper, or further away, from an organization's operating ambit which then come to impact on an organization's strategic choices. We describe these groups and their potential to influence an organization's strategic success or failure below.

External dependent groups

Important **external dependent stakeholders** have the following relations: (1) economic (lenders, customers, suppliers, competitors, distributors) where stakeholders can influence the value creation process; (2) advisory (non-executive Directors, consultants, gurus, business schools, lawyers, accountants); and (3) sociopolitical (local authorities, unions).

1. Economic relations with the firm can be influenced by lenders, who can withdraw funds if a firm acts in ways that are not approved. Or it may be that firms are unable to secure loans for strategies that do not fit with the lenders' views. Substantial customers and suppliers can influence the firm through the withdrawal of orders and supplies or the imposition of less attractive terms and conditions, such as payment terms. Competitors can influence the firm through their actions as well as public statements of intent. For instance, Airbus Industries made public the amount of resources it put into its new super-jumbo aircraft and the contracts it has been awarding for this purpose. This "signaling" is clearly intended to influence its major competitor, Boeing, into reconsidering whether it really wants to compete head on with such a commitment of resources.

2. *Advisory relations* influence the firm by providing ideas and solutions to problems. Non-executive directors perform an important role in having sufficient senior experience to comment on the affairs of the firm but have no management say in the day-to-day running of the organization. Their semi-independent status is an important characteristic to ensure impartiality, and so they should not have a commercial or other interest in the organization beyond drawing a modest remuneration for their time. A key issue, however, is that the company chooses who to appoint.

   Around 90% of Britain's top companies now employ outside consultants to advise them on strategy (a percentage that is typical throughout the Western world). These consultants are part of an industry now worth some $40bn world wide. The executives who pull strings are also increasingly from consulting backgrounds. For instance, the alumni of McKinsey's include the heads of America's Boeing, IBM, Levi-Strauss, and American Express, France's Bull, Germany's BMW and in the UK, Asda, HSBC, Jones Lang LaSalle, Vodafone, the Confederation of British Industry, and the Foreign Secretary in the UK's government. With their connections, consultants are able to collect impressive data and are well placed to tell firms which companies are doing best. They perform an important role as creators and disseminators of information and, in particular, are associated with communicating "best practice." This message is both pervasive and persuasive, although generally relies on clients fearing being left behind in the competitive race rather than staying ahead. Many companies worry about how frequently they use consultants and so we provide some guidance about whether you use them too much in Figure 2.3. The way that consultants look at strategic problems thus also influences the way their clients see the world. For example, McKinsey's philosophy of "Everything can be measured, and what gets measured gets managed" tends to place the emphasis on certain "hard" generic characteristics and generally leads to less of a focus on the unique "softer," more distinctive, or less tangible, aspects of a firm's competitive advantage,[6] like those discussed in Chapter 6, Corporate Identity and Chapter 7, Organic Strategy.

3. *Sociopolitical relations* can have an influence at the local level through different types of business and planning regulation. Unions can influence the firm through organizing employee action.

Internal dependent groups

Internal dependent stakeholders may not have very much influence on top management and company strategy as individuals unless they are a particularly valued resource. For instance, they may have (a) particular skills or knowledge, such as research scientists, (b) a substantial reputation that can move markets, or (c) control of a vital customer relationship. A negative example of this was the

---

ARE YOU ADDICTED TO CONSULTANCY? TEST YOURSELF.

Ask yourself the following questions to find out whether you're over-using consultants:

1. Can you say when you expect your consultant will be leaving the premises permanently?

YES / NO

2. Do you have a good reason for not using somebody internal or not taking someone on as staff to fulfill the consultant's role?

YES / NO

3. Do you have a defined objective for the consultancy you've employed?

YES / NO

4. Do you ask your consultants for advice on matters other than the task for which you hired them?

YES / NO

5. Do your employees refer to the consultant as the "owner" or "manager" of the initiative?

YES / NO

Answer "yes" to the first three questions and "no" to the last two and you're likely to be using consultants sensibly. "No" to the first three and "yes" to the last two means you're using consultants as a crutch rather than as a defined and useful part of your business.

Adapted from "Lost the ability to think for yourself?" by Guy Clapperton, *The Guardian*, 27 October, 2006.

Figure 2.3 Consultancy addiction test

leaked e-mails from the University of East Anglia which threw into doubt claims about climate change. Recent research by Angwin and Paroutis has also shed light on significant C-level executives who are central to many change initiatives in large companies. These Senior Strategy Directors (SSDs) deliberately interface between CEO initiatives and different internal interest groups in order to facilitate change amongst conflicting parties. They also have a boundary spanning role in linking external stakeholders with multiple internal levels of the company, acting as critical links across different social networks. In the words of one SSD, "we are the lubricant in the machine."[7]

Internal stakeholders often achieve greater power where they can group together to achieve collective bargaining power. In France, for example, surgeons grouped together and came en masse to England as a protest to the Government about their terms and conditions of work in France. Internal stakeholders may also align with an external group, such as a union, when internal grouping is insufficient to exert pressure on employers. In the United Kingdom the current strike actions of the Union UNITE, and subsequent interactions between it and the British Airways organization, has caused the British Airways performance and reputation to suffer. It is not unusual for external stakeholders to actively seek linkages with internal stakeholders to achieve their aims. For instance, suppliers may link with purchasing officers, or customers with marketing managers, to represent their interests.

Non-dependent groups

Standing above the stakeholders who are dependent on the firm are **non-dependent stakeholders**, stakeholders who can influence the firm but are not themselves dependent on it. These stakeholders include: (1) governmental bodies, which may be at the industry, regional, national, and supranational levels; (2) technical organizations; and (3) opinion influencers.

1. *Governmental bodies* can influence the firm by setting up regulators to protect interests. For instance, within countries such as the UK, "watchdog" bodies have been set up to represent customer interests. Examples include the Office of Fair Trading (OFT) for protecting the consumer and Ofwat to regulate the price of water supply. More recently a new body has been set up to monitor the quality of schools, and has been nicknamed "Off-Toff"![8] More general frameworks have also been used, such as the Citizen's Charter Initiative in UK public services to raise performance standards on "customer service." In the US, Congressional legislation has been bolstered. In the wake of the collapse of WorldCom, George Bush set up a Corporate Crime Taskforce and gave extra money to the Department of Justice and the Securities and Exchange Commission to pursue corporate wrongdoers. In 2002, Sarbanes–Oxley legislation was rushed into law in response to the Enron scandal. These rules involve an annual assessment of internal controls over financial reporting and certification by the CFO and CEO that the financial statements and accounting practices are accurate. This should remove the "aw, shucks" defense used by lawyers in Bernie Ebber's trial (and used by former Enron bosses), claiming that, as a former milkman with no formal training in accounting, he was incapable of spotting fraud. Although the amount of detail required to satisfy this legislation is perceived as extremely onerous for US companies, it does force them to "comply or explain" and there is evidence that investors are demanding such explanations.

   There are also international bodies that monitor standards, such as Transparency International, which publishes a "perceived corruption index" of countries. This sort of information can influence the decisions of firms to invest abroad and the extent to which they might risk trading in such areas.

   It is interesting to note that following the recent wave of mega-mergers, there are now a number of sizable firms which generate such large amounts of tax revenue that the government cannot be seen as a non-dependent stakeholder. In the UK for instance, BP, Vodafone and Tesco have paid billions of pounds in tax and it is inconceivable that this huge contribution to the Treasury has not given these firms some bargaining power.

2. *Technical organizations* can influence the firm where independent credit rating agencies, such as Standard & Poor's, can directly affect the ability of the firm to raise funds through the direct costs of borrowing as well as influence on share price. With the current oil spill crisis in the Gulf of Mexico, BP's credit rating has been downgraded as investors wonder whether the firm can survive the pressure being put on it by the US Government. Other standards agencies may determine appropriate technology

47

standards for a market. For Business Schools there are several accreditation agencies such as the AACSB, AMBA and EQUIS that exert significant influence on the strategies that can be followed by MBA programs through the promotion and policing of global standards.

3. *Opinion influencers* can have an impact on the firm's strategy by providing the latest ideas and concepts. Here the role of gurus, consultants, and business schools is well documented. The power of thinkers such as Clayton Christensen, Sumantra Ghoshal, Gary Hamel, C.K. Prahalad, Michael Porter, David Teece, and ideas such as the Boston Box, Best Practice, Blue Ocean Strategy, Bottom-of-the-Pyramid, and the Business Process Reengineering to influence management initiatives is clear to see in both profit and not-for-profit organizations (see live Case 2-7 on Fad Power).[9]

Deeper social influencers

In addition to these three main groups of non-shareholding movers and shakers, there are a number of less categorizable opinion influencers that good strategists should not ignore. These include campaigners for broader social issues, such as fighting poverty in Africa. High-profile media stars like Bob Geldof and Bono have organized events, such as Band Aid and Live 8 (mentioned in the introduction to this chapter), which propel issues onto the public stage. At the moment, through tireless campaigning, Geldof among others is attempting to influence the banks of the First World to rescind African debt. Underlying such campaigns is a strong view of what is right and ethical behavior for companies. While it is by no means clear that everyone agrees on what is "right" and "ethical" behavior, as the world consists of very diverse cultural norms and beliefs, there are mounting pressures for socially and environmentally responsible behaviors to be viewed as synonymous with good management and embedded in a firm's strategy. This "corporate social responsibility" (CSR) point of view is gaining ground. There is growing evidence of firms now producing CSR documents and, as we shall see in Chapter 10, Sustain Ability, altering their behavior as a consequence of a backlash from, for instance, consumers disapproving of the use of child labor.

CSR focuses on the embeddedness of the organization in a wider set of social conditions and recognizes that business affects society as well as depending on a set of social conditions, such as quality of workforce, government regulation, etc. to be able to operate and compete. Michael Porter suggests that, at the **generic (or highest) level**, business has little effect on broad social issues. He gives the example that despite a laudable donation from a US software firm in aid of the HIV/AIDs pandemic in Africa, there is little impact either way in this sort of action. However, in terms of focusing on the **value chain** or **operating level** of the firm, he perceives substantial impact in the way that a firm might modify its operations to mitigate harm and improve sustainability. He also perceives overlooked value at the **competitive level**, where the firm's philanthropic efforts can create social change while improving the environment for long-term corporate success. In his view, for firms to be effective and socially responsible, they need to move beyond generalized concepts of good citizenship and set strategic priorities for strategic philanthropy.[10]

How Can Different Stakeholder Interests be Managed Strategically?

The expectations and interests of each stakeholder will differ and often be in conflict. The classic conflicts that may exist include:

- short-term results to suit equity markets versus long-term investments to secure the future success of the firm;
- improve efficiency versus substantial job losses;
- the need for professional managers versus the loss of family control;
- reduce costs versus providing a social necessity;
- public share ownership versus need for more openness and accountability;
- operating locally in one country versus parent ways of operating and expectations located in a different country.

Conflict among stakeholders can be particularly difficult to manage in not-for-profit situations, where there can be much greater diversity among stakeholders and the interactions among them. The greater diversity of providers, resources, recipients, and public/private values produced and a richer set of interactions with the environment all serve to present formidable challenges to not-for-profit senior managers (see live Case 2-6 on Britain's National Health Service). Nevertheless they, like all organizations, need to make decisions (and not doing anything with regard to stakeholder conflicts is still a decision but generally not a very good one!). It is useful, therefore, to map these multiple interests to understand political priorities. This can be done using the tree shape we outlined in Figure 2.2 and thinking through which stakeholders/roots can seriously damage or enhance the health of the organization; or through a power/interest grid, which identifies the level of power a stakeholder has to influence the firm and the level of interest it has in supporting or opposing a particular strategy (see Figure 2.4).

By debating the positioning of different stakeholders and categorizing them graphically on the power/interest matrix, it becomes possible to identify which ones are likely to be key supporters or blockers of a strategy, and to create priority lists, engage in scenario thinking (see Chapter 1), and develop action plans. Moreover, it can help to sharpen ideas about the best means of communicating with the various stakeholder groups (e.g. whether they need only be informed of what an organization is doing after strategic decisions have been made, or whether they must be involved early in the strategy-making process).

A major tool for tending to stakeholders in this regard is lobbying, and most major companies employ specialists, such as public relations officers, relationship managers, or stakeholder relations managers, for the purpose of understanding and potentially influencing key powerful interested parties such as Governments and legislators. Lobbying also exists on a much more micro level as a direct activity, carried out person to person, such as wining and dining a favored client, as well as an indirect one, creating alliances with support groups or significant people in order to bring pressure to bear on a specific stakeholder. For example, despite seeming a long way removed from eBay's business, Geldof and Live 8 were able, through their ability to lobby media attention and public

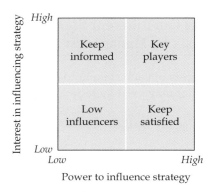

Figure 2.4 Stakeholder power/interest matrix (adapted from Mendelow, 1991)

popularity for their cause, to influence eBay's strategy. They had a lot of power to influence the management of eBay, so the firm had to respond to their concerns. If we look at the other example from the beginning of this chapter though, we can say that the New Zealand Rugby Union (NZRU), while keen to influence what TradeMe were doing, lacked either the necessary public sympathy or clout to influence TradeMe's activities. Hence, TradeMe issued some lukewarm warnings about checking the terms and conditions of rugby tickets before seeking to sell them on and kept the NZRU informed of what was happening on its sites as a courtesy, but the company felt little further compulsion to act.

Categorizing stakeholders on the power/interest grid raises issues of how to manage those who have power and interest. Through the careful use of information, bartering, or negotiation, objections that these stakeholders may have to a strategy may be removed on the grounds that concessions are given on other fronts. This can raise ethical issues for top managers over whether they are, or should be, weighing up the conflicting expectations of stakeholder groups; whether they are answerable to one group, and then work to make those interests acceptable to others; or whether they are really acting in their own interests and managing stakeholders to suit their own purposes.

This returns us to our opening problematic issue of whether CEOs are good agents of shareholders, stewards in looking after the best interests of the firm (and not necessarily prioritizing shareholders) or an agency problem.[11] It is in response to the excesses of some "Imperial CEOs" that there has been a recent rise in legislation and an emboldening of boards of directors and shareholders. They are now beginning to make a difference. Top executives Carly Fiorina (HP), Hank Greenberg (American International Group), and Michael Eisner (Disney) have departed and Sumner Redstone (Viacom) was forced into an extreme downsizing of his firm. In the eyes of some observers, these events mark a very dramatic shift in the balance of power between CEOs and their firms' stakeholders. However, recent research[12] has now begun to question the primacy of shareholders in for-profit firms in Anglo-American business models. Investigating legal theory, these researchers find that shareholders do not own the corporation, which is an autonomous legal person. Indeed when directors go against the wishes of shareholders, courts generally support the directors even when there is a loss in corporation value. In other parts of the world, primacy is not given to shareholders with some governance systems explicitly recognizing the importance of employees in workers councils for instance. Nevertheless other researchers have found that directors may cut down mature forests or release dangerous toxins in order to maximize shareholder wealth.[13] This raises interesting questions about the role of the institutional context in shaping directors' roles – the interplay between institutes of directors, lawyers and business schools in communicating and educating directors on their real roles, as it is the acting out of these roles that can seriously affect strategic decisions. For instance, in the recent acquisition of Cadbury – the venerable UK chocolate maker, by the giant US food giant, Kraft Foods – conventional wisdom tells us that management sold out to maximize shareholder value. However, if directors should give more weight to the futures of their employees (Kraft subsequently sold a factory and dismissed employees), the health of communities, and possibly the longevity of deeply embedded corporate values, then the sale may not have been the best outcome. Following public and political pressure the UK government is now considering whether the takeover rules should be changed to enable longer term interests to be considered more fully.

Movers and Shakers Key Learnings Mind Map

Having read and reviewed the chapter outline what do you believe to be the key learnings from the chapter and the relationships between these on the notes pages below.

2-1 Disney: Disney versus Disney

On May 9, 2005, following the appointment of Robert Iger as the CEO designate and successor to Michael Eisner, former Directors Roy E. Disney and Stanley P. Gold filed a lawsuit in the Delaware Chancery Court against the Walt Disney Co. and certain members of the Board of Directors of the company alleging that the Board made false statements to the company's shareholders about its CEO search. This represented the latest salvo in the corporate governance battle between Disney and Gold and the management and Board of Directors of the company.

The roots of this battle can be traced back to 1984 when, following a long period of relative decline reflected in both its stock price and profits, a power struggle at the company was eventually won by a group of shareholders led by Directors Roy E. Disney (nephew of Walt Disney and son of Roy O. Disney, the co-founders of Walt Disney Productions) and Stanley Gold (Disney's close friend, attorney, and financial adviser). The existing management was replaced by Michael Eisner (Chairman and CEO) and Frank Wells (President). Both were equals in the sense that they reported directly to the Board, with Eisner seen as the "creative talent" and Wells the "businessman."

Over the next 10 years the stock price rose 6,000%, the company opened EuroDisney, made numerous successful films and TV shows, expanded Disney World, and purchased a number of TV stations and sports franchises. Eisner was lauded as one of the great CEOs of the 1980s and 1990s. The partnership tragically ended in April 1994, when Frank Wells was killed in a helicopter crash.

From then on the company, dominated by Eisner, who temporarily held the positions of President and Chief Operating Officer along with Chairman and Chief Executive Officer, entered a period characterized by management changes, poor investments, and an underperforming stock price. In 1994 Jeffery Katzenberg, the executive responsible for the most successful animated film ever – *The Lion King* – left after a clash with Eisner, eventually receiving a payoff worth $275m. The following year, Michael Ovitz became Disney President, only to leave 14 months later, with a $140m severance package, once again following a disagreement with Eisner.

In 1996, Disney purchased Capital Cities/ABC for $19bn – the largest media takeover to date and the second largest acquisition of a US firm. When it was acquired, ABC owned the leading television network in the United States but, by 2002, it was ranked third among the three leading television networks. Other notable failures included a botched plan to build an American history theme park; the loss of millions of dollars on a new California Adventure attraction at Disneyland; and a $1bn loss attempting to replicate Yahoo!'s internet portal. The acquisition of Fox Family Channel in 2001, for $5.3bn, was widely perceived to be at an exorbitant price.

At this time, Disney's Board of Directors included Eisner's friends Sidney Poitier (the actor), Robert A.M. Stern (the architect who designed many Disney properties), and George Mitchell (the former Senator, who consulted for Disney). The Board's judgment was seen as particularly questionable with regard to the compensation packages it approved for Eisner, who in the 20 years of service following his appointment received total compensation worth almost $1bn. In the eyes of Roy Disney and Stanley Gold, these questionable decisions around remuneration as well as group strategy were enough to prompt them to begin a campaign in 2000 to force the Board to become more independent of Eisner and to develop a plan for his eventual succession.

During November 2003 Roy E. Disney resigned from the Board because he was not included in the list of Directors for the next election. In his open letter of resignation, in which he claims the company has lost its creative direction, Disney blames Eisner for micro-management and the refusal to establish a clear succession plan. He concludes by saying: " . . . it is my sincere belief that it is you who should be leaving not me. Accordingly, I once again call for your resignation or retirement" (www.savedisney.com/letters/red_resign_letter.asp).

The following month Stanley Gold resigned from the Board and also published his letter of resignation. He criticizes the Board for " . . . not actively engaging in serious discussions regarding the Company's flawed plans and management's unmet projections and unfilled promises" (www.savedisney.com/letters/spg_resign_letter.asp).

Of course, it may be that these negative comments from disposed Directors are sour grapes, but in February 2004, Comcast announced a hostile bid for Disney worth $54 bn in stock. The bid was rejected and Comcast did not pursue it further. However, the annual shareholder meeting that followed saw 45.37% of shareholders withhold their vote for Eisner. Later in the day it was announced that Mitchell would replace Eisner as Chairman of the Board.

In September, Eisner announced that he would retire when his contract expired in September 2006. This 2-year transition period was heavily criticized for being too long, increasing uncertainty, handicapping the development of corporate strategy, and creating a "lame duck" CEO. Eisner also made it clear that Robert Iger was his personal choice as successor. Company President and Chief Operating Officer, George Mitchell, who led the search for the new CEO, also announced that Robert Iger was the only internal candidate for the post.

Iger was appointed Eisner's successor on March 13, 2005 and, after a 6-month period of working in tandem with Eisner would then assume the post of CEO. Eisner would remain on the Board until September 2006.

According to Roy Disney and Stanley Gold, although the Board promised shareholders that it would conduct the CEO search with "open minds" and with no predeterminations or preconditions, in reality, the Board's CEO selection process precluded serious and effective consideration of external candidates. In particular, they were dissatisfied with Michael Eisner's presence, or expected presence, at the interviews of external candidates and by reports that the Board interviewed only one external candidate, delayed notifying her of any decision, and did little to dissuade her from withdrawing her candidacy. They claimed that the Board had failed to properly fulfill its corporate governance responsibilities, including its paramount task – the search for a CEO – and that it was not appropriate for Eisner, who had already decided who his successor should be, to participate in the candidate reviews.

1. *What are the problems with Eisner holding several offices in this case?*
2. *How should the Board have gone about appointing a new CEO?*
3. *How should an independent Director be defined and how should Directors be appointed to the Board?*

◄◄◄ Disney vs. Disney: Some ideas toward a "model answer"…

Disney vs. Disney raises a number of issues of importance to the ongoing debate about corporate governance. Although the Board should not be involved directly in the management of the business, it is responsible for the company's overall strategy and should approve any major changes in the company's strategic direction and management structure. This case provides a good example of what can happen when a company's Board lacks the independence to effectively separate itself from the company's management.

Although common in the USA, the same individual holding the position of both Chairman and Chief Executive Officer can create problems (see question 2 above). In addition, many of the Board's members were appointed to the Board by Eisner (see question 3) and/or had a business relationship with the company (e.g. Robert A.M. Stern, architectural work; Senator George Mitchell, consulting). Roy E. Disney and Andre Van de Kamp – two Directors who were critics of Eisner – were forced to leave the Board.

This led to claims by Stanley P. Gold that Disney has "… an insular Board of Directors serving as a bulwark to shield management from criticism and accountability." It could be argued that the Board had become little more than a rubber stamp, automatically endorsing Eisner's actions. In the 5 years up to August 2002, Disney was the worst performing stock among the 30 companies that make up the Dow Jones Industrial Average. However, the Board did nothing to question Eisner's judgment regarding unsuccessful investments during this period, including the acquisitions of the ABC TV network and the Fox Family Channel, and the loss of more than $1 bn invested in the go.com internet portal.

The role of the Board in awarding Eisner a total compensation package worth $737 m in the 5 years up to 2001, a period in which company profits fell and the company's stock underperformed the overall market, raises questions about the criteria used to decide his remuneration.

Another key role of the Board of Directors is to ensure that an appropriate succession plan is in place covering the key executive positions in the company. This was not the case at Disney. Potential successors to Eisner – Katzenberg and Ovitz – were both forced out by him at great expense to shareholders. There was an absence of a succession plan should Eisner leave the company and he resisted any attempts to implement one. The Board should have challenged him about this and through the Nominations Committee identified a potential successor.

Finally, it can be argued that Eisner's role in the appointment of Iger as his successor as CEO reduces Iger's credibility, making a difficult job even harder.

1. What are the problems you see in the case with Eisner holding several offices?

From his appointment in 1984 until March 2004, Michael Eisner was both Chairman of the Board and Chief Executive Officer of Disney and for a short period following the death of Frank Gates he also held the positions of President and Chief Operating Officer. Although, unlike the UK (where the corporate governance code recommends against it), it is not uncommon in the USA for the same person to be both Chairman and CEO, it does mean that the responsibilities of the head of the company (the Chairman, who leads the Board and looks after shareholders' interests, and the Chief Executive

Officer, who leads the executive, who manage the company on a day-to-day basis) are held by the same person. This has the potential for conflict if the Chief Executive's interests differ from those of the company's owners – the shareholders. Many commentators argue that the most important task a company's Chairman will be called upon to perform is to "fire" the Chief Executive Officer. Obviously, if the Chairman and CEO is the same person, this is unlikely to happen.

As in the case of Eisner, when he held four key positions, the question has to be asked: How is it possible for one person to have sufficient time to undertake the responsibilities of these positions effectively?

2. *How should the Board have gone about appointing a new CEO?*

The search for a new CEO should be undertaken by the Nominations Committee, which, in the UK, would normally be headed by an independent Director (possibly the Chairman). It should decide on the balance of skills, knowledge, and experience required and prepare a description of the role and capabilities expected of the new CEO. In most cases, the company would then appoint a specialist external search consultant – "headhunter" – to identify and make the initial approach to potential candidates. The next stage would be for all members of the Board to meet, preferably on an individual basis, with a shortlist of candidates determined by the Nomination Committee based on the search consultant's recommendations. After considerable discussion, the Board members would then vote on the appointment, hoping that a split among the members would not become apparent. Should a member of the Board have strong reservations concerning the successful candidate, it would be necessary for him or her to consider whether it was possible to remain as a member of the Board.

3. *How should an independent Director be defined and how should Directors be appointed to the Board?*

The definition of an independent Director varies internationally. Generally, to be "independent," a Director must have no connection to the company other than a seat on the Board. This excludes full-time employees of the company, family members of employees, and the company's lawyer, banker, and consultants. Some definitions include people with connections to the company, such as suppliers, customers, debtors, and creditors. Others include direct or indirect recipients of corporate charitable donations. The latest version of the UK Combined Code on Corporate Governance (2003) states that a Director is not independent if he or she:

(a) has been an employee of the company or group within the last 5 years;
(b) has, or has had within the last 3 years, a material business relationship with the company either directly, or as a partner, shareholder, Director or senior employee of a body that has such a relationship with the company;
(c) has received or receives additional remuneration from the company apart from a Director's fee, participates in the company's share option or a performance-related pay scheme, or is a member of the company's pension scheme;

(d) has close family ties with any of the company's advisers, Directors, or senior employees;

(e) holds cross-Directorships or has significant links with other Directors through involvement in other companies or bodies;

(f) represents a significant shareholder;

(g) has served on the Board for more than 9 years from the date of their first election.

In the USA and the UK, the nomination of individuals for election by the shareholders to the Board of Directors is normally handled by a Nominating Committee. This is largely, if not entirely, made up of independent Directors. They make recommendations concerning potential Directors to the full Board of Directors who, if they agree, then ask the shareholders to approve their nomination. In theory, the Nomination Committee should work independently of the other Board members, including the CEO. However, as this case study shows, this is frequently not the case, with the CEO and/or Chairman often making "recommendations" to the Nominations Committee.

In the UK, a separate section of the annual report should describe the work of the Nomination Committee, including the process used in relation to Board appointments. An explanation should be given if neither an external search consultancy nor open advertising has been used in the appointment of a Chairman or a non-executive Director.

▶▶▶

Case Notes:

2-2 Safeway: Changing the face of industry

On January 9, 2003, Wm Morrison, the UK's fourth largest food retailer, announced a £2.9bn offer for its larger rival, Safeway PLC. Morrisons was concentrated in the north of England while Safeway's chain of stores was located mainly in the Midlands and the south of England.

UK consumers buy 80% of their food, 75% of fresh vegetables and fruit, 65% of fish and meat, and 50% of their milk from the five largest supermarkets. The supermarket industry as a whole is worth some £100bn a year. However, overall growth rates had slowed to 2.9%, which was equal to the growth of the economy as a whole. In the last few years, overseas supermarket giants had entered the industry, with Wal-Mart of the USA (the world's largest retailer) purchasing Asda in June 1999 and discount operators Aldi, Netto, and Lidl setting up their own operations. To compete in this more difficult market and with these global players, the UK supermarkets had to become more powerful and larger.

It may not be surprising, then, that just 1 week after the Morrison bid, J. Sainsbury confirmed its interest in Safeway, followed by Asda registering its interest and delivering details of its bid, except the price, to the Office of Fair Trading. Meanwhile, rumors that Kohlberg Kravis Roberts, the American buyout giant, was interested were also confirmed just as Safeway's broker of 10 years, CSFB, swapped sides to help the bid. It was also rumored that the entrepreneur Michael Green was looking closely at the opportunity. The retail giant Tesco, however, was thought unlikely to bid because it would then have 35% of the UK market and this would undoubtedly be blocked by the regulator on the grounds of it being anti-competitive.

With potential overconcentration in the supermarket industry about to occur, the Office of Fair Trading (OFT) referred the takeover bid (Morrisons) to the Competition Commission, whose role it is to protect the public interest and ensure that excessive concentration in an industry will not result from a merger and potentially damage consumer interests. Rivalry between companies is viewed as a healthy virtue by the regulator as it encourages competition and innovation and allows the possibility of new entrants into the industry. In looking at the overall concentration of the supermarket industry, the Commission realized that while the overall market share of the supermarkets was 69.2% for all stores, for stores over 2,300 m^2 it was 95.2%. Calculating the weighted Herfindahl–Hirschman Index (HHI) for industry concentration gave a figure of 2,672, which is very high given that scores above 1,800 are considered indicative of concentrated markets.

Crucial to whether an industry is concentrated is the definition of the industry itself. In 2000 there had been an inquiry into the concentration of the supermarket industry and the distance the consumer had to travel for choice between competitors was a critical issue. A 15-minute driving time rule had been developed as a test and now this was used again to assess shopper choice in their immediate neighborhood.

To assess the likelihood that a further acquisition in the sector might damage the public interest, the Competition Commission requested submissions from interested parties at the Haberdasher's Hall in London. In this grand City setting, packed with Chief Executives, Directors, bankers, and lawyers, with combined personal wealth of tens of millions of pounds, the hearing took place.

Morrisons: "We need the merger to enable us to compete effectively with the larger players. We would "leap-frog" to third place in the sector, running a close race with Sainsbury's. Combining with Safeway will increase our market share to 16%, which is below the threshold of 25% at which the OFT would normally investigate. Combining with Safeway would have the least effect of potential supermarket bidders on the HHI. There are very few geographic areas where we overlap with Safeway. Unfortunately, since the bid, our share price has plummeted, wiping 15% off the value of our bid."

Sainsbury's: "Amalgamating with Safeway will confirm our position as number two and help us resist global players. It would result in significant industry concentration. Our sales proposition is different to Safeway's low price strategy. However, we do realize that a successful bid would heavily indebt the group and since announcement our share price has already fallen 11%."

Asda: The bookies' favourite, Asda argued that the deal would make it number two in the UK. "With a combined market share of 26%, together with Tesco, we would control over 50% of the market which the Competition Commission would see as against the public interest." A substantial sale of many Safeway stores in the North and Scotland, where both groups were strong, would be likely. There would also likely be a ferocious price war with Tesco post-deal.

Philip Green: "I have a lot of experience in clothes retailing through my ownership of clothing retailers BHS and Arcadia. Owning Safeway will allow me to sell clothing through those outlets which currently have few non-food items. My bid does not trigger market concentration issues."

KKR: "Safeway is underperforming. We could run it for 5 to 7 years to improve operations and then sell it off. We do not trigger market concentration issues."

Consumers' Association: "The reduction in the number of major supermarkets will reduce the overall level of competition in the industry. There will be a reduction in product offering and that may lead to price increases. Consumer interests will be damaged."

Smaller supermarkets: "Most supermarkets now offer a wide range of items, including newspapers, dry-cleaning, pharmacies, post-office outlets, petrol, and a huge range of "non-grocery" items such as clothes and electronics. The overall effect has been to decrease the number of smaller and independent operators."

Small and convenience stores: "Further amalgamation will damage our businesses even more. Already many convenience stores have closed, unable to compete with the scale economies of supermarkets. Further amalgamation would drive them out of business. During the last 10 years, 425 superstores have opened and 25,000 corner shops have closed."

Paul Rhodes: The pig farmer of the year and Chairman of United Pig Marketing told Sir Derek Morris's panel of competition experts that the supermarket slogan of "every day low prices really stands for every day less pigs." In 1997, pig farmers received 50% of the value of the pig. This has gone down to 38% and more than 35% of the pig industry has gone out of business. Since 1998, the production of pigs in the UK has halved but consumers have not reduced the amount they eat, so the gap is filled from abroad. The industry is in intensive care.

Somerset cheese farmers: "The increasing scale of purchase by supermarkets has given them enormous bargaining power. This has greatly depressed our margins to the point of driving some of us out of business. If this trend continues, further exits are inevitable and to attempt to avoid this situation, the prices charged to convenience businesses will have to rise to compensate."

Makers of branded goods: "The Competition Commission enquiry in 2000 recommended that sharp practices be curbed – where supermarkets force a supplier to cut the price of one of its best-selling lines in order to win shelf space for a new product. There have been no complaints since then, because who would complain against their biggest customer?"

Friends of the Earth: "The 2000 report's Supermarket Code is not working and suppliers are being leaned on. No mergers should be allowed."

In considering these submissions, the Competition Commission also considered that it would probably have to formulate a remedies statement requiring the successful bidder to take certain actions to avoid problems they identified. For Sainsbury's, such a remedies statement would probably require the disposal of some 90 to 130 Safeway stores to avoid prejudicing customers. A potentially awkward consideration was that Lord Sainsbury is a major shareholder and a Minister within the Department of Trade and Industry, which has overall responsibility for the bid. For Morrisons, around 30 stores would probably need to be divested and for Asda, assuming that the bid could succeed, the number would be very substantial. Another important consideration was whether the merger would make it more difficult for other new players to enter the industry. Table 2-2.1 provides key data on market share, turnover, profitability and size by major supermarket companies. Their competitive position is illustrated in a growth share matrix analysis shown in Figure 2-2.1.

Table 2-2.1 Supermarket industry (April 2003)

	Market share (%)	T/O (£bn)	PTP (£m)	EPS (p)	Employees	Stores (UK)
Tesco	25.8	26.33	1,401	13.98	296,000	730
Sainsbury's	17.4	18.20	571	21.5	173,000	463
Safeway	10.0	9.40	335	24.4	92,000	480
Asda*	15.9	n/a	810 (est)	n/a	117,000	258
Morrisons**	5.9	3.92	243	10.0	46,000	119

* Owned by Wal-Mart (US), T/O £150 bn, PTP £7.6 bn
** Only in North England

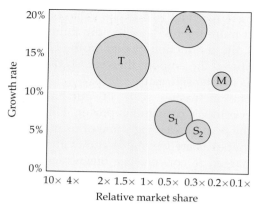

Key: T = Tesco, A = Asda,
S₁ = Sainsbury's, S₂ = Safeway,
M = Morrissons
Size of circle = profitability

Figure 2-2.1 Growth share matrix

1. Why did the takeover battle come about at this time? And what, or who, were the drivers for this battle and how are they moving or shaking Morrisons' strategy?
2. Using the stakeholder power/interest matrix, discuss the main issues the regulator should consider. Which issues should determine what bidder(s) can proceed?
3. If you were CEO of Safeway, what would you have looked for in a deal? If you were CEO of one of the bidding companies, and you thought that you wouldn't win the battle, what would you have done next?

Case Notes:

2-3 Carlton: Shareholder revolution

As Carlton and ITV rival Granada pursued a $7.5bn merger, an extraordinary battle of wills blew up between institutional shareholders and top management, threatening to undermine the deal. A group of institutional shareholders wanted the removal of Michael Green (Executive Chairman and founder of Carlton TV) while non-executive Directors insisted that they would not be forced to jettison him without detailed negotiations.

Sir George Russell, the Deputy Chairman of Granada and its Senior non-executive Director, chaired an emergency meeting of the Granada Board that lasted for 3 hours and focused on Mr. Green stepping down as Chairman of the merged companies of Carlton Communications and Granada Group. Sir George was reported to have never seen such shareholder power massed against a single executive and, in the words of Will Hutton writing for *The Observer* newspaper, "it was, in truth, the loudest attack on a company chairman I have ever witnessed." Granada's Board's backing of rebellious shareholders, who held 33% of Granada's and 36% of Carlton's shares, calling for an independent non-executive to be appointed as Chairman of the enlarged company, extinguished Mr. Green's ambitions. The Board said it wanted to go forward "with the full support of its shareholders." Although Mr. Green, founder of Carlton TV, had presided over the firm's growth, through multiple acquisitions and mergers, to its current size of £4.6bn, many investors perceived him to be arrogant, overpaid, and incompetent. He was reportedly capable of incandescent rage like few other people and he was often at odds with shareholders, which earned him a reputation for indifference to the wishes of the company's shareholders. In terms of overpayment, he latterly received a salary of £843,000, an annual bonus of £670,000, benefits of £47,000, had taken £100m out of the company by selling shares, and currently held 10.2 million Carlton shares worth £22.5m (October 2003). Mr. Green also owned five types of share options with those in the money being worth £4.3m, was entitled to a pension of £134,000 from age 60, could be awarded severance pay, and had the right to a cash bonus of £707,000. His supposed incompetence related to the loss of $2bn in the ill-fated attempt to give ITV a digital broadcasting platform, On Digital. He was also blamed for the loss of advertising revenue and pre-tax losses of previous years.

Once the Competition Commission cleared the way for Granada to take over Carlton and deliver ITV as one integrated television contractor, the big shareholders were able to call for new leadership. The "quiet assassin," Tony Bolton, manager of US fund-managed Fidelity Group in £2.6bn Special Situations Fund and leader of the shareholder campaign, issued an ultimatum for Mr. Green to step down, saying it would call an extraordinary general meeting of shareholders if its demands were not met on Tuesday, October 28, 2003. Michael Green was removed unwillingly from his post.

In an attempt to appease Fidelity and other disaffected shareholders, Carlton offered a three-point plan to avert a shareholder revolt. This included making Mr. Green non-executive Chairman in May 2005; the appointment of an independent Deputy Chairman and to seek two other non-executives for the ITV Board. Mr. Bolton found this proposal counterproductive and disappointing and felt there was a window of opportunity for change.

The implications of such shareholder activeness are that the success in removing Mr. Green may give investors the appetite for outright confrontation with other management Boards in the future rather than behind the scenes negotiations. These fears may be justified in the light of a number of controversial decisions. Investors are reported to be unhappy with: Matt Barratt, CEO of Barclays, aiming to become Chairman after a disastrous performance in front of the Treasury Select Committee; the elevation of James Murdoch, 30, to the Board of BSkyB, where he may be more interested in representing the interests of the 35.4% holder, The News Corporation, rather than other investors; and the intention of Sir Peter Davis to step up to Chairmanship of Sainsbury's after the Group's poor performance.

1. Why did a group of institutional shareholders want the removal of Michael Green, and how did they engineer Green's demise?
2. Why does Tony Bolton have such interest and such power?
3. What can other CEOs do to avoid a similar fate to that of Michael Green?

Case Notes:

2-4 Lafarge and Blue Circle: Repel borders

On January 21, 2000, the giant French buildings materials group, Lafarge, launched an all-cash hostile bid for Blue Circle PLC, the sixth largest cement producer in the world. At 430 pence per share, the offer valued the target at £3.4 bn and represented a premium of just 1.4% over Blue Circle's closing middle market price. At the time, the dot.com bubble was in full swing and fund managers were desperate to release money tied up in unfashionable "old economy" stocks, which appeared overvalued. Lafarge was the only real bidder for Blue Circle and was confident after an earlier acquisition. The slim premium offered seemed a shrewd move. If the takeover bid succeeded, Lafarge would become the largest cement company in the world.

Lafarge attacked Blue Circle for mistakes made in the past, including the diversification strategy of the 1980s and early 1990s which resulted in a number of subsequent losses on disposal. Blue Circle had then not expanded internationally through cement acquisitions to the same extent as its competitors and was now heavily dependent on too few countries, which meant its profitability was inherently volatile. Its new CEO, Rick Haythornthwaite, appointed in July 1999, argued that Blue Circle's recent expansion into Asia was an enviable achievement, but he was also conscious that just after taking office he had had to announce a profits warning, which had affected Blue Circle's share price.

For Blue Circle the first critical issue was what value to put on the firm. The valuations prepared by City analysts were generally around 500 pence. Blue Circle's adviser's valuation was in line with this and seemed reasonable provided profit forecasts in the business plan were achievable. Haythornthwaite recognized, however, that the firm tended to achieve actual results lower than planned, and instructed them to reduce their profit forecasts, which led to a revised valuation of the business at a relatively conservative 486 pence.

Blue Circle's first formal response to Lafarge's offer document was to assert that the offer undervalued the company and to claim that the bid was a "quest for our Asian assets, which justifies our investment strategy." The final dividend for the year was raised to 10.95 pence per share, which was now in line with the industry. Assets were revalued and a profit forecast issued for the Asian businesses to convince shareholders that those investments would pay off in the short term.

On April 6, Blue Circle announced its operational improvements program (OIP). The document announced details of the projected benefits arising from such cost savings and included forecasts of £116 m of benefits per annum to be achieved by 2002.

The final salvo in Blue Circle's defense was on April 11, 2000. Blue Circle announced that it would return £800 m to shareholders in advance. The first tranche of £400 m was to take place by way of a tender offer for Blue Circle's shares. This return of capital was in effect a down payment to shareholders demonstrating the confidence of management in delivering the promises they had made. Blue Circle's gearing increased significantly (17.2% in 1999 to 107.7% in 2000) and free cash flow available for future projects was reduced dramatically.

At the same time Haythornthwaite reviewed a number of other options. "Many were dismissed because they did not give cash to shareholders, and because of the reluctance of other parties to get involved." The pressure from shareholders for cash was palpable: "The only consideration of shareholders was cash. They were not interested in any wider responsibilities to the company and there was a total lack of engagement," said an Executive Committee member.

Options considered but rejected were a management buyout, a large acquisition, a white squire defense (where another firm would invest in new Blue Circle equity), and a white knight (where a friendly company would take them over). For various reasons, no other companies wished to be involved in this way.

On April 19, day 46 of the bid, Lafarge launched a dawn raid and picked up 19.9% of Blue Circle directly and a further 9.6% through its bankers. Lafarge then increased its offer to £4.50 per share and was confident of victory.

During the last 10 days of the offer period, Haythornthwaite and his Finance Director held a number of meetings with institutional investors to persuade them to back management and reject the bid. As day 60 approached, the lobbying of shareholders paid off when Schroeder's Bank publicly backed the incumbent management and other shareholders followed. On May 3, the bid lapsed as Lafarge's acceptances and holdings totaled 44.5% of Blue Circle shares. This was the first all-cash bid for a FTSE 100 company to fail for 15 years.

Collomb, the Lafarge CEO, was severely shaken with the failure and the defeat was seen by many as a personal failure. It is highly unlikely that he would have launched another hostile bid for Blue Circle in 2001 as he would not have been prepared to risk failure again.

Haythornthwaite was widely fêted by commentators for his successful defense of Blue Circle. "The smile on Rick Haythornthwaite's face says it all. His success in beating off a cash bid in a market where cash was clearly king has propelled a little known executive into prominence. With the target having seemed doomed at the outset, the escape was seen to be a considerable personal victory for Rick Haythornthwaite" (*Financial Times*, May 6, 2000).

Blue Circle was left with a major competitor effectively owning 32.2% of the firm. To remain independent, a major acquisition was needed but, with such a large minority shareholder, potential partners were not interested. The group also had to deliver on defense promises, which analysts suspected might have been too ambitious. Haythornthwaite also realized that forecast operating profits were significantly below analysts' estimates and earnings quality appeared to be deteriorating.

Haythornthwaite presented three strategy options to the Board to deal with Blue Circle's relative short-term strength but medium-term weakness: (1) achieve an early deal with Lafarge; (2) make an acquisition to move out of Lafarge's reach; (3) execute a merger with another party. Considerable time and resources had been devoted to evaluating acquisitions of or mergers with various parties but the Board decided that negotiations should begin with Lafarge. Lafarge offered £4.70 with no dividend but Haythornthwaite needed to present the deal as being worth over £5.00 per share in order to recommend it to shareholders. The advisers to both sides worked in the period up to and over Christmas, finally agreeing a deal at £4.95 per share plus a final dividend. A Board meeting on Sunday January 7, 2001 recommended the offer to shareholders.

The vast majority of Blue Circle's shareholders were institutions and readily agreed to the bid, which was regarded by analysts as being "a sensibly priced deal." However, many individual shareholders, who were mainly ex-employees with an emotional attachment to the firm, voted against the takeover, as they saw Blue Circle as a "British Institution." Nevertheless, the deal was completed and Lafarge's shares responded favorably. As for Haythornthwaite, he left Blue Circle on July 11, 2001 and on July 24, 2001, it was announced he would become CEO of Invensys PLC.

1. *Why was Blue Circle bid for?*
2. *Was it in the interests of Blue Circle's shareholders for the hostile bid to fail?*
3. *Were the defense strategies adopted by Blue Circle consistent with reducing the chance of takeover but not prejudicial toward its shareholders? Did Haythornthwaite act in his own best interests or those of his shareholders?*

Case Notes:

2-5 Brasila: Brazil's New Diplomatic Power

Much has been made in recent years about the rise of the so-called BRIC nations (Brazil, Russia, India, and China), but of these four countries Brazil's rise has attracted the least attention. Its apparent lack of indigenous global brands may have helped Brazil to "fly under the radar," although a closer look reveals growing corporate strength: Petrobras is a giant on anyone's terms; Embraer is now the world's third largest manufacturer of civilian aircraft; and Havaianas flip-flops are now prevalent on beaches across the globe.

So how did a country that lacks the sheer economic size, military muscle, strategic location at the center of the world's population, and obvious world-leading companies, come to be a member of this new club of movers and shakers. A good portion of Brazil's success in this regard may be related to the skillful recalibration of its Diplomatic Corp and to that Corp's subsequent ability to successfully lobby on Brazil's behalf. A recent article in *Monocle* magazine attributed Brazil's rise to seven key (or "corp") steps:

1. Creating and generously funding a special school for grooming Brazilian diplomats

Since President Lula took power in 2002, Brasilia's Rio Branco Institute has been turning out over 100 new Brazilian diplomats a year (before this it only produced 25). As a consequence, there are now 1,400 Brazilian diplomats around the world, 40% more than a decade ago. In addition to having excellent grades, prospects have to pass a tough public exam to gain entry. Many will spend several years just preparing for the test. From the day they are admitted students are not called students; they are called diplomats. After graduating from the two-year program, graduates will be fluent in Portuguese, English and at least one other language

2. Having a foreign minister with serious clout

Foreign Minister Celso Amorim may be Lula's closest ally and confidant. Many assume that he will be his leader's choice to succeed him as President. If an organization wants to promote the importance and influence of a particular element of its operations, be it diplomacy for a government or marketing for a business, then the head of that department must have a seat at the highest table.

3. Investing in new and uniquely Brazilian-looking embassies

An unprecedented embassy building boom emphasizing Brazil's unique architectural heritage (most obviously personified by the work of Oscar Niemeyer) has seen Brazil's network of influence extend over a whole new range of countries. And this reaching out is being reciprocated. In the eight years since President Lula came to power, almost 40 new embassies have opened in Brasilia.

4. Developing and building its own fleet of diplomatic planes

Brazil's diplomats are helping out local industry through its contracting of Embraer to build a special fleet of diplomatic corp planes to facilitate the growing number of air-miles being clocked up by its ambassadorial staff.

5. Championing a "new view of world politics"

Unencumbered by alliances shaped around historical poles such as East versus West, Brazil has been actively building new alliances and offering a "third way" in world diplomacy providing a focal point for those disaffected by or tired with the old ways of seeing things.

6. *Using Brazilian culture to woo new friends*

Brazilians and Brazil's vibrant culture are loved the world over. Brazil's diplomats are schooled in this and they seek to use it and Brazil's non-threatening image to its advantage.

7. *Showcasing a new purpose-built foreign ministry*

Brazil's Ministry of External Relations, or the Itamaraty Palace as most people call it, is larger that any of the other ministries in Brasilia – and so is its power. When foreign dignitaries visit, they often comment on the "Palace's" grandeur.

While many of these elements may seem airy-fairy, they are being pursued with a serious intent to clear strategic goals: which include Brazil's key aim of winning a permanent seat at the United Nation's Security Council. Many are now seeing this goal as within their grasp, and are talking up Brazil and relating its potential clout on the world stage to that of China.

While Brazilian diplomats are pleased to be recognized as increasingly important, they are also keen to point out that Brazil is different from its other BRIC-mates. The country's economic and social system may seem chaotic to outsiders, but its human-rights record and working conditions appears superior to those found in many parts of the other BRICS. Brazilians will proudly point out that the Havaianas Company recently explored the possibility of moving production to China, before realizing that the essence of the brand was inseparable from its Made in Brazil label and unique Brazilian rubber.

Since the team led by Rio de Janeiro's mayor Eduardo Paes won the bid to host the 2016 Olympics a growing number of commentators have suggested the '10s may be "Brazil's Decade," but there is still much work to be done. The *Monocle* concluded its editorial for its "Brazil Issue" by suggesting some ways that Brazil's diplomats might further move and shake the wider world's perception of "Brand Brazil":

- Create a global, public service new organization broadcasting in Portuguese and other languages (like the BBC) and staff it with the smartest and best-looking people Brazil can offer.
- Help to promote a new Brazilian architectural language.
- Make Brazil synonymous with excellent service across all sectors.
- Turn a Brazilian airline into a global mega-carrier to match the emergence of the gulf airlines like Emirates.

---

1. *Do you think that lobbying prospective partners and other stakeholders is a key skill in developing effective strategies and achieving strategic goals?*
2. *If so, what might other organizations learn from the Brazilian Diplomatic Corp?*
3. *What advice would you add to that given by the editors of Monocle to further build Brazil's strategic influence in the world?*

2-6 The NHS: Merry men and Virgins

As a means of demonstrating how students of strategy, like management consultants, or anyone else for that matter, can bring assumptions based on their own experience to bear on problems that may require a different mindset, we often use a little exercise based on Robin Hood and his merry men. Robin has a problem, which is described below. The question we pose to students is: Robin has hired you as a management consultant; what would you advise him to do?

Robin Hood's revolt against the Sheriff of Nottingham began as a personal dispute. But Robin knew that he could do little to exact his revenge without the help of others. So, he set out to find allies – men with similar grievances that he could unite under a common cause. He did not have to look very hard, and as he looked back on the first year of his operation he was still surprised at how quickly he had gathered around him able men who shared his personal hatred of the Sheriff and his overlord – the brutal Prince John, who ruled, unjustly in Robin's eyes, in the absence of Richard the Lionheart.

There had been little structure or routine to the establishment of the band of merry men that had emerged. Robin asked few questions of his charges and their motives and only required that they trusted his ultimate decision-making authority and gave their all in pursuit of what had become their motto: "rob from the rich and give to the poor." Under Robin's rule, a simple structure had evolved with particular tasks delegated to those who Robin saw as his most able lieutenants, such as Will Scarlett, Little John, and Friar Tuck.

But, as the legend of the merry men spread, so the number of recruits from further afield increased. Some came with a taste for adventure; others with a desire, or need, to live outside of the law. As the band grew larger, what was once but a few tents was turning into an established camp with an increased range of ancillary services attached. More and more men spent more and more time sitting around waiting to be organized and waiting for adventure. The cost of maintaining this organization was on the rise.

In the meantime, revenue was declining. The rich were becoming more adept at avoiding capture by Robin's less than nimble organization and the Sheriff and Prince John were becoming more skillful in anticipating and combating Robin's raids. Moreover, in response to Robin's opposition and stirring up of the region's common folk against them, they had worked hard to shore up their own defenses and political alliances, so as to make their overthrow – which had, at one point, been Robin's driving ambition – increasingly difficult.

As he moved into the second year of his campaign, Robin was confronted with some difficult problems. Was his strategy effective? How should he organize his forces? What did he need to change and what should he seek to retain? One thing was clear, however: he did not know the answers to these problems himself. He would need to consult with others. "Perhaps," he mused, "I could benefit from hearing more about the latest thinking in these domains."

Students don't tend to begin by imagining the particular "macro-context" within which Robin operates before thinking of solutions that would fit with this. Hence, they tend to unthinkingly provide modern answers to Robin's problems. For example, from a modern management consultant's perspective, what Robin should do is decentralize, devolve responsibility, empower those beneath him, or franchise. However, in Robin's cultural setting – where his forceful, charismatic, almost divine leadership is the core that holds everything together – such solutions would likely be seen as a sign of weakness, that Robin is losing his "mojo," or that he is no longer committed to the cause. They would likely leave the organization in a greater state of malaise than when the consultants came in.

Many believe that a similar overlaying of generic solutions that did not take account of the particular operational context occurred when consultants from the Virgin Group, famous for revamping maturing consumer product and service markets like air and rail travel, cola, vodka, and banking, were called in by Government ministers to write a report on Britain's hospitals at the beginning of the year 2000. In an article in *The Sunday Times,* the Secretary for Health, Alan Milburn, described Britain's publicly funded NHS (National Health Service) as "a 1948 system operating in a 21st century world. That is why," he explained, "I have now asked Sir Richard Branson's award-winning Virgin Group to advise us on how hospitals can be made consumer friendly. It is about transforming the very culture of the NHS to make it a modern consumer service." Press releases claimed that the Prime Minister, Tony Blair, would use the report to follow up on accusations made by his Health Secretary of the dire "forces of conservatism" within the NHS and "the gross inefficiencies built into the system."

The consultants visited nine hospitals and several GPs' surgeries over a 26-day period and composed a damning report. They wrote of "over-centralization," "too much red-tape," "chaotic booking-arrangements," and "poor management." They concluded that "the patient is required to fit into the system, rather than the other way around," and that the "dead hand of bureaucracy seems to stifle imagination and flair." However, on the up side, they claimed that "most [staff] are probably decent people who just need a little leadership and direction." The actions they believed should be taken to remedy the situation included the sort of ideas that have become commonplace in many organizations: "empowering workers to be more innovative," making hospitals more "consumer friendly," and increasing transparency and accountability. (One recommended means of doing this was to allow patient representatives to go behind the scenes and carry out "snap inspections.") There was also talk of snack trolleys and making hospitals "more fun."

However, NHS employees were critical of the Virgin report and the Government's handling of it. Doctors felt they were being blamed for poor public perception of the NHS, which, they argued, was caused by lack of funding. Stephen Thornton, the Chief Executive of the NHS Confederation, accepted that declining standards needed to be addressed but challenged "the Virgin team to show me what they describe as a suffocating bureaucracy. Where on earth do they get ridiculous figures that imply there is one administrator to every two clinical staff?" Of all NHS staff, only 3% were managers/administrators, compared with 44% nurses, 8% doctors and 17% clerical, he said, asking "I wonder how many backup staff it takes Virgin to get one pilot into the air." In any case, he continued, "many administrative and clerical staff undertake critical patient-related tasks. It is disingenuous to suggest these people hinder rather than help the treatment of patients." Peter Hawker, Chairman of the British Medical Association's Consultants' Committee, similarly suggested that he was "all for improving the services to patients but we need real resources, not an exercise in spin [doctoring]."

These criticisms sparked a wider debate about the Blair Government's use of consultants. A survey by the *Independent on Sunday* showed that it had spent almost a billion pounds hiring private consulting firms in its first three years in office. It was revealed that The Department for Education and its agencies spent almost £10 m between 1997 and 1999. In response, Nigel de Gruchy, General Secretary of a prominent teaching union, claimed that: "The money could be much better spent. The Government paid Hey McBer consultancies £3 m to come up with criteria for what makes a good teacher. We could have told them that for nothing."

The Department of Health's spending on consultants in the same period was two and a half times that of Education. According to one source, this could have paid for 2,327 heart bypass operations, 4,421 hip replacements, 737 full cancer treatments, and the wages of 1,133 junior doctors. A spokeswoman for the Unison health union said: "It's an awful amount of money to spend on consultants, particularly if those consultants are at the expense of money going into front-line care. We generally know what the problems are, the difficulty is getting the Government to listen to the people who are on the ground."

1. *Why were consultants from Virgin used to advise the NHS?*
2. *What are the advantages and disadvantages of hiring management consultants to move or shake a company's strategy?*
3. *Having read this case, how would you now approach the situation if you were asked to act as a consultant advising Robin Hood about the best way to deal with the predicament outlined in the first part of this case?*

Case Notes:

2-7 Management gurus: Fad power

Business process reengineering (the 1990s' most pervasive strategic management mantra) and the Mozart effect (the idea, which also became popular in the 1990s, that babies who are exposed to classical music grow up to be more intelligent) might seem worlds apart but, according to Michael Skapinker, management columnist for the *Financial Times*, the similarities between both phenomena are many.

Where did the classical music and babies theory come from? In 1993, the science journal *Nature* published a study that showed that college students (i.e. not babies) who listened to a Mozart sonata for 10 minutes increased their performance on a subsequent spatial intelligence test. This became known as the "Mozart effect."

Subsequent studies produced mixed results, at best. In 1999, an analysis of 16 such studies, also published in *Nature*, concluded that the overall effect of playing music on spatial intelligence was in fact negligible. In another article entitled "The Mozart Effect: Tracking the Evolution of a Scientific Legend," Adrian Bangerter and Chip Heath of Stanford University analyzed both why people projected what had originally been a study of students on to infants, and why the story achieved such wide currency (in US surveys, 80% of respondents had heard of the Mozart effect).

Bangerter and Heath concluded that the reason the nature of the original study shifted from students to babies was because infants are the focus of so much uncertainty and anxiety. All parents worry about whether they can do more for their children and this seemed to give them something to do that would temporarily assuage their anxiety. They also noted that media references to the Mozart effect had now tailed off. This was partly because of the subsequent scientific studies questioning the link between music and intelligence, and also because it had lost its novelty. Parents' attention switched to newer fads.

Skapinker claimed that reading about the rise and fall of the Mozart effect reminded him of several other frenzies, involving companies rather than children: business process reengineering (BPR), the dash to go on-line, and, now, locating the organization's core competence and outsourcing everything else. As he explained in his *FT* column: "Reengineering is particularly apposite because, like the Mozart effect, it began with a founding text. When Michael Hammer and James Champy's *Reengineering the Corporation* was published in 1993, it caught US and Western business at a low ebb, very scared of what appeared to be frighteningly efficient Japanese companies selling high-quality goods at low prices."

In an uncertain business environment most companies were desperate to cut their costs (just as parents are desperate not to deny their infants any advantage). BPR seemed to show them how. Most never read Hammer and Champy's book, or understood what it was based on, or whether it was founded on solid science, but "the idea" of it, they believed, told them what to do: reexamine every business process as if they were setting it up from scratch; ask whether they really needed all those employees; slash their workforces. Subsequently, and at great long-term cost, middle managers, deemed worthless and superfluous because what they did (communicate, for example) could not be easily quantified, were dispatched with particular vigor.

Reengineering the Corporation was not as simple-minded as that, Skapinker pointed out. It actually advocated looking at each encounter from the customers' point of view and designing processes to ensure that those particular customers were best served. This could have involved merging departments that were previously separate, but it required taking employees' abilities more, rather than less, seriously. But, all that was drowned out in the stampede to follow the simple mantra of "downsizing." And when the rush was over, companies were left to rue the experience and expertise they had lost. Indeed, all the factors that lay behind the Mozart effect were there, too: anxiety, weakness, and misinterpretation of the original writing.

Skapinker also saw Mozart effect parallels with what he terms "dotcom madness," where so many companies were panicked into believing that they would be overtaken unless they made the internet the core of their future development – whether it suited their particular competitive advantage and business environment or not.

Perhaps the current craze to outsource to and get established in developing countries will play out the same way? As Skapinker's column concludes: "Of course there is an Indian and Chinese challenge – and opportunity [in this respect]. These are potentially huge markets that are just beginning to open up. In the same way the internet was extremely important – it was just [in reality] not very clear why that was. But there is more than one method to deal with any new situation. When everybody believes they have found the way to do it, there is a good chance that everyone is wrong."

1. *Why might a company's strategies be so easily moved or shaken by fads and the management gurus that issue them?*
2. *What are the dangers of following fads or trends like BPR?*
3. *What could you as a manager do to help your company to resist following the latest fads blindly?*

Case Notes:

> When an industry with a reputation for difficult economics meets a manager with a reputation for excellence. It is usually the industry that keeps its reputation intact.
>
> *Warren Buffet*

> The field of business strategy offers a contrary view: it holds that the most important impediments are not the property of collections of firms, but arise instead from the unique endowments and actions of individual corporations of business-units.
>
> *Richard Rumelt*

3

Industry Dynamics

Why is it that some *industries*[1] seem to be consistently more profitable than others?

Table 3.1 shows a selection of industry sectors and their average annual return on invested capital (ROIC) from 1992 to 2006 (Porter, 2008)

The soft drink industry, for example, dominated by the duopoly of Coke and Pepsi, has been clearly more profitable than the poor old airline industry, which consistently fails to earn its 7-8% cost of capital year in and year out. These patterns of industry returns arise because of the differences in each industry's characteristics, dominant structure, evolutionary phase and underlying competitive and cooperative forces. In other words, "industry dynamics."

Strategic Hell – Perfect Competition

For strategists, hell is a set of (industry) dynamics that combine to remove any options other than to do what everyone else is doing. This culminates in an organization being forced to take the industry price (i.e. be a *price taker*) rather

Table 3.1   Annual average ROIC[2] 1992–2006 selected industry segments

Industry segment	Average annual ROIC (%)
Security Brokers and Dealers	40.9
Soft Drink Manufacturers and Distributors	37.6
Packaged Software	37.6
US industry average	*14.9*
Hotels	10.4
Airlines	5.9
Catalogue and Mail Order Houses	5.9

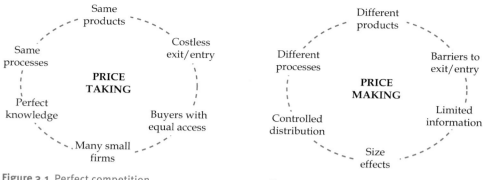

Figure 3.1 Perfect competition

Figure 3.2 Imperfections

than having discretion to set a different price (i.e. be a *price maker*) through innovative products and services or through having proprietary ways of reducing costs. The epitome of such hell is *perfect competition,* illustrated in Figure 3.1.[3]

In perfect competition there are many sellers and hence no scope for coordination of market pricing. The businesses are too small to achieve any firm-specific advantages through economies of scale and, as they all use the same technology and production techniques, no cost advantages are available at the process level. They all sell products that, in the eyes of their buyers, are the same and those buyers can easily switch from one supplier to another. On both the demand and supply side there is informational transparency and hence swift dissemination of any innovation in product or process.

In this environment businesses are forced to take the prevailing market price. If an organization increases its prices above the market it sells nothing and there is little point in setting a lower price as it is already selling all it can at the market price. As such average long term profits trend towards being equal to the cost of capital wherein the business can earn just enough to compensate for the level of risk in the industry – what economists call *normal profits.* If profits move above this level, new firms enter the industry to grab their share and, if profits fall, then some businesses will exit to pursue other opportunities and overall profitability returns to the normal level. Note that if high exit costs exist, as is the case in many capital intensive industries, firms will be trapped into staying in the industry even though they are making poor or negative returns as the cost of staying in is less than the cost of leaving.

To achieve returns greater than the cost of capital industry *imperfections* must exist. These imperfections (like those illustrated in Figure 3.2) are the opposite of the factors driving perfect markets and include product differentiation, entry barriers, switching costs, and so on. If a firm can develop and exploit such imperfections better than its rivals, then it will outperform the average of its industry returns and have competitive advantage. This advantage will be sustained as long as those imperfections, and the firm's unique ability to exploit them, last. One view of strategy then, is that it is the ongoing quest for returns greater than the cost of capital through the establishment and exploitation of firm-specific imperfections. While some industries are born nearly perfect some become that way over time due to the underlying, evolutionary forces. It is to these industry-shaping forces that we now turn our attention.

The Industry Life Cycle⁴

Industries are born, they grow, mature, and in some cases eventually die. At each stage of this cycle each industry has its own critical success factors (CSFs) that all firms must address in order to be successful. Those win-the-game (WTG) attributes that give a competitive edge initially become a standard in-the-game (ITG) requirement as competitors imitate and improve on the original offering or capability. Japanese manufactures stole a march on their international rivals in the 1980s with the quality and reliability of their products, but these features are standard for durable consumer goods like cars, washing machines and televisions in the 21st century.

In the early, introductory or innovative phases of the life cycle (Figure 3.3), profitability and cash flow are often sacrificed to gain a foothold for the future. The life cycle is a description of the past and not a predictor of the future and there is no straitjacket forcing specific dynamics to emerge at each stage. For example, industries can be de-matured by innovation or new thinking as the airline industry was de-matured in terms of passenger growth by the development of the low-cost operator. Or macro-environmental forces can shift to see a product or service become popular again (e.g. the rise of AIDS led to the rejuvenation of the condom industry). Or a determined mover and shaker can reignite an industry (e.g. Mat Hoffman in BMX, as described in live case 3-6; or Stelios Haji-Ioannou in European Airlines, as in the live case on easyJet in the next chapter). Such shifts can result in a "dolphin tail" effect where the downward curve on the right of Figure 3.3 can be rejuvenated back up again. However, the ILC gives a general indication of the different strategies that organizations might follow to be successful at different stages (Figure 3.4).

- **Introduction:** At the early stage of industry development the features, benefits and functions of the *product* are the CSFs. Most product industries go from birth to death rapidly as the new product fails to generate sufficient customers. Those that do find sufficient acceptance grow rapidly once a critical mass of consumers develops.
- **Growth:** As the industry grows there tends to be a convergence to a dominant set of product features. These become standard ITG requirements as, for example, all TV, mobile phones, personal computers, financial products, etc. offer the same set of features and benefits. Now the foundations of ongoing success rest on superior *marketing* (distribution channels, brand, reputation) and *operating processes* (production, logistics, service).

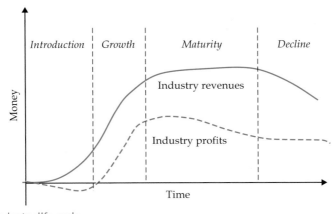

Figure 3.3 The industry life cycle

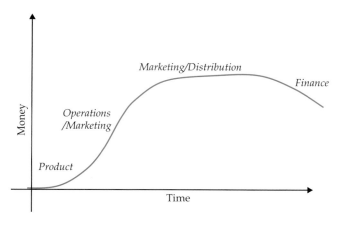

Figure 3.4 Generic Critical Success Factors across the industry life cycle

- **Maturity:** As growth slows consumers have become more knowledgeable, and processes as well as products have become common across all players. Product/process development continues and products around the common standards proliferate as companies seek to cover all the bases and gain an edge where they can. However, any improvements disseminate rapidly throughout the industry and parity is soon restored as competitors emulate and imitate the innovators.[5] Increasingly it is superior *marketing and distribution* that separates the successful from the average. Cost reduction, to counteract increased price competition, is now an essential ITG factor for long-term survivors. Most industries in the industrialized world are mature with growth rates at about the same level as GDP. Accelerating sales in less-developed countries becomes the prime source of real, industry growth. Hence industry **consolidation** through merger and acquisition, a fanatical focus on brand and marketing and relentless cost-cutting, become essential to ensure profitability. Industries can be de-matured and grow to new levels through innovation so, for example, the low-cost airlines have markedly increased the number of people flying in Europe and America or sometimes through a macro-environmental change – hence war is not good unless you are part of the armaments industry and a publicized increase in sexually transmitted diseases boosts the sales of condoms.
- **Decline:** In this phase the skills of the financial undertaker come to the fore. Consolidation of now-cheap businesses and, hence, management of overcapacity, minimal investment, and a controlled milking of the product to its final demise or niche existence are the basis of success. Whether the declining industry is profitable – such as cigars or quality fountain pens – or not – such as prepared baby foods – depends on how well surplus capacity is adjusted and also the extent to which resilient niches of price insensitive demand remain among the general decline.[6]

Industry Structure

Mature industries are characterized by an overall structure that dictates to a large extent the nature and scope of the competitive advantages or imperfections theoretically available for companies to exploit. Economists have suggested four generic structures, each of which carries different implications for the firms comprising the industry:

1. **Perfect Competition** has been discussed above and by definition there are no sources of competitive advantage. One of the most important strategic implications in such markets is that companies are forced to *take the market price*. Regardless of other factors, commodity producers – e.g. steel, wheat, oil – take the market price whether that price is high, low, or medium and so at the *product* level these are examples of perfect competition.

2. **Monopolistic competition** exists where most of the other conditions of perfect competition hold sway other than the fact that each seller offers a slightly differentiated product, i.e. each seller has a monopoly in its own products. Sellers can charge different prices as individual price differences are not noticed by the many other sellers who, because they have differentiated products and hence relatively loyal customers, do not respond. Restaurants, doctors, hairdressers are all examples of such structures. In such industries firms do not have carte blanche pricing discretion but can *price to what their market (segment) will bear*.

3. **Oligopoly** occurs when significant demand side economies of size are available to bigger companies and where there are many opportunities to differentiate. The industry coalesces to a few companies that become big enough to leverage the cost reduction and have differentiation options. Pharmaceutical, soap powder, supermarket, and aircraft industries are examples. It is in such industries that pricing is truly "strategic" in that *the potential response of the other players is a critical input to the pricing decision*.[7]

4. **Monopolies** are firms that have no, or at least very limited, competition for their products and hence *can raise or lower prices without taking into account the responses of other firms*. Market-based monopolies, as contrasted with government legislated ones, can form where there are substantial economies of size and limited options for differentiation. The cost of getting big enough to compete with the entrenched incumbent is too high for potential rivals. So-called natural monopolies are industries where economies of size are large and where the minimum efficient size (MES[8]) is greater than 50% of the market. MES indicates the minimum level of output that is necessary to capture the lowest level of costs. If the MES is 50% or more, the first one to get to 50% market share gains such a cost advantage that others cannot catch up, and hence the first one moves on toward the other 50%.[9] Power and water utilities and railways are examples of such monopolies in most countries.

Industry Forces

Driving the final industry structure as it evolves are the underlying industry forces. Figure 3.5 is likely the most famous strategy diagram ever published. It is Michael Porter's encapsulation of decades of industrial organization economics research and theorizing into a framework that captures the fundamental ideas for non-economist managers. Three broad dynamics, *power, entry, and rivalry*, interact to contribute to the potential profitability (attractiveness). These dynamics all influence the degree to which firms have control over pricing, particularly in terms of being able to increase prices to lift margins or even just to compensate for increased costs.

Power – the horizontal axis

Despite pious talk of partnerships the buyer supplier relationships are power-based struggles focused on capturing as much long-term value for the firm as possible while giving enough to the other buyer or supplier firms to keep them in business. There are many characteristics that interact to determine which party is the more powerful. These include relative size, switching costs and whether either party is able to backward/forward integrate.

The balance of power varies over time. For example, in the relatively recent past the major brand name suppliers such as Coca-Cola, Unilever, and Procter & Gamble held pricing power over their supermarket customers. They were bigger, i.e. were more concentrated than their customers, and had more pull-through power with the brand-sensitive end consumer. Now, with the growing credibility of the supermarkets' own label products and the increasing consolidation of the worldwide supermarket industry, the power has shifted. The pain that a Wal-Mart might feel from not stocking Coca-Cola is now potentially less than the pain that Coke would feel from being delisted.

Power is related to the degree of switching costs that is incurred in changing from one supplier or product to another. High switching costs promote *lock-in* wherein having made the initial choice the customer has made an investment that now becomes costly to undo. Switching from one brand of toothpaste to another is a costless choice that can be made in the face of an opportunistic discount offer. However, switching from one MBA program to another once you have taken the initial courses is more difficult. The search behaviour of customers and the marketing ploys of companies reflect this. Customers take far longer to evaluate high switching cost goods before making purchase commitments and companies design low-cost entry but high-cost exit pathways to lock customers into their phone contracts and house mortgages.

Power is one thing, but the inclination to use that power is quite another. This inclination is referred to as *price sensitivity* and indicates that customers are more sensitive to changes in prices of some products or services than of others. The factors that contribute to price sensitivity are mainly components of the extent to which a price rise from one firm takes value away from the other. Rich buyers who can easily pass on cost increases to their own customers tend to be relatively insensitive to price increases, particularly for a product/service that, while a low

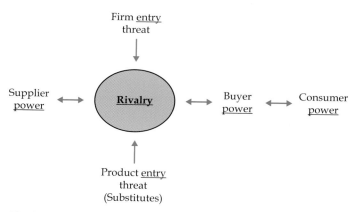

Figure 3.5 The Five Forces of Industry structure (adapted from Michael E. Porter (1985) *Competitive Advantage*. NY: Free Press, p.6)

part of their overall costs, is important to their own product/service in terms of function or quality. However, buyers who are struggling to make money and/or whose own customers will not accept price rises, tend to be much more sensitive to the impact of a price increase. This is particularly so for purchased inputs that constitute a relatively large proportion of the buyer's total costs and are not critical to the quality or performance of the final product.

Entry/substitution – the vertical axis

The vertical axis covers two areas: the entry of other firms trying to get some of the industry value for themselves and the potential substitution by other products offering similar benefits. These both act to keep a cap on *industry* pricing.

If an industry is very profitable and earns well above its average cost of capital, then other firms will be tempted to enter. Their willingness to attempt an entry will be lessened if:

1. New entry will reduce prices and hence profitability. This can be due to such factors as increased capacity or the aggressive responses of incumbents. There are many point-to-point travel connections in the airline industry that are profitable to the one airline that operates the connection, but would be loss-making for both if another airline entered that route.
2. The existing players have large advantages in such things as brand, locked in distribution or scale-based low costs that are very expensive for a new player to match, i.e. there are high entry costs. Coke and Pepsi are protected from entry into their lucrative duopoly by over a century of brand investment.
3. There are very high exit costs, e.g. very costly asset-specific investments which must be written off on leaving the industry. A semi-conductor fabrication plant costs billions of dollars to build but has no application for anything else if you decide to leave the industry.

Industries are defined in terms of products that are close substitutes for each other and so the boundary between what is regarded as a competitor product and a substitute product is blurred. Substitutes have positive cross-elasticities of demand: as the price of product A is increased, the demand for substitute product B increases. Competitive products demonstrate very direct and swift cross-elasticities whereas more distant substitutes show longer term relationships. Hence if a cinema chain puts up the prices of its tickets it will quickly lose customers to cinema chains that have lower prices.

However, if cinema tickets in general increase in price, the demand for substitute forms of entertainment, such as bowling, football, and live theatre may increase but at a slower rate. Despite this slower rate the price of these substitutes still acts as a cap on cinema ticket prices even if rivalry does not exist between cinema chains. The main driver of the growth of the plastics industry was value-adding substitution. It replaced various packaging materials such as paper, cardboard, glass, metal, and structural materials such as timber and steel. Nowadays in many packing and structural applications plastic is a competitor product for other materials more than a substitute, and vice versa.

Rivalry

This middle force of the five, which is also engaged in both the horizontal power play and the vertical entry play, captures the impact of the ongoing direct competition between industry participants. The more that the industry reassembles perfect competition the fiercer becomes the price competition and the more unattractive or unprofitable it becomes. Rivalry is driven by more than industry structure as managers with different personalities and from different local and international cultures have different goals and different ways of dealing with competition. Some prefer an ongoing knock-down-drag-out-fight while others favour a more genteel way of doing business. Hence, while pharmaceutical oligopolies engage in marketing wars, French hypermarkets engage in price wars and the attractive returns of some are gained at the expense of others.

Industries are not necessarily homogeneous with respect to rivalry. In some cases there are clear demarcations between sets of competitors adopting similar strategies aimed at similar customer segments. These *strategic groups* can have high *mobility barriers* that prevent companies moving in the same way that entry barriers deter movement into an industry. Department stores, for example, compete more directly with other department stores than they do with supermarkets, although both are in the retailing industry. Mobility barriers, however, erode or can be overcome and so French hypermarkets now sell luxury goods; and the formerly down-at-heel "pile it high and sell it cheap" Tesco of post-war Britain – which was firstly admired then emulated – now dominates Sainsbury's, its former up-market rival. Tesco overcame the substantial mobility barriers between the "deep discount" strategic group which targeted the low-income consumer and the "value for money" group targeting the middle class.

Cooperative Forces

The overriding goal of business strategy is to *create value* for the firm's stakeholders. With this in mind, we can see that, while *competition* over your share of the value pie might be an inevitable consequence of being in business, there is also much to be gained by *cooperation* with other firms in increasing the *overall size* of that value pie. Figure 3.6 captures this idea by explicitly identifying the role of complementors.[10]

Complementors

Complementors are companies from which customers buy, or to which suppliers sell, products that are *complementary* to the company's products. A complementary product is one that makes customers more willing to buy it or suppliers more willing to supply it. Hence, manufacturers of games consoles and designers of games are in a complementary relationship in that increased success of Play Station, for example, is of value to the designer of Play Station games. Similarly Microsoft (X-box) would cooperate readily with a games designer who promised a "killer" X-box game.

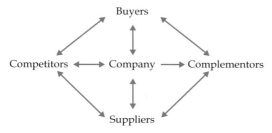

Figure 3.6: The value net (Source: Adam Brandenburger and Barry Nalebuff (1996) *Co-opetition*. NY: Currency Doubleday)

Complementary products have negative cross-elasticities of demand: as the price of Product A increases the demand for its complement, Product B, decreases. A recent example of this was the impact that sharply rising gasoline prices had on the demand for the complementary products of cars in the USA. As gasoline prices rose the demand for gas-guzzling SUVs declined to be replaced by demand for cheaper, more fuel-efficient vehicles. For car companies like Toyota, which made the same profit margin from one SUV that they made from 10 small cars, the impact of complements was significant.

Functional necessities such as games and consoles, CD/DVDs and players, pens and paper, etc. are obvious examples of complementary products/relationships. But so too is the relationship between roads and cars, yet initially the major car companies in the USA had to build seedling roads to encourage public pressure on government to develop highways – a lack of roads would have discouraged many from buying a car.[11] The Michelin restaurant guide, by encouraging gastro-nomically inclined car owners to drive to distant restaurants, also encouraged tyre wear and purchase – hence restaurants become complementors of tyre companies.

Competitors can also be complementors by increasing the market size for the product. Hence although the low-cost airlines in the Western world have certainly caused major problems for the full service flag carriers, they have also generated a significant increase in the number of people who are flying. In the long term this may prove to be very valuable to the major airlines once they have reduced their operating costs in line with the low-price industry in which they now operate.

Co-opetition

The competitive and cooperative tensions in a complementary relationship are captured by the term *co-opetition*, first used by Brandenburger and Nalebuff. As well as helping to increase the size of the value pie through complementarity, firms become increasingly able to compete to grab more of it if they

- become substantially bigger than their complementor(s);
- have a greater influence on pull through of customers;
- have more credible threats of integration into their complementor's functions than their complementor is able to muster;
- have customers who find it more costly to switch from the firm's product than from the complementor's offering.

81

For example, in the complementary relationship between PC manufacturers and software developers, Microsoft's share of the bundled value of hardware and operating system has not diminished as prices of PCs have tumbled over the past two decades. A quick run through of the above factors will help to explain this.

Heightened awareness of complementors has been a factor in mergers between content and channel providers such as Sony with Columbia Pictures and AOL with Time Warner. In these examples the complementarity was seemingly obvious but subsequent value was not, e.g. Sony wrote off 3.2 billion dollars at the end of its complement-driven acquisition.

We started this chapter by asking why it was that some industries are more profitable for companies and investors than others. As discussed in the sections above some of the reasons for this lie in the interacting forces of the industry and the different stages of its evolution. While some industries have product – process – buyer interrelationships that lend themselves to multiple opportunities for advantage over other firms; others have dynamics that constrain the ability of firms to outpace their rivals. The strategic hells of near perfect competition, augmented by overcapacity in some capital-intensive industries, can be contrasted with the strategic heavens of differentiated oligopolies or brute monopoly power.

Industry dynamics are demonstrably important, as are the other environmental forces covered in the discussion of the macro-environment in Chapter 1 and the description of the role of key movers and shakers in Chapter 2. However, environmental considerations are neither the sole, nor necessarily the most important, determinants of the individual organization strategic fate. Some businesses consistently outperform their industry rivals as well as other businesses in more attractive industries. Levers of successful strategy are in the hands of the managers, and it is to these levers that we turn our attention in the next part of the book, which deals with corporate strategy, strategic positioning, corporate identity, and organic approaches to strategy development.

Industry Dynamics Key Learnings Mind-Map

Having read and reviewed this chapter outline what you believe to be the key learnings from the chapter and the relationships between these on the note pages below.

3-1 Sportswear: Power is money[12]

In the 1960s a change took place in the sporting apparel and footwear markets. Until then, by far the most important consumer had been the amateur and professional athlete who wore the shorts, tops, tracksuits, specialist shoes and other paraphernalia necessary for his/her particular sport. Of this group, the largest segment comprised the millions of amateur sports enthusiasts throughout the world. Direct promotions to these consumers and promotion via endorsement by top athletes made a performance enhancing proposition, i.e. "wear our kit and be a winner". Then, in the "swinging sixties", pop groups like "The Rolling Stones" began to wear "trainers" (i.e. running shoes) as a counter-cultural symbol of youthful rebellion; and so Reebok, Nike, Adidas, etc. became fashion as well as sports brands.

The wholesale global sportswear industry is worth more than $60bn per year and nearly $150bn at retail. The top two brand companies, Nike and Adidas/Reebok, share 40% of the branded market (29% of the total). While these firms retain the core competitive functions of marketing and design, manufacturing is outsourced to the lowest cost sources in a long global supply chain (Figure 3-1.1), e.g. market leader, Nike[13] (20% of the branded market. See Nike in Chapter 10 Sustain Ability) has over 700 suppliers worldwide.

The targeted sportswear consumer, particularly teenage and young adult segment, is fashion sensitive and relatively price insensitive. Wearing what is "in"

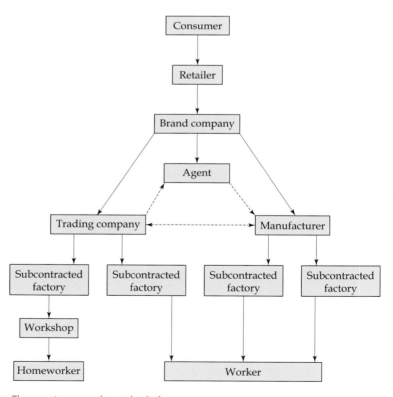

Figure 3-1.1 The sports apparel supply chain

is more important than wearing what you have until it is worn out. High-profile sports teams are aware of this dynamic and regularly change the design of their (branded) playing shirts (their "strip") to profit from loyal fans who "must have" the latest shirt with the name and number of their favorite player added at extra cost. Sporting teams, however, pale into retailing insignificance compared with giant consumer distributors like US-based Wal-Mart or France's Carrefour. While 80% of athletic footwear sales and 75% of sportswear are sold under brands, retailers understand that even fashion conscious, price insensitive customers will, if given the choice, pay the lower of two prices for their chosen branded item. So being able to offer that lower price is a key competitive weapon. As they thrust and parry with price reductions the retailers constantly put pressure on their suppliers for compensating cost reductions to ensure that retail margins are maintained.

While retailers set the consumer price, the brand company infuses the product with its "value." Creating image-based value means that marketing is *the* major cost as both saturation media coverage and celebrity endorsements are expensive. In making over $1bn profit in 2004, Nike expensed nearly as much on marketing. Yet, while nothing is spared on value-creation in design and marketing, things are entirely different at the production end. Here the watchwords are "efficiency" and "cost reduction". These watchwords are passwords for the agents, trading companies and manufacturers seeking access to "manufacture and supply" orders.

Some of these intermediaries themselves are large multinationals but, like the myriad of smaller companies and the even smaller subcontractors that supply them, are dependent for their corporate lives on winning the orders of Reebok, Adidas, etc. As well as pressures on product cost, this level of the supply chain must manage complex forecasting, inventory and logistics algorithms as retailers respond to variable consumer demand by giving shorter lead times for more frequent but smaller orders. Hence these suppliers bear most of the risk and costs of inventory management as well as the challenge of continuous cost reduction.

Flexible low-cost manufacture in a labor-intensive product demands flexible, low-cost workers. Hence the supply chain ends in countries like China, Cambodia or Indonesia, the comparative advantage of which lies in an abundant supply of low-cost (i.e. poor) workers. On April 1, 2010 the official minimum wage for full-time workers in Shanghai, one of China's most dynamic and modern cities, rose by RMB 160 to RMB 1120 ($164) per month with the wages of hourly paid workers moving from RMB 8 to 9 ($1.31) per hour. On Nike's official website the price of shoes ranged from a low of $45 for a sandal to $110 for the top of the range, customizable pair of runners.

1. *Explain the power relationships in this supply chain.*
2. *How might these power relationships predict the winners and losers in terms of ongoing profitability?*
3. *What advice would you give to the governments of developing countries that the sportsware manufacturers have used to manufacture shoes, like Indonesia or Cambodia?*

◄◄◄ Power is Money: Some ideas toward a "model answer" . . .

Price is the final manifestation of the ongoing power struggle for value between suppliers and buyers throughout the supply chain. In the "supply chain", i.e. the horizontal dimension of the five forces diagram as it is represented in the text, it is **price sensitivity** that determines how keenly price gains and reductions will be sought and **relative power** that determines which "partner" bears more of the ensuing cost. "Winners and losers" should perhaps more accurately be denoted as "winning and losing" at the downstream (i.e. more toward the consumer) end of this industry because there tends to be an ebb and flow of who is "on top" as the big guys (large manufacturers, brand companies and retailers) arm wrestle each other. But, like all power hierarchies, the less power you have the more dependent you are on the largesse of others and the final upstream "supplier," i.e. the worker, captures value consistent with his/her low power.[14]

Consumers – winners

The individual consumer is powerless to change the price of the retailer, no matter how price sensitive he or she might be. Even if many consumers are price sensitive they lack power because they cannot effectively coordinate with other like-minded consumers to act together to threaten to shift their custom if price reductions are not forthcoming. However, **transparent pricing** (transparent through advertising and word-of-mouth) effectively acts as a **coordinating mechanism** and forces retailers to deal with consumers as if they were a coordinated group rather than a bunch of separate individuals. While *a* consumer lacks power *the* consumer is powerful in the context of retailer price rivalry. Big retailers know that if one of them decides to price a particular pair of Nike trainers at $42.50 against a prevailing price of $50.00 then *the* consumer will tend to take this offer and hence it must be matched.

Retailers – winners

The retail industry is increasingly **concentrated** and hence has enormous power as the major distribution outlet (and point-of-sale promoter) for the brand companies. Given the consumer "traffic" through Wal-Mart in the USA, for example, it would be a brave marketing manager who would risk being de-listed by this giant retailer. The retailer is price sensitive to the extent it cannot pass on price increases to the consumer but the force that most deters retail price increases is **rivalry** between the retailers themselves. Hence retailers are always seeking "exclusive product" arrangements with major brand suppliers (although such arrangements flirt with illegality in several countries). Despite their power the retailers cannot push the brand companies too far. They are dependent on the heavily promoted brands to generate traffic through their stores and so it would be an equally brave Wal-Mart buyer that chose to de-list Nike for example. Nike spends a lot of money creating brand loyalty and these brand loyal Nike buyers would buy the "swooshe" and perhaps other products at the same time, at a Wal-Mart rival. Not stocking the major brands would result in lower sales for Wal-Mart even if it also hurt the brand.

Brand companies – winners

The reciprocal power relationship between the retailers and the brand companies has been mentioned above. Unlike their retailers these firms do not want to compete with each other on price. They are all in need of high margins (supported by high price) to support the marketing/promotion that goes into creating their value proposition that in turn drives the high price that consumers are prepared to pay. This is a battle of marketing where **barriers to entry** (need for a brand and guaranteed distribution) are high and **substitutes** few. Hence with relatively price insensitive final consumers and equality of power with retailers there is no need for price wars and the inevitable erosion of profits that result. However the other side of the margin equation is cost and here the brand companies are ruthless.

Trading companies, manufacturers, agents – win some; lose some

This sector is **less concentrated** than its buyers, cannot **forward integrate** and lacks **unique assets or capabilities**. **Barriers to entry** are low in that there are many trading companies/agents with the necessary skills/infrastructure than can enter the industry and develop contacts or already have the necessary connections. Even large manufacturers that supply multiple brands can be bypassed by an agent/trading company willing to coordinate subcontractors. These firms are under constant pressure for cost reduction, quality improvement and increased inventory efficiency with the (implicit) threat from the buyer that "if you can't do it I'll find someone who can." As these intermediaries get bigger they are, paradoxically under more pressure, as the loss of a big order can result in ongoing losses and potential bankruptcy. Most are locked in to their customers but the converse does not apply.

Subcontracted companies – win some; lose more

By now you can see the picture. At this level power is limited. These are the last structured parts of the system. The financial penalties imposed for late deliveries, poor quality often end up here passed down from "above" as do the consequences of delay and obsolescence should the retailer not want the stock after all. And if these organizations don't want the business, **new entrants** from around the globe of underdeveloped countries as well as a myriad of rivals in their own backyard are queuing up to fill the gap. With no power to make a price these companies exert the only power they have to make a profit; on their controllable "costs" – labor.

The worker – losers

These "suppliers" face numerous **competitors** (replacement workers) in their own neighborhood and numerous potential **entrants** in other countries. They tend to have a relatively **low skill base**, to act as individuals rather than collectively and to have no alternative "customers" to whom they can tender. While the price (wages) might be low and constantly subject to being lowered (through non-payment of holiday pay, increased piece work rates, etc.),[15] the options that exist tend to be at the level of "take the 'price' reduction (and be hungry) or leave it (and starve)."

As the title of the case suggests, power is money in the supply chain, and where you find power you find money, and where you find no power . . .

Case Notes:

3-2 Carrefour: The price of entry

As the takeover battle for Safeway PLC, Britain's third largest supermarket chain, was being waged in 2003, there was widespread speculation that the French superstore giant, Carrefour, might enter the fray. For them the question was whether the UK supermarket industry was sufficiently attractive to enter.

The UK supermarket industry as a whole was worth some £100bn a year. The main activity of these supermarkets was food and drink retail, although most had also added petrol stations to their outlets and had also begun to branch into clothing retail with significant success. The primary activity, however, remained food and drink retail and UK consumers bought 80% of their food, 75% of fresh vegetables and fruit, 65% of fish and meat, and 50% of milk from the five largest supermarkets. These supermarkets, in order of market share in 2003 were: Tesco (25.8%), Sainsbury's (17.4%), Asda (15.9%), Safeway (10.0%), and Wm. Morrison (5.9%). Pre-tax profits for these companies mirrored their size, with Tesco generating £1.4bn, Sainsbury's £0.57bn, Safeway £0.36bn, and Morrisons £0.24bn. Asda's figures are not known because it had been acquired in 1999 by the world's largest grocer, Wal-Mart of the USA. Despite this profitability, the overall growth rate for the industry had slowed in recent years to 2.9%, which was equal to the growth of the economy as a whole.

The main suppliers to the industry were farmers and fast-moving consumer goods (FMCG) companies. Located around the world and supplying thousands of products, the number of farmers involved was huge. Colossal improvements in transportation in terms of both lower costs and refrigeration had opened massive sourcing opportunities for the supermarkets. With increasing levels of competition, farmers attempted to work together through cooperatives to improve their negotiating position *vis-à-vis* the supermarkets. However, unless the product was particularly valued by the supermarkets, these organizations had little effect on the terms of trade achieved by the farmers. The FMCG companies, however, such as Kelloggs and Heinz, operated on much larger scales than the farmers, but still faced a challenge in finding opportunities for large volume sales in the UK. While their brands protected their margins, the supermarkets had been investing in their own brands with mixed results. Some FMCG companies were willing to supply stores' own brands alongside their own, despite some cannibalization of their products, whereas others, such as Kelloggs, refused to manufacture anything other than their own branded product. At the time of writing, a very large merger was announced between Procter & Gamble and Gillette – two large FMCG companies.

The main customers of the supermarkets are ordinary people in the UK. Everyone is within around 15 minutes' driving time from at least one supermarket. Many people use the supermarkets for large volumes of shopping and may go once a week or less frequently, but spend well over £100 each time. Most supermarkets operate a reward scheme so that consumers gain points on their store card relative to the amount spent. This can be redeemed against later in-store or petrol purchases. Most regard the supermarkets as an efficient way to buy a wide range of foods and essential household products. In an increasingly time-poor society, this efficiency is attractive to many shoppers. However, there are also good café facilities for those with more time to spend, such as older people or those with children. The supermarkets have also launched home shopping, where customers set up their order preferences on the internet and are then able to order whatever they want for a specific delivery time. Although it is time consuming to set up the initial order, home shopping is proving increasingly popular. Despite the heavy use of supermarkets, both in-store and home delivery, supermarket shopping is not really much of a topic for conversation among shoppers and it is fairly rare for them to compare these sorts of shopping experiences.

The prime competition for supermarkets is the corner shop, which has fared very badly in recent years. However, trade magazines suggest that the local shop is fighting back by focusing on more specialty products. Delicatessens, wine shops, butchers, and cafés are all beginning to flourish again as consumers enjoy taking time choosing among high-quality produce. Another source of competition is from farmers' markets. Mindful of the huge profit margin that supermarkets are making on products sourced from the UK, English farmers are setting up their own farm shops and also attending farmers' markets where they can sell fresh produce at prices significantly below those of the supermarket. Interestingly, Sainsbury's recently announced the opening of its own farmers' market shop in central London, to much disapproval from consumer groups.

For Carrefour, the UK supermarket industry would be a significantly different environment that in France. There are strict planning regulations for the building of large out-of-town supermarkets, and very few stores of this appropriate size are now allowed anywhere. The best sites are also taken. Carrefour also does not have a reputation in the UK and it was also mindful that the French are not always well regarded in the UK. Carrefour was also aware of the frustrating tactics that the UK supermarkets used in their attempts to prevent discount operators Aldi, Netto, and Lidl from setting up their own operations. Through lobbying Parliament, these low-cost retailers had to operate initially as clubs, requiring a membership fee from new customers. With all of these factors to consider, Carrefour needed to decide whether to try to enter the UK supermarket industry and whether a bid for Safeway was an appropriate step to take.

---

1. *Using the Five Forces model, determine whether the UK supermarket industry is generally attractive (i.e., will it allow higher than average margins to be made) in 2003.*
2. *Should Carrefour seek to enter this industry by taking over Safeway?*
3. *Analyzing the power dynamic that runs across the horizontal axis of the Five Forces from supplier to buyers for this industry, give evidence to show how the main groups of players are continuously wrestling for greater bargaining power.*

3-3 McDonald's: The Golden Arches[1]

Twoallbeefpattiesspecialsaucelettucecheesepicklesoniononasesameseedbun

McDonald's advertising slogan first used in 1975

White Castle, started in 1921 by Edgar Waldo "Billy" Ingram and hamburger bun inventor J Walter Anderson was the first US hamburger chain. Selling hamburgers at 5 cents each, along with French fries and cola, it grew rapidly. Nearly 20 years later, on May 15, 1940, Richard "Dick" and Maurice "Mac" McDonald opened their first hotdog stand that evolved over time into a barbeque restaurant. In 1948 they sketched out a new, octagonal-shaped layout on a tennis court and opened a restaurant of that design in San Bernardino, California. This new outlet incorporated their "Speedee Service System"; an assembly line approach based on a restricted product range of hamburgers, cheeseburgers, French fries, and drinks only. It encouraged customers to place their orders at a window and eat in their cars, as the restaurant had no tables. It also made use of innovative preparation techniques such as Multimixers – machines that mixed six milkshakes simultaneously – to enable a faster throughput of customers.

The mass production system proved a winner. Dick redesigned the restaurant with the, now famous, "golden arches" going through the roof and sloping to the front and in 1953 the brothers began to franchise their operations. They commanded an upfront fee and an ongoing percentage of sales from new operations in Phoenix (Arizona) and Downey (California), both built on the San Bernardino model. Intrigued to find out why the brothers were ordering so many Multimixers from him, Ray Kroc visited San Bernardino. He was so impressed that he became a McDonald's franchise seller before opening his own store in Des Plaines, Illinois on April 15, 1955.

People flooding into Kroc's restaurant to buy the 15 cent burgers and 10 cent fries were often amused to see the cleanliness-obsessed owner scraping chewing gum off the surrounding footpaths with a putty knife. He introduced further streamlining and other initiatives to ensure a total focus on timely, efficient, and clean service, and "Q.S.C. & V" (Quality, Service, Cleanliness, and Value) became the company motto in 1957. The 100th McDonald's opened in Chicago in 1959. In 1960 the company was renamed "McDonald's Corporation" and one year later Kroc bought out the brothers for $2.7m. Then, insisting on the same look, food, and attention to cleanliness in all outlets, and backed by a huge marketing and branding campaign based on the friendly clown "Ronald McDonald," he set out to grow by opening new restaurants. The first non-US franchises opened in Canada and Puerto Rico in 1967. By the 1990s the company was opening a new store every 18 hours somewhere in the world. Today

[1]Sources: Various newspaper and magazine articles and a number of websites including McDonald's company website and www.mcspotlight.org

over 30,000 McDonald's restaurants serve over 47 million people in 122 countries every day.

Ray Kroc, when asked why McDonald's was so successful, replied, "We take the hamburger business more seriously than anyone else." So seriously, that in 1961 the McDonald's "Hamburger University" was opened in Elk Grove, near Chicago. Here, each year, handpicked "undergraduates" from the thousands of McDonald's stores worldwide go to learn and compete for honours in the "Hot Hamburger" competitions. Despite such commitment, McDonald's was not alone in growing rapidly in the fast food industry. Kentucky Fried Chicken opened in 1939 and licensed its first franchise in 1952. In hamburgers, Burger King opened in Florida in 1954 and Wendy's in Columbus, Ohio, in 1969. By the start of the 1990s there were 12,000 McDonald's, 6,300 Burger Kings, and 3,700 Wendy's in the USA along with a host of other hamburger chains and other fast food outlets selling everything from chicken, pizza, tacos, and sandwiches to sushi and noodles. More lately "Subway," boasting sandwiches with fresh, healthy ingredients and an ever-changing menu, has entered to challenge the dominance of the "Big Mac."

After its public flotation in 1965 McDonald's enjoyed 35 years of perpetual profit growth. However, between 1997 and 2003 it lost 3% of its US market share and in December 2002 declared its first loss as a public company. The interacting dynamics seen to contribute to the decline had been evolving for some time. Increased rivalry was an obvious feature with McDonald's entering a price war in the US and UK markets with the 99 cent (99 pence) burger. Environmentalists (e.g. Greenpeace) had targeted the fast food industry, and particularly McDonald's, in terms of animal welfare, environmental integrity, advertising, censorship, etc. Nutritionists had also taken aim through film makers (Morgan Spurlock's *Super Size Me*), authors (Eric Schlosser and *Fast Food Nation*) and US lawyers mounting lawsuits on behalf of obese "junk food addicts." Added to this was the expensive loss of a lawsuit mounted by the owner of several franchises for damages done by other stores being opened in close proximity.

In response to its first ever loss the Board dispensed with the existing CEO and recalled retired veteran Jim Cantalupo. His first instinct was to continue with the 2,000-store annual building rate. However, figures showing that more than 100% of the McDonald's sales growth came from new stores, convinced him that the major problems lay with current store performance and he focused strategy at this level. Store grading had fallen into disuse and was re-established; menus were revamped; nutritional and environmental information was placed on tray mats' and a host of incremental improvements such as stronger forks, thicker straws, and competitive tendering for marketing funds was complemented by McDonald's first global marketing campaign "I'm Lovin' it."

These "back to basics" actions reversed the downward trend. The focus on getting more customers into existing stores, continued by the company after the untimely deaths of both Cantalupo and his successor Charlie Bell drove the company's same store sales, profits, and share price upwards. By 2004 McDonald's was back at the forefront of the global fast food industry as an operator and investment vehicle and it remains there today.

McDonald's history is a good example of how a company's strategy, its successes, and its failures are reflections on how well the company addresses the changing demands of its industry environment. What wins the game today might not even be good enough to keep you in the game tomorrow.

1. How could you use the theoretical models in this chapter to explain the developments in this case?
2. Use the industry life cycle to explain McDonald's problems in the 1997–2003 period?
3. How might the managers of McDonald's have been able to predict the potential problems if they had applied the models?

Case Notes:

3-4 Dell: High-tech hell

Many of the technology giants of Silicon Valley are under threat. The rise of low-cost computing caught out Sun Systems, HP, and IBM. Technology standardization and overcapacity acted together to drive prices down. The standardization of information technology, exemplified by the emergence of low-cost computers running the open source Linux operating system on mass-produced hardware, is a problem for big technology companies with huge R&D spend and massively expensive sales forces.

There is also massive change in the software industry, with open source software programs produced by worldwide communities of volunteers bringing low-cost alternatives to branded products. There are also cheaper ways to produce and distribute software, from web-based delivery to techniques for building applications from reusable software "components."

The choice for the technology giants is whether they should strive to produce high-technology products that command high profit margins or compete on lower priced products from a lower cost base. Initially, the most competitive player in this market was Dell, with sales of $50bn and a growth rate of nearly 20% per year up until 2006. It had little R&D to support, and it sells direct to consumers rather than distributors. Its overheads were less than 10% of sales compared with 18% at HP and 47% at Sun.

What are the giants to do? IBM is seeking an optimal business mix. Seeking to sell its personal computer business to Lenovo of China was a further move in redefining Big Blue, who could see bigger margins in related areas, such as information systems and consultancy services. HP and Sun have abandoned parts of their high-tech business to compete more directly with Dell, but this has put their earnings under pressure and their market share has fallen. Standardization and commoditization are leaching profits out of the businesses. The problem of standardization is that it makes it harder for companies to differentiate their products and demand premium prices. It also makes it easier for customers to shop around and frees them from "lock-in."

Overcapacity gave customers the power to influence manufacturers into giving them interchangeable products. IBM, HP, and Sun responded by offering cheaper and more flexible products. By purchasing Compaq, HP hoped to take the lead in low-cost servers, even though this cannibalized their existing business in corporate computers. Although HP did see its sales rise strongly, its profits and revenue failed to follow. Part of the reason is that HP has been selling this new low-price technology using its traditional expensive sales techniques. Although there were efforts by Ms. Fiorina, HP's CEO at the time, to adjust salespeople's compensation, this is widely perceived as too little, too late.

By 2009 this strategic hell had even caught up with former star player Dell. Increased commoditization and the rise of savvy Eastern players like Lenovo and Acer meant that customers found it hard to differentiate Dell's products from those offered by Acer, for example. Cloud computing meant that bigger storage drives (one of Dell's big selling points) became less of a concern, and there was a shift toward notebooks as the primary use of a computer for many was becoming as a communication device. Furthermore, Dell was struggling to grow in new markets such as India and China, where an unwillingness to purchase on-line using credit cards and the lack of reliable parcel delivery networks made Dell's traditional business model difficult to roll out. Founder and former CEO Michael Dell felt compelled to return to the helm of the company, but he and every other commentator agreed that keeping Dell out of the strategic hell that was engulfing the established players in this industry was not going to be easy.

---

1. *Why do large parts of the technology industry appear to be turning into strategic hells of low profit margins?*
2. *Draw a Five Forces diagram to show the industry forces that led to Michael Dell's decision to seek to change tack by embracing a greater emphasis on services and design.*
3. *What would you advise Dell to do to pull itself out of the strategic hell that they seemed to be being drawn into in 2009?*

Case Notes:

3-5 Ranbaxy: Ranbaxy's Rise, Big Pharma's Demise?

This is how it used to work: "Big Pharma" companies came from developed Western countries, with names that people (in the West at least) knew and trusted: GlaxoSmithKlein, Merck, Shering Plough, Pfizer, Novartis, AstraZeneca. They employed the best scientists and patent lawyers. They paid low prices for ingredients from suppliers in developing countries like India. And, they dominated the world pharmaceutical markets with their global brands and respected salesforces. These companies controlled the industry terrain. But now they don't. The rise of Ranbaxy shows how the terrain has changed and gives some clues as to why.

Ranbaxy Laboratories Limited was founded in 1961. It began, like many Indian pharmaceutical companies, as a producer of ingredients. But, unlike most, it saw that the future was about moving up the value chain from supplying to competing with drug manufacturers, and it understood the value of overseas expansion. It started a research program, directing its scientists to perfect reverse engineering techniques that could drive the production of "generic drugs" (drugs with the same composition as branded drugs that have come off patent). From such moves emerged a strategy that current CEO, 34-year-old Malvinder Mohan Singh, describes as "low-cost, high-tech."

Ranbaxy established its first overseas subsidiary in Nigeria through a joint venture in 1977 with the express aim of exploiting its "process advantage by supplying cheap drugs to the unmet demand in a developing country" and in 1984 it expanded operations to Malaysia.

Ranbaxy entered the USA in 1995 by acquiring an FDA-approved manufacturer and in 1996 it started a joint venture with another US-based firm. In 1998 Ranbaxy established a 100% subsidiary in the USA and started marketing products under its brand name.

Within just four years of starting its US operations, Ranbaxy had achieved $100m in US sales. The firm also began expanding its production facilities in Europe by setting up a subsidiary in the UK (1994) and establishing a manufacturing plant in Ireland (1995), providing a base for Ranbaxy's forays into other European markets.

In recent years Ranbaxy has pursued an aggressive acquisition strategy to drive further internationalization. In 2004, the company acquired the fifth largest generics company in France. In 2006, Ranbaxy acquired two generic companies: Terapia in Romania, where Singh's winning of the deal surprised many (he under-bid his rivals on price but sealed the deal with his impassioned presentation of the "better fit" between Ranbaxy and the Romania company); and Ethimed in Belgium; before buying the large unbranded generic product portfolio of Allen SPA in Italy.

Ranbaxy's internationalization has resulted in a mix of revenues from emerging and developed markets far more balanced than the traditional Big Pharma companies. Which is handy, given that predictions are that pharmaceuticals sales growth will increasingly come from the "Emerging 7" (China, Brazil, India, South Korea, Mexico, Turkey, and Russia) and the "Rest of the World" rather than the traditional markets of the USA, the EU, and Japan.

For the future, Ranbaxy is gearing up its legal and R&D skills to move further along the value chain. In order to protect its competitive advantage, Ranbaxy is now applying for innovative process patents worldwide. Singh claims that the experience gained here is helping to develop the regulatory skills needed to obtain approval for its products under the "Abbreviated New Drug Applications" (ANDAs) scheme in the USA. And, on the R&D front, while Singh is clear that "our bread and butter is going to come from generics. Beyond 2012, I want to see Ranbaxy emerge as a strong hybrid player with substantial revenue flow from proprietary drugs."

In 40 years Ranbaxy had grown into India's largest pharmaceutical company. It produces what it calls "a wide range of quality, affordable generic medicines, trusted by healthcare professionals and patients across geographies." It has a presence in 23 of the top 25 pharmaceutical markets of the world, manufacturing facilities in 8 countries and customers in over 125 countries, a 12,000 strong multicultural workforce comprising 50 nationalities, a pool of over 1,200 scientists, and has recently signed collaborative research programs with GSK and Merck. In 2009, the company recorded global sales of $1,519m.

Then came a move that shocked many in the Indian business world. Ranbaxy was sold to traditional Japanese pharma company Daiichi Sankyo in June 2009. To some astonishment Daiichi valued Ranbaxy at 20 times its EBIDTA and 4 times its total sales and paid $4.6bn for a controlling stake. But the Japanese may still have got good value. It has bought a sound business with potential to grow, good access to growing developing markets, at a time when the Japanese government is looking to deregulate its own drugs market in an attempt to create competition and cut its own costs. The percentage of generic to branded drugs is about one third of the ratio in the USA and the UK.

Meanwhile, while Ranbaxy was growing in strength and influence, how was the industry environment opening up to provide them with opportunities for expansion?

Nils Pratley, financial correspondent from *The Guardian*, calls the 1990s the "glory years" for Big Pharma. In the period 1993–2003 the industry averaged a 14% return on investment in the US. During the same period, US Treasury Bonds paid 4.3%, the Hotel industry 5%, and the Mining and Oil sectors 9%. How did pharmaceuticals offer such good margins and good returns?

- After so many years in competition together, the Big Pharma companies had carved out their niches and they respected (to some extent at least) each other/s territories. *Competitive conduct* was fairly "gentlemanly."
- For many years the *buyers* of drugs – governments and insurance companies – had respected the authority of the Big Pharma companies. When Big Pharma put prices up, these customers tended to pay up, and to pass the burden on to taxpayers and insurance premiums.
- *End users* (i.e. patients) had high switching costs if they wanted to find alternatives. Complementary medicines or generics were generally not funded or covered by buyers, nor were they encouraged.
- This reduced the number of viable *substitutes* that could compete with conventional medicines.

- Patent laws and government regulations (again, partly out of respect to Big Pharma company advocates), and the value that end-users placed on the advice of established medical professionals and the branded drugs they had always prescribed, created very high *entry barriers* in the way of potential new competitors.
- The basic commodities that went into drugs could be bought quite cheaply from *suppliers* in developing countries whose own governments were often not well organized economically and desperate for foreign currency. Buyers and end-users paid little attention to the integrity or ethics that might be associated with a pharmaceutical supply chain.

But think about how these things have changed over the past decade.

By 2010 margins were getting tighter and tighter for the traditional Big Pharma companies. The good news was that decades of healthy margins had left most with some cash reserves: but what should they do with that cash to fight back? Some alternatives were already emerging when this case was written:

- Develop further legal expertise to re-establish legal barriers to entry, through tactics such as "patent clusters" (filing lots of new patents closely related to the patents that apply to nearly off-patent drugs, to confuse or intimidate potential copycats) or using out of court settlements to delay when generic manufacturers can effectively enter new markets.
- Achieve economies of scale through mergers and acquisitions.
- Partner in, or develop their own, generic manufacturing expertise.
- Reinvigorate their risk-taking in R&D (which their bureaucratic cultures may have stymied in the past).
- Acquire, or partner with, small innovative start-ups as a way of tapping into new potential breakthroughs.

---

1. *Draw a 5-Forces of Industry diagram that enables you to explain how the conditions for Ranbaxy's growth in the 1990s and 2000s emerged.*
2. *Do you think the acquisition of Ranbaxy puts Daiichi Sankyo in a stronger position? If so, how?*
3. *What advice would you give to traditional Big Pharma companies trying to compete in the new pharmaceutical industry environment?*

Case Notes:

3-6 BMX: From "Joe Kid" to ESPN

Look at any strategy textbook for a view of how an industry should evolve and the most likely image is the smooth incline and fall of the Industry Life Cycle (ILC). It begins with profile growing and revenue and profits coming on stream in the "Introduction" phase, climbing steeply during "Growth," leveling off during "Maturity," and dropping away in "Decline" (see Figure 3.3). But often real life doesn't run so smoothly. In reality, the macro-environment and various individual "movers and shakers" can insert speed bumps, dips, and unexpected climbs.

For example, sales of condoms dipped to nothing in the 1980s until the AIDs virus changed things, while social changes such as an emphasis on enjoying youthful activities or memories for longer have created what we might call a "nostalgia cycle" – whereby old products make a comeback as retro versions of their former selves: vinyl record albums and the sports shoe and car industries are some of the more visible examples of this. At the same time, key individuals can play a large role in what actually happens to an industry: think of Barrack Obama and US auto manufacturers.

While the basic phases of the ILC play a role, the shape of most industries' evolution may actually appear more like a BMX, or Bicycle Moto-Cross, track. An interesting example of this kind of undulating reality is provided in the recent documentary film called *Joe Kid on a Stingray,* which charts the history of BMX. The film tells the story of the birth and rebirth of that sport and its associated industry.

BMX probably began in 1963, when Schwinn produced a smaller, lighter bike called the Stingray, which enabled young kids to race and do tricks like their motocross heroes. Kids with bikes started to come out of their homes in the burgeoning suburbs of the western United States and look for tracks to race on.

A teenage entrepreneur called Scott Breithaupt started a series of BMX races in Long Beach, California, at around the same time as Palms Park in Santa Monica began to offer races and small amounts of prize money. Breithaupt and others began to form teams and then the teams started to go on the road. In an enthusiastic but ramshackle fashion, these teams headed west in their summer school holidays in old buses, with little money for food, and put on small exhibitions in cities and towns to the east.

Touring teams attracted a lot of interest from curious youths and, in turn, bicycle manufacturers as sponsors. New companies like Mongoose sought to work with the riders to develop stronger, better bikes that, in turn, led to better racing.

After a number of good years and growing professionalism, by the late 1970s interest began to wane. Until one BMX rider with unusually good control of his bike, Scott Haro, started noticing that people wanted to watch the funny little hops, jumps, and other tricks that he was perfecting. By 1980 Breithaupt's brand of BMX had bottomed-out, but Haro's "Freestyle" was on the rise.

One of the most important changes was that Freestyle tapped into changes in the American suburban environment. Freestyle teams toured shopping malls, giving displays in car parks dressed like "new wave" or glam rockers; a far cry from the dirty brushed shirts of the original BMXers on their edge-of-town dirt tracks. This attracted a new range of sponsors ready to endorse Haro and other teams. The new style, and new sponsors, also fueled further developments in bike technology with new products, such as shock-absorbing springs, foot pegs, and lighter frames.

At the time, Breithaupt thought they were a bunch of posers and weirdos, but, in the grand scheme of things and with the benefit of hindsight, he admits that Haro and the Freestyle movement were good for the sport – they gave it a new lease.

By 1988, Freestyle was in decline. But it morphed into two further evolved forms: Half-Pipe, which took advantage of the facilities provided by skateboard parks and ramps, and Street, which was about riding and doing tricks in an urban environment. These movements were relatively short-lived, however, and by 1992 sales of BMX-type bikes hit their lowest point since the 1960s. Most said that the sport was dying, if not already dead.

But Mat Hoffman wasn't going to let it. As he says in the film: "Everyone was saying it was dying, that was hard to take, it's not like they were just saying that your sport was dying, this was and is my life and I was like "I'm not dead!" This is my life and soul, all my love went into this. How can they say that. Even if it killed me I was going to show the world what my sport could be about."

And it nearly did. Hoffman, seeing the writing on the wall for Half-Pipe, left Team Haro to form his own team and began touring under the label "Bicycle Stunt Series." He and the community who joined him back on the tour circuit broke many bones pushing the jumps, twists, and flips from earlier styles to new extremes (the danger played well with a new group of teenagers and the musical styles of the mid-1990s).

Hoffman is no Obama, but his efforts, and the efforts of those who gathered round him, rejuvenated the industry and led to ESPN looking to promoting the sport on television. In 1995, the first ever ESPN-sponsored X-Games was held, and over the next few years the X-Games Tour became established as a multimillion dollar series of worldwide events.

Looking back, the riders from different eras show respect for each other, the industry as a whole, and the series of chapters within it that they had shaped. Even the down slopes played a role, explained rider Kenan Harkin: "During the down times . . . the riders got better, the technology got better, so that when it eventually got put on TV it wasn't just guys hopping on their tires. . . there was something great to watch."

The X-Games are now over a decade old, so what's next? "Where will it go?" laughs Harkin, "They've been asking that since the 70s. The technology gets better, the riders get better, the imagination never stops, so the sky is the limit."

According to rider Steve Swope, the answer to "what's next?" is "It's up to the next generation. It's up to them to get it done."

---

1. *Draw the Industry Life Cycle of BMX as outlined in this case. How do you account for the difference between its shape and the shape of the generic ILC from Figure 3.4?*
2. *Do you think that knowledge from other strategy pathways, such as the "Macro-Environmental" and "Movers and Shakers" frameworks, need to be incorporated into an industry evolution analysis such as this? If so, how?*
3. *What do you think might happen next with BMX?*

3-7 Royal Air Maroc I: Crumbling palaces

We have often found that students are good at extracting data from cases and filling in models. However, in many cases, far less ability is found in interpreting these analyses and synthesizing results. The following case about Royal Air Maroc, a North African airline, therefore consists of the following tools and frameworks already deployed and largely completed:

1. An industry analysis using Porter's **Five Forces framework** (Figure 3-7.1)
2. A competitor analysis looking at service quality and scope or coverage (Figure 3-7.2)
3. A macro-environmental analysis using the PESTLE framework (Figure 3-7.3)

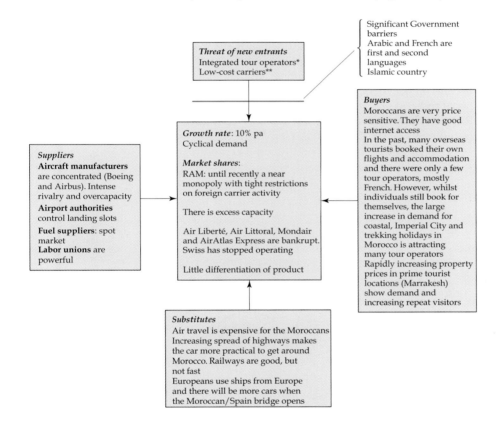

Threat of new entrants
Integrated tour operators*
Low-cost carriers**

Significant Government barriers
Arabic and French are first and second languages
Islamic country

Suppliers
Aircraft manufacturers are concentrated (Boeing and Airbus). Intense rivalry and overcapacity
Airport authorities control landing slots
Fuel suppliers: spot market
Labor unions are powerful

Growth rate: 10% pa
Cyclical demand

Market shares:
RAM: until recently a near monopoly with tight restrictions on foreign carrier activity

There is excess capacity

Air Liberté, Air Littoral, Mondair and AirAtlas Express are bankrupt. Swiss has stopped operating

Little differentiation of product

Buyers
Moroccans are very price sensitive. They have good internet access
In the past, many overseas tourists booked their own flights and accommodation and there were only a few tour operators, mostly French. However, whilst individuals still book for themselves, the large increase in demand for coastal, Imperial City and trekking holidays in Morocco is attracting many tour operators
Rapidly increasing property prices in prime tourist locations (Marrakesh) show demand and increasing repeat visitors

Substitutes
Air travel is expensive for the Moroccans
Increasing spread of highways makes the car more practical to get around Morocco. Railways are good, but not fast
Europeans use ships from Europe and there will be more cars when the Moroccan/Spain bridge opens

*Integrated tour operators	**Low-cost carriers
UK: FirstChoice	Corsair
Germany: TUI	AirEurope
Belgium: Jetair	Air Horizon
Spain: Globalia	easyJet
France: TUI France	Virgin Express
Italy: Alpitour	GB airways
	Hapag Lloyd and Air Berlin
	Neos
	RyanAir

Figure 3-7.1 Industry analysis (2004)

The exercise is for you to interpret them and to construct an argument toward answering the questions posed at the end.

1. Industry analysis (2004)

Note that free access in Morocco to low-cost airlines (easyJet, RyanAir) has recently been agreed.

2. Competitor analysis (January 2004)

- RAM (Royal Air Maroc) is the flagship carrier for Morocco. Created in 1957. It now has a capital of some MAD 1.5bn (16 MAD = £1). The main shareholder is the Moroccan Government with 94.39%. The remaining shareholders include Air France and Iberia.
- RAM operates scheduled flights on domestic routes and over 40 international destinations. It has a fast-growing fleet consisting of Airbus A321-220s and new Boeing 737s. RAM conveys 3.7 million passengers per year and runs 150 flights per day. It operates out of Casablanca, which is the main hub for international flights in Morocco.
- RAM has a partnership with Regional Airlines, in which it leases them the aircraft and decides on networks, products, and markets. RAM deals with distribution and operational costs.
- RAM has obtained the first international certificates in Africa for technical skills, including ISO 9002, ISO 9001.

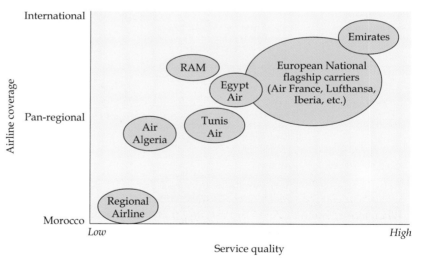

Figure 3-7.2 Competitor analysis (January 2004)

Political	Moroccan Government's priority is the growth of the tourist industry through '2010 Vision'; to reach 10 million tourists p.a. This involves the investment of 3bn euros in hotels and the opening of five new sea resorts
	The Government is also encouraging foreign tour operators to come to Morocco
	In 2001 Morocco approved an open sky agreement with the USA as well as other European countries
	Morocco is requesting integration into the EU sky. EU regulations and technical controls are being applied increasingly
	The Government has signed the liberalization programme between Arab countries. Complete liberalization is intended for November 2006
	9/11 raises need for increased security through pre-flight identification
	Iraq war
	Terrorist bomb in Casablanca
Economic	The currency is tightly controlled and stable against major world currencies
	Rising petrol costs
	Iraq war
Sociocultural	The Moroccan communities in Europe are important and make regular trips to Morocco for holidays
	Religious events, such as pilgrimage to Mecca and "Omra" generate significant traffic from Morocco to MEA
	While Arabic and French are the first two languages in Morocco, English is spreading rapidly in major tourist areas
	Morocco has realized that the hospitality of shop owners insisting on inviting tourists into their shops is often perceived in a negative way by foreigners and this "pestering" is now more tightly controlled
Technological	New channels of distribution are evolving rapidly with internet technology
	Although statistics show relatively low per-head use of the internet in Morocco, each terminal has a large number of users
	The growth in worldwide demand has led to the development of high-capacity aircraft
Legal	The air transport sector is being liberalized at the national and pan-national levels – scheduled and chartered activities are effective February 2004

Figure 3-7.3 Impact matrix using key ESTEMPLE elements

3. Macro-environmental analysis

NB: You can develop the issues discussed in this case further by reading "Royal Air Maroc II: Red, green, and blue" (Case 4-7) in the next chapter, Corporate Strategy.

1. *Looking at the frameworks above, discuss the challenges facing the Moroccan airline industry.*
2. *Is there anything that you would add to these frameworks, based on your own research or changes since this case was written?*
3. *What actions should RAM take resulting from your conclusions?*

Case Notes:

Part II The Strategic Organization

Why Does the Multibusiness (M-form) Exist?[1]

Historically, companies in the USA were configured as a "Unitary" whole, divided into functional responsibilities. The CEO's major strategic role in managing this U-form was to coordinate the efforts of the various functions of the business (see Figure 4.1). However, the weakness of the U-form became apparent as firms grew in size and complexity and attempted to adjust to environmental changes. CEOs became overly involved in routine matters and neglected their longer term strategic role. Functional managers saw their function as an end in itself. Coordination between increasingly stand-alone "functional silos" became more demanding and less fruitful.

Facing such problems, the large US companies Sears Roebuck, DuPont, General Motors, and Jersey Standard moved to the "Multidivisional" (M-form)[1] structure in the early 1920s. They were divided into semi-autonomous profit centers, later known as **"strategic business units" (SBUs)**, responsible for a stand-alone segment of the firm's operations, such as a particular product, brand, or national/regional market. In this structure (see Figure 4.1) the new business managers were able to specialize in the operations of their particular competitive arena and engage in **competitive strategy** – managing the customer/competitor dynamic as the ultimate source of profit. This freed corporate managers at the center of the firm to focus on the overall strategic direction of the company, or **corporate strategy**. Here the concerns are the **scope** of the product markets, industries, and geographies addressed by the firm and how value may be added above the sum of the component parts.

By the late 1960s over 80% of the Fortune 500 companies were structured in this way with similar trends in other industrialized countries. Now the M-form company is the most prevalent structure among large businesses. It has established a new layer of management, the corporate office, and with it, *corporate strategy*.

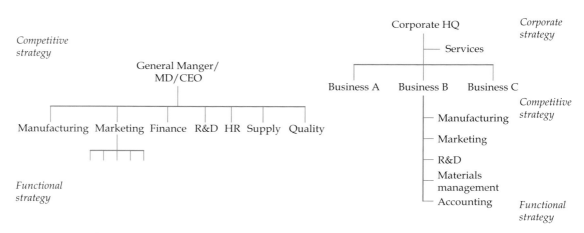

Figure 4.1 The U form (left) and the M-form (right)

108

What Scope of Businesses should they own?

The original M-form adopters had a relatively narrow product-market focus. Their component businesses had similarities in terms of products, processes, markets, underlying capabilities, or some other important attribute. These businesses can be described as **related**. However, companies faced limits to growth in their original product markets and, over the past 80 years, other factors encouraged further increases in product market diversity:

- Many firms had significant levels of free cash and managers tend to reinvest rather than return money to shareholders – this is linked to the fact that managerial salary and perks are often positively related to the size of their business empire.[2]
- The concept of the company as a portfolio of risky assets became popular in the 1970s and the risk of the bundle could be reduced by diversifying into different assets.
- The M-structure made the acquisition and divestment of business units easier than before as the messy tie-ups with other products/regions had been cut.

These factors encouraged expansion through **related diversification**, which is typically manifested as **vertical** and/or **horizontal integration** beyond the original narrow product-market focus.

Firms **vertically integrate** by buying other businesses upstream in their value chain (i.e. they buy into their supplier base) or downstream (i.e. they buy into the customer end). The original Ford Motor Company was integrated from the forests supplying the wood for the dashboard facia to the dealers selling the final, black, product. Essentially vertical integration can be characterized as the "make" side of the **"make or buy" decision**. The benefits of vertical integration lie in the reduction of **transaction costs**. In particular, where businesses are dependent on one supplier or customer, then they are vulnerable to being held to ransom and hence might be better off buying that supplier or customer.[3]

Horizontal integration means buying businesses with products, processes, or services that are **complementary** to those of other businesses in the portfolio. Typical manifestations are when firms buy other businesses selling the "same" products in the same industry (e.g. Daimler buying Chrysler in the automobile industry) or buy other businesses with complementary skills (e.g. Procter & Gamble buying Gillette on the basis of complementary consumer branding capabilities). The value from horizontal integration lies in optimizing **economies of scale and scope**. These kinds of gains are what managers often mean when they justify an acquisition on the grounds of "**synergy**" (more on synergy later). A firm might also gain through an increase in **market power** through being able to exert increased pressure on suppliers or customers or by simply reducing competitive rivalry by acquiring rivals or complementary firms.

Where businesses are brought into the corporate portfolio and have no common characteristic, they can be described as **unrelated diversifications**. *In extremis* these are **conglomerate** companies of which GE (of Jack Welch fame) is a classic example. Unrelated diversification initially emerged as a means for corporate growth when anti-monopoly legislation prevented related diversification.

It was also encouraged by developments in the practices and theory of corporate strategy, particularly those emphasizing the value of general management and the risk reduction of diversified portfolios. The value logic of unrelated diversification relies on the corporate center acting as a better-informed and powerful shareholder. In stand-alone businesses, managers can maximize their "on-the-job consumption" by, for example, taking business trips to exotic locations with their wives. They can also disguise or hide poor performance. As part of a corporation, the business is subject to the frequent reporting and use of auditing functions to maintain the integrity of information. Managers are paid at market rates but are compelled to perform to high standards to maintain their position, and the corporate level can intervene at an early stage to correct poor performance.

As the number of multidivisional firms grew, so too did the interest in their financial performance, with the debate generally centering on the differences between related and unrelated diversifiers. In an early study, Richard Rumelt[4] came up with the intuitively appealing conclusion that, in terms of value creation, related diversifiers outperformed unrelated diversifiers – intuitively appealing because **synergy** seems more logical among related businesses. Subsequent research has not unanimously supported this finding and it seems that the characteristics of the business and its industry, the skills and imagination of management, and the corporate strategy being implemented all have impacts on performance.

With these strategic options available to corporate centers, there was a need to make decisions about which direction of development was most desirable. This corporate strategy question of "where should we expand/invest?" gave rise to portfolio management tools, the most famous of which was the growth–share matrix or, more colloquially, the **Boston Boxes** (from its origins with the Boston Consulting Group). Beginning life in the early 1970s, as a doodled framework for the Mead Paper Corporation, the Boston Box evolved into the now-famous **cash cows**, **dogs** (initially "pets"), **question marks**, and **stars** (Figure 4.2). It combined insights about the cost-reducing effects of the **experience curve** (and hence the importance of relative market share) with the notion of **sustainable growth** and fostered the orientation that cash-generating cows provided funds for cash-needy question marks so that they might become cash rich and growing stars. This virtuous cycle is illustrated in the figure. Dogs were either run down for cash or sold off.[5]

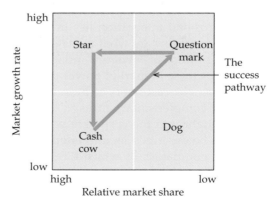

Figure 4.2 The growth-share matrix

Other more complex matrices followed.[6] McKinsey, through its association with GE, developed the **GE/McKinsey Business Screen** – a well-known, nine-cell portfolio planning matrix with an "industry attractiveness" axis in place of the "market growth rate" and the business unit's "competitive strength" instead of "relative market share" (Figure 4.3). The **industry attractiveness** axis combines an aggregate weighting[7] of factors deemed important in the organization's industry (e.g. market size, projected growth, structure, profitability) while the **competitive strength** axis aggregates such factors as market share, advertising effectiveness, experience curve effects, and others deemed relevant.

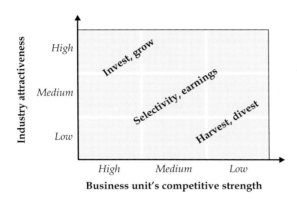

Figure 4.3 The GE/McKinsey Business Screen

Both matrices generated strategic imperatives (such as "invest," "divest," "harvest," and "manage for cash") that depended on a business unit's position in the matrix. Through these matrices the corporate direction of the firm could be established.

By the end of the 1970s, nearly half of the Fortune 500 companies were using portfolio planning as a driver of their corporate strategy. What had begun as an analytic aid to one corporation had become a strategic model for all multibusiness companies. Corporate strategists believed in the need for "balance" in their portfolio of companies, where balance extended to risk,[8] cash generation, geographical spread, etc. This logic legitimated the acquisition of businesses outside of the parent's core activity and gave rise to a huge wave of diversifying mergers and acquisitions during the 1970s and 1980s. Share markets responded positively and rewarded diversification moves through increased stock prices. Businesses were treated as financial instruments to be bought and sold in the context of an existing portfolio of assets rather than to be *managed*. The stand-alone dynamics of the M-form structure facilitated this orientation, as did the movement toward controlling business units through financial outputs rather than managing them through behavioral inputs.

Unfortunately the search for cash and risk balance brought more and more unconnected businesses together under one corporate umbrella, and the complexity of managing these different businesses became too much for even the most capable corporate office. As a result the share market began to devalue conglomerates and the stock value of the firm became lower than the sum of the market capitalization of the separate businesses – the so-called **conglomerate discount**. The corporate raiders of the 1980s benefited from this by recognizing that the sum of the parts of these conglomerates greatly exceeded the value of the whole. They borrowed huge amounts to buy these conglomerates and then un-bundled the component businesses, paid back their borrowings, and became even richer on the proceeds.

By the end of the 1980s, the academic, business, and investment worlds had largely turned away from portfolio management as a viable corporate strategy. Even though debate continues as to the relative merits of *related* versus *unrelated* acquisitions, the overall picture is that most corporate acquisitions destroyed rather than created value (see Angwin 2007 for a review of performance). As Goold et al. (1994) pointed out, companies had to overcome the **beating the odds** paradox, in that the probability of value-adding success through acquisition was empirically low.

While the portfolio technique was a major approach to determine which businesses to own, it became clear that the corporate center had to provide inputs to add value to these businesses. Without group-based value, shareholders should invest in the separate businesses themselves without the imposition of expensive corporate overhead. This raises the questions, then, of how to achieve synergistic value between the businesses in excess of their value as individual units and how the corporate center can bring about such added value.

Corporate Strategy as Adding Value – the Whole Worth More than the Sum of the Parts

The beginning of the chapter described the problem that ICI was forced to consider as a consequence of Hanson's hostile bid – how can the firm justify not breaking itself up into separate stand-alone businesses in which shareholders can invest as they see fit?

There are two important, interrelated questions here for those managing a multibusiness firm (and for those planning to invest in multidivisional firms):

1. *What is the added value created by having a set of businesses in one business?*
   To make sense from an economics/financial perspective, any multidivisional business must have a greater ongoing value (V_c) than the sum of its component, stand-alone businesses (A_s, B_s, etc.): i.e. $V_c > A_{s+}$, B_{s+}, C_s. This is the age-old corporate dynamic of **synergy**. In non-economic terms, authors have expressed the quest for synergy in terms of a **dominant logic**[9] (the concept that a unifying idea links the unit) and/or in shared **core competences**[10] (a unifying set of resources or capabilities that underpin the value-generating processes or product of all business units).
2. *How should this grouping be managed to develop and maintain this added value?*
   The answers to this question lie in the organizational processes of corporate strategy, with a particular focus on the role and activities of the corporate center.

In addressing these questions, Michael Porter[11] suggested four mechanisms of value-creation. Michael Goold and his colleagues also identified four routes to **parenting advantage**,[12] which, although named differently, are congruent with

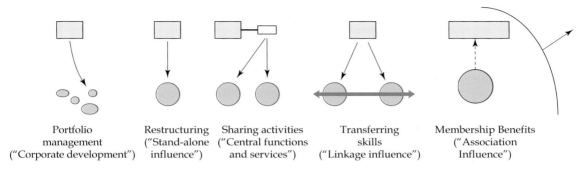

Portfolio management ("Corporate development")   Restructuring ("Stand-alone influence")   Sharing activities ("Central functions and services")   Transferring skills ("Linkage influence")   Membership Benefits ("Association Influence")

Figure 4.4 Value-adding approaches of the center

Porter's classification. These mechanisms (Goold et al.'s version in brackets) are as follows:

- Portfolio management ("Corporate development")
- Restructuring ("Stand-alone influence")
- Sharing activities ("Central functions and services")
- Transferring skills ("Linkage influence")

These four styles require specific managerial action but there is a further way in which being part of a group may add value.

- Membership benefits ("Association influence")

These five styles can be represented diagrammatically as shown in Figure 4.4.

Portfolio management (corporate development)

Despite the negative view of the portfolio-based conglomerate, this does not mean that it no longer exists as a business technique, or that those that use it inevitably perform badly. In the five years to the end of 2009, which incorporates the beginning of the global financial crisis the DHIA (Dow Jones Industrial Average) had lost 3.3% of its value while the broader S&P 500 (Standard and Poor's 500) index was down by 8%. The share prices of most conglomerates did worse than these indices. For example, GE's share price was down by nearly 60% over that time with Newell Rubbermaid off by 38% and Ingersoll Rand down 11% (all values adjusted for stock splits). But not all conglomerates did badly as 3M's share price was 1% higher. However, as any investor can develop its own portfolio; the corporate center needs to do more than be a proxy for that investor if it is to attract investment funds.

Restructuring (stand-alone influence)

In its purest sense, **restructuring** relies for its value-adding potential on (1) the insight of the corporate office in spotting and buying an underperforming business at a low price, and (2) its capability to then address the weaknesses of the business and bring it to its full potential (and then resell it at a higher price commensurate with its new value). The sale rarely happens in practice and this form of corporate strategy more generally entails the corporate layer (including the

CEO) exerting *ongoing* and direct *stand-alone influence* on the actions and decisions of otherwise autonomous business units.

Business units may still be fully autonomous with respect to other business units, but they are subject to strategic and operational direction and control from above. Influence occurs through a variety of mechanisms, ranging from direct commands ("do this!") to indirect control through policy manuals, pronouncements, or a set of prescribed targets ("achieve this!"). The frequency, intensity, and focus of interaction depends on the culture of the corporation and the personality of the CEO, and varies from the "light touch" of strategic reviews to the "blowtorch" inquisition of every negative variance.

The classic **restructurer** was ICI's predator, Hanson PLC. Along with its arm in the USA (Hanson Industries), this company made a practice of acquiring companies in mature, asset-based industries providing essential goods and services. To meet the Hanson criteria for purchase, the business needs to have a leading position (and, hence, a good cash flow) and a well-known name in its market. But, most importantly, it must be performing at a level below its capability. Having acquired the business, a Hanson team immediately began to lift operating efficiency, reduce waste and excess overhead, cull non-profitable products and customers, divest non-core assets, and identify strategic focus and new management. The local management then ran the business in a completely decentralized way, although heavily incentivized through substantial bonus payments or the threat of dismissal, to meet fiercely demanding operating and growth targets "agreed" with the parent body.

In this category of corporate strategy, the center is an *active* manager of its businesses rather than the passive investor of the portfolio management approach. However, it is still difficult for the center, having completed any restructuring, to add value on an ongoing basis over that of a motivated, informed set of business managers. Goold et al. (1994) refer to the **10 percent versus 100 percent** paradox, wherein it defies logic that "part-time" corporate managers can, by spending only 10% of their time in the business, do better in terms of business performance than the dedicated business managers spending 100% of their time on the same issues. If this were to be the case it would suggest a chronic incapability in the business managers and the solution to that problem is obvious.

Sharing activities (central functions and services)

Parenting advantage, or core competence, from this category of corporate strategy arises from functional or process experts at the corporate level. These individual or departmental experts either **augment** the existing expertise in the business or **substitute** for it.

In an **augmenting** structure, the central resources have the time and resources to develop world-class capability in their functional expertise whereas the business function, through time and resource restriction, must focus on the day-to-day operations. One corporation in the automotive components industry in the UK has a **Kaizen** (continuous improvement) team in each of its businesses but also has a corporate team that brings best practice Kaizen processes to the businesses. In a corporation with an augmenting orientation, the business units may still have autonomous capability but be subject to compulsory oversight by the corporate function (an influencing relationship) or may have a voluntary consultancy or customer–supplier relationship. A classic example of a mix of compulsory/voluntary inputs is the corporate manufacturing services function of the American company Cooper Industries. New businesses acquired by Cooper underwent a compulsory process of "Cooperization" by the Manufacturing Services group, who worked with the operations staff of the acquired business to transfer Cooper's processes and know-how. Once businesses had become fully fledged members, however, the Manufacturing Services group intervened only on invitation from the Division Manager.[13]

Substitution means that particular functions or facilities are taken out of the businesses and centralized at corporate level. As well as the standard service functions, such as taxation and legal offices, more strategic functions, including distribution, branding, quality, R&D, finance, manufacturing, and others, have been centralized by various M-form companies around the world. Synergistic value is added through economies of scale, benefits of functional specialization, and increased focus on a smaller number of key processes at operational level. Businesses are no longer completely autonomous in their overall day-to-day functioning but rely on "sharing activities" with the corporate function to function as a business. A typical example of substitution took place at a UK multibusiness automotive company that, since 2002, has centralized the purchasing of steel. The corporate center realized that autonomous purchasing by the businesses was not exploiting the potential supplier power that concentrating the buying might bring. Annual savings of over £3m were achieved by this consolidation.

To truly add value at the level of sharing activities, Goold and his colleagues (1994) emphasize that the corporate center has to overcome the **beating the specialists** paradox. Stand-alone businesses are free to outsource any function or process to outside specialists who have greater capability and/or higher efficiency in that arena. This is happening on a worldwide scale, as companies outsource call centers, software writing, manufacturing, and other functions to Eastern Europe, Mexico, India, China, or any other country with comparative advantage. To justify its place as the external provider of a business function/process, the corporate center needs to show that it has a sustainable competitive advantage over other external providers. The fact that the corporate center can provide a central service *better than the businesses can do separately* is only one part of the corporate strategy question. An increasingly important second part is: can the corporate center provide that service better than a world-class specialist?

Transferring skills (linkage influence)

Corporate strategy in this category is based on interactions *between* the businesses. The primary source of parenting advantage lies in the transfer of knowledge-based best practice and competitive capabilities and occurs in practice through such mechanisms as staff transfer, cross-business work teams, and shared objectives. Economists describe this as facilitating economies of scope wherein related business units share specialized physical capital, learning and knowledge, management expertise, and so on. Of all of the categories of corporate strategy, this is the level that seems to have most theoretical support as having the potential for adding value beyond the individual businesses through the development of **core competences** that transcend business boundaries.

Canon's capabilities in optics, mechanics, and electronics transcend its product–business boundaries in printers, cameras, copiers, faxes, etc. as does Sony's focus on miniaturization and Wal-Mart's complex capability in logistics. Honda's complex matrix structure in Europe aims to exploit a core competence in engine design as well as economies of scale across all its country-based businesses and its product groupings of motorcycles, lawn mowers, and cars. Similarly 3M's obsession with innovation is primary whereas the product groups resulting from this obsession are the secondary consequence of this competence. Large corporate staffs often manage these pan-corporate competences; they require ongoing effort, commitment, and expense. Another requirement is to do battle with business/country/product managers, who rarely relinquish their autonomy without a fight – a fight they continue to engage in even when the benefits of sharing seem well established.[14]

Goold et al. (1994) suggest that the paradox to overcome here is one of **enlightened self-interest**, wherein the managers of stand-alone businesses could link with other businesses equally well outside of a corporate framework. While such sharing is theoretically possible for stand-alone businesses, it is unlikely because these (related) businesses would normally be competitors and the risk of opportunistic exploitation is difficult to eliminate. The risks are particularly acute where the sharing involves knowledge-based competencies. Once the knowledge is transferred from one party there is little incentive for the other party to reciprocate or to maintain the relationship unless there are significant ongoing and/or future gains that are contingent on continuous dealing. Many well-intentioned alliances flounder when one or other party begins to feel that the outcomes from the engagement are minor compared with those of its partner. Once businesses are part of the same corporation, however, these issues of exploitation theoretically disappear because all parties are on the same team and therefore have a mutual interest in the overall value of the interactions.

Hence, corporate strategy at this level offers the potential for substantial value creation, but the power of a corporate hierarchy is generally needed to ensure the development and maintenance of pan-business capabilities, as business units cease to be autonomous in the conventional sense of stand-alone operation. While not necessarily dependent on other units or functions for day-to-day operating, they become strategically interdependent on one another or on a corporate function or activity they all share. The businesses are participants in or users of important strategic resources that they cannot unilaterally direct or control. Their delegated, stand-alone activities are fewer and narrower and performance measurement is more ambiguous. Rarely do the managers in the businesses become completely comfortable with these constraints and rarely do they totally cease struggling against them.

Membership benefits (Association influence)

Parenting Advantage is about value creation through active management from the corporate center. However, benefits do accrue to subsidiaries from simply being part of a larger group. This may allow them to raise capital more cheaply, increase their borrowing capacity, and obtain other material inputs on better terms if the credit worthiness of the parent company is better than their own. Ownership by a large corporation, especially one with a high reputation and strong finances, may allow increased new subsidiary bargaining power with consumers who may draw comfort that their supplier is backed by a robust parent. For this reason after a merger it is not unusual for a new subsidiary company to add a parent brand name/logo to their products/services in order to encourage confidence in potential purchasers. For example, after the acquisition of Skoda cars by Volkswagen AG, subsequent advertisements showed a Skoda badge or product in the foreground with a Volkswagen shadow behind. This graphically showed that a larger, stronger, technically advanced and trusted company was standing behind Skoda and this was successful in substantially raising consumer confidence in their new cars.

Corporate Strategy and the Role of the Center

The unwelcome bid by Hanson for ICI, which opened the chapter, asked a pertinent question of a multibusiness firm: is the value of the whole greater than the sum of the parts? Directly this questions whether the corporate center is adding value beyond the intrinsic components of the firm.

If we viewed ICI as an unrelated group of businesses, then corporate managers should be better-informed shareholders who have access to their businesses in a way that outside shareholders do not and they can intervene earlier if there are signs of underperformance. Being closer to the businesses, they can ask more relevant questions of local managers and replace those who are unable to achieve. The corporate center is also able to allocate resources and capital more efficiently than external markets. Clearly Hanson did not perceive the corporate center to be adding any value through these mechanisms that couldn't be achieved by the businesses standing alone.

If we viewed ICI as a set of related businesses, then we would expect to find value added from the sharing of activities and linkages between the businesses. The corporate center would provide centralized facilities – **coaching** at both general and functional management level and **coordinating and driving** the inter-business relationships. Hanson, however, believed that the corporate center was not better than an outsourced specialist supplier at providing facilities or better at developing business value through developing linkages than motivated, competent, self-interested business managers.

Hanson's bid poses a generic question for all multibusinesses: why should their portfolios not be floated and become truly autonomous without the encumbrance of an additional layer of expensive management? Although ultimately unsuccessful in its bid for ICI, the de-merger of Zeneca shortly afterwards suggests Hanson's question was a good one.

Corporate Strategy Key Learnings Mind Map

Having read and reviewed the chapter outline what do you believe to be the key learnings from the chapter and the relationships between these.

4-1 Z Enterprises: Parenting problems[15]

Chen Song, the CEO of Z Enterprises, had a dilemma. Although Z was profitable and growing it had failed to achieve a number of operating targets for the most recent financial year. The key among these were *Quality, Inventory* control and product *Cost* reduction (Table 4-1.1). The US based board, on which Chen Song sat, had expressed their disappointment with these shortfalls and had asked him to prepare a report detailing how he planned to get these measures back on track for the following year.

Z is a corporation made of three businesses which design and manufacture parts for the domestic and export automotive industry. They all use capital intensive processes in value-added manufacture and have to meet the same quality, cost and delivery standards. 70% of the Original Equipment Manufacturer (OEM) customer base is common to all three with over 90% being common to at least two. The managers and technical staff and many of the senior shopfloor personnel have expertise in a variety of the processes that contribute to increasing productivity and quality such as total quality management (TQM), business process reengineering (BPR) and just in time (JIT) inventory control. The Managing Directors (MDs), along with the Corporate Finance Office and a small Human Resources department report to Chen Song as part of the Corporate Management Board (CMB) which meets monthly, hosted by each business in turn (Figure 4-1.1).

A in Table 4-1.1 was the original business of Z enterprises. It had originally been a State Owned Enterprise (SOE) making parts for agricultural machinery but had been bought by an overseas group and switched to manufacturing exhaust systems for automobiles after China's acceptance into the WTO. Chen Song had been the Managing Director of A when it was acquired. He had impressed the new owners with his energy and dedication and the way in which he had transformed the culture and operations of A from an inefficient, bloated, rundown SOE to a productive, lean, state-of-the art company.

A, a Shanghai-based operation, now employs 530 people (down from over 2,000). The MD, Wu Min, who had risen through the engineering function to become Chen Song's understudy, is regarded as a tough but fair manager who engenders a shared passion (and expertise) for cost reduction in all employees. B and C were acquired in the past three years. They had both been start-up companies aimed at cashing in on the growing automotive industry. B, located near Guangzhou, has 370 employees engaged in the manufacture of various pressed metal components. MD Yu XiuBao, part of the original start-up syndicate, is an aggressive, entrepreneurial woman who believes that inventory is the basis of all (manufacturing) evil. C, close to Beijing,

Table 4-1.1 Selected operational outcomes (targets) for latest financial year (best in **bold**)

	A	B	C	Z
Quality* (%)	6.12　(4.5)	4.54　(4.0)	**3.03　(3.5)**	4.51　(4.0)
Inventory (turns)	16.34　(20.0)	**22.18 (20.0)**	15.17 (24.0)	18.23 (22.0)
Cost (%)	**−7.24 (−5.0)**	−2.1 (−4.0)	0　(−6.0)	−3.5 (−5.0)

*These measures are aggregates: i.e. *quality*, expressed as a percentage of output that is faulty, combines production and customer reject figures; *inventory* measures all stock (i.e. raw material, components, work in progress (WIP), and finished goods (FG)) and is expressed as stock turns; and *cost* is the real (i.e. inflation adjusted) decrease in overall direct product costs for the year.

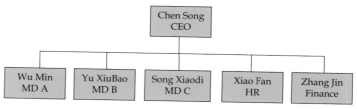

Figure 4-1.1 Organizational structure of Z's Corporate Management Board

employs 250 people in generating the highest margins in the corporation from its high-technology components for sophisticated "vision systems" ("mirrors"). MD, Song Xiaodi is well-liked but has a reputation for sometimes favoring analysis over action, except when it comes to his obsession with quality. The managers of C feel superior to their counterparts in A and B. This sense of superiority is well known by the others and is strongly resented.

In addition to a salary, each MD earns a significant bonus based on a percentage of his/her business's profit. Business (and hence corporate) profits had initially grown rapidly but the industry was maturing, sales growth had plateaued and there was increasing pressure on price. Hence it was clear to Chen Song that more returns needed to be squeezed from internal processes. The businesses currently operate as stand-alone, autonomous units with the only structured contact being between the MDs at the monthly CMB meeting. As well as direct instruction to the MDs at these meetings (and individually) Chen Song had often pointed out to the group that each of the businesses was excellent at some things but poor at others (Table 4-1.1) and that it would benefit everyone if this "best practice" was shared. "We have islands of excellence – we need bridges!" he exhorted. The MDs insisted that they did share knowledge but in reality inter-business relationships were highly competitive; there had been too many examples where managers had "forgotten" to pass on necessary knowledge to the counterparts outside of their own business. Even Chen Song's practice of rotating the CMB meetings between businesses was to avoid charges of a "Shanghai" bias that would arise from meeting in his office in Pudong (Shanghai).

Chen Song pondered his dilemma. When he was a business MD he had vehemently defended business autonomy and the right to manage "his" business without corporate interference. "Let me run it and if you're not happy – sack me" was one of his typical responses. He knew that his own MDs would be just as aggressive. Despite this he could see clearly that without some corporate intervention the business improvement in their areas of weakness would take far too long. Having thought about it for some time he could see a variety of options, each with its own benefits and challenges.

What are the options, their strengths, and weaknesses, and what would you recommend?

1. *What are Chen's options?*
2. *Outline what you believe to be the strengths and weaknesses of each of these options.*
3. *What would you recommend that Chen should do?*

◄◄◄ Parenting Problems: Some ideas toward a "model answer". . .

Chen Song faces a dilemma that confronts many who are in charge of multidivisional companies. The businesses and their MDs are fiercely autonomous and want to stay that way, but this desire for separateness, what Prahalad and Hamel (1990) refer to as the "tyranny of the SBU" (Strategic Business Unit), prevents the development of pan-corporate competencies and/or the sharing of best practice. From Table 4-1.1 in this case we can see, for example, that business A is the best at cost reduction. Hence the corporation can benefit from A sharing its expertise with B and C while at the same time benefiting from their knowledge of inventory control techniques and quality management, respectively. Similarly, B and C will improve by sharing with each other and A. Note that although each business is meeting its target on one of the measures, the corporation as a whole is not meeting its targets on any measure. Chen Song has three major options (and, of course, any mixture of the three) each of which has advantages and disadvantages:

1. Use direct influence on stand-alone units

In this corporate style Chen Song would be a "guru." He would work directly with each MD to improve the areas of shortfall. So, for example, he would work with Wu Min to improve A's quality and inventory management. This might involve such things as changing the bonus structure to incorporate more measures than just profit (i.e. an internal "balanced scorecard"), insisting that A hired more experts or used outside consultants to focus on those areas, or merely threatening to replace Wu Min if improvements are not forthcoming.

The advantages of this approach are that it maintains the focus of the businesses on their particular product/market/customers and their particular problems (what the economists would call "optimizing economies of specialization"). Also, it does not add to corporate overheads and keeps the MDs happy in that they are running autonomous businesses. The disadvantages are that it does not promote any pan-corporate competences but maintains the "islands of (different) excellence." It also puts Chen Song in a "supervisory" role and will take up all his time. It is unlikely that he is an expert in all three processes, therefore the potential for conflict between him and his subordinates is high, particularly if business priorities change and he is forced to change focus.

2. Develop corporate centres of excellence

In this option the corporate centre develops competence in a process or function. For example, Chen Song could hire a Corporate Quality Manager who would put together a team of experts to form the Corporate Quality Department. There are three general mechanisms by which such corporate services operate:

(a) As advisory experts to the business function to be called on when needed by the business or to be imposed if targets are not met.
(b) As a centralized function wherein the responsibility is at corporate level, not at business level. Functional employees, although perhaps located in the business, are controlled and administered from the corporate level.

(c) As a matrix-like amalgam of (a) and (b), whereby the business function reports to both the MD of the business and the corporate department. This is a very common structure for the finance function for example which often reports to both the local business manager and the corporate finance function.

With arrangements of this sort the corporate centre becomes a facilities manager. The advantages are such that Chen Song can be more confident that business functions will be directly focused on corporate level targets without him having to try to influence this through the MDs and spending a lot of time on it. The corporate level functions, free from the grind of day-to-day operations, can maintain a world-class capability by visiting and benchmarking world leaders and attending training events. They can then pass this expertise on to the business level through normal interactions (tacit knowledge is shared by interaction). The disadvantages lie in the added costs at corporate level (and the MDs are always very sensitive to allocated overhead costs) and the fact that it may engender an "us (business) versus them (corporate)" dynamic. Mr Chen would need to be sure that the benefits would outweigh the added cost (including the costs of the turmoil of "start up") because he can be sure that the MDs and his corporate bosses will notice if they don't.

3. Broaden the responsibility of the businesses[16]

With this approach Chen Song changes the roles of the MDs. Currently they "own" their business and are rewarded in both monetary and psychological terms for championing their own causes. It is the sense of what they "own" that needs to change under this approach. The MDs need to see themselves as "stewards" of the businesses and (part) "owners" of the corporation. Some mechanisms for moving to this approach include

(a) Changing the bonuses of the MDs from being based on business results to being based on corporate results, or a combination of both (e.g. the bonus is based on business results but is only triggered if the corporation achieves its targets).
(b) Making the MDs accountable for overall operating processes (i.e. corporate level) rather than just the business processes. So Song Xiaodi might become the corporate quality manager, for example, as well as the MD of C. In this way he has a vested interest in sharing his expertise around the other businesses because his quality responsibilities have been broadened. In a similar way the MDs of the other businesses can be given corporate responsibilities.
(c) Ensuring that robust inter-business processes, such as regular meetings, exchange of employees, co-located functions (i.e. multi-site), shared databases, joint presentation to customers, etc. are established and maintained.

In this approach the corporate centre (Chen Song) acts as a "boundary rider" ensuring that fences are being knocked down and not rebuilt. It has the advantages of developing truly pan-corporate best practice across a number of dimensions and getting the MDs (and eventually all employees) to have a broader perspective. Its disadvantages lie in the additional costs, including those of complexity and hassle and the strong possibility that by getting managers to focus on both the business *and* the corporation they will not focus sufficiently on either. As somebody once said "more than one objective is no objective".

So now what would you do?

4-2 GE: A conglomerate by any other name?

In 1879 Thomas Edison invented the electric light bulb and by 1890 had organized his various businesses into the Edison General Electric Company – now the General Electric Company (GE). GE is the sole survivor of the Dow Jones index of 1896 and was number 4 by revenues in the 2009 Fortune 500. While in the top ranks by revenue, the company has failed to translate its revenues into returns to shareholders. For the 2009 financial year its total return to shareholders was a loss of 0.4% (ranking the company 404th in the top 500). Over the ten-year period up to 2009, GE had *lost* an average of 8.9% per year for its shareholders, which ranked it in 351st position. A lot of this underperformance is attributable to the company's high exposure to financial markets during the Global Financial Crisis. Nevertheless such performance levels do not look good for Jeff Immelt who, in 2001, was appointed GE's 9th CEO as successor to the legendary Jack Welch who, in his 20-year reign as CEO, had overseen the growth of the company from $13 bn to several hundred billion and was famous (notorious?) for managing steady income growth.

GE comprises 5 segment divisions made up of various businesses (Table 4-2.1). On the basis of 2009 sales revenue, the smallest of these divisions (Consumer and Industrial) ranks at 243 as a stand-alone company in the Fortune 500, above such firms as Eastman Kodak and Yahoo. The largest (Capital Finance) is at number 40 in line with such well-known companies as Dell, Goldman Sachs, and Pfizer. Jeff Immelt, however, like his predecessor, has always denied that GE is a conglomerate "a conglomerate generates returns by trading in and out of businesses; it's basically a gigantic mutual fund. By contrast, GE generates returns by undertaking projects that only it has the wherewithal to undertake: the biggest, the most difficult, the longest term. Scale is one of GE's traditional strengths." (*Fortune Magazine*, 05/04/04.)

In its report of its 2009 performance, GE does refer to its "portfolio" and shows how the composition of that portfolio has changed from "early in the decade" to "now" then to the "future" as a consequence of an overarching corporate strategy (Tables 4-2.2, 4-2.3, 4-2.4). The report also indicates how the majority of future profits are seen to come from "Infrastructure," and while "ongoing NBC–Universal

Table 4-2.1   GE's 2009 segments (GE Annual Report)

Division	*Products/businesses*
Capital Finance	CLL, Consumer, Real Estate, Energy Financial Services, GEGAS Revenues: $50,622mil Profits: $2,344mil
Consumer and Industrial	Appliances and Lighting, Intelligent Platforms Revenues: $9,703mil Profits: $400mil
Energy Infrastructure	Energy, Oil & Gas. Revenues: $37,134 mil Profits: $6,842mil
Technology Infrastructure	Aviation, Healthcare, Enterprise Solutions, Transportation Revenues: $42,474 mil Profits: $7,489mil
NBC-Universal	Revenues: $15,436 mil Profits: $2,264mil

CORPORATE STRATEGY

123

Table 4-2.2 GE portfolio and strategic orientation: "Decade ago"

Segments:	Insurance
	Capital Finance
	Infrastructure
	Plastics, Media and Consumer & Industrial
Corporate Strategy:	*Reduce Risk and Investment*

Table 4-2.3 GE portfolio and strategic orientation: "Today"

Segments:	Capital Finance
	Infrastructure
	Media and Consumer & Industrial
Corporate Strategy:	*Reposition, Simplify & Invest*

Table 4-2.4 GE portfolio and strategic orientation: "Future"

Segments:	Capital Finance
	Infrastructure
	Consumer
Corporate Strategy:	*Growth & Value Creation*

investment" is foreshadowed, this is in the context of operating via a subsidiary relationship rather than full operational ownership, as NBC was classified as "held for sale" at the end of December 2009.

Given the diversity and size of its past and ongoing operations, and its acquisition/divestment approach to managing its past, present, and future strategy, it is difficult to see how GE is *not* a conglomerate even in the terms of its current CEO (see Jeff Immelt's quote above).

---

1. *Do you think GE is a conglomerate?*
2. *How does having such a disparate collection of businesses make value-adding sense?*
3. *Does the latest reorganization change anything? Should GE be broken up further and, if so, why; if not, why not?*

4-3 Golden Promise: Star Bright?

You are part of the corporate team of Golden Promise Inc. which is a diversified conglomerate.

The portfolio of your firm and some relevant data are shown in Table 4-3.1.

Your investment bankers Wewantyourmoney Inc. have notified you that Bright Inc. is a potential acquisition. Bright Inc. is a rapidly growing business with sales of USD 240m in the last financial year in an industry showing an average 8% growth rate over the past five years. It is the third largest player in the market with 12% market share, with the largest player being Shiny Inc. with sales of USD 360m and a market share of 20%. The figures supplied by your advisers indicate that Bright Inc. has been gaining on the two leaders for the past three years. The bank believes that in the current climate you can obtain Bright Inc. at its current market capitalization (i.e. with no premium) provided you make an all-cash offer.

Your latest strategic plan carried the following goal statement under a heading "Key Points for Future Success": "The company is seeking growth opportunities as the latest forecasts for average GDP growth over the next five years is 2.8% and merely matching this is not sufficient to meet our commitments to our shareholders."

Table 4-3.1 Portfolio (and selected data) of Golden Promise Inc.

Strategic Business Unit	Turnover (USD millions)	% market share (industry rank in brackets)	5 year. industry growth (%)	% market share of industry leader (2nd in brackets)
Forever Inc.	750	24 (1)	1.7	24 (12)
Double Inc.	400	15 (3)	5.3	20 (17)
Pastoral Inc.	350	8 (4)	1.5	24 (16)
Devos Inc.	320	12 (3)	6.9	18 (15)
Harris Inc.	300	15 (=1)	2.8	15 (15)
Faraday Inc.	270	7 (5)	11.4	14 (12)
Lester Inc.	250	18 (1)	2.0	18 (16)
Amber Inc.	180	6 (5)	1.5	15 (12)
Jackson Inc.	100	30 (1)	9.0	30 (20)
Total	**2,920**			

1. *What is the structure of your current portfolio in terms of the growth/share matrix (i.e. the Boston Boxes)?*
2. *What are the strengths and weaknesses of adding Bright Inc. to that portfolio?*
3. *What advice would you give to your CEO?*

4-4 easyGroup: Easy does it?

In 1995, Stelios Haji-Iannou, just 27 years old and with a loan from his family, launched easyJet. Starting with just six hired planes working one route, by 2003 it had 74 aircraft flying 105 routes to 38 airports and carrying over 20 million passengers per year. easyJet by then had a dense point-to-point network, linking major airports with large catchments with very frequent flights. The fleet of aircraft is now large, modern, and relatively environmentally friendly. The brand is very strong, with a high degree of consumer awareness of the company's orange color and logo.

easyJet aims to be the lowest fare on a route and a low-cost philosophy permeates throughout the business. Tickets are not issued to passengers and around 90% are purchased on-line. Because 100% of sales are direct to consumers, easyJet does not pay intermediaries. The fare system is dynamic: "the earlier you book, the less you pay." There are no free in-flight refreshments, although they can be purchased. Travelers are expected to clear up after themselves and this helps to reduce the amount of time aircraft need to remain on the ground. There is no distinction between economy or business class.

While easyJet goes from strength to strength, Stelios has also been starting up other new ventures. This dynamic, serial entrepreneur, as he describes himself, is a highly energized presence, a terrific talker, and full of ideas and reasons. His mission is to "paint the world orange." easyCar resulted from his observation that the cost of renting cars from airports that easyJet served was a "rip-off." With easyCar, a Mercedes A-class, in the trademark orange of the group, can be rented for a very competitive price. Other ventures include easyInternet café, easyCruise, easyBus, easyHotel, easyMobile, and easyCinema.

easyCinema follows the familiar Stelios mission of identifying industries where a new venture can compete on low cost, innovation, and fun. In cinema, Stelios observed asset underutilization – with only one in five seats on average being sold – inflated prices, which also did not reflect that films become less valuable over time, and overpriced popcorn and coke for sale. Stelios felt that an "easy" makeover was called for. He searched for a location to offer a cinema based on easyGroup values. Eventually, he found an aging multiplex in Milton Keynes, a large conurbation some 40 miles north of London.

The interior of the once lavish multiplex was ripped out and the whole complex painted a bright orange, much to the annoyance of passersby. Gone were the popcorn, drink, and ticketing facilities. In the words of his posters, "If you really want to eat popcorn, bring your own, but don't make a mess!" Tickets are purchasable over the internet. Through payment by credit or debit card, the customer can print out a bar code for use at the entry scanners in the multiplex. Prices start at 20p per ticket, compared with around £4.60 per ticket at neighboring cinemas.

With just 2 weeks to go before opening, Stelios did not have films to show at his new cinema. The only major blockbuster to open near this time was *The Matrix Reloaded*. However, none of the four major film distributors was interested in supplying Stelios with their films when they heard that he would be selling tickets for just 20p per person. He received many criticisms over the lack of staff at his facility, concerns over public order and health and safety, and whether piracy could be avoided. Stelios interpreted these as stalling tactics as the film distributors were not happy with his intention to have low prices. To remove the potential loss distributors might incur through low box-office takings, Stelios decided to offer them a £2,000 cash lump sum for a week for a film three weeks post-opening, which he had calculated to be the entire box-office takings for such a film at this stage in the USA. He did not receive acceptance and so still had to find films for his cinema. Fortunately, he was able to procure films from a leading independent producer, Pathé. While Stelios was unsure that *The Little Polar Bear* would really provide competition for *The Matrix Reloaded*, which would be showing across the street at the same time, it was, at least, a new release.

With film distributors controlling 90% of the market, Stelios had to find a way to deal with these large players. On their part, they could not be seen to collude against him because that would be anti-competitive and illegal. However, Stelios's lawyers suggested that their uniform action to date could be deemed to be evidence of tacit collusion. When this observation was sent to the distributors in a formal letter, the net result was that they then provided Stelios with some films. Although not the blockbusters he had hoped for, they were, nonetheless, new releases.

Just days before launching the new cinema, easyGroup and Stelios launched a public relations offensive, with widespread advertising on radio, internet, and television, as well as the prominent display of provocative orange posters on buses, taxis, and billboards. Stelios himself walked around Milton Keynes with a billboard proclaiming: "The end of rip-off cinema is nigh!" Followed by television cameras, he entered shopping malls and the foyers of competitor cinemas where he was forcibly ejected. There is little doubt that the people of Milton Keynes were aware of Stelios's enterprise and many would have met him or at least heard of his evangelical tirade.

Despite a few technical difficulties on the opening night, customer volumes during the first week were good, despite only having a "little polar bear" rather than a "matrix." Even when customers were in their seats, the Stelios offensive continued. Although they had entered for as little as 20p per ticket, Stelios explained that the film distributors were forcing him to pay £1.30 per person. Could they put a further contribution into the bucket he was passing around? The goodwill of the customers was evident as people did contribute. Stelios then announced that these funds would in fact be donated to a local hospice. The point, however, had been made: Stelios was trying to protect his customers by providing entertainment at a reasonable cost.

Despite a slackening in demand at easyCinema in the ensuing weeks, there is evidence of an underlying level of support. However, Stelios realizes that for the project to really take off, he needs to be able to show the new blockbusters. To gain leverage over the distributors, Stelios has engaged US competition lawyers (if you lose litigation in the USA, you do not pay the other side's costs). The lawyers have found a 1950s legal precedent in favor of a cinema exhibiter who faced producers ganging up against him. Stelios is now considering opening further cinemas in London to extend the concept.

However, observers are beginning to wonder if Stelios is struggling. easyJet was floated in 2000, with the easyGroup – although still the largest shareholder – taking more of a back seat. Stelios stepped down as chairman in 2005: (1) easyCinema can't seem to get the films it needs; (2) the internet cafés at one point were losing

£3m per month; and (3) the easyCar business is still losing money. And yet the group continues to expand. The year 2005 saw the launch of easyMusic.com, where users can download tracks for as little as 25p, and easyMobile, which offers voice calls for a flat rate of 15p per minute and SMS text messages for 5p each (rates that were due to fall by June 2005). The group plans to keep costs low by only selling over the internet and by not subsidizing sales of handsets. The mobile giant Orange has now sued the group over the use of the color orange, but Stelios's response was: "I have been using this color for ten years and I will not stop using it now for anyone. Let the battle commence."

1. Why has easyJet been a corporate success? And why have the national flagship airline operators struggled to imitate easyJet's corporate model?
2. Is the cinema industry a good addition to the easyGroup portfolio? Where would you place it in the BCG matrix?
3. Does the easyGroup parent company add value to its subsidiaries? What would you recommend to Stelios for the future of his group?

Case Notes:

4-5 Telco: Pendulum swings. . .

Like many organizations over the past two decades, public and private, Telco bought into the decentralization revolution. In 1988, its annual report described the way in which it had "adopted a new business philosophy." It explained: "With the centralized demands of a centralized head office, the company was slow and unresponsive. [However], a decentralized organization structure is now being adopted to improve Telco's operating performance."

In 1989's report, it reiterated that: "A bureaucratic organization with centralized control could never function effectively in a competitive marketplace. The new organization structure is now in place." Although 1990's annual report stuck to the same script, it was less gung-ho about the task having been completed: "The former system of centralized and bureaucratic controls added to overall costs and inhibited the development of a market-reactive business. However, the company is now capable of functioning efficiently in a competitive environment. The restructuring of Telco is largely completed."

Three years later, Telco representatives announced that the Company was "reverting back to centralized control." With hindsight, it was claimed that the rationale for decentralization was that it was simply "a phase in the Company's development, designed to achieve what the head of a prominent union involved in the process called the 'creation of a new culture'."

Whether or not this was in fact the plan, many practicing managers will find the story of a company seemingly on a pendulum, swinging back and forth from centralization to decentralization, very familiar. Interviewing many of Telco's senior managers in 1991 and 1992 – the period between the wholehearted embrace of decentralization and moving back to centralized control – revealed some interesting insights into the process.

The then Marketing Director explained the logic behind the move in 1988 as follows: "Essentially we used to be a very bureaucratic organization, with everything centrally controlled and directed, and the restructuring concept was to create a much flatter organization with decision making much closer to the customer base and a substantial degree of autonomy in each of the operating companies."

The Director of New Ventures was more to the point: "We had a very big problem with what was called Head Office. You couldn't order a rubber [eraser] out of Auckland unless you actually got a bit of paper from Head Office. So, we went through a very deliberate breaking up of Head Office."

Telco's corporate office was scaled back, or "emasculated" in the CFO's words. As the GM of Accounting explained, "we had to move very quickly, so the way to do that is to break up the bureaucracy into autonomous responsible divisions."

The head of one of the newly autonomous operating companies summed up his own philosophy, and that of the other new power-brokers that had been brought in to shake up the organization, thus: "Any holding company or any corporate office or any central group should be minimized as much as possible." However, later on this manager would admit that: "There is not the same degree of performance across the operating companies that we would like. I guess a lot of this is because we have taken an organization that was totally centralized and said 'we have to be decentralized – quickly'."

Other managers spoke of the impact of the move to decentralization going too fast, and too far:

> **CFO:** "They wanted to concentrate on getting stuff down close to the customer. But in the process they all started inventing things that actually ended up with entirely different approaches ... I mean it's swung too far .... the operating companies were getting the feeling that they had autonomy in a number of areas, and of course they ran off in a number of different directions ... There is this tendency for people to run off and invent their own bloody systems because they have got their own agendas one way or the other."

> **Head of Corporate Strategy:** "The problem with that kind of responsiveness is the anarchy. And I'll give you a piece of day-to-day responsiveness. You know when someone has a rush of blood to the head, decides to change the numbering plan in the Hill region, so Countytown vanishes from the toll network. OK. You need that coordinated thing, because we are in a network business."

> **Director of New Ventures:** "As is often the case we went too far in practical terms by devolving to the regional operating companies too much autonomy. What tended to happen was we saw a breaking up of direction. We heard of some, who were a division of arseholes, going in that direction; another going in this ..."

> **GM of Accounting:** "In fact, you ended up with a whole series of different strategies ... you had one regional unit that believed they were in the customer premises equipment market. Another believed they weren't. And another one that wasn't but believed we should be because of what they perceived to be our corporate image. It all depended on individuals ... you didn't have a common policy."

> **Head of Technology Strategy:** "I think there needs to be a lot more standardization of processes. The example I use at the moment, which I really find quite frustrating, is the fact that information systems are purchased and the project managed in a totally different way to other technology contracts."

The Head of Corporate Strategy summed up the views of most in explaining what went wrong and prefacing why Telco would now seek to recentralize: "We went from extreme centralization to extreme decentralization very rapidly and because we are a network business, by taking the heart out of the organization like that, a lot of the coordinating mechanisms were broken."

In 1991, new committees were formed to cut across the regional operating companies and were empowered to develop common policies in functional areas like human resources, marketing, and technology. This was rationalized in the following ways:

- GM of Accounting: "We had to bring back the control aspect that was missing."
- CFO: "There clearly needed to be brought back a common approach throughout the organization."
- Director of Marketing: "I think we had to reduce some of the devolved responsibility."

The committees grew quickly.

By the time the company formally announced it was reverting back to full-blown centralized control there were murmurings that the early recentralization initiatives were already showing signs of being taken too far. One senior manager was resigned: "There is a danger that the pendulum will swing back too far as a reaction. Yes. It will happen." In the CFO's words: "You just hope that the pendulum doesn't swing too far, [but,] well, it's inevitable; the pendulum swings and then we are up the creek." He expanded on this with an example: "Telco is becoming strikingly similar to the old organization – run by committees. I mean when the first schedule of the meeting came out, 25% of the nominal working year was taken up with bloody committee meetings. They are pretty much a waste of time anyway – I tend not to go now."

"I don't think we have solved the central versus decentral item yet," said another manager in conclusion. "We have swung the pendulum from one extreme to the other. We are now on the way back, and we haven't got to a stable end point yet."

Despite the swings and roundabouts, many, perhaps most, of the managers interviewed did reflect that perhaps the notions of centralization and decentralization did not really constitute an either/or choice. The CFO mused that, "it's a paradoxical situation – you provide much more computer ability now to the individual than was ever possible before, but you have to do that within a common framework or else there will be no meaning." One regional operating company head offered that: "In actual fact, to some degree, all of the tasks we have, have a central element and a decentral element in them." The GM of Accounting concluded by saying: "I have been one of the biggest catalysts in making decentralization happen. But at the end of the day a decentralized environment really didn't make any sense to me, so I began to talk about 'centralized decentralization' – that's my phrase word – and it's not stupid because I can't afford to have, as we have had, 14 computer sites and 14 different configurations, and heaven knows how many sets of accounts."

1. *Why did Telco move away from centralization towards decentralization, and then move back again?*
2. *Why do firms often get confused about how the center can best add value and swing from one approach to another?*
3. *Does the concept of centralized decentralization make sense to you? How would you make it work?*

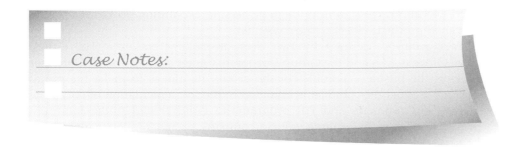

Case Notes:

4-6 Tata: "Steeling" itself for the future

The acquisition of Corus by Tata Steel, part of the Tata group of companies, is the largest overseas acquisition to date by an Indian company. It shows a new and dynamic feature of the global investment landscape – the international expansion of large companies from emerging economies. They are assisted by the progressive relaxation of foreign exchange controls and political support from Government. Most deals are directed at more advanced markets, as Indian companies are increasingly driven by cost advantage, production efficiency, managers' willingness to take on risk, and exposure to overseas competitors. Founded in 1874, by Jamsetji Nussewanji Tata with a single textile mill, the group currently comprises 96 operating companies employing 330,000 people and generating revenues of USD 28.8bn (2006/7). The group plays a central role in the Indian economy, being responsible for about 2.9% of India's GDP. Tata is active in 54 countries and exports to 120 countries around the world. It has 7 areas of business: Information Systems and Communications (ICTS); Engineering; Materials; Services; Energy; Consumer products; Chemicals with the three main areas of activity being: (1) Materials (mainly steel) which became the largest group after the Corus acquisition; (2) Engineering (including automotive) and historically the largest activity; and (3) ICTS, which has emerged as the fastest growing segment in the group (36% growth every year for the five years 2003–2008). In fact its consultancy segment first championed the "global delivery model" deploying India's cheap but sophisticated workforce to write software and manage IT/IS systems for companies in the West.

The governance of the group traditionally left considerable autonomy to individual operating subsidiaries where professional management ran them as fiefdoms. However they fell back on the Tata name when it suited them for raising funds. Despite this confederation of loose entities, there was a lot of activity among Tata companies in the form of intra-group loans, cross shareholders and interlocking directorates. Since 1993 Ratan Tata has been trimming lines of businesses and increasing Tata Sons stakes in the companies along with strengthening the corporate center with enough power to enforce discipline on the operating units. This enabled the exit of some old businesses, entry to new ones such as telecoms, and improved efficiency in traditional areas: Tata Motor's break-even point for capacity utilization is one of the best in the industry; improved management of materials at Tata Steel in 2000, restructuring, timely upgrading of equipment and halving of its workforce made it one of the world's most efficient steel producers with lower production costs that China's steel majors. Tata Steel also followed a plan of "de-integration expansion" – reinforcing upstream output in low-cost locations close to iron ore deposits and expanding downstream with more finished products closer to the consumer.

The Tata group is defined by two decision-making bodies – The Group Executive Office (GEO) and the Group Corporate Center (GCC). The GEO defines and reviews the business activities of the group. Its aim is to make the group activities more synergistic and so is involved in the implementation of corporate governance, environment, and HR programs to build shared understandings. Specifically it assesses the unique value a company brings to a particular sector as well as what the group can bring to its particular business. The GCC works closely with the GEO and guides future strategy and direction of the group.

The Tata group has a set of five core values: integrity, understanding, excellence, unity, and responsibility. Coordination is helped by Tata Administrative Services (TAS), which traditionally grooms promising young Indians for life-long opportunities and to be a talent pool. Recently TAS has focused upon facilitating the mobility of talent across companies. In 1996 a "Brand Equity and Business Promotion Agreement" was introduced. For a fee, businesses can use the Tata name but are also forced to adhere to the Tata Code of Conduct and the Tata Business Excellence model – a Baldridge style quality management system.

Although the Tata group has had an international outlook from the very start, by the late 1990s international sales only accounted for 12% of group turnover. However, in 2000 Tata Tea made the largest takeover of a foreign company by an Indian one with its acquisition of Tetley in a USD 432m leveraged buyout. Until this date, Tata acquisitions have been small relative to the group. However, in 2004 Ratan Tata, in an interview with *Business Week* (26.07.04) stated the need "to internationalize in giant strides, not in token, incremental steps." Since then there have been much larger acquisitions with the purchase of Anglo-Dutch firm Corus by Tata Steel in 2007 for USD 11bn – the largest deal out of India to date and the fourth largest ever in the steel industry. In 2008 Tata Motors purchased the Jaguar and Range Rover car brands for USD 2.3bn.

Most of Tata's companies are growing through acquisition. Tata Chemicals has become the world's third largest manufacturer of soda ash after acquiring three plants of Brunner Mond and complementing it through acquiring cheaper sources of natural soda ash from Magadi Kenya where the unique operation makes it one of the lowest cost producers in the world. Tata Power has purchased two major equity stakes in major Indonesian thermal coal producers. TCS acquired Swiss-based TKS-Teknosoft to possess marketing and distribution rights to the QUARTZ® platform for wholesale banks to add new products in the private banking and wealth management space as well as its record of successful implementation of large complex technology financial projects. Tata Steel's acquisition of Corus allows access to EU markets and high quality steel products and the acquisition of Singapore's NatSteel and Thailand's Millennium Steel helped strengthen its presence in higher value finished products. This also helps avoid tariffs on imported finished steel products. Sometimes the pressure for overseas acquisitions has come from pressures within India. In 2007 VSNL's monopoly on international long distance voice in India, which accounted for nearly 90% of revenue, came to an end. In response the company entered new domestic businesses such as enterprise data and internet telephony as well as acquiring submarine cables under the Atlantic and Pacific Oceans and more than 200 direct and bilateral agreements with leading voice carriers. Its software system which facilitates the location of roaming mobiles, is in use at 95% of telecom operators in the world and VSNL is now the third largest carrier of voice minutes in the world.

Tata companies have tried to develop an ability to understand the culture of the country where their acquisitions take place in order to be able to manage their acquisitions skillfully. Contrary to Corus expectations, the post acquisition period did not result in massive upheaval and change but a laissez-faire approach.

A Strategic Integration Committee (SIC) chaired by Ratan Tata was formed to facilitate integration and create a **virtual organization** across the combined business. The group focuses upon the sharing of best practices, manufacturing excellence, cross-fertilization of R&D and the rationalization of costs across businesses which are coordinated by a Program Office. Joint teams, formed from both organizations, work together to identify areas for change. This presents a paradox of how an emphasis on collaboration rather than control as an adaptive model allows the distinctiveness of the Tata Brand to persist.

With mergers and acquisitions being of increasing significance to the Tata group, it is salutary to examine the integration of Corus. Ratan Tata, Chairman of the Tata group that owns Tata Steel, was keen on Corus because of its sophisticated steelmaking technologies, its broad customer base in Europe and its size which was four times bigger than Tata Steel in terms of shipments. The deal made Tata Steel the world's 8th biggest steel producer. At the time of the transaction Tata Steel was one of the world's strongest steelmakers in terms of profit margins, while Corus's profits record over the past decade had been decidedly patchy and indeed at one point the firm nearly collapsed.

Unfortunately Corus became one of the biggest European casualties of the global recession starting in late 2008. Corus made EBITDA losses of more than $1bn in the first nine months of 2009 and more than 5,000 jobs were cut, mostly from UK plants. For the financial year 2009/10 Corus's dire financial state has had a big impact on Tata Steel's overall profits. Although the company's India-based operations have been relatively unscathed by the recession, thanks to robust domestic growth allowing earnings before interest, tax, depreciation and amortization of $1.3bn for the nine months, Corus provided a $643m loss. Nevertheless in the final three months Corus recorded positive EBITDA of $142m, causing some industry observers to say that "even though there are short-term problems, over a longer period the Corus deal will turn out to be a wise move for Tata."

One London-based banker is less enthusiastic about the deal. He says: "Mr Tata badly wanted to do this acquisition but in my view he paid a very full price for Corus. It also diverted the company from other possible approaches [to building up its steel business], especially in Asia. I don't see this as a positive move from either a financial or a strategic point of view." There are also questions over whether Tata has been correct to run Corus essentially as a stand-alone operation, with its management left very much to Mr Adams. Also, confusingly for many outsiders, H. Nerurkar, who became Tata Steel Managing Director last September, does not have any responsibility for Corus but instead has power only to direct the company's operations in India, Thailand and Singapore. One India-based consultant criticizes the absence of anyone with direct management responsibility on day-to-day matters for the whole of Tata Steel. "I think the company should have done a lot more to try to integrate its [Indian and European operations] rather than the Indian management adopting a largely hands-off approach. There are a lot of people in the company who should be working together but are at cross purposes." This argument is rejected by Lord Bhattacharyya, Director of the Warwick Management Group at Warwick University in the UK and a confidante of Mr Tata. He says it is right for Tata Steel to keep the identities of its Indian and European operations separate, given a big difference in their size and characteristics. "People do talk to each other from the different parts of the company, so in this sense there is a sufficient amount of integration going on," he says. "The management of Corus is doing a good job and I think over the longer term the deal will be seen as being a sensible and positive move for Tata."

1. *Diversification is generally recognized to be a risky and inefficient strategy for creating value for shareholders. Explain why the Tata group has traditionally pursued diversification, and continues with this strategy.*
2. *The Tata group recognizes that post acquisition integration is a major reason for the failure of acquisitions and that this is a critical risk for the firm. How does Tata manage its acquisitions and how does this create value?*
3. *It seems that a lot of Tata's success is based upon efficient low cost operations. The world's attention was recently attracted by Tata's announcement to build the Nano, a USD 2,500 car – a low cost product targeted at the "bottom of the pyramid". How does this fit with Tata acquiring two of the most luxurious brands in the motor industry, Jaguar and Land Rover?*

Case Notes:

4-7 Royal Air Maroc II: Red, green, and blue

Compagnie Royal Air Maroc was founded in 1957. It had 443 employees, a fleet of three DC3s, and was able to draw on the facilities and expertise of Air Atlas, which was developed after World War II primarily to ship freight on Junkers JU52s between Morocco, Algeria, Spain, and France. Royal Air Maroc now flies over 44,000 flights per year to 60 destinations in 30 countries in Europe, Africa, North America, and the Middle East. The Moroccan Government holds about a two-thirds stake of the company's capital.

The company is extremely proud of its "Royal" status, not surprisingly in a country that reveres and has great respect for its royal family. The proudest moments listed in its corporate history often involve the opening of facilities, or blessings of events, by members of Morocco's Royal family. It also takes its status as the "national flag carrier" (hence the colors of Royal Air Maroc: red and green) very seriously.

Royal Air Maroc's strategy is thus closely tied to the Moroccan Government's national strategy. In November 2001, Royal Air Maroc initiated a strategic vision with the objective of turning the company into a national multiple service entity and driving force tied to Morocco's economic development. Its website (www.royalairmaroc.com) proudly states that it is "fully aware of the citizen role [we] should play, Royal Air Maroc actively contributes to the economic development of Morocco and its international image" and that Royal Air Maroc's strategy is "intimately linked to the economic and industrial dynamism of our country." Furthermore, Royal Air Maroc sponsors almost all of the major Moroccan cultural and artistic events, such as the Fez Sacred Music Festival, the Rabat Festival, Essaouira Festival, and the International Film Festival at Marrakesh.

The Royal Air Maroc Group is organized around six "principal growth activities" that relate to its core expertise in air transport and allied activities. There are three "basic areas," as the company describes them (Regularly Scheduled Transport, Tourist Transport, and Air Cargo), and three "allied areas" (Hospitality, Industrial Activities, and Service and Innovation).

Over the past few years, Royal Air Maroc has been growing nicely, with the "basic" divisions performing especially well, despite a business environment that has been difficult for airlines. The restructuring of these divisions' activities around Casablanca's airport (named after King Mohammed V) toward establishing "Casa" as the international airline hub linking Europe, Asia, and the Americas into Africa has been particularly successful. This development has seen a great expansion in the number of services offered in and out of Morocco, through strategic partnerships formed with airlines such as Air France, Spain's Iberia, Delta Airlines from the USA, Saudi's Gulf Air, Tunisair, and Emirates, and through growing Royal Air Maroc's own services (the company opened up 11 new routes in 2004 and had added a further 15 by October 2005). Africa has been the biggest growth area, and Royal Air Maroc is seeking to play a leading role in developing further growth in the region. Toward this end, it recently created Air Sénégal International, a subsidiary based at Dakar, with 51% of the stock held by Royal Air Maroc and 49% by the Government of Senegal. This growth has seen Royal Air Maroc recently top four million passengers per year, 7bn dirhams in turnover, and acquire four new Airbus jets toward a planned fleet of 45 aircraft by 2010.

Royal Air Maroc's latest advertising campaign subsequently promotes a strong message of confidence in the company's future. It claims that: "in a turbulent marketplace, Royal Air Maroc affirms its assets and consolidates its strong position: this is an airline company passionately Moroccan, eager to participate in solving the big challenges facing the Kingdom, [and] modern and effective in its goals of developing tourism and industry in Morocco." In the words of Royal Air Maroc's own press statements: "this is an airline company perfectly armed to battle the economic 'war of the skies'."

However, despite this claim to be "perfectly armed," in 2004 Royal Air Maroc announced the creation of a new subsidiary called Atlas Blue that would compete with Royal Air Maroc in the passenger air transport arena. Royal Air Maroc management explained that: "The creation of [Atlas Blue as] the low-cost air carrier of Royal Air Maroc fits into the Governmental vision of initiating in our country a strong national tool geared to the development of tourist transport. This national tool will make it possible to strengthen the competitiveness of the air transport industry in our country and to turn it into a major vector for the growth of tourism in the framework of the Vision 2010 program."

Perhaps the African continent's first purpose-built, low-cost airline, Atlas Blue, was established with the expressed purpose of "flying certain routes from Moroccan provinces [at present Marrakesh and Agadir are the two airports served] and to and from tourist issuing markets [initially France, Belgium, Italy, Holland, England, and Germany – with research currently being done into developing Russian services] with point-to-point service."

Atlas Blue would draw on Royal Air Maroc knowledge, facilities, capital, maintenance and other services, as well as Royal Air Maroc's HR training facilities. But many other aspects of Atlas Blue would be separate:

- The primary distribution channel for Atlas Blue's reservations and sales operations would be direct selling through stand-alone websites and call centers.
- Marketing: its advertising slogan is "Atlas Blue … Morocco at unbeatable prices." Atlas Blue's "corporate colors" are sky blue with ochre, to represent the sea and the distinctive mountains of Morocco's inland districts (testing had shown these to be enduring images for tourists to Morocco).
- Atlas Blue's head office would not be in Casablanca but in Marrakesh, Morocco's premier tourist destination.

Atlas Blue's initial fleet comprises six B737-400s with the company planning to add two further aircraft each year until 2012.

---

1. *Royal Air Maroc seems to be doing well, so why create Atlas Blue? Why could they not have simply expanded Royal Air Maroc's own services rather than incurring all the cost associated with establishing a new identity?*
2. *How can Royal Air Maroc – or the "corporate center" – best add value to Atlas Blue?*
3. *Given that Royal Air Maroc sponsors Moroccan cultural events, what should Atlas Blue sponsor?*

> Competitive advantage, whatever its source, ultimately can be attributed to the ownership of a valuable resource that enables the company to perform activities better or more cheaply than competitors.
>
> *David Collis and Cynthia Montgomery*

> If a man write a better book, preach a better sermon, or make a better mouse-trap than his neighbor, tho' he build his house in the woods, the world will make a beaten path to his door.
>
> *Ralph Waldo Emerson*

5
Strategic Positioning

In Chapter 3 we found that industry dynamics mattered for both investors and managers in terms of the returns that can be made, i.e. different industries make different returns.[1] However, in most industries some companies seem to consistently outperform their rivals in generating value for shareholders. Over the ten years 1998–2008, incorporating just the start of the Global Financial Crisis, those who invested in GM and Ford at the beginning of that decade saw average annual losses of 22.3% and 21.2% respectively (i.e. from 1998 their total investment, including reinvested **dividends**, diminished on average by one fifth each year for ten years). On the other hand, those who had the luck or foresight to invest in Oshkosh, a manufacturer in the very same industry, would have been far happier. They made average annual *gains* of 5.9%.

Why is it, then, that some firms, in the same industry consistently perform better or worse than others? Some of the answers to this question lie in an understanding of **competitive advantage** and **competitive strategy** and the links between the better products on offer (the better mousetrap) and the better resources employed (inventing and manufacturing mousetraps).

Competitive Advantage

Industrial rivalry benefits customers and consumers but harms industry's profitability as, for example, marketing/development costs go up, and/or selling prices come down. All firms, with the exception of monopolies, must compete with other businesses for customers. Even not-for-profit organizations increasingly must compete for the hearts and minds of the communities within which they operate by showing how they create a value that is greater than the alternative means of providing similar products, services, or experiences.

Those organizations with a **sustainable competitive advantage** will do so more profitably, or by adding greater value, than others with less to offer. Competitive advantage is the unique set of assets, capabilities, positions, and environmental circumstances that enable an organization to consistently outperform its competitors in its chosen strategic outcomes. In industry terms (as we saw in Chapter 3), competitive advantage means that an organization exploits industry imperfections better than its rivals or reaps the benefits of organization-specific imperfection(s).

There are two generic forms of competitive advantage:

1. **Cost advantage**: an organization can do the same things as its rivals but do so at a lower *delivered cost*, i.e. total costs – not just product/service costs. Such organizations exploit economies of scale, scope, and learning (or experience) effects and are obsessed with efficiency and cost control.
2. **Differentiation advantage**: an organization offers something of value that is unique or sufficiently better than rivals to be seen as unique. These organizations create a form of monopoly in that nobody else can deliver the same product/service-based value to the target market. Their obsessions centre on protecting and improving their uniqueness in brand, product, process, etc.

And, although exceptions may exist, we can state the general facts that:

- Organizations with competitive advantage are more profitable, or create more value, than their rivals.
- Organizations that consistently demonstrate higher profitability or value than rivals have competitive advantage(s).
- Organizations may be very good but may not be better than the others with which it is competing. Consequently, many organizations do not have a competitive advantage.
- The degree to which an organization can achieve competitive advantage is constrained, to some extent, by the dynamics of its industry.

Competitive Strategy

Competitive *advantage* is a measure of the relative superiority of a few organizations over others, whereas competitive *strategy* comprises the ongoing decisions or actions that each company undertakes to achieve its goals – a major one of which is competitive advantage. Definitions of strategy are legion and rather than attempt to reinvent the already reinvented we will stick with the non-controversial and classic definition by Alfred Chandler for the purposes of this chapter. This is that strategy is:

> . . .the determination of the long-run goals and objectives of an enterprise, and the adoption of courses of action and the allocation of resources necessary for carrying out these goals.

Such strategies generally manifest themselves in two ways:

1. The **position** an organization adopts in terms of its stance relative to its competitors (be they other companies in a for-profit arena or alternative investments of time, money, etc. by key stakeholders in a not-for-profit arena), its products or services and its choice of buyer segments. This incorporates the broad **value proposition** that the organization is offering compared to rivals and the customers to whom the value is offered.

2. The **resources and capabilities** underpinning the positioning of the organization. This incorporates the patterns of activities, routines, investments, systems and so on that combine to give the organization its unique ability to **exploit** existing resources and **explore** new opportunities, compared to its rivals.

An organization with a competitive strategy should be able to describe its **business model**, or its expression of how it adds value, using either or both of these two approaches. We explore them further in the paragraphs that follow.

Strategy as Positioning (or "Fit")

As industries grow and evolve the requirements for strategic success (i.e. **critical success factors** or CSFs) also change. Each firm, in order to survive, must (a) ensure a *fit* between its strategy and the CSFs of the industry and (b) strive for competitive advantage over rivals who are also striving for the same thing.[2] In this sense, all businesses have a *strategy* – whether this is a formally designed set of goals and plans, or an unspoken consistency in a stream of decisions/actions does not really matter. However, as indicated above, only a few businesses have *competitive advantage(s)*.

The generic strategy matrix

Unfortunately the traditional use of the same generic terminology (e.g. cost and differentiation to describe both advantage *and* strategy) can lead to confusion.[3] We can see how this can happen by looking at the most commonly used strategic positioning framework, Michael Porter's Generic Strategy Matrix (GSM), where strategic choices between cost and differentiation (which Porter labels the Competitive Advantage axis) are combined with a choice about the scope of attack; whether to compete across a broad front (a wide range or target market), or focus firepower on a narrower segment or niche. This creates the four generic strategy categories that can be seen in Figure 5.1.

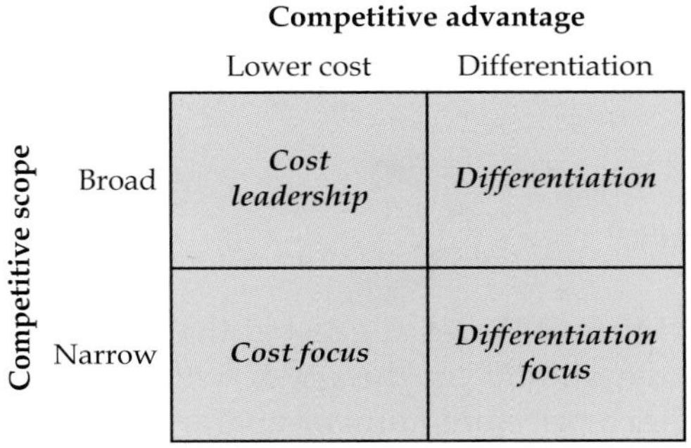

Figure 5.1 Generic competitive strategies (Source: Adapted from Michael E. Porter (1985) *Competitive Advantage*, NY: The Free Press)

141

The confusion here between advantage and strategy is potentially damaging to your wealth as the differences between generic *strategies* and *advantages* are critical. Strategic *advantages* protect the firm against rivals and reduce the power of buyers/suppliers and the threat of entry and substitution – generic *strategies*, per se, may not. So, simply placing a company or a brand in a category (e.g. GM with its focus on scale in 'cost leadership'; BMW with its focus on broadening the appeal of its engineering innovations in 'differentiation'; Land Rover with it narrow range and market segments in 'differentiation focus'; and Hyundai with its small range and generally lower prices in 'cost focus') does not mean that it has a competitive advantage by being in that box. Hence it is dangerous to assume that because your strategy will place you in one or other category your organization will be safe. Other factors will dictate whether that strategy confers an advantage in an industry. For example, historical factor conditions and a string of poor investment decisions meant that GM in 2009 certainly did not have a competitive advantage; whereas Hyundai's home conditions in Korea, aligned with their skill in deploying their low-cost strategy, combined with how this nicely "fits" with an increased sense of frugality in times of global financial crisis, would indicate that Hyundai at that point in time did have a competitive advantage.

One of the strengths of the GSM is its simplicity. This makes it a useful starting point for discussions about strategy, positioning, and advantage. However, simplicity can be a weakness too, and it can blind users to other options. It can be helpful, therefore, to also think about positioning in relation to other complementary frameworks. We describe four such frames below.

Four different scope strategies

In a more detailed description of competitive *scope* dimension depicted in the GSM, Henry Mintzberg[4] suggests that there are four generic approaches:

1. *Unsegmentation*: the firm offers the same products across a broad range of market segments, e.g. Coca-Cola, Wal-Mart, Google.
2. *Segmentation*: the firm still addresses a broad range of market segments but designs different products for those segments, e.g. Honda, Dell, British Airways,
3. *Niche*: the firm focuses on one segment of the market, e.g. Ryanair, LVMH Group, Mothercare.
4. *Customization*: the firm focuses on individual customers and shapes their offering to the unique requirements of that buyer, e.g. up-market homes, event organization, golf course design.

The strategic "clock"

In his original work Michael Porter suggested that it is a major problem for any firm to be "stuck in the middle" of the GSM, with neither sufficient differentiation advantage to claim a price premium or guarantee customer loyalty, nor sufficient cost advantage to underpin superior margins at prevailing prices. However, other authors are not so sure that this is such an either-or choice and point to

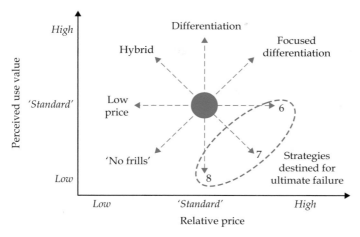

Figure 5.2 The strategic clock. (Source: Cliff Bowman (1988) *Strategy in Practice*, Harlow: Prentice Hall)

the success of Japanese car companies such as Toyota or Honda in offering high-quality, highly and flexibly featured vehicles produced at low costs with substantial brand equity. Another generic strategy framework that does acknowledge the possibility of a high-value/low-cost strategy is the strategic "clock" (Figure 5.2). This suggests that viable strategy options depend on how the firm's offering is perceived by the market in terms of its *price* relative to other offerings and its relative *perceived use value*. Whereas a *low price* strategy offers a standard perceived use value at a low price, a *differentiation* strategy offers a high perceived use value at a standard price.

The strategic clock goes further, however, and acknowledges the viability of high-value/low-price "hybrid" (e.g. the Japanese car manufacturers on entry to the USA or Tesco, as in the live case later in this chapter) high-value/high-price "focused differentiator" (e.g. luxury goods) and low-value/low-price "no frills" (e.g. low-cost airlines) strategic options. Both the no frills and the focused differentiator options are consistent with Porter's focus quadrants. As with the GSM the differentiators can leverage their differentiation through price premiums or increased volumes/market share. Those operating in the low price arena will tend to experience price wars that will put pressure on margins and encourage cost reductions that will push them toward the no-frills segment. The remorseless pressure of imitation and competition meanwhile will tend to pull the hybrids into the competitive orbit of the differentiators

According to the strategic clock, the strategies that are doomed to ultimate failure are those where the offering ends up being perceived to have low relative use value but standard or higher relative price. Marlboro (cigarettes) and Compaq (computers) were able to maintain high relative prices over a long period. However, as they fell out of fit with the wider environment and their perceived, relative "use value" declined, they ended up in the lower right-hand quadrant and sales declined accordingly. Significant price decreases were needed to save them from extinction.

Six different differentiation strategies

You will have noticed that Bowman's strategic clock has made a subtle but significant reorientation to *price* as an advantage rather than cost (it is important in strategy to remember that these are not the same or necessarily even related; think about how Nike, for example, succeeded for many years with a low-cost/high-price strategy). Another Henry Mintzberg framework endorses this stance in suggesting that all strategy and advantage is based on some form of differentiation *of which price is one variant*. It takes Porter's simple differentiation column on the GSM and suggests 6 different forms of differentiation strategy (Figure 5.3). Any of these may or may not lead to sustainable competitive advantage depending on (a) the value the customer places on the chosen option and (b) how much better the firm is than its rivals in delivering this option.

A useful insight from these 6 options is the fact that many firms basically do the same as each other – *they are undifferentiated*. They offer similar products at similar prices with similar service, etc. and still make enough money to earn an acceptable return on the capital invested – just how differentiated is one financial services institution from another, for example? Note that whether a strategy is actually undifferentiated or not may depend on who you ask – most if not all organization are *trying* to adopt a different position. The less differentiated they actually are is generally correlated to a need for "gaming" to "improve their strategic position."

Gaming for position

When there are very few competitors (as, for example, in an oligopolistic industry), or many undifferentiated competitors, strategic moves must explicitly take into account the potential (and likely) responses of rivals. **Game theory** is that branch of economics/strategy that analyzes decision processes and outcomes when each actor makes decisions – for example, pricing, capacity, product introduction – based on the anticipated actions and reactions of its rivals. Delving into the

Strategy	Description
Low price	A lower price than rivals e.g. the no frills airlines verses the big national carriers in the US and Europe
Image	A brand or reputation e.g. Coca Cola, Mercedes, Gucci, Harvard Business School, etc.
Support	Provision of back-up or after sales service e.g.Dell
Quality	A more durable or reliable product or one with higher performance, e.g.digital cameras (pixels)
Design	Different product functions, e.g. pharmaceuticals, mobile phones
Undifferentiation	Same as the others, e.g. Car rental firms, financial service firms, petrol stations, steel companies etc.

Figure 5.3 Six basic differentiation strategies. (Source: adapted from Mintzberg, 1998)

full intricacies (and mathematics) of game theory is beyond the scope of this text but the following example gives a flavor of the sort of reasoning in a game theoretic decision.

Suppose that a capital-intensive industry, dominated by two main, equal-sized and not very differentiated companies called Caesar and Brutus, has demand that exceeds current supply. The CEOs of Caesar and Brutus are contemplating expanding capacity, but the nature of the manufacturing process is such that capacity can only be expanded in relatively large and expensive lumps. The CEO of Brutus has a financial model that shows her the following profit figures for her company depending on the expansion outcomes:

1. No expansion by either – Brutus's profit: US$360 million per year (i.e. maintaining current profits).
2. Brutus expands and Caesar does not – Brutus's profit: US$400 million per year.
3. Brutus does not expand but Caesar does – Brutus's profit: US$300 million per year.
4. Both expand – Brutus's profit: US$320 million per year.

But she knows that the CEO of Caesar has exactly the same set of figures for his company. So what should she do?

John Nash (made popularly famous through the film *A Beautiful Mind*) won a Nobel Prize in economics for his analysis of such situations. His insights demonstrated why the most likely outcome in such cases is that both companies expand (i.e. outcome 4 above – a worse outcome than Brutus doing nothing). One way to understand why this is so is to put yourself in the place of either CEO and answer this question: "Given you do not know what the other firm will do, what is the decision you can make that you will never (financially) regret *whatever* your opposite number does?" You might also further understand why tacit or even explicit (generally illegal) collusion is so tempting in oligopolistic competition; and why it has become popular to develop **"blue-ocean" strategies** (strategies that enable you to get clear of the bloody red ocean where the undifferentiated pack is fighting it out at close quarters – see Chapter 11).

Strategy as Resources (or "Capabilities")

Value-creating activities

Industrial organizational theorists stress the importance of establishing a close fit between the strategy of the firm and the CSFs of the environment. This emphasis has tended to deflect attention from the fact that establishing an advantageous position depends on performing combinations of competitively valuable activities better than rivals or alternatives. Michael Porter describes this through the value chain framework (Figure 5.4).

Whether an activity is merely a necessary cost or a potential contributor to competitive advantage varies between different firms across different industries. Marketing via branding is the key value differentiator for Coca-Cola, whereas operations and outbound logistics, i.e. making and delivering the cola, are operations to be made as efficient and as cost-effective as possible. For Federal Express,

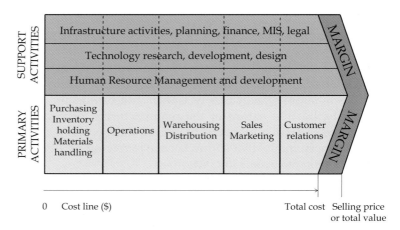

Figure 5.4 The Generic Value Chain. (Source: adapted from Michael E. Porter (1985) *Competitive Advantage*, NY: Free Press)

however, operations and logistics comprise its core differentiating offering. In any event, one need not respect the sections of the chain as Porter drew it. Many modern organizations don't have purchasing or warehousing or inventory in the way that companies did in 1980 when the chain was first drawn (think of Google, for example). It is better to use the broad outline of the chain to express your organization's business model, thinking through and drawing the things it does to convert inputs into outputs of a market value greater than the cost of conversion. If an activity in the chain is not a necessary cost or does not add value greater than its cost, or the added value is relatively low in relation to other activities in the chain, then you have to ask whether it is worth continuing with it. Maybe there is a case for outsourcing such an activity if a provider can achieve the same or better, reliably and at lower cost. This sort of thinking has driven a great deal of outsourcing in the financial services industries to low-wage economies such as India and China. In Formula 1 motor racing the Williams team outsources the parts of its racing cars, preferring to rely on the world-class engineering skills of a wide variety of component suppliers. Williams provides a critical set of skills as a strategic assembler of components.

In some instances, however, it may be preferable to keep an activity in-house as it is deemed strategic to the organization as a whole. Keeping it in-house may be linked to protecting core capabilities and resources and maintaining organizational flexibility. This is the thinking of Ferrari who prefer to carry out nearly all of its engineering in-house. Maintaining an activity may also be part of a loss-leader strategy, whereby you make a loss on one activity (e.g. Formula 1 racing), to promote value elsewhere in the business (e.g. the perception of a brand as "high performance"). Or it may be that you need to face up to a long cherished activity becoming uneconomic!

Resources and capabilities – the resource-based-view (RBV)

What the value chain does make us do is to focus on the underlying activities and capabilities, and the relationships between these, which are the prime source of developing and maintaining an advantageous position.

Subsequently, a reaction to the dominance of the generic positioning frameworks outlined in the previous section, but in fact a logical complement to them, emerged in the 1980s and developed rapidly to become a major influence on strategic thinking. Building on insights first developed in the 1950s,[5] RBV proponents emphasize that competitive advantage stems from the uniqueness of a firm's resources as one of our opening quotes suggests. While resources refer to the usual tangible factors of production such as plant and equipment and more intangible assets like brand, they also include the various capabilities/competences[6] the firm possesses for exploiting existing resources such as the **innovation** capabilities of Apple or the marketing capabilities of McDonald's. Moreover the business's abilities to learn, improve, and change these capabilities to enable the exploration of new untapped resources (i.e. its **dynamic capabilities**) are also part of its long-term resources. This approach links with the positioning frameworks as the cost advantage of a business stems from its capabilities in cost reduction, or success from a brand depends on its capabilities in brand development and management. Even if luck[7] plays a part in getting a firm to an initial position of advantage, the constant erosion of that advantage by competitors can only be held at bay by superior learning competencies embedded in the social fabric of the firm.

For a valuable resource to offer long-term competitive advantage it must have two key characteristics[8]: it must be *competitively superior* and it must be *scarce*. Even then an organization must be able to appropriate or extract value from that resource or capability.

Competitive superiority, Scarcity and CASIS

To be valuable a resource must fit with the CSFs of the industry. However, to be competitively superior it must do so better than the resources of its rivals. It must increase value through higher prices or volumes or through lower costs than the competition. Dominoes are good at making and delivering pizzas but no better than their opposition and so it is only superior marketing that can offset the trend toward low price as the default strategy in the delivered pizza industry. The problem in this industry is that great marketing capabilities are still at the mercy of the 2 for 1 pricing offer as these pricing attacks must be matched.

However, the competitive advantage from a valuable resource will be short-lived if that resource is not scarce (rare). Some physical resources are actually rare; sometimes due to natural circumstances such as with viable, low-cost oil fields or due to government fiat such as with the champagne-producing region of France. In the main however, physical rarity as a durable competitive advantage is itself rare. The most common threats to scarcity lie in the standard competitive dynamics of *imitation* and/or *substitution* by another resource offering the same benefits to the user/consumer.

Imitation

Over decades the fabled Toyota Production System (TPS), a complex organizational capability in quality and cost control, gave that company a significant productivity advantage over its US competitors. However the gradual dissemination of knowledge enabled the others to *imitate* the TPS. So in 2007 Chrysler was achieving the same person-hours per vehicle rate as Toyota (37.3) with Honda, GM, Nissan, and Ford less than 3.5 hours per vehicle behind.[9] The pressure of the chasing pack eventually told on Toyota as the company was forced into humiliating and costly recalls in 2009/10 – the fable had ended.

If legal blockages cannot be established through patents or copyrights, then imitation can only be prevented or slowed if a number of *isolating mechanisms*[10] are in place to protect the valuable capability. Such isolating mechanisms include the following:

1   It is *expensive* to develop (e.g. semi-conductor fabrication planets) – and/or
2   It will take a long time and involve a lot of prior learning (**path-dependency**) (e.g. Coca-Cola's branding expertise) – and/or
3   There is little understanding of the processes underlying the capability even in the business with the capability (causal *ambiguity*); e.g. Southwest Airlines low-cost capability; everyone knows the parts – the internet booking system, the fast plane turnaround, the lack of onboard services, etc. – these have been extensively examined, written about and imitated. However the implicit, cultural "glue" that makes up the whole, and which is much more the key to financial success, has proven much more difficult for its US rivals to copy.

Substitution

The threat of substitutes is an industry level force we discussed earlier in this book and normally this is couched in terms of replacement of products (e.g. plastics as a substitute for steel). However, resources can diminish in value as substitute capabilities emerge. For example, the big broking houses found that their in-house capability for research and analysis in stock investment became less valuable as low-price, internet broking-only services encouraged investors *to do the research themselves*. Buyers developing the expertise and doing it themselves is an ongoing substitution threat to in-house capabilities in any expertise-based industry like education, consultancy, brokering, house repairs, restaurants, etc. Even the physical scarcity of large, low-cost oilfields won't sustain competitive advantage if high prices encourage the development of viable substitution by other energy sources such as nuclear, wind power or hydrogen cells in cars.

Appropriabilty

Appropriability is a term from economics which denotes that a resource can only underpin competitive advantage if the value from that resource can be gained ("appropriated") by the business. If the resource is an individual or group of individuals then almost invariably a bargaining process for the value created begins between the firm and those individuals. The ongoing threat to the firm is that their human resources can be tempted away by other firms or can set up in opposition themselves. This dynamic is most obvious in professional sports teams, financial firms, consultancies, etc. where the star players garner more and more of the income for themselves. However, the increasing size of remuneration packages for CEOs of large corporations across the Western world suggests that more value is being appropriated by the stars of the board room that can leave to manage the competition if their wants are not met. Note that the size of the remuneration package is bearing less and less relationship to company performance and more and more to the perceived scarcity value of the star. Unfortunately shareholders pay for the star but not necessarily his or her best game.

It can be a useful checklist to think of the idea described in the sub-sections above in terms of the acronym **CASIS**. Checking off whether the resources and capabilities that contribute to a strategy are: *Congruent*, or fit, with the CSFs of the industry; *Appropriable* by the organization; *non-Substitutable* and *non-Imitable;* and, finally, are the resources *Supported* or encouraged by the organization. (An alternative acronym is **VRIO**: i.e., are the resources and capabilities Valuable, Rare, Inimitable, and Organizationally supported?)

Linking Corporate and Positioning Strategy

Whether corporate strategy (discussed in Chapter 4) should follow positioning (often referred to as competitive strategy) is like asking "which came first, the chicken or the egg?" They should continually replenish one another. So while a book requires that the two be presented in a particularly linear order, it is important to look back at how they can be effectively linked. A simple way of doing this is through Cummings and Angwin's Value Chimera (see Figure 5.5). This takes the basic shape of the value chain but gives it many "heads" to depict a strategic reality for most organizations of any size: their "corporate stables" will have different "horses for courses," or brands or products that will require different positioning strategies for advantage in market places.

It can be useful to think of how an organization's different product lines are positioned to meet different target markets on the right-hand side of the Chimera (e.g. think about where the Volkswagen group's Audi, Seat, Skoda, and VW might sit in the GSM) and then analyze how the organization's corporate strategy enables, for example, costs to be combined or saved earlier in the Chimera so that the left-hand side can generate significant economies of scale. For corporate strategists the trick is to achieve competitive positions in market places, scale economies among suppliers, and manage tensions throughout the value chain in order to enable expertise to be transferred across different "horses". Effective strategic positioning of the whole value chain should enable greater value to be created than the collective costs of running these many activities.

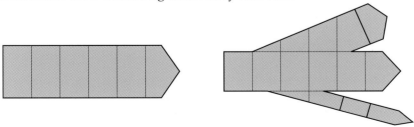

Figure 5.5 The value chimera as a way to link corporate and competitive strategy

149

The long-term superior profitability of a firm depends on how much better that firm's strategy fits with environmental forces *relative to its rivals* and its greater skill in developing and marshaling *unique* resources to maintain and improve that position. Oshkosh Truck, the star performer in the US automotive industry, has done just that by outperforming its rivals and its industry average for 10 years. We also know that others in the industry are attempting to wrest away Oshkosh's advantage, because that is what happens as industries mature. Macro-shocks, such as a significant technological advance – e.g. electricity, the telephone, the internet – can batter down the existing advantages of incumbents but, in the main, advantages are slowly eroded by the prevailing winds of *imitation* and *substitution*. In line with the quotes at the beginning of the chapter, the driving quest of all organizational strategy must be for the development and maintenance of *unique, valuable* positions and/or capabilities and, hence, an ongoing battle to avoid imitation and substitution. Being better than others at the same thing is highly unlikely to remain unique (advantageous) in the long term. You have to muster your resources to stay ahead of the pack. Strategists must stay vigilant and be paranoid – the competition is out to catch and overtake you!

Strategic Positioning Key Learnings Mind Map

Having read and reviewed the chapter, outline what you believe to be the key learnings from the chapter and the relationships between these.

5-1 Tesco: The train pulling in is Tesco[11]

In 1997, Tesco, the UK's largest retailer and its biggest private employer, announced its intention to establish a 2,508 square-meter supermarket at the train station of the village of Gerrards Cross in the county of Buckinghamshire, southeast England. Gerrards Cross is an affluent village with a typical house price costing almost four times the national average. Most of the 7,342 villagers were horrified at the thought of a mass-market retail outlet and, citing concerns about increased traffic and the impact on local retailers, the district and county planning offices refused permission for the store to be established. Tesco management appealed that decision to the highest level of government. Their appeal was approved and, from November 2005, Tesco, with 2004 revenues of over £31bn, would become a big part of little Gerrards Cross.

On hearing of the success of the company's appeal, the village greengrocer relet his property to a betting shop. He recognized what many had found out before – when Tesco comes to town, local food retailers leave. In 1950 there were over 260,000 independent grocery stores throughout the UK. Sixty years later that number was less than 40,000, with even some of these being Tesco outlets. The modern-day Tesco not only has over 30% share of the overall UK grocery market through its stores and on-line services, it also has significant presence in the petrol retail market and a growing position in a variety of other areas, including clothing, home goods, and personal finance. Combining this with its growing international ventures in Europe, the USA, and Asia makes Tesco an irresistible retail force.

Ironically Tesco itself started as a *very* small store. Returning to his family home after serving as an air force mechanic in WWI, Jack Cohen, son of a Polish-Jewish tailor, made a living by selling cans of food from a market stall in London's East End. He began by buying £30 of army surplus rations, taking them to the Well Street market, and selling them for a profit of £1. As well as army surplus food stocks, Cohen's low-cost purchases included unlabelled tins from salvage merchants who had themselves bought the products as reject batches from large manufacturers. Cohen would relabel the dented cans and sell them on at very low prices to grateful customers living on tight post-war budgets; customers who could not afford the prices charged by the established "high street" retailers like J. Sainsbury and Marks & Spencer.

By 1930 Jack Cohen was operating a string of stalls across markets all over London and, such was his increased purchasing power and acumen, had become a wholesaler to other stall holders. The dubious sourcing strategies of some of their supply channels meant that he and his nephew still had to rebadge cans with new labels to disguise their brand origins. One day, needing a new label for a batch of tea, Cohen combined the first three letters of the supplier's name with the first two letters of his surname and "Tesco" was born. He opened his first store in 1931. By taking advantage of the post-war housing boom outside London, and paying low rents to grateful developers, he had 100 stores by 1939. Tesco's profits came from high volume sales driven by low prices ("pile it high, sell it cheap") based on Cohen's obsession for low-cost inputs that included low employee wages. On a 1946 visit to America he found a mechanism that both increased throughput and reduced (employee) costs – self-service. Tesco stores became self-service "supermarkets."

By the early 1960s, as J. Sainsbury opened lavish new premises that focused on offering well-presented quality products (at higher prices) to its middle-class customers, Tesco had expanded to over 400 outlets through the acquisition of cheap stores. In 1961 it opened a new-look store in Leicester combining food and non-food items and providing undercover parking for 1,000 cars. Its new format caused further clashes with the brand-name manufacturers. They had often taken the company to court for setting its own retail prices in defiance of the "resale price maintenance" laws under which the supplier set the retail prices. Tesco fought these laws and eventually, by one vote, the British Parliament struck them down; price wars were now legal between competing chains. Over the next decade they grew rapidly as thousands of small stores, stripped of price protection, closed throughout the country.

In the mid 1960s Tesco increased sales further when it introduced "Green Shield Stamps." Customers collected these, based on the value of their purchases, and traded them in for goods when they had collected the stipulated amount. Its up-market rival J. Sainsbury was disdainful of such inducements and campaigned unsuccessfully for their removal. In the 1970s, with Britain in the grip of national union action and the working week reduced to 3 days, Tesco sales and profits declined. In response the company dispensed with stamps and slashed prices to reflect the £20m annual cost savings. The shoppers returned and sales surged ahead once more.

Throughout the next two decades Tesco expanded its product range, store size, and polished a new image as it wooed consumers, employees, and local authorities. It introduced share incentive programs for workers. Its small, crowded, untidy, "pile it high" stores were closed to make way for spacious, tidy supermarkets, hypermarkets, and specialty shops catering for the increased affluence and mobility of its customer base. High end brands shared shelf space with (cheaper) Tesco branded products across an increased range of products. This enabled the brand conscious consumer to shop alongside her more price-sensitive companion. In 1995 Tesco overtook J. Sainsbury to become the largest retailer in Britain.

Tesco remains price competitive as it must but the reality is that all supermarket chains use their buying power to manage costs and so the actual price differences between the majors are minimal. In 2007 a trolley of 100 common items bought at Tesco for £173.97 cost just 74p less at Asda, a large but more downmarket rival (data from *The Grocer*). Comparing bigger shopping baskets of 10,000 items yielded a similar result with Asda and Tesco charging the same for almost three-quarters of their goods. What price differences exist in reality are too small to be noticed by most shoppers and hence it is perception that becomes critical, and here Tesco's budget for branding (perception shaping) is much larger than that of any of its rivals.

Tesco is a classic "small to huge" success story.

---

1. *In terms of strategic positioning and capabilities how might we account for the rise of Tesco?*
2. *Outline Tesco's strategic strengths today.*
3. *What strategies might J. Sainsbury have pursued to combat Tesco's success?*

◀◀◀ The train pulling in is Tesco: Some ideas toward a "model answer"...

Beginning in an era when many people suffered great financial hardship, Jack Cohen's market stall sold damaged cans of food at very cheap prices. This is the ultimate in **no-frills** (strategic clock), **cost-focus** (Porter) or **low-price** (Mintzberg) strategies. His **competitive advantage** was based in **low costs** derived from his buying acumen (a **capability**) and his willingness to use (legally) dubious sources. In contrast, the more traditional high street retailers such as J. Sainsbury and Marks & Spencer were firmly in the category of broad based **differentiators** offering **quality** of goods to underpin their higher prices. Even after the stall became "Tesco" Cohen continued to focus on price rather than quality or product range as his main profit-generating approach. His stores were small, untidy, and crowded with goods. In a sense they were mini warehouses staffed by a few people to take customers' money (and finally by even fewer people following the move to self-service).

The move to "Green Shield" stamps was both a form of **price discount** (added value for the same price) and a mechanism for **locking in** customers who were tempted to add more and more points to gain higher value "rewards." While this value-adding ploy was in effect, Tesco still offered low prices and no-frills products/services. Dumping the stamps and slashing prices was Tesco's last major initiative as a **"no-frills"** retailer.

Throughout the 1970s and 1980s Tesco's consumers became increasingly affluent and less in need of *lowest* prices. They began to move up-market in their food and drink tastes and, while perhaps shopping for basics at the cheaper Tesco, began selectively purchasing higher value items at J. Sainsbury and Marks & Spencer. Although strongly resisted by Cohen,[12] Tesco began to follow its customers up-market as it moved from a **no-frills** to a **low-cost** (strategic clock) strategy (more broadly targeted **cost leadership** in Porter's terms). Its stores became bigger, cleaner, and brighter and offered a more pleasant shopping environment; although the prices were still keen.

Gradually Tesco crossed the major **mobility barriers** between its **strategic group** (the "pile it high and sell it cheap" retailers) and the "quality and service" strategic group made up of such stores as J. Sainsbury and Marks & Spencer. It did so by adding a perception of value without sacrificing the inducement of price. Its "strategy" **emerged** so gradually that its competitors did not notice the gradual erosion of the barriers.

Note that it is doubtful that Tesco management ever articulated a **formal (design) plan** to "take on" J. Sainsbury – they just followed their customers. The danger of an **emergent strategy** is that if even the company does not "know" that this strategy is in place the competitors may also remain ignorant and not respond until it is too late.

Today Tesco's strategic strength emanates from its **"hybrid"** position on the strategic clock. On the one hand it offers a wide range of branded and own brand products in modern, clean, efficient supermarkets with parking, facilities for children, and other on-site specialist services, but it still offers (or at least appears to offer) lower prices. It underpins these low prices with **low costs** which it enjoys because of its **buying power**. With many suppliers Tesco enjoys **"monopsony"** power in that it takes most (if not all) of the supplier's product (readers are probably more familiar with the term "**monopoly**" which is where the supplier dominates the market). Note, however, that Tesco does not necessarily have the *lowest* costs but it certainly has at least equal low costs as its major competitors and much lower costs than its smaller rivals.

Tesco continues to grow into various other segments of consumer goods and as it grows so too does its **relative buying power** and its ability to **differentiate i**tself through branding. Price is the key competitive weapon for broad-based retailers stocking the same goods. Any retailer with a structural cost advantage that offers the same (or better) perceived value as its competitors is a formidable competitor. The Tesco train will take some stopping!

▶▶▶

Case Notes:

5-2 Tele2: How to position Tele2?

Russia is one of the largest and fastest growing mobile phone markets in the world. Recent estimates (for the year end 2007) put the total revenue generated in the Russian mobile market at nearly EUR 14 bn per annum. Penetration rates (113.3% in 2007 – meaning that on average there were 1.13 mobile phones for each potential customer) were the highest in Eastern Europe apart from the Ukraine, and rising fast (the estimate by 2010 was 134%). Analysts have predicted that strong growth will continue with total mobile subscriptions increasing from 187.8 million in 2009 to 276.4 million in 2013.

However, until recently, no foreign provider has sought to enter this potentially lucrative market. This may be partly because of the vagaries and risks associated with such a large, geographically and culturally diverse, politically charged, and customer savvy environment (for one thing Russians have never bought into the idea of needing to purchase SIM cards for their phones). But it may also be because, since the fall of communism and the rise of capitalist free markets in Russia, the market has evolved to comprise three main players covering three distinctive generic strategic positions: MTS, VimpelCom/Beeline and MegaFon.

MTS is the most established and the largest of the three. It was the state-owned telecom company under communism and while it has been criticized (as have other formerly state-owned telecoms around the world) for being sluggish and overly bureaucratic, it has undergone substantial reforms and with an injection of new management expertise has emerged as a formidable competitor. Its network is the most comprehensive across Russia's vast landmass and it continues to remain the network of choice for many business people. As at 2009, MTS had a 35% share of the market. The nearest competitor was VimpelCom/Beeline, 11 points behind. MTS can be seen, in classic Porterian terms, to be following a broad cost strategy.

Beeline has always defined itself as something different from MTS: trendier, cleverer, and technologically more advanced. Owned by the well-resourced VimpelCom Corporation it was one of the first private organizations to emerge after the fall of communism (the first Russian company to float on the New York Stock Exchange in 1996) and has been seen as something of symbol of the new vibrant and entrepreneurial Russia. The Beeline brand has won numerous awards and accolades. For example, in 2009 Beeline was ranked at number 72 in BrandZ Top 100 Most Valuable Global Brands survey, with an estimated brand value of USD 8.9 bn and was named in the same survey as one of the world's top 10 most valuable telecom brands. Beeline was also listed as "Most Valuable Russian Brand" by the European Brand Institute and showed the highest brand contribution index of any brand in Russian, demonstrating its effectiveness in driving business earnings. In Generic Strategy Matrix parlance, Beeline is a Broad Differentiator (like MTS, Beeline is also a significant ISP or Internet Service Provider).

MegaFon is third in terms of market share (22% in 2008, versus MTS's 35% and Beeline's 24%), but it is growing fast. In terms of new subscribers across an 18-month period from the beginning of 2007 until the middle of 2008, the number of new subscribers being added by MegaFon grew by 23% as against 19% added by MTS and the 10% added by Beeline.

Unencumbered by a history of state-ownership or maintaining its image as a flagship designer brand, MegaFon has been able to take advantage of the falling cost of mobile network provision and has quickly and cleverly improved the quality and reach of its network while maintaining its reputation as the most cost effective option for many Russians. In GSM terms, MegaFon is a cost focus company currently seeking to move broader from a narrow position.

The three companies' websites provide a good visual representation of their relative strategic positions. MTS (www.mts.ru) is smart, solid and comprehensive. Beeline (www.beeline.ru) is quirky, clever, and colorful. MegaFon (www.megafon.ru) is simple, no-nonsense and functional.

Each company appears to occupy a different segment of Porter's Generic Strategy Matrix. The fourth segment, focused differentiation, may have been occupied by smaller regional players in the past but these companies have been gradually acquired by the main players as they have sought to solidify their positions. As such, the competitive landscape in Russia is now similar to the layout of Telecom brands in many other countries, where a former state-owned company is seeking to hold a broad cost position, others fill the cost focus and broad differentiation segments and there seems little scope for focused differentiation strategy.

There has been some movement in recent years, perhaps in line with the mobile operators having almost exhausted regional expansion through acquisition as a route for growth, with Beeline in particular feeling the effects of a "squeeze." MegaFon has improved its network quality and its marketing has aggressively gone after the "young and innovative" customers that had traditionally favored Beeline; while MTS has shaken off some of its fusty "State" image and improved its customer service and marketing campaigns to present a more premium image.

And the Russian triptych was finally challenged a Swedish-based Tele2 (www.en.tele2.ru) entered the market aggressively. But, as the market is now populated by three well-developed and well-managed organizations with extensive local knowledge, it is still unclear whether Tele2 can significantly challenge the established home-grown players.

1. *Where would you seek to position the Tele2 brand on the GSM as it enters Russia and through what kind of initiatives? What advice might you give the other three companies to combat Tele2?*
2. *In a case such as this, where the nature of the industry appears to preclude the existence of focus differentiators, would you seek to redraw the GSM to aid analysis? And, if so, how?*
3. *Do you think that this case highlights the continued usefulness of the GSM, or its limitations as a strategic framework in a changing world?*

5-3 Mother's Preference:
The power of the customer

You are the managing director of Mother's Preference, a manufacturer of baby furniture (things like high chairs, play cots, etc.), pushchairs (prams/strollers), and child restraints (safety devices in cars). The Target chain of discount stores is your largest customer, taking 30% of your sales and contributing about USD 19 m of margin (i.e. revenue – variable costs) to your business. Louis is Target's new 23-year-old nursery buyer and he is determined to make his mark and progress quickly up the company. You are about to go into session to draw up the contract for next year's orders from Target.

In a stagnant market you hold about 25% total market share. Your closest competitor, Mother's Hope, holds a similar share. Two or three other smaller competitors have around 10–12% each. Both you and Mother's Hope have well-established brand names and similar product ranges that are sold exclusively through retail outlets. Although you have active advertising programs, the most important influences on the buying decision are point-of-sale and word-of-mouth. Due to the top-of-mind nature of the two major brands, the large chain and department stores tend to use one or other of you as a loss-leading traffic generator on the front of their catalogues (i.e. to lure customers into the store in the hope that they buy other, higher margin items while picking up their cheap pushchair or child-seat).

After each major promotion by a retailer, this loss-leading strategy always causes your phone to run hot as other buyers demand to know: "How the hell can our competitors afford to offer those prices? You must have given them a discount that you are not giving us. So you better give it to us or else."

Despite your generally truthful assertions to the contrary, you are rarely believed and never sympathized with, and all of your customers continue to demand preferential discounts in a downward spiral as they claim that "there's no margin in your product!"

A couple of years ago you were the clear market leader, but Mother's Hope has recently gained ground by taking share from the lesser brands. Your industry contacts suggest that this has been achieved by significant discounting cleverly disguised as either "contribution to advertising," "consignment stock," "volume rebates," "early payment discounts," or "payments for buyers to visit supply factories in Taiwan" (via Hong Kong for shopping and/or hours of pleasure – depending on the buyer). But when you had the opportunity to confront the MD of Mother's Hope about this, he vehemently denied any such underhand behavior.

"So, here's the deal," says Louis. "For the supply contract next year I need an 8% reduction in your delivered price across each of the three major product groupings. Oh, and by the way, my assistant is outlining the exact same proposal to your chief competitor across the hall."

At this point you start to wail about the effects this will have on your children and the children of the employees you will be compelled to "retrench" with one day's pay. But Louis is unrepentant. He offers three possibilities:

"If one of you gives me the reduction and the other doesn't, then the one who does gets all the business" (which you currently split with Mother's Hope

50/50 in all the product categories). "If you both give me the discount I'll leave the share split as it is for next year. If neither of you gives me the discount, I am forced to leave it as it is for next year, but I will begin to look for some other suppliers who we can work with."

You are pretty sure that this last point is a bluff. He could not afford to delist both of you. However, he can easily afford to delist one of you although he would probably prefer not to if he was honest.

"I will not negotiate any other price, and here, in writing, is my contractual commitment to go by the decisions that you and your competitor make. Decide what you will do with furniture first; pushchairs second; and child restraints last. I will send my assistant for your first decision (on furniture) in fifteen minutes. He will let you know what your competitor has decided on this category. Then we will do the same thing for the second and then the third categories."

You had been expecting something like this from Target and had worked out the approximate losses/gains based on various combinations of price reduction and share of the Target account (Table 5-3.1). Gaining all the Target account, even with an 8% price reduction, is very attractive because the additional gains from volume-driven efficiencies in the factory and supply chain would off-set the price drop.

Table 5-3.1 Contribution in USD millions under various pricing and volume conditions

Product Category	Current contribution (half the Target account)	Contribution with 8% price reduction and half the Target account	Contribution with 8% price reduction and all the Target account
Furniture	5	4	10
Pushchairs	5	4	10
Child restraints	9	8	18
Totals	**19**	**16**	**38**

1. *So when the assistant comes back for your decision on furniture pricing what are you going to do? Are you going to reduce price or not?*
2. *How will the result of your first decision influence your next decision?*
3. *What does being in this position tell you about your relative competitive advantage with respect to your major competitor?*

5-4 Taytos: Out of the frying pan. . .

Tayto's Crisps have dominated the Irish savory snack market for 40 years. Every week the Tayto Group produces and sells 8 million packets of potato crisps (chips) and snacks in a country with a population of fewer than 4 million people. This means that, on average, every Irish person consumes almost 100 packets a year.

However, Tayto's position is now under threat. British company Walkers, backed by the muscle of its parent company Frito Lay and Frito Lay's owner, the giant Pepsico Corporation, launched the UK's most popular brand of crisps in the Republic of Ireland on March 17, 2000 (St. Patrick's Day). According to Andrew Hartshorn, Walkers Brand Manager for Ireland, Walkers intends to capture a "substantial share of the [Irish] market quickly." Indeed, Walkers appears to not only want to eat up market share, but to change the way Irish consumers see potato chips. While Tayto's generally come in dinky 25-gram bags, replete with the skin shavings and blemishes of the potatoes they once were, Walkers is a crisp without blemish. They come with a minimal trace of vegetable oil in bigger servings with a modern foil bag decorated in the global Frito Lay format.

While Walkers is now backed by an American parent, Tayto has recently gone the other way, returning to Irish ownership after US firm TLC Beatrice sold it to the Irish drinks company Cantrell & Cochrane.

All of Ireland's crisps were imported from the UK until Mr. Joe Murphy from Donabate, County Dublin, founded the Tayto Company in 1954. Murphy's biggest claim to fame was his invention of cheese and onion flavored crisps (prior to this the only "flavoring" option was salt). Cheese and onion is now the top selling flavor in Ireland and in the UK, where Murphy's innovation was quickly copied. Originally, Tayto's were produced by hand using two sets of deep-fat fryers, but the company grew quickly, aided by the financial association with Beatrice, who first acquired a stake in the company in 1965. Factories were built in Rathmines, Harold's Cross, and Coolock, all in the Dublin area. Tayto now employs over 250 people and boasts a low staff turnover as testimony to the family atmosphere of the company.

Tayto's supply and distribution chains go deep into the Irish fabric. It only uses Irish potatoes grown under contract by farmers with whom Tayto has been associated for many years, and it has developed an intricate distribution network. Tayto's distributes its crisps through one of the largest direct van sales operations in the country, with ten regional depots located through the country supporting a roving fleet of 35 Tayto's vans. This provides a 99% domestic distribution level – a quite remarkable feat given the still rural nature of large parts of Ireland.

To further consolidate these channels a central distribution center was created in 1996 in Ballymount, Dublin. The center is fully automated and contains 10 automated loading bays, with the capacity to hold in excess of 150,000 cartons of crisps. All types of outlets are serviced by this system: supermarket chains, pubs, newsagents, garage forecourts, off-licenses, and independent owner-operator stores, and Tayto guarantees that each customer receives fresh product through weekly service calls.

The result: almost every shop in Ireland – from the biggest supermarket to the smallest independent corner grocer and the most remote petrol station – prominently displays Tayto crisps, a big factor in a market where it is estimated that approximately half of all sales are impulse purchases. Finding an Irish person, or anybody with a connection to Ireland, who is unaware of the brand is a difficult task. Indeed, the way in which some Irish speak of Tayto crisps seems to indicate a kind of spiritual attachment. In a recent survey of brands, Tayto was rated the third biggest Irish brand and first in the grocery sector.

While Tayto holds a domestic market position enjoyed by few indigenous consumer brands (in 1999, it held 60% of Ireland's crisp market, and the second highest selling brand, King Crisps, is also owned by Tayto), it has no official export business in an increasingly global savory snack market. However, there are what could be called "independent initiatives" that bring Tayto crisps to the world. It is often claimed that there are more Irish living outside of Ireland than within, and packets of Tayto are regularly dispatched to Irish emigrants from friends and family at home. Martin McElroy, an Irishman now living in Philadelphia, has developed an agency that now orders over 100,000 bags of Tayto a week which he sells through local wholesalers. "It's wonderful to see the reaction of all the Irish people here when they walk into a shop and there is a box of Tayto Cheese & Onion," claims McElroy. "But the Americans are really developing a taste for them too. In fact I can see that Tayto will be regarded as the luxury import in the same way that many American products such as nachos are regarded at home [Ireland]." The crisps are retailing for $1 a pack, twice what they sell for in Irish stores.

Walkers can also trace its history back 50 years. As a local pork butcher in Leicester in the English midlands, Walkers began producing crisps as a way of utilizing staff and facilities in its small factory while meat was heavily rationed after World War II. It began to expand into other British regions around 20 years ago. In recent years, with the backing of its new parents and the help of a big marketing budget wisely spent, particularly on television advertisements featuring British soccer stars, it has become the UK's second most powerful grocery brand after Coca-Cola. Walkers now boasts annual sales of well over £300m and a 65% share of the UK potato chip sector.

Walkers/Frito-Lay/Pepsico is taking the Irish launch of its products very seriously. It has given away more than a million free packets of crisps and made an Irish variation on its theme of soccer-star television advertisements starring Roy Keane, who was one of the highest paid Irish players in the English football league, Andrew Hartshorn explains that the huge marketing budget that Walkers is currently using to push its crisps in Ireland is a "long-term investment" – a strategy that is part of a bigger global picture. Success in Ireland, Europe's fastest growing economy and Walkers' first overseas target, will help the company to develop the knowledge, experience, and confidence necessary to launch into other European countries.

Evidence from Northern Ireland does not bode well for Tayto. While the Tayto brand (owned by a different company in the North) is still well regarded, Walkers replaced it as the best-selling crisp in just 3 years. However, there are many cultural and business factors that make the Republic a different market – not least of which is the clout of the myriad smaller independent stores which still contribute a much higher percentage of sales than in Britain or America and with whom Tayto's has long-standing relationships. Tayto's Managing Director, Vincent

O'Sullivan, subsequently believes that Tayto can compete against the might of the multinational threat: "We're not going to give away market share to anyone," insists O'Sullivan. "What [Walkers] are going to find out is that it's a very competitive market with strong local brands."

1. *What resources and capabilities might Tayto's have that will be difficult for Walkers to replicate?*
2. *If you were CEO of Tayto's, what strategies would you use to protect the company's competitive advantage?*
3. *If you were CEO of Walkers Ireland, what strategies would you employ to build a competitive advantage?*

Case Notes:

5-5 IBB: Mirage?

In August 2004, the Financial Services Authority granted a banking license allowing the Islamic Bank of Britain (IBB) to open its first retail branch in London, promoting *sharia*-compliant products. Islamic law (the *sharia*) bans the payment and acceptance of interest – fundamental concepts in Western banking. In early 2005, IBB opened a branch and head office in Birmingham, a lower cost location than London, and one where a substantial proportion of the country's Muslim population resides. Other branches followed in London and Leicester, with further branches planned for other areas of high Muslim concentration (www.islamic-bank.com). However, start-up costs on branches and direct banking widened losses to £3.1 m in the first 5 months to December 2004. IBB is imprisoned by its fixed costs and has to grow to escape its constraints and compete with the huge cost-reducing scale economies of its giant conventional competitors. Is this quest to become the first fully fledged Islamic bank in the UK and Europe really chasing a mirage?

Muslims are the second largest religious group in Britain and, with 2 million followers, there is clearly a potential market for an Islamic bank. However, there are two problems facing IBB: (1) Muslims avoid banks if they want to retain their beliefs; and (2) the Islamic banking model may not be competitive in the mature UK banking market.

Islamic beliefs

In Islam, human beings are God's co-managers on earth and the well-being of the community must be considered when it comes to economic actions. Wealth should be neither hoarded nor wasted on unproductive ventures. Money should not be created from money, but through investment in useful activities. Interest is opposed on several grounds, but from a social perspective, it is the poor and needy who are forced to borrow whereas the rich have money to save. Interest therefore penalizes the poor and rewards the rich. The accumulation of wealth through interest is deemed a reward without productive effort and is therefore selfish. On this basis, conventional banking is not appropriate for Muslims.

Islamic banking

The essential feature of Islamic finance is that it is interest-free. *Sharia* explicitly prohibits interest (*riba*) and excessive risk or uncertainty (*gharar*). The prohibition of interest does not mean that money may not be lent under Islamic law, it simply rules out what might be considered unearned profit. Indeed, the provider of capital should be allowed an adequate return by having a stake in the undertaking, but is not permitted to fix a predetermined rate of interest. Money is not considered a commodity in Islamic economics, but rather a bearer of risk. There should be a price for time, but not fixed in advance. Owners of capital can share the profits made by the entrepreneur based on a profit-sharing ratio rather than a predetermined rate of return. This means that the borrower and lender share risk and work more closely together to ensure the business's success, which is more productive for society and provides cohesion between social classes because finance is available equally to anyone with a productive idea.

Two of the most popular types of "compliant" business in Islamic banking are: (1) *murabaha*, a contract for purchase and resale that allows customers to make purchases without having to take out loans and pay interest; and (2) *mudarabah*, an investment on your behalf by a more skilled person who shares part of the profits in return for time and effort (see case note below for further details).

IBB offers the following products to both Muslim and non-Muslim customers and stresses the fact that it tries to make all transactions with the bank simple for customers in terms of delivery and understanding.

1. *Current account* – includes the same facilities as conventional current accounts but no interest is paid or charged and a credit balance preferred.
2. *Saving account* – offers term structures and operates on a *mudarabah* basis, with the clients sharing in the bank's profits, the rate being reviewed monthly.
3. *Treasury deposit account* – for high-net-worth clients. The minimum deposit is £100,000, with fixed periods. Structured on a *murabahah* basis, the depositor obtains the profit from the purchase and sale of commodities.
4. *Masjid (mosque) proposition* – a free overdraft of £1,000 to mosques for a maximum of 30 days. This is very successful because mosques are major influences on local communities. When Muslims see their mosques dealing with IBB, this boosts their confidence in the bank and its Islamic nature.
5. *Sweeping facility* – transfers money automatically from the customers' saving accounts to their current accounts to avoid the latter getting overdrawn.
6. *Other products* – home finance, Islamic credit cards, internet banking in 2006. In the horizon of 3 to 5 years, the bank plans to introduce mobile banking, to offer investment and insurance products – possibly through the establishment of a UK subsidiary – and to establish physical continental European branches.

The banking market in the UK is highly consolidated, with the top six players accounting for 83% of the total market for financial retail services. The market grew at 10% (2002–3) and the banks have been posting record profits, aided by aggressive reduction in costs through the use of technology. At the same time there has been a reduction in customer satisfaction in the level of service received.

Within the UK market of 65 million, there are over 2 million Muslims. Of these, 62% are drawn from the Indian subcontinent and 21% from the Middle East and Africa. There are high concentrations in urban areas, with half living in London, and this promotes strong social cohesion. Unemployment among Muslims is almost three times the national average and the quality of their housing is among the lowest in the country. The young and the old show strong religious devotion, with 250,000 attending mosques regularly. Although strongly influenced by British society and culture, the majority of the young are proud of their Muslim identity. Many Muslims have small businesses and an increasing proportion of young Muslims are joining the professional classes. The estimated pool of savings of Muslims in the UK was £1 bn in 2003.

The recent spate of terrorist attacks has raised anti-Muslim sentiment in Britain. However, no Islamic bank has been linked in any way to these activities.

Interestingly, the effect upon Muslims has been to cause them to turn more to their religion, and Islamic banks in general have witnessed a huge surge in business when their links to terrorism were shown to be unfounded.

Competition for Muslims worldwide has been rising rapidly. Many of the key players in conventional banks, such as HSBC, now provide Islamic offerings targeted at institutional clients and overseas high-net-worth individuals, rather than Muslims in Britain. Other competition comes from the providers of ethical banking such as the Co-operative Bank and Islamic institutions operating in the UK as subsidiaries owned by offshore operators such as Pakistani and Bangladeshi banks. These latter banks also provide reliable and trustworthy communications channels for British Muslims with families in the Indian subcontinent. However, this service may be more valuable to first generation immigrants rather than younger generations with weaker overseas ties. Also these banks are limited in their product range, such as money transfer.

IBB feels the increasing competition may make customers more aware of this type of banking practice and help to sell the concept and "grow the cake." However, they think these Islamic offerings are not really Islamic in either manner or essence of operations. For instance, HSBC Amanah in raising money can borrow this informally from the parent, which is a non-Islamic channel. From a conservative Islamic point of view, this money is tainted.

There is no doubt that IBB differs significantly from conventional banks:

1. Although there are similar types of risk, they are run at higher levels because of extensive trade and investment activities. However there is no interest-rate risk.
2. Liquidity management is a problem owing to the lack of *sharia*-compliant liquid assets and no "lender of last resort facility" with the central bank. Conventional banks' treasuries place the excess funds overnight in money markets, lend the surplus in the interbank network, or invest in Government securities. IBB cannot utilize these options, and is obliged to hold relatively large amounts of non-income-generating cash (www.islamicbankingnetwork.com).
3. Islamic banks' focus of financial accounting information is on asset allocation and return from investments and trade rather than interest rate spread, provision of loan portfolios, and maturities of liabilities.
4. In theory, Islamic banks should guarantee neither the capital value nor the return on investments; these banks basically pool depositors' funds to provide professional investment management. This is similar to the operations of investment companies in the West. However, for investment companies the public are entitled to voting rights and can monitor the company's performance. In IBB, depositors are only entitled to share the bank's net profit (or loss) according to the profit/loss sharing ratio stipulated in their contracts, and they cannot influence IBB's policies. However, under English law, IBB is required to provide guarantees to depositors' capital.
5. In cases of default, there is no ambiguity about control of the assets under Islamic mark-up contracts because the financial institution retains title to the asset until the agent makes all payments.

Being an Islamic bank poses internal challenges. Firstly, the bank has had to establish an Islamic *Sharia* Committee to assess whether its activities are in accordance with Islamic law. This is time-consuming, costly, leads to confusion about what Islamic banking really encompasses, and hinders its widespread acceptance. It also makes it difficult for Western regulators to understand the idea of Islamic banking. This lack of understanding, coupled with lack of regulation, causes tension between Islamic banks and British regulators, and affects the regulators' willingness to support such organizations. Indeed, the collapse of BCCI in 1991, a conventional bank but with many Muslims on its Board, prompted significant tightening of banking regulations in the UK, which caused Al-Baraka International Bank, IBB's predecessor, to close down. Today, Western regulators require Islamic banks to maintain higher liquidity requirements because their operations are riskier than those of conventional banks. Until recently, the British tax system was unfair to Islamic banks because interest is tax-deductible, whereas profit is taxed. However, IBB has recently claimed a major victory in the battle with the authorities since changes in legislation have been announced.

There are few professional courses and training tailored for Islamic banking and this has resulted in a lack of qualified staff for IBB and it has to resort to recruiting staff from conventional banks. However, such staff find adjusting difficult. In addition the lack of trained staff slows innovation in Islamic products and means unqualified management.

Against a very competitive background, and the lack of awareness of what Islamic banking is, IBB was pleasantly surprised at the launch of its Whitechapel Branch in London, when 60 accounts were opened within the first 4 hours.

---

1. *Has IBB identified a new strategic position in the market, or is this really a mirage?*
2. *How can IBB compete with the large well-resourced incumbents and protect its competitive advantage?*
3. *What should IBB be prioritizing to make the most of its resources and capabilities: focus on increasing its product range (or scope), opening new branches; creating of an online banking facility; or something else?*

Case note: The *sharia*-compliant products are:

1   *Murabaha* – a contract for purchase and resale, which allows customers to make purchases without having to take out loans and pay interest. The financial institution purchases the goods for the customer, and resells them to the customer on a deferred basis, adding an agreed profit margin. The customer then pays the sale price for the goods over installments, effectively obtaining credit without paying interest.

2   *Mudarabah* – refers to an investment on your behalf by a more skilled person. It takes the form of a contract between two parties, one who provides the funds and the other who provides the expertise. They agree to the division of any profits made in advance. In other words, Islamic Bank of Britain would make *sharia*-compliant investments and share the profits with the customer, in effect charging for its time and effort. If no profit is made, the loss is borne by the customer and Islamic Bank of Britain takes no fee.

Two decades ago, the Browerij Huyghe was in trouble. The brewery was founded in 1906 by Leon Huyghe, a brewery worker married to a brewer's daughter. It grew steadily by producing pils and basic "table beers." By the 1960s, it was supplying its own chain of 300 pubs in addition to filling several big Government contracts, most notably to provide beer for hospital restaurants and railway workers. However, things went against Huyghe in the 1970s and 80s. There had been as many breweries as there were villages in Belgium, but consolidation now meant that Huyghe did not have the relative economies of scale necessary to compete on cost in the pils and table beer segments. Advances in distribution networks made competition less regionalized and subsequently fiercer. Government organizations like hospitals and railways began to question whether supplying their workers with beer, the traditional Belgian drink, was necessarily a good thing. In fact, it is doubtful that the brewery would have survived if it were not for the discovery of *Delirium Tremens*.

According to brewery manager Alain De Laet, the creation of Delirium Tremens was "coincidental." De Laet explains how in 1988 a distributor asked for a strong blond beer for the Italian market. Brew engineer Patrick De Wael made a first experimental batch on December 26, 1988. "It was dead on target," claims De Laet. "The process hasn't been changed a bit ever since. "

The distinctive features of Delirium's packaging also emerged serendipitously. The grey speckled bottle was the remnant of a failed campaign. Painted by a German company and three times more expensive than normal bottles (too pricey to fill with pils or table beer, where the margins are far lower), these had been intended for a "Grand Cru" for a German customer. After this deal fell through, they sat in storage and were due to be destroyed – until a bottle was used for the trial batches of Delirium.

Another part of the eclectic but distinctive packaging mix is the label with its pink elephants, and brightly coloured monsters and birds. The formulation of this is the subject of folklore. The story goes that De Wael, excited by his creation, immediately brought it to a small meeting of Huyghe staff and family members. After tasting it and agreeing it was good they sat down to drink more. After four bottles, one of the group said, "if I drink much more of this I'll start to see pink elephants." After seven, eight, nine, somebody else said, "if I drink any more of this I'll be seeing monsters." After eleven, somebody said they'd start to see those birds from Alfred Hitchcock's movie *The Birds*. (It is worth pointing out that the beer contains a hefty 9% alcohol.)

Jean De Laet, Alain's father, who was running things at the time, remembers it slightly differently: "Initially, the label showed a skull, to clarify the link with the disease." (Delirium tremens is an acute disorder following withdrawal from alcoholic intoxication and, because seizures can last up to six days and involve terrifying hallucinations and violent tremors, it can be fatal.) "But a student working with us once drew the now well-known Pink Elephant, and bingo!"

The name Delirium Tremens (born when an inspector from the Excise Office tasted the new beer and said, "If I drink too much of this, I'll get a delirium") is unlikely to have been approved by a multinational corporation, but it works for Huyghe.

In the company's view: "The most important thing is that people really remember the beer." In a market where there are hundreds of alternatives, this is crucial.

Delirium has subsequently been "remembered" by some very influential people. In 1997, beer guru Stuart Kallen surprised aficionados by declaring Delirium Tremens the world's best beer, despite the fact that it would make his life more difficult: "If I simply mentioned a beer everyone had heard of, without the name of a drinker's disease, I would get more peace," he wrote. In 1998, it won at the World Beer Championships. Subsequently, sales are booming. About two-thirds of the Huyghe's output is now Delirium. The vast majority of this is sold outside of Belgium, where it attracts a premium price.

Despite the prospects for small breweries being seen as bleak by many commentators (their cost structure makes it extremely difficult for them to compete against increasingly large conglomerates), Huyghe's management is upbeat, claiming that the company has certain advantages. "What we can do is when a buyer comes to us from Guadeloupe – or wherever – he comes and visits us and talks to us. It's a nice trip for him. Then if he only has a small shop we can make up a mixed pallet, half a crate of this and that, whatever he wants. So, he walks away with a ready-made shop of specialty beers. Big companies like Interbrew can't do that," explains Wim Van Mannem, Huyghe's accountant.

More than just tailor-making pallets, Huyghe will also tailor-make beers to suit particular clients' needs – a claim proved by a quick look around the warehouse piled high with surplus labels for different niche-fillers. Alain De Laet sums up Huyghe's philosophy as "meeting the demand of the customer as good as possible, and as it were, providing 'made to measure.' Important customers asking us for a new beer must be able to get it. We are open to all possibilities."

Interbrew is an altogether different Belgian brewery. Interbrew's operation is state of the art. The new factory, all polished steel vats and piping, produces around 10 million units of Stella Artois, Interbrew's flagship brand, each day. There are very few people to be seen, apart from the computer operators in the control room. Across the road, the old plant is now producing smaller runs of specialist brands, like the famous abbey beer Leffe, which are now an integral part of the Interbrew "family."

Interbrew has grown very big and very global very fast, having made 24 acquisitions in 14 countries in the 10 years to 2003. According to CEO Hugo Powell, Interbrew's seemingly paradoxical aim was to become "the world's local brewer. Our global approach is based on strong regional platforms and supported by our great ability to adapt to local markets and cultures."

Ludo Degelin, director of operations and manager of international technical support, explains the approach in greater detail. He begins by reviewing some of the approaches favored by Interbrew's competitors. Anheuser-Busch (AB), the world's largest brewing group, tends to buy up local production facilities (important given the high distribution costs associated with beer) that can then be converted and standardized to produce their global brand – Budweiser. "It's a good strategy that has worked well for them, but it works because they started from such a large base and they have a huge global brand. We start from a different position and in any case I don't think their approach suits us," Ludo explains. Guinness attempts to match local tastes (and take advantage of different licensing laws) by varying their recipe. Hence, the Belgian Guinness is stronger than in Britain, where the excise regime is a lot stiffer, and the African brew is both stronger and sweeter than the Irish. A lot of mileage can be got out of one brand in this way. However, Ludo believes this strategy is becoming problematic as drinkers increasingly move across national boundaries and are confused by the variation in what they assume to be the same product.

Interbrew, by contrast, looks to acquire breweries with brands that have a strong local identity and are market leaders, and, unlike AB, they expect to develop these brands. "It is difficult to recreate the emotional attachment that local people already have for these beers," claims Johan Robbrecht, who works with Ludo on aspects of packaging development, "they are deeply rooted in the community, linked to particular sports and so on." However, Interbrew does change some things. In Ludo's words, while they do not alter the taste of a local brew too radically, they do seek to "clean up the production, using our technical experience and expertise, and then effectively relaunch it. Once this is done we offer the local management the opportunity to brew Stella, which we are building as our global flagship brand. However, [unlike Guinness] they must be able to produce it using the Belgian recipe so that it tastes as close as possible to the Stella brewed in Leuven. And, importantly," Ludo adds, "it must come into the local market at a premium price in keeping with a premium brand."

Over time, Interbrew aims to operate high-volume local brands that generally tap into that area's traditional masculine sporting culture in tandem with Stella as the premium more refined brand "over and above these," to use Ludo's words. In this way, Ludo believes that Interbrew avoids pitfalls such as those encountered by its competitor Heineken as it attempted to penetrate Eastern Europe. In one country in particular, its approach was to discontinue local brands and replace their production with Heineken. This caused local resentment, with Heineken seen as a foreign intruder even though local people produced the beer. Then, because of Heineken's global branding, it had to be sold at a price that very few drinkers in the East could afford (any lower would diminish the value of the product in neighboring countries).

Ludo sees the way that Heineken now follows the same approach to international development as Interbrew as a vindication of Interbrew's strategy. However, he stresses that tolerance for local difference must have its limits. Just adding more and more brands to the portfolio creates logistical and organizational problems, and the cost savings that can be made by discontinuing brands that are not performing must be realized in a company of Interbrew's size. Plus, it has to be admitted that some of the local brews are not, in Ludo's diplomatic words, "as good as they could be." Indeed, Corporate Marketing Director Johan Peeters points out that there are some global constants in beer. "For example, if a beer is colder people will drink more of it: physiologically this is true, and this is why Guinness is brewing colder now. And all people appreciate a beer that is more consistent and technically better brewed." However, Ludo and Johan agree that beer is also connected to human emotions and traditions. So, if you are going to change production approaches, recipes, or temperatures, it must be done gradually. That local people do not like to see their traditional tastes trashed appears to be another "global constant."

Despite the challenges associated with its rapid internationalization, Interbrew has little option but to grow quickly given the nature of developments in the brewing industry. Analysts predict that three or four players will dominate the world market in the 2010s. Stefan Descheemaeker explains the situation with a simple diagram, with *profitability* on the vertical axis and *size* on the horizontal. Between the axes he draws a "U" shape. "In the future, only the smallest micro-breweries and the largest groups will exist. You cannot survive in the middle."

Postscript:

Since this case was written Interbrew has grown further through acquisition to become the world's largest brewing group. It is now called InBev.

1. Use the value chimera to sketch out Interbrew's (or InBev's if you want to do this case in real time) strategic business model, and the value chain to draw that of Huyghe.
2. Define the respective strategies of Hugyhe and Interbrew,. Do you think these companies have competitive advantages? If so, what are they?
3. What advice would you give Huyghe and Interbrew for the future?

Case Notes:

STRATEGIC POSITIONING

5-7 World Cities: Clashing Megalopoli

Increasing globalization and the pervasiveness of information technology has meant that geographically distant organizations that never before had to think of themselves as in competition with one another and, subsequently, had not had to consider strategic positioning in relation to each other, now do. For example, cities now compete head to head to be centers of excellence – to be key airline transport hubs for a geographic region; centers of learning; the focus of fashion, to host major sporting and cultural events such as the Olympic Games and Expo. One highly contested territory is to be taken seriously as the world's financial capital. Prime contenders include New York, Hong Kong, Singapore, London, Frankfurt, and Dubai.

While there may be more than one winner in this race, it has been postulated that the same trends compelling these cities to jostle for position and compete for the best hearts and minds (globalization, seamless communication) will eventually lead to a clearly defined top tier of three centers. The earth's rotation means that three may be all that's needed to keep the financial world whirring across the time zones.

New York, given the fame of Wall Street and its long distinguished history, allure to "high flyers," and position in the world's largest free market, is favourite to hold the number one spot for the foreseeable future. It is also likely that a European city will fill out one of the other two podium places, and here it seems to have reduced to a contest between London and Frankfurt. Frankfurt stands spatially at the center of Europe; London, geographically and politically, stands somewhat aloof, although it has other benefits: a very long and distinguished history as a financial center and the location of the headquarters of a number of the world's largest companies. Moreover, apart from the high octane levels within and around the financial heart of the City, it also has many cultural and historical attractions to draw the best minds among the highly mobile international financial class. City of London boosters often remark, "if you were a dynamic young professional with options, where would you rather live: Frankfurt or London?"

The city to round out the top three is harder to pick. Dubai is at the center of the oil wealth of the Middle East with a government that will bend over backwards to make business run smoothly. Singapore too has a strong and stable pro-business government leading an ordered highly educated and highly motivated population in a self-contained city-state. It is positioned at the center of the world handily half way between New York and Greenwich Mean Time. And it is relatively close (geographically, politically, historically, and culturally) to the booming economies of China and India.

Like Dubai and Singapore, Hong Kong also seems to possess a number of factors congruent with the critical success factors in this competition: proximity to wealth and big business; agreeable governance; a good position geographically. But talking this competition through with a group of MBA students at the Chinese University of Hong Kong revealed a confidence that a number of other unique resources could sway the race in Hong Kong's favor. Some of these are obvious: Hong Kong is, like Singapore, in a great time zone; it is in China but it has Western institutions; it can draw on the best of Eastern and Western traditions and education systems; it is pulsating, dynamic, edgy, and fun (in other words, more attractive than Singapore or Dubai to those "high-flyers" mentioned earlier).

However, others aspects may be less obvious, at least to an outside observer, or an economist. The students insist that perhaps the best thing that Hong Kong has going for it is its home-grown talent (in addition to its ability to attract the best financial brains from East and West). This is because of the heady mix of three interconnected factors that feed into the Hong Kong "mindset": a passion for mathematics, a love of trading, and a keen interest in gambling. The latter two dimensions are certainly apparent if anybody spends any time in Hong Kong, even as a tourist. The former may not be so apparent, but it certainly can be seen if one spends time in Hong Kong's schools. And if supported well institutionally (by Hong Kong's governors and regulatory environment), these three socio-cultural aspects, with the other critical success factors and resources that Hong Kong can draw upon, may well be non-appropriable, non-imitable, and very difficult to substitute by its competitors.

Indeed, it seems that it is not just cities aiming to be leading centers of finance that will be competing with one another to attract the mobile creative class that is now seen to be a key driver of innovation and wealth creation. A recent book called *Who's Your City?* by Richard Florida claims that all cities must seek to understand and position themselves in relation to their unique "psychological profiles" – profiles shaped by the dominant personality traits of the people who live and work within them. This is a theme that we will expand upon in greater detail in the chapter that follows: Corporate Identity.

1. *Why has "strategic positioning" come to be seen as an imperative for many cities? What has led to these changes? Do you agree with Richard Florida that cities should seek to understand their "psychological profiles" and use this understanding to drive their strategies for the future?*

2. *Which cities do you predict will be the world's main financial centers by 2025? Why and which strategies would you be promoting if you were advising the government and city council of Hong Kong? Singapore? Dubai?*

3. *Do you think that conventional positioning models like the generic strategy matrix or the strategy clock can be used to analyze traditionally not-for-profit entities like cities. If so, do they need to be adapted? If not, what type of new frameworks might be useful?*

Case Notes:

These days, building the best server isn't enough. That's the price of entry.

Ann Livermore, CFO Hewlett-Packard

This land is me
rock, water, animal, tree,
they are my song.

Aboriginal tracker in the 2002 Australian film **One Night the Moon**
by Kev Carmody

6
Corporate Identity

In the late 1990s, many organizations, like Hewlett-Packard, developed campaigns to promote their distinctive corporate character as a reflection of the "land" or geographical setting from which the company emerged. HP put considerable effort into understanding and promoting the values of its founders, Bill Hewlett and Dave Packard, their individualistic pioneering spirit, and the company's subsequent history of significant innovation. HP articulated what it termed "the rules of the garage" – partly an expression of the beliefs shared by Bill and Dave as they toiled away in their little inventor's shed in Palo Alto, California, and partly a devotional rallying call to today's stakeholders in the company's fortunes. These "rules" were boiled down to one underlying characteristic – "Invention." Subsequently, the company has ensured that wherever one sees the HP symbol, it stands upon the word "Invent."

Why would a company that essentially makes technology for the present and the future put so much effort into celebrating its past identity? The answer, to a large extent at least, lies in the quotation from HP's CFO, Ann Livermore. Thanks to the increasing speed with which knowledge flows, the increasing ease with which the technical aspects of a company can be reverse engineered and copied, and the increasing homogeneity of the processes of corporations and their consultants, everybody's technology is good: a "first-rate server" just gets you into the game. So, what else can a company utilize to make it stand out as an entity that people choose to do business with over its competitors? Not only is HP's identity a key point of differentiation (in that it is unique to it), this character also is inimitable (in that it, unlike technology, cannot be "reverse engineered" or copied by its competitors). For this reason **corporate identity** has become a key element steering the development of a sustainable competitive advantage for an increasing number of corporations.

In this chapter we compare a corporation's identity to its "character." There are many definitions of character in the *Oxford English Dictionary*, but the following two best describe this chapter's focus. The first stems from natural science: "character is the aggregate of the distinctive features of any thing; its *essential peculiarity*." The second connects with the peculiarly human aspects of character: "the

173

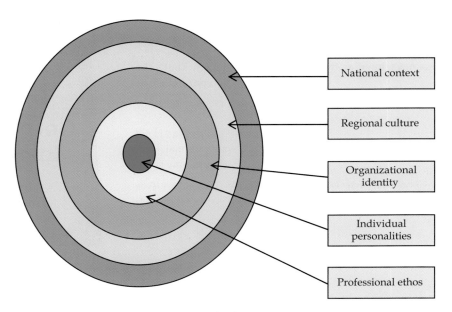

Figure 6.1 Layers that contribute to corporate identity

sum of the moral and mental *qualities* which *distinguish* an individual or a race; the *individuality* impressed by nature and habit on man or nation."

This kind of character or corporate identity is deeply rooted and multi-layered. Figure 6.1's onion shape outlines some of the layers that create a distinguishing corporate identity to illustrate this. We can apply this onion model to better understand why the HP character described above works. Moving from the outer layer in, we can say that HP's identity draws on the *national context* of the USA. This is the country in which the context that led to the computer industry, as we know it, emerged. HP's character draws on US traits, such as individualism and entrepreneurial spirit. It also connects to California's *regional culture*, something that one might characterize as a combination of a pioneering spirit, a hard-work ethic, and a free-thinking nature and the *professional ethos* of those early computer programmers whose shared values and beliefs drew them to Northern California (in other contexts strategists must be mindful of the professional values or oaths of doctors, accountants, or even MBA students).[1] And, HP seeks to enact an identity embodied in the *individual personalities* of Bill and Dave, in a garage, working hard, challenging conventions, and doing things that people thought couldn't be done. HP consequently has an *organizational identity* that draws from all of these elements and builds upon this the added historical dimension of being a long-established innovator in its industry. The sum of these essential qualities is something unique to HP and hence should distinguish the company and its strategic trajectory from others.

Whereas the previous chapter examined how an organization's activities can be positioned to meet different marketplace needs, this chapter looks at how an organization's corporate identity can extend out to find markets or even create new ones. Building on some of the later elements of Chapter 5, which outlined how positioning should be related to emerging and difficult to replicate unique resources, this chapter goes deeper into the importance of national context, organizational culture and individual personalities in shaping those resources.

The Impact of National Context and Culture

Perhaps the best-known framework for analyzing how a nation's context, and the identity that stems from it, can influence a region's natural competitive advantage is The Porter Diamond.[2] Michael Porter and his team of researchers at Harvard developed The Diamond of International Competitiveness as a means of better understanding why, for example, the best watches seem to come from Switzerland, the first computer companies were American, or why Hong Kong might be a key financial center or the best equipment for racing yachts might be made in New Zealand. He claimed that the answer lay in distinctive background provided by the interrelationships between the following four contextual elements that make up the corners of the diamond:

1. context for *firm strategy and rivalry* (vigorousness of competition)
2. *demand conditions* (whether customers are sophisticated and demanding)
3. *factor conditions* (quality and cost of factors such as labor, natural resources, capital, and physical infrastructure), and
4. presence of *supporting industries* (is there a critical mass of capable suppliers?).

And two outlying, but important, elements (see Figure 6.2):

1. *government strategy* (government can influence all four of the major factors listed above through subsidies, education policies, regulation of markets and product standards, taxes, and antitrust laws), and
2. *chance* (which can nullify advantages and bring about shifts in competitive position through new inventions, wars, shifts in world markets, and political decisions).

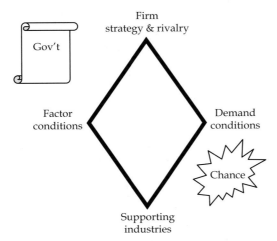

Figure 6.2 The Porter Diamond of International Competitiveness (adapted from Porter, 1990)

Table 6.1 The national context underpinning Belgium's competitive advantage in brewing

Factor conditions	Belgium's breweries lie close to some of the best natural ingredients for beer, while long established apprenticeships and training programs, combined with the traditional high status afforded brewers in Belgium, ensures a good supply of quality human resources.
Demand conditions	Beer is Belgium's national drink and consumers are consequently knowledgeable and discerning. They will not tolerate bad beer.
Related and supporting industries	As mentioned above, Belgium's breweries benefit through close proximity to quality hop farmers. Moreover, with the major cost involved in selling a bottle of beer being distribution, it helps that Belgium is a hub for many major distribution networks and companies.
Firm strategy, structure, and rivalry	There are perhaps more breweries per capita in Belgium than in any other country. While they are all fiercely competitive, they also have a history of collaborating when in the collective best interests.
Government strategy	The Belgian Government has supported the beer industry throughout many centuries. It has supported the industry's training programs and its low-excise regime for beer makes it very inexpensive in Belgium relative to other parts of the world. More recently, the Belgian Government has actively sought to become the center of the European Union.
Chance	Belgium happens to be well placed as a lynchpin between major powers such as France and Germany (see above) and at the center of the world's greatest beer-consuming bloc – Europe.

Using Porter's framework we can explain, for example, why many of the world's great beers come from Belgium (Table 6.1). The constellation of these elements, which have emerged over time to provide the context within which Belgian brewers operate, is unique and inimitable. No other region's contextual background provides quite the same positive environment for making great beer.

While the elements that make up the Porter Diamond might reflect the harder or more economic side of corporate identity, we might gather the softer, but no less influential, aspects of identity under the heading of *culture*. There have been innumerable attempts to define culture. These range from Geert Hofstede's austere "culture is the collective programming that distinguishes one group of people from another" to Linda Smircich's plainly put "culture is the specific collection of values and norms that are shared by people in a corporation that control the way they interact with each other and with stakeholders outside of the corporate body."[3] However, it is unlikely that any definition has approached the clarity of the colloquial expression that culture is "the way things are done around here."

The focus on how culture can differentiate what a corporation does entered the mainstream strategy literature in the late 1970s, as people began to question what had enabled Japanese companies to emerge as such a potent force. Books appeared urging Western managers to embrace Japanese management practices such as *kaizen* (continuous improvement) and quality circles (and, subsequently, total quality management), approaches that had emerged out of a distinctive

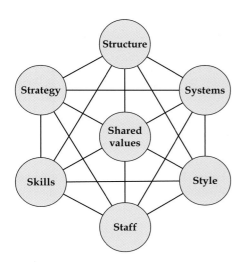

- **Strategy:** What is it and how is it implemented?
- **Structure:** How is the company organized? What processes does it employ to get things done?
- **Systems:** How the company operates on a day-to-day basis.
- **Skills:** Core competences of the organization vs. key competences.
- **Staff:** "Demographic" description of important personnel categories within the firm.
- **Style:** Symbolic behavior of management – what does it consider important?
- **Shared values:** Company culture and corporate identity.

Figure 6.3 McKinsey's 7-S framework (adapted from Pascale and Athos, 1981)

Japanese way of thinking and doing: a way that emphasized community, harmony, slow patient increments (rather than "quick fixes"), and a long-term view.

Perhaps the most widely used framework for understanding culture – the "Seven S's" – was developed at this time (see Figure 6.3). Hatched by four McKinsey & Co. consultants (Anthony Athos, Richard Pascale, Tom Peters, and Robert Waterman), the 7-S's formed the basis of Pascale and Athos's book, *The Art of Japanese Management*. This argued that whereas US managers focused on *strategic* plans, organizational *structures*, and *systems* of control, Japanese managers embraced the "soft S's" – a concern for *staff, skills* development, their corporation's *style*, and greater or *superordinate* goals (which would later be rephrased as "shared values").[4] This, according to Pascale and Athos, was why Japanese companies were more successful than those from other nations.

Beyond contrasting American and Japanese cultural practices, Dutch academic Geert Hofstede examined the cultures of 53 different nations and categorized them according to five dimensions of: (1) power–distance, (2) individualism versus collectivism, (3) masculinity, (4) uncertainty avoidance, (5) long-term versus short-term orientation (these are described more fully in Chapter 8, Crossing Borders).[5]

These different orientations can be seen to affect many things that relate to strategy: from the type of management theories that one nation develops or favors (Hofstede was particularly concerned to show how American management theories might not apply outside of the US) to the way staff behave and develop and implement strategy, to a particular nation's customer values. Herein lies an explanation why a company's advertising for cooking products will show male and female partners cooking together in the Netherlands while the same ads are adapted to feature two female friends in Germany[6]; and why some argue that Marlboro cigarettes were more successful in Asia than Camel because the Camel symbol represented a lonely figure whereas the Marlboro cowboy was implicitly part of a group.[7]

While many interesting discussions have stemmed from this sort of analysis of national character and how it affects corporations, there is always the danger that simple categorizations lead to stereotypes and, subsequently, inaccuracies. To better understand character one must look deeper at organizational particularities.

Building on the success of Pascale and Athos's application of the 7-S's to Japanese management, Tom Peters and Robert Waterman used the framework as a basis for learning about the characteristics of high-performing firms. They found that successful firms emphasized the softer S's, particularly shared values.[8] In their famous book, *In Search of Excellence*, they claimed that these firms tended to exhibit a particular type of culture, namely one that exhibited eight traits: a bias for action; being close to the customer; valuing autonomy and entrepreneurship; emphasizing productivity through people; being hands-on and value driven; sticking to what they know best; having a simple structure and lean workforce; and being simultaneously centralized and decentralized. While time has seen many of the companies that *In Search of Excellence* promoted fall by the way-side and subsequently many of the specific traits it advocated (e.g. sticking to what they know best, having a simple structure) were problematic as general rules (identity, as we are seeing here, should help us to recognize that it is difficult to generalize about successful organizations), others have built on those elements of *In Search. . .* that have stood the test of time to fashion other cultural "guidelines." For example, Chris Bilton and Stephen Cummings suggest that successful creative organizations tend to exhibit:

1. A strong, but adaptive, culture
2. Meritocratic politics
3. Deutero learning (learning that questions established ways of thinking)
4. Drawing on good ideas from inside *and* outside the organization
5. A multitasking workforce
6. Ambidextrous architecture (i.e. a combination of open plan and traditional office space)
7. Poise (i.e. they are not static or frenetic but are always poised for change when it is required to maintain environmental alignment)[9]

Another useful framework for analyzing the components of a corporate culture is "the cultural web" developed by Johnson, Scholes, and Whittington (see Figure 6.4). By describing the distinctive rituals, stories, symbols, power, and organizational structures, and control systems that contribute to the organization's paradigm (or world-view), one can more clearly characterize an organization's culture.[10]

The "symbols" of an organization are broad ranging (e.g. from the clothes staff wear, the logo or brand, to the buildings in which the organization is housed) but particularly telling with regard to culture. For example, much has been written on how the dominant architecture of a period characterizes the sensibilities of a particular society, and for organizations it is no different: an organization's architectural choices say a great deal about the organization's identity. Sir John Harvey-Jones, the famous British television management guru, once exclaimed that an experienced observer can tell a great deal about the culture of a firm by entering and looking at their premises. For instance, if one went to almost any town in the UK during the early 1990s, bank branches were grand affairs located in prestigious high street positions, with ornate stone exteriors and beautiful interiors of rosewood-paneled counters, marble floors, and expensive brass fitments,

Figure 6.4 The cultural web (Source: Johnson, Scholes and Whittington, 2005)

all symbolizing permanence, prosperity, and importance. If one looks at the stunning new steel, chrome, and glass buildings in big cities today, many occupied by professional service firms, a strong message is being stated.

Peters and Waterman concluded that "without exception, the dominance and coherence of culture proved to be an essential quality of excellent companies," a finding endorsed by Collins and Porras's more recent investigation in *Built to Last*, which went on to claim that the key factor in sustained exceptional performance is a culture so strong that it is not dissimilar to a "cult."[11] However, a culture that is so tightly knit can be both a curse as well as a blessing. While a strong unified culture can help people to act quickly and efficiently, it can blinker companies from rethinking their assumptions as the environment changes, as we explained in Chapter 1 (remember the Icarus Paradox), and present difficulties when needing to integrate with other companies. Duncan Angwin (2007) reports high failure rates when two organizations come together through merger or acquisition or other form of interorganizational alignment such as joint venture. These failures are commonly attributed to culture clash – a contest for dominance by one culture over another. The live cases "Pharmacia: Vikings and Anglos" and "MojoMDA: Sydney chainsaw massacre," later in this chapter, show how superficial similarities between national and industry cultures, may conceal deep-seated fundamental differences in corporate identities and lead to severe post-deal consequences.

Attempts to characterize organizational cultures turned over much fertile ground and caused a whole generation of managers to take what Peters and Waterman described as the "softer side" of strategy seriously, there emerged a tendency to believe that there was one best type of culture. This led to attempts to ape Japanese approaches in the West, approaches that only made sense within the deep context in which they emerged, and attempts to try to insert new culture into organizations as one might insert a new carburetor or air conditioner into a car.

179

Needless to say, most of these attempts failed, and when the new culture did take hold it generally succeeded only in making companies more like those they were competing against – something that goes against one of strategy's main tenets and runs contrary to what corporate identity should bring to a business.

The Organization as Reflective of an Individual Personality

One method of moving beyond this tendency to "sameness" when thinking of character is to use the analogy of an individual: to think of an organization as if it were a human identity, or a personality, having its own distinctive soul or spirit or ethos. This is particularly helpful, because while we might tend to aggregate and look for *similarities* in national and organizational cultures, terms like "identity" focus us on *differences*. In this view, just as we all have – and should nurture – a unique personality, a distinctive spirit, or a particular ethos, so too should an organization.[12] This notion can be related to Aristotle's view that the man who tries to be friends with all will not be seen as a friend by any – implying that organizations, like people, must make difficult choices about who and what relationships they really care about and subsequently which they must prioritize. It supports the view that strategists will have a clearer understanding of the choices they should take if they have a good understanding of the organization's *ethos* (defined as "the characteristic spirit, prevalent tone of sentiment, 'genius' or distinctive spirit of a people or institution"). Sometimes founders (as at HP) or entrepreneurial leaders (such as Richard Branson at Virgin) can provide a personality around which a corporate identity and thus a set of strategies can coalesce, but such characters are not necessary. People can still gain strategic insight by thinking of their organizations as people.

A clearer understanding of an organization's ethos can be gained by thinking of it as if it were a living personality (or even a proxy for a personality like a brand of car or a band – see live case 6-5), and then by asking questions like:

- If our organization was a person (or a car), what sort of person (or car, or musical group, etc.) should it be?
- What sort of characters would our competitors be?
- How are we different from those characters?
- What sort of actions should this different character, or ethos, encourage us to take in order to be consistent to ourselves?

The Expressive Organization, by Schultz, Hatch, and Holten Larsen, examines similar themes, claiming that successful organizations are those that understand their distinct identity and their brands but also regularly and consistently express their identities internally and externally through their actions.[13]

This analogy of the organization as an identity brings us into some fairly "soft" areas not usually considered part of the realm of strategy. But given that these sorts of ideas are increasingly being taken very seriously by those whose job it is to design products and services, strategists should be thinking this way too. Steve Jobs, founder of Apple, is often quoted as saying that "Design is the fundamental soul of a man-made creation [and] we don't have a good language to talk about

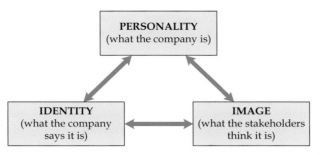

Figure 6.5 Elements of corporate reputation

this kind of thing." By implication, we need to think more about how we might express the soul of a product, a service, or the brand or company that delivers these things. A recent *Business Week* review of the automobile industry concluded that after a decade-long drive to close quality and engineering gaps, the number one selling point is now a car's particular personality and the emotional response that this elicits. Consequently, it claims that the number one *strategic* element in car manufacture is design.[14]

Such notions bring strategy into close contact with marketing concepts like branding and image. However, it is important to recognize that while branding is an increasingly important strategic consideration, an effective corporate character must reflect a consistency between the external face and internal reality of an organization. One way of understanding how these elements can be joined *and* differentiated is shown in Figure 6.5, adapted from Davies and Miles's *What Price Reputation?*[15]

The Expressive Organization makes a similar distinction between image and identity, seeing the former as relating to external stakeholders, the latter to those within the corporation. But both works identify the key requirement as maintaining a good fit between an organization's projected image and actual identity. These distinctions illustrate that, for a corporation's character or personality to effectively drive its image and **strategic planning**, it must be authentic. Lewis and Bridger make this point in their book *The Soul of the New Consumer*.[16] They explain that today's consumers are very savvy to corporations "selling their image." If a company is going to make claims about its identity, they will only be respected and taken seriously if they are clearly linked to real places, times, and events. Hence, HP can authentically claim the character described at the outset of this chapter, but another company could not do so to good effect.

This emphasis on the organization has encouraged some to even encourage applying the five human senses to better articulate an organization, product, or brand's character. In the book *Lovemarks*, Kevin Roberts explains why we should focus on understanding the distinctive taste, feel, sound, look, and even smell, of an organization to ensure we have a character that stands out.[17] While this may sound far-fetched at first hearing, reflecting on this can bring to mind some compelling examples:

– The millions spent by car manufacturers trying to achieve the right feel of a leather trim, or the right sound a glove compartment or car door makes when it is opened and closed;

- Harley-Davidson's attempt to patent the sound that its motorcycles make (to prevent other firms replicating this key element of its competitive advantage);
- Crayola's awareness of the importance of how its crayons smell (it's the 18th most recognized smell in America – coffee being first, peanut butter second – so Crayola will do anything to protect and preserve it);
- The "perfume" that some leading hotel brands, such as the Langham, will emit in their lobbies around the world to create a feeling of distinctive luxury and positive brand association upon entry.

The importance of the connection between how products or services look, sound and feel, how these human senses and memory link into corporate identity and, ultimately, strategic success, is also increasingly plain to see (or hear or smell!).

Vision, Mission, Values, and Beliefs

The focus on seeing the firm as a living character has also encouraged the trend toward developing compelling and unique **visions**, **mission statements**, and **core values** that guide and inspire strategy.

A vision articulates a view of what the company wants to achieve or the future it is aiming for. Good visions generally adhere to five principles:

- *brief* (not long-winded "hero sandwiches of good intentions," as Peter Drucker complained many vision statements were);
- *true to the particular company's identity and focus*;
- easily *understandable* to all employees;
- *inspirational*; and
- *verifiable* so that progress and, ultimately, success can be determined.

Starbucks successfully drove its strategy with the vision: "2000 stores by the year 2000." Henry Ford's vision, published in 1907, is considered a classic: "To democratize the automobile. To build a motorcar for the great multitude. It will be so low in price that no man making a good salary will be unable to own one. The horse will have disappeared from the highways and the automobile will be taken for granted."

Mission statements should also adhere to the tenets above. But there is a subtle but important difference between a mission and a vision. The root of the word vision is the Latin *vide* (to see) whereas mission's root means "to send." Consequently, a mission is not so much a goal or a picture of where you want to get to in the future, but rather a philosophy, or way of moving toward the vision in the present. Organizations can therefore have both a vision and a mission. For example, LEGO's vision is "Inventing the future of play," while its mission is to "Inspire and develop the builders of tomorrow." Other classic missions include Walt Disney's "To make people happy" and Tesco's "Every little helps."

In addition to statements of vision and mission, organizations now often list a number of core values, beliefs, or principles that guide its decision making.

A decade ago these were often derided for being bland and generic (see the beginning of Chapter 11 for an example), but organizations are now striving to make these more specific, more interesting and, hence, more useful from the point of view of encapsulating a corporate identity that can drive a strategy. Good examples include engineering company BECA's "Partnership, Tenacity, Enjoyment, Care"; Apple, whose principles in recent times have included "people with passion can change the world," "we believe in the simple, not the complex," and "we believe in saying no to thousands of projects so that we can really focus on the few that are truly important and meaningful to us"; or Air New Zealand's, listed below:

- We will be the customers' airline of choice when travelling to, from, and within New Zealand.
- We will build competitive advantage in all of our businesses through the creativity and innovation of our people.
- We will champion and promote New Zealand and its people, culture, and business at home and overseas.
- We will work together as a great team committed to the growth and vitality of our company and New Zealand.
- Our workplaces will be fun, energizing and places where everyone can make a difference.

In assessing corporate identity and how it might be related to strategy, the key appears to be understanding the nature of an organization's identity, its elements, where it came from, and how this might add to an organization's differentiated competitive advantage if properly harnessed. Strategists must realize that character runs deep and so be careful to avoid dealing with it mechanistically. Crucial in harnessing character for strategic advantage is attempting to nurture what is unique and inimitable about the organization and letting its identity drive the corporation's strategy in a way that ensures that the company's unique individuality is authentically and consistently developed. Tina Brown, renowned magazine editor, expresses the importance of this "consistent individuality" in describing her key test for any good magazine: "You should be able to throw a magazine on the floor [have it land] at any page and know [just from looking at that page] what magazine it is." By the same token, every encounter with an organization should be indicative of its identity and that identity should be indicative of its strategy.

Given the growth of multinational organizations, and multibranded business, this is becoming increasingly challenging for strategists. However, just as the value chimera enabled us to integrate the core concepts from Chapters 4 and 5, it may also be useful to reflect on it's shape – a single body with multiple heads – here too. Just as the multibranded firm may target a portfolio of markets with its positioning strategies while seeking to achieve underpinning synergies with its corporate strategies, with regard to corporate identity strategists they may have to consider "families" of different identity branching off from the one underlying central identity that holds across their business (the examples of the BBC in the last live case in this chapter, and of HSBC in the final case in Chapter 8, provide good illustrations of this).

Having read and reviewed the chapter, outline what you believe to be the key learnings from the chapter and the relationships between these.

6-1 Pokemon:Pokemon versus The Little Engine That Could

Examining how the national context influences a company's strategic development has been commonplace since serious studies of strategy began. However, in 1992 Virginia Hill Ingersoll and Guy Adams published a paper that looked far beyond the sort of contextual factors generally seen as important environmental considerations. This paper, entitled "The Child is 'Father' to the Manager," argued that traditional national or regional tales shape the perceptions of children, and that these perceptions may continue to influence the way adult managers perceive work, organization, and strategy.

For example, the focus in American children's stories on equal opportunity, clear links between individual attitude and effort and particular outcomes, and individual achievement and fulfillment against the odds through making tough choices and sacrifices, practice and hard work, underlie many widespread American preconceptions with regard to business. They also relate these preconceptions to what is often referred to as The American Dream. Stories from "The Little Engine That Could" (where a small steam train who is roundly dismissed and put down by his bigger peers reaches his particular "mountain top" – which is, in his case, actually steaming to the top of a particularly steep mountain – through secret training and single-minded determination) to the Rocky movies and other Hollywood fables sponsor and reinforce widely held American values.

Japanese children's stories generally have a very different focus. They tend to involve different characters bringing together particular skills to restore harmony by solving a problem that affects a whole community. Being an esteemed member of the team sees each character's status reinforced and enlarged. This is obvious in traditional Japanese fables, but it also underlies more modern Japanese tales. A recent article in *The Economist*, entitled "Pokemania v Globophobia," wrote of how Pokemon's "little monsters still teach distinctively Japanese values about the importance of team-building and performing your duties. The only way to succeed at the game is to cooperate with others – and the easiest way to fail is to neglect to care for your charges." Japan has a history of such tales from traditional myths to Manga comics to Bakugan Battle Brawlers. German tales are different again, traditionally emphasizing the importance of sticking to the known path – dark things happen to those who wander off the beaten track, who go it alone into the forest. Mexican stories for children often emphasize the importance of having fun and Polynesian stories stress the importance of community and extended family.

What might all of this have to do with management and strategy? Well, take a popular management theory like Abraham Maslow's *hierarchy of needs*. Maslow's hierarchy, developed in the United States in the 1940s and 1950s, will be familiar to any student of management or sociology and it is still taught as explaining the universal essence of human motivation. One can see how its scale of needs, starting with the satisfaction of basic physiological needs, such as food and water, and moving up to safety, belongingness, status, and finally self-actualization as the pinnacle (see Figure 6-1.1) makes sense in an American context.

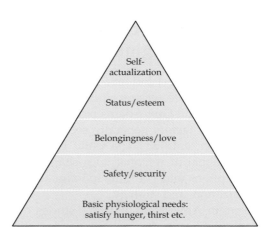

Figure 6-1.1 Maslow's hierarchy of needs

However, by focusing on the context set by children's stories, one can also see how such attitudes might be relative. Many people from Asian backgrounds, for example, accept the framework when it is taught to them, but will later confess to be perplexed by the idea that "self-actualization" could be more important than "status" within one's community. Polynesians might alternatively see belongingness, particularly with regard to the extended family, as the pinnacle. The implications for how one might manage strategic human resources or goal-setting in different social contexts, for example, in the light of this deep-set relativity, could be profound.

Perhaps the particular values inculcated through stories could also shed light on one of the most controversial assertions in strategic management in recent times. In a *Harvard Business Review* paper in 1996, American strategy guru Michael Porter argued that "Japanese companies rarely have strategies [as they] rarely develop a distinct strategic position." In 2001 Porter went further, claiming in the *Wall Street Journal* that the Japanese are inherently "bad at strategy." However, Porter's classic American view of strategy is one where the heroes are strong managers who take the lead in setting off down one path or another, a focus on cost or a focus on differentiation, for example. The Japanese view, on the other hand, is generally one that sees strategy as something that emerges slowly over time out of the collective interactions of many employees and which seeks a harmony between cost and quality rather than choosing a focus on one over the other.

> 1. *Do you think that the values promoted in different nations' or regions' popular tales could influence different views of strategy?*
> 2. *Can you relate the American children's stories described above to Hewlett-Packard's corporate character described at the beginning of this chapter? Can you relate the different American and Japanese stories outlined above to Hofstede's cultural dimensions?*
> 3. *Which do you think is the better view of strategy: the mainstream American view, represented by Porter, or the Japanese view?*

◀◀◀ Pokemon versus The Little Engine That Could: Some ideas toward a "model answer". . .

1. Do you think that the values promoted in different nations' or regions' popular tales could influence different views of strategy and what is important at work?

While this is difficult to prove scientifically, the national stories do seem consistent with Hofstede's widely regarded analysis of national cultural differences, and they can be related to the conventional American view of strategy as being about vision, planning, and positioning and the mainstream Japanese view of strategy as a more communal and emergent practice. Thus, it would be useful for strategists to at least consider the influence that such traditional tales might have on national and thus corporate character. Indeed, it might be useful to think yourself about some of the popular children's tales in your region and how these might influence particular attitudes to work and strategy in later life. Other elements that could influence national or regional character could be: traditional notions of asset ownership (e.g. individual or community based; communist or free-market); key historical events (e.g. wars; previous eras of strength or weakness); geographical and weather characteristics (e.g. mountainous or flat; arid or wet; hot or cool); beliefs about what's important in life (e.g. financial security or having a good time in the present; extended family or nuclear family); and views of time (e.g. punctuality). And there might be others that you can think of.

2. Can you relate the American children's stories described above to Hewlett-Packard's corporate character described at the beginning of this chapter? Can you relate the different American and Japanese stories outlined above to Hofstede's cultural dimensions?

Yes, indeed, the Bill and Dave story is quite close to "The Little Engine That Could" or "Rocky." A couple of nerds that one might expect not to succeed work hard, are resourceful, inventive, and determined, try and try again and succeed, bringing themselves great fame, fortune, and self-actualization. As explained at the beginning of this chapter, it is because the HP story, and thus character, fits so well with its regional and national value system that it is authentic and works extremely effectively.

Three of Hofstede's cultural dimensions in particular can be related, with varying degrees of ease, to the American and Japanese stories. First, on individualism versus collectivism, they reflect America's propensity to value individual achievement and Japan's propensity to value communities working together. Second, on uncertainty avoidance, we might relate the desire to act individually to an American being more likely to take risks and the Japanese value of gaining consensus as related to being more risk averse. Third, although less obviously linked to the stories described, one could relate games like Pokemon's ongoing or never-ending character to a long-term focus and Rocky or Little Engine's focus on the achievement of a single goal to a more short-term orientation.

3. Which do you think is the better view of strategy: the mainstream American view, represented by Porter, or the Japanese view?

If one takes the themes in this chapter seriously, the answer must be both or neither. Their national characters shape the conventional Japanese and American views of strategy and one cannot say objectively, or with certainty, that one nation's character (and thus approach to strategy) is inherently better than another's. As the conclusion of this chapter explains, it is likely to be more advantageous for strategists to recognize the differences, understand from where these differences stem, see the merits of each, and be able to work with and apply them both where they are best suited to the situation.

Case Notes:

6-2 Pharmacia: Vikings and Anglos

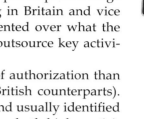

A few years ago, we were discussing strategic decision making with the senior managers of a Swedish–British company (a steel-making organization). In many respects the merger was highly successful. They had joint HRM policies, had agreed on a common organizational structure, and had put in place a large number of cross-postings, with Swedish managers working in Britain and vice versa. However, it was when strategic decisions were presented over what the core business was and the extent to which the firm should outsource key activities (for example) that difficulties began to emerge.

The Swedes took significantly longer to get to the point of authorization than the British (generally, at least 6 months longer than their British counterparts). They spent longer negotiating and analyzing any problem (and usually identified a few additional problems in the process). "We like to achieve both high participation levels and consensus," one Swedish manager told us, "so we invest time in working the problem before we commit ourselves, then we can implement the decision quickly and without much further conflict or negotiation."

The British managers approached the same problems by seeking closure at every meeting. They wanted to narrow down the alternatives quickly so that the decision could be about a choice between a very small number of alternatives. The Swedes, on the other hand, specialized in opening up the number of alternatives at the same meetings and, in turn, raising fresh problems. This was one of the commonest causes of frustration and conflict between the British and Swedish managers. The tensions thus caused were a key factor in the eventual demerger of the organization only a few years after the merger had taken place.

* * *

In addition to the obvious organizational culture clashes that can frustrate corporate mergers, the huge increase in cross-border M&A activity has highlighted how differences in national culture can also influence the way in which mergers unfold. This is not just a recognition of differences in language but an acknowledgement that, at a fundamental level, firms are embedded in their social contexts and this influences behaviors and assumptions over how business is done and for what purpose. Unfortunately, however, oftentimes (particularly in acquisition situations) managers tend to believe that there is one right way of doing things, which tends to ignore the reality that the acquired or merged business is probably heavily customized to its operating environment. This is a prime reason for the fear felt by local employees and communities when foreign firms move in, and underlies the argument that cross-border acquisitions are corrosive of the local social and economic fabric.

A classic example of a post-merger situation that was heavily influenced by national differences is that between pharmaceutical firms Pharmacia of Sweden and Upjohn of the USA in 1995. Many rows ensued following this merger, with great falls in productivity, because of the Americans banning alcohol at lunchtimes and scheduling meetings during the Swedes' national holidays, which caused uproar. There was additional friction between the two decision-making styles as the Swedes preferred open and full discussion of issues at meetings to arrive at consensus whereas the Americans preferred short meetings to rubber-stamp decisions made informally in advance. As distrust between the two sides grew, a new corporate head office was established in London – supposedly neutral territory. But neither the Americans nor the Swedes would close their own "head offices" so the result was another layer of management that duplicated existing structures and increased inefficiencies – a somewhat ironic outcome when one of the primary reasons for the merger in the first place was to increase efficiencies.

1. *Use the Porter Diamond to outline why Sweden and the USA could have an international competitive advantage in the production of pharmaceuticals.*
2. *Use Hofstede's dimensions to explain why the Swedes and the Americans have such different corporate characters and perspectives.*
3. *What strategies would you have employed to make this merger run more smoothly?*

Case Notes:

6-3 Mojo MDA: Sydney chainsaw massacre

Two of Australia's best-known advertising agencies, Mojo and Monahan Dayman Adams (MDA), merged to form Mojo MDA. Mojo brought with it a reputation as the most dynamic "boutique" agency in Australia, while MDA was larger, more established, and more low key. John Singleton, the well-known advertising man, described the merger as being akin to the Beatles combining with the post office.

Mojo's offices were in Paddington, entry being via a long, narrow, paved driveway lined with ferns, which then opened out into a large courtyard with willow trees and a fernery. The offices surrounded this courtyard. Those on the ground floor opened on to the courtyard, while those on the upper level opened on to a wisteria-covered balcony that overlooked it. MDA's offices were quite different, located in the concrete and glass high-rise area of north Sydney.

The agencies had also brought to the merger quite different staffing structures. Mojo's practice was to employ mainly highly paid senior staff that were given a high level of independence. They operated with a flat organizational structure of few hierarchical levels. This arrangement has been described as being "like free-lancing under the umbrella of a company with the bonus of the companionship of like minds." MDA had a much more traditional pyramid structure of a few senior staff supported by large numbers spread over several hierarchical levels.

Mojo had a reputation for being undermanaged. For example, no one holding a position in the company had a clear job description specifying the duties and responsibilities for that position; there was no such thing as formal meetings, and the use of written memoranda was just not an acceptable practice. Some people, including many in Mojo, interpreted "undermanaged" to mean poorly managed. Consequently one of the attractions of the merger with MDA for such people was that MDA had a reputation as a well-organized "professional" company. For MDA, the parallel attraction was the highly regarded skills of Mojo's creative staff. Together they constituted the largest Australian-owned agency. Size was also a major consideration in the merger. Both agencies were proud of their independence from foreign ownership and wished to maintain this situation while also enlarging to a size where they felt they could successfully take on the advertising giants of New York and London.

Mojo MDA was building a new office at Cremorne which would house all its staff, but until that was completed it was decided that all creative staff (copywriters, art directors, and production staff) would move to Paddington while all management staff (the "suits") would be located at the north Sydney offices. One of the Mojo people required to move was its Finance Director, Mike Thorley, who moved to north Sydney where he was to work under Stan Bennett, MDA's Finance Director, who had been put in charge of finance for Mojo MDA. He describes the situation and what followed.

Thorley was one of the original Mojo employees and, as such, did not really think of himself as an employee, more as a partner. That he was not a partner was brought home forcefully at the time of the merger. Like the rest of the staff he had no warning that Mojo was going to merge with MDA and was shocked and angered by the announcement.

Thorley was referred to as the shop steward of Mojo: he looked after the staff, molded them into a team, and was at least partly responsible for giving the agency its character. However, after the merger he was banished to north Sydney to work for Stan Bennett. He did not go quietly.

To try to make the Paddington people feel at home in north Sydney at MDA, management installed a bar so the staff could follow their usual custom of a few drinks after work. But it was a modern black laminate structure running around the edge of the room. It looked like some up-market suburban pub. It was nothing like the solid white bench in the kitchen at Paddington and it seemed to Thorley that it summed up the differences between the two agencies: it was a symbol of how Mojo had let its people down. In an act of defiance he took a chainsaw to the work one morning and cut the bar in two.

---

1. *Draw two Cultural Webs (Figure 6.4), one outlining what you might think MDA's Rituals, Stories, Symbols, Power and Organizational Structures, and Control Systems were before the merger, the other doing the same thing for Mojo.*
2. *Having done this, how would you describe the paradigms of MDA and Mojo before the merger?*
3. *Knowing the deep differences in the characters of the two firms, how might you have sought to manage this merger?*

Case Notes:

6-4 John Smith's: From Jack Dee to 2-D and back

In the early 1990s Jerry Goldberg, Brand Manager at Scottish Courage Breweries, oversaw the appointment of an up-and-coming deadpan comedian Jack Dee as the spokesperson for John Smith's Bitter. "When John Webster at DDB [the advertising agency responsible for the campaign] suggested Dee, we weren't worried about whether he'd be big," reflected Goldberg. "The fact was that his personality suited the brand's 'no-nonsense' positioning." Five years later, the Jack Dee campaign, with 50 awards to its name, was widely regarded as having helped propel John Smith's from number 16 to number 4 in the UK beer market, toppling Tetley's from its market-leader perch in the Bitter segment for the first time. In December 1995, John Smith's sales were almost two percentage points behind Tetley's. Three years later, they were 4.5% ahead.

In 1998, Scottish Courage decided to replace Jack Dee as the personification of John Smith's.

The Jack Dee campaign had re-energized a beer with a long, solid history; a beer that had personified the honest, straight up, "no-frills, just good taste" ethos of a bitter first brewed in Tadcaster, Yorkshire 240 years ago. Now a new creative team from the agency GGT came up with *No-nonsense Man*, a cardboard cut-out synthesis of the essential "average bloke" pictured, in various guises, silently holding a pint of John Smith's. Jerry Goldberg's successor as Brand Manager explained that the new No-nonsense Man campaign would take "the 'no-nonsense' proposition one step further – our new frontman is the ultimate no-nonsense celebrity." Scottish Courage's Marketing Manager claimed, "No-nonsense Man aims to show the beer's down-to-earth positioning in an involving way. It conveys all the product values. It has the potential to become a cult star."

Even though Jack Dee was by no means everybody's favorite comedian, the momentum generated by the Jack Dee image had helped to put John Smith's in a position where it looked well placed to leapfrog Guinness as the UK's third top-selling beer (after Carlsberg and Fosters). However, after the launch, a survey by *Campaign* magazine showed that 67% of people thought that the No-nonsense Man image was less effective than Jack Dee. A year on and the general consensus among industry and media commentators was that No-nonsense Man lacked the impact of the previous campaign and that, despite Scottish Courage not giving up on him, he was not catching on. No-nonsense Man had not become a cult star. John Smith's had not overtaken Guinness.

In a twist of fate, Jack Dee was chosen to host the British Advertising and Design Awards in 1999. One magazine's review of the night describes how "the audience loved it when he riffed about 'the days when John Smith's advertising used to win awards' and baited 'Anyone here from GGT?' with a 'You haven't won anything'."

Four lean years after ditching Jack Dee, Scottish Courage returned to the comedy circuit for a human face to replace No-nonsense Man. They selected the up-and-coming North-of-England comic Peter Kay, who, while different in many facets, in many ways represents a Jack Dee for the new decade. With

No-nonsense Man folded away, Kay was shown taking a no-nonsense "blokey" approach to sports. The first ad, called *Ball Skills*, shows a group of young soccer players earnestly warming up by practicing their "keepy uppy" skills. After each player keeps the ball up for a time he effortlessly passes it on to the next man, until it reaches the solid figure of Kay – who promptly "wellies" the ball into a neighbor's garden while exclaiming "'ave it!" The ad closes with Kay overlooking the half-time orange segments and going straight for a can of John Smith's instead. "Research shows that John Smith's enduring association with a no-nonsense attitude plays a big part in its appeal to consumers and everything about Peter reflects this," said John Botia, the new Powerbrands Director at Scottish Courage.

The Peter Kay campaign returned the brand to the limelight. It has received a string of awards, including best British campaign of the year for 2002/3. The judges described the ads as "a brilliant campaign that has entered people's everyday lives while boosting sales and winning fans, plaudits, and column inches galore in the process." Analysts enthused that: "The Peter Kay campaign created massive awareness. It successfully communicated the brand's positioning in a way that people could really engage with. As a result people feel closer to the brand, which ultimately has had a positive impact on sales. The TV commercials have been talked about in offices and pubs across the country, and sayings such as "ave it!' have entered the everyday vernacular."

Postscript:

History may have (almost) repeated itself in recent years with Peter Kay being replaced with a more generic series of John Smith's ads before making a triumphant return as the face of the brand in 2010. Go to YouTube or Google to check out John Smith's advertisements and images.

1. Use the 7-S framework with Jack Dee or Peter Kay at the center to represent John Smith's shared values, and then build up a picture of the corporate character of the brand by filling in the Style, Skills, Staff, Systems, Structures, and Strategy that these values should promote.
2. Why do you think Jack Dee and Peter Kay were helpful in determining and developing the corporate identity of John Smith's, whereas the cardboard cutout No-nonsense Man wasn't?
3. While Jack Dee and Peter Kay are popular comedians, they were probably not the most popular comedians or actors of their age. Would John Smith's have been even better served by choosing the most universally popular comedian's image to represent its identity?

6-5 Hyundai: Striking a chord?

It is likely that people personalize their relationship with their car more than with any other material possession. And automobile designers have been concerned with how potential customers perceive the "character" of their cars for many decades. Increasing competition in what is seen as a declining market has only intensified the focus on intangible factors like the perceived identity of car brands, and even new players from countries often thought of simply focusing on low-cost products have become extremely sophisticated in these "arts."

In keeping with the way that people anthropomorphize cars, Europe's biggest selling auto magazine, *Car*, includes in its monthly review of all car brands a link to a band that, by analogy, seems to capture the identity of a particular brand, alongside the more normal performance measures and ratings. A selection of these brand/band relations are shown in Table 6-5.1 and related to changes in UK sales performance over the first part of 2009 relative to 2008.

At first glance it does appear that those marques that have outperformed the industry average in a very tough year (where sales declined by 28%) are associated with bands that have also sold well, have made a successful comeback or have high visibility. It's not so much that a brand needs to be associated with a "cool" band to do well. But it does appear that an association with musicians with a clear identity who are selling well to a particular market could be some indicator of success.

Take Hyundai as a case in point. This is the only brand to have increased sales in the UK during the period. Busted may not be at the cutting edge of musical excellence or even particularly distinctive but they seem to be fun and effectively shift product. And, like their stable-mates (Kia/Leona Lewis), they may appear bland and manufactured, but they seem harmless and are not without credibility, range, and power. In fact, it may be that they are typical of what tends to go down well in this era.

Also doing well, relatively, were effective niche fillers like Suzuki (Madness), Ford (Kylie), Audi (Coldplay), Toyota (Daniel O'Donnell), and Jaguar (Tony Bennett). Mazda, like the Prodigy, do well by being on the edge of mainstream. In the middle, are MOR, or middle class, favorites like Dire Straits (Mercedes), ABBA (Volvo), Dido (Volkswagen), and Elton John (Vauxhall). Nissan, like Amy Winehouse, are a mixed bag. And Fiat too suffers from a lack of consistency.

Underperformers include the increasingly irrelevant Lexus/Kraftwerk; the random Mitsubishi/Utah Saints; and the "used to rock" Renault/Roxy Music and Subaru/Chilli Peppers. Bringing up the rear, are American brands to which the UK authors of *Car* seem to delight in ascribing tragic musical doppelgangers.

But it may not be so clear cut – some brands have seen significant declines despite band analogies that would seem to be positive. For example, BMW (Kanye West) and Porsche (Rolling Stones) saw sales decline significantly. Perhaps we should be cautious about seeing brand/band identity as an isolated performance indicator.

Table 6-5.1   UK new-car market sales SMMT analysis – January to May 2009 vs 2008

Marque	2009	% market share	% change	change relative to industry change of -28%	Band
Hyundai	14,534	1.94	+8.00	36	Busted (bubblegum stuff, but not without cred)
Kia	14,119	1.89	−7.36	20	Leona Lewis (characterless but gaining popularity fast)
Suzuki	9,987	1.33	−16.97	11	Madness (a lot of fun)
Ford	129,287	17.27	−17.48	10	Kylie Minogue (honorary Brit, hugely popular, great chassis)
Audi	39,180	5.23	−19.41	8	Coldplay (slick, unstoppable, slightly annoying)
Toyota	40,265	5.38	−20.20	8	Daniel O'Donnell (your Gran's favourite)
Jaguar	7,602	1.02	−20.29	8	Tony Christie (surprising us after years in wilderness)
Mazda	17,646	2.36	−23.19	6	Prodigy (on the edge of mainstream)
Mercedes-Benz	27,137	3.62	−23.63	6	Dire Straits (men of advancing years love them)
Volvo	11,397	1.52	−23.73	6	ABBA (middle class, middle of the road)
Volkswagen	62,892	8.40	−26.20	2	Dido (loved by the middle classes)
Nissan	24,093	3.22	−26.64	1	Amy Winehouse (good range, but all over the place)
Vauxhall	101,023	13.49	−29.46	−1	Elton John (decades of uncool, but still standing)
Honda	31,423	4.20	−30.59	−2	David Bowie (keeps pushing new stuff but we want CRX back)
BMW	34,098	4.55	−32.12	−4	Kanye West (brash, borderline genius)
Citroen	25,788	3.44	−32.49	−4	Oasis (was massive; always threatening comeback)
Mini	12,757	1.70	−32.42	−4	The Cheatles (a Beatles tribute act, of course)
Peugeot	39,164	5.23	−33.52	−5	Tight Fit (as in *The Lion Sleeps Tonight*)
Porsche	2,259	0.30	−33.24	−5	Rolling Stones (thoroughbred, bankable, cool, peerless)

(Continued)

Table 6-5.1 UK new-car market sales SMMT analysis – January to May 2009 vs 2008 (*Continued*)

Marque	2009	% market share	% change	change relative to industry change of -28%	Band
Fiat	17,197	2.30	−33.88	−6	Paul Weller (veers from highs like The Jam to Style Council lows)
Land Rover	11,287	1.51	−40.37	−12	The Clash (utterly brilliant, but people spit at them)
Lexus	3,115	0.42	−41.93	−14	Kraftwerk (highly technical, largely forgotten)
Saab	4,517	0.60	−45.79	−17	Robbie Williams (no proper hits since 1990s)
Cadillac	42	0.01	−46.15	−18	Garth Brooks (loved in America, ignored elsewhere)
Subaru	1,265	0.17	−52.16	−24	Red Hot Chilli Peppers (used to rock, losing edge)
Renault	21,139	2.82	−57.22	−29	Roxy Music (once at cutting edge, now plain & cosy)
Mitsubishi	3,628	0.48	−61.32	−34	Utah Saints (marries tech with raw appeal and a random, sporadic back catalogue)
Dodge	778	0.10	−65.94	−37	New Kids on the Block (unwelcome comeback tour underway)
Chrysler	857	0.11	−75.43	−47	Bon Jovi (living on a prayer)
Total	**748,691**	**100.00**	**−27.89**		

1. *Do you think that Table 6-5.1 indicates that there may be a link between ascribed corporate identity and strategic performance?*
2. *While it is easy to link personalities to cars, do you think any potential link between identity and strategy could be relevant in other products or services? Give examples.*
3. *Based on this case, what strategic advice would you give to automobile manufacturers?*

6-6 NZ Police: Safer communities together

The New Zealand Police have a reputation as being one of the least corrupt law-enforcement bodies in the world. Up until the early 1990s, this simple ethos or mission guided them:

"To work with the community to maintain the peace."

Generations of policemen and women took great pride in living up to this ideal.

However, as was often the way with public service organizations in the 1990s, the New Zealand Police Force was increasingly encouraged to become more "professional," to employ modern management thinking to bring it into line with approaches used in the private sector. The Force was urged to utilize external consultants to help it move closer toward "best practice," to develop more rigorous methods of managing performance, and be seen to be more "accountable."

One of the first services that such consultants generally offered was the creation of a new mission statement. Hence, after much development work, 1992 saw the launch of NZ Police's new mission:

"To contribute to the provision of a safe and secure environment where people may go about their lawful business unhindered and which is conducive to the enhancement of the quality of life and economic performance."

Curiously, while the later statement is five times longer it says no more of substance than the first (indeed, by making no mention of how, or by what strategy, its stated aims should be achieved – contrast "To work with the community." with "To contribute." – it says less). Subsequently, the second statement is far less memorable and more confusing in terms of how it might be operationalized.

According to members of the Force it was not a great success. Many policemen and women on the ground now claim that it confused rather than guided them and admit that they paid little attention to the new mission, instead continuing to look up to the earlier statement and the ethos that it embodies. It is perhaps not surprising then that recent times have witnessed a reappreciation of simpler times. The New Zealand Police's new vision is: "Safer Communities Together," which says more or less the same as "To work with the community to maintain the peace." However, it is even easier to paint on to the side of a police car!

1. *Apply the five principles of a good vision described in this chapter to the NZ Police's original motto, and then to the mission statement developed in 1992.*
2. *Why do you think the NZ Police's original mission might have been more effective than that developed by consultants in 1992?*
3. *Why might using consultants in this way actually diminish rather than add to an organization's corporate identity?*

Channel 5, Britain's newest terrestrial (non-cable) television channel, had a problem. It, unlike its competitors, did not have a clear identity. Consequently, viewers did not know what to expect from it and, subsequently, seem less likely to tune in or build a relationship with it.

British researchers have recently demonstrated that viewers tend to have clear images in their minds about the identity of the television channels they watch. BBC1 was seen as staid and establishment, but reliable – "the Queen Victoria of channels." BBC2 was seen as an "enthusiastic educator – something between an old professor and a trendy teacher, with a touch of social worker keen to save the world." ITV was seen as jolly, lively, and "more normal," but also a bit "dodgy," with something of a "used-car business" about it. Channel 4 was identified as a "Richard Branson" – entrepreneurial, dashing, and risk-taking, often pushing the boat out a bit too far, but then this suited its character.

The researchers also found that people do not apply the same standards to each channel. For example, it appeared that one reason for making a customer complaint was if a program delivered something at odds with the customer's anticipations of the channel's personality, thereby causing dissonance that led to the relationship between viewer and channel to be questioned. A racy program shown on Channel 4 would receive fewer complaints than the same program shown on BBC1 – partly because of the profile of the people tuning in to each (those watching Channel 4 were likely people who had already decided that their ethos was okay with them), but also because of viewer expectations. Using the same logic, when Channel 4 recently took over the rights to show cricket matches from the BBC, it knew that it would have to show them in a more dynamic, less traditional way – otherwise viewers would wonder "what on earth is happening to Channel 4?" The message seems to be that, as with the people in their everyday relationships, customers will tolerate difference between different companies far more than inconsistent behavior from one company.

Channel 5's problem in this regard is that their programming seems particularly inconsistent: an unruly mix of half-baked game shows, soft-porn, and 1960s wildlife programs. It is hard to see any positive pattern to it and thus it is hard for any significant segment of the population to connect with it. This is partly due to circumstances beyond its control. It is young and it could be said that it is still finding its way – no infant arrives with a personality completely intact. Plus, just after a highly successful launch, when the Spice Girls were used as the channel's spokespeople (indicating a bright, optimistic, youthful image), the five Spices became four, and those four seemed to go their own separate ways, making it difficult for Channel 5 to build on the initial success of the launch.

Eighteen months after the "personality research" described above came out, confusion still prevailed regarding what 5's character should be. Channel 5 executives recently announced that the channel was going to reposition itself dramatically – moving away from its salacious programming to become a "family broadcaster emphasizing popular entertainment." However, this did seem to have been compromised somewhat when one Channel 5 senior executive was reported to be demanding that his channel be allowed to show more explicit sex.

Channel 5 is not the only channel that is working on its personality. ITV has recently launched separate cable-only channels, with related but slightly different

CORPORATE IDENTITY

personalities, that will allow it to show a more diverse range of programming without compromising its flagship identity, and the BBC is reportedly not entirely happy about the staid Queen Victoria image. The BBC's public service remit is to "serve all people" and, in response to what its own research defines as an increasingly fragmented and multicultural market with different delivery methods and more consumer choice, it is currently asking itself how BBC1, in particular, should change its personality to better match the new environment.

Postscript:

By the end of 2002, Channel 5 did seem to be beginning to establish an identity in the market. In the *Independent Review*, critic Thomas Sutcliffe wrote the following: "Evidence that even the most incorrigible miscreants can mend their ways was also available on Channel 5, which formally relaunched itself after months of stealthy self-improvement. The [garish] 'Dolly Mixture' logo [around the number 5] has now gone to be replaced with a classy sans-serif text [of the word 'five']. Even more mind-bogglingly, it has been running a series of documentaries on ecclesiastical art and architecture [called *Divine Designs*], presented by a genial anorak called Paul Binski. It's as if you were to go on an 18–30 holiday and find that the pool-side entertainment was a lecture on 14th-century choir-stall carving. On Tuesday night, Binski referred to the medieval church's attitude to its congregation: 'We're actually sinful, vicious, oversexed, greedy, stupid creatures,' he said – a perfect summation, as it happens, of the world-view which appeared to govern Channel 5's early schedules. Now [this appears to have] given way to a [blend] of the high minded and cheap and cheerful. *Divine Designs* is not finely wrought television. The final credits list just 13 people in total. In television terms, this is one man and a dog he's borrowed for the day, but that hardly matters. Binski overflows with enthusiasm for his subject. Some medieval historians might have winced at the suggestion that church gargoyles were 'the 14th-century equivalent of *The Simpsons*,' but it got the point across – and you won't find such a conjunction anywhere else on television. The Channel 5 button on my remote control has remained in factory condition until now – I have a feeling it might be getting shinier." Sutcliffe's comments were typical of a number of other favorable reviews of the relaunch of Five.

Since this case was written the BBC has expanded its portfolio of channels. This now includes additional channels such as BBC3, BBC News 24, BBC Children's, BBC History, and a number of others.

1. *Why do you think 5's initial attempts to develop an effective corporate identity failed? Why might the direction that Five is now following (outlined in the postscript) be more successful?*
2. *Do you think that the BBC should seek to replace its "Queen Victoria" identity?*
3. *What can we learn from the 5 to Five case about the link between corporate identity and strategy?*

There is no such thing as society. There are individual men and women, and there are families.

Margaret Thatcher

[The myth of individualism] gets in the way of understanding how the world actually works. And in doing so it lowers our chances of success, depresses our pay, limits our promotions, decreases the value we create, reduces our ability to get things done, and even jeopardizes our health, happiness, and welfare. And it closes off all the great possibilities of life.

Wayne Baker

7
Organic Strategy

Having learnt much from the previous decade (where conservative right-wing political parties held sway), Bill Clinton's wily advisor James Carville focused his boss's 1992 presidential campaign around a simple slogan: "It's the economy, stupid." It became one of the most remembered catchphrases of the early 90s. By the later 90s, however, the slogan and the idea that people's most important concern was their individual economic well-being, had fallen out of favor. While most leading management thinkers up until the late 20th century would have supported Carville's words, at the beginning of the 21st century, management guru Tom Peters was winning plaudits for turning it on its head – "It's relationships, stupid," claimed Peters.

Peters' phrase spoke to a growing recognition that while economic considerations were important for living beings, they were no more primary than the social. Living beings rely on, are sustained by, and are fulfilled by relationships. In this light, Thatcher's notion that there is no such thing as society, an increasingly popular view in the 1980s and early 1990s, now seems rather archaic. If anything, it seems to make more sense nowadays to speak of there being no such thing as an individual. "No man is an island," to borrow a popular saying.

This chapter on organic strategy takes up the notion that organizations are relational and social. Whereas the previous chapter looked at organizations as having individual identities, this chapter takes the next step to look at how these identities are interlinked by and criss-crossed with human relationships. Subsequently, we should think of strategy as an organic thing rather than a mechanistic one. We look at how strategy is shaped by the relationships that are so much a part of everyday life and the social capital that can grow out of them. Managed well, these relations can make strategic progress seem effortless; managed poorly, and they can place insurmountable barriers in the way of success.

Four recognitions have led the shift from a focus on economics and mechanical views to seeing organizations as living beings and relationships:

1. Organizations, like living organisms, need to learn. Machines can't learn.
2. Organizations, like living organisms, live in the world and they are subject to multiple layers of influence from which they cannot be separated (e.g. the individual is

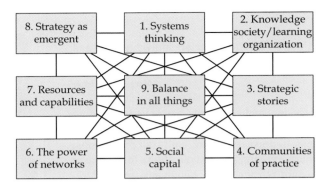

Figure 7.1 Organic strategy: strategy development through living relationships

part of a team, which is part of a division, which is part of a company, which is part of an industry, which is part of a society).

3. An organism's past, present, and future are closely interwoven. The same is true for organizations. They are "thrown" by their pasts in particular directions that shape their future aspirations and possibilities.[1] Points 2 and 3 mean that the being of an individual living organism (and thus an organization if we think of it as a living organism) exists within a complex system of relationships.

4. Finally, the points above mean that living organisms are greater than the sum of their parts: they are not just discrete independent individuals. In other words, they have a metaphysical as well as physical dimension. The problem, according to Jesper Kunde, is that: "Most executives have no idea how to add value to a market in the metaphysical world. But that is what the market will cry out for in the future. There is no lack of 'physical' products to choose between."[2]

These recognitions have led to the development of new interrelated themes for exploring how to add value in organizations by seeing them as organic beings (Figure 7.1). These are outlined in the sections below.

Systems Thinking

Perhaps the most influential systems-thinker to affect how we look at strategy is Peter Senge, author of *The Fifth Discipline*.[3] Senge identified five interrelated "disciplines" required to build a learning organization: (1) personal visions; (2) surfacing the often implicit models currently used for decision making; (3) developing a shared vision; (4) team learning; and finally, (5) the fifth discipline: **systems thinking** to understand how the relationships and interactions between the elements of the organization and the environment affect the whole. This systems thinking should entail:

1. seeing interrelationships and processes rather than things and snapshots;
2. recognizing that individual "cogs" are not to blame for poor performance – they can only do what the system allows them to do;
3. distinguishing which parts of the system have high impact on strategy and which are only minor details;
4. paying attention to (3) and focusing on areas of "high leverage" – the 20% of things that will make 80% of difference (sometimes this is referred to as **the 80/20 rule**);

5. looking beyond solving *symptoms* and *outcomes* through popular quick fixes or applying generic buzzwords – poorly performing systems require systematic solutions.

The Knowledge Society and the Learning Organization

Senge credits much of his development as a systems and strategic thinker to Arie de Geus, author of *The Living Company*.[4] De Geus's thesis is quite simple: "We are living in a new *knowledge society*. This requires that companies must learn and adapt quickly to remain successful. But, we tend to see companies as machines. Machines can't learn. Only living beings can. We must change the way we perceive companies."

De Geus describes the historical development of the **knowledge society** as follows. Basic economic theory suggests that there have always been three sources of wealth: land and natural resources, capital, and labor. Up until the late Middle Ages, the critical factor was land. Those who possessed and controlled land controlled the accumulation of wealth. But a shift began as nation states became concerned with corporate expansion, and the capital to finance endeavors became the most valuable commodity of production. During this time, the modern company was developed, as capital was made available for the wealth-creating processes of the medieval tradesperson. At the same time, the break up of old craft guilds and their evolution into competing companies gave the speculative owners of capital great control over human resources. In the language of economics, capital was far more scarce and worth far more than labor.

Over the past 50 years, however, the world of business has shifted from one dominated by capital to one based on knowledge. Capital has become less scarce. After World War II, a huge capital accumulation began and individuals, banks, and companies sought to be more skillful and forthright in maintaining and building their investment portfolios. Technological advances made capital easier to move around, share, and invest. And, with capital more easily available, labor (or, more correctly, the knowledge held in the heads of labor) became the most valuable component. Increasing cross-border competition and the subsequent complexity of work fed a need for people to be a source of inventiveness. With globalization making capital easier to obtain and the possession of land less of an issue, those who had knowledge and knew how to apply it would henceforth be the wealthiest. The shift has become visible in the rise, since the 1950s, of traditional asset-poor but knowledge-rich companies such as international auditing firms, management consultancies, advertising and media businesses, and IT providers.

This changing nature of the economics of the firm, combined with globalization and the growth in information technology, has meant that organizational knowledge is now not only the most valuable commodity, it also moves more quickly than ever. Hence, an organization cannot survive for long unless it continually adapts and reshapes its knowledge and thus itself. And, adaptation to a changing environment requires learning: the ability to manage change by changing oneself. A simple model of the elements of the learning process is mapped out in Figure 7.2.

De Geus then suggests that there are two ways in which this learning process can happen: (1) **learning by assimilation:** perceiving changes for which the learner already has structures in place to recognize what is being taught (e.g. skilled bank strategists are well set up to recognize and respond to a change in

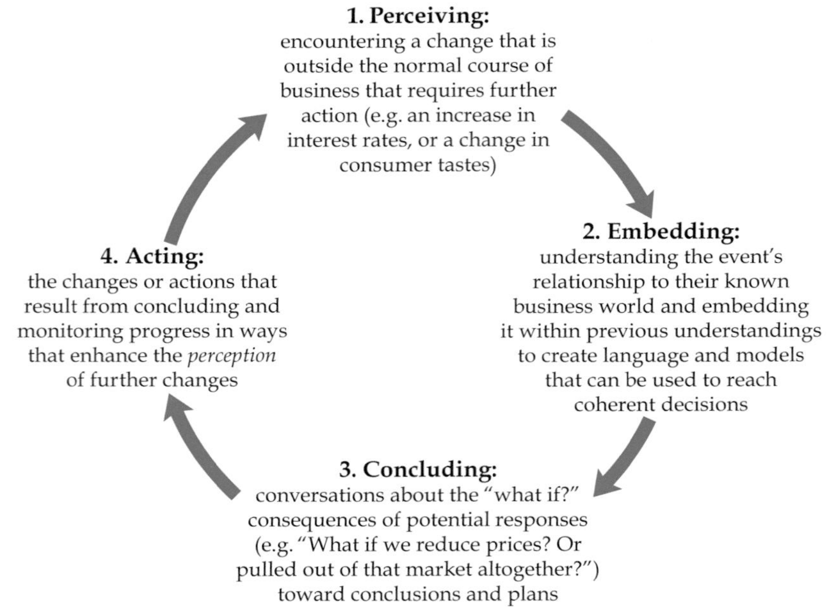

1. Perceiving:
encountering a change that is
outside the normal course of
business that requires further
action (e.g. an increase in
interest rates, or a change in
consumer tastes)

4. Acting:
the changes or actions that
result from concluding and
monitoring progress in ways
that enhance the *perception*
of further changes

2. Embedding:
understanding the event's
relationship to their known
business world and embedding
it within previous understandings
to create language and models
that can be used to reach
coherent decisions

3. Concluding:
conversations about the "what if?"
consequences of potential responses
(e.g. "What if we reduce prices? Or
pulled out of that market altogether?")
toward conclusions and plans

Figure 7.2 A learning process cycle (Adapted from de Geus, 2000)

interest rates); (2) **learning by accommodation:** changing one's learning process to remain in harmony with a changed environment (e.g. only a few banks have picked up on a shift in customer preferences for a bank that seems more like a retail environment and reconfigured accordingly (see live case 7-3)). Whereas learning by assimilation is generally a mechanical process, with change constrained by predetermined parameters, learning by accommodation becomes a living attitude and the possibilities for change here are infinite. Given the increasingly fast-paced and unpredictable nature of the knowledge society, there is no doubt that learning by accommodation is the more important of the two types of learning for organizations to master.

In summary, de Geus defines the successful living company, or **learning organization**, as having four aspects:

1. *Sensitivity to the environment* – an ability to learn and adapt.
2. *Cohesion and identity* – an ability to build a personality and a community for itself.
3. *Tolerance and decentralization* – awareness of its ecology, its ability to build constructive relationships with other entities, within and outside itself.
4. *Conservative financing* – an ability to govern its own life and evolution effectively.

James Collins and Jerry Porras's book, *Built to Last,* came to similar conclusions.[5] It claimed that the most admired companies combined a powerful drive for progress that enabled them to change and adapt without compromising their core ideals, a strong sense of identity, and sensitivity to their ecology. And, they found that while financial gain was also a secondary objective for these companies, financial gain tends to follow from focusing on long-term survival.

Many others have also looked at the importance of knowledge and learning to strategy. A particularly influential stream of research is that developed by Ikujiro Nonaka. This looks at the importance of turning tacit knowledge into explicit knowledge through a cycle of *socialization* (sharing of tacit knowledge between individuals); *externalization* (articulation of systemization of this into explicit knowledge); *combination* (putting this knowledge together with existing knowledge in useful ways); and *internalization* (converting this knowledge into new organizational and individual **routines**).[6]

The Power of Strategic Stories

Human beings can learn by accommodation through two practical means: by being changed by personal experience, or through encountering other people who communicate stories encapsulating other experiences. Given the inherent limitations of personal experience, stories are invaluable for the learning organization. In the words of Annette Simmons, "When you tell a compelling story, you connect people to you or what you are trying to achieve." While stories have for some time played a role in conveying complex marketing messages to customers (e.g. the identities of Unilever's main ice cream brands have been organized around the following storylines for many years: Solero – stories of refreshment; Magnum – self-indulgence; Carte d'Or – sharing), they are now playing a part in the way that many companies think about leading strategic development.

In 1998, "Strategic Stories: How 3M is Rewriting Business Planning" was published in the *Harvard Business Review*.[7] It clearly struck a chord, becoming one of the *HBR*'s best-selling offprints. In the article, 3M ascribed much of its success to the company's "story-intensive culture" and how this has changed the way it "does strategy." 3M attributes its new approach to two things. First, a recognition that traditional bullet points and list-making approaches to communicating strategic plans are too generic, leave critical relationships unspecified, and subsequently do not inspire thinking or commitment. Second, a recognition that communicating and developing the same ideas through stories enables people to see themselves and their business operations in complex, multidimensional ways, helping them to explore opportunities for strategic change and form ideas about future success. "When people locate themselves in these strategic stories," the authors concluded, "their sense of commitment and involvement is enhanced."

There are more scientific reasons why stories, or conversations about **strategic stories**, are important for organizations. Psychologists have established that lists are much harder to remember than stories because of "recency" and "primacy" effects. People mainly remember the first and the last items on a list but not the rest of it. Also, lists enable "selective memory" as people tend to select the individual points that they like and focus on those, forgetting about the whole and the many integrated parts that make this up. Language researchers have found that when they translated history textbooks into the story-based style of *Time* or *The Economist*, students could recall up to three times more information. Cognitive scientists have examined how the stories we hear in childhood enable us to imagine a course of action, imagine its effects on others, decide whether or not a particular direction should be taken, and plan accordingly.

If a picture paints a thousand words, then a story or an anecdote about a company can connect up a thousand threads and give a corporation a flexible focus that can launch a thousand initiatives that both encapsulate and build core values (see Chapter 6). In the words of Gardner and Laskin, authors of *Leading Minds: An Anatomy of Leadership*: "Stories of identity – narratives that help individuals think about and feel who they are, where they come from, and where they are headed – constitute the single most powerful weapon in the leader's arsenal."[8] Tom Peters even has a term for a management style based on this type of thinking: **MBSA** – "management by storying around." It is interesting that human beings can communicate and learn an incredibly complex system of meaning through a whole series of convoluted stories, yet be unable to remember a vision statement, code of ethics, or list of policy objectives. In a knowledge society, where learning organizations are imperative, many organizations are taking stories seriously. At the time of going to press, a nice example was provided by the Scheaffer company, who's website (www.sheaffer.com/stories/) linked to a number of video clips where customers connected their Sheaffer pens to signature moments in their lives as a way of expressing the company's strategy of promoting the idea that a "Sheaffer is more than a writing instrument."

Communities of Practice

Communities of practice are informal networks bound together by shared expertise or experiences and a passion for a particular joint enterprise. They tend to be self-selecting, self-organizing, self-reinforcing, and self-renewing, attracting new members through the strong sense of self-identity that they convey. They are held together by strong relationships and have a shared value system, memory, and knowledge base.[9] According to proponents of the view, it is these communities of practice, rather than senior planners and consultants, that really drive strategy. They can spread knowledge, develop professional skills, retain and recruit talent, and generate new lines of business. And, what they do is more likely to stick because they are organic beings, not manufactured policies. It is little wonder, therefore, that strategists should be aware of, identify, and get onside with the key communities of practice within their organization and the external communities that might either help or hinder the achievement of the company's strategic goals. A good example of a community of practice is provided in the case on "Team Schumacher" described in Case 7-1.

Social Capital

Social capital refers to the resources generated through personal and business networks. One might see it as the outcome of the emergent communities of practice described above. The word *social* is used to emphasize that key personal and business resources (e.g. ideas, opportunities, promising leads, access to financial capital, power and influence, emotional support, good-will, trust, and cooperation) are not owned by any single person, but reside in interdependent networks of relationships. The word *capital* emphasizes that resources like these can, and increasingly must, be used to create value and achieve business goals. The main insight offered to strategists by social capital theory is that most organizations and individuals within organizations need to build more entrepreneurial networks (i.e. larger, more diverse, and outwardly focused).

Strategies for achieving social capital include: encouraging rising managers to partake in external education programs (such as a high-quality MBA); sending delegations to interesting conferences; arranging staff exchanges with allied companies; allying with key influencers in other related industries; or arranging business forums and meetings for companies and other key stakeholders in an industry.[10]

The Power of Networks

These ideas about the power of communities of individuals and networks in shaping effective strategic directions are not that new. In 1982, Peters and Waterman's *In Search of Excellence* saw the advantages of "simultaneously loose-tight properties" or organizations as coalitions of individuals and belief systems, rather than machine bureaucracies, as a key to business success.[11] In 1993, two articles in the same issue of the *Harvard Business Review* looked at ways of rethinking business processes in terms of networks. Normann and Ramirez's "From Value Chain to Value Constellation: Designing Interactive Strategy" argued that a **value constellation** of relationships was a better metaphor for understanding how firms really add value than the traditional linear value chain. Krackhardt and Hanson's "Informal Networks: The Company Behind the Chart" claimed that one needs to see behind the formal hierarchies outlined in an organization's official chart to find the networks or communities of practice that really influence strategic direction setting.[12] Evans and Wurster's "Strategy and the New Economics of Information" went further, demonstrating how this new thinking about the loose–tight nature of interdependent relationships and communities, combined with advances in information technology, was changing the economics of the firm. The future, they argued would be one of **hyperarchies**: fluid networks and temporary coalitions of different, but like-minded, bodies rather than clearly stratified hierarchies.[13]

While articles like these have demonstrated the importance of looking at strategy as influenced by a wider network of internal and external influences than was traditionally thought to be the case, they often present an overly rosy view of the effects of these influences. Networks, and tightly knit communities of practice, are not always good for sponsoring effective strategies. Just like strong cultures, strong networks can become conservative, unquestioning, and resistant to outsiders and changing by learning through accommodation.

This is not a new idea outside of the management literature. Philosopher Michel Foucault developed the term **power/knowledge** to express the inescapable link between the two. Those who have power also to a very large extent determine what is knowledge, or at least what is valuable knowledge. Foucault also challenged preconceptions about power and networks by arguing that power does not exist in "bodies of authority" (e.g. government, the police, the media, the education system), but in the relationships (tangible or otherwise) between these bodies. Hence, protesting through directly confronting such bodies may cause the network to organize knowledge against the protest and make traditional conservative bonds stronger.[14] The best form of resistance is therefore to organize alternative networks of like-minded individuals who can help a cause behind the scenes. In similar vein, William Foote Whyte's 1943 study, *Street Corner Society*, diagrammed interactions between individuals to understand relationships between group structure and individual performance. Whyte found that the most successful and influential people were those with the most key "connections."[15] The recognition of the power of communities of practice, social capital, and networks, has led some strategic human resource experts to argue that the traditional approach of attempting to improve performance is by headhunting key individuals. The future may, however, lie in "heads-hunting": identifying effective relationships teams and seeking to lure whole teams.[16]

Resources and Capabilities

This brings us back into contact with the **resource-based view of the firm**, which was introduced in Chapter 5.[17] The RBV argues that each organization is made up of a constellation of tangible and **intangible resources**: *physical* resources like land, offices, and machinery; *financial* resources like access to capital; *human* resources like experience and expertise; and *organizational* resources like reputation, culture, and traditional relationships. (The ideas of Kunde and de Geus expressed earlier in this chapter would suggest that the human and metaphysical resources are key. This indicates why HR has come to be seen as such a strategic issue. No amount of cutting-edge technology or state-of-the-art business processes can compensate for a lack of human skill and teamwork. Hence, top-performing companies are up to four times more likely than the rest to pay what it takes to prevent losing top performers.[18]) When these resources are networked together in ways that enable the effective performance of a task or activity, they become capabilities. And, when these capabilities are superior to those of a firm's competitors they become a competitive advantage. In fact, the RBV approach suggests that an analysis of the firm's network of resources, rather than the external environment, is a better place from which to begin to understand a company's strategic potential.

The constellation of relationships between resources, and the knowledge embedded within them, suggests that the whole will always be greater than the sum of the parts, and indicates such constellations cannot be engineered – they have to grow organically. Because a system of relationships is an organic living being, it is reflective of a particular geography, history, and emergent relations between employees within the firm, and then between them and suppliers and customers and so forth. Therefore, each organization's RBV constellation will likely be rare and difficult to imitate. This is important to recognize, because in an age when firms have become very good at copying what they can copy through best practice benchmarking and reverse engineering, it may be claimed that tacit resource and knowledge webs will become the key to an organization's sustainable competitive advantage.

Strategy as Emerging from Processes and Practice

The living strategy view described above reinforces the importance of the **emergence view of strategy** championed by Henry Mintzberg and a new breed of strategic thinkers. We may believe that strategy is a rational and analytical activity resulting in plans and predetermined objectives that are then acted upon and achieved, but the emergence view suggests that strategy is in reality more about being adaptive enough to bend to follow opportunities and possibilities as they crop up. Here strategy is as much about the patterns that emerge as life unfolds as it is about planning.

Mintzberg's views are supported by Andrew Pettigrew's research, which suggests that the content or outcomes of a company's strategy (e.g. its plans, vision, or positions) is more a function of the particular processual patterns by which strategy emerges than by rational design. Hence, to understand a strategy's content, one should first consider the organizational context and processes. This **process view of strategy** has been developed further in recent times by the **strategy as practice** perspective.[19] The practice perspective builds on the strategy as process view, but looks at the particular behaviors and activities of individuals and groups who may influence strategy rather than organizational processes. For instance, what managers say or don't say, their choice of language, how they communicate through "technology" (such as Lotus Notes or Microsoft software), how meetings are conducted, the use of flip charts to control and steer discussion for instance, and the role of away-days are all of great interest as "micro-practices" in how strategy may be formed. Valuable insight can be gained by looking at strategy in this way. For example, we can recognize how middle managers are key gatekeepers of strategy: their communications can undermine or translate and promote the strategies espoused by those at the top of an organization or disrupt or facilitate the ideas of those below. Individuals within the organization who impact upon strategy are also likely to be connected across the organizational boundary both vertically and horizontally, perhaps with links to key suppliers and customers, or to institutional bodies. Recent research by Angwin and Paroutis (2009) has identified a pivotal role in the work of Senior Strategy Directors in bringing about significant organizational change through their diverse social networks. Viewing organizational boundaries as permeable raises interesting questions of how external parties, such as consultants, can and do influence the internal workings of the firm and also how internal strategy workers may shape external opinions. Strategy-as-practice allows us to focus on how managers, in practice, actually work with, adapt, and work around the "clean lines" and tidy categorizations of the classical frameworks depicted in the previous chapter.

The focus on strategy as emerging organically in an organization has taken on increasing importance as it is realized that such strategies are more difficult to replicate than conventional approaches, which saw strategy as about explicit plans and positions issued from the top of the bureaucracy. Generally speaking, the more emergent, organic, and embedded an organization's strategic processes and practices are, the more difficult it is for competitors to replicate the strategies that emanate from these processes.

This focus on the RBV and strategies emerging organically out of particular processes and practices should not imply that strategists are powerless to plan, design, position, and lead change. Indeed, as opportunities emerge in the life of an organization, it is up to strategists to seize on them and get the corporation behind them. Just as a human being must face two directions at once (both taking stock and moving forward; carrying on traditions yet taking up new directions), the living strategy perspective requires the strategist to be agile in facing both backwards and forwards at once. The metaphor sometimes used to express this attitude is "surfing." Because strategists cannot engineer waves or relationships, they must instead surf or work on the most favorable ones that already exist and be open to harnessing new waves, or promising practices, as they emerge.[20] We shall develop this idea further in Chapter 9, Guiding Change.

Balance in all Things: the Balanced Scorecard

As the paragraph above indicates, organic strategy, like life itself, is about balancing competing desires. Just as people must balance acknowledging past relationships, enjoying the present, and planning for future well-being, organizations too must achieve a similar balance in determining their strategies. One approach that has become an extremely popular means of helping an organization to achieve a balance between financial performance in the past, customer satisfaction in the present, and developing organizational capabilities for the future is Kaplan and Norton's **balanced scorecard** approach (see Figure 7.3). This encourages the use of multiple criteria beyond the financial measures that have generally been used to assess performance.

By using a balanced scorecard, organizations can, on the horizontal axis, consider and match assessments about:

1. what is our differentiated corporate identity or "How do our customers see us?" with. . .
2. how do we meet, exceed or change these expectations or "What must we excel at?"

In effect, this can help an organization to balance the classic positioning approach of identifying target customers or markets and more recent ideas about the importance of being true to an emergent and distinctive corporate identity (the two ticks and one cross on this axis in Figure 7.3 depicts an organization that is performing well on two dimensions but needs to be clearer about its identity while improving internal processes to match this on another). And by focusing on the vertical dimension organizations can seek to balance decisions about short-term financial dividends and investments in future resource or capability development (the 3 ticks versus 2 crosses on this axis in Figure 7.3 depicts an organization that appears to be performing well in the present but is consequently underinvesting for the future – a lack of balance that will probably come back to haunt it). The measures used for assessing balanced scorecard achievements on each of these four dimensions can be metrics, such as return on capital employed or return on net assets, or such factors as employee attitudes, extent of customer awareness and satisfaction, or the development of knowledge or skills within the organization that can help to drive innovation and new product development.

Building upon the classical views of strategic management promoted in Chapters 4 and 5, which grew out of the more mechanistic discipline of industrial economics, Corporate Identity and Organic Strategy have introduced a series of new and human-centered ways of thinking about developing strategic direction. All of the four pathways that make up part two of *The Strategy Pathfinder* (see Figure 2 in our Introduction on page xviii) provide a useful means of achieving and increasing an organization's strategic orientation. The next two chapters, Crossing Borders and Guiding Change, examine how new animation and movement can build upon this greater sense of orientation.

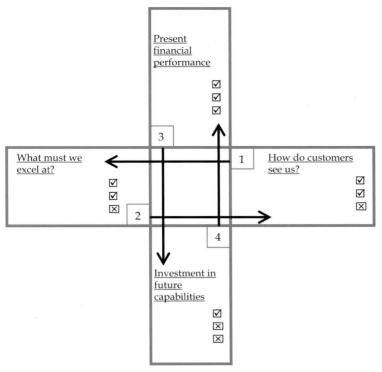

Present
financial
performance

☑
☑
☑

3

What must we
excel at?

☑
☑
☒

2

1

How do customers
see us?

☑
☑
☒

4

Investment in
future
capabilities

☑
☒
☒

Figure 7.3 The balanced scorecard framework (adapted from Kaplan and Norton, 1992)

Organic Strategy Key Learnings Mind Map

Having read and reviewed the chapter outline what you believe to be the key learnings from the chapter and the relationships between these.

7-1 Formula 1: Schumacher's success. . .

Perhaps the most popular story used to illustrate the power of relationships is that of Michael Schumacher's move to Ferrari. In 1996, Schumacher left the Benetton Formula 1 racing team – which he had helped to lead to unprecedented successes – to join Ferrari, the world's most powerful team. Many thought the world's best driver, combined with the richest team, would be invincible, but it was not to be. In 1996 Schumacher only recorded three wins and the team finished second behind Williams.

The next year, Ferrari's 50th anniversary, the story was much the same: Williams first, Ferrari second. But something very important happened at the end of that season. Ferrari lured Technical Director Ross Brawn and Chief Designer Rory Byrne from Benetton. The old Benetton team was reunited. Apparently it took some time for the Brawn–Byrne–Schumacher team to bed in to the Ferrari community, and while 1998 was encouraging, Ferrari still finished second, this time to McLaren. But in 1999 everything clicked. At the time of writing this, Ferrari had won every Formula 1 championship since 1999, and by increasingly grand margins.

For Schumacher, winning races has seemed to get easier and easier. But he is not stupid. Listen to him being interviewed and he will always credit the team, the relationships, the innate combinations, the camaraderie, the instinctive knowledge of what each other needs and what must be done for the team. It is the relationships that keep Schumacher winning and enjoying things so much that he wants to keep coming back for more, even though many commentators believe he has nothing left to prove.

Postscript:

Michael Schumacher did eventually retire from Formula 1 at the end of 2006, lauded as perhaps the greatest driver ever. However, a few years later he began a comeback, reuniting with Ross Brawn (but Rory Byrne had gone his own way) at the Mercedes team. At the time of going to press (late 2010), however, Schumacher had been unable to even come close to matching the performances of his former glory days. Many commentators have suggested that at 41 he may now simply be too old.

1. *Using Figure 7.1 as a guiding framework, outline the living strategy dimensions that you believe have contributed to Team Ferrari's eventual success.*
2. *If you were managing an F1 team, what would your approach to recruitment be to ensure that you achieved the best value for money?*
3. *Is Schumacher's failure to match his past stellar achievements in his comeback simply due to his age, or might there be other contributing factors?*

◄◄◄ Schumacher's success: Some ideas toward a "model answer". . .

Although Case 7-1 is brief, you should be able to use the information it provides, in combination with your own and others' knowledge (you might do a search on Schumacher and Ferrari to find out more information), to contribute something from all of the nine living strategy dimensions outlined in Figure 7.1, and described in this chapter, and answer question 1 above.

1. *Systems thinking*: While Schumacher might be "high leverage" (i.e. the 20% that can make 80% of the difference), he can only be as good as the system that he works within. Schumacher is integral, but on his own he was no "quick fix" here. Ferrari's success lies in the interrelationships (and processes that have developed out of those interrelationships) over time.
2. *Knowledge society/learning organization*: In a knowledge society, human capital is more valuable than other more tangible assets. This seems to be true in motor racing at the highest levels. All of the top teams have access to capital and technology – it's the human factors, like the knowledge that exists in Schumacher and his associates' heads, that make the difference. Recognizing this, Ferrari showed willingness to learn from and adapt to their previous poor performance and the success of others.
3. *Strategic stories*: While there are no explicit examples of this mentioned in the case, a lot of the power surrounding the Ferrari brand, and its ability to attract such people as Schumacher and Brawn, is provided by the stories and myths of characters like Enzo Ferrari and the "tifosi" (Ferrari's ultra-loyal fans).
4. *Communities of practice*: Schumacher, Brawn, and Byrne form a community of practice. They are bound by similar passions and values and know each other so well that they can learn, act, and effectively adapt in unison, without the need for time-consuming deliberation. They, more than the company's strategic planners, are the people who drive Ferrari's success.
5. *Social capital*: As this community of practice began to embed into Ferrari's broader network of alliances, these relationships began to produce social capital – a form of capital that is very difficult for Ferrari's competitors to replicate.
6. *Networks*: The old Italian Ferrari network seemed resistant to change. For many years the idea that a German would lead Ferrari would have been resisted. However, the new Ferrari is a more open network in which information flows quickly across the organization to where it is needed without having to follow the old hierarchies and power structures. This makes the organization more adaptive, while it still holds true to Ferrari's core ideals.
7. *Resources and capabilities*: Ferrari now comprises a network of physical resources, financial resources, and organizational resources like reputation, culture, and brand (which it has had for some time) with the best human resources. Networked together, this has led to the development of capabilities that contribute to its competitive advantage.
8. *Strategy as emergent*: While some, in hindsight, might put Ferrari's recent success down to good planning, the team's success has emerged gradually over time through Ferrari becoming open to adapting to emergent opportunities as they have presented themselves, and then letting Schumacher, Brawn, Byrne, and others get on with things, developing processes and practices that would shape effective strategic plans.
9. *Balanced scorecard*: For an F1 racing team it should be obvious that short-term victories or financial success is only one measure of performance. These must be balanced against keeping fans, clients, and sponsors happy, maintaining the capabilities that will enable new developments and future success, and keeping a clear sense of how the team identity is distinct from others so as to protect the brand that helps to sell merchandise and add to the brand value of the company's production automobiles.

And finally, returning to systems thinking helps us to understand that Ferrari's real strength lies in the interrelationships between all of these nine dimensions.

With respect to question 2 (managing an F1 team), reflecting on the ideas expressed in this chapter relating to networks, social capital, and communities of practice should suggest that one should be cautious of just head-hunting and transplanting in star drivers without investigating who some of their key "team-mates" are and looking to see if one might recruit the team. Or, by taking the vertical dimension of the balanced scorecard, one could examine whether it may be better to forgo short-term performance in the interests of growing your organization's own team relationships for the future – relationships that would be difficult for your competitors to poach or replicate. And while answering might depend on your level of knowledge and interest in F1 and your personal views of Michael Schumacher, we would hope that the reader would be able argue that success or failure, from an organic strategy perspective, is always the result of a system of factors, rarely just one.

▶▶▶

Case Notes:

7-2 The Band: Better together

As well as a decision analyst, I am a guitarist and I play music in a band (an organization). The latter is often more enjoyable than the former! The band's decision-making processes with regard to what material we play is heavily influenced by what might be called *intersubjectivity*. "We" only play particular material and, by definition, not other sorts of material. "We" articulate this to audiences who might ask for a tune that does not fit our repertoire – "we" say "we" don't play that song. However, this is completely different from saying "we" *can't* play that song.

As individual players, we are quite capable of playing a wide variety of music and styles. Yet, as an organization that is constantly evolving by adding new material, "we" play only selected material and in a style that conforms to (and is created by) the shared meaning and interpretation of the band's members. Change the band, of course, and you will also change the shared collective consciousness. But it too will evolve into a new shared intersubjectivity that will, consciously and unconsciously, take the organization's decision making down a particular lane of things that the organization will, and will not, do.

Reflecting on this history of popular music over the past few decades, this view that there is some intersubjectivity (or "magic") that emerges organically to make the whole of a good band much greater than the sum of its parts, appears to be backed up when one contrasts the outputs, collectively as a band and individually in the band members' solo projects, of, for example: The Beatles, The Rolling Stones, Simon and Garfunkel, The Sex Pistols, Nirvana, Public Enemy, Guns 'n' Roses, Crowded House, Soundgarden, Smashing Pumpkins, Rage Against the Machine, The White Stripes . . . and the list goes on.

1. *Apply Senge's five disciplines, and any other frameworks you think appropriate, to analyze what makes a group of musicians successful.*
2. *Why does a group produce music that is different from, and often superior to, that produced by the individuals who make up the group?*
3. *Can you relate your answers in questions 1 and 2 to how you might want to develop strategy organically in an organization?*

Case Notes:

7-3 Washington Mutual: Bringing back the branch?

A recent survey on international banking by *The Economist* began with the headline that "Banks have rediscovered the virtue of knowing their customers." Smaller banks probably never lost sight of this fact, but now even the biggest banks are rediscovering the value of the personal touch.

Until recently, the trend was to cut costs through automation. Branches fell out of fashion because the accountants deemed buildings to be too expensive and people too expensive and too unreliable. Banks found numerous ways of discouraging customers from bothering their tellers (such an antiquated term now), from charging them for the privilege, to removing staff or branches altogether, to incentivizing the use of web-based banking through discounts or prizes.

In addition, a bank's call-center might put an inquiry from Wolverhampton through to Mumbai. With the decline in the cost of telephone calls, increases in English language capabilities, and weaker union agreements making it easier to have people work odd shifts that correspond to business hours in countries many time zones away, it's certainly now much cheaper to operate in this way. And the customers probably wouldn't even be able to tell the difference; and, if they could, they probably wouldn't care. Or so the banks thought.

While telephones and computers are fine for checking bank balances or making fund transfers, they are much less good at selling products of any complexity. According to *The Economist*'s review: "Most people prefer to discuss mortgages, mutual funds, and so forth face-to-face. Moreover, banks these days want potential customers to do more than open a new current account. They aim, in the industry jargon, to maximize their 'share of wallet' by selling a whole portfolio of services. People are much better at that than machines are."

According to Charles H. Green, author of *Streetwise Financing for the Small Business* and Vice President of Atlanta's Sunrise Bank: "As big became bigger, the fate of smaller banks was written off many years ago. But the fact is that [the mega-banks] never really threatened community banks. More often than not, they have been outgunned by smaller, more focused banks that have chosen to stay true to their primary business of meeting customers' real needs."

Take banks like the Seattle-based Washington Mutual or New Jersey's Commerce Bank who have adapted their practices to suit customers' needs and wants rather than trying to funnel them into using less labor-intensive channels such as the internet.

At Washington Mutual (or WaMu as it is widely known) branches sell coffee and chocolates and piggy banks shaped like footballs, and there are play areas for young children. Some branches have given away the (somewhat tongue-in-cheek) "Action teller" dolls dressed as WaMu staff. There are no counters and no ropes to funnel people toward glass bound tellers. It looks more like a shop than a bank, which isn't surprising when you learn that WaMu managers are seeking to model themselves on leading retailers such as Wal-Mart and Home Depot rather than other banks.

Its marketing is similarly innovative. When they launched in Chicago employees handed out WaMu wallets containing $1.50 to advertise that they would not impose the usual surcharge on other banks' customers to use its ATMs. To announce their arrival in New York, WaMu bought out Broadway theaters for a day and gave the seats to the City's teachers. Both gestures won customers.

WaMu's assets have doubled in the past 7 years and now stand at $275bn, making it America's seventh-biggest bank. In mortgage lending it now jockeys with Wells Fargo for the No. 1 spot in the US market.

Vernon Hill, who founded Commerce Bank in 1973, claims to "love it when other banks merge." The growth in deposits at Commerce surged after the last two big mergers on his patch. Acquisition, says Hill, "is a good way to lose customers. It dilutes your model, dilutes your culture, distracts your firm, and dilutes your brand. No great retailer ever grew by acquisition."

Hill insists on calling himself a retailer, not a banker, and also extols the likes of Wal-Mart and McDonald's. Indeed, Commerce's business hours are much more like those of a retail store than a bank. Branches are open from 7.30 AM to 8.00 PM on weekdays and from 11.00 to 4.00 PM on Sundays. Somebody greets you as you enter a branch and Commerce's interiors are designed to be more homely than the austere surroundings one encounters at traditional banks. There are no screens to separate customers from tellers (a rarity in the New York area) and there are "penny arcades" where you can convert your loose change and maybe win a small prize.

Commerce has been growing at a furious pace. The increase in like-for-like sales (or deposits to use banking terms) has been close to 30% for the last few years. At the end of 1998, it had 96 outlets and $4.9bn in deposits. It has now spread from New Jersey into Philadelphia and Manhattan and has 275 branches and $20.7bn in deposits. By 2009, Commerce plans to have 700 branches.

But it's now not only smaller banks that are trying to play the relationships and communities cards. Bigger banks are seeking to configure themselves in ways that are far less impersonal. The HSBC's attempts to configure itself as "The World's Local Bank" and Barclays Bank's retraction of its advertising campaign that told people that what they really wanted was a "Big Bank," of Robbie Coltrane proportions, are good examples (see Case 8–7). Moreover, in the USA the number of bank branches has been on the rise for several years (up from around 69,000 in 1992 to 80,000 in 2003) and much of this rise is now coming from big banks reopening branches. "In 1999 and 2000," says Todd Thompson, CFO of Citigroup, "conventional wisdom was that branches were bad. What we understand [now] is that stores are good. People like to go to a real physical presence. It feels safe. It feels solid." Bank of America currently has plans to open 350 new branches and Bank One is adding new branches for the first time in over 5 years. It is also building in "teller towers" and waiting areas for customers' children.

In other countries, overall branch growth may be stagnant or declining, but banks all over the world are beginning to rethink how branches could be used. Given the increased recognition of the importance of long-lasting relationships that engender trust, for example, they are certainly less inclined now to whisk promising managers off to head office and more willing to leave them in the field.

"The wake up call for the mega-banks may be this," explains Charles H. Green: "As long as there are people who want to deal with people rather than an 800 number, a website, or a standard computer scoring program, there will be a demand for community bankers. It's relationships, stupid."

However, some commentators may point to the recent demise of WaMu as evidence that a focus on borrowing ideas from other industries and making bank environments more fun and friendly was a step too far. But, at the same time, innovations in making banks less austere and easier for customers to relate to continue to be rolled out: Metro Bank (the first new bank to open on the UK's high streets for more than a century) recently announced that it would open on Sundays and that it would provide not only complementary mints for humans but also dog biscuits for customers' pets, who would also be made most welcome at its branches.

1. Why might branches staffed with living beings (as opposed to other, technological banking interfaces) become more important in a "knowledge society"?
2. What learning and social capital might accrue from these local branches? How could you feed this learning and social capital into strategy development?
3. Do you think that WaMu's focus on making the customer or client environment more relaxed and friendly was a factor in their demise? If so, how might you seek to balance a demand for friendly customer relations with the need for professionalism and seriousness in an industry such as banking?

Case Notes:

7-4 The Prudential: Helping old people eat

Like all big companies, Prudential had a formal statement of purpose:

> Prudential plc provides retail financial products and services and fund management to many millions of customers worldwide. Our commitment to the shareholders who own Prudential is to maximize the value over time of their investment. We do this by investing for the long term to develop and bring out the best in our people and our businesses to produce superior products and services, and hence superior financial returns. Our aim is to deliver top quartile performance among our international peer group in terms of total shareholder returns. At Prudential our aim is lasting relationships with our customers and policyholders, through products and services that offer value for money and security. We also seek to enhance our company's reputation, built over 150 years, for integrity and for acting responsibly within society.

While CEO Mark Wood recognizes the necessity of such a statement, recently he has been trying to bring what it means to life through the sharing of stories about the company. Below are some extracts from his "Prudential Story" which he presented to a conference of Pru managers in 2003. Wood's story has two key chords.

First, is the attempt to take the best of the company's history into the future. The Prudential was founded 150 years ago in London with a purpose to offer life assurance and loans to the middle and working classes. It took its name and corporate symbol from the form of Prudence, one of the four cardinal virtues, and developed a new system for providing insurance based on door-to-door agents supported by actuarial tables to enable them to provide personalized advice and simple explanations of its products. The Prudential – affectionately known as "the Pru" (probably the only nickname of a multinational company to have become an official part of the English language) – and its calling salesmen, affectionately referred to as "The Men From the Pru," became a part of the fabric of everyday life in the UK. By the 1900s, the Pru's values of security, plain-speaking honesty, value for money, integrity, and the ensuing emphasis on sound and solid investments and innovations that made things simple for ordinary people had led to Prudential insuring one-third of the UK population. However, by the 1990s shifts in the way in which financial services could be sold had made the Pru's door-to-door distribution channel unworkable. The company's strategic response: to update the Man From the Pru to "Plan From the Pru."

Second, Wood has a keen ear for the stories shared between employees that characterize what the Pru aims to be about. For example, a story was told of a young telephone operator in Scotland who made a regular follow-up call to a lapsed customer. He turned out to be an elderly man who told her that he always meant to fill in the forms that were sent to him to renew and update his Pru policy, but he found them to be too long and confusing and so never completed them. He said that when the Man From the Pru used to call at his door, they would fill out the forms together over a cup of tea. So, the telephone operator said to the gentleman that she was going to take a tea break in ten minutes. If he liked he could go and make himself a cup of tea and by the time that was done she would have hers and she would call him back and they would fill out the forms together. He liked the idea very much. They filled out the forms and a satisfied member of the Pru was back in the fold. You will see the influence of this story in Wood's.

"I want to tell you a story – a story about our business, the place where we work, where we are each investing our time, where we are building our careers. My purpose in telling this story is to describe my ambition for our part of the Pru over the next 1,000 days and indeed into the next century.

"What has shaped our future success? Cost reduction? No, but it played a big part in getting us to where we need to be; it has been the price to be paid to enable our business to prosper but it is only a first step. We have become a low-cost operator. By knocking out all the obvious areas of duplication while simultaneously making more significant moves, including the transformation of our customer service operation and the development of our Indian service center, we have shifted from the old high-cost model to low-cost, fast-delivery, and enhanced service. We have combined this with working hard to maximize the return on our customers' savings, and to providing the best possible service and incentives to our distributors. Our long-term future is dependent on the profit we accrue day by day, week by week, month by month. This determined approach has resulted in the achievement of our doubling of intrinsic value.

"However, the preservation and increase of our reputation – our *brand* – have been much more important. Underpinning the financial strength I've just described is the way we do things – *our values*. We are a friendly place, approachable, concerned to correct mistakes, but generally known by our customers for being careful, caring, and conscientious. The Pru is a place for consistent good value over the long term rather than the best rate for a short period of time. The Pru is prudent rather than expedient. We believe that if it seems too good to be true, it probably is. We would rather be criticized for cutting bonuses and maturity values than risk our financial strength. Our speed of service, while prompt, is not unsustainably or flashily fast. We are a place where you talk to real people at the end of the telephone rather than one of those computer thingies; if you are a bit muddled in your thinking about your finances at the Pru, you will find somebody, using words you understand who will take you through what you need to do and in a straightforward way. You will not find us talking in jargon. We are a place where, whatever the purpose of your call, you'll get a professional and sympathetic ear – someone concerned to ensure that your confidence in the Pru grows with every contact.

"To double our intrinsic value we knew that we had to have the right priorities. We made some tough decisions. We stopped some big projects. We have placed increasing importance on return on capital. This meant that we decided not to pursue some profitable opportunities. They required too much capital. We disappointed, irritated, and confused people. Some decided to leave us because they did not enjoy our disciplined pursuit of return on capital. But we knew we were focusing in the right place, on our brand, our product strengths, on our distribution channels, and on our costs and our financial strength. We focused on our product strengths in Group Pensions, Bulk Annuities, and our capability within the With Profits and Annuities markets. Our clear view and a particular focus on managing our scarce capital and long-term financial strengths dictated our priorities. Nonetheless, on several occasions we acted tactically. Without notice we changed tack, spotting an opportunity, moving swiftly and decisively, often against competitors, following rapid analysis and assessment to pounce and to profit. We have ceased to be a thinking organization enjoying debate for its own sake, insisting on perfection rather than delivery. We have become prone to action, valuing 'sooner rather than perfect,' earning the right to exist by charting a pragmatic course and having something to show for it.

"So at the end of these 1,000 days what has changed? Well in 1,000 days we, each of us individually, will be here because we want to be. The pulse rate of the organization has quickened. The acceptable standard of performance has risen. The error rate has dropped. Decisions result from analysis not opinion. Effectiveness counts more than seniority. We like the people we work with. We can depend on each other as we work to a common set of clear, defined, stretching – but achievable – 90-day deliverables. We trust each other based on our experience of working with each other.

"But there is something else beyond all this. We have shown each other what happens when we pull together. We have realized that one plus one can equal three. We understand that we are interdependent. This has made our teamwork more effective – we are listening to each other, analyzing what we hear, checking, and then taking action. We are developing a sense of balance between working for today and learning for tomorrow. We are recognizing that what we put into the organization will be reflected in what the organization achieves and in how we are rewarded. When something is being developed, changed, and implemented, we run as a project. When we are chasing new business, somehow, we are all aware of it, and we hunt as a pack. We now have a head office that feels more like a college library than a corporate bureaucracy; we have meetings standing up, we informally gather around open-plan tables, we pop round to see each other rather than sending an e-mail. We are on the move. We are constructive. We are optimistic.

"But smooth interfaces, effective products, excellent investment performance, fast decisions, competitive pricing and commissions, even financial strength, are just 'hygiene factors.' Our key differentiated product and service is The Plan From the Pru. The Plan From the Pru has transformed the way in which people think about their savings. Now they understand what they are doing. With the Plan From the Pru as their guide, they have set themselves financial objectives. We work relentlessly to simplify our products to ensure that our customers understand what they are buying, how the product works, what the promise is, what they can expect, and what they are risking.

"We have disregarded unnecessary processes, duplicate activities, restrictive bureaucracy, valueless overheads, pretentious practices; these will never have a place in our business. Grand offices, layers of management, ponderous meetings, lengthy decision making, hesitant procrastination, ineffective delegation, and the avoiding of individual responsibility have no place with us. But there is more to it than that, something more fundamental. Above all else we have worked, first and foremost, to ensure that our customers, in their old age, can afford to eat, to heat their homes, to take the style of holiday they are used to, to replace worn-out clothes, and continue to tend the garden they love and live in the home in which they are comfortable.

"Thus, the job we have chosen to do is among the most valuable in society. Doctors and priests, depending on your outlook, have more worthy roles in our community – they deal with our physical and spiritual well-being. We are the custodians of people's material well-being. We provide the foundation for a civilized society. Civilization, a society that can afford leisure, depends on a secure store for savings protected for the future. We provide that secure place. We have an obligation to perform at the highest possible level in every aspect of what we do. People trust us; we must be worthy of that trust. Prudential is a mighty business."

The second last paragraph already has a good deal of folklore around it. Wood has become well known throughout the company for touting "Helping Old People Eat" as the Pru's true calling or mission. While the conventional vision outlined at the head of this case remains, the far more unlikely sounding Helping Old People Eat (and the ensuing acronym HOPE) is striking a chord with an ever-increasing number of employees.

1. What is the strategic value of Mark Wood and Prudential's story-telling approach outlined in this case?
2. What does the HOPE mission provide that the conventional Pru vision described at the beginning of the case does not?
3. Place the HOPE mission in the middle of a Balanced Scorecard diagram (see Figure 7.3). Now figure out how this might apply to the projection of differentiated identity to customers, how that might suggest particular internal process strategies, and interesting questions about balancing short-term financial performance with long-term learning and investment.

Case Notes:

7-5 Deutsche Bank: The power of the WEB

When Heinz Fischer arrived as head of human resources at Deutsche Bank he found that women accounted for fewer than one in six at the managerial level despite making up half the bank's workforce. Experience had shown him that companies that pursue diversity enjoy better performance, largely because their strategies subsequently reflect a cross-section of society rather than just one particular category and because putting different types of people together in teams often sparks creative solutions to business problems. So, Fischer invited 30 women employees to a workshop to discuss the obstacles they faced. The most critical barrier the women identified was the lack of informal networks of the type used by men, such as the golf course or the drink after work.

Pilar Conde, a Managing Director at JP Morgan, claims that networking is a key in any individual or group achieving their goals. He says that people often misunderstand networking: "They ask: 'Why do I need a network to be successful? If I do my job well, my manager will recognize me.' But everyone in a position of power has used a network." Women, or any underrepresented group, will thus find it difficult to influence agendas as they emerge from the lower levels of an organization, or steer strategies as they are handed down from the top, because they lack the "common-interest" networks drawn upon by others in corporations to grease the wheels. Directly confronting these networks can often create counterproductive "underground" forms of resistance. So, perhaps the best solution is to form alternative networks.

In response to the problems outlined by Heinz Fischer above, Deutsche Bank encouraged the establishment of a "women's network" within the European arm of the company. This network then decided to extend its web beyond the organization. A group of the bank's female executives organized and hosted, and Deutsche Bank funded, the first Women in European Business (WEB) Conference in Frankfurt in March 2000. Four hundred delegates were anticipated; more than 1,000 women attended. The success of this conference led to it becoming established as an annual event sponsored by Deutsche Bank.

Deutsche Bank now links WEB to a collection of other women's networks. Within the firm, operating across the three main centers of London, Frankfurt, and New York, is the Global Partnership Network for Women (GPNW). This network actually began life in 1991 when it was established by a group of women at the American organization Bankers Trust prior to it becoming part of the Deutsche Bank group. GPNW sponsors an American equivalent of the WEB conference: Women on Wall Street (WOWS), something that Deutsche Bank was very keen to continue. WOWS is now attended by over 2,000 men and women annually, from across the Deutsche Bank group and beyond, from all parts of the wider business community.

Speaking about a recent WOWS conference, Karen Meyer, Head of Global Diversity at Deutsche Bank, claimed that it "demonstrated the company's commitment to providing forums which foster the personal and professional development of women, where they can have access to role models, learn from peers, and continue to build their professional networks."

Deutsche Bank sees these developments as being very good for business. Annette Fraser, the Chair of the Executive Committee organizing the 2003 WEB conference and an executive with Deutsche Asset Management, noted that while the growth of these networks is important to women with the bank "it is also good for Deutsche Bank itself, which is now seen as a leading promoter of diversity in the workplace." And the bank seems to be able to back this promotion up: Deutsche Bank was named one of the top 100 companies for working mothers by *Working Mother Magazine* in 2002, and received a score of 100% in the Human Rights Campaign (HRC) Corporate Equality Index 2003 report.

---

1. *What strategic benefits might accrue to the members of the WEB network?*
2. *What strategic benefits might accrue to Deutsche Bank through its involvement in developing and helping to maintain this network?*
3. *Can you foresee any negative effects that might emerge as WEB becomes more established? How would you manage these?*

Case Notes:

7-6 American Association of Scientists: Practice above content

While we often tend to focus on the explicit outcomes or content of strategy, much of the value in developing strategy comes as people engage in the process and practice of strategy making, articulating, challenging, and adjusting views as people communicate with others. The two examples below may seem disappointing in terms of the outcomes or impure in terms of the application of theoretical frameworks, but from a "strategy as practice perspective" they can be seen as interesting success stories in this regard.

In March 2001, a spokesperson for the American Association for the Advancement of Science's (AAAS) campaign for an oath to set global ethical standards for scientists announced that they were "dropping the future pursuit of it." It wasn't so much a lack of interest in its pursuit or failing to see it as an important issue that had brought things to a halt, as the inability of the many bodies concerned to agree the wording of a common code. Having collected 101 different proposed or existing codes of ethics from science groups worldwide, Vivian Weil, Director of the Center for Study of Ethics in the Professions at the Illinois Institute of Technology, told AAAS members at a recent meeting in San Francisco that agreeing a common oath that could be practically applied was proving to be a problem.

Interest in a common pledge, seen as the scientist's equivalent of the Hippocratic Oath, was kindled by Sir Joseph Rotblat advocating such an oath during his Nobel peace prize acceptance speech in 1995. He suggests that "[such] a pledge is becoming more important because the impact of science, with the cloning of humans and genetic modification of food, is becoming so much more direct." Subsequently, Rotblat has admitted that the ongoing disagreement over such an oath or common code was a big blow.

However, the cloud hanging over the scientists' common code may contain silver linings. Rotblat is heartened by the grass-roots support for the oath that had emerged from young scientists keen to embrace such a standard. And, as one executive director of a leading scientific research society reasoned: "While I'm skeptical about the practicality of an oath that can be widely applied, the spirit of the discussions that led toward an oath may be more important than the oath itself."

* * *

Power's, a pub/restaurant group, has grown fast through successful acquisitions. It now owns many big-name brands, including Mr. Beef, M.J.'s, and Pizza Court. To aid the company's coordination as it grows, managers need to think through how the various elements of the growing company relate to one another. The diagram in Figure 7-6.1, and the dialogue below, came about as the result of encouraging them to use Michael Porter's classic strategy frameworks to express their own ideas about where the company was going. The diagram, a conglomeration of Porter's Generic Strategy Matrix, Five Forces of Industry, and Value Chain, is one group's analysis of Mr. Beef and the presentation and debate that followed.

Manager 1: "Basically we saw Mr. Beef as being a family pub/restaurant, but a bit better than the competition – differentiated. However, over time this

ORGANIC STRATEGY

225

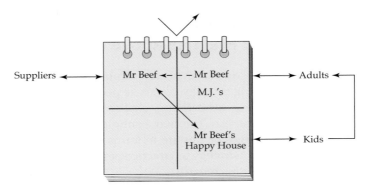

Figure 7-6.1 Analysis of Mr. Beef sketched on a notepad

has been kind of forgotten. It's been easier to focus on cost reduction and it's drifted back into the broad-cost segment. The interesting progression is the development of Mr. Beef's Happy House [Mr. Beef's Happy House is a children's restaurant/playground that had been established within a number of Mr. Beef pubs]. These have proved really popular and are differentiated and focused on kids, obviously. So, what do we do? Perhaps we need to revamp Mr. Beef and move it into the differentiated end again?"

Manager 2: "Maybe, but there it's almost directly competing against M.J.'s."

Manager 1: "And surely Mr. Beef is such a big chain now that we should be in the broad-cost segment. If you add in that part of Porter's Five Forces of Industry, that's where we can really exercise power over suppliers by using our size as a buying strength."

Manager 2: "But what about the disparity between Mr. Beef and Mr. Beef's Happy House? If we continue with your bringing in the Five Forces and look at the other side of things, buyer power, we all know that for family pub/restaurants it's kids who often make the buying decision. We can't afford to damage that link by letting Big Steak Wacky Warehouse slide the way of Mr. Beef."

Manager 3: "Sure, but if we realize the difference and the relationship between the two then surely we can benefit at both ends of the value chain – a strong link into key suppliers and a key hook into a special type of buyers."

Manager 4: "Yeah, in a way, if we could do this, and get the best of both sides, then this could be a source of competitive advantage hard to replicate. It would create a real barrier to new entrants up at the top of the box there."

1. *Although the scientists did not arrive at an official "all-purpose" oath, what learning and social capital might have accrued from the process of seeking one?*

2. *Even though they did not apply Porter's frameworks in the manner that they are generally presented, why might Power's managers have benefited from the "practice" they engaged in as described above?*

3. *Why might the process and practice of discussing the development of strategies with staff and other stakeholders be important in orienting and animating an organization?*

7-7 The Dalai Lama: On the Global Financial Crisis

Everybody seems to have an opinion on what caused the global financial crisis of 2008, and as the GFC continued on into 2009 journalists cast their net beyond the traditional market analysts often called upon to comment on such matters in search of broader insights. In the middle of 2009, the Dalai Lama was interviewed by German magazine *Die Welt* and American magazine *Business Week,* both seeking the spiritual leader's guidance on the economic meltdown.

As one might expect of a Buddhist leader, he saw what financial analysts tended to see mechanistically in terms of living beings. "Companies are living complex organisms and not profit machines," he was quick to point out. Not only this, but they are made up of living beings who make value judgments, over time.

Part of the problem, the Dalai Lama explained, was to see this as an economic problem or a failure of the market and look for short-term solutions rather than examine the root causes. And, getting to the root required recognizing that "the financial crisis is no crisis of the market economy itself, but a crisis of values." While it was easy to blame the mechanisms of capitalism, this overlooked the fact that the market is made up of humans.

Rather, the Dalai Lama identified a gradual narrowing of human values by some individuals as a root cause. "Those people [became] only concerned with money . . . Of course money is important. Without money you can't survive. However, it is not the only measure of value. We have other values: the happy family, compassionate family, the family full of affection . . . this crisis reminds us you should find some other values. Money value alone is a limitation."

And, as with any living being's decline, the Dalai Lama saw the seeds being sown many years previously. "According to Buddhism," he told *Business Week* journalist Steve Hamm, "these things happen due to their own causes and conditions. Through years or through decades this present crisis developed. All the causes and conditions were fully ripe. No force could stop it. It [became] the natural law."

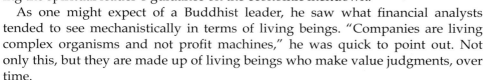

1. *Do you think the global financial market can be seen as a living being?*
2. *If so, what characteristics might we observe that we might not see when thinking of the market as a mechanism?*
3. *Would a more "organic" view of the market enable people to better foresee and prevent future crises?*

Part III Strategic Advances

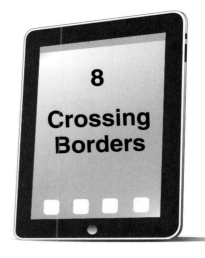

8

Crossing Borders

You may say I'm a dreamer, but I'm not the only one; I hope some day you'll join us, and the world will live as one.

John Lennon

When I am at Milan, I do as they do in Milan; but when I go to Rome, I do as Rome does.

St. Augustine

During the 1990s, James Dyson, a British inventor, created a revolutionary new vacuum cleaner that didn't use a dust bag and was significantly more efficient than competitor products. It was an immediate hit in the UK market and soon Dyson was selling his product overseas. Dyson followed this triumph by inventing a revolutionary washing machine containing two contra-rotating drums to give greater performance than other models. Such successful entrepreneurialism earned Dyson national recognition and his company "cult hero" status in Britain. So, imagine the shock when, in 2003, he announced that his factory in Malmesbury, England, was to close and all manufacturing moved to Malaysia. There was widespread outcry in the UK press and from the trade unions. "This latest export of jobs by Dyson is confirmation that his motive is making even greater profit at the expense of UK manufacturing and his loyal workforce. Dyson is no longer a British product" (Derek Simpson, joint General Secretary of Amicus; Neil Collins, *The Daily Telegraph* (August 25, 2004)). Not only would 865 jobs be lost, but this also seemed to symbolize so much of British industrial history: the loss of yet another world-beating product overseas. Why would Dyson, a hero of British entrepreneurialism, risk the wrath of his countrymen for the sake of profit?

Dyson is just one example of a company that rapidly succeeds in its home market, quickly begins to export its products, and then moves production overseas to reduce costs and/or to be closer to other markets. This raises a number of questions central to international business strategies. Why do countries specialize and organizations trade across national boundaries, and how recent is this phenomenon? Why do some organizations leave their home country for another? What are the obstacles to crossing borders? What strategies are used for competing internationally? Which borders should be crossed? What methods can be used to enter different countries? How might an organization make a strategic retreat? And, how can firms structure themselves for competing across borders?

Why Do Countries Specialize and Organizations Trade Across National Boundaries?

Although a relatively new academic subject, international business itself is not new. Evidence survives of the Phoenicians mining for tin in Cornwall, England in 500 BC. The Cistercian monks engaged in pan-European wool trading in the 13th century. In the 15th century, the rise of the city republics, such as Venice, saw substantial integration into international trade. Soon afterwards, in the Age of Empires, the Portuguese, Spanish, Dutch, French, and British controlled and traded with many far-flung countries. The political power of these countries rested upon the economic power of trade, which came to be dominated by trading companies such as the East India Company (India), Hudson Bay Company (N. America), and Inchcape (Asia).

In essence, trade results in a higher level of economic well-being for its participants. This logic at the level of the parent nation was articulated famously in Adam Smith's **theory of absolute advantage**: "If a foreign country can supply us with a commodity cheaper than we ourselves can make it, better buy it off them with some part of the produce of our own industry, employed in a way in which we have some advantage."[1] Each nation, then, should specialize in producing goods in which it has a natural or acquired advantage. For example Scotland has an absolute cost advantage over Spain in producing whisky. In Chapter 1 we outlined how Nike has benefited from the absolute advantages of different countries as it is carrying out R&D in the USA; fabric, rubber, and plastic shoe component production in Korea, Taiwan, and China; and assembly in India, China, the Philippines, Thailand, and other low-wage locations.

What if a country has no natural advantages? To address this question, in 1817, David Ricardo developed a **theory of comparative advantage**, which examined the relative costs of production between goods in each country.[2] On this basis, countries should produce and trade in goods that they are best equipped to produce, even though their cost of producing other goods may still be lower than the countries with which they are trading. Traditionally, these theories focused on natural resource endowments, population, and capital, but critical roles are now recognized for social and cultural factors such as human capital and management capabilities.

To improve on the rather static nature of the early theories, a more dynamic model was proposed by Hecksher (1919) and Ohlin (1933). Their **HOS model of factor endowments** argues that as a country specializes in a particular product, the main factor of production, such as land, labor, or capital, becomes increasingly scarce and expensive. As a consequence, countries that may have a large labor force, encouraging labor-intensive production, are likely to experience rising wages. To compensate for such pressures, countries need to develop other advantages. In order to explain the development of Japan and the catching-up process of industrialization, Kaname Akamatsu coined the term "The flying geese pattern of development." This model was presented to the world's academic audiences in 1961. It explains Japan's post-war transition away from cheap labor, through acquiring technology and developing capabilities, as reflected in changing industry emphases on textiles, chemicals, ship building, cars, and electronics. It also explains the rapid rise of NICs (newly industrialized countries) by recognizing that comparative advantage shifts across countries over time. Such Tiger economies, including Singapore, Taiwan, Malaysia, and Korea, have grown organizations that are beating Japanese industry in many areas and some, such as Samsung, can now claim to be world leaders at the forefront in several product areas.

Why Do Organizations Leave Their Home Countries?

Within these broad national trends, organizations attempt to adjust to changing contexts such as those identified by ESTEMPLE (see Chapter 1). For organizations such as Samsung, with growing demand for its products in overseas markets, direct investment in production capacity abroad becomes increasingly attractive to reduce logistic costs. As the product becomes standardized, production may be moved to areas where manufacturing costs are low. This dynamic is captured in Raymond Vernon's article "International Investment and International Trade in the Product Life Cycle." Vernon suggests an **international product life cycle**[3] theory to explain why the location of industries changes. "As production and consumption increase, production costs decline and markets expand, so exports increase. With increasing competition, price cutting forces production to shift to cheaper countries." On this basis we have an explanation for the transfer of Dyson's manufacturing as well as the cataclysmic decline in traditional British industries such as mining, shipbuilding and textiles

Some organizations may be more likely than others to internationalize. Organizations that own hard-to-replicate proprietary advantage, such as technology, brand name, or distribution, may come to dominate the home market and later overseas markets.[4] This does not fully explain all differences between organizations and industries. For instance, Tesco, which has been the undisputed leader in the UK supermarket industry for some years, is still primarily a domestic operation. This oligopolistic theory was refined in John Dunning's **eclectic theory**, which centered on **ownership**, **location**, and **internalization** (OLI). The organization has to: have some ownership of specific unique assets that can be transferred (O) and which will offset the additional costs of competing overseas; locate where cheap capital, labor, and other resources can be obtained and where logistics costs can be minimized in terms of transportation and tariffs (L); be able to make transfers internally to retain control of revenue generation (I). Those organizations that derive most from internalizing activities will be the most competitive in foreign markets. The eclectic theory suggests that where an organization's OLI advantages are high, organizations are more likely to prefer an integrated mode of entry across borders.[5]

Organizations, then, are motivated to cross borders to exploit new market opportunities and to reduce labor costs. They may also be motivated by needing lower cost supplies and/or securing procurement such as key raw materials. The rising costs of R&D and technology may need investment greater than can be sustained in the domestic market. Having operations in overseas countries may reduce the risk of fluctuating exchange rates and also allow arbitrage benefits by using resources in one country to benefit another. The "Californianization of society," or globalization of tastes, increases pressure for universal brands and products. This can be as much at the personal level, with products such as mobile phones and iPads, as with business consumers wanting similar service and products around the world for all their subsidiaries. Such standardization suits high-tech products with low cultural content, and encourages economies of scale and scope in producers. Other pressures encourage the integration and coordination of operations in different countries. When the blockbusting film *The Matrix* was launched, it had the distinction of being the first film to open simultaneously around the world. Where there are short product life cycles, such as with movies and computer software, it is now essential to have coordinated global product launches to reduce the time for competitive response and illegal copying. Microsoft's Windows, for instance, now launches simultaneously worldwide. Coordination also allows learning through the transfer of best practice, people, and information. These advantages of gaining new markets, reducing costs, timing benefits, learning, and arbitrage opportunities are real but have to generate a competitive advantage for the organization. Specifically, crossing borders must offer value propositions more attractive than available at home. Even if opportunities seem to satisfy this criteria, numerous obstacles exist which may impair their realization.

What Are the Obstacles To Crossing Borders?

Obstacles can be classified into four types: (1) political and legal barriers, (2) commercial factors, (3) technical issues, and (4) cultural factors.

Political and legal barriers occur through the use of regulation, duties, and quotas that can limit free flow of people, cash, and products. For instance, to impede the importation of Japanese electronics, the French required all imported goods of this type to go through a single customs point, located in the mountains. Ownership policies, such as refusing total ownership (particularly if the industry is perceived as strategic) and only allowing joint ventures, for instance, may disrupt attempts to improve international coordination of business.

Commercial factors may include limited access to distribution networks, the need for customization, and differentiated approaches to sales and marketing.

Differences in technical standards can increase costs and transportation difficulties can reduce the benefits of economies of scale and standardization. There may also be a spatial need to be present locally, for instance in the provision of health care.

Cultural barriers may exist as differences in social attitudes, beliefs, and norms and in terms of language, etiquette, and way of interacting. These may hamper interactive communication and reduce the benefits of standardization. For instance, the British are notorious for using language in an opaque way. Where the British say "I hear what you say," foreigners will understand this to mean "He accepts my point of view." In actual fact, what is meant is "I disagree." When the British say "that's an original point of view," foreigners will tend to think that their ideas are interesting and liked, whereas what is meant is that "you are crazy, or very silly." In some countries, great emphasis is placed on getting to know the people one is negotiating with, whereas other countries focus more on the transaction. For one large UK company that recently acquired a firm in Spain, the UK Director decided to visit the Spanish MD for a discussion about strategy. As time was tight, and in order to be efficient, the UK Director requested a working lunch over sandwiches. The Spanish MD regarded this as a personal slight as removing lunchtime also removed the time, necessary in his eyes, for the building of relationships – critical for doing business in Spain. Furthermore, where was the Spanish firm to get sandwiches from?

From our examples, one can perceive many different aspects of national culture. Studies aimed at crystallizing such differences have concentrated on: (1) ethological perspectives, such as Hall's study[6] on silent differences such as the importance of time, social and physical space, material goods, friendship, types of agreement, and the relative importance of context versus content; (2) country cultures such as Huntingdon's work[7] identifying civilization clusters by language, religion, beliefs, and institutional and social structures; (3) economic cultural differences such as Whiteley's work,[8] which examines business systems and forms of capitalism; and (4) country cultures based on managerial values. Probably the most famous, and certainly the largest survey into managerial values, is by Dutch academic Geert Hofstede, who surveyed 116,000 IBM employees across 53 different nations to assess national cultures based on work-related values.[9] With subsequent refinements, Hofstede categorized them according to five dimensions:

1. *Power-distance*, or the degree of inequity among people that a country's population sees as normal. Countries such as the USA, Germany, and the Netherlands scored low on power-distance, while Russia and China scored high.
2. *Individualism vs. collectivism*, or the degree to which people prefer to act as individuals rather than as members of groups. Countries or regions such as Hong Kong, Indonesia, and West Africa scored low on individualism; while the USA and the Netherlands scored high.
3. *Masculinity vs. femininity*, or the degree to which values often labeled masculine (e.g. assertiveness, competitiveness, performance orientation) prevail over those often labeled feminine (e.g. relationships, solidarity, service). Scandinavian countries, the Netherlands, and Russia scored low on masculinity; Japan, and Germany scored high.
4. *Uncertainty avoidance*, or the degree to which people preferred structured rather than unstructured situations. Countries such as Hong Kong, Indonesia, and the USA scored low, while Japan, Russia, and France scored high.
5. *Long-term vs. short-term orientation.* Countries such as Japan and China scored high on long-term orientation, whereas the USA and Britain scored low.

These different orientations can affect many things that relate to strategy, from the type of management theories that one nation develops or favors, to a nation's preference for certain types of action over others, to the way staff behave, develop and implement strategy.

While Hofstede's work has been criticized for focusing on a single organization, other researchers, such as Laurent,[10] have sampled more broadly and still identified systematic patterns of national differences among managers in their assumptions concerning power, structure, roles, and hierarchy. Later research by Fons Trompenaars and Hampden-Turner, following in Hofstede's footsteps, has identified cultural discriminators[11] by examining value-oriented differences.

Dimensions such as those identified by Hofstede are amenable to further empirical testing. They have been used extensively by international business researchers to understand variations in implementing strategies in different national contexts.[12]

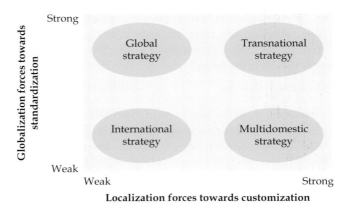

Figure 8.1 Global integration/local responsiveness grid (Adapted from Prahalad and Doz, 1987)

The four categories of obstacles to global integration identified above push organizations away from standardization towards local customization. While this means that scale advantages are harder to achieve, there are benefits of being focused more locally. These include being more responsive to customers, enabling a better understanding of their needs and being able to adapt more quickly to their demands. A useful framework for capturing this tension between the attractions of globalization and localization is captured in Prahalad and Doz's global integration/local responsiveness grid (see Figure 8.1).[13]

What Strategies Can Be Used For Competing Internationally?

First outlined in 1965, Igor Ansoff's Growth Vector Components Matrix is perhaps the first, and still one of the most useful, frameworks for thinking about development options in strategic management. Figure 8.2 shows an adapted version of the matrix with its four generic growth choices: diversification, product innovation, market innovation, and market penetration. There is a suggestion that for risk-averse companies the best pathway to adopt is to expand through market penetration as the organization is well versed in the dynamics of competition in its own sector. It is only when this route for growth becomes limited, that alternative directions should be pursued and for risk-averse companies this often means market innovation – expanding into new markets, perhaps in overseas territories but selling current products. Organizations may then wish to begin product innovations, although these can be riskier and longer term propositions than overseas expansion and finally when these avenues are becoming exhausted organizations may engage in diversification (sometimes called conglomerate diversification) – entry into new markets with new products, which is widely perceived as the riskiest growth pathway. More recent versions of the policy matrix tend to focus more upon the deployment of current capabilities and competencies but the fundamental idea of staying with what you know before expanding into the unknown, remains true. From this one can gather that overseas expansion, potentially offers a riskier route to growth than just growing in domestic markets. However if growth objectives cannot be met at home then overseas expansion is likely.

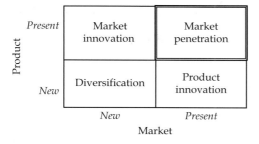

Figure 8.2 Strategic development options matrix (adapted from Ansoff, 1965)

Another way of thinking about strategic options for acquisition is to consider Figure 8.3, an adapted version of the **five forces of industry** (first outlined in Chapter 3). This shows how an acquisition can help an organization to bridge borders between itself and potential competitors, customers, suppliers, substitutes or new unrelated opportunities.

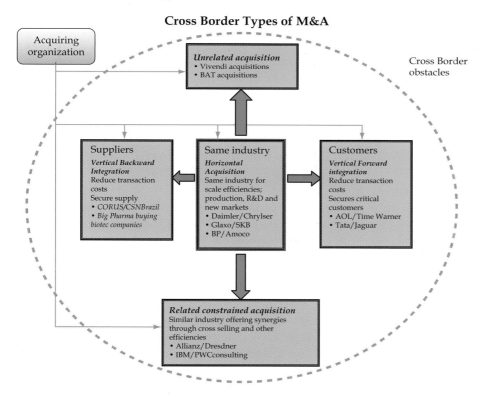

Figure 8.3 Cross border types of M&A

The degree of pressure from globalization forces requiring standardization and localization forces requiring local cultural richness will determine the strategies that organizations will adopt. Figure 8.1 identifies the following four dominant styles. **International strategy**, where organizations have (a) just begun to expand overseas but do not perceive a dominance of either dimension and (b) no need to customize a product, and its high and distinctive value gives few incentives to invest in scale economies. This may be a pre-competitive state, so new competitors may force choices. **Global strategy**, which emphasizes economies of scale through the standardization of products and services. This strategy lends itself toward high-volume production and very efficient logistics and distribution systems. A weakness is geographic concentration of such activity and isolation from target markets. **Multidomestic strategy**, which emphasizes differentiating products and services through adapting to local market needs. Customization, through tailoring packaging and service at the point of sale, incurs greater costs but there are advantages in greater flexibility and responsiveness to local demands, as well as allowing differential pricing across different markets. **Transnational strategy**, seeks to optimize the tradeoffs between global and multidomestic strategies by dispersing the organization's resources according to their most beneficial location. Typically, activities close to the customer are more decentralized and those further away are more centralized as less adaptation is required. The potential risk is whether the value of local adjustment is really realized as the successful melding together of two organizations' resources, processes and structures is needed. This requires a "recombination" capability which is vital for creating and capturing value. Successfully managing this capability is the highest order competitive advantage of the MNE and yet is very difficult to achieve as it presents a paradox – strong organizational routines are key for efficient organizational processes and yet their rigidity can also be detrimental to agile recombination. These internal tensions and their criticality are highlighted in Cummings and Angwin (2004) where different organizational approaches to the paradox are illustrated.

Which Borders Should Be Crossed?

With forces pushing organizations to expand overseas as well as opportunities attracting them to other countries, organizations need to decide on where to expand or move to, and what method(s) to use. Through entering another country, organizations ought to earn a return higher than the risk-adjusted weighted average cost of capital (**WACC**). This focuses attention on both the opportunities, in terms of market prospects and competitive conditions, as well as the risks of operating in that territory.

Analytical techniques outlined in Chapter 1 can be used to assess the dynamics of the macro-environment of a new country. There exists considerable macro data on economic variables (e.g. GDP per capita, disposable income, investment rates), social data (e.g. urbanization levels, socioeconomic distribution), demographic factors (e.g. population profile), and institutional variables (e.g. government spending, quality of infrastructure) on websites of the Economist Intelligence Unit (www.eiu.com), the World Bank (www.worldbank.org), and Business Environment Risk Intelligence (www.beri.com). These data allow regression analyses to identify drivers of spending/potential spending patterns. For instance, one important relationship recognized through this approach is the **middle-class effect**, which shows that an increase in GDP per capita can have a disproportionately larger positive effect on middle-class disposable income. A small increase in GDP, therefore, can result in great increases in spending on aspirational goods, such as digital cameras and flat screen TVs, by the middle classes.

Further insight into a country's competitive advantage can be gained through the application of Michael Porter's country Diamond.[14] The framework (introduced in Chapter 6) is based on the principle that the national environment exerts a powerful *dynamic* influence on the performance of the organization. The level of domestic rivalry in particular is critical for promoting improvements in other local factors – such as skilled labor, R&D capability, and infrastructure – and geographical concentration magnifies the interaction between these factors. The framework, while useful, has received criticism for being based on data for ten countries with greater economic strength/affluence than most countries in the world. The roles of chance and government seem to be presented in a positive way, but chance is unpredictable and both can act against the interests of business. While the Diamond is presented as a technique for national analysis, it must be applied in company specific terms because "firms, not nations, compete in international markets."[15] Porter contends that only outward foreign direct investment (FDI) is valuable in creating competitive advantage and that inbound investment or foreign subsidiaries are never a solution to a nation's problems. This conclusion has been challenged empirically.[16] The model also does not adequately address the role of the multinational enterprise (MNE) and perhaps this ought to be listed as the third outside variable. For MNEs, their competitiveness is more influenced by the configuration of Diamonds outside of their home countries and this may impinge on the competitiveness of home countries.[17] For different countries, then, different Diamonds need to be constructed and analyzed.

For smaller countries, such as Canada, Finland, and Norway, there could also be a case for using a "double Diamond."[18] Canadian organizations, for instance, needed greater economies of scale than could be obtained entirely within the domestic market. They now produce for the North American market as a whole and so are in direct competition with organizations operating in a Diamond of their own in the USA. They can no longer rely entirely upon their home country's Diamond and natural resource base. For corporate strategy this means that the two countries of Canada and USA are integrated into a single market and for this reason a Canadian/US double Diamond is appropriate.

Porter suggests that countries, and regions within countries, can form clusters that are attractive for business development. Examples of such clusters might be Silicon Valley in the USA, Sassuolo near Bologna in Northern Italy for ceramic tiles, and around Banbury, Oxfordshire, England for Formula 1 racing cars. Clusters promote competition, concentration, and reinforcement. Networks of businesses and supporting activities in a specific region, where flagship organizations compete globally, may include private and public sector organizations, think tanks, support groups, and educational institutions. It is no surprise that high-tech clusters have formed successfully around universities in the UK such as Cambridge and Oxford.

What Methods Can be Used for Crossing Borders?

Having decided on which country to enter, the organization has to decide on an entry strategy and its timing. The entry strategy will be determined by, among other things, the organization's resources and capabilities for establishing an overseas presence and the transaction costs of negotiating, monitoring, and enforcing agreements, the costs of transportation, and information costs.[19] The least exposure or involvement in the overseas country would involve licensing; a contractual arrangement whereby products/process technology are transferred to a licensee for commercial exploitation for royalties. Other methods used where direct investment is not justified include **franchising** and the use of agents and distributors. The latter two are frequently used by small and medium enterprises (SMEs), the former for the logistics of stocking, transporting, and billing, the latter more for taking orders and as a salesperson. Where low intensity of investment remains but greater ownership is required, a representative office is used. This is also a popular method, being perceived as a stepping stone for future and greater engagement. Where greater investment is intended, although ownership is limited, then the organization may engage in a **strategic alliance**, which can include a **joint venture** or being part of a **consortium**. Joint ventures are the main form of foreign direct investment in emerging markets and are often encouraged by the governments of the overseas country so that their citizens can engage in industrial development without loss of control. For the entering organizations, they gain local market knowledge and contacts with decision makers. Often joint ventures have a limited life-expectancy and can end up being wholly owned by one of the founding companies. A useful typology of joint ventures can be found in the book by Dussauge and Garrette[20] and suggestions for effective management in Hamel, Doz, and Prahalad's paper "Collaborate with your Competitors – and Win."[21]

If organizations entering a country are prepared to make a substantial investment in order to gain greater control of a cross-border development, then they may either opt for a wholly-owned subsidiary or an acquisition. Setting up a wholly-owned manufacturing facility, a green field site, is the way that Dyson, our opening example, has gone. While this is expensive and can take time, through complete ownership, the quality of production can be controlled and the Dyson vacuum cleaner can benefit from the lower cost labor force – provided local obstacles are navigated. A more popular approach, primarily because of its speed advantages, is to acquire a pre-existing local operation.

While it is easy to see how a cross-border acquisition can potentially add value it is always important to be aware of the common pitfalls that lead to such values being overestimated and underachieved. Apart from the generic reasons why acquisitions may underperform, such as inadequate due diligence, lack of integration planning, over payment, hubris, cross-border acquisitions can present additional difficulties related to the acquired organization operating in quite different political, social/cultural, economic environments. Physical distance may present coordination difficulties and finding ways in which the new organization can operate in a synchronous way across very different social/cultural landscapes can be a massive challenge. Even the most apparently trivial issues can be symptomatic of deep differences between organizations and can cause untold trouble. For instance when setting a time for a meeting, in some cultures executives will arrive well before hand in order not to miss out whereas in other cultures it would be remarkable if they managed to arrive within an hour of the prescribed time – indeed in some extreme cases, they may not even believe they need to arrive on the same day! The implications are that in order to manage cross-border acquisitions acquirers must take into consideration an additional layer of fundamental issues in order to hope for success. For a more detailed discussion of cross-border pitfalls in post-acquisition integration, see Angwin's book *Implementing Successful Post-acquisition Management*.[22]

The timing of border crossing is especially important because organizations can either aim to gain first-mover advantages or wait and become fast followers. The problems with first movers are significant investment and having to handle all uncertainties without guarantees of sufficient return. However, first movers can pre-empt resources, establish their presence in terms of brands and standards, and have a head start in understanding local needs. Fast followers often need substantial resources and different strategies from first movers. They are unlikely to be the only entrants, so competition is greater. However, they are in a position to learn from the experiences of the first mover and so reduce their risks.

How Can Organizations Retreat and Retrench Back From New Markets?

In recent times, events in Iraq have caused military, political, and even business commentators to stress the importance of having a good exit strategy. A senior CNN correspondent summed up the military lessons learnt from Iraq in the program *Crosstalk* in December 2009: "Always have a clear goal, always go in with as much force as you possibly can have [and] always have an exit strategy. Or as somebody else once said: 'You got to know when to hold 'em, know when to fold 'em, know when to walk away and know when to run'." And since the global financial crisis of 2009, this has been especially true in business strategy where the skillful management of retrenchment and divestment have become increasingly important strings to the effective strategist's bow.

Sell offs and disposals have always been part of the MNEs strategic arsenal as it competes in a game of global chess, adjusting its portfolio of commitments to reflect changing macro conditions and the actions of competitors. For larger organizational restructuring, there may be demerger where the organization breaks itself into two companies. An example is the creation of Astra and Zeneca from the company Unilever when it became apparent that separating the parent into two businesses would result in greater value than these businesses combined. More frequently large businesses see that their operations in one geographic area are beginning to underperform relative to other parts of the group, or that the operations no longer fit with the group's strategy and the decision is made to divest. This might be thought of as a proactive strategy of continuously renewing the group. It can also be that the parent is suffering from financial distress, as some large companies have undoubtedly been experiencing during the recession, and may divest in order to prevent itself from going into liquidation. Whilst the advantages of disposal are clear for the parent company the effect upon the disposed of organization may be less certain as it may have become very dependent upon resources from the parent group. There may also be significant effects upon the local overseas economy, with loss of jobs, investment, technology and economic contribution. For instance for one automotive component supplier based in Tunisia, the exit of the German owner, who was also a major customer of the business, left the local managing director with a major problem of finding new customers and paying specialized employees who could not find similar work locally. With no welfare state to support the unemployed, he felt a strong personal obligation to try to keep his workforce in employment. For large divestments local effects on employment may be severe if there had been substantial population migration to this organization in the first place as these workers may not be able to migrate back to their place of origin and re-engage with earlier activities. In many cases however large companies do not aim to brutally sever links with former subsidiaries and take significant care over trying to ensure that they can remain as viable businesses for the foreseeable future. They also have a vested interest in keeping local governments content as they may wish to engage with the country again in the future.

How Can Organizations Structure Themselves for Competing Across Borders?

As companies spread around the world, new organizational challenges arise. The need for coordinating and controlling, as well as adapting to local demands, places organizations under tension. The relative importance of each will vary depending on the nature of the industry. Where the need for global standardization (and, so, centralized control) is dominant, a centralized hub form is an ideal structure. Where local responsiveness is more important than global standardization, a decentralized federation is likely.

To reflect an equal emphasis on being global and local, a hybrid form was developed by ABB. The "matrix" structure was very popular at the end of the 1990s, with its dual command structure, in its simplest form, allowing employees to respond to both regional and product managers. However, its complexity led to internal confusion over responsibilities and absorbed a great deal of time in meetings and discussions necessary for coordination. Organizations have begun to move away from the matrix form and even ABB has now abandoned this structure. Bartlett and Ghoshal suggested an alternative for the global/local dilemma.[23] They proposed a "transnational" design, which combines functional, product, and geographic designs into networks of linked subsidiaries (see Figure 8.4). Within the network are nodes for coordination. The important feature of the transnational design is that it doesn't focus on structure but on management processes and culture. Managerial behavior is more important to them than structure and so a particular form is not prescribed.

At the heart of crossing borders, a paradox remains for managers: whether the international context is moving towards Leavitt's conformity or whether this is something of a myth, as argued by Douglas and Wind, and it will remain fragmented. Should businesses anticipate and encourage **convergence** and aim to realize global synergies, accepting some local value destruction, or exploit local diversity at the expense of global efficiencies? To some extent the answer to this question lies in the cultural richness of products and it is here that Dyson's decision, discussed at the beginning of the chapter, is seen to be based on products with little cultural richness. The opportunities to reduce costs for Dyson outweighed the value of localization. Dyson also recognized that global business is dynamic and that all organizations have to continue to fight to preserve, re-animate, and grow their strategic advantages, not just in pastures old, but also in pastures new.

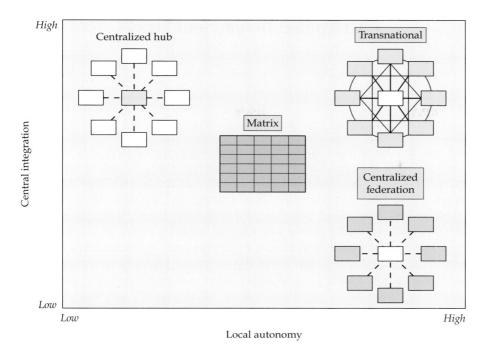

Figure 8.4 Border-crossing designs (adapted from Bartlett and Ghoshal, 1989)

> ## Crossing Borders Key Learnings Mind Map

Having read and reviewed the chapter, outline what you believe to be the key learnings from the chapter and the relationship between these.

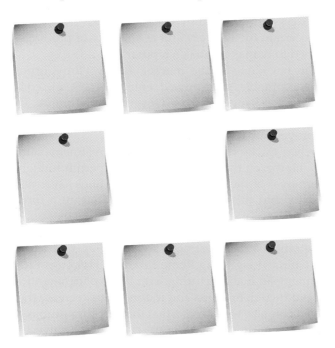

8-1 Kodak: Do you feel lucky?

"When the tiger comes down from the mountain to the plains, it is bullied by the dogs."
Chinese proverb

When you are out of your element, your power/influence is greatly diminished and yet crossing borders is about taking strategic risks. Kodak faced this challenge in 1997 when it considered how to expand further in China. In its home markets it had been experiencing slow growth and the incursions of a major competitor, Fuji. The strong dollar helped Fuji adopt a policy of aggressive price reductions and also had the effect of making Kodak's products more expensive abroad. For the fiscal year 1997, Kodak's full year earnings were down 24% and it was estimated that they had lost 3% of the consumer photo-film market.

At the same time China's photo film market was perceived to present a huge opportunity: China had a population of 1.2 billion, a GDP per head which had increased by 36% between 1990 and 1995, and increasing disposable income (as the Chinese Government covered major costs such as health and housing). Fewer than one in ten households owned a camera, and the average purchase of films was only 0.1 rolls per head, compared with 6 in the USA. The Chinese were also very brand conscious and perceived foreign goods as superior quality.

Kodak seemed well placed to take advantage of this demand. It had experience of conducting business in China since the 1920s and had been awarded a specific technology transfer project in Xiamen in 1984. However, Kodak was suffering in the market as it had to rely on a Hong Kong regional shipping company to ship products to Chinese distributors, which meant a loss of control over product quality. The excessive transit differences also increased the rate of spoilage and rendered less certain the delivery and availability of products. Such practical obstacles threatened to damage Kodak's reputation.

Kodak was also not alone in the market. Lucky Film Corporation, China's largest and most profitable state-owned enterprise (SOE), controlled 25% of the Chinese market and benefited from Government support. The Ministry for Internal Trade helped Lucky set up a national sales network to market its products and also approved substantial loans and grants.

Kodak approached Lucky by proposing large investments and taking a large share in the firm. However, the Chinese refused to permit foreign majority ownership and the removal of the Lucky brand name. Lucky was also a supplier to the Chinese military and this strategic importance meant a foreign owner was unlikely.

The other main competitor at the time was Fuji, which had adopted an aggressive market penetration and investment strategy. Fuji had a solid distribution channel through China-Hong Kong Photo Products Holdings Ltd and had made significant investments in manufacturing with the explicit intention of shifting all compact camera production to China and Indonesia to decrease the costs of manufacture. However, it was also well known that the long tumultuous history between China and Japan meant that the Chinese community (investors, consumers,

Government officials) would rather trust *Meiguo* (America/beautiful) than *Riben Guizi* (Japanese devils).

Kodak CEO, George Fisher, an executive passionate about China and with direct experience of FDI projects in his former role at Motorola, knew that Kodak had advantages over Fuji and had to expand into China, but what were the risks? Would they be lucky?

> 1. *Why is Kodak considering expanding into China?*
> 2. *In what ways might Kodak be a "tiger" in relation to local Chinese competition and why might it be that, as the Chinese proverb suggests, "although you may be a superior force, in unfamiliar territory you may be weaker than local forces"?*
> 3. *Outline the strategy that you think Kodak should pursue using insights gained from models in this chapter.*

◀◀◀ Do You Feel Lucky? Some ideas toward a "model answer"...

1. Why is Kodak considering expanding into China?

There is a mixture of push and pull factors acting on the firm. Contextual factors, such as the strengthening dollar, were favoring Kodak's competitors' aggressive pricing strategies. The overall industry was also stagnating. The evidence of the pressure was Kodak's decline in profits. In contrast, China offered a vast, largely untapped market with strong consumer demand for foreign products. The recent strong growth in GDP per capita can be assumed to have greatly increased middle-class incomes and their aspirations for Western goods meant that the sale of cameras would be likely to increase substantially.

2. In what ways might Kodak be a tiger in relation to local Chinese competition and why might it be that, as the Chinese proverb suggests, "although you may be a superior force, in unfamiliar territory you may be weaker than local forces"?

Kodak has considerable strengths as a company with international operations. Its state-of-the-art technology was superior to anything owned by the Chinese, and the firm was well resourced financially. However, operating in the Chinese market was causing Kodak's capabilities to be undermined. The practical difficulties of getting its products to the consumer in a fit state were damaging its reputation. Even though Lucky, the main player in the Chinese market, was inferior to Kodak, it had close and preferential links with the authorities, which allowed it to be subsidized and sponsored. The fact that the Chinese also did not permit foreign ownership also removed Kodak's strength as a well-resourced company to influence the situation. Perhaps in attempting to purchase a substantial share of Lucky, Kodak had been acting as a tiger?

It is worth noting that, for China, having Kodak and Fuji as two tigers was beneficial: as they fended off each other to claim the coveted venison, the Chinese deer slowly transforms into a dragon, which neither of the two can defeat – the Chinese would continue to support Lucky.

Kodak clearly began to make much more progress when they approached the Chinese situation in a culturally more sensitive way. This approach was undoubtedly helped by having a CEO who had prior experience of FDI projects in China and who was passionate about the country.

3. *What strategy should Kodak pursue?*

Given that Kodak should expand into China, there are a number of options that might be pursued. Kodak can continue to attempt to link strongly with Lucky either as a major investment partner or through some form of alliance, or indeed continue to try to persuade the Chinese authorities that some sort of merger might be in Lucky's and China's best interests. If a major commitment could be put in place, this might give Kodak a major advantage over Fuji in terms of market share as well as close links with Chinese authorities. However, there is also the risk that a major tie up may cause Kodak to be severely hampered in how its Chinese operations would actually function, and once such a large commitment was made, it might be difficult to reverse.

Kodak might decide to try to do something different and arrange joint ventures or other types of alliance with other Chinese partners. As these firms were small in size, many such alliances might be necessary to gain scale and this could take a lot of time to put in place and take considerable efforts to manage/coordinate effectively. It is unlikely that this approach would really provide robust competition for Fuji, although the size of the Chinese market and its growth rate mean that there is considerable scope for competitors at this time.

Ideally Kodak needed a step change in the size of its Chinese operations and needed to control every aspect of product quality and distribution process. While a greenfield site was not politically acceptable, negotiations with the Chinese authorities might allow a compromise that would be better options to the ones considered above. In terms of an optimal strategy, if something along these lines could be worked towards, Kodak should also be continuing talks with Lucky to prevent the chance that Fuji might take this opportunity and completely dominate the market.

Hofstede's dimensions suggest major differences between American and Chinese cultures (see Figure 8-1.1).

Substantial differences are clear for power-distance, individualism, and long-term orientation. These differences should be taken into account by the Americans (on the basis that this deal is in a Chinese context). Kodak will need to adapt its negotiation style to recognize that, for the Chinese, building trust and aiming for long-term relationships are important, underlining the key issue of long-termism. For the Americans, where there is greater emphasis on rapidity and a focus on getting a contract signed, learning to be patient is important. They must recognize that for the Chinese this is more about building a long-term relationship. The American top-down decision style and use

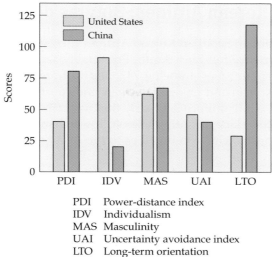

PDI   Power-distance index
IDV   Individualism
MAS   Masculinity
UAI   Uncertainty avoidance index
LTO   Long-term orientation

Figure 8-1.1 Geert Hofstede's 5D model comparing China and the USA (source: www.geert-hofstede.com/hofstede_china.shtml)

of only a few specialists in a negotiation team will be faced, provided that the negotiation is important, with a large Chinese delegation among whom decision making is consensual. To Westerners, the opaqueness of the Chinese decision-making approach will necessitate the use of Chinese experts and contacts to make headway.

▶▶▶

Case Notes:

8-2 Korean Airlines: Biggles does Korea

Flying from London to Seoul on Korean Airlines turned out to be a very interesting cultural experience for Tony Smith. Predictably for such a long flight (some 13½ hours), the aircraft was a Boeing 747, and in Korean Air livery. Passengers were greeted in Korean and English by smart and courteous cabin staff, in neatly pressed blue and white uniforms. Clearly the cabin crew was of Asian origin but while seated on the plane, awaiting takeoff, it was hard (for a Westerner) not to note the many unusual clues on-board as to the Asian-ness of the aircraft and its service.

However, after the aircraft took off, and after being lulled into this authentic Oriental ambience, Tony was suddenly subjected to a rude awakening as a clipped English public school accent punctured the air: "This is Basil your captain here. Spiffing weather today at our cruising altitude of 32,000 feet. Hope you enjoy the flight. Toodle pip!" It was hard to fathom. Surely, nobody today actually speaks like that – it was as if Biggles, the 1920s fictional flying ace, was captaining the aircraft!

The rest of the flight continued in this rather bizarre fashion, with cabin staff moving quietly, efficiently, and discreetly around the aircraft while abrupt "English toff" style interjections periodically came from the flight deck. In attempting to make sense of this incongruous mixture, Tony determined that Korean Airlines might be using a tape recording to make English-speakers feel more at ease. However, in attempting to make the commentary as English as possible, they had alighted upon a rather over-dramatic actor for impact. Why would the airline have gone to such trouble?

In the late 1990s, people became increasingly concerned about the poor safety record of Asian airlines. Of the five airlines that have had four or more serious crashes in the last decade, four of them are Asian. And researchers identified Korean Airlines as having the world's worst safety record. The airlines with the best records were mostly from Anglo-Saxon English-speaking countries like Britain, Australia, Canada, Ireland and, particularly, the USA. In 1998, *The Times* ran a story on this research with the headline "Asian culture link in jet crashes." One can begin to understand why an Asian airline might want to promote Anglo influences.

However, things may not be as clear as the first cut of the data might suggest. One London-based expert specializing in risk assessment claimed: "It is notoriously difficult, even misleading, to try to draw meaningful conclusions from 'snapshots' in aviation." And many commentators are quick to point out that the Japanese, with a similar socio-cultural background to some of the worst performers, have one of the world's best safety records. Despite these warnings, some analysts have begun to look at the extent to which national cultures affect pilot performance by comparing flight data with cultural characteristics.

Research done by Dutch academic Geert Hofstede in the 1970s and 1980s demonstrated that Asian nationals scored higher on dimensions of collectivism, power-distance, and uncertainty avoidance than their Western counterparts. Those groups that score high on *collectivism* recognize their interdependent roles and obligations to group consensus, aspects indicative of a "strong" culture. Those on the high end of the *power-distance* scale expect and accept that power is distributed unequally, accept the necessity of hierarchies, and are less likely to challenge authority. Members of high *uncertainty avoidance* cultures prefer rules and set procedures to contain and resolve uncertainty, whereas low uncertainty avoidance cultures tolerate greater ambiguity and prefer more flexibility in responding to situations.

Aviation researchers have identified that total reliance on the autopilot facility is dangerous in potential crash situations, that captains can make fatal errors of judgment that can often be corrected by other crew members, and that the speed and decisiveness of decision making is usually vital. A more recent study carried out by psychologists from the University of Texas indicates that 100% of Korean pilots claim to prefer deferring to the autopilot and always used it (the highest percentage of the 12 countries surveyed), and showed greater shame when making a mistake in front of the crew than pilots from other countries.

---

1. *Why was Tony surprised by the voice of "Biggles" during the flight to Seoul? Why would Korean Airlines be hiring British pilots?*
2. *Why might culture have been part of the explanation for the poor safety record of Korean Airlines? What other factors may also play a part?*
3. *What alternative solutions could you suggest for this safety and communication problem?*

Case Notes:

8-3 Vodafone/Mannesmann: Cultural icebergs

Vodafone PLC, under Chris Gent, chose Christmas 1999 for the launch of the biggest ever hostile takeover – an offer of DM 135bn (£83bn) for Mannesmann of North Rhine Westphalia, Germany.

The announcement of the takeover was met with something approaching hysteria in Germany, which was living through the agonies of BMW wrestling with the "English Patient" (namely, Rover Cars). At the political level, the German Chancellor, Schröder, announced: "Hostile takeovers destroy corporate culture." Similarly, Jurgen Ruttgers, leader of the CDU in the North Rhine Westphalia, said, "an unfriendly takeover *does not fit* with the rules of the social market economics which have been very successful for 50 years." Others remarked that "we should hold on to our culture and that implies our business culture as well." Indeed, drastic action was taken in the past when foreign companies aimed to buy German firms; for example, when the Austrians were close to buying the Salzgitter steel company from Preussag in North Rhine Westphalia, the regional government stepped in with DM 1bn of public money (its budget for 2000 was DM 90bn). Comments and actions such as these were bluntly criticized by European Central Bank President, Wim Duisenberg, who said they did not enhance the image of being an increasingly market-driven economy across the Euro-area.

Klaus Esser, Mannesmann's Chairman, took a contrary view, believing that national culture and historical foundations were unhelpful: "We could really do without the national pathos; it doesn't suit our time." Esser was seen as a new breed of German CEOs who were used to acquisitions, understood the concept of shareholder value, and saw the advantages of Anglo-American financial markets. Controversially, Esser publicly stated that he would fight a clean fight and would concede victory if Vodafone secured more than 50% of votes – even though in theory he could still frustrate the bid. By eschewing court actions, white knights, poison pills, and other US-style defense tactics, Esser laid the foundations for one of the cleanest, fairest, and most investor-friendly takeover battles.

For Esser, the case for keeping Mannesmann independent was based largely on the strengths of his own company's prospects. However, he also attacked Vodafone's strategy and commented on the volatility of its share price.

Esser's road show through the USA argued that Mannesmann was growing more rapidly than Vodafone (forecasting a 39% compound earnings growth for 2000–3 versus 24%), controlled leading mobile operators in three of Europe's four largest markets, and was well placed to be European partner of choice. The offer would also involve replacing Orange with Vodafone's UK business despite the former substantially outperforming the latter. In essence, Esser was arguing predominantly for **organic development** coupled with strategic alliances.

Gent decided to make the offer under German takeover rules rather than UK rules because this allowed Vodafone to raise its all-stock offer at a later stage, although Vodafone stated it had no intention of so doing. His case for the deal was that, even if Mannesmann remained independent, it would soon have to merge with a large US player to be able to compete in a fast-moving global industry. Indeed, there was concern over Vodafone's continued independence if the deal did not go through. Standing alone and waiting for some future alliance would take time in a world of mobile data and internet time, where time is of the essence. On this basis, acquisition is the only sustainable approach to growth as organic growth is too slow.

Esser lost some of the early initiative in the deal because some big Mannesmann shareholders were also concerned to protect their investments in Vodafone, which would suffer if the bid failed. In addition, the concerns of shareholder power were not as strong as in the UK and the USA, where many investors were based. Throughout the battle, there was controversy over the amount of Mannesmann shares held in Germany, with Mannesmann suggesting the figure to be around 40% whereas Vodafone believed it to be nearer 25%.

Although Mannesmann revealed excellent preliminary figures on January 7, 2000, showing a 70% rise in earnings (EBITDA) to €2.2 bn, which it argued represented outstanding results for shareholders, they were perceived as being in line with analysts' expectations and appeared to offer little additional support for Mannesmann.

To avoid falling foul of the European competition authorities, Vodafone announced its intention to spin off Orange, the UK wireless carrier.

As this was unfolding, the sentiment in the stock markets was bullish and, at the same time, a blockbusting deal between AOL and Time Warner was announced. As the elapsed time of the bid increased, both Mannesmann's and Vodafone's shares increased in value. This proved problematic for Esser, as Mannesmann's defense document stated that Mannesmann was worth €250 a share, and he was on record as saying a fair price would range from €300–350, and now they stood at around €350 a share; an increase of 46% on the price at bid launch. He therefore switched focus toward the amount of shares in the combined company that Mannesmann shareholders would receive, arguing for 58% rather than the 47.2% being offered.

On February 4, 2001, Mannesmann capitulated, with the Vodafone offer valuing Mannesmann shares at €353 and the German group's shareholders taking 49.5% of the combined company. Esser became an Executive Director on Vodafone's Board until summer and then became a non-executive Deputy Chairman. In Chris Gent's words, "It's been a long run, but it's been a pretty friendly hostile. Mannesmann – a great company – will be better with Vodafone." The new Vodafone emerges as Europe's largest publicly traded company and the world's largest telecoms group – a global giant to compete with NTT DoCoMo of Japan, WorldCom and AT&T in the USA, and Deutsche Telecom in Germany. As the undisputed champion of the European telecoms sector, it stands at the center of the continent's wireless internet revolution.

1. *Why did Vodafone launch its hostile bid to acquire Mannesmann rather than engage in an alternative strategy for cross-border growth into Germany?*
2. *Why was there German outcry at the prospect of Vodafone acquiring Mannesmann? And why did Mannesmann lose the contest anyway?*
3. *Was this a good outcome for the main stakeholders?*

8-4 Coca-Cola and Toyota:
Cola, burgers and cars

Coca-Cola's iconic worldwide campaigns – like "I'd like to buy the world a Coke," "Always Coca-Cola," and "You can't beat the Real Thing" – represented an age of global standardization and homogenization. However, Coke's new millennium began with its CEO Douglas Daft announcing the abandonment of its worldwide campaigns and global policies. According to Coke's British head of external affairs, Ian Muir, "We used to say that we thought globally and acted locally. Now we are thinking locally and acting locally." Events in Britain provide a good example of why Coke now feels the need to move this way. Perhaps the most successful soft drink in the UK in recent times has been Tango, a brand spurred on by campaigns determined to connect to the quirkier aspects of British humor. (Anyone who has seen the ads will recognize that they would not go down well in most other cultures.) Coke's global campaigns appeared bland and pallid by comparison.

Moreover, American Cola giants like Pepsi and Coke are suffering from some local consumers taking a political stand against them. Witness the growth of *Mecca-Cola* launched at the end of 2002. (Sales pitches for the brand include: "No more drinking stupid, drink with commitment" and "Don't shake me, shake your conscience.") The brainchild of French businessman Tawfik Mathlouthi, Mecca-Cola is now imported into a growing number of North African states. The first African bottling plant, recently opened in Casablanca, locally produced and sold 300,000 units in its first week and there are plans for more such operations. Similar "ideological" opponents to Coke, such as *Muslim Up* and the British-based *Qibla-Cola*, are also doing well. More humorous in its approach, but also doing well on the back of anti-American sentiment, is Turkey's *Cola Turka*. A new series of ads starring Chevy Chase show the American becoming more and more Turkish (sprouting a mustache, cooking stuffed grape leaves, and bursting into rousing Turkish songs) the more he sips on a Turka. This new campaign coincided with what was seen as the heavy-handed seizure of Turkish soldiers by US troops in northern Iraq. Cola Turka's share of the Turkish cola market is already 10%.

In response to these sorts of local uprisings, Daft's first move when he took over at Coca-Cola was to send executives out of Atlanta and closer to local customers and give creative leeway to branches to produce their own promotions. On March 27, 2000, Daft outlined his vision for the company:

> "Even though our historical strength came from operating as a 'multi-local' business that relied heavily on the insight of our local bottling partners, we knew we had to centralize control to manage expansion. [Thus], we have headed in a direction that had served us very well for several decades, generally moving toward consolidation and centralized control. That direction was particularly important when we were 'going global.'
>
> "The world, on the other hand, began moving in the 1990s in a different direction . . . as globalization accelerated, many national and local leaders understandably sought to ensure sovereignty over their political, economic, and cultural identities. As a result, the very forces that were making the world more connected and homogeneous were simultaneously triggering a powerful desire for local autonomy and preservation of unique cultural identity.

"Consequently, what we learned was that the next big evolutionary step of 'going global' now has to be 'going local.' In other words, we had to rediscover our own multi-local heritage. We must lead a Coca-Cola that not only has the expertise and structures required for success in a globalized economy, but which is also able to act nimbly and with great sensitivity in every local community where our brands are sold.

"So, we are placing responsibility and accountability in the hands of our colleagues who are closest to individual sales. We will not abandon the benefits of being global, but if our local colleagues develop a strategy that is the right thing to do locally, then they have the authority and responsibility to make it happen. Our local people are ready to take on their shoulders the authority and accountability that naturally belongs to them.

"In our recent past, we succeeded because we understood and appealed to global commonalities. In our future, we'll succeed because we will also understand and appeal to local differences. Think local, act local. The 21st century demands nothing less."

But while Coca-Cola goes local, that other American icon, McDonald's, recently surprised analysts by bucking localizing trends with its new standardized global advertising campaign.

Over nearly 50 years McDonald's knitted together one of the world's most recognizable brands on the back of campaigns created by its regional agencies that each expressed the character of the country it was marketing in. But, at the end of 2003, it unveiled a global tagline ("I'm lovin' it") and supporting series of ads for the very first time. McDonald's Executive Vice-President and Global Chief Marketing Officer, Larry Light, claimed that: "This first-of-its-kind borderless approach will let us capitalize on the powerful energy of our worldwide system."

However, some observers are questioning the merits of McDonald's adopting a global line. "People are reacting to US cultural imperialism, and what McDonald's is doing is responding by being more culturally imperialist than ever before," says one agency executive. Furthermore, Sydney-based food marketing consultant Gawen Rudder says McDonald's global campaign "is a complete disconnect" from its latest local image in Australasia. "Recently there has been a completely new look," he says. "It's a healthier, more logical, less energetic approach to the brand that has been encapsulated in Salads Plus. In the face of the debate over obesity it has been absolutely admirable." But, Rudder says, the global campaign will force two identities on the local market. "It is nice branding, slickly done, but I now have two conflicting personalities to think about. Then again, McDonald's don't make too many mistakes."

Australian marketing manager Nick Rodd is quick to downplay simplistic suggestions that the overarching borderless approach necessarily means that regional McDonald's initiatives will be stymied. "We will still do Australian campaigns," he says. Recent McDonald's advertising in the region has borne this out with the "I'm loving it" series being supported by parallel campaigns that are very local in both their form and content. Indeed, Larry Light stresses that the point of the global campaign is to give the brand a "consistent message" while at the same time allowing tailoring to regional markets to continue. In other words, the company must "Think global and local; act global and local."

Another global icon, Toyota, may represent a happy medium in this regard. After a period veering toward the world-as-one end of the scale, with an aim for "world cars" and global best practices, it is now seeking what the company sees as a perfect balance of loose and tight (or, to use their terms, integration and expansion). They describe their forces for organizational integration that stabilize the company's expansion and transformation, as being: values from the founders; up-and-in people management; and open communication. And their forces of organizational expansion in order to animate the company to instigate change and improvement as: setting impossible goals; encouraging local customization and promoting experimentation. This balance dovetails with the company's newly espoused strategy of "learning local and acting global" as they look to increase the self-reliance of overseas manufacturing facilities and to develop good ideas from anywhere.

1. *Why did Coke decide to "go local" in 2000, and what effect might that strategy have on Coke's organization structure?*
2. *Why has McDonald's persisted with a global approach and what risks does McDonald's face with this strategy?*
3. *Where would you position Coke, McDonald's, and Toyota on the global integration/local responsiveness grid? Which company do you think has adopted the best position?*

Case Notes:

8-5 Banque du Sud: Building a pan-regional actor?

In 2005 Banque du Sud (Tunisia) was acquired by AttijariWafa Bank (Morocco). This was the first time in the Tunisian privatization process that there was an acquisition into Tunisia from a south Mediterranean country (i.e. Morocco). The stated aim of this acquisition was to develop different synergies between Morocco and Tunisia in terms of expertise and know-how.

The Tunisian economy has seen sustained rises in GDP over the last few years (see Table 8-5.1) largely as a result of greater engagement with the global economy and through adopting policies designed to promote free competition with foreign markets, i.e. the Investment Code 1994 substantially improved, standardized, and codified incentives for foreign investors. Wealth in the economy at the national level has allowed the funding of large infrastructure projects in particular, and at the individual level has increased the purchasing power of Tunisia's upper and large middle class.

The signing of the *Agadir Agreement for the Establishment of a Free trade Zone between the Arabic Mediterranean Nations* (Tunisia, Jordan, Egypt, Morocco) in Rabat, Morocco February 2004, aims at establishing a free trade area as a possible first step toward establishing a Euro–Mediterranean free trade area. This agreement is widely perceived as a likely driver for regional business development and may also result in the modernization of sectors.

For some time the Tunisian Government has been actively encouraging selected foreign direct investment (FDI), particularly for export-oriented industries. It screens potential FDI to minimize the impact of the investment upon domestic competitors and employment.

A large part of this FDI has been from Tunisia's privatization program which sells off state-owned or state-controlled firms. The program began in 1987 with the sale of the smallest and least viable public sector enterprises, but now includes

Table 8-5.1 The Tunisian economy (Tunisian dinar = TND)

	2003	2004	2005
GNP constant value			
(TND millions)	19,348	20,517	21,384
GNP growth rate	5.6%	6.0%	4.2%
Inflation rate	2.4%	3.6%	2.0%
Investment (TND millions)	7,536	7,913	8,410
Savings (TND millions)	7,122	7,799	7,968
Exports	10,342	12,054	13,607
Imports	14,038	15,960	17,101
Tourism revenue	1,902	2,290	2,564

CROSSING BORDERS

major state assets such as Tunisie Telecom and there has been partial sale of the national petroleum distribution company (SNDP), the State automobile manufacturer (STIA), and a planned sale of 76.3% in Magasin General, the Government's 43-store supermarket chain. Every year the Ministry of Development and International Cooperation and the Foreign Investment Promotion Agency (FIPA) hold an investment promotion event, the Carthage Investment Forum, to introduce Tunisian business opportunities to global investors. In 2006 total FDI amounted to USD 15 bn, contributed to the creation of over 2,600 companies and some 250,000 jobs. Total FDI in 2005 was USD 750 m.

The largest single foreign investor to date in Tunisia is British Gas, developing an offshore gas field for USD 1.1 bn. Many of the worlds largest multinationals are also invested in Tunisia, i.e. Siemens, Sony, Philips, Pirelli, Fiat, Nestle, and Citibank. Spain continues to be a big investor in Tunisia and in order to achieve a more level playing field for US companies, the USA has begun a process of establishing a Free Trade Agreement (FTA).

The mobilization and allocation of investment capital is still hampered by the underdeveloped nature of the local financial system. The stock and bond markets find it hard to attract investor interest and are currently flat. Foreign investors can purchase shares in Tunisian firms but they have to do this through authorized brokers or indirectly through established mutual funds. Capital controls are still in place.

The banking system is considered generally sound and is improving as the central bank has begun to enforce adherence to international norms for reserves and debt. Recent measures include strengthening the reliability of financial statements, enhanced credit risk management and improved creditors' rights. There are now tighter rules on investments and bank licensing and the required minimum risk-weighted capital/asset ratio has been raised to 8%, consistent with the Basel Committee capital adequacy recommendations. Today 13 of the country's 14 banks conform to this ratio (compared with just 2 in 1993). Despite these strict new requirements, many banks still have substantial amounts of non-performing or delinquent debt in their portfolios. The Government has established debt recovery entities to buy up these non-performing debts but there is no information on how successful this has been.

Despite privatization, the Government remains dominant in the banking sector controlling 11 out of 20 commercial and development banks. However, foreign participation in the capital of banks has risen significantly and now stands well over 20%.

The Banque du Sud was set up in 1968 and at the end of 2005 had a registered capital of 100 million dinars (USD 1 = TND 1.25 approximately). The bank had 89 branches throughout Tunisia and held a 10% market share. Turnover in 2002 was TND 129 m, resulting in after-tax profits of TND 10.2 m. It was recognized at the time that Banque du Sud had a substantial branch network and a large and diverse customer portfolio. It had a large presence in international trade and this offered significant potential for future development. Banque du Sud was engaged in every customer segment but it also had a high proportion of doubtful or uncertain credits and its ratios had been declining for some time as the competition in the banking sector was increasing. Although the bank was in a poor financial situation it did have devoted employees. However, the management of these human resources appeared weak with bad communications and poor or old systems. For instance, there were no assessment systems to evaluate the competency and skill of employees. Whilst under state control the level of investment in information systems had been low and there had been little need for clear direction for the bank. However, now with a deregulating economy and the likelihood of increasing bank regulations in the future, the Banque du Sud faced a major challenge.

By international standards, Morocco's banking system is reasonably well developed and regulated. Recently consolidations have resulted in six large banks (Attijariwafa, CPM, BMCE, BMCI, SGMB, CDM) controlling 80% of loans and 88.3% of total deposits. The banking sector is divided into four categories:

1. Deposit taking banks: the five large privately owned banks; Attijariwafa; BMCE; BMCI; SGMB; CDM
2. Credit Populaire du Maroc: a mutual company and the leader in deposit taking from Moroccans living abroad (the State is the majority shareholder)
3. Specialized financial institutions: CIH; Credit Agricole du Marcoc
4. Niche banks: Bank Al Amal; Media Finance; Casablanca Finance.

Foreign banks are strongly present in the private banks holding significant share stakes, i.e. BNP Paribas controls 65.1% of BMCI; Société Générale de France owns 51.6% of SGMB; Grupo Santander holds 14.6% of Attijariwafa.

With assets of 146.8 billion Moroccan Dirhams (MAD) (equivalent to USD 16.7 bn with MAD 8.8 = USD 1, as at June 30, 2006), AWB is Morocco's largest private sector bank. Attijariwafa Bank was formed in June 2004 in course of the restructuring of the banking sector by a merger of Wafa Bank and Banque Commerciale du Maroc. With over one million customers, the bank claims a domestic market share of some 25%.

AWB is listed on the Casablanca stock exchange and is the second largest firm by capitalization. It is fully owned by private Moroccans and foreign investors. The biggest stakes are held by Groupe ONA (33.1%) and Banco Santander (14.6%). Groupe Ona is controlled by the Moroccan royal family.

AWB is a Universal bank with strengths in corporate banking and subsidiaries in consumer and mortgage lending (where it has 27% and 20% of the market respectively), leasing, factoring, asset management and investment banking. AWB has a domestic branch network of 540 branches. AWB also has a presence in Senegal (it acquired Banque Senegalo-Tunisienne in late 2006) and is currently looking to expand into Algeria. AWB has a presence in Europe through a 100% owned subsidiary and this gives good access to Moroccan expatriates. They have 360,000 customers with total deposits of MAD 24 bn as at June 30, 2006.

Since its merger with Wafa Bank and tougher economic conditions in Morocco, AWB has had to book large provisions over the last three years but since 2005, higher credit volumes, stronger earning diversification and better cost control has improved profitability and asset quality. AWB is now well placed in retail banking to capture additional earning streams from the emerging lucrative consumer banking segment in Morocco. This should help to reduce the bank's concentration for risk in corporate lending. The bank's funding and liquidity profile is strong due to good access to retail deposits, including Moroccan expatriates and large government bond holdings.

AWB has completely rethought its organizational structure to place the customer at the heart of its concerns in order to enhance cross-selling, to improve levels of service and to develop specialist expertise. The group is organized now in six independent business units each with its own resources. The main guiding principals are: strengthen management; develop a performance driven culture; encourage employees to take more responsibility; increase powers of delegation; make the execution process more professional by better internal controls.

AWB has two main objectives:

1. Enhance the bank's position in Morocco, especially in retail and small and midsized enterprise segments as well as investment banking.
2. Strengthen its position outside of Morocco, mainly in the expatriate segment but also North and West Africa.

AWB plans to increase its branch network to 900 branches and 2.5 million customers by 2010 and wishes to control one-third of the Moroccan mortgage and personal loan segments. AWB plans to consolidate its relationship with large firms, enhance cross selling and fee rich transactions – this might help improve the quality of its loan portfolio and profitability.

To develop its strong position outside of Morocco, AWB plans to further enhance its share of expatriate business through its French subsidiary. It already has 26.4% of expatriate deposits which provides AWB with a comparative advantage. It also intends to expand its mortgage business by offering loans to customers wishing to purchase property in Morocco. Having an international presence helps AWB to serve the needs of some of its larger clients. AWB has a more developed appetite for expansion in North and West Africa than its competitors but its presence in these countries has never been tested by an economic downturn. The credit culture in these countries remains weak and there could be problematic exposure to credit and foreign exchange risk.

In 2005, Attijariwafa with Santander bank acquired 53.54% of Banque du Sud capital, in Tunisia, as part of its expansion plan. Approximately USD 45 mn was paid for the state's 34% share of the bank's capital and a further 17% was purchased from a private Tunisian group. "We and our strategic partner Santander bought the stake from the Tunisian government under privatization," said Wafa Guessous, Attijariwafa Bank's Public Relations Manager. "We want to make Banque du Sud a leader in retail banking and in financial and trade flows between Morocco, Tunisia and Spain," she added.

The new Managing Board of the bank now ordered an exhaustive audit of the acquired bank to identify priorities and to strike a balance between shareholders, customer and wage earner interests. They aimed to create a strategic plan which would make the bank a "famous local actor". Through this plan the bank wants to participate in the economic development of Tunisia and to adopt the logic of economic cooperation between Maghreb countries. However despite these well intentioned broad aspirations, the Board knew it had to take specific actions in order for the acquisition to be successful. There were questions to consider about all aspects of the business – who would lead it? How would know-how transfer actually take place? How would AWB really benefit from the acquisition? Why did AWB think it could manage Banque du Sud better than it had been managed before?

Tunisian Banking Industry Comparative data

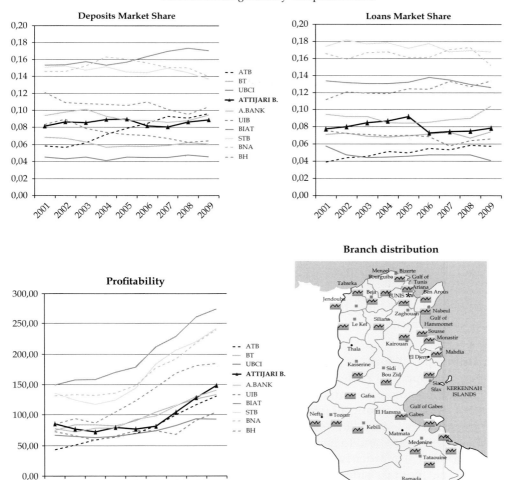

Figure 8-5.1 Tunisian banking industry: comparative data

1. *Why did AWB want to acquire Banque du Sud? Why were the Tunisian authorities happy to let the purchase take place?*
2. *How should AWD go about integrating Banque du Sud? What key actions should they take in the integration process? On what basis can they decide what needs to be done?*
3. *Has the acquisition been successful?*

CROSSING BORDERS

8-6 Red Cross/Red Crescent: Humanitarian movement across boundaries

The Red Cross is one of the world's most recognizable symbols alongside corporate brands like Ford, Coca-cola and Apple. However, the organization that it symbolizes is not a single multinational structure under the command of CEO and a Board of Directors. Indeed, the often heard "International Red Cross" is something of a misnomer as no official organization bearing that name actually exists. Rather the Red Cross "Movement's" nearly 100 million volunteers and 12,000 full-time staff spread around the world are coordinated by a number of distinct and legally separate organizations that are united by common basic principles, objectives, symbols and statutes.

At "the sharp end", as it were, is the International Committee of the Red Cross (ICRC), a private humanitarian institution whose 25-member committee has unique authority under international humanitarian law to protect the life and dignity of the victims of armed conflicts. The ICRC is the lead organization in coordinating humanitarian relief in armed conflict situations.

On the ground are the 186 national Red Cross and Red Crescent Societies, each of which works in slightly different ways according to their specific circumstances and capabilities but all of which are united by the Movement's seven fundamental principles, which are summarized below:

Humanity   We act to prevent and alleviate human suffering wherever it may be found; to protect life and health and to ensure respect for the human being; to promote mutual understanding, friendship, cooperation and lasting peace among all peoples.

Impartiality   We relieve the suffering of individuals, being guided solely by their needs, and to give priority to the most urgent cases of distress.

Neutrality   In order to continue to enjoy the confidence of all, the Movement may not take sides in hostilities or engage at any time in controversies of a political, racial, religious or ideological nature.

Independence   The National Societies must always maintain their autonomy so that they may be able at all times to act in accordance with the principles of the Movement.

Voluntary service   A voluntary relief movement not prompted in any manner by desire for gain.

Unity   There can be only one Red Cross or one Red Crescent Society in any one country. It must be open to all.

Universality   The International Red Cross and Red Crescent Movement, in which all Societies have equal status and share equal responsibilities and duties in helping each other, is worldwide.

Under the Geneva Convention, relief workers from National Societies bearing Red Cross and Red Crescent authorized symbols are protected under international law and must be granted free access to people in need of help.

And, in the middle of the Movement there is the IFRC (International Federation of Red Cross and Red Crescent Societies). The IFRC manages and coordinates the activities of the National Societies. It is also the lead organization in missions not related to armed conflicts and organizes interaction and cooperation with the ICRC. The IFRC is primarily funded by contributions from the National Societies. Its executive body is a secretariat led by a Secretary General supported by four division heads but the highest body in the IFRC is the General Assembly which convenes every two years with delegates of all the National Societies.

The Red Cross Movement began in 1862, when Geneva businessman Henry Dunant had a global idea. The resources of the many Red Cross Societies that had emerged in different countries by this time could be pooled to provide humanitarian assistance in peacetime and not just to provide medical aid in times of war. Dunant wrote that "These Societies could also render great services, by their permanent existence, in times of epidemics, or of disasters such as floods, fires or other natural catastrophes."

Further impetus was given to this idea by Henry Davison, president of the American Red Cross War Committee. In December 1918, responding to US President Woodrow Wilson's call for ideas as to how the world might be better managed after World War I, Davison proposed a league of the world's Red Cross Societies as a parallel to the League of Nations that Wilson had advocated. On May 5, 1919, the governors of the Red Cross Societies of France, Italy, Japan, the United Kingdom, and the United States signed the original Articles of Association.

Perhaps the thorniest issue for the IFRC as it has expanded its reach, relates to its identity, or what a for-profit organization might more readily call its "brand." The red cross on a white background was the originally adopted symbol declared at the 1864 Geneva Convention, In terms of its color it is a reversal of the Swiss national flag, a meaning that was adopted to honor Dunant's, and the Movement's, Swiss heritage.

However, this symbol raised issues as early as 1876 when members of the Turkish Society took the view that the red cross (redolent of the Christian Crusades in medieval times) would alienate Muslim soldiers during the Russo-Turkish war and adopted the Red Crescent symbol as an alternative. When asked by the ICRC, the Russians agreed to respect the sanctity of people under the Red Crescent banner and the Ottomans reciprocated by accepting the sanctity of those operating under the Russian Red Cross. After this local declaration of the equal validity of both symbols, the ICRC declared that it should be possible to adopt an additional protection symbol for non-Christian countries, and the Crescent was formally adopted in 1929 when the Geneva Conventions were amended. Currently the Red Crescent is the symbol used by 33 of the Movement's 186 National Societies.

However, wary that further proliferation of symbols could be problematic (both in terms of the unity of the Movement and of people being able to recognize and respect those acting under its banner and its principles), the ICFC and the IFRC have since rejected a number of further applications to incorporate different symbols into the Movement, such as the Red Archway proposed by Afghanistan in 1935, the Red Lamb proposed by the Republic of Congo in 1963, and the Red Wheel proposed by India after Indian independence. In such instances, following the rejection of their claims, each of the National Societies concerned has agreed to use either the Red Cross or the Red Crescent as their symbol.

More problematic though, was the Israeli Society's (known as Magen David Adom – MDA) Red Shield of David. The ICRC and the IFRC's rejection of the Red Shield (in the shape of the Star of David) and MDA's desire to keep it, led to the ICRC and IFRC not officially recognizing MDA as part of the Movement for many decades. In protest at their exclusion, the American Red Cross Society had been withholding its financial contribution to the IFRC since 2000. By 2008 this had amounted to USD 45 m.

The impasse was only resolved in 2008 when an alternative third symbol, the Red Crystal (effectively a red diamond shape in outline) was proposed and voted in by over the required two-thirds majority by delegates at a Red Cross and Red Crescent assembly conference. At the same time Magen David Adom and the Palestinian Red Crescent Society (which had been excluded previously by the statute that only societies from sovereign nations be allowed to join the IFRC) were officially admitted to the Movement.

The Red Crystal can be used by any relief teams in areas where there is sensitivity about Christian or Muslim symbols. Members of MDA will be able to work across borders under the Red Crystal banner. On their own territory – or with the agreement of other states participating in relief operations abroad – they will be able to fly a flag with the Red Shield of David within the Red Crystal shape.

Discussions are now taking place as to whether other National Societies may use their own local symbols within the Red Crystal on their home territories.

1. *What advantages do you think have accrued in pursuit of the Red Cross Movement's global aims by allowing individual societies to choose whether they wish to use the Red Cross or Red Crescent symbols? Are there any disadvantages?*
2. *Do you agree with the decision taken in 2006 to allow the Red Crystal as a third symbol and as a way of allowing Magen David Adom to become a fully fledged member of the IFRC? Give reasons for your answer.*
3. *What insights do you take from this case about how organizations might project a consistent corporate identity across national borders?*

Case Notes:

8-7 HSBC: The world's local bank

From humble beginnings as a regional bank established in 1865 to finance international trade along the coast of China, HSBC (Hong Kong Shanghai Banking Corporation) has grown astronomically over the past decade. It has grown both organically and through astute acquisitions to become one of the world's biggest companies. From its early history as a collection of banks connected through British Empire or Commonwealth ties (early principal members included The British Bank of the Middle East, The Saudi British Bank, and the Cyprus Popular Bank), HSBC now employs over 200,000 staff based in 87 countries and territories. The recent growth spurt can be traced to 1991, with the formation of HSBC Holdings, a holding company for the entire group with its headquarters in London and its shares quoted in London, Hong Kong, and New York.

Unusually for a company of its size, however, HSBC has always championed the importance of local diversity rather than the importance of scale. In the words of Group Chief Executive Stephen Green, "We do not aspire to be a unicultural company." This is down to the belief that, according to former Group Chairman John Bond: "People do not appreciate the one size fits all approach commonly associated with global corporations."

But how do you continue to grow and coordinate and focus a company that operates across so many borders? One way was to adopt a unified brand. This brand, featuring the letters HSBC next to a red and white hexagon (a stylized version of the original 19th-century HSBC flag based on the cross of St. Andrew) was launched in 1998. Within a couple of years, this symbol and the letters HSBC were well recognized, but according to HSBC's then Head of Marketing, Peter Stringer, people were not really sure what the letters stood for. They weren't sure about the values or the character behind the HSBC name and symbol.

At around about this time, a group of UK-based HSBC executives on an executive development program settled down to discuss the ethos of their corporation and its current strategy. As part of an exercise they began to think of the HSBC in terms of its personality. In other words, to think on the question: "If our company was a person, what kind of person could it and should it be?"

While this was not an easy task, one thing that surfaced very quickly in the ensuing discussion was that these executives were sure that one of their leading competitors had recently got its "personality" all wrong. Barclays Bank had just launched a media campaign extolling the virtues of its "bigness." Celebrities like Anthony Hopkins and Robbie Coltrane told the camera that "people want things 'big' – and they want a big bank." According to the HSBC executives, while people may have wanted some of the benefits that a big bank offered, they also liked the idea of dealing with a bank that "felt" small and valued particular personal relationships.

Eventually, having split themselves into three smaller groups, each group came up with a possible personality: James Bond, the current CEO of the Bank, and Michael Palin.

After some discussion, Palin was thought best. Although the idea of Bond appealed to many, particularly the male members of the team, it was quickly decided that while his British, suave demeanor and his unruffled "shaken not stirred" character could fit nicely, his risk-taking and attitude to women (an interesting character to have a "fling" with, but not a very safe long-term bet) probably did not fit the image the bank wanted to present. Many thought that having a well-liked CEO step forward and lead the company from the front, in the spirit of Victor Kiam or Richard Branson, would have been particularly powerful. However, others countered that his personality could be problematic given that it was not well known to those outside the company and that the "heart" would be pulled out of the corporation when he, eventually, left. So, in the end it was Palin – the decent, good-humored, charitable, stoic, and curious ex-Monty Python turned world-traveling documentary maker – who won out. (If you are unfamiliar with Michael Palin, you may want to consult www.palinstravels.co.uk/.) He was British, but had made a second career of combining this very British nature with embracing foreign cultures and appearing completely sympathetic to their differences. His TV shows were the epitome of the "when in Rome..." ethos. He was also, said one manager, "a nerd, but with a broad good nature and a sense of humor underneath it – unlike James Bond you can associate this with a bank. Particularly with our bank."

The executives placed Palin firmly in the middle of the conventional competitive advantage distinction between costs and differentiation. "It's a very Palin-like position," said one manager. "He just understands different perspectives." This was something also indicated by his wide-ranging appeal ("you can watch his show with the kids and even teenagers kind of like him because of the Monty Python connection").

"I guess this fits with our strategy," another manager continued. "Like all banks we're increasingly having to cut processing costs. Globalization is increasingly giving up opportunities to do that. At the moment we're switching a lot of our data processing and clearing stuff to India and places like that."

Another interjected: "But we maybe have to be careful about this, what with concerns with business ethics and so on."

"Sure, sure, we can't abuse different people – maybe the Palin image can help us to formulate our approach to that. No matter what, though, we have to cut costs to compete. But, at the same time, one of the strongest things our market research is telling us is that most of our customers like having a branch. They like the idea of a branch manager or someone they can talk to in a branch about what concerns them. So, one of the ways that we are going to try to differentiate ourselves increasingly is by having a strong local branch presence while others are closing theirs down. So I guess what I'm saying is that we have to look both ways – toward new suppliers for cost saving and to existing and new customers to differentiate, even though keeping the branches open and staffed costs us a lot."

There was general agreement about this logic. Another manager expanded on it: "And we do, through our traditional presence on the world's high streets, have a broad appeal – in fact we have to cover a lot of fixed costs so we really have to be broad to shift the 'units' needed to perform."

Nobody present knew whether Mr. Palin would have been available to approach with a proposal that could have led to these ideas being used in a public arena. But perhaps this didn't matter. A group of managers had a clearer idea of what their organization was and what it was not and could, from there, begin to think about how they would move into the future.

And, indeed, future developments at HSBC, while not involving Mr. Palin, did increasingly seem to bear the stamp of his spirit.

In 2002 a new advertising campaign was developed, with the strap-line "HSBC: The World's Local Bank." This campaign, with which you are probably already familiar, focuses on how things are done differently, or how the same things can mean different things, in different local contexts. The television ads in particular follow a travelog style and ethos that is very Palin-esque. Thus, they illustrate the importance of HSBC's "local knowledge and tailored service" approach. According to Head of Marketing, Peter Stringer, the campaign "makes a clear and powerful statement of what we stand for . . . we think the world is a diverse place, full of interesting people, and it is these people that we want to help go about their business." Beyond these initial campaigns HSBC advertising has continued to play upon the way that different people in different places see and do things differently and how this makes the importance of global reach and local knowledge key. These ads are perhaps most recognizable in airports around the world with HSBC perhaps more than any other company seeking to be the most visible advertiser in these trans-border locations.

On a more practical level, too, the Palin ethos of respecting and learning from local cultural norms seems to be ringing true. For example, recent initiatives include:

- having specialist branches in the UK for Indian businesses;
- establishing a north London branch, situated among a large orthodox Jewish population, that opens on Sundays;
- being the only UK high street bank to offer a *sharia*-compliant mortgage for Muslim customers;
- operating a number of women-only branches in Saudi Arabia.

Moreover, the past few years have witnessed HSBC increasing its investment in local philanthropic initiatives. For instance, it spent over USD 34 m on a wide range of educational and environmental projects in 2003.

And finally, in introducing the publication of a new history of HSBC in 2004, Group Archivist Edwin Green emphasized that "We are international in a way very few companies of any kind can claim. What is distinctive about the group is not how early it gets into markets, but that it stays with them through thick and thin: crises, wars, emergencies, social upheaval, HSBC has seen them all."

1. *HSBC has grown primarily through acquisitions. What are the virtues of this approach?*
2. *Why was Michael Palin the best choice of corporate identity for HSBC?*
3. *In 2001, British retailer Marks & Spencer developed the tagline "exclusively for everyone" which was widely criticized for being illogical and impossible to live up to. Can HSBC really compete effectively by championing local diversity and yet proclaiming itself as a global bank?*

California sunlight, sweet Calcutta rain,
Honolulu starbright, the song remains the same.

Led Zeppelin

You can never step into the same river twice.

Heraclitus

Wisdom lies neither in fixity nor in change, but in
the dialectic between the two.

Octavio Paz

9
Guiding Change

Any strategic development will, of necessity, involve managing some degree of change to structures, technologies, products, services, culture, or processes. But over the past two decades the flow of change that organizations have sought to keep pace with has increased dramatically – to the point, indeed, where commentators like Christopher Bartlett and Sumantra Ghoshal have claimed that the levels of change have in many instances outpaced the human capability to cope with change.[1] While organizations must move to keep pace with a changing environment, the strategist must also ensure constancy and consistency with regard to stakeholder relationships and corporate character, among other things. The change management challenge paradoxically requires ensuring both movement and stability in optimal measure.

Since the 1980s there has been a dramatic expansion in the number of ideas and frameworks to deal with guiding change. These can be divided into two camps: conventional or straightforward "one-best way" methods, or frameworks that promote more nuanced or differentiated approaches.

Conventional or 'Straightforward' Approaches to Managing Change

Despite a great expansion in numerical output, a review reveals a similarity among conventional approaches to managing change. This can be seen by the way that John Kotter's method, currently the most widely used framework for managing change, replicates most of what has been said in applied management fora on this subject.[2] Kotter claimed that a successful change process goes through a series of **eight steps of change**. These steps are shown at the top of Figure 9.1. Other commentators may have outlined their ideas about managing change in other ways, but they are easily assimilated into Kotter's steps.[3]

The main reason for the homogeneity of conventional change management theories in the 1980s and 1990s may be history. In the early 1950s, Lewin discovered what textbooks to this day call the three basic steps that summarize what's involved in the process of changing people and organizations: unfreezing → moving → refreezing.[4] Figure 9.1[5] shows how others (all the way up to Kotter in the mid-1990s) would subsequently follow Lewin's lead, building on his classical approach, adding details or splitting levels but maintaining Lewin's three simple steps. This homogeneity is underpinned by a number of assumptions about change:

- Change is a generalizable linear input → process → output process: hence we can determine "one-best way" approaches to it.
- Change comes from the top or outside in and then works its way down. In Kotter's (1995) words, top people must firstly provide a vision for change.
- We can break down the complexity of change into its "component parts" that can then be ordered into a series of steps.
- Change and constancy are seen as an either/or choice: conventional approaches would have difficulty comprehending the quotation by Octavio Paz at the head of this chapter.

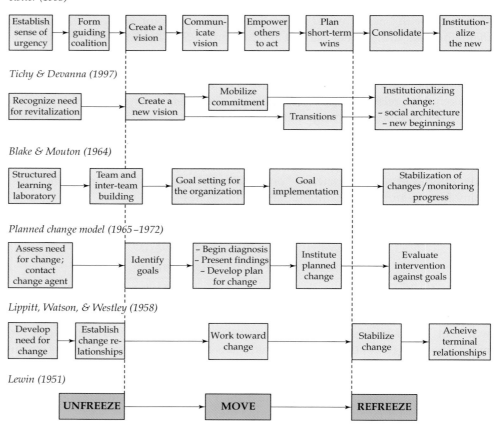

Figure 9.1 The incremental development of conventional change management frameworks since 1950 (Source: Cummings, 2002)

While almost all of the authorities mentioned above and in the related notes are American, Kotter's eight steps seemed to also ring true with the best of European theory. Pettigrew and Whipp's *Managing Change for Competitive Success* presents ideas very similar to Kotter's eight steps. In a study of competitive change in a number of UK industries, Pettigrew and Whipp identified nine key aspects: (1) building a receptive context for change, legitimization; (2) creating a capacity for change; (3) constructing the content and direction of change; (4) operationalizing the change agenda; (5) creating a critical mass for change within senior management; (6) communicating the need for change and detailed requirements; (7) achieving and reinforcing success; (8) balancing the need for continuity and change; and (9) sustaining coherence.[6] Of these nine steps, the only thing that the American works generally do not incorporate is the notion of "balancing continuity and change."

All of these straightforward general models can be used effectively to develop and communicate change programs. However, given that we can now see them as somewhat similar, and hence limited, perhaps we should look at additional frameworks that may inspire us to think about managing strategic change differently.

Unconventional, or Nuanced, Frameworks for Guiding Change

The frameworks for guiding the management of change outlined in the section above are both useful and heavily used. They are used because they are simple, easy to remember, and easy to communicate. However, often managing change is not so straightforward. No two change initiatives are exactly the same and the following differences are worth investigating:

- Change occurs at *different* organizational and conceptual levels.
- There are often *different* needs and objectives that organizations are seeking to achieve and subsequently *different* styles of crafting change.
- Change can be instigated by *different* types of individuals or groups.
- Change initiatives meet with *different* forms of resistance that the skillful strategist will want to take account of.
- Finally, human nature and capabilities require that change be combined with continuity, to *different* extents, depending on the circumstances.

These complexities, which require good managers to take a more dexterous or nuanced approach, rather than just implement an eight- or nine-step plan, are explored in more detail in the sections that follow.

Different Levels of Change

Change can occur at different conceptual or practical levels. Mintzberg and Westley's framework (see Figure 9.2) provides a useful means of separating out, and seeing the interrelationships between, the more organizational versus the more strategic aspects of change and relating these to different levels of thought

	Changes in organization	Changes in strategy
More conceptual (thought)	Culture	Vision
↕	Structure	Positions
	Systems	Programs
More concrete (action)	People	Facilities

Figure 9.2 Strategic changes related to organizational changes (Source: adapted from Mintzberg and Westley, 1992)

versus action.[7] For example, changing an organization's vision for the future will necessitate changing the organization's culture if this new vision is to be achieved, all of which will require a lot of conceptual work. This should then trickle down to more practical, but congruent, actions relating to the organization's facilities and people or human resources to ensure consistency of corporate identity.

Degree of change	Level of change	Characteristics
Status quo	Can be both operational and strategic	No change in current practices. A decision not to do something can be strategic as well as operational
Expanded reproduction	Mainly operational	Change involves producing "more of the same" goods or services etc.
Evolutionary transition	Mainly strategic	Sometimes radical changes occur but they do so within the existing parameters of the organization (e.g., existing structures or technologies are retained)
Revolutionary transition	Predominantly strategic	Change involves shifting or redefining existing parameters. Structures, processes and/or technologies likely to change.

Figure 9.3 Levels of operational and strategic change (Source: adapted from Wilson, 1992)

It can also be useful to develop a clearer understanding of whether what is envisaged is a more strategic- or more operational-level change, and what differences of approach this might necessitate before embarking on the change. For this purpose David Wilson's framework, pictured in Figure 9.3, is very helpful.[8]

Different Change Needs and Styles

Different organizations in different settings have different needs for change. For example, organizations in industries or societies that are quickly undergoing fundamental changes may require a complete *revolutionary* **transformation**,

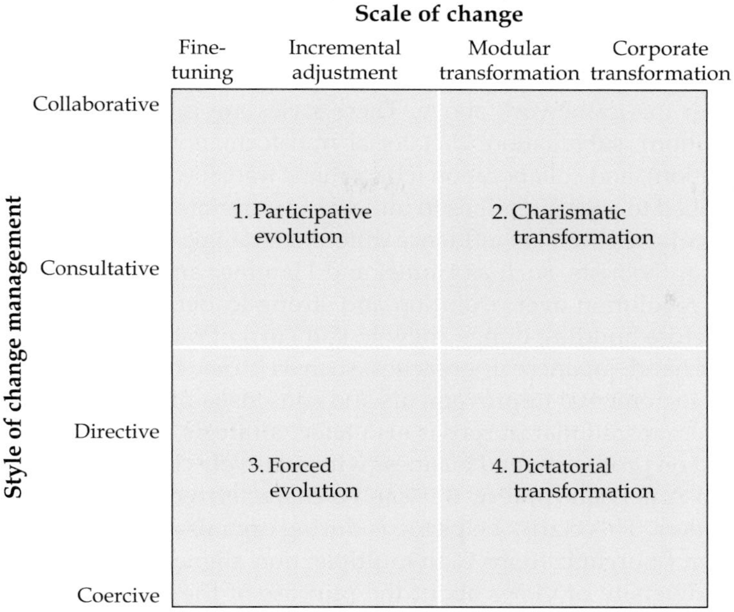

Scale of change

Figure 9.4 Different scales and styles of change (Source: adapted from Dunphy and Stace, 1990)

a change program that is broad in scope, necessitating sharp changes to most if not all of its procedures. Where the firm is facing collapse, its turnaround would necessitate revolutionary change – a complete rethinking of the nature of the business and how it competes, and radical and immediate surgery for survival.[9] In a calmer setting or a more conservative industry, a more *evolutionary* **transformation** and some fine-tuning to just a few aspects of the organization's activities will be more appropriate. Figure 9.4 provides a useful means of characterizing different change needs and then thinking through the sort of management approaches and programs required to satisfy those needs.[10]

There are four main styles of change:

1. **Participative evolution** is appropriate when the organization is either "in fit" with its environment, or it is "out of fit" but time is available, and key interest groups favor change.
2. **Charismatic transformation**, led by a popular **change agent**, is appropriate when the organization is out of fit, the need to change is urgent, and key interest groups or stakeholders support substantial change.
3. **Forced evolution**, driven by a strong leader, is appropriate when the organization is either in fit but needs minor adjustments or is out of fit and, although time is available, key stakeholders oppose change.
4. Widespread **dictatorial transformation**, imposed from above, is appropriate where the organization is out of fit, time is short, and key stakeholders oppose change.

A particular context where there are varying needs for change is *post-acquisition* integration. The target company has been acquired but will have different degrees of organizational and strategic fit with the acquiring company and varying amounts of time available for change. Duncan Angwin (2000)[11] has developed a contingency framework based on post-acquisition change in UK mergers and acquisitions and suggests **four types of post-acquisition integration style** which resonate with the framework above. These styles are isolation (which would be forced evolution), subjugation (dictatorial transformation), maintenance (participative evolution), and collaboration (charismatic transformation). Figure 9.4 can be usefully applied to such situations to indicate appropriate styles of change.

Different cultures can also influence different strategic change styles. For example, American theorists, such as Hamel and Hammer and Champy, have tended to advocate revolution over evolution and strong leaders wiping the slate of the past clean before building things anew to suit current rather than former needs.[12] On the other hand, Japanese approaches, such as *kaizen*, have favored slower evolutionary or incremental improvements and consensus-driven change.[13]

Different organizational purposes also affect strategic change styles. So far we have focused on profit-oriented business with relatively clear objectives and aims – in the Anglo-American context, this can be characterized as the pursuit of profit for shareholders. This clarity helps focus during organizational change. However, for not-for-profit organizations with multiple, non-aligned stakeholder pressures, reflecting a diversity of views about the purpose of the organization (where the customers are not so much the marketplace as the provider of funds), this coherence may not be achievable, raising huge challenges for organizational change. If there is any doubt about the massive complexity and difficulties involved in changing not-for-profit organizations, one only has to look at the agonies of the UK National Health System, the problems of improving state education, and the consequences of privatizing the national railway system.

Different Instigators of Strategic Change

We tend to associate strategic change initiatives with those at the top of an organization. While executives and the roles they play do have a large influence on how change is enacted in an organization, the dexterous manager of strategic change will recognize that change can also be driven by individuals with unique insights at lower levels of the organization, or by groups or communities rather than individuals.

That 'managers shape change' seems an obvious statement. However, different managers manage in different ways, and different organizational situations require different **styles of change**. The Leavy and Wilson scale (shown in Figure 9.5)[14] is an excellent means of thinking through what type of management locus will best suit the challenge faced.

Perhaps just as often, however, innovative individuals who can see beyond current conventions and practices and create new visions of the future are often the drivers of change. Writers and artists such as James Joyce and Picasso challenged established beliefs and in turn transformed our understanding and appreciation of literature and art. Political figures such as Luther and Gandhi overturned the establishment in similar ways. While it is tempting to think of organizational executives as drivers of change in much the same manner, such figures, in the mold of Richard Branson for example, are in fact remarkably rare.[15] This is probably inevitable. Corporations themselves have become incredibly analytical, seeking to

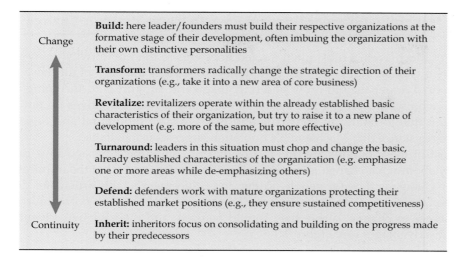

Change

Build: here leader/founders must build their respective organizations at the formative stage of their development, often imbuing the organization with their own distinctive personalities

Transform: transformers radically change the strategic direction of their organizations (e.g., take it into a new area of core business)

Revitalize: revitalizers operate within the already established basic characteristics of their organization, but try to raise it to a new plane of development (e.g. more of the same, but more effective)

Turnaround: leaders in this situation must chop and change the basic, already established characteristics of the organization (e.g. emphasize one or more areas while de-emphasizing others)

Defend: defenders work with mature organizations protecting their established market positions (e.g., they ensure sustained competitiveness)

Continuity

Inherit: inheritors focus on consolidating and building on the progress made by their predecessors

Figure 9.5 The locus of influence of leadership related to change versus continuity (Source: adapted from Leavy and Wilson, 1994)

mitigate risk by doubting their hunches, passion, and gut-feelings and employing sophisticated logarithms to plot their course instead.[16] Moreover, the higher up the establishment people are, the less likely they may be to question the very processes that enabled them to get where they currently are. It is important to remember that the likes of Joyce and Gandhi did not employ managerial risk analysis techniques and were nowhere near the top of their fields or societies when they began their transformational quests.

The same is true in business organizations. Often the people with the most innovative ideas, the ones that could really shake-up or change an organization for the better, are not those who have been in senior management positions for a decade or more. For example, it is doubtful that any of 3M's executives would have developed Post-It Notes. Some times the best ideas for new products and process that go on to define a companies future come from research scientists, shop-floor workers, designers or lower-level managers. However, what 3M executives did do was create an environment in which people from all over the organization had the confidence and systems in place to enable them to contribute innovative ideas that could drive change in the organization.

Creating an environment where bodies other than executives can drive change is also important when it comes to unleashing the change potential of communities of practice – those informal networks of influential people that we discussed in Chapter 7, Organic Strategy. Communities of practice can be powerful drivers of change because they can solve complex problems quickly; they facilitate the transfer of new practices; they continuously develop professional skills and the knowledge base of the organization; they can help attract and retain new people. The best communities of practice tend to form naturally, but skillful managers can also encourage their emergence. However they come to be, it is crucial that they are supported by an adequate infrastructure. Because they tend to lack the legitimacy and budgets of more formal groups, communities of practice can be vulnerable without this kind of support.

Managing Different Forms of Resistance to Strategic Change

One of Machiavelli's most often quoted lines gets to the nub of why many well-planned change initiatives fail: "The innovator makes enemies of all those who prospered under the old order and only lukewarm support is forthcoming from those who would prosper under the new." Many change initiatives do not gain traction due to failing to anticipate and manage such individual and organizational resistance that Machiavelli's quotation suggests is inevitable.

Most of these failures are due to insufficient communication and thus uncertainty about what change is coming, why it is coming, and what the implications of the change will be for people. Kotter and Schlesinger's table articulates different communication strategies that can be used to work through normal forms of **resistance to change**, where they should be used, and their relative advantages and disadvantages (see Figure 9.6).[17]

The Leadership of Strategic Change: Blending Change and Continuity

Leadership, is currently one of the 'hot topics' in business, and it particularly intersects with strategy where change is concerned. People often ask: what is the difference between "strategic change" and "change in general"? Our view is that strategic change requires a deft leadership that blends and balances a seemingly paradoxical mix of change *and* continuity. This is true now more than ever before, for two reasons. First, there are now very few completely bad organizations.

Strategy	Commonly used	Advantages	Disadvantages
Education + communication	Where there is a lack of information or inaccurate information and analysis	Once persuaded, people will often help with the implementation of the change	Can be very time comsuming if lots of people are involved
Participation + involvement	Where the initiators do not have all the information they need to design the change and others have power to resist	People who participate will be committed to implementation. Any relevent contributions can be integrated	Can be very time consuming if partici-pators design an inappropriate change
Facilitation + support	Where people are resisting because of adjustment problems	No other approach works as well with adjustment problems	Can be time consuming, expensive and still fail
Negotiation + agreement	Where somebody with considerable power to resist will lose out	Sometimes a relatively easy way to avoid major resistance	Can be too expensive if it alerts others to negotiate for compliance
Manipulation + co-optation	Where other tactics will not work or are too expensive	Can be a quick, inexpensive solution	Can lead to future problems if people feel manipulated
Explicit + implicit coercion	Where speed is essential, and the change initiators possess considerable power	Speedy, and can overcome any kind of resistance	Can be risky if it leaves people mad at the initiators

Figure 9.6 Dealing with resistance to change (Source: adapted from Kotter and Schlesinger, 1979)

Increased global competition has run them out of business or forced them to improve. Almost every company does one or a few things well and these should be built on or surfed. Second, research now suggests that good employees are having difficulty keeping up with, and are consequently frustrated by, the change programs that they feel they have no control over. And, we know that these days companies cannot afford to disengage good people. Despite the need for change, people crave continuity. It is this dialectic – the interplay between forces for consistency and forces for change – that the successful strategist must lead. This reconnects us with that one element of Pettigrew and Whipp's nine steps for managing change that was substantially different from conventional change frameworks: "balancing continuity and change." Paradoxically, then, it may be that the most important question with which to begin a strategic change program is: "What aspects should we preserve and maintain?"

The Strategic Leadership Keypad, outlined in the book *Creative Strategy*, can be a useful guide in this regard (Figure 9.7). Here the authors argue that, with an increase in the value and power of the engaged "knowledge worker," leaders of strategic change need to become less "command and control" oriented and be more facilitators, enablers, mentors, and coaches. Whereas traditional business, government, and military models would see the leader at the top; and the previous chapter made a case for strategy and change emerging from the "bottom-up." *Creative Strategy* argues that the strategic leadership of change should be positioned at the middle, or in the centre of things, providing a hub for the creative band of brains and networks to latch on to: a gravity that connects and respects the diversity and dynamism necessary for change while ensuring that things don't spin out in conflicting orbits.

Around this middle the Keypad distils four key elements for effectively leading continuity and change across: linking; sussing; promoting and mapping. Successful leaders of change should be able to "toggle" between the four keys, between inside and outside, past, present and future, between emergence and top-down leadership.

The first key, active or interactive *linking* with the external environment, means defining who the key external stakeholders are, and being a lynchpin that helps

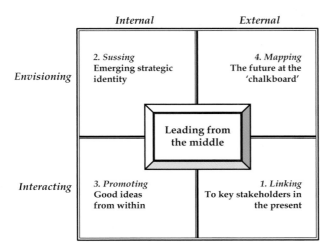

Figure 9.7 The strategic leadership keypad (adapted from Bilton & Cummings, 2010)

to connect them to key internal stakeholders. It also often means being the public face of the organization, explaining it, promoting it, and if necessary defending it. Taking these roles frees the creative minds within to get on with creating value. A.G. Lafley enabled strategic change at Procter & Gamble by clearly defining the key stakeholders that employees and team members respectively should have in mind: customers. He saw P&G's most meaningful results come from two critical points of contact with the outside: first, when customers choose to buy a P&G product over others and, second, when they use the product at home. Subsequently, Lafley came to see the importance of innovations being born not only in the lab: they should be driven by consumers, or, more accurately, from the interaction between P&G employees and consumers. Hence, almost every P&G office and innovation centre now has customers working inside with employees.[18]

Second, strategic leaders must be able to step back and envision, or *suss*, the essence of the organization: to distil and embody or exude the organization's strategic identity. To make the strategy simple and tangible so that people don't have to spend time wondering whether a new creative idea, development, or interpretation, can be made to fit, add to, or recalibrate the organization's strategy – they just know if it isn't and get on with it if it is. One of Bill Campbell's (the guiding force behind many of Silicon Valley's most creative companies: from Apple to Google to Jasper Wireless) "signature moves" is convincing CEOs to remove, or move aside, a CFO that has become lodged in the centre of things thereby distancing a CEO from an ability to keep their finger on the pulse and thus their ability to know and communicate "the suss" on what their companies are about.

Third, strategic leaders understand the value of stepping in to find and *promote* good "waves" (emerging ideas, values or people) from "lower echelons" quickly up the organization. They know that higher level employees do not have a monopoly on good ideas, that game-changing practices are likely to come from those not yet inculcated, and that just the sense that good ideas will come from everywhere in the organization keeps people higher up on their toes and motivates those further down. The Post-It Note example described earlier is a good example of leading change through promotion; as is Billy Beane's promotion of scramblers and "uglies" at the Oakland A's, described in live Case 9-5.

Fourth, strategic leaders must be able to externalize a vision: so as to *map* the path ahead or provide a picture of where the organization is heading. This need not be accurate. Things change. The purpose is rather to give confidence about what good movement will look like and lead to, and that momentum will be maintained – even if things don't emerge as planned, movement and momentum motivate creative people and make them more ready and able to adjust and change in any event (more on this in Chapter 11).

Duncan Angwin and Sotirios Paroutis have recently argued that Senior Strategy Directors (SSDs), sometimes called Chief Strategy Officers (CSOs), fulfill many of the roles necessary in bringing about organizational change by being the missing link in connecting up strategy – from the shop floor to the boardroom. They argue that as organizations need to be strategically agile, able to be nimble and flex rapidly, while also making strong choices and resource commitments over the long term, this places increasing strain upon the connectivity of companies internally and across organizational boundaries. SSDs act to identify tensions and rifts in order to bridge them through translation and brokering skills. They perform a critical role in providing leadership and necessary structural ties vertically and horizontally throughout organizations and with external stakeholders, binding different social networks in a dynamic way to facilitate organizational realignment. In order to succeed as an SSD, impressive social skills and strong technical competences are key to being a credible strategic leader of change to a wide range of audiences.

While there is no shortage of frameworks that can be used to enhance the chances of successfully navigating change, it is important to realize that many of the conventional mainstream frameworks draw on quite similar assumptions and are consequently fairly simplistic. Blending a following of these approaches with a leadership that understands the unique setting or context in which the change initiative must work, and some of the other less-straightforward ideas related here, will enable you to be a more effective leader of strategic change.

Referring back to our organizing schema (Figure 2 on page xviii), we can see that having covered the third part of this book by examining two pathways, Crossing Borders and Guiding Change, that can help to animate an organization as it builds upon the orientation provided by the four pathways outlined in Part II we now move on to look at two final pathways. Sustain Ability and Maverick Strategies point the way to new and, as yet, not fully charted strategic futures.

Guiding Change Key Learnings Mind Map

Having read and reviewed the chapter outline what you believe to be the key learnings from the chapter and the relationships between these.

9-1 Pringle: Hanging by a thread

Pringle of Scotland is a knitwear company with a long and proud history. Established in 1815 in the Scottish Borders and based around the town of Hawick, its trademark argyle sweaters and golf-wear became increasingly popular in the middle of the 20th century, when it found fans among the early "Sweater Girls" – who included sophisticated leading ladies like Jean Simmons, Deborah Kerr, and Margot Fonteyn – and the dapper Edward, Duke of Windsor. However, the later part of the 20th century saw a decline in the company's fortunes. A perceived "stale-ness" of the brand and falling sales saw a company that once employed 4,000 people in the region shrink to a quarter of that size. In June 1998, a further 720 jobs were shed with the closure of two factories in Scotland. With just 200 employees left at the Hawick factory, and Nick Faldo seemingly entrenched as Pringle's poster-boy for the past 20 years (a good golfer but hardly a fashion icon any more), many feared that Pringle was not cut out for the modern world of business. The company was put up for sale.

Kenneth Fang of SC Fang & Sons, a Hong Kong Knitwear manufacturer, bought Pringle in March 2000 and immediately poached a young manager from Marks & Spencer's to head up the company. Kim Winser was responsible for trebling the turnover of aspects of M&S's clothing business, but she recognized that Pringle presented a much tougher challenge.

On a positive note, however, the recent post-modern love affair with things retro has seen the successful resurrection of a number of "former glories" like Pringle. For example, Daks – the label that introduced the first self-supporting waist-band for women's trousers – has adapted its style to changing times. Recently, the label invited fashion students from the Royal College of Art to give it a 21st century makeover: with the proviso that its trademark shades of camel, vicuna, and black were kept to the fore. LVMH, whose portfolio includes brands such as Dior, Givenchy, and Louis Vuitton, has gone from strength to strength under the impressive Bernard Arnault. Burberry is another label that has enjoyed a renaissance after new managers and new designs were introduced in 1997, and successful diversifications were made into other product ranges. Since then, celebrity devotees have helped regenerate Burberry's image.

Indeed, the recent craze for all things vintage has given such companies an inimitable source of advantage: an ability to recreate their iconic lines. Boucheron, the haute jewelry company, launched its Vintage Limited Edition collection in 2002, re-releasing designs from the 1970s. Its creative director, Solange Azagury-Patridge, plans to add vintage pieces from the 1980s in the next few years. "Boucheron is 150 years old and has a really rich archive, with pieces that are so great and so appropriate that it is a shame not to revisit them again," she says. However, this new trend to revisit the old is not simply about scoring some quick sales; it is also a clever external marketing and internal strategy initiative. Azagury-Patridge points out that "reissuing pieces from the past is a way of conveying the essence and character of the brand." In other words, it is an "event" that can create a buzz and whip up enthusiasm for customers jaded by the homogeneity of global shopping, while raising awareness of what the company stands for and the standards it is trying to achieve and maintain.

GUIDING CHANGE

However, there seem to be just as many failures as success stories with attempts to rejuvenate luxury brands. Since fading into obscurity in the 1980s, Jaeger has made repeated attempts to update its image by redesigning product lines and ranges. However, these attempts did not win enough new customers and traditional followers felt alienated. Shares in the cash-strapped Luxury Brands Group, which owns the Hardy Amies brand, were recently suspended because of a rumored takeover bid and shares in Printemps-Redoute, the French retailer that is the majority owner of Gucci, fell over 50% in the first half of 2002. Prada, the fashion house, has had to cancel its float three times for fear of a poor response from the market. The effect of September 11 and wealthy tourists staying away from Europe has been blamed for adding to the struggles of smaller businesses of a similar ilk. Dawson International, the cashmere company, issued profit warnings in 2002 at about the same time as Chester Barrie, the Savile Row tailor, had to call in the receivers. Even traditional stalwart Fortnum & Mason, the "Queen's grocer," which was privatized in 2001, is fighting for its life. It has frozen staff pay and been forced to open its doors on Sundays – something previously unthinkable – in an attempt to revive its fortunes. Managing Director Stuart Gates told staff, "The company has to face hard decisions critical to the future of the store."

Maceira de Rosen, an analyst at JP Morgan, says that the luxury goods labels that remain intact will be those that have a strong brand that is "balanced geographically, whose sales are spread over regions, like Burberry. It also helps to have good management with experience of tough times and capable of flexibility in terms of cost-cutting."

So, what has Kim Winser overseen in her first 2 years in charge at Pringle? She began by finding out, and then explaining, just how dire the situation was. She characterized her and her staff's task as: "Rescuing the heritage of a great British brand."

Following this she instigated an aggressive trimming of existing product ranges (out went lesser quality lambswool jumpers and underwear, for example). "We only make beautiful cashmere knitwear," she explained. She then sought greater efficiency in the Hawick factory. The potentially infinite number of different Pringle jumpers on the market – a function of allowing some retailers to order alterations to colors, buttons, and sleeve lengths – has been discontinued, with Winser claiming that "we must have one very clear range, one message, which must not be broken. If people don't like our sleeves or our buttons I suggest that they don't buy Pringle."

While a strategic decision has been made to continue and invest in the factory in Hawick (at a time when so much manufacturing is being relocated out of the United Kingdom to the Far East), the existing Factory Manager was relieved of his duties. Winser promoted a younger more energetic character from the floor to take his place and then worked closely with him to improve processes and facilities.

While the previous Pringle design team was retained, new blood was also injected. The first collections under Winser's reign showed a heavy emphasis on updating the signature argyle knits and promoting the traditional Pringle Lion logo in interesting new ways. The new head designer drafted in to breathe further life into Pringle's venerable history is Stuart Stockdale, a 33-year-old with diverse credentials. Stockdale graduated from Central Saint Martins in London before completing an MA in womenswear design at the Royal College of Art. Since then he has covered both ends of the fashion market, working as assistant to the Italian designer Romeo Gigli before cutting his teeth in commercial design with J Crew – purveyor of basic casual-wear to the US masses. This experience gave him a great understanding of the American market – a market that is crucial to Winser's plans for resurrecting Pringle. Since returning to the UK, Stockdale has set up his own label in London as well as launching Jasper Conran's first luxury menswear collection. Now he works for Pringle. "When I first saw the archive, I was totally inspired," Stockdale claimed. "There is so much potential. There was nothing else like Pringle on the market. My challenge is to break out from the knits, yet everything I design must come from the heritage of the knit-wear." Stockdale is well placed to understand what he is taking on. He was born just a stone's throw away from Pringle's Hawick home.

Winser set her staff tough targets. Within 12 weeks of her joining the company, she reversed a previous decision not to show a new Pringle range at the world's biggest menswear fair in Florence, and soon after this wanted to launch completely new menswear and womenswear ranges in Pringle's first live catwalk shows since the 1950s. While it was a close-run thing, both targets were met successfully, providing a tremendous boost to staff morale.

Nick Faldo has been removed as the personification of Pringle's identity (although he has been retained to promote golf-wear in certain markets). David Beckham has been identified as an appropriate update of Faldo, and American anglophiles such as Madonna and Julia Roberts reinforce his British presence. The aim of these changes is to refocus the company identity around an "old-world take on modern elegance."

Pringle's London headquarters has been moved from Savile Row, which Winser saw as too fusty and not fashion-oriented enough anymore, to a setting described as "retro-chic" – a converted 1960s warehouse just around the corner. A new emphasis on retailing has been signaled with Pringle "signature stores" being developed in Milan, New York, Tokyo, and London. The latter will replace Emporio Armani's flagship store in Bond Street. Bill Christie, who played a significant part in the successful regeneration of Burberry, has been employed as the new head of retail. Mr. Christie is promising VIP customers complimentary single malt Scotch whisky in the "libraries" within these stores, where the men's range will be displayed.

The signs, so far, are positive and Winser is proud to communicate the company's recent achievements. Sales are up by a third. Many new high-fashion retailers are now buying Pringle. The number employed in Hawick is up by a quarter. The American market is still tough, but Winser claims that Pringle is not suffering like some and that "we're well placed for when things pick up." It is speculated that Winser has even begun to cast her eye over some of Pringle's traditional competitors (like those mentioned above) which have fallen on hard times, but she claims to be holding back at the moment: "I think it's best to focus on [the brand that] we have already." However, new international licensing deals are now enabling Pringle to take the label into related diversifications such as leather goods, children's clothes, and home-wear, and increase production quickly and effectively.

The *Sunday Times* has described Pringle's progress as "a great British success story." Winser herself is more circumspect: "Is the company saved? Not completely. But we've made a very good first step."

> 1. What do you think some of the key elements of leading strategic change in the luxury brands sector might be?
> 2. Where would you have placed Pringle in terms of the locus levels outlined in the Leavy and Wilson framework (Figure 9.5) at the time that Winser joined the company?
> 3. What has made Winser such an effective manager of change at Pringle?

◄◄◄ Hanging by a Thread: Some ideas towards a "model answer" . . .

1. What are the key elements of managing strategic change in the luxury brands sector?

While the effective management of change will require an understanding of the particular organization in question, this case seems to suggest at least one general characteristic in this sector. It seems important to be very cautious about revolutionary change because a luxury brand often relies on a mystique created by its associations and relationships with the past – and this must be preserved at all costs. Often the guardians of these relationships are long-serving staff or suppliers or customers, so they must be treated with care. However, often these firms have fallen out of fit with the modern business environment, and subsequently on hard times, by not questioning old processes, inherited inefficiencies, or outdated production methods. Managing change in this sector appears to require a very dexterous change agent who can effectively blend evolutionary and revolutionary approaches, going through each item of the value chain, asking what should be preserved and what should be changed, and asking if every item does actually contribute to a great enough extent to justify its costs.

2. Where would you have placed Pringle in terms of the locus levels outlined in the Leavy and Wilson framework (Figure 9.5) at the time that Winser joined the company?

To begin, the company is probably in the revitalization category. As the case goes on it moves down the Leavy and Wilson scale toward requiring an increasing emphasis on continuity and a lessening emphasis on change. Correspondingly, Winser combines Revitalizer, Turnarounder, Defender, and Inheritor loci.

3. What has made Winser such an effective manager of change at Pringle?

One can quite easily break down Winser's success using a straightforward change framework like Kotter's eight steps. Using this we can see that Winser:

1. emphasizes the urgency of the situation
2. works hard to form coalitions (with the existing design team and the new Factory Manager, for example)
3. expresses a clear vision, both in word and in deed
4. communicates the change with everything she says and does

GUIDING CHANGE

5. sets tough targets and then lets people get on with achieving them
6. uses these targets, once achieved (e.g. the fashion shows), as exemplars of short-term wins
7. communicates to consolidate these successes
8. recognizes that the current success is just a start and that there is more change to come.

However, this sort of analysis only tells part of the story. As the ideas for the previous question suggest, managing change in this sector requires a dexterous approach that blends different types of evolutionary and revolutionary methods. In this light, it is interesting to look at how Winser exhibits a number of different change management styles in this case. For example, she exhibits a number of Dunphy and Stace's four change styles at different phases, and on different issues, when appropriate (as is often the case new leaders can take advantage of the uncertainty and new opportunities that a change of leadership brings to start out more dictatorial and move toward more participative styles). Consequently, she also uses different strategies to manage resistance.

She seems to focus strongly on the importance of consistency across the operational and strategic levels, and the culture and the strategy of the organization, to preserve the corporate or brand identity. Moreover, in terms of the strategic leadership keypad, she identifies buyers as the key lynchpin to the outside and seeks to improve relations here while not allowing buyers to customize items and hence dull the key identity that she has sussed: (e.g. "Rescuing the heritage of a great British brand"; "We only make beautiful cashmere"). Her deeds here are backed up by promoting certain pre-existing aspects from below: the Scottish/British heritage; sporting/aristocratic traditions through bringing through the likes of David Beckham and Madonna; the traditional argyle; and the promotion of the new factory manager from the floor; and her clear mapping of a more positive future of building upon the traditional knits and getting to new customers.

Finally, she acknowledges that the change program is not over. No matter how successful these early steps have been, they are still first steps on a long onward journey.

▶▶▶

Case Notes:

9-2 Reliant: The plastic pig

During the 1970s, Reliant was the second largest independent British producer of cars in the UK, with 360 cars a week coming off its production line. Reliant was noteworthy for the three-wheeled Reliant Robin as well as the up-market sports car estate, the Scimitar, once favored by Princess Anne. The three-wheeled Robin consisted of a fiberglass body and an 850 cc aluminum engine capable of 60 miles per gallon, all of which was made in-house.

After a long period of decline, Reliant went bust three times during the 1990s. (A brief history of the firm and its cars can be found on www.3wheelers.com/reliant.html.) While in administration, Jonathan Haynes, an ex-Jaguar engineer, decided to attempt a rescue of the ailing firm. Haynes's father had been famous for designing the E-type Jaguar, a famous racing car, and son, like father, also had a passion for sports cars. He was attracted by Reliant's illustrious past even though sports cars hadn't been made since the early 1990s. Just before Reliant entered administration, the firm was only producing the Robin, which had been dubbed "the plastic pig." To get the factory working again, Haynes would have to focus on production of the Robin and postpone any thoughts of a more glamorous future. How could he possibly turn the tide?

On arriving at the site, he found total disarray as the administrators had left the site in a real mess. The machines had lain idle and had seized up and rusted. One employee commented that it was a good collection a museum would be proud of. Haynes' first task in getting production restarted was to hire back the original engineers, as they knew how to make the Reliant Robin. It was a testimony to their loyalty to the car that they even considered this very uncertain future.

Suppliers proved very awkward. They had lost money when Reliant went into administration. Even for such small items as bulbs costing 10 p each they wouldn't supply until Reliant's cheque was cashed. There were other demands on working capital as well. Employees needed to be paid and, to get production moving as soon as possible, Haynes had to pay for large amounts of overtime.

Reliant Robin customers are passionate about their cars. Around 44,000 were registered and many had bought seven or eight cars over a sustained period of time. The Reliant Robin had a strong image at the time, as it featured in a favorite BBC comedy *Only Fools and Horses* and was also the object of many jokes by the comedian Jasper Carrott. Although laughed at for its quirkiness and down-market image, many also regarded the Reliant Robin fondly – indeed, the jokes were seen as free advertising. Part of the attraction may have been the unusualness of a three-wheeled car, and the camaraderie of an ownership club. The car was certainly popular among market traders and farmers. The loyalty of the customers meant a continuous demand for spare parts and updates, although many competitors were filling this demand.

Haynes forecasted that the firm had to build 50 cars per week to pay his rehired 60-strong workforce and to balance the books. Fortunately when he took charge, he had discovered 14 Robins in nearly complete form. With little effort these cars were finished and sold.

One of Haynes' early priorities was to meet with the dealers to hear their views on what the customers wanted. Throughout the first year, Haynes was close to the dealers, but also demanded quick and prompt payment from them.

At the factory he placed a salesman into a position that he regarded as the most important in the firm – to sell off spare parts to generate £2,000 per day. This target was soon doubled. In his words: "Sell anything! Sell, sell, sell!"

Haynes was conscious that traditional attitudes in the company had to change. Many employees had lived through the previous three collapses and were very cynical that anything would really change. In the day-to-day operations of the business, Haynes detected the attitude of "The answer's no, but perhaps we can do it, but the answer's no!" In response he would quote John Neil of Unipart: "The answer's yes – now what's the question?"

Haynes was worried by his 20 employees involved in making the bodies of the car, entirely by hand. This seemed overly labor intensive and outdated, as chopper guns existed which could do the task more quickly and would require fewer employees. In forceful discussions with his production manager they agreed to test out the new technology.

Haynes underachieved his target of 50 cars per week, producing 36 cars at the deadline. Reasons included reliance on new employees who had to be taught the job. However, support from Haynes' backers continued. A special edition Reliant Robin was launched in racing green and was well received by customers. At this time Haynes also hired a designer to draft images of a new sports car.

At the end of the first year, Haynes relaxed at his farm and reflected on the trials and tribulations of his first year. At one stage they had almost come close to bankruptcy, with just £400 in the bank. He had pushed all his employees hard with long hours, tough discussion, and with only the promise of an uncertain future. Indeed, his own farm had suffered as he put all his attention into Reliant. However, it seemed now that Reliant was back onto a firm footing and Haynes savored the prospect of the unveiling of his new four-wheeled sports car at the Birmingham motor show the following month.

1. *What barriers or resistance to change did Haynes encounter?*
2. *Why was Reliant declining prior to Haynes' arrival and why do you think Haynes' change strategy appears to have been successful.*
3. *Why was Haynes' initial approach more revolutionary or transformational approach than evolutionary? Despite this, what aspects of Reliant's past would you continue with into the future?*

Case Notes:

9-3 Baraka: Development from the grass roots

In an article in the *New Republic* at the beginning of 2000, Joseph Stiglitz, former Chief Economist with the World Bank, offered a stinging critique of his former organization and the IMF (International Monetary Fund), "fixer" of the economies of poor countries. Wrote Stiglitz: "Critics accuse the institution of taking a cookie-cutter approach to economics and they are right. When the IMF decides to assist a country, it dispatches a mission of economists. These economists frequently lack extensive experience in a country; they are more likely to have first-hand knowledge of five star hotels than of the villages that dot its countryside. They work hard, poring over numbers deep into the night. But their task is impossible. In a period of days or, at most, weeks, they are charged with developing a program sensitive to the needs of the country. Needless to say, a little number-crunching rarely provides adequate insights into the development strategy of an entire nation." Given their limitations, Stiglitz claims that country teams have been known to "compose draft reports before visiting. I heard stories of team members copying large parts of the text for one country's report and transferring them wholesale into another. They might have got away with it, except the 'search and replace' function on the word processor didn't work properly, leaving the original country's name in a few places."

The views of Tony Smith, Principal of Baraka Agricultural College, appear to support Stiglitz's. "The models used by the IMF and World Bank," he explains, "tend to judge development in terms of industrialization. So, if countries like ours want funding, they have to show how it will be channeled into big industrial projects." Not only are such projects potentially damaging to the sensitive ecosystems within the countries that the IMF seeks to help; Tony explains that they are often simply not feasible in countries where the infrastructure – electricity, clean water, roads – is not yet able to support existing needs. At present, for example, the college has to make preparations for at least three lengthy power-cuts a week.

Baraka College was founded in 1974 by a group of Franciscan Brothers. Its ends are more or less the same as the IMF: "to respond to the needs and aspirations of the poor." However, its stated philosophy indicates very different means: "Baraka promotes sustainable agriculture and rural development through education, training, and extension programs that focus on recognizing the environment, natural and human resources as the foundation of economic and social activity. In the current demographic, economic, environmental, and social realities of East Africa, the most appropriate response is that of *Sustainable Agriculture and Rural Development.*"

From humble beginnings, Baraka now attracts students from all over East Africa. It seeks to train these students to get more out of their land, and enable them to spread this knowledge when they return to their homes. In contrast to some of the grander IMF-sponsored projects, Baraka's latest initiative is the promotion of and training in beekeeping. This is an activity that is easily set up, does not take away resources from soil crops (indeed the bees' activity improves yields of traditional crops such as coffee, bananas, and sunflowers), and provides small farmers with invaluable extra income. In a land where subsistence farming is still very much the way of life and the dominant mode of production, the college believes that this sort of from-the-ground-up development is far more practical and beneficial to local people at this point in time than industrialization imposed from on-high.

* * *

At the beginning of the year 2000, Robin Cook, the British Foreign Secretary, approved a new campaign to "rebrand" Britain. Twelve new posters were designed to replace decorations in British Embassies and Councils that had not been updated since the 1960s. While calculated to show that traditional images of Morris Dancers and crooked teeth, flatulent beef-eaters, and glossy Kodachromes of Castles have been eclipsed, the posters sought to illustrate a sense of continuity with the past. Each is split down the middle, connecting *Old England* with *New Britain*. A frock by Sir Hardy Amies, the Queen's most respected couturier, is cut in half and joined with the right half of an outfit by John Galliano, the flamboyant Englishman who designs for Christian Dior. Julie Christie, the face of the "swinging sixties," fades into Kate Winslet. Sir Geoff Hurst, in his 1966 World-Cup-winning England kit, kicks at a ball that is melded with the one being chased by England's most recent international football sensation, Michael Owen. The late Benny Hill is paired with Mr Bean, and a horse painted by George Stubbs in the 18th century is "cross-bred" with Damien Hirst's infamous 1990s *pickled sheep*. Embassy staff and the general public have welcomed the campaign, as has Mark Leonard, who writes on national identity for the independent "think-tank" Demos. "It is a good use of money," says Leonard. "We could do with some of these posters at British airports and the Eurostar [train] terminal, too, just to remind us – as well as visitors – what Britain is about."

* * *

Hewlett-Packard was founded by Bill Hewlett and Dave Packard in a garage in a small mid-western town in the United States at the height of the Depression in the 1930s. Along with IBM, it grew to become the most successful computer company in the world, and, all the while, the company's existing employees and its new recruits were inspired by the circulation of what were called "Bill and Dave stories." However, in the 1980s and 1990s the company fell upon relatively hard times and appeared to be losing its focus in a market where differentiation was becoming increasingly important. On November 15, 1999, under the leadership of new CEO Carly Fiorina, HP announced a new global campaign. "We must reinvent ourselves," proclaimed Fiorina. At the heart of this reinvention was a theme of "going back to the garage." Advertisements featured a small wooden garage at twilight with a light burning inside, over the top of which were printed messages such as: "The original company of inventors started here. It is returning here. The original start-up will act like one again."

* * *

A former state-owned enterprise in New Zealand had just been privatized and bought by an American corporation. The new controllers brought about many changes. They needed to if the organization was to be successful in its new guise. Most managers were gung-ho about the structural changes that had been put in place and felt that the culture of the organization would not take long to catch up. "From a structure point of view, there's very little left to do," claimed one senior manager. A senior director claimed that, "We have a people and a 'mind set' problem. We were 25,000; we are now 15,000. Of those 15,000, 13,500 worked for the old organization. We don't have a structure problem."

However, things did not come around as quickly as they had hoped. "From a culture point of view," said the first manager quoted above, "there are quite a lot [of problems] because the people who are still here from the old organization are not in tune with the new direction and the values that the new management has put in place. Theirs is a culture that does not work in a trading organization – sorry, full stop, end, not any of it. It has to be completely new."

A year later, many believed that, on reflection, a lot of the teething problems that the organization suffered in the first 2 years after the change were caused by the original assumption that "everything must go" – that the old culture held nothing within it of use to the service organization of the future. Staff members expressed their frustration and disappointment at the way things had developed by faxing cartoons to one another, like the ones pictured in Figure 9-3.1. (Spot the Dog, an agreeable little terrier who would go anywhere and do anything to help people out, was the company's "spokesperson".)

The Head of Corporate Strategy, a veteran with the company and one of the many we interviewed, summed up the feelings of many looking back – with the benefit of hindsight – at the change process:

Figure 9-3.1 Cartoons drawn by staff of the New Zealand organization a year after the takeover by the US firm

"The old organization had a very strong ethic; a strong sense of 'family.' There was a strong sense of public responsibility and I think many who stayed in the organization over a long period of time stayed because of these values and a sense of service . . . I think at the moment the family sense is shattered or strained. I think the sense of service, the spirit of service, is not there because too many issues are being reduced to issues of profitability, accountability, and incentivization, and this emphasis is devaluing those things."

1. *Why can evolutionary approaches to strategic change be more successful than revolutionary approaches?*
2. *If you were involved in managing change in these organizations how would you look to incorporate "strategic stories" (see Chapter 7) from the organizations' pasts as they move into the future?*
3. *Why do managers of business organizations often favor revolutionary rather than evolutionary approaches to change, and more tangible things like structures or technology than less tangible things like stories?*

Case Notes:

9-4 Church(es): Three in one

The new vicar of St. Margaret's rose to address the assembled congregations of St. Margaret's, St. Barnabus, and Trinity church.

St. Margaret's vicar: "I'm pleased to see so many of you here this afternoon to discuss the future of our three churches and how we may move forward as a unified body. Our churches already work together in a number of ways, such as a shared parish newsletter, occasional shared services, and the rotation of priests on a bi-monthly basis. This is very much in the spirit of the Church of England's wishes that ecumenicalism, the working together of different branches of Christianity, is the road we must follow. When I was appointed to my position at St. Margaret's, it was made clear to me by the bishop that we must embrace our differences as a source of strength. With this vision in mind, we must also confront the practical challenges of everyday existence in our parish. Our congregations are aging and dwindling and we have very significant costs in the upkeep and running of three church buildings. We are also expected to increase our contributions to the diocese from our collections and bequests. The vicars of St. Barnabus and Trinity have had many meetings on this subject and this evening are proposing that we consider worshiping more closely together under fewer roofs. This will also have the welcome effect of reducing our costs.

"As you know, St. Barnabus's is a grade 1 protected listed building and so cannot be changed in any way. The focus of attention is therefore on what we should do with St. Margaret's and Trinity church. Trinity is located on the main street of our town and a large number of people pass daily. Local interest is evident in the very successful coffee mornings held on Saturday. However, Trinity is in very poor condition and will need a complete restoration in the next few years or a rebuild – I believe some architects have been contacted informally and they recommend the latter course of action. Needless to say either course is very expensive even taking into account the subsidy we may receive via the bishop. St. Margaret's is a very large Victorian building with a seating capacity of 700. It is less well located, being set in attractive memorial grounds, in a quiet leafy side road some way from the town center. Apart from regular Sunday morning services, its large seating capacity makes it attractive to local schools for their special events. St. Margaret's size is also a drawback as the older members of the congregation complain that it is cold and there is no doubt that it costs a lot to heat.

"I would now like to ask all of you for your thoughts on how we might go forward in realizing our aims of greater ecumenicalism, and reducing our costs."

Trinity church's vicar: "Thank you for your opening words, vicar. I would like to suggest that the forces of St. Margaret's and Trinity combine to create a stronger, unified congregation. I believe either church would be large enough for this to happen. The arguments for making Trinity our preferred option are its excellent location and it could be rebuilt to be a striking new presence on the high street. St. Margaret's, on the other hand, could be redesigned to suit the needs of an enlarged pluralist congregation."

Congregational member of St. Margaret's: "When you say 'redesign St. Margaret's,' what do you mean exactly?"

Trinity church's vicar: "Well, our style of worship at Trinity is more intimate than that of St. Margaret's. We prefer a more conversational style in smaller spaces, rather than the, dare I say it, 'pomp and splendor' of the high church style of St. Margaret's. I would like to suggest that architects are employed to see how St. Margaret's could be partitioned into a series of meeting rooms and glass screens used to separate the main worship space from the body of the church."

Congregational member of Trinity church: "Because St. Margaret's has such large spaces, microphones and amplification have to be used. We oppose the use of such 'technology' – it interferes with the word of God!"

Organist of St. Margaret's: "If you partition St. Margaret's, you will be losing the finest acoustic in the county. I don't know the actual revenue figures, but a number of chamber orchestras and other instrumental groups use the building on a regular basis to make recordings for CD and radio broadcasts. They also hire the organ and piano, both of which are outstanding instruments. These fees help maintain them and the building."

Accountant to St. Margaret's: "I'm surprised to hear that St. Margaret's is financially unhealthy. Although our congregation is dwindling, our receipts from bequests are actually increasing and, as the building is in superb condition, I don't anticipate any capital expenditures for years to come."

Congregational member of St. Margaret's: "Of course the congregation of St. Margaret's would welcome the congregation of Trinity church if they chose to join us."

Congregational member of Trinity church: "Thank you for your welcome, but we would need to be sure that we could have our normal service, led in our own way at 9.30 a.m."

Congregational member of St. Margaret's: "Well I'm not sure that's possible as our service starts at 10 a.m., so your service would have to start at 9 a.m. or 11.30 a.m."

Congregational member of Trinity church: "Why should we have to adjust our service times? We are the ones who would be sacrificing our building to move to your building. We also have many very elderly members in our congregation and getting to church for 9 a.m. on a wet winter's day would not be possible. Why can't St. Margaret's move its services?"

Vicar of St. Barnabus's: "Before we get into the detail of changing St. Margaret's, maybe we should think about St. Margaret's congregation moving to Trinity church. Rebuilding Trinity with a modern design in a prime location is bound to attract attention and visitors. Now that businesses can open on Sundays, the church has to face competition for its services. St. Margaret's is really too far from the center of town. A new Trinity church would be an excellent visible statement of the progressiveness of the church. To fund this new building, I suggest that St. Margaret's be sold off for development, as it is a large area of land in a very desirable residential area, where there is a shortage of parking space."

At this point, an elderly lady struggled to her feet, her outstretched arm shaking with rage.

Elderly lady: "Do you mean to tell me that St. Margaret's would be turned into a parking lot – how dare you even suggest such a thing?! My husband is buried in those memorial gardens, as are the loved ones of many people in this meeting. How can you even think of building over them?!"

Congregational member of St. Margaret's: "I agree – how can you consider demolishing St. Margaret's? I have worshiped there all of my life – for 60 years. I was married there and my children christened there. You cannot destroy St. Margaret's. Anyway, who are you to say what should happen to St. Margaret's? What has your congregation got to do with it? You don't worship there – you don't care!"

Later that evening, the new vicar of St. Margaret's reflected on the situation and despaired. She had had no idea of the difficulties that "working together" would entail. There was even a question mark over her future already. Why would there be a need for two vicars in the same church? She was the most recent arrival and the other two vicars seemed to be against her. The telephone rang:

Congregational member of St. Margaret's: "Sorry I couldn't be at the meeting this afternoon, vicar. I gather it didn't go very well – I bet the other two churches ganged up on us? Anyway, I have great news. In anticipation of those problems, I have applied to have our church listed as a building of important architectural interest – so it may be protected after all from change . . ."

The caller continued, but all the vicar could think about was tomorrow morning's meeting with the bishop and his parting words from the last meeting:

"We really have to move things on, you know. Your parish is in the vanguard of change – everyone will be looking to see how you have handled this highly desirable move towards our ecumenical goals. I really hope you can tell me what steps you are taking towards this aim and the progress you have made when we next meet. Don't let me down."

1. *What are the drivers for change at the three churches?*
2. *What are the barriers to change?*
3. *What ways forward can you suggest for the new vicar?*

9-5 The Oakland A's: Billy Beane's leading ugly

Over the past decade the Oakland Athletics have regularly outperformed the bigger, richer teams in the professional baseball. They did this with a team of misfits and mis-shapes, passed over by the scouts from the other clubs. How? The answer may be a rather unconventional leader of change: Billy Beane.

As a promising young player, Beane was a "five tool" guy. He ran fast, threw strong, fielded skillfully, hit well, and he could hit with power. In the mind of the scouts who selected players for the major league clubs, he was the full package. The icing on the cake was that he looked great: tall, lean, square-jawed. The scouts had a term for this: Billy Beane had "the good face". He joined the New York Mets straight from high school. The Mets considered him as a better prospect than Daryl Strawberry, who they signed in the same draft. And then Beane's playing career slowly fell apart. After toiling away between various major league club rosters and their feeder teams for nearly 10 years, he ended up with the A's.

He then walked a path seldom trod, from the field to the front office. And there Beane found the Oakland A's GM, Sandy Alderson. He asked Alderson an unheard of question: could he hand in his glove and become an advance scout, going out on the road ahead of the team to watch and report back on future opponents. Alderson liked Beane. Beane treated him with a respect that baseball people often didn't afford somebody who hadn't played pro ball. Plus, Alderson admitted, "I didn't think there was much risk in [it] because I didn't think an advance scout did anything." By 1998 Beane was in Alderson's job.

Beane drew lessons from his own travails and his unique collection of perspectives. He was the first major league GM to have been a future all-star, a failed player, an advance scout and intensely curious about things outside of baseball. This enabled him to suss that certain types of players and skills were overvalued in baseball. Others, on the other hand, were not valued highly enough.

Beane failed as a player because he didn't have it in the head. He was so good as a young man that he'd never really failed at anything. Subsequently, he crumbled under the pressure of the big leagues. He seemed unable to make minor adjustments that might have helped him, and became, in turns, paralyzed by over-analysis and engaged in making wholesale changes that confused himself and his coaches until his self-confidence was sapped.

Such an embedded deficit was not apparent to a scout watching a high school star. As a player, "I was sort of misjudged," Beane would later explain. "[T]hey were measuring the wrong things, like running speed and strength, and they were undervaluing guys who actually did things (such as get on base and score runs) that contributed to winning games. . . There were a lot of guys who maybe weren't the natural athlete I was, but they were much better [pro] baseball players."

Beane's emerging views about what was over- and undervalued in baseball, and his elevation within the A's front office, emerged at a fortunate time. Former A's team owner Walter A. Haas Jr. was prepared to sink his own fortune into keeping up with the big club's spending. New owners Stephen Schott and Ken Hofmann weren't. As a business proposition, pumping millions into a team that relatively few people supported (the population of Oakland is just over 400,000) made no sense to them. Scott and Hofmann made innovation a matter of urgency. Beane was the right leader in the right place at the right time to revolutionize the A's strategy, and, subsequently the way professional baseball teams are led.

Together, the new owners and Beane worked out a new approach, and what seemed a source of perennial shame became a rallying call for the underdogs: "We can't do the same things the Yankees do," Beane said. "Given the economics, we'll lose." Unable to *join* them, or follow what was best practice for the big clubs, Beane set about seeing if they could *beat* them at a different game: trading.

He would assemble a team that would sign the players nobody else wanted – "fat guys who don't make outs." After buying low, Beane would look to sell high as his players became established and successful, by which time he would have another "ugly" and cheap cohort rising through the ranks. This was the strategy, but achieving it would require promoting a number of things that baseball insiders currently didn't value, and, subsequently, demoting a number of others that had long gone unquestioned.

Beane's former boss Alderson had introduced him to Bill James, a little-known amateur publisher of pamphlets of statistics that most baseball insiders considered unimportant. Beane saw in these numbers an ability to map something that he had been gradually sussing for some time. James provided proof that what matters most in terms of winning baseball matches were the ugly things: primarily scrambling to first base by whatever means, particularly through walks. Consequently, the stats that most people in baseball did focus on, like batting average (which does not include walks), were the wrong ones.

Alderson could see this and the consequent arbitrage possibilities it might afford, but found it hard to push the envelope without a baseball pedigree and under Haas' free-spending ownership. The stars aligned far more favourably for Beane to build upon his mentor's insight and put James's numbers into practice.

But there was still a battle to be fought against the old baseball thinking. Whereas the kingpin at a baseball club was generally the first team manager or coach, the A's new owners supported Beane's installation of a different kind of man in this role. Coach Art Howe was put in place to follow Beane's strategy. This team would be led from the front office, not from the dugout.

Beane then set about dismantling the monopoly that the scouting team had on recruitment. The secret weapon in Beane's armoury was Paul Podesta, a Harvard graduate with a laptop. Beane subtly promoted Podesta, a statistician with no track record in the game, into the mix when prospective new players were being evaluated and when the front office was deciding who to buy ahead of the draft.

These discussions had as their focal point a big white board with the names of players to be ranked in order of desirability. Beane would begin by listening to the scouts outline their top picks. Then he would use Paul's stats to critique their ideas.

Podesta and the influence of Bill James led Beane to begin by promoting a particular kind of prospect: college players. Scouts tended to be enamored with high-school stars and measured themselves on picking those high school prospects who had then gone on to achieve a potential that only the wizened scout could have foreseen – no matter how long the odds of this were. As Beane would say, "We [used to] take fifty guys and celebrate if two of them made it. In what other business is two for fifty a success?" Because college players played in leagues with a large number of games played to a good standard, they had meaningful stats. Podesta used these stats to assess the investment risk.

So, down came most of the high school players from the white board. Unlike other clubs, the A's no longer saw those potential stakeholders as key. Then, Beane would set about critiquing what was left and introducing his own players.

In 2002, Jeremy Brown provided a case in point. Brown was an "ugly" catcher from Alabama who just made the last page of the lists of hundreds of possible players compiled by the scouts. Where the scouts saw only "a bad body catcher," Paul's laptop enabled him to counter that "He's the only player in the history of the SEC with three hundred hits and two hundred walks." Beane moved Brown's name from obscurity to the top of the list. And a new map began to take shape.

By the end of the discussion, Beane had a list of eight players on the white board very different from the list of names the scouts had started with, but gradually some of the scouts started to appreciate Beane's vision and buy in. "We've got three guys at the top of the board that no one has ever heard of," said one, with a trace of pride. "There isn't a board in the game that looks like this one," said another.

All the scouts and players and coaches, from the top team to the dozens of feeder teams that contributed to the A's franchise, were now expected to understand the significance of the diagrams and the numbers churned out by Podesta's laptop – even if it looked ugly, getting a free walk to first base was as valuable as a spectacular hit. Players were taught to play to a new creative strategy, a new percentages game, not just to swing and hope to be a hero.

Beane's revolution redefined talent in baseball. What looked good on the field did not win games. He sussed out that while appearances could be deceiving, certain statistics gathered over a long enough period of time, generally weren't.

Beane took the A's from also-rans to perennial contenders. They won 91 games in 2000, 102 in '01 and 103 in '02, more games than any other club in baseball (except the big-spending Atlanta Braves), and they made it to the play-offs three years straight. While the Beane revolution has now spread and other teams have caught up by learning the A's lessons, for a period of four or five years, Beane's strategic leadership put his team well ahead on baseball measures, and on some seemingly obvious but seldom applied "business measures" too, like dollars spent on players per win. At the top of this scale the Texas Rangers were paying nearly $3 million per win. The A's were paying $500,000, or 6 times less.

1. *Use the Strategic Leadership Keypad to outline how Beane led change by linking to new people outside of baseball, promoted those who were undervalued, sussed what the A's strategy should be and communicated or mapped out the sort of players that would contribute to this strategy.*
2. *Where would you place him on the Leavy and Wilson continuum of change and continuity?*
3. *What contributed to Beane's overcoming the initial resistance to change?*

9-6 elBulli: Innovative HR practices driving strategic change

elBulli may be the world's most famous restaurant. Owned and run by Ferrán Adrià and Juli Soler since 1990, elBulli was established in 1961 by Hans Schilling and his wife Marketta. Schilling, a homeopathic doctor, and his wife arrived from Germany in Rosas 10 close to the French border in the northeast of Spain, where they decided to set up their restaurant. Since its inception, the owners have employed the approach to hiring that has helped elBulli become one of the most innovative and in-demand organizations in the world.

Every year, elBulli receives approximately 2 million reservation requests but can only satisfy around 8,000 of these requests over the 160 days a year the restaurant is open. Why not open longer? Why only 160 days? According to Ferrán Adrià, "The restaurant [only] opens six months a year... because you need more time to create."

Adrià and elBulli's creative team work the other six months in a Barcelona workshop in which they continuously develop new cooking techniques and concepts.

"Cooking is not difficult. Creating, however, is another thing altogether," notes Adrià. "While you create you need to get out of the routine and be aware of creative rhythm. This creative rhythm tells you when you have to change, explore or exploit things.. A definition of creativity, given by the chef Jacques Maxim ("Creativity means not copying"), inspired Ferrán Adrià to a new radical approach to human resources to help feed the desire for creativity.

At elBulli there are 30 to 40 chefs depending on the season. Of these, 13 are full time and the rest are "stagers." The stagers are chosen from over 5,000 talented applicants from around the world.

Stagers must have a very high level of culinary skill ("we need to level up the members of the team so that experience is balanced out" says Marc Cuspiera, elBulli's Personnel Manager), but this is certainly not the only and maybe not even the most important selection criteria. Stagers are selected from many countries so that the kitchen can benefit from the diverse knowledge and experience of their native countries. And teamwork, generosity, openness, and engagement are also critical aspects for being selected as an elBulli stager.

Each new technique at elBulli is documented and published. The idea behind this is that the discoveries made at elBulli can help worldwide cuisine evolve and develop. "Creativity here never stops, one idea develops and we move forward. In this context you will not say 'this is mine,' we expect people to work for the same objective. Generosity is critical to be part of this team."

"My secret is not to have secrets" – comments Adrià in the book 'elBulli desde dentro'. At elBulli we are moved by creativity and our wish to innovate.

Cuspiera further underscores the importance of having the right talent: "It would be a mistake for someone to come here if he or she believes that the first day they will learn and take just recipes. That person did not understand that this is an organization in which we share time, generosity, and knowledge. And it would have been our mistake to have hired such a talent because that individual talent is not leveraging the organizational talent we need to develop."

This team dynamic applied to the endless search for new gastronomical techniques and concepts has resulted in dozens of major discoveries and hundreds of minor developments: frozen savories, non-pasta ravioli, sperification (tiny flavored spheres of vegetables or fruits), new foams, hot jellies and many more. Almost single-handed elBulli has created what is considered a new cuisine, la cocina de vanguardia (or the new vanguard). It has changed the way the world thinks about what is possible in gastronomy.

1. How does elBulli's innovative approach to HR facilitate strategic change?
2. What insights does this case provide into how strategic change may be facilitated or disabled?
3. Do you think that other organizations could learn from what elBulli has done or would it be unrealistic to transfer or adapt elBulli's approach to other more conventional organizations?

Case Notes:

9-7 Little Chef: Big Chef = Big Changes?

Little Chef, a British chain of roadside restaurants, was established in 1958. Founder Sam Alper, a caravan manufacturer, wanted to develop the restaurant on roadside eateries he had seen in the USA. And the opening of the first Little Chef coincided with Britain's first US-style motorway.

By the 1980s, the chain was ubiquitous on Britain's motorway network. About 440 restaurants with the famous red and white "Fat Charlie" logo beckoned hungry families and business travelers. The concept was to provide traditional British food quickly in a US-style diner environment. Popular menu items included: a big English fried breakfast called the "Olympic," haddock or cod with chips, beefburgers, steaks, and tea.

With its familiar red and white decor and wipe-clean menus, Little Chef became, according to the *Sun* newspaper "a national institution," serving up 10 million cups of tea every year as well as 13 million sausages, 15 million rashers, and 15 million eggs. The chain became a firm favorite with kids. Any youngsters leaving a clean plate at the end of their meal would receive a free lollipop. Such was the popularity of Little Chef and its Fat Charlie logo that an attempt to slim him down caused outrage among fans, with 15,000 complaints forcing the chain to keep Charlie as he was.

But by the end of the 20th century, Little Chef's fortunes were in decline. While there had been little roadside competition in the UK in the first few decades of its existence, by 1990 US franchisers like Burger King and KFC were aggressively seeking to expand along motorway sites. A trend toward healthy eating had begun. Refurbished service stations had expanded their stores to include coffee chains and sandwiches. And, traditional pubs had begun to incorporate restaurants and new chains based on the pub/restaurant concept, such as Brewers Fayre, were established.

Higher prices had earned Little Chef a new nickname: "Little Thief" and at the same time more and more customers were complaining about poor quality food. The chain was now owned by huge conglomerates, firstly Trust House Forte, then Granada, then Travelodge Hotels Ltd, and Little Chef restaurants appeared increasingly shabby and run down, leading to suspicions that the variety of new owners were extracting too much money from the business while investing too little.

By 2005, the number of Little Chef restaurants had declined to around 230. New owners, The People's Restaurant Group, planned to modernize, introduce self-service, and slash prices in what was marketed as a "Little Chef's price crash." But this just resulted in lower revenue. By the end of 2006 the firm was thought to be losing £3 million a year and it was reported that Fat Charlie would be hanging up his hat, with the loss of around 4,000 jobs.

But the brand was rescued in January 2007 by RCapital, a UK private equity group who bought 197 of the remaining outlets for less than £10 million. The new owners said they were going to modernize (as most new owners do). Then they did something surprising. They hired Britain's most notoriously avant garde chef: Heston Blumenthal; and asked him to redesign not just the menu but a refit of the restaurants. Blumenthal's quest was filmed as a documentary series for Channel 4 called "Big Chef Takes on Little Chef."

Wikipedia refers to Blumenthal as "famous for his scientific approach. . . [and] perennial runner-up to Ferran Adria of elBulli [see the previous case] in the [chef] world rankings." His Fat Duck restaurant was voted best in the world in 2005 by *Restaurant* magazine and best in the UK by *The Good Food Guide* in 2007 and 2009. His signature dishes include snail porridge and bacon and egg ice cream. His recipe for "The Perfect Black Forest Gateau" took two years to perfect and the dish can take two days to construct.

The Channel 4 documentary shows that Blumenthal is serious about the challenge. Labeling the chain as "iconic," he says the invitation is "A big honour." And a big risk: "If I get it right it would be a fantastic achievement. If I fail it will be a disaster. . . it will be a complete humiliation."

"There's a big chunk of Britishness about Little Chef nostalgia" claims Blumenthal. He outlines that the key words for him in this challenge are "Britishness and excitement. . . bringing excitement back to the brand."

But upon entering a Little Chef restaurant for the first time in 20 years, the scale of the brand's decline is greater than Blumenthal expected. He is confronted with a huge menu – over 60 dishes referencing a wide variety of culinary traditions. Blumenthal counts them off: "Thailand and America and Jamaica and Maryland. . . and everywhere else other than Britain!. . . [It] wants to take every country in the world and be everything to everybody. . . This is the menu of a company in a panic." The décor of the Little Chef restaurants he visits across the country is tired and shabby, kitchens are poorly fitted out, the corporate menu allows for "no creativity, no excitement, no passion," and the food that he and his Fat Duck chefs taste is in their words "unbelievably awful."

However, Blumenthal finds Little Chef's staff positive about the brand. They are saddened about the company's decline and very keen to get behind him and turn things around.

Blumenthal tells Little Chef Chief Executive Ian Pegler, who brought Heston in to turn things around, that the old menu must go. In its place, Blumenthal will create an entirely new menu that will "reinvent British classics for the 21st century." Pegler enthusiastically agrees and outlines his vision. He wants to see "a taste explosion in every single thing that you do [Heston]. . . a menu that will *wow* the public." "Think as wide as you can. . . take the core product and explode it. . . Use blue sky thinking. . . but without alienating our current customers who like the food we currently serve."

Emboldened, but somewhat nervous about what Pegler wants, Blumenthal worries about Pegler's vision. Thinking through it as he drives away from meeting with Pegler back to the Fat Duck where the new menu will be developed, he muses that it "doesn't actually make sense, it's almost as if he's contradicting himself. . ."

"Heston's Menu," as it comes to be called, contains dishes such as scrambled eggs with Lapsang Souchong and Earl Grey tea infusions, pea and ham soup, a Lancashire Hot Pot but with oysters and rosemary oil added, and chocolate ice cream with mandarin steam. It will be trialed in a "flagship" Little Chef site in Popham, Hampshire. Popham manager Michael Cook has worked at Little Chef for 25 years, and is passionate about the company. He desperately wants the turnaround to work, but is nervous about Heston going too far and alienating customers. At Popham the restaurant is divided in half with two of Heston's Fat Duck chefs offering the Heston menu on one side, and the Little Chef chefs offering the traditional menu on the other. If Heston's menu proves popular it will begin to be rolled out across the chain.

But first, Ian Pegler and his management board members are invited to a tasting with Heston. Pegler and the board leave deeply disappointed. They are not "wowed." It's underwhelmingly ordinary, Pegler thinks, lecturing Heston that "we could have got this from any celebrity chef. . . the reason we chose you was because you are so different. Where is the blue sky thinking?"

Meanwhile, Heston's menu bombs in Popham. Customers prefer the traditional menu by a ratio of 5:1. A culture clash has developed between the Fat Duck chefs and the Little Chef people. At one point Michael Cook barks at the Fat Duck crew "don't think you're better than me, because your not."

"I think they look down on Little Chef," Cook later says to the camera. "What made them think that these dishes would work at Little Chef. . . Little Chef is not about fancy food, it's about quick food in and out."

When Blumenthal watches customer reactions to his dishes on tape later on, Cook's views are backed up. His food is described as "too rich," "too expensive," "too slow," not "making sense," and "a bit poncy." It's "a let-down," another customers claims. "Once the mandarin steam is gone, it's just chocolate ice cream."

For a disappointed Blumenthal it's an unprecedented failure and one that he takes personally. "As a chef I seek to give people pleasure through food. . . and it's clear that I haven't given these people pleasure. . . It feels like being kicked in the stomach, but I can't dismiss it. . . I've got to try and pull something out of this. At the end of the day my menu was wrong for Little Chef." With his relationship with Pegler straining to breaking point he outlines what he believes to be the best way forward: "I've got to find out what British people want to eat. . ."

---

1. *Outline what you believe Blumenthal did well and what he did not do well in seeking to manage the strategic change of Little Chef.*
2. *How would you seek to manage this process from the point at which the case finishes (YouTube may be a source of interesting clips that show how this case developed)?*
3. *There seems to be a clash between what customers appear to want and Ian Pegler's "wow" vision. How would you seek to manage this conflict and any resistance that either party may put up against Heston's attempts to turn things around?*

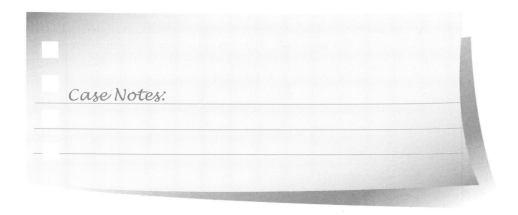

Case Notes:

Part IV   Strategic Futures

> "...businesses have done more than any other institutions to advance prosperity, turning the luxuries of the rich, such as cars a century ago and computers today, into goods for the masses."
>
> *The Economist*

> Capitalism is the astounding belief that the most wickedest of men will do the most wickedest of things for the greater good of everyone.
>
> *George Maynard Keynes*

> It's almost like seeing a guy show up at the soup kitchen in a high hat and tuxedo – couldn't you have downgraded to first class or something, or jet-pooled or something to get here?
>
> *House of Representative's Member Gary Ackerman to carmaker CEOs who arrived via private jet in Washington in November 2008 to plead for bailout funds for their stricken companies*

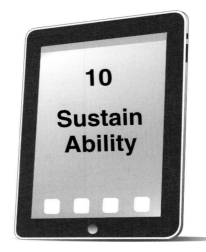

10
Sustain Ability

The first decade of the 21st century has not been a good one for the public image of business. On June 29, 2009, Bernie Madoff was sentenced to 150 years in prison for defrauding investors of over \$65bn through the mechanism of a giant Ponzi scheme (i.e. a scheme that promises high returns but uses the investment funds of subscribers to pay other subscribers). Mr. Madoff was no fly-by-night conman. His investment company had started in the 1980s and he had risen to become a highly respected member of the investment community with positions on several prestigious non-profit boards as well as serving as Chairman of NASDAQ. He was a trusted pillar of the business society. He turned out to be a crook.

Such individual examples aside, the latter part of the 00s has been dominated by the Global Financial Crisis (GFC). A combination of factors including: the over use of debt to leverage returns; the assumption that bundling and splitting risk somehow removed it and the underpricing of risk in general, etc. led to a big bang and the collapse of financial institutions and other companies around the world. Huge bailouts by governments were necessary to keep large institutions afloat and prevent an even more catastrophic outcome. There is a strong sense among many that the causes of the crisis emanated from the greedy, cavalier managers who, while quick to demand the rewards for their entrepreneurship in good times, were equally quick to demand that society, in the form of government, throw them a lifeline when all their bets were losing ones. The audacity of some of these titans of industry who rolled up to beg for handouts in private jets with their assistants carrying their begging bowls brought howls of protest, as exemplified by the quote at the top of this chapter.

Society has always had an ambivalent relationship with business and business people. We benefit from the invisible hand of public good that arises from self-interested trade. The quote from *The Economist* at the head of this chapter gives a succinct modern statement of Adam Smith's original concept. However, we are less enamored of the all-too-visible hands of some senior executives appropriating shareholder wealth for their own enrichment, or the apparent privileging of shareholder wealth over the integrity of the environment that all have to share. Lord Maynard Keynes' satirical take on the invisible hand (above) reflects a degree of cynicism that is shared by many.

Mr. Madoff's breach of trust and the sharp practices that contributed to the GFC are sadly not the only issues that have lowered people's view of the role of corporations and their leaders in recent years. Consider, for example:

- The high level chicanery at firms like Enron and World.com aided and abetted by auditors with equally questionable values;
- The exploitation of gullible investors by "entrepreneurs" and analysts with vested interests during the dot-com bubble;
- The egregious level of financial compensation conferred on senior executives while they are in the job and when they are sacked;
- The cavalier attitude to consumer health demonstrated by various tobacco, pharmaceutical and building companies as they orchestrated silence and deception about the effects of their products;
- The blind eye turned to the exploitation of off-shore workers, including children, by some of the most famous branded goods companies in the world;
- The connivance with corrupt officials and governments by some extraction companies keen to protect valuable leases and mining rights;
- The popular movies and books, such as *The Corporation* or Michael Moore's works, which have presented these sorts of infamy to an increasingly receptive audience;
- The sub-plots of popular movies from *Wall Street* to *Avatar* that "big business" is sinister and an exploiter of innocence;
- BP's pollution of the Gulf of Mexico in 2010 and its seemingly lackluster response (of which we'll say more at the conclusion of this chapter).

These, and many other examples, raise questions about the corporate world. Are these merely examples of rogue companies or is this the tip of a large rubbish dump wherein the best that can be said of the remainder is that they have not yet been caught? Society's answers to these questions and the actions and attitudes adopted by business in general, and individual organizations in particular, will have a significant influence on the degree of strategic freedom enjoyed by firms for the remainder of the 21st century. The clamour for increased government oversight and regulation grows louder and more insistent with each new Enron or Madoff or Global Financial Crisis. Is it sufficient that the contract for wealth enhancement between companies and society can be grounded in the side effect of the invisible hand or should a more explicit compact about the more general role of business be formulated?

In this chapter we explore sustainable development, or "sustain ability," a convergence of several as yet not fully defined paradigms which is reshaping the role of the firm and capitalism. Sustainable development, according to some of its most zealous advocates, goes beyond dealing with how organizations should look to protect and sustain their competitive advantage across the long term and how they should act as good citizens concerned with sustaining or preserving our shared environments for the future. It goes to the heart of what an organization strategically is.

Students and practitioners of strategy are familiar with the concept of sustainability in the context of a **sustainable competitive advantage**. Advantage is sustainable if the underpinning sources are not substitutable or imitable. The durability of any advantage is a function of the isolating mechanisms impeding copying (see Chapter 5 Strategic Positioning). However, the concept of sustainability has taken on broader connotations since the World Commission on Economic Development (WCED) drew attention to the need for **sustainable development** as ". . . development that meets the needs of the present generation without compromising the ability of future generations to meet their own needs."[1]

This rather loose definition has likely contributed to much of the rhetoric about sustainability lacking clarity, with sustainability becoming a rather amorphous catch-all term used to incorporate everything from corporate social responsibility, only using renewable resources, and organic farming, resulting in arguments with cross-purposes. Hence, while we believe that strategists must take the force of feeling behind sustainability seriously, they would also do well to be clear about what aspect of the phenomena they are actually implying in their arguments. Table 10.1 presents a range of related but different ecological concerns that could be grouped under the sustainability banner (we shall pick up on some of the social aspects of sustainability further on in this chapter).

Table 10.1   Ecological concerns related to sustainability

Biodegradable – A product that will decompose into the earth without having a negative effect on the environment.

Carbon footprint – The amount of greenhouse gases released into the atmosphere by manufacture, transport, materials, activities, etc.

Carbon neutral – Human activities that do not increase the amount of CO_2 in the atmosphere, or if they do are offset by activities that reduce CO_2.

Ecological footprint – The amount of land needed by a person or population to sustain their lives with the consumption of natural resources, calculated and compared to the earth's ability to generate these resources.

Energy efficiency – Achieving the same outcome with less energy, such as achieving the same light from a lower wattage light bulb.

Organic – An alternative farming method which removes toxins, manufactured chemicals, synthetic additives, genetically modified organisms (GMOs) and provides products which are biodegradable.

Waste neutral – When the weight in kilos/pounds for products that are to be recycled is the same amount as the weight of products to be made from the recycled products.

Recyclable – A product or packaging that can be recycled when the end of its lifecycle has been reached (e.g. cans that can be broken down into their pure matter and made into new cans).

Renewable materials or energy technology – Natural raw materials (e.g. timber) that can be replenished over time or using natural and perpetual energy resources such as water, wind and sun.

Remanufacturable – When a product reaches the end of its lifecycle, it can be manufactured for a second time using the parts which remain functional (e.g. refillable printer cartridges).

Repurposable – A product or material which is used for another purpose once its original purpose has completed (e.g. packages such as glass jars which can be used for home storage).

Reusable – A product or material which is used again and again for the same purpose, such as milk bottles.

While present views of sustainable development may be somewhat muddled, the broad concept as it relates to corporations (or **corporate sustainability (CS)**) results from the convergence of the principles of **environmental integrity**, **economic prosperity**, and **social equity** (see Figure 10.1). This convergence denotes a significant socio-economic shift.

Historically, economic development through firms was viewed as being a tradeoff with environmental concerns and social equity. Pollution, logging, land abuse, etc; have been viewed as negative externalities or collateral damage of the value creating process. The underpayment of women and minority groups has been seen as necessary in the interests of shareholders (see Chapter 2 Movers and Shakers). Public, media-driven shaming, or direct control though legislation and hence prosecution have both been used to ensure that firms give more weight to the public and environmental good.

Another change that had been evolving before the WCED report, but was further stimulated by it, was an increasing focus at a lower level of analysis. Sustainable development had traditionally been discussed as an intraglobal issue at the level of the nation state. So it is nations which sign or do not sign the Copenhagen accord on greenhouse gases, for example, even though it is organizations within nations that do the emitting, and it is nations which make trade and tariff agreements although firms do the trading. It is also nations which were first measured on a sustainability index. However, in modern industrialized nation states the firm is becoming (willingly or not) a focus for sustainable development rather than an involved but not necessarily committed bystander. This seems logical to some commentators because "corporations . . . control most of the resources of our global society. If we are to have effective leadership of the sustainability movement, then much of the movement must come from the corporate sector."[2]

There has been a paradigm shift in that businesses are being asked to become manifestations of the planet's requirement for environmental integrity *and* economic prosperity *and* social equity, rather than maintain an uneasy equilibrium of tradeoffs. This mirrors the evolutionary biologist's perspective that ecology and economy are interdependent and inseparable dynamics.[3]

Corporate environmental integrity emphasizes a firm's responsibility to manage its processes and products so as to minimize their impact on the physical

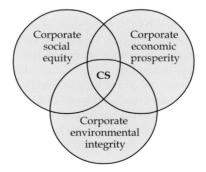

Figure 10.1 The three legs of corporate sustainability (CS)

environment. At the most reactive end of the continuum, this calls for businesses to simply act responsibly in the way they dispose of the waste and by-products of their processes. A more progressive approach, however, involves seeking ongoing improvements and/or innovation, to reduce and eventually eliminate such pollution ("pollution prevention").[4] Further on from this, "cradle to grave" responsibility encourages firms to design products for minimal energy usage both in manufacture and in use, to use less material and components, and to use material least harmful to the environment both as an input and with regard to eventual disposal. Some predict that legislation will increasingly demand that firms accept the disposal ("grave") end of the product process as their responsibility. As an example, the "take-back" law in Germany already makes auto manufacturers responsible for disposing of their products at the end of their useful life.

Much of the language of the above paragraph reflects a "do no harm" and "minimize depletion" orientation and would be familiar to most managers today. Many claim, however, that true sustainability demands a more constructive response whereby companies actively seek to *improve* the world's environmental integrity. The concept of an "ecological footprint" captures the daunting scale of this problem.[5] It takes a footprint of 10.3 hectares to supply the basic needs of the average US citizen compared with 0.8 hectares in India – yet even India's total footprint is larger than the country itself. If the remainder of the world comes to enjoy the same level of consumption as the USA, then the known resources of the world would need to triple to accommodate that growth unless a major reorientation takes place in those companies fulfilling that consumption. Logging companies who plant more trees than they chop down are a simple example of this sort of reorientation. (Note that genetically modified (GM) food is not problem-free in this regard and Monsanto, for example, has many virulent critics with respect to their development of GM, as live Case 10-2 illustrates.)

The **corporate social equity** leg of the corporate sustainability stool often manifests itself as *corporate social responsibility*[6] (CSR) or *corporate citizenship*. The discussion around this dynamic, associated with the older concept of business ethics, dates back at least to the governing bodies of the ancient Greeks.[7] From one extreme, it is argued that a firm's social and ethical responsibilities are fully discharged in maximizing long-run returns to shareholders and are captured in the aphorism "the business of business is business."[8] *The Economist*, for example, is unapologetic in asserting that "managers … ought not to concern themselves with the public good: they are not competent to do it, they lack the democratic credentials for it, and their day jobs should leave them not time even to think about it. If they merely concentrate on discharging their responsibilities to the owners of their firms, acting ethically as they do so, they will usually serve the public good in any case."[9] The diametrically opposing perspective is that "social responsibility is the managerial obligation to take action to protect and improve both the welfare of society as a whole and the interests of organizations" and, within this perspective, maximizing shareholder value is *neither a necessary nor a sufficient component.*[10] Hence, while *The Economist* stresses "acting ethically" when pursuing shareholder value, others suggest that it may be the pursuit of shareholder value per se that is the problem.

These arguments are often expressed in terms of the relative gains and losses of various **stakeholders** and the extent to which the needs of some *direct stakeholders* *of the firm* (e.g. shareholders, senior managers) are privileged over the needs of others, who may be directly or indirectly involved (e.g. employees, customers, local community, and society in general). The heat in the argument is generated most when the actions of businesses harm some stakeholders while pursuing the interests of others. *Roger and Me*, a 1989 film by the ever-controversial producer Michael Moore, captured this dynamic by showing the negative economic and social consequences for Moore's home town, Flint in Michigan, when General Motors (then under the stewardship of Roger Smith) closed down its Flint manufacturing facility with a loss of 30,000 local jobs. Current arguments along this line concern such matters as putting local people out of work by "off-shoring" their functions to lower cost countries, the sale of socially harmful products (e.g. high-sugar and high-fat foods), the use of child labor, and dealing with corrupt regimes.

Beyond the level of the individual firm, there are a number of typologies of CSR. Some suggest a longitudinal pathway from one general orientation to another while others indicate a continuum of similar dynamics coexisting in different ways in any cross-section of businesses. Table 10.2 illustrates a historical perspective with different phases of social responsibility having emerged because of different pressures at different times.[11]

An alternative suggestion is that while social change – for example, in the form of increasing pluralism and global awareness, and a far wider share ownership – has indeed forced a change in orientation in business in general, it is more realistic to view different organizations as having different perspectives contingent on their specific histories and contexts. Like people, companies can range from socially responsible to irresponsible, from being careful to preserve a legacy for tomorrow's citizens to being cavalier with that heritage in optimizing today's benefits.[12] Table 10.3 describes an evolution in firm orientation in this respect, with each higher level "type" incorporating and developing on an earlier level.[13]

The table should also be taken to suggest that each firm has elements of each of the four types and so both context and firm character are important in determining which characteristic predominates. In underdeveloped countries, where most businesses may be type I (through competitive and other contextual forces), there will be some that are higher up the social responsibility scale. The increased proportions of firms in the II–IV categories in developed countries may say more

Table 10.2 Development of sustainability orientation in developed countries

Phase	Time	Orientation
I: Profit maximizing	Post-Industrial Revolution	Maximize profits within the law
II: Trustee management	1920s–1980s	Equitable balance among competing claims of internal and external stakeholders
III: Quality of life management	1980s–now	Broad economic, social, and environmental responsibility

Table 10.3 Business types and societal roles

Type	Societal role
I: Profit maximize	An *economic entity* with the sole objective of making legal profits. Labor is an input factor to be bought and sold like land and capital
II: Good employer	A *human development entity* with obligations to develop and use employees to their fullest capability by providing a stimulating work environment and meeting both the hygiene and motivational needs of its workers
III: Good citizen	A *civic entity* with obligations to support its local community with money and effort and to be fair and open in its dealings and not engage in deceptive or unsafe market or product practices
IV: Social worker	A *societal entity* with obligations, within and beyond its local context, to actively protect and enhance both the physical environment and social equity

about the local political and social context than about the fundamental "personality" of those businesses. And so companies that might otherwise be classified as type IV (e.g. Nike and Royal Dutch Shell in the past) have been accused of turning a blind eye to labor exploitation (Nike's Asian suppliers)[14] or corrupt dealings (Shell's links with the Nigerian Government)[15] when outside their home markets (contexts). Cynics suggest that inside every (socially constrained) type IV firm there is in fact a type I genie bursting to get out!

Corporate economic prosperity (i.e. creating value and prosperity through producing and selling goods and services) is the fundamental rationale underpinning the existence of firms and the capitalist system. The value created is shared between the business and other direct stakeholders/members of society dependent on the extent to which the price obtained by the firm is greater than the overall economic costs of creating and distributing its offerings. In some intensely competitive industries, businesses are forced to sell at prices below economic costs for long periods and hence value is transferred to consumers (airlines and mass-producers of cars have been placed in this position over various business cycles). When prices exceed costs, then the firm captures the value it creates and is able to enhance the prosperity of managers, shareholders, and other direct stakeholders.

While this might seem the "no-brainer" leg of the corporate sustainability stool, a more controversial aspect is captured in the idea of using it to develop a business case for corporate sustainability. A "hook" for the "greed is good" business community, some social/environmental champions have dangled the bait of making money from being "good" by showing, for example, how environmental opportunities can become a major source of revenue growth (e.g. "... few executives realize that environmental opportunities might actually become a major source of *revenue growth* ... most companies fail to recognize opportunities of staggering proportions")[16] It has been noted that the combination of high shareholder returns and a strong focus on social welfare has long been a characteristic of outstanding companies.[17] In line with this, the Dow Jones Sustainability Index – which tracks the share prices of international companies considered leaders in sustainable development – has often outperformed the Dow Jones Global Index. This seems to offer prima facie evidence that corporate sustainability is indeed a function and a driver of corporate economic prosperity, corporate environmental integrity, and corporate social equity (Figure 10.1). Three broad theoretical thrusts, all with some empirical support, propose reasons behind this relationship.[18]

1. **The organizational slack perspective** – those firms which earn good returns can devote more resources to social equity and environmental integrity.[19]
2. **The positive synergy perspective** – combining the idea of resource availability and good management, the advocates of this view suggest that, along with all the other things they do well, good managers in firms with available resources also do well in terms of social equity and environmental integrity.[20]
3. **The social impact hypothesis** – the actual costs of social equity and environmental integrity are small compared with the higher risk entailed by failing to meet these requirements. Increasingly those firms that are indifferent to broader stakeholder demands will pay a price in terms of reputational disadvantage and/or a higher risk premium on debt/equity.[21]

These models can be contrasted with the "tradeoff" approaches mentioned earlier in which social equity and environmental integrity are claimed to entail additional costs that will financially disadvantage the "do-gooder" against more opportunistic and less principled competitors. This is most often expressed by regretful companies attributing their loss of integrity to the lack of a "level playing field" whereon all competitors must play to the same ethical and environmental "rules." It is more subtly expressed in terms of a review or renewal of "the contract between business and society."

The argument that sustainability authors make against the business case orientation is that it is inherently a contingent concept, as captured in: "The business case is not a generic argument that corporate sustainability strategies are the right choice for all companies in all situations, *but rather something that must be carefully honed to the specific circumstances of individual companies operating in unique positions within distinct industries*"[22] (emphasis added). This orientation puts economic prosperity at the top of the company's agenda and other aspects of sustainability, such as environmental integrity and CSR, will follow *when and if* it is economically sensible for them to do so.[23] Corporate sustainability is not a contingent concept; it makes economic prosperity, environmental integrity, and social equity equal and ever-present partners (Figure 10.1). There is no "if … then" relationship (e.g. "*if* it is good for shareholders *then* we will do it"); there are no "ors" (e.g. "we can be socially responsible *or* we can maximize shareholder value"); there is only "and" (e.g. "we will make profits *and* improve society *and* improve the environment").

The Triple-Bottom Line

In response to the convergence outlined above, businesses are demonstrating a commitment to sustainable development (or at least its language and reports) through reporting on the so-called **triple bottom line (TBL)** of economic, social and environmental performance. Economic reporting relates to the traditional

Table 10.4 A "worked example" of TBL thinking from Longmount (Colorado) City Council

Street sweeping

Economic factors:

- – Cost of equipment, fuel and maintenance over the life of the equipment
- – Replacement cost.
- – Cost of labour.
- – Lower cost of preventing water pollution as compared to other treatment methods.
- – Lower medical costs associated with improvements in air quality.
- – Economic benefits to businesses – customer perception.

Environmental factors:

- – Reduction in pollutants such as sediments and nutrients in streams and rivers (offsets the costs of providing treatment for these pollutants).
- – Reduction in particulate air pollution (improvement in public health).
- – Lower emissions and fossil fuel usage.

Social factors:

- – Increased sense of pride in community.
- – Improved sense of safety (cleaner neighbourhoods = safer neighbourhoods).
- – Improved bicycle and traffic safety.

(*Source*: www.ci.longmont.co.us/city_council/agendas/2010/documents/033010_4C.pdf)

balance measure of financial performance, environmental performance relates to the sorts of concerns listed in Table 10.1 and social performance tends to be used to report upon employee and community well being (see Table 10.4 for an example of the sort of things that might be thought through and inputted into a TBL analysis of a particular activity).

A lack of clarity around how the social and environmental bottom lines might be balanced, measured or related to the financial bottom line of an organization means that often the social and environmental sections of TBL reporting are simply lists of intentions or commitments, targets and achievements. However, reporting and publicizing commitments and achievements with regard to the three bottom-lines is becoming commonplace, with laggards under more scrutiny to explain their lack of transparency. To some companies, TBL is no more than dealing with one of the "pests" of PEST, or ESTEMPLE, but to others it is seen as a strategic necessity, not only in terms of diffusing potentially hostile political and social forces, but also in terms of potential reputational disadvantage in the minds of environmentally sensitized customers. Indeed, quotes such as the following by Bill Ford in 2005: "My great-grandfather's vision was to provide affordable transport for the world. I want to expand that vision for the 21st century and provide transportation that is affordable in every sense of the word – socially and environmentally, as well as economically"; are a good example of how these three bottom lines have become a part of today's strategic language.

Table 10.5 Alternative measures of performance that are linked to reputation. (All information from Fortune.com)

2010 performance ratings	"Fortune 500": America's biggest companies by annual revenue	"Fortune 100 Best Companies to Work For" (based on employee surveys)	"Fortune World's Most Admired Companies" (based on surveys of people external to each company)
1.	Wal-Mart	SAS	Apple
2.	Exxon Mobil	Edward Jones	Google
3.	Chevron	Wegman Food Markets	Berkshire Hathaway
4.	General Electric	Google	Johnson & Johnson
5.	Bank of America	Nugget Market	Amazon.com
6.	Conono Phillips	DreamWorks Animation SKG	Procter & Gamble
7.	AT&T	NetApp	Toyota Motor
8.	Ford Motor	Boston Consulting Group	Goldman Sachs Group
9.	J.P. Morgan Chase	Qual comm	Coca-Cola
10.	Chase	Camden Property Trust	Microsoft

While there is growing awareness of TBL, some commentators, notably Jeffery Pfeffer, have noted that the intense debate around ecological sustainability may have diverted attention away from human and social sustainability, particularly with regard to employees.[24] However, new league tables focusing on employee engagement and "best-places to work" should ensure that this does not get lost in the wash. Indeed, one thing is certain, at a time when organizations are increasingly concerned with how their corporate reputation can positively or negatively impact on their likelihood of survival there are an increasing number of ways that performance and reputation are being measured, beyond the traditional singular emphasis on financial performance (see Table 10.5).

Business Ethics and Corporate Integrity

The developments outlined above have helped to re-ignite debates about business ethics by making it increasingly untenable for organizations to simply stand behind Milton Friedman's famous claim that a company's responsibility is only to conduct "business in accordance with [shareholders'] desires, which generally will be to make as much money as possible while conforming to the basic rules of the society." While it is impossible to do justice to the burgeoning field of business ethics here, we do offer two sets of key ethical approaches below that we think all strategists should be mindful of.

SUSTAIN ABILITY

Two ethical orientations

Since at least the time of the Ancient Greeks there have been two different ethical strands.

The first is often termed a **deontic** approach (*deos* meaning "duty" in Ancient Greek, and, more commonly now in modern Greek "fear"). This is an "outside-in" approach based on aspiring to universal Platonic ideals. For organizations, this kind of ethics is generally manifest in written codes outlining acceptable conduct, standards, responsibilities and corporate duties which can be referred to when ethical questions arise. A famous example is Johnson & Johnson's "Credo," which you may like to Google.

The second is an approach often traced back to Aristotle, where ethics is related to individual and particular virtues which can be discerned "inside-out," from self-reflection on one's particular role within a community. This approach is often termed **aretaic** (*arête* meaning "virtue") and in organizational terms is closely related to the open and honest portrayal of the organization's corporate identity that the company will adhere to (see Chapter 6). So, for example, a low-cost airline that markets low price as their primary virtue cannot be accused of being "unethical" if they only adhere to minimum industry standards in other respects: they are being consistent with their well-publicized virtue of being 'low-cost'. In modern times we might regard an aretaic approach more like an "ethos" than ethics.

Three ethical principles

1. "Do not do to others what would anger you if done to you by others." This quotation is from Isocrates, but it is a sentiment that dates back to ancient Babylonian texts and is captured in the often expressed aphorism: "Do unto others. . ." From an organizational point of view this might be applied by asking questions like "do we treat our staff (or customers etc.) as we would like to be treated"?
2. "Act only according to that maxim whereby you can at the same time will that it should become universal law." This is Immanuel Kant's famous "categorical imperative." In an organizational setting, this might encourage reflections such as: "I could cut corners with this trade, but what would be the result if this "cutting corners" became the norm?"
3. "The moral worth of an action is determined by its utility in providing happiness or pleasure as summed among all beings." This is the founding principle of Utilitarianism of whom Jeremy Bentham and John Stuart Mill are the most famous proponents. It is often described using the phrase "the greatest good for the greatest number of people." In an organization, one might reflect on how much good a particular decision might bring to stakeholders relative to other potential course of action.

Whether one favors a deontic or aretaic orientation, or both; the categorical imperative, utilitarianism or another ethical principle, the aim should be fidelity and *reflection*: *fidelity* to the chosen orientation and the principles and statements that emanate from them; and, at the same time a willingness to reflect upon and respond to changes in social, ethical, legal and ecological beliefs in the wider environment (the S E L E of ESTEMPLE outlined in Chapter 1). While the term **integrity** has been bandied about in business circles, it has been used fairly loosely and without a clear sense of what it really entails (Enron listed integrity as one of its core values). Strategists would do well to give clearer meaning to integrity by understanding it in these terms.

The Good Corporate Citizen or Green-washing: In Pursuit of "and"?

In the year 2000, British Petroleum relaunched itself as "Beyond Petroleum," proclaiming its concern for the environment and championing its efforts in developing alternative energy sources. The move was widely criticized. In an editorial entitled Oil Slickness, London's *Sunday Telegraph* pointed out that: "less than 1% of BP's revenues come from renewable sources of energy and well over 90% of its income still comes from fossil fuels and derivative businesses such as chemicals and petrol retailing." "Beyond Petroleum," they scoffed, "it's beyond belief." Other media commentators and the general public also didn't buy it, and the Beyond Petroleum marketing was quickly scaled back while the company rethought.

At the end of 2002, Beyond Petroleum bubbled back to the surface as part of the company's new "It's a start" campaign. This featured "ordinary people" sharing their concerns for our environmental future before BP explains what it was doing about these concerns. For example, one billboard announces: "Our goal is to make solar a $1 billion business by 2007 . . . it's a start." *The Times* of London remarked that it seemed "astonishing that the company should plug 'beyond petroleum' after the roasting it received from the press in July 2000 when it announced the rebranding." Its article explained that while steps such as the installation of windmills at some service stations to generate electricity for the fuel pumps "may seem more of a gimmick than a business opportunity for a company that sells petrol … BP is not like that; it has invested $200 million in a solar power business that has yet to turn a profit. It was the first oil company to state publicly that climate change was a problem linked to carbon emissions. It declared its support for the Kyoto Protocol and set itself a more aggressive target – to reduce carbon emissions by 10% below 1990 levels."

While other commentators have not been so positive (e.g. Daniel Gross on MSN's *Moneybox* program slated the new campaign as audacious and dishonest), public opinion saw something more authentic, and thus viable, about BP's words this time. Most of the reader feedback posted to Gross's MSN column gives BP the benefit of the doubt, with one reader responding: "Gross's point [that] BP is still a carbon-belching behemoth trying to garner some mostly undeserved cachet with a mostly superficial eco-marketing campaign and some small forays into alternative fuels, is absolutely true. But still . . . it's a start. I'd rather have big oil companies do what BP is doing than actively fight against alternative energy – by lobbying against tax breaks and government incentives – or do nothing at all, which is what some companies are doing."

But that was before the deep-sea drilling disaster of 2010 . . . Based on the ideas, developments and principles outlined in this chapter, and what might be learnt from the initial failure of Beyond Petroleum (seen as just a "green-wash") and then its partial success, what else *should* BP have been doing as it advanced their "Beyond Petroleum" virtue. And what would *you* do if you were appointed BP's CEO now to put the company on a more sustainable footing?

The occasional Bernie Madoff or Enron chicanery has led to relatively muted outcries in the past. These have been viewed as idiosyncratic flaws not representative of the general run of managers and businesses. The Global Financial Crisis that began in 2008 has changed the mindset of society. The collective result of vast arrays of businesses pursuing their own logical ends was a systemic blow to society as a whole – society will strive to not allow that to happen again. Subsequently, the most intriguing aspect of this major new arena is that there is little or no disagreement as to the desirability or validity of the general importance of sustainability, even though what this means exactly is still being worked out. A major divide remains however between those who firmly and genuinely believe that the corporate world, through enlightened self-interest and a desire to be good corporate citizens, will embrace and drive sustainable development (left-hand column in Figure 10.2), and those who believe that any appearance of this is merely **green-washing** (companies "spinning" their products and policies as environmentally friendly), that in the business world the profit imperative of the individual firm will inevitably undermine any collective will toward sustainability. But on one point there can be no debate. The days of businesses claiming not to care, or not wanting to engage with these issues, are gone. At the very least, the wider community will expect that all organizations consider, develop, and defend a view of where they stand with regard to sustainability. The two poles of sustainable development *or* profitability are now a false choice as they have become two sides of the same coin. Sustainability *and* profitability are now coexistent – an organization's Sustain Ability is what counts.

Business will promote sustainable development	**Business will not promote sustainable development**
The long-term viability of a business and its ability to deliver ongoing shareholder value is contingent on a viable social and physical planet. Hence the enlightened self-interest of business managers will promote global well-being in much the same way as new products have enhanced quality of life as an unintended side-effect since the Industrial Revolution. In terms of table 10.2 all that is required for social and environmental welfare is for firms to be diligent Type Is and then, for their own and everybody else's good, to evolve to Type IVs. The vastly increasing wealth, health, and general well-being of the world thus far is evidence that the system works	Due to free-rider problems (wherein one selfish firm can benefit at the expense of many enlightened ones), the pressures of "sub-goal optimization" (wherein the urgent, short-term imperatives of business – such as achieving this month's budget – inevitably drive out the long-term sustainability goals), and the inevitability of "moral hazard" (dishonesty) from some companies, the world cannot rely on businesses to embrace sustainable development as a natural consequence of profit optimization. Continued deforestation, global warming, dwindling fish stocks, pension mis-selling, and many other examples of firm self-interest dominating the well-being of society is evidence that legislation and surveillance are essential for the planet to thrive and that the current dalliance with CSR is failing

Figure 10.2 Poles of opinion regarding the relationship between corporations and the current emphasis on sustainable development and corporate sustainability

315

Having read and reviewed the chapter, outline what you believe to be the key learnings from the chapter and the relationships between these.

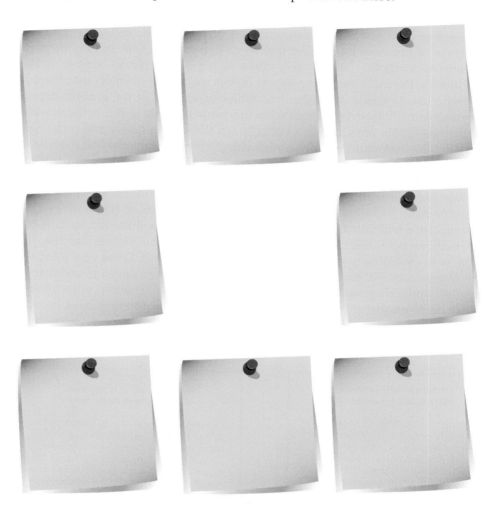

10-1 McDonald's: McAttacked

I'm lovin' it
McDonald's 2005 tag line

As one of the most famous brands in the modern world and *the* foremost emblem of "fast food" in the 21st century, McDonald's is only ever one overcooked French fry from controversy. In 2002 the company conceded defeat in a class action claiming that beef flavoring was used in preparing its French fries, whereas McDonald's had always claimed that only pure vegetable oils were used. In August 2005 California's Attorney General asked for a court order requiring McDonald's and eight other restaurant chains to warn customers that the same fries may contain the potential carcinogen acrylamide. A by-product of the chemicals and heat in cooking, acrylamide is found in low levels in several foods but at higher levels in fried offerings such as fries and potato chips. Such stories, whatever their truth, dent the reputation of well-known brands more than their lesser known rivals. Since 1984, when James Huberty killed 21 people in San Ysidro, California, by raking one of its restaurants with gunfire, McDonald's have come to understand that there *is* such a thing as bad publicity.

From its earliest marketing campaigns using the lovable clown Ronald McDonald, McDonald's implicit characterization of itself has been one of good, clean, fun-like wholesomeness. This was symbolized in the innocence of the children in its advertising, operationally embodied in Ray Kroc's obsession with cleanliness and friendly service in its restaurants and is the essence of the basic "bread, meat, and potatoes" of its products. The company has spent enormous sums developing and maintaining this image and has been famously litigious in protecting it from encroachment and debasement. An Australian rugby supporter, Malcolm McBratney found this out in 2005 when he tried to register his nickname "McBrat" which he was using as a (clothing) logo in his sponsorship of his local team. McDonald's opposed this on the grounds that it owned the "McKids" (toys) trademark and that there would be confusion between the two. In an earlier case the company sued a Scottish cafe owner called McDonald for infringement in using the name "McMunchies," even though it was a family business dating back well over a century.

The company took umbrage again in 2003 when the word "McJob" – defined as "low paying and dead-end work" appeared in the Merriam-Webster Collegiate Dictionary. As well as the implications for the morale of workers in its 30,000+ restaurants, a spokesman pointed out that "McJobs" was the company's trademarked name for its training program for handicapped people. McDonald's eventually chose not to pursue this line of attack being perhaps mindful of the negative publicity generated from the UK "McLibel" trial. This began in June 1994 when the firm chose to sue two British protestors for libel contained in pamphlets that the pair were distributing outside McDonald's outlets in London. After 314 days the longest libel action in British legal history concluded with £60,000 damages awarded to the company (later reduced on appeal to £40,000).

SUSTAINABILITY

The judgment was widely viewed as a pyrrhic victory due to two and a half years of negative press coverage and the fact that the judge did not dismiss the allegations of environmental, work, and health malpractice as untrue, but merely that the protesters could not prove their claims. In a further blow to the company's image the European Court of Human Rights found that the laws under which McDonald's were successful, breached the protestors' rights to a fair trial and freedom of expression. The UK Government changed the laws accordingly.

More importantly for McDonald's, the issues at the heart of the McLibel case, and in particular the criticisms of its major products, have refused to go away. In 1999 the veteran French activist Jose Bove achieved international exposure when he was jailed for three weeks after leading a group of farmer-activists in the destruction of a branch of McDonald's. He thus became a martyr for both the anti-globalists (Ralph Nader invited him to the Seattle WTO conference) and the opponents of the industrialization of food production. His attack on "mal-bouffe – bad food," although perhaps aimed at protecting French farming interests, resonated on a number of fronts with a mounting tide of condemnation of McDonald's-style food across the USA and Europe.

So-called "lifestyle" related illnesses from smoking, drinking/drugs and in particular, obesity, are the most significant precursors of health problems in the industrialized world. While people are living longer in general, they are at the same time manifesting health problems that are costly to society as lost productivity, diminished quality of life, and, what cynics suggest is the major issue, ballooning healthcare expenditure. The fast food industry, epitomized by McDonald's, has been targeted by governments and, in the USA by lawyers, as being at least partially "responsible" for the modern "epidemic" of obesity and obesity-related illnesses. In a move reminiscent of the tobacco industry, obese US plaintiffs began a series of court actions claiming their obesity to be the responsibility of McDonald's and seeking (astronomical) payments in compensation and damages. In 2004 the US House of Representatives passed the "cheeseburger bill" (The Personal Responsibility in Food Consumption Act) banning such actions.

While seemingly protected from obesity law suits, McDonald's is still faced with the fact that increasingly it is seen as a purveyor of unwholesome products to customers whose eating habits the company has influenced since their childhood. The fate of the potential McDonald's "addict" was dramatized in the documentary "Super Size Me," in which the film's producer, Morgan Spurlock, ate nothing but McDonald's food for 30 days. This resulted in: liver toxicity, a 55-point increase in blood cholesterol count, a 25-lb weight gain, depression, and loss of libido. Through such high-profile challenges the restaurant chain is being forced to address the question of its degree of responsibility for the food its customers eat both in terms of its ingredients and quantity. Proponents of healthy eating have proposed that, like tobacco and alcohol suppliers, fast food outlets should be offering "health" warnings to customers in their restaurants. These warnings should specify such things as the amount of saturated fats and salt in the order compared with the recommended daily average and indicate that fast food should not be eaten more than once or twice a week.

A stock response from McDonald's spokespeople has been that what people eat "is all about personal responsibility and individual decisions." But as more headlines appear like "McDonald's Salads Fattier than Burgers," "Shock News: McDonald's Makes You Unhealthy," and "The Invisible Extra with a Happy Meal McCarrot" (revealing that carrot sticks are kept "health looking" by being dipped in hydrogen peroxide) the company comes under increasing pressure to respond with more than "caveat emptor."

---

1. *To what extent do you think companies like McDonald's are responsible for the eating habits of their customers?*
2. *What do you think may be the major sustainability issues (broadly defined) facing McDonald's over the next ten years?*
3. *What should McDonald's do about these?*

◄◄◄ McResponse: Some ideas toward a "model answer"...

There is no doubt that for McDonald's and other fast food restaurants the issues touched on in this case are significant political and social forces that must be systematically dealt with as part of their ongoing non-market strategies. It is unlikely, for example, that the House of Representatives passed its "cheeseburger bill" without at least some lobbying from industry representatives. It is also logical that new menus be developed with healthier options, calorie counts for all the items on the menu be provided (in some McDonald's restaurants these are on the tray mats), and that cooking styles be (publicly) modified as McDonald's has done by switching to vegetable as compared with beef fat in its frying. Notwithstanding these strategic responses, there remains the question of the extent to which McDonald's can or should be held accountable for the eating habits of its customers. Although this might be argued to be a generic "ethical/legal" issue for all companies, it is particularly emotive for those companies, like McDonald's, that target children as a critical market segment.

On one side of the **corporate social responsibility (CSR)** continuum it can be argued that as the company targets children in their formative years it takes on more than a customer–supplier relationship with these **stakeholders.** In sponsoring such programs as Sesame Street and idealizing eating in their restaurants, the companies are doing more than inviting informed consumers to trade with them (the standard trading relationship). By shaping the tastes, expectations, and aspirations of children they have no choice but to also take on some of the parental responsibilities to prevent those children unwittingly harming themselves by developing poor eating habits with negative health consequences in their adulthood. In the same way that liquor companies, for example, are increasingly required to promote responsible drinking and to not glamorize alcohol to the young, so too should fast food companies be made to face up to their broader social responsibilities

On the other side there is an argument that children do not walk into these restaurants by themselves and, as with skateboards, video games, baseball bats, or chocolate sweets, it is parents who train and shape their children into being good citizens and having appropriate self-regulation when it comes to eating or behaving of any kind. The company must of course not provide products that are harmful in themselves but as any food is harmful in excess it comes back to parents, and not the company, to instil this lesson. If a child spends 20 hours per day watching television, then this is unlikely to be good for its long-term social development and yet the television company is not held to account for such excessive viewing – parents are.

Others emphasize the role of government in regulating both consumers and industries. It is often forgotten, for example, that "hard" drugs like heroin and cocaine were once legal. With legal "drugs" such as alcohol and tobacco the government regulates who can buy and sell and how (or even if) these products can be advertised. Whilst minors are not allowed to purchase alcohol the onus remains on the seller to ensure that the customer is the legal age – others buying alcohol for children are also held legally liable. This sense of legal liability for the actions of others is spreading so that with the problems associated with drink-driving, for example, many countries have enacted legislation putting the legal onus on serving staff (and their hotel/restaurant) to not sell alcoholic beverages to customers already showing signs of inebriation. While the juxtaposition of food and drugs/alcohol may seem a "stretch" it has in fact been suggested by some of the more extreme critics that McDonald's, through overuse of fats, salt and added flavouring creates a form of addiction in the young consumer who may develop a preference for fast food over a more healthy (but less "tasty") diet. Could we see a time when a fast food restaurant will be held liable for selling fat enhancing foods to already obese patrons?

Whatever McDonald's does, it is aware that these complex issues are not going to disappear overnight. The fact that companies (or people) firmly believe themselves to be paragons of moral and ethical conduct can sometimes blind them to the obvious fact that such judgments are always made in the eyes of the observers – *no matter how unfair those judgments may seem*. McDonald's probably sees itself selling nutritious meals to willing customers whilst being unjustly attacked by gold-digging opportunists citing one-sided "junk science". There are equally sincere opponents who are horrified at what they see as McDonald's unfettered, capricious purveyance of addictive junk food to vulnerable consumers who lack the capability for informed choice and stand in need of protection. And between those two extremes lie a plethora of positions that shift with each new headline. McDonald's recognition of the politics of such issues and a need to manage them head on is reflected on its main website www.mcdonalds.com where a large section is devoted to "good works" and various reports and accounts of the company's sustainability initiatives. The firm also confronts some of the more trenchant criticisms of its marketing and products on such sites as makeupyourownmind .co.uk.

10-2 Monsanto: Growing the future?

Monsanto is an American-owned international agrochemical and food conglomerate with 2009 revenues of nearly $12bn and profits of $2.1bn.

*"**Monsanto** is an agricultural company. We apply innovation and technology to help farmers around the world be successful, produce healthier foods, better animal feeds and more fiber, while also reducing agriculture's impact on our environment."*

(www.monsanto.com)

Monsanto's perspectives[25]

"Sustainable development is going to be one of the organizing principles around which Monsanto and a lot of other institutions will probably define themselves for years to come."

"We can't expect the rest of the world to abandon their economic aspirations just so we can continue to enjoy clean air and water. That is neither ethically correct nor likely to be permitted by the billions of people in the developing world who expect the quality of their lives to improve."

"...current agricultural practice is not sustainable...You have to get twice the yield from every acre of land just to maintain current levels of poverty and malnutrition ... new technology is the only alternative to any one of two disasters: not feeding people... or ecological catastrophe."

"If economic development means using more stuff then those who argue that growth and environmental sustainability are incompatible are right."

"We can genetically code a plant...to repel or destroy harmful insects. That means we don't have to spray the plant with insecticides. Up to 90% of what's sprayed on crops today is wasted. Most of it ends up on the soil...Can we develop plants that will thrive in salty soil... create less thirsty plants suited to a drier environment?"

"Because of Monsanto's history as a chemical company, we have a lot of employees – good people – with a recurring experience like this: their kids or their neighbours' kids or somebody at a cocktail party asks them what kind of work they do and then reacts in a disapproving way because of what they **think** we are at Monsanto. And that hurts."

"At Monsanto we're trying to invent some new businesses around the concept of environmental sustainability."

The perspectives of others[26]

"Monsanto is in the process of acquiring and patenting their newest technology... 'Terminator Technology'. If used by Monsanto on a large-scale basis, it will inevitably lead to famine and starvation on a worldwide basis...seeds have been genetically engineered so that when the crops are harvested, all new seeds from these crops are sterile... This forces farmers to pay Monsanto every year for new seeds...half the world's farmers are poor and can't afford to buy seed every growing season, yet poor farmers grow 15 to 20% of the world's food..."
(www.ethicalinvesting.com)

SUSTAIN ABILITY

"Recent research is beginning to confirm that dairy foods produced using Monsanto's genetically-engineered Bovine Growth Hormone (rBGH) may speed the growth of human breast and prostate cancers." (www.ethicalinvesting.com)

"Monsanto is part of the Chemical industry. . . . It is important to expose the unethical practices of specific companies as their behavior is often indicative of the entire system." (www.mcspotlight.org)

"Monsanto is not held back by any considerations of ethics and it hides the reality of its sordid machinations behind a wall of secrecy. Everything Monsanto does is exclusively with the intent of increasing its own profit – everything else be damned. If left to its own devices it will most certainly destroy the livelihood of millions of farmers – a process begun a decade ago in India and certainly in many other countries as well. The planet's ecosystems will be seriously threatened by unnatural ways of changing agricultural patterns." (www.smokymountainfarm.com)

"Recently, a study by the *International Journal of Biological Sciences* revealed that Monsanto's Mon 863, Mon 810, and Roundup herbicide-absorbing NK 603 in corn caused kidney and liver damage in laboratory rats. Scientists also discovered damage to the heart, spleen, adrenal glands, and even the blood of rats that consumed the mutant corn. A 'state of hepatorenal toxicity' the study concluded. This hasn't slowed down Monsanto's profit machine. In 2008, Monsanto cleared over $2 billion in net profits on $11 billion in revenues. And its 2009 is looking equally as excellent." (www.walletpop.com)

1. *What do you think about Monsanto's position expressed in this case?*
2. *Where do you stand on this issue?*
3. *What would you do if you were CEO of Monsanto today?*

Case Notes:

10-3 Marcos: Codes and conduct

Enrico Marcos gazed ruefully at the Code of Conduct poster on the wall of his office in his factory in the southern Philippines. The output of the Ethical Team of the biggest customer for his sporting footwear, it comprised five points making up the acronym "'WORTH" (Figure 10-3.1). Enrico had worked in a factory in his youth and hence could only applaud the sentiments behind the poster. Excess working hours, often in the form of compulsory and unpaid overtime, had been the norm for himself and his parents. Resigning was out of the question, as even the meagre wages on offer were better than nothing, and to complain only increased the verbal and physical abuse from harried supervisors. While forced into excessive, underpaid efforts during peak periods workers would be told to stay at home or were not paid when orders dried up. The occasional foolhardy firebrands who attempted to enforce their legal rights, or to form a union of other brave rebels, soon found themselves out of a job and often in detention at the local police station.

When Enrico had started up his own small workshop 14 years ago he had vowed that if ever he became an employer he would not be one that allowed the same conditions that made his factory life so miserable. His workshop was soon employing others as his diligence and attention to detail garnered him increasing numbers of repeat customers. After 6 years he had rented a cheap, disused building on the outskirts of town and started up his own factory. Sales grew and the Marcos Company enhanced its reputation as a reliable supplier of quality products and a place of work where employees were treated with fairness and respect.

Although the Ethical Team visited every 2 years or so, members of his customers' Buying Team were in his office at least every quarter and often more frequently. The team comprised aggressive, ambitious young executives all intent on fast-tracking their careers through performance that was noticed by superiors. They mocked the Ethical Team as "ETFAP," i.e. "ET — From another Planet" and declared that they were interested in "value" not WORTH. Their guidelines were the " 5F's.".

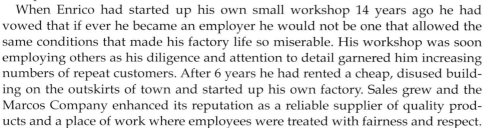

The Marcos Company recognizes the **WORTH** of all its workers and their rights to dignity and security in employment. The owners and management acknowledge their responsibilities to all staff and commit to working within the **WORTH** guidelines, which they accept to be minimum standards of conduct.

Working hours will be reasonable
Overtime will be voluntary
Rates will be fair
Trade unions will be accepted
Harassment will not be tolerated

Signed: Enrico Marcos, CEO

Figue 10-3.1 The acronym WORTH

They needed Fast delivery times to meet the needs of their giant retailer customers as well as Flexibility of response should things change – as they always did. If suppliers did not meet their deadlines and targets the costs would be passed onto them as Fines for poor performance. Finally, and most crucially, they needed increasingly Frugal pricing to keep margins high enough to sustain the payments to celebrities whose endorsements were essential to sell the product.

"You said there were five F's," Enrico pointed out. "That's only four."

The smartly dressed buyer 20-something smiled her dazzlingly white smile,

"That F is what happens if the other four don't work; we will be Finished with the supplier, but I'm sure that will never apply to you Enrico."

Enrico could not pinpoint exactly when it was that conditions in his factory began to change but change they certainly had. The incessant pressure for price decreases had forced him to save in the only place he could and that was in labour costs. As he was required to supply more items for lower prices he passed this onto his workers in higher piece-rate targets. Initially he had asked his workers to work overtime only for special rush orders and they had been happy to help, particularly as the extra hours were paid. These days the extended working day was the norm and the fines from customers, often for things outside of Marcos control, had eaten into the funds available to pay for extra time. As the workers worked faster they made more mistakes; in response the supervisors had instituted a practice of off-setting quality costs against the worker's pay where the individual who made the error could be identified. To further reduce ongoing costs the company now hired workers on temporary contracts and rotated the labour frequently to avoid paying the entitlements due to permanent employees. It had also found that female workers tended to be more compliant with extra work loads and lower pay and so females now made up the vast majority of the workforce. Complaints from some of his longer staying workers made Enrico aware that some supervisors were bullying workers to hit their targets and to maintain their silence about working conditions – he felt ashamed.

He felt ashamed also about how he had systems in place to keep the factory working in the way that it was while reporting a different ethos. Audited once every two years by the Ethical Team, the Marcos Company had become adept at keeping false time records to hide the excessive hours as well as two payroll records, one that reflected actual pay and the other to satisfy the WORTH requirements. Each audit was announced well ahead of time and, in preparation for the inspection and the interviews, the factory was thoroughly cleaned and painted and selected workers were trained in how to deal with the interviewer's questions. Some of these interviewees were given extra money, but for most the threat that the factory might be closed down if the audit results were negative was sufficient inducement. The Marcos factory was an unpleasant place to work but the pay was enough to prevent starvation – the only other available option.

1. *Discuss the 'causes' of the mal-treatment of workers as presented in this case.*
2. *What can Enrico do?*
3. *How can these problems be overcome?*

10-4 Handi Ghandi Curries: No worries?

There are many chains of Indian takeaway restaurants throughout the world, and the chain created on Australia's Gold Coast is not too different from most of them – apart from its quirky name and catchy advertising.

Handi Ghandi Curries has grown quickly through franchising and there are now stores using the Handi Ghandi Curries name and logo being opened in Australia's major cities. The company, which primarily delivers a large range of Indian-style curries in American-style Chinese takeaway boxes, uses the slogan "Great curries . . . No worries," has a logo featuring a cartoon image of Mahatma Gandhi tucking in to a Handi Ghandi box, and a jingle featuring a man singing "I am Handi Ghandi, eat my curries" in an accent like that used by the actor Ben Kingsley in the popular film version of Gandhi's life.

However, as the company has grown, its exploits have attracted more attention and it turns out that the Mahatma's family is not at all pleased with this use of his image. His great-grandson Tushar, managing trustee of the Mahatma Gandhi Foundation, was outraged that the Gandhi name had been used to sell meat curries (even though it had been misspelled). Mr. Gandhi described the act as offensive, saying it went against all the renowned vegetarian's beliefs. Especially offensive was the sale of beef curries by Handi Ghandi, as cattle are considered sacred to Hindus.

On June 16, 2005, *The Calcutta Telegraph* reported the story as follows:

> The Mahatma has been many things to many people. But when an Australian company portrayed him as a cook to sell beef curry, his great-grandson decided things had gone too far. Tushar Gandhi today requested Prime Minister Manmohan Singh to take up the matter with the Australian Government and stop the New South Wales-based Handi Ghandi Pvt Ltd from abusing the Mahatma's memory. Tushar Gandhi would have had no problems as long as the Mahatma sold the company's samosas, vegetable curries, parathas, naans, chutneys, salads, and biryanis. It was the Beef Madras, beef vindaloo, lamb rogan josh, Bombay Fish, and butter chicken that got his goat.
>
> "I have nothing against non-vegetarian food," the relative said, "but using Bapu's [Gandhi's] image to sell meat curry is too much. I probably would not have raised the issue if the company had promoted vegetarianism and health food."
>
> The great-grandson has written to the Prime Minister's Office, the Ministry of External Affairs, and the Union Law and Judiciary Department to take the issue up at a diplomatic level with Canberra."Bapu's image is protected by the Indian Constitution," he said. "It is the equivalent of a national flag or any other Indian emblem (in sanctity)."

Although Mahatma Gandhi's name and image are protected under India's Constitution and national emblem laws, they are not protected outside of India, so legal action could not be taken in Australia. Indeed, the Handi Ghandi brand and logo were approved by and registered with the Australian trademark authorities. However, in response to the Gandhis' protests, the company issued the following statement on its website and announced the change of its logo from a drawing of Gandhi to a caricature of a more generic Indian man.

"A recent press release distributed with comments from Tushar Gandhi, the great-grandson of Mahatma Gandhi, stating his concerns over the use of a caricature contained in our company trademark has been viewed widely around the world. Our company has never at any stage intended any offence or disrespect to the great Mahatma Gandhi or his family and Indian nationals. In a sign of good faith our company has decided to alter its corporate logo."

Handi Ghandi hoped the alteration of its logo would placate the Gandhi family – but it didn't. The *Lismore Northern Star,* a local paper in the area where Handi Ghandi was established, reported Tushar Gandhi's response on June 25:

THE great-grandson of Mahatma Gandhi has called on Northern Rivers residents to boycott Handi Ghandi takeaway restaurant chain if it refuses to alter its name. If the restaurant complied, Tushar Gandhi said he would eat the Lennox Head-based company's curries himself. In an email interview, the Mumbai resident said he was sending an appeal to the residents.

"To those of you who work for Handi Ghandi and for those of you who are their clients, prevail on them . . . to change the name, remove the mis-spelt but still related name of my illustrious great-grandfather . . . from their brand name and stop the use of the very offensive jingle," he said.

"May peace and joy be your eternal neighbours."

International protests have been sparked by the company selling curries in the name of vegetarian pacifist Mahatma Gandhi. A caricature logo of the leader attracted complaints from Australian Indians and the Mumbai-based Mahatma Gandhi foundation. Even Indian Prime Minister Dr Manmohan Singh has joined the protest, adding his name to a letter demanding the company drop the use of the image and change its name.

The protesters won a partial success last weekend when Handi Ghandi decided to change its logo; swapping an image of Mahatma Gandhi for a picture of a bearded man in Indian garb. But the company co-owner and managing director Troy Lister said the name would not change. "It is a legally registered tradename," Mr Lister said.

Mr Lister has said the name of the takeaway franchise was deliberately mis-spelled to prevent it relating directly to Mahatma Gandhi.

Mr Gandhi [also] wants the people of Ballina to know that the Handi Ghandi jingle parodying the Indian accent is demeaning to Indians. "It is a racist image of the Indian accent," he said. "[The Handi Ghandi promotion] is as offensive to us as if the name and images of Jesus [were used] to sell products or, for the British, if the Queen's image as a sales woman [was used]." [However, Mr Ghandi] said he would be the first to thank Handi Ghandi if they complied. If Handi Ghandi changed its name "I would not hesitate to patronize their business," he said.

Some Western media did not take these protests quite so seriously, however. Under the heading "What's Next, Martin Luther Burger King Jr.?" *CMO Magazine*'s Constantine von Hoffman made light of the situation: "The family of Mahatma Gandhi is upset just because some Aussie company is using the great guy's name and image to sell curry. Some people are just sooo sensitive."

And, the *Calcutta Telegraph* did point out that Tushar himself had faced public criticism in 2001 when he was accused of trying to sell the Mahatma's image to a US-based licensing company for use in a film advertisement for a credit card. CMG Worldwide had offered $51,000 per year for the use of the image.

1. *Why do you think Handi Ghandi Curries is so resistant to changing the name of the company?*
2. *What do you think Handi Ghandi Curries should do now?*
3. *Can you think of a way that the company can satisfy the Gandhi family, be seen as a good corporate citizen, and help develop its sustainable competitive advantage?*

Case Notes:

10-5 Il Ngwesi: Eco-warriors

Tourism is currently the world's largest growth industry. But with a growing number of tourists comes increasing pressure on natural resources, and an increasing number of international investors in the industry looking to make quick returns rather than foster sustainable development. Recognition of the need to preserve and protect natural environments for the long term has led many countries to focus on ecotourism. The United Nations is also seeking to promote ecotourism, not only in terms of managing the impact of tourism on the natural environment, but also because of the positive effects it can have on human environments. In other words, the UN believes that encouraging local communities to conserve their wild surroundings, and educate visitors about the value and fragility of their land, can lead to a greater respect for and promotion of their own well-being and cultural legacy. Recognizing the global importance of this sort of initiative, the United Nations designated the year 2002 as the International Year of Ecotourism.

Ecotourism aims to conserve the environment while benefiting local communities in sustainable ways. It generally takes place in poorer, less-developed areas that attract a higher proportion of independent travelers, and often involves smaller companies with more local commitment. However, even with smaller local companies in charge, ecotourism can reduce local access to natural resources, disrupt community groups, and have a damaging effect on the livelihoods of poor people in the area unless the process is properly managed.

Just a few hundred kilometers from Baraka College (see Case 9–5), one of the UN's exemplar ecotourism projects is going from strength to strength. Il Ngwesi is a communally owned ranch that combines sustainable farming, local development, and ecotourism. The local Maasai people of the Samburu region run the Il Ngwesi Community Conservation Area (INCCA) in central Kenya. They have built a 16,500-acre group ranch owned collectively by the 499 pastoral households, comprising 6,000 people that inhabit its diverse environment. It operates as a community-owned trust with a Natural Resource Management Committee responsible for land management.

On one portion of this ranch, people have moved their cattle off the land in favor of wildlife. On this site in 1996, an exclusive ecotourism facility, Il Ngwesi Lodge, was established – Kenya's first community-owned and managed tourist destination. The lodge, built using funds donated through the Kenya Wildlife Service, was constructed using materials from the local area. It employs 28 people from the local community, half of whom work in the lodge looking after visitors while the other half work as Il Ngwesi's ranger force, providing security for the animals and people in the region. From the lodge, visitors can spot elephant, buffalo, bushbuck, kudu, and the occasional big cat. The local Samburu community who live there and run the lodge now earn much more revenue from tourism than they ever did from cattle. Although the original construction of the lodge was funded by donors and built with the assistance and support of the Lewa Wildlife Conservancy (www.lewa.org/IlNgwesiGR.htm), Il Ngwesi is now financially independent.

Earnings from the lodge are dispersed as wages to employees and as dividends to members. For these workers and their families, these wages provide security and consistency. The lodge operates as a separate company but revenue from the lodge and other ecotourism activities is also put back into the community in a variety of other ways: to pay for education, infrastructure, and medicines, measures to bring an end to cattle rustling and banditry that meant losing valuable assets and income, and access to better emergency healthcare through a new radio and vehicle to provide emergency access to the nearest hospital.

Ten years ago, it was unsafe to travel through this area of Kenya because of the risk of attack from armed bandits. Today, thanks largely to the security infrastructure funded through the increased revenue from ecotourism, Il Ngwesi is a safe and peaceful place for tourists to visit, while the local community no longer has to fear that their village might be raided at any time.

The stable conditions created through the Il Ngwesi Trust and the clear responsibility to protect and maintain the wilderness area have resulted in the lodge going from strength to strength. A Water Use Association has been established to deal with misuse, overconsumption, and pollution in the area, and this, combined with the use of solar power for water heating and electricity in the lodge rather than wood or fossil fuel, has added to Il Ngwesi's reputation as an ecologically sound tourist destination. Meanwhile, protection from logging, overgrazing, and poaching of wildlife such as elephants and zebra, thanks to enhanced security, has helped Il Ngwesi to become a recognized safe haven for wildlife. A collaring and monitoring program for lions and elephants has been established and the Kenya Wildlife Service is now beginning to translocate various game to enhance the present diversity near the lodge, including an endangered hand-reared black rhino.

And, beyond already being an internationally acclaimed tourist destination, Il Ngwesi is also sharing its experiences with others through educational tours that are helping other communities to see just how it is done. Indeed, it recently featured as one of five such ecotourism projects in a television series made by TVE (The Television Trust for the Environment) and hosted by Anita Roddick. The TVE website provides more details (www.TVE.org/network.html).

This website also provides a summary of the key aspects that can be learned about implementing successful ecotourism strategy from the Il Ngwesi experience. These are paraphrased below. Ecotourism projects should:

- ensure that all partners are involved in the development of an ecotourism strategy from the outset, especially local villagers (particularly important for villages near protected wildlife areas because local villagers have traditionally been the custodians of natural resources and have specific skills and knowledge to take on responsibilities within the development of ecotourism);
- encourage local people to be involved in staffing the project;
- hold democratic communal meetings to discuss revenue distribution, management policies, registration of new members, and election of a management committee that carries out day-to-day management;
- ensure that benefit-sharing between ecotourism partners is equitable, with established legal agreements that should address issues of respect toward the local culture and indigenous knowledge of the community;
- ensure that at least a portion of revenue should be used for the development of social services, bursaries, self-help groups, etc.;
- be supported by national policies that encourage community-owned, sustainable ecotourism activities, as well as provide incentives toward the development of ecotourism initiatives;

- be market driven and commercially viable, in addition to being environmentally sound and supportive of local communities;
- aim to become self-sufficient as quickly as is practically possible;
- seek to encourage a sense of pride among local people about their local culture and environmental legacy.

1. *Why do you think Il Ngwesi's strategy has been so successful?*
2. *Why do you think "ecotourism" is a growing industry?*
3. *The Il Ngwesi's sustainable competitive advantage is obviously connected to sustainable development. But do you think this is necessarily the case for all corporations these days?*

Case Notes:

10-6 Air New Zealand: Greening the skies

After a poor start to the decade which saw its share price dropping to a desperate NZD 0.24 and it requiring national government assistance to stay afloat, Air New Zealand overcame the challenges of being the world's most distant major airline to be in a strong position by 2010. It turned a profit of NZD 99 m from a revenue of NZD 4,502 m in 2008/9, a tough year for airlines. And in recent years, it has been recognized through international awards for its passenger service, IT, its loyalty program and its website, and an Air Transport World "Public Relations Award." It was named 2009 Readers Digest Most Trusted Airline Brand as well as Top Airline for Innovation 2009 (The World Traveller – China), Best Transpacific Airline at the 26th OAG Airline Industry Awards, and voted "Best Airline" by Vacation.com in the USA and Best Value Long Haul (Conde Nast Traveller Awards 2007, UK). It has also received several awards for its advertising, marketing, and sponsorship, including an MTV award in 2007. It soared even further in 2010 by winning four best airline awards from Air Transport World, Skytrax, and UK-based *Which*? (ahead of favorites like Singapore Airlines and Emirates).

Air New Zealand's vision is to "strive to be number one in every market we serve by creating a workplace where teams are committed to our customers in a distinctively New Zealand way, resulting in superior industry returns." Sustainability initiatives are seen as matching this.

Air New Zealand is not alone in pursuit of environmental initiatives in the airline industry, with most of its direct full-service international competitors also offering carbon offsetting programs (typically through partner organizations), publishing sustainability reports, and pursuing fuel efficiency programs such as special wingtips on selected aircraft. This may not be surprising, given that aircraft are estimated to account for about 3% of the global total CO_2 emissions. In response, some individuals have decided to avoid air travel altogether because of the impact they perceive it has on the environment and ozone layer. Concerns about air travel carbon emissions are also affecting fresh produce cargo, as the local food movement encourages shoppers to only purchase locally grown produce.

However, Air New Zealand may have gone further down the "sustainability track" than any other airline. As societal concerns about the impact of air travel on global warming and climate change began to rise, the company launched a broad organizational initiative to address the airline's "carbon footprint". Air New Zealand's sustainability report in 2008 stated: "For an isolated island destination such as ours, air travel is critical. As a country, we are dependent on tourism and trade. Our future as New Zealand's national carrier is also reliant on the protection and enhancement of our unique and treasured environment. This makes effective, sustainable air travel a priority. As the only airline in the world dedicated solely to destinations to, from and within New Zealand, we need to endorse this country's clean, green reputation. If we don't continue to innovate, New Zealand is in danger of losing its appeal as a place to visit and a country to trade with."

Air New Zealand's initial moves to address its emissions included directly providing the option for travellers to offset their personal emissions from their flight (through the Air New Zealand Environmental trust). These have since been expanded to a company-wide Environmental Management System, based on the

ISO 14001 international standards. More than 2,500 employees are now part of Air New Zealand's "Green Team," which, since 2006, has launched a number of other initiatives. First, the company has committed up to NZD 2bn to enhance its fleet of aircraft in 2008, reducing the average age to about 6.5 years by 2013 (8.2 in 2010). These newer planes are up to 20% more fuel efficient than older planes. In addition, existing planes are being refurbished with aerodynamic packages that include being an early adopter of special wing tips that reduce drag and fuel usage significantly. These actions are complemented by other moves to more accurately match fuel loads to plane weight, reducing plane weight by removing onboard humidity from insulation, adjusting pilot flight operating techniques and flight routes, using ground-based energy sources (rather than less-efficient on-board auxiliary generators) while at the gates, and just-in-time refueling. Air NZ aims to be a world leader in examining every aspect of flight operations to reduce CO_2 emissions by saving fuel. It has instigated more than 40 projects in the past four years, reduced emissions by over 90,000 tonnes per year and now has one of the lowest fuel burn rates in the global Star Alliance network of airlines.

The airline also intends to source 10% of its total annual fuel needs from sustainable fuel by 2013. In taking a leadership role in searching for alternative jet fuels, Air New Zealand has partnered with Boeing, Rolls-Royce and Honeywell UOP. One promising option appears to be producing biofuels from jatropha seeds, with sustainable fuels potentially reducing CO_2 emissions by 50% on a lifecycle basis in comparison to other biofuels sourced from crops such as corn or soybeans. Jatropha meets "social, technical and commercial criteria for an environmentally sustainable fuel, because it doesn't compete with existing food stocks; the fuel looks like it will be at least as good as the product we use today; and finally, it has the potential to be cheaper than existing fuel supplies and is readily available." A "world first" test flight by a commercial airline using one engine of an Air New Zealand 747 commercial flight was completed in 2008.

Air New Zealand's Environmental Management System has also generated initiatives to reduce energy use throughout the organization and to reduce waste associated with air travel (both on the ground and during flights). And the company is also contributing to its environmental trust to offset the travel incurred by its business executives as they travel during their work. To top things off the company has recently been awarded an Enviro-Gold accreditation (the highest rating under the Qualmark Green responsible tourism criteria).

1. *To what extent are Air New Zealand's new sustainability initiatives likely to provide it with a sustainable competitive advantage?*
2. *Why do you believe that Air New Zealand's management have been so motivated to promote sustainability: because it is good business, because they want to be good global citizens, or both? Does it matter what their motivations are?*
3. *If you were advising Air New Zealand what would you suggest they do to build on their recent strategic successes?*

10-7 Post Office: Sustaining Postman Pat?

In December of the year 2000, the British Post Office announced that its corporate figurehead, Postman Pat, an animated character whose television show has been entertaining children in Britain and other parts of the world for decades, would be dropped from its promotional and charity work. (If you are not familiar with Postman Pat you may want to check him out at www.postmanpat.co.uk.) Among other measures, Post Office employees will no longer be encouraged to visit local schools, fêtes, and children's wards dressed as Pat. Instead their volunteer work will be directed toward a new campaign to encourage literacy. In the Post Office's defense, a press officer said that it was nothing personal: "We're not anti-Pat. We're just reassessing our priorities."

These are certainly challenging times for the Post Office. Courier companies, many of them well-known global corporations, are eroding market share in what once was largely a monopoly for the Post Office. Society's values are also changing. However, David Thomas of *The Independent* has put up a spirited defense for the long-serving Greendale-based postie:

> I realize, of course, that judged by the ruthless, market-driven standards universally prevalent today, Pat is a hopeless case. From the moment when, just as the day is dawning, he climbs into his bright red van, his life is a catalog of professional misconduct. The Post Office was quick to confirm that his habit of letting Jess, his black-and-white cat, ride in the front of his van was a blatant contravention of health and safety procedures.
>
> Similarly, the incidents [from his television and book adventures] that repeatedly cause post to be lost, misdirected, or damaged (one thinks, for example, of the occasion when Pat entrusts the school mail to young Bill Thompson, who promptly drops it in a puddle) would be matters requiring disciplinary action. "This is a very serious matter for a postman," said my source.
>
> But his most persistent failing is his seemingly incurable habit of allowing his close relationships with local folk to distract him from the swift delivery of the mail. "We do like a postman to be community minded," I was told by the Post Office spokesperson. "But he's there first and foremost to do his job."
>
> This is something that Pat would do well to remember. No one could deny his fundamental enthusiasm. He's determined to do his deliveries, come wind, rain, or snow. He has been known to use methods as various as inline skates, sledge, and motorized super-speed scooter to help him on his rounds. But there's no escaping the degree to which other matters are liable to intrude.
>
> In Postman Pat's Washing Day, for example, he begins his rounds with the observation that Granny Dryden has neglected to hang out her washing, despite the sunny, breezy weather. He stops to discuss the matter with the rheumatically afflicted pensioner, who reveals that her washing-machine has broken. Taking her dirty togs, Pat promises to deliver them to Mrs. Pottage. He then drives to see Dorothy Thompson, with whom he has tea and a slice of cake, before discussing laundry issues with the Rev. Timms, Ted Glen, Miss Hubbard, and George Lancaster.
>
> On the following morning, Pat delivers Granny Dryden's laundry to Mrs. Pottage and stops for yet another cup of tea, only for his uniform jacket and hat to be thrown into the washing-machine along with the old biddy's unmentionables. This is by no means the only occasion on which Pat causes damage to his uniform (one remembers, with a shudder, the white paint he left all over his trousers on the occasion

333

of Granny Dryden's redecoration), despite being contractually responsible for its upkeep. But the fact that Pat has to complete his round in a tweed jacket and deerstalker hat belonging to Mr. Pottage is far less significant, in the great scheme of things, than the blatant time-wasting that has gone on beforehand.

Here is a man with no concept whatever of productivity or time-and-motion. And he is not alone. Consider Ted Glen, the local handyman. Pat visits him during his search for Katy Pottage's lost doll. Ted has agreed to mend toys, television sets, cookers, cake-stands, bikes, roller-skates, farm machines, and house machines, "more than you could count." Yet he has no idea when he will fulfill these contractual obligations. Even when he does, his service is abysmal. Among his goods is a watch of Miss Hubbard's, of which he remarks, "She brought it to be fettled, last Christmas."

The service economy has made little headway on Greendale. But is the region's apparent refusal to move with the times really so counter-productive? Here we have a rural community that can sustain both a sub-post office (run by Pat's superior, Mrs. Goggins) and Sam Waldron's mobile store. At a time when households are shrinking and the increasing autonomy of individuals as social and economic units is producing side effects of isolation and alienation, Greendale folk evince a strong sense of community.

When Granny Dryden's ceiling needs painting, Miss Hubbard provides dust sheets, Dorothy Thompson donates spare time while both Pat and Ted Glen volunteer their time to do the job for free – a task rewarded by cake and tea.

This is a world which has no need for social workers, a world that looks after its own. When Ted Glen's design for Pat's scooter causes chaos, people do not sue or seek compensation. Instead they take the matter to PC Selby. He, in turn, talks to Mrs. Goggins. She has a quiet word to Pat, who abandons his machine without complaint, secure in the knowledge that Dr. Gilbertson is having words with his superiors in Pencaster to ensure that they get him a proper trolley for his parcels.

People feel better living in a world like that, and there are clear economic benefits. The Government spends £120 bn on social security, much of which could be saved if people were empowered to take local voluntary community action.

Pat and Ted's working methods are less wasteful than they may appear to corporate accountants, who seem incapable of seeing the financial wood for the budgetary trees. In a country plagued by the longest working hours in Europe, staff everywhere find themselves burdened with ever greater responsibilities, while being offered diminishing professional security. No wonder that more than two-thirds of TUC safety representatives identify stress as the greatest health and safety concern in the workplace.

Stress is now the single biggest cause of absenteeism, and costs corporate Britain anything between £9 bn and £19 bn per annum in compensation payments, quite apart from the mammoth cost of lost days of work. The Government spends about £8 bn in incapacity benefits every year, quite apart from the drain on NHS resources.

If more of us were more like Pat – or if we were allowed to be – the social and economic benefits would be enormous.

Beyond the decision to drop Pat and the publication of Thomas's defense of Pat's worth, there has been good and bad news with regard to the Post Office's maintenance of its traditions. In a bid to sound more global and meaningful and relevant to today's business world, the Post Office changed its name to Consignia. But it changed it back again in 2002, after 2 years of public confusion as to what Consignia stood for and public dismay that terms that they had become familiar with, like "the Post Office" and the associated "Royal Mail," could have been discarded so brusquely and without discussion. Not long after this, however, on June 20, 2003, it was announced that the Post Office branch that had inspired Postman Pat was to be closed. The author of Postman Pat, John Cunliffe, reportedly wrote the books after listening to conversations in the Beast Banks branch in the Lake District town of Kendal. *The Independent* reported that Beast Banks would be one of 350, mostly rural, Post Offices that would be closed in 2003.

---

1. *Do you think the Post Office's management should have handled the relationship with Pat differently?*
2. *How might the association with Pat be a part of the Post Office's sustainable competitive advantage?*
3. *Develop a strategic rationale for bringing back Pat as the symbol of the Post Office's virtues.*

Case Notes:

> You can't be remarkable by following someone else who's remarkable . . . The thing that all great companies have in common is that they have nothing in common.
>
> *Seth Godin*

> Creativity means not copying
>
> Jacques Maximin

> We sold more books today that didn't sell at all yesterday than we sold today of all the books that did sell yesterday.
>
> *An employee of Amazon.com explaining how the rise of the "long tail" affects his company*

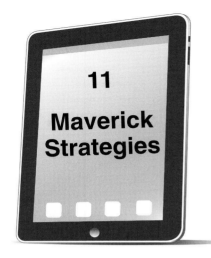

11
Maverick Strategies

A few years ago we were asked to advise a medium-sized financial services company. This company had hired a management consultancy to develop a set of "core values" for them. The list was as follows: integrity, respect, commitment, professionalism, teamwork, creativity, humor. Unsure of the worth of this list, their CEO wanted us to carry out a survey comparing it to the core values of its competitors. We found that all of the first five values were common to all of this company's main competitors. About half also listed creativity. The CEO's first response was: "If everybody is espousing the same values then they are just 'hygiene factors.' What we need are some added-value values."

For Jesper Kunde, many companies in the early years of the new millennium became "more or less identical" thanks to the rise of best practice benchmarking and copying, often facilitated by bringing in management consultants.[1] Correspondingly, Clayton Christensen's highly regarded work suggested that many companies that increased their investment in getting strategy right in the 1990s tended to copy "best practice" and became homogeneous with their competitors.[2] Indeed, in the late 1990s, sensing that strategies were becoming less concerned with differentiation, Michael Porter published a paper in the *Harvard Business Review* which argued that strategy – which Porter defined as about "performing different activities from rivals" or "performing similar activities in different ways" – was being confused with operational effectiveness (or "performing similar activities better than rivals").[3]

The rise of "risk management" and "accountability" may have added to this strategic homogenization. As managers were increasingly held to account for performance in the short as well as long term, they sought to mitigate their risks, and they increasingly turned to management consultants who employed similar generic techniques as a kind of "quality guarantee" (or as a cynic might say a way of "passing the buck"). Warren Buffett liked to use the following metaphor which may explain the phenomenon: "As a group, lemmings may have a rotten image, but no individual lemming has ever received bad press." David Koepp, co-writer of *Jurassic Park*, believes that a similar logic explains the growth in movie sequels: "Approving a sequel is a non-fireable offence. If a sequel doesn't work, they can still say, 'It wasn't my fault! It was a no-brainer'." Others have blamed the Global Financial Crisis of 2008/9 on a lemming-like homogenization of strategies with regard to lending practices.

Subsequently, the "surplus society" of the 1990s and early 2000s, as it was labeled by Kjell Nordstrom and Jonas Ridderstrale, produced "a surplus of *similar* companies, employing *similar* people, with *similar* educational backgrounds, coming up with *similar* ideas, producing *similar* things, with *similar* prices and *similar* quality."[4] Instead of daring to be unorthodox, most companies, in keeping with "leadership" coming to be seen as the next big thing with millions spent on studies into what made a leader and leadership courses, followed whoever their external advisers identified as "the leader." All this despite the obvious tautology: *following* best practice means you are a *follower*, not a leader.

However, there are a number of reasons why this decade, in contrast to the last, should see the rise of the mavericks, the companies not afraid to go their own way. First, research by Philip Nattermann has now shown that companies in industries where best practice benchmarking was seen to be good strategy generally suffered from declining margins, as product or service offerings become similar, consumers struggle to differentiate between competitor offerings and increasingly buy on price.[5]

Second, and relatedly, with the Internet opening consumers up to an unprecedented myriad range of choices from around the globe, companies must either be the lowest cost producer or stand out in some other way. And, as Tom Peter's puts it: "You can't compete with Wal-Mart on price, and you can't compete with China on cost."[6] Indeed, an interesting study by the UK Design Council suggests that the only way you can compete with companies that benefit from the lower factor costs of "developing" or emerging economies is through being creative. Figure 11.1 tracks the share index of the FTSE and FTSE top 100 companies

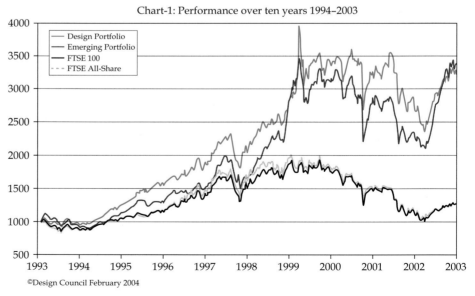

©Design Council February 2004

Figure 11.1 Relative share price performance: FTSE All-share, FTSE 100, Emerging Markets Portfolio and Design Portfolio (roughly the same) with a portfolio of companies based in emerging economies. Keeping pace with the emerging index is what it known as the "design portfolio." This is made up of companies who have won recognized design awards.[7]

A third (also related) factor is the rise of what has been termed the "long tail." In an article in *Wired* magazine and a book called *The Long Tail: Why the Future of Business is Selling Less of More*, Chris Anderson argued that while globalization may have led to a greater frequency of demand that could be grouped together (or placed in the centre of a bell curve), what was more interesting was that the tail of that curve was getting longer and longer. Demand here was becoming increasingly individualized and difficult to categorize. In many markets there are more people wanting something different rather than a majority of consumers happy with the same – the point made by the Amazon employee at the head of this chapter. So, from a strategic perspective just copying best practice isn't enough, being creative in thoughtful and directed ways (e.g. good design) does pay, and there are significant numbers of consumers looking for something outside the norm. We may be entering a new age of maverick strategies.

While an emphasis on thinking differently or creatively to add value in strategy is becoming increasingly seen as crucial to securing an organization's future, there are many who argue that such things cannot be taught. There is a famous story about Anita Roddick (a great maverick strategist) beginning a guest lecture to an entrepreneurship class at a famous business school by saying that if any of them were actually cut out to be entrepreneurs they would not be sitting there being taught how to do it – they'd be out there doing it. However, researchers like Kim and Mauborgne are less dismissive. Their database of many of the world's highest performing companies, shows that those that created new markets generally followed a systematic path.[8] While you cannot be a maverick by following a formula, organizations can develop systems and cultures that help to instill a maverick orientation and help animate people to engage in maverick acts. We believe there are some general lessons as to how effective maverick strategies can be encouraged and we describe seven of these below.

1. Build Awareness of Maverick Strategies and Their Value to the Organization

It is important to convey a sense of how an organization's health depends on maverick strategies. There are many now famous examples of organizations that did not fall into copycat traps that can help to bring this home.

- Anita Roddick's Body Shop went against traditional ways of how cosmetics are developed and sold by challenging the industry's previous assumptions.
- Cirque du Soleil, a Canadian circus troupe in a dying industry, effectively collapsed two industries into one: theater and circus. This saw Cirque open up entire new venues and a new audience (who were prepared to pay higher prices).
- Swatch challenged the assumption that a watch was a luxury or high-tech item that people only needed one of. It sold watches as collectable fashion accessories.

More recently, Kim and Mauborgne's research, published in the book *Blue Ocean Strategy*, shows that while 86% of business or product launches are line extensions, or incremental improvements, they only account for 62% of corporate revenue and 39% of profits. Value innovations (the remaining 14% of launches) account for 38% of revenue and 61% of profits.

A prominent framework that makes the case for new strands in an organization is the **S-curve**, introduced in Richard Foster's book *Innovation, the Attacker's Advantage*.[9] It shows how a product will hit a plateau where further improvement will either be impossible or prohibitively expensive. Corporate performance over the long term thus requires different products, markets, or approaches being brought into the picture – even though they will take time to pay off and may even fail.

At the same time, it is important to convey that maverick strategies are not just about innovation for its own sake. They can come from simply connecting old thinking from different spheres or re-looking at an existing product from an unusual perspective. This is a theme of Kim and Mauborgne's promotion of value innovation – an approach that ensures that maverick strategies focus on providing added value to customers rather than just invention. Hence, the selling of books without bookstores, or nappies that are disposable, or flights that operate more like buses, are as much "value innovations" as the iPod. Thus, maverick strategies can be developed by anybody – you do not need to be a "creative type." Indeed, Kim and Mauborgne suggest that value innovation can be advanced by any manager asking structured questions like:

1. What factors could be eliminated that an industry has taken for granted? (For companies like Egg and First Direct it was that banks need branches.)
2. What product/service elements could be reduced below the industry standard? (For Ryanair and Southwest it was complementary food and baggage services.)
3. What elements could be lifted above the standard? (For Dyson and Alessi it was that things like vacuum cleaners and teapots could have designer styling.)
4. What should be introduced that the industry has never offered the customer? (For Swatch it was the idea that you could launch watches like fashion collections.)
5. Could a new offering win buyers without any marketing hype? (The Smart car or new Mini created demand simply through people seeing them on the streets.)

2. Promote Your Organization's Particular Maverick-ness

Because companies have become used to looking to what other companies are doing for the answers, engendering maverick-ness thus firstly requires that this mindset be deprogrammed. Each organization should be aware of, and actively develop, its legitimate strangeness, to use a term promoted in Stephen Cummings' book *Recreating Strategy*. This partly reflects social trends (for the first time ever, Nike is finding that young people in its surveys claim to aspire to being "themselves" rather than Michael Jordon or Michael Johnson, which indicates that customers are increasingly seeking difference and individuality) and this is partly because it makes good business sense (recent studies show how continually chasing and measuring oneself against the competition leads to declining performance).[10]

Promoting a maverick approach to strategy requires a shift from following the leader to continually getting better at being yourself, a theme developed in

Joe Calloway's book *Becoming a Category of One: How Extraordinary Companies Transcend Commodity and Defy Comparison*.[11] As Jerry Garcia of *The Grateful Dead* put it: "You do not merely want to be the best of the best: you want to be considered the only ones who do what you do." Fostering this maverick attitude requires some changes in emphasis:

- moving away from following customers ("*We have focus groups*," explains James Dyson, "*but I take a perverse delight in ignoring them*"; *while* Steve Jobs claims that Apple does "no market research. . . we just want to make great products." "Companies should be idea-led and consumer informed," claims Doug Atkin, Director of Strategic Planning at advertising and branding consultancy Merkley, Newman, Harty, because the world is moving too fast for consumers to understand what is possible and following focus groups can only result in averages and incremental developments);
- questioning strategic supplier relationships (Wayne Burkan's *Wide-Angle Vision* claims that suppliers who make you question your practices are more likely saviors than those designed to fit efficiently into your existing modus operandi);
- and, as we have already described, moving away from an emphasis on promoting best practice copying.

In advocating this last point, however, Chris Bilton and Stephen Cummings acknowledge that it is not enough to simply dismiss best practice as an approach to developing. Consequently, they promote four alternative maverick strategy generating foci in their book *Creative Strategy*:

- Focus on understanding and discussing situations where you or your competitors have messed up, or **worst practices** – according to David Snowden of the think-tank Cynefin "striving to avoid failure is more compelling than imitating success"; and according to James Dyson "children should be marked by the amount of mistakes they make at school because it is through these mistakes that we come up with new ideas" (the fact that the Dyson vacuum cleaner was the result of over 5,000 prototypes indicates that Dyson practiced what he preached in this regard!).
- Focus on promoting different types of **good practice** – encourage your team to debate the particular merits of other organizations' (or your own) good practices and decide which; or better yet develop a hybrid.
- Focus on identifying particular **promising practices** – seek them out, they may be bubbling up in your or other organizations, and promote, incorporate and develop them with gusto.
- Focus on **next practice** – instead of seeking to catch up with last year's success story (who no doubt has already moved on) think about leapfrogging best practice and defining your organization's view of the next level.

Simply put, an organization's people need to understand and be animated to act on a particular maverick orientation. According to Seth Godin, if you can't explain such an orientation "in eight words or less, then you don't have one"[12]; But some claim that an organization's maverick-ness should be even easier to see. Jean-Marie Dru's book *Disruption* claims that the following companies are greatly aided because their names imply a single unique and inspiring verb. It is widely understood that Apple *opposes*, IBM *solves*, Nike *exhorts*, Virgin *enlightens*, Sony *dreams*, and Benetton *protests*.[13]

3. Diversity

According to Arthur Koestler, "Invention or discovery takes place by combining ideas. The Latin verb cogito for 'to think" means 'to shake together.'. . . the creative act, by connecting previously unrelated dimensions of experience, is an act of liberation – the defeat of habit by originality."[14] Koestler's philosophy underpins the recent promotion of diversity management: the idea that if you want to encourage inventive thinking in an organization you need a dissimilar workforce who will look in different ways, then challenge and shake up one another's habits. An inspiring anecdote in this regard is that of Andrew Higgins, who was charged with building landing craft for the American army in World War II. He turned out 20,000 craft (that Eisenhower credited with winning the war) by hiring all sorts of people in addition to the obvious engineering graduates. Higgins argued that they spent too much time teaching you what you can't or shouldn't do at engineering school.

A number of Bob Sutton's ideas in *Weird Ideas That Work* are also useful spurs here. Sutton claims that you should: hire people that make you uncomfortable; use job interviews to get new ideas, not just to screen candidates; never try to learn anything from people who seem to have solved the problems you face; decide to do something that should fail, then convince the people working with you that they will succeed and see what happens; or simply hire people you don't seem to need.[15]

Furthermore, it is worth questioning the norm that most senior positions in organizations are occupied by people from law, engineering, and accountancy backgrounds. Such fields are generally concerned with compliance, with being mindful of past precedent, general standards, and established practice. This makes them unlikely mavericks or supporters of maverick-ness. People from backgrounds such as design, advertising, human resources, or even strategy, may be better able to understand the importance of uniqueness, the particular emotional ties that a brand or product can convey, and of standing out from the crowd. Companies would do well to bring them into the boardroom.

4. Space + Urgency

Sutton's last point implies that maverick-ness requires "slack" – mavericks need to be provided with time and space with which to think. This may be as simple as giving people time out to try new things (Post-it Notes, for example, emerged from a research scientist doing his own experiments in the 15% of work time that 3M allocated to employees exploring their own new ideas; more recently Google have employed a similar "free-time" philosophy); or to actively encourage the prototyping of new ideas. "Effective (i.e. quick) prototyping may be the most valuable core competence an innovative company can hope to have," claims Michael Schrage – because "*Innovation occurs as people see, deconstruct, and rebuild prototypes.*"[16] Thus, mavericks need to be encouraged to try, fail, learn, and try again.

Good thinking tools that can encourage maverick thinking include scenario planning, which we discussed in Chapter 1, and "blue ocean" thinking. Blue ocean strategy is a term developed by Kim and Mauborgne in an attempt to get beyond strategy's "wrong-headed militaristic foundations." These foundations suggest that firms, like armies, are competing for finite pieces of territory. Mavericks look beyond such territorial boundaries and blue ocean thinking encourages managers to think across and beyond established industries, traditional buyer groups or suppliers, or the traditional functional or emotional orientation of an industry. Apple's PC revolution in the 1980s stemmed from this sort of thinking. By assembling a group of employees that IBM would never have hired, Apple took a new type of computing (fun, stylish, cheap, easy to operate) to a group of buyers that the industry hadn't really paid much attention to.

However, and perhaps ironically, effective slack generally requires a parallel sense of urgency. Indeed, you may recall John P. Kotter's eight steps for managing change from Chapter 9. The first step is "establishing a sense of urgency." In recent times, having been struck by just how much everything else stands or falls on achieving this first step, Kotter has returned to focus on just how urgency can be encouraged. In his recent book, *A Sense of Urgency*, he describes a range of innovation-spurring urgency tactics such as sending employees out of the organization and bringing other stakeholders in, looking for opportunities in crises, using unusual media (if your people are used to PowerPoint Presentations, then unplug the computers and tell them a story), and disseminating surprising, dramatic, counterintuitive data to staff to see how they respond. It is for this reason that many commentators regard a recession as fertile ground for innovation. Necessity, or at least urgency, may be the mother of maverick strategies.[17]

5. Entrepreneurial Thinking + Financial Flair

Maverick strategies require people to be entrepreneurial rather than just accepting what has passed for a good product or strategy before. It is hard to define an entrepreneur, but one way of doing so is to think of a person with an ability for innovation, a vision or "memory" of the future (that is, an ability to see the future as a different place requiring different things), and a desire to take risks. These innovative, risk-taking, and visionary characteristics, if effectively combined, have an ability to inspire and instill confidence in others to follow these entrepreneurs on their maverick path. Such entrepreneurs may be CEOs like Richard Branson or Rupert Murdoch, or inventors like Steve Jobs or James Dyson, or even people operating at lower levels of companies (who are often termed "intraprenuenrs" – people who are entrepreneurial within an organization). Susan Segal-Horn suggests that lower level employees can become entrepreneurial if they cease to be "implementers of top-down decisions" and become instigators of corporate actions. Often, because these people go against the grain, they are seen to be odd or misguided. A few organizations recognize this – Tait Elder at 3M famously said that "we expect our champions to be irrational." However, companies need them if they are to seize or create new opportunities and growth. Moreover, they need to fund them – new ideas seldom get off the ground without sponsorship. But deciding to back such people and their ideas generally means using judgment and taking calculated financial risks rather than following rational financial criteria to the letter.

Perhaps the most influential new trend in business thinking in the past few years has been the promotion of design-thinking. This has been interpreted in a number of different ways, and covers far more than space allows us to comment on here, however, perhaps the key aspect with regard to maverick strategies may be design thinking's promotion of **abductive logic**. According to Roger Martin, author of *The Design of Business*,[18] traditional companies tend to reward only two types of thinking:

- inductive logic, whereby the aim is to prove that something can actually work (e.g. a new product idea or production process); and
- deductive logic, proving that something exists (e.g. a new market opportunity, investor interest).

But Martin argues that a third way:

- abductive logic (or positing that something might be and then reaching out beyond what is already known to understand and develop something new), is necessary to inspire substantive innovations.

The most heroic example of abductive thinking in modern times may be John F. Kennedy's pledge to get a man to the moon, but it's also true that lower order innovative strategies, like Apple's initiative to create a device to enable portable personal music collections, would not have happened if people had to prove that an iPod could work or prove that a market existed for it, before the plan was approved.

7. Develop Strategy Representations That Convey Your Own Organization or Industry's Uniqueness

While the traditional view was that structure followed strategy, more recently experts have suggested that strategy follows structure too. Consequently, if structures shape strategy we must innovate with the structures that inform strategic thinking. In a 1999 *Harvard Business Review* article titled "Organigraphs: Drawing How Companies Really Work," Henry Mintzberg advocated moving away from representing companies with standard prototype organization chart hierarchies, toward an individualized approach of drawing the unique things that each organization does and how it does them.[19] Figure 11.2 provides an example of an organigraph for a marketing strategy consultancy, outlining its strategy of aligning a brands core "beliefs" with key media to radiate out to a particular audience at a number of levels. One can see how thinking of an organization in this particular way would be more likely to encourage the development of tailored strategic thinking connected to its specificities, rather than perceiving it as an organization chart.

The promotion of the individual organigraph over the organization chart as a maverick strategy driver relates to a further aspect promoted by some interpretations of design thinking: the notion of visual "boundary objects," material prototypes

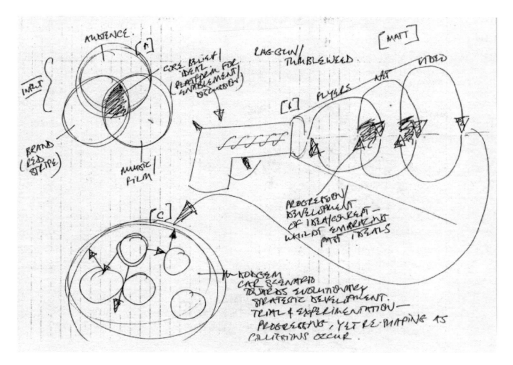

Figure 11.2 Organigraph of a marketing strategy consultancy

or graphical drawing as important aids that help developers to see, gather around, test drive, learn from, and manipulate. The equivalent of the prototype in strategy may be "the strategy framework" many examples of which we have discussed in this book. And, just as the good designer would expect to adapt and manipulate a prototype, the good strategist (and especially the maverick strategist) should be bold enough to innovate with existing frameworks and templates.

In Chapter 2 we described how leading theorists and their frameworks can act as movers and shakers but that overreliance on these can blinker independent thought. For example, ask MBA students how many forces there are in an industry and they will generally tell you "five." Ask them why and they will cite Porter's Five Forces. In reality, of course, the world is a more diverse and open-ended place, and a maverick approach is more likely to come from manipulating such blinkers. Asking, for example, what Apple's iPod is in relation to the music industry (a buyer, a new entrant, a competitor, a substitute, a potential supplier, or all of the above, or does it represent something new – another force?) and subsequently adapting the five-forces framework will lead to stimulating discussion on new approaches to strategy. Some industries can be analyzed effectively in terms of a five-forces diagram and this can be amended to include other drivers where appropriate, such as government or technological change to create a seven-forces drawing to aid strategic thinking. In strategy, a picture really can paint a thousand words, and any approach to drawing, adapting, sharing, and communicating a strategy framework (or what we have elsewhere termed **stratography**) can help to provide innovative prototypes that can strategically orient and animate people in your organization.[20]

345

Further examples of graphical framework development include the value chimera which we outlined in Chapter 5, and the customization of the value chain promoted in Bilton and Cummings' book *Creative Strategy*.[21] They argue that while a lot of emphasis is now placed on organizations being creative, often this does not result in improvements to an organization's strategy. One way to effectively join creativity to strategy is to creatively redraw the classic input–process–output shape of the value chain. And in doing this, Bilton and Cummings outline "6 degrees of strategic innovation (see Figure 11.3)."

The first and most obvious degree is *value innovation*, where products or services perceived to have greater value to a market are invented or extended. Value innovation does not need to be a grand invention like the light-bulb or iPad, small additions to a value proposition can have major effects. Sony shifted the value chain in their industry by adding *portable* to music. Momofuku Ando was named Japan's inventor of the 20th century. He added *instant* to noodles (a highly significant value innovation when one considers that 86 billion servings of instant noodle are consumed each year). Indeed, asking what adjective or verb you should be putting ahead of your product or service can be a very good way to inspire strategic innovation in an organization. Progressive completely reorganized its business model around a revised view of the value they provided to customers: it wasn't insurance, it was *speed*; in other words, providing customers with insurance quickly, so that they could get on with other things.

The second degree, *cost innovation*, increases margins by the creative reduction of costs. Recent examples include the fashion companies that recognized that putting on full-blown catwalk shows during a recession was not good for their image, developed online viewing opportunities, saved money and benefited from enhanced viewer feedback. Other organizations, such as Tata and One Laptop Per Child, have completely changed the view of how much a car or a laptop could cost by setting audacious targets and reengineering traditional processes from the ground up.

The third degree, *volume innovation*, is about creating ways to get more into or out of the value chain. A classic example is Henry Ford's combination of the "$5 dollar day" and the conveyor production line, outlined in this chapter's first live case. A more recent example is the concept of **crowdsourcing**, where organizations put out a call for potential solutions on the web and award prizes or contracts to the "winning entries."

The fourth is *market innovation*, which is about devising new ways of relating to the market by focusing on innovative means of delivering or experiencing the product. Elias Howe invented the mechanical sewing machine but quickly went under because of his insistence on selling them full price. Isaac Singer recognized that the productivity benefits of the new machines were difficult for factory

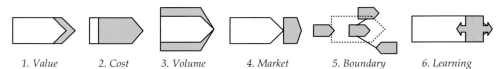

1. Value   2. Cost   3. Volume   4. Market   5. Boundary   6. Learning

Figure 11.3 Bilton and Cummings' 6 degrees of strategic innovation (adapted from Bilton and Cummings, 2010)

owners to fathom. So he gave them away and charged rent for them. Very few people today have heard of Elias Howe. In the music industry, bands like Radiohead and Nine Inch Nails are changing the way consumers relate to music by giving away free downloads, inviting customers to remix and upload their own versions of songs, and generating revenues from concert tickets, customized services and special events instead of relying on declining CD sales.

Boundary innovation, is about finding ways to break down traditional boundaries between sectors, or customers or suppliers and an organization, and consequently breaking up and reconfiguring the value chain. The sixth and final degree of strategic innovation is *learning innovation*: figuring out how the organization can learn better about its capabilities and its potential customers. Good examples of the last two degrees of strategic innovation are provided in this chapter's second live case on IRL, Levis and Land Rover.

The seven maverick elements described in this chapter reinforce Godin's and Maximin's statements with which it began: leading firms will increasingly seek to do strategy in different ways – ways that suit their particular resources, capabilities, and contexts. Rather than sticking to the norm they will be taking risks on the "bleeding edge," on the boundaries or the unexplored intersections, like Circe de Soleil (theater/circus) or Swatch (fashion/watches) or Body Shop (sustainability/cosmetics) or, the firm that provided the very first example in this book on page 1: Apple (computer hardware/internet/design). As Kurt Vonnegut put it, "out on the edge you can see all kinds of things you can't see from the center."[22]

8. Epilogue

In recent times, Henry Mintzberg has published another new book bemoaning the traditional MBA degree's role in churning out the "similar" people described in the quotation with which this chapter began and who subsequently diminish the likelihood of maverick-ness.[23] Similarly, Roger Martin, advocate of "design thinking" has come out against the traditional business school: "We're telling students that the big bucks are made by administering linear improvements – getting better and better at doing essentially the same thing. . . But the real challenge lies in getting better and better at a different thing: devising clever solutions to wickedly difficult thinking."

However, it is important to recognize that Mintzberg and Martin are not critical of MBAs or business students per se, but rather the notion of a generic and limited business education that can dull people's ability to think independently and to take risks if one does not guard against this. And *The Strategy Pathfinder* has been developed to avoid this "dulling" of the mind. The philosophy behind the live and open-ended cases in this book, and behind learning frameworks, is not so that they can just be consumed and regurgitated, but adapted and applied skillfully to particular situations. *The Strategy Pathfinder* is designed to encourage creativeness in readers in order that the "creative strategists" that Mintzberg's wonderful work has championed, emerge, as strategy matures, to become perhaps the most influential of all business disciplines.

Thus, the maverick strategist, indeed the expert strategist in general, should not forgo the conventions and theories of strategy; he or she must learn from them, and become expert. They provide a language for engagement and a conceptual toolkit from which the strategist should draw to skillfully create endless different combinations. These will provide greater insight into live (and wicked) strategic problems and enable clever solutions to be devised. True experts, such as Senior Strategy Directors however, are not bound by frameworks but are masters in their creative application to their own particular situations and circumstances. Picasso, for example, became a great artist by first learning well the conventions he would later knowingly twist around and adapt to suit his own particular maverick approach. The skilled strategist, the "strategy pathfinder" if you will, must similarly be both a traditionalist *and* a maverick.

Maverick Strategies Key Learnings Mind Map

Having read and reviewed the chapter, outline what you believe to be the key learnings from the chapter and the relationships between these.

11-1 Apple and Ford: 6 degrees of strategic innovation

Perhaps the world's most significant new products at the beginning of the 20th and 21st centuries cover all of the six degrees of strategic innovation described in this chapter at one time.

Henry Ford's Model-T was clearly a value innovation. It was quite simply better than its competition in terms of durability, reliability, maneuverability, flexibility, simplicity and "fixability" (i.e. one didn't need to be a master mechanic to keep it on the road). Ford recognized that these value-adding attributes were very important, given the state of the roads in the USA at the time, particularly outside the cities on the frontiers where America was growing quickly. But, the T also ticks off all of the other five degrees of innovation. Through design innovation Ford simplified parts and reduced their number making his revolutionary production line concept workable. This, and limiting consumer choice as to variations, significantly reduced production costs. Offering new value that a new breed of car consumer wanted, at a lower price, opened up huge new markets for the T. It made owning a car not just the preserve of the wealthy, but of the farmer and the middle manager too. But it would have been pointless to create this demand and not be able to match it with the sort of volume innovations that we attributed to Ford in Chapter 7. Cost innovations and volume innovations combined led to a drop in the time needed to produce a T from 12 hours 8 minutes to 1 hour 33 minutes a year later in 1913. The price went from $900 in 1912 to $440 by 1919.

Ford was also a marketing pioneer, arranging races where he would drive a "souped up" Ford against more expensive cars and better drivers, attracting unprecedented publicity. But perhaps Ford's most significant market innovation was the rigorous selection of dealers. The dealers were imbued with a sense that it was their responsibility to keep in close and regular contact with customers and prospective customers alike, and acted as a valuable "information system" for Ford. Because of the T, there was no shortage of capable dealers wishing to "buy into" Ford. This made it a seller's market for the company who only accepted those dealers who would agree to pay cash, up front, for factory deliveries. This unheard of practice also acted as a great motivation to dealers to get out and sell cars quickly in order to recoup their outlay.

This blurring of the line of the border of the company may also be seen as a boundary innovation, but on the 5th degree of innovation Ford was also actively looking for ways to combine insights from a burgeoning electrical industry with his mechanical knowledge in order to add new value to an automobile. Furthermore, Ford was an active learner. As the letter T designation indicates, a great deal of prototyping and responding to the market happened between 1903, when the company was incorporated, and 1908 when the first Model-T was being rolled out.

This would suggest that Ford was able to create innovations through learning from *worst practice*. Indeed, one of his more famous aphorisms was that "Failure is the opportunity to begin again, more intelligently." But he also kept abreast of *good practice* throughout the industry of which he had been a part since the late 1800s (he paid particular attention to Henry Leland's development of precise machine tooling and interchangeable parts – which would make Ford's own cost and volume innovations possible), and he was a great stimulator of *promising practices*. As a manager he was fond of claiming that "I don't do so much, I just go around lighting fires under other people." Or, as one shop worker put it "He'd never say, 'I want this done!' He'd say; I wonder if we can do it, I wonder.' Well, the men would just break their necks to see if they could do it. They knew [broadly] what he wanted [and] they figured it was a coming thing." And what came *next*, which nobody else but the Ford Motor Co. at that point of time could have brought home, was the Tin Lizzie.

Ford's innovations also point to the importance of other aspects of creative strategy – Ford's leadership on the shopfloor connects with the kind of "leadership from the middle" we discuss in Part IV of this book. The organization was tightly run but there was also an openness to new ideas, at least at the design concept stage of production. And Ford was an entrepreneur who applied himself diligently to improving the process of production, but was enough of a dilettante to pick up other people's innovations as well as implementing his own.

Before the iPod, MP3 players competed on the basis of technology, in particular on data capacity. Apple recognized that the majority of consumers did not need several thousand songs on the move, and that attractive design and consumer interface were more important than data capacity or even sound quality. This moved Apple from red ocean competition (competing on technology) into a market of one (competing on design), where the best-selling alternative to an iPod is another form of iPod. This was the first degree of the iPod's innovation – a value innovation or discovery which redefined the product and the market in which it operates.

Another key innovation was Apple's coupling of the iPod with iTunes, the music download service which uses a proprietary format uniquely compatible with the iPod. Consumers were thus locked into a hardware–software package which allowed Apple to cross-subsidize iTunes while increasing sales of iPods. Here Apple used second and third string innovation (increasing volume and reducing costs of its music downloads) in order to achieve market dominance, and thereby outflanking the record labels' belated attempts to develop their own music download services.

The iTunes innovations on inventory and price thus complemented the iPod's value innovation, allowing the iPod to command a premium price for a desirable product even as iTunes cut the cost and increased the total market. The decision to base the business model on hardware (sales of iPods) rather than software (sales of music through iTunes) was later borne out by the discovery that only around 2% of the music on iPods has been purchased online – consumers were using their iPods to copy, store, or organize music collections, not to purchase new music.

Apple used its own best and worst practices to develop the iPod. Apple had succeeded in the personal computer market by prioritizing elegant design and user-friendly customer interface over technical specifications, and this "best practice" was reapplied to the iPod (and subsequently the iPhone). Indeed, the creation of the iPod and iPhone helped Apple to rediscover its core strengths and reinvigorate its other computing products – so the cycle of discovery and creation continued to fuel innovation across the company's range.

Apple also learned from its own mistakes – an example of "learning innovation" (6th degree) – and from the mistakes of its competitors ("worst practice"). Apple's first entry into the mobile phone market was the Rokr, a mobile phone produced by Motorola which was compatible with iTunes. The device was expensive: most mobile phone companies subsidize the cost of the phone through service charges, and customers are often given the phone for free in return for signing the service contract. The Rokr did not benefit from this cross-subsidy, because iTunes had to be purchased separately from the service contract and mobile networks were consequently unwilling to subsidize a product where a large part of the revenues were flowing back to a separate organization. And the collaboration with Motorola meant that Apple's distinctive "look and feel" were missing, thereby alienating Apple's loyal customer base who might have adopted the product at a premium price and drawn in other customers.

The iPhone reversed these mistakes – it was a distinctive, branded Apple product, marketed to iPod users and Apple loyalists first before diffusing to later adopters. Apple can now afford to diversify its market, offering other types of iPhone just as it has developed new formats of iPod (Shuffle, Nano, Mini, Classic) and opening up to new partners and customers.

Finally, the iPod/iPhone exemplifies "boundary" innovation (5th degree) connecting together different competences and attributes and bridging several markets (personal computer, phone, MP3 player, portable video) within a single product. The vision to move sideways from Apple's core expertise (computers) into the music download market is another boundary-crossing innovation, reconfiguring and redefining its new and existing markets. This required an imaginative recasting of the existing market based on "next practice" – recognizing that what had been a piece of technology, appealing to a few enthusiasts, was now a lifestyle accessory, customized to a variety of users. In doing so, the iPod has joined that exclusive family of products (Biro, Hoover, Google) where a brand name becomes a generic term for the entire market.

1. *What do you think enabled Henry Ford and Steve Jobs to be such maverick strategists?*
2. *Can you think of or invent any further degrees of strategic innovation, in addition to Bilton and Cummings' six?*
3. *Apply the ideas from this chapter with regard to worst, good, and promising practice to outline what you think might be the future (or next practice) strategies for automobiles or computing in 2011 and beyond.*

11-2 IRL, Levis and Land Rover: Maverick ways of learning

When Shaun Coffey joined Industrial Research Limited as CEO, he identified one major area he wanted to help IRL to develop – its connection to the community it was established to serve: New Zealand Industry. IRL is a state-owned corporation whose purpose is to provide research and development expertise to New Zealand businesses. IRL did not lack for clever people – indeed it may have boasted the highest percentage of PhDs per capita of any organization in New Zealand, but seeing a relative lack of commercial "nous" as a hindrance to its achieving its full potential, one of the first things that Coffey did was seek to establish a leadership program and identify innovative minds from throughout the organization to be a part of it.

A core part of this program was a "Dragon's Den" exercise. Groups of around four participants were required to develop a new business venture for IRL and then present this to a panel comprising captains of industry and government and chaired by Coffey. The objective was to impress upon the panel the need for IRL to provide the group with the resources to pursue their "Den Project." A number of interesting projects grew out of the exercise, but one presentation was to have a particular impact on IRL. This was "What's Your Problem, New Zealand?"

Picking up on the issue of IRL's need to build upon its connections with New Zealand industry, a group of four young scientists came up with an idea for a competition, open to all businesses in New Zealand. The prize: up to NZD 1 million of free research from IRL for the company with the most interesting business problem. The group outlined how this would not actually cost IRL that amount of money – spare organizational capacity could be used, for the most part, and what IRL's research time was priced at was, obviously, more than what it cost to provide. But having just experienced something akin to a collective "eureka" moment, the panel were more interested in the benefits. The following Monday, Coffey met with the group and began to mobilize significant resources to get WYPNZ up and running as quickly and as effectively as possible.

Domain names were secured, a structured online questionnaire for entrants was developed, IRL project teams to help companies to prepare their entries were established, and media outlets and ministers were debriefed about the initiative.

WYPNZ was launched to a great fanfare by the Minister for Trade and Enterprise at a major function with many leading lights in NZ business and government in attendance, and hundreds of entries poured in. A judging panel, chaired by Coffey, whittled these down to a short list of 10 and these were coached by IRL project teams, the commercial law firm, and contest sponsor AJ Park, as they prepared presentations for an independent panel of scientific and business luminaries.

The finalists covered a broad spectrum of business problems from a wide range of industries, but the prize was awarded to Resene, a paint company with a project to develop a waterborne paint that was based on resins made of 80% sustainable ingredients, breaking the long-term reliance on gas and oil for high-performance paints. Resene Managing Director, Nick Nightingale, commented after the announcement was made that "this competition presented an amazing opportunity for Resene to team its commercial experience with world-leading science and revolutionize an industry. We're committed to sustainable developments and we took a bold idea to the judges and showed them how it can be realized with IRL to ensure that the financial benefits continue to flow to New Zealand."

In a similar vein, Levi's have recently been rethinking the way it conceives its value chain. Using the conventional linear, step-by-step, input–process–output view of adding value embodied in the conventional generic value chain, clothes manufacturers take inputs like fabrics and fixtures, use the company's information systems and knowledge to subject these inputs to value-adding processes (such as design and assembly), and distribute outputs to customers who pay for the finished product and then go on their way. Levi's has attempted to deconstruct these assumptions and look at ways in which it can *involve* its customers in the value-adding process so that they become part of the company, and part of the "Levi's community," rather than an anonymous body beyond the company walls.

Flagship stores, such as those in San Francisco and London, developed a "Levi's customization area." Here customers can photograph themselves and input these images into computer terminals that allow them to see what various outfits from the Levi's range would look like on them. Then they can become part of the value-adding design team by testing out how customized alterations (different cuts, or washes, or buttons, or pockets, or rips, or stitching, or patches and so on) would look on them. Finished designs can then be taken to an in-house construction team that works with the customer to develop what is wanted. Information on individual customers can be kept for return visits and aggregated to provide insights into popular trends.

Moreover, the London store was refurbished into a combined store and club/arts venue, incorporating a "chill-out" area, internet stations, plasma screens, ISDN links, a suspended two-tier DJ booth designed by DJ Paul Oakenfold, and a record outlet called Vinyl Addiction. It can be transformed into a 500-capacity venue with facilities to host club nights, live music, fashion shows, film screenings, comedy nights, and exhibitions. It can create and sustain "value" in many more ways than the traditional, "go in–browse–buy–leave" retail outlet.

Land Rover Australia has attempted to achieve similar aims with its Land Rover Club. One of the main strategic issues that the brand has faced in recent times is the decreasing switching costs of that growing set of customers who have never driven off-road who are buying SUVs not on performance but on "looks." To keep Land Rover drivers connected to the brand, the Club seeks to link Land Rover customers to one another and involve them in the value chain – by learning from them about the problems and fears that prevent inexperienced off-roaders from trying or enjoying off-roading. New owners are provided with free weekends away at resorts with new Land Rover drivers from nearby post-codes as well as being invited to off-road rallies, other special events, and "adventures." The weekends include free off-road driving lessons where driving behavior can be observed, learned from and incorporated into the way that Land Rover designs its vehicles and instruction manuals.

1. Why might WYPNZ be a good learning innovation for IRL and how might it lead to other degrees of innovation?
2. Draw a value chimera incorporating Levi's value chain for its conventional product offering and the customization offshoot. Given that the two parts of the business are at opposite ends of the "S-curve," how might each of these two heads of the value chimera support one another?
3. Draw organigraphs to depict how IRL's and Land Rover's strategic innovations described above might help to create more effective engagement with clients or customers.

Case Notes:

11-3 Synear: Dumplings to Villas

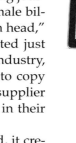

Synear Quick-Frozen Food Company was founded in 1994 in China's southern provinces by a group of young and ambitious Chinese mavericks, including journalism graduate Li Wei (who has recently become one of China's first female billionaires). Synear began as a manufacturer of dumplings. China's "dragon head," or leading player, in the quick-frozen food industry, Sanquan, was located just 1 mile from Synear's base. As a newcomer with little experience in the industry, Synear's founders perceived this "dragon head" as a model and aimed to copy Sanquan's factory layout, administrative systems, training processes, supplier relationships, and recipes, as nearly as possible. They set out to become, in their words, a "mini-Sanquan."

While this approach enabled Synear to get its operations off the ground, it created a number of problems. Perceiving Sanquan as "best practice" and duplicating its products made it hard for customers to differentiate the two companies' offerings. Inevitably, this led to a price war that Synear, given its much smaller operating base, was in no position to win. Synear management found that the only way it could shift sales in this environment was to offer its dumplings on credit, but the difficulties associated with deferred payments by customers led to a serious cash-flow problem.

Synear responded in two ways. First, to improve cash flow, it integrated forward into restaurants that utilized Synear products but enabled bigger margins and improved cash receipts. Second, it began to think about how it could differentiate its dumplings from those of Sanquan. This it did in two ways that might be seen as contradictory by followers of classic Western strategic management theory.

On the one hand, Synear abandoned what it described as "high-income" customers and focused instead on those with middle or low incomes who would sacrifice some degree of quality for a lower price. This enabled it to focus on every step of the processes it had copied from Sanquan and examine how costs could be cut. For example, Synear decided not to sell its dumplings to wholesalers and stores in traditional small packets, but in bulk cartons from which shoppers could pick the amount they wanted and pay by weight at lower prices. Synear was soon able to market its wares as the lowest priced dumplings on the market, knowing that Sanquan, whose success was wedded to its broad appeal to all income groups and traditional dumpling manufacture techniques, would find it difficult to follow.

On the other hand, however, Synear sought to differentiate its dumplings in ways that appealed to younger people like themselves. Synear's managers had watched with interest the emerging awareness of environmental issues among younger consumers. To match these interests they decided to go after the newly developed Chinese "green product certificate," which assured customers that a product was made of natural or organic ingredients and that the manufacturing process did not pollute the environment. Additionally, it introduced natural dyes to some products to create green dumplings in addition to the traditional white color. This made Synear dumplings stand out in the marketplace and attracted attention to the green policy. A yellow coloring was also added in honor of the Yellow River, "being" of great cultural and spiritual significance in the region.

MAVERICK STRATEGIES

While its lack of experience in frozen foods had been seen as something of a hindrance when Synear started life, it was now beginning to use the fact that its people weren't ingrained with traditional approaches and could therefore think about making and selling dumplings in new and different ways. Other innovative approaches that Synear developed included:

- Convincing Sanquan to develop an alliance that would give the companies added muscle to jointly procure produce at lower prices.
- Using some of its underutilized frozen food facilities to develop a range of ice cream.
- An alliance with a local sales agent willing to put money into the company. This agent became the company's second largest shareholder. The cash injection enabled dumpling and ice cream production to double.
- Another alliance with a regional agent who had a strong hold over the market in three provinces in China's southwest region, provinces where companies like Sanquan had yet to establish a presence. This provided a ready market for the increased production described above. While ensuring this agent's cooperation required an agreement to sell to him at little more than cost, his networks enabled Synear to dominate the frozen dumpling market in these provinces within a matter of months.
- Broadening its portfolio by buying the recipes for proven products (a particular regional black sesame dumpling, for example) from smaller companies that lacked the finance to develop the market for such items.
- A commitment to developing very good and very professionalized relationships with banks and government agencies – relationships that, over time, would help with obtaining the capital and permits required for further developments. This was something that traditional and less entrepreneurial Chinese companies had generally not focused on.

The development of these new strategies meant that business was getting much better for Synear, but as time went by the partners became increasingly aware of the relatively low margins that the dumpling and restaurant businesses provided. It was time to diversify further. However, once again the direction the company took might be seen by some to make little sense when analyzed using classical Western decision-making models.

Synear's managers made the decision to enter the real estate business. However, this time they realized that they needed to differentiate themselves from the competition from the outset. There were literally tens of thousands of property development businesses in China and most of them much the same as one other, but Synear sought to mark itself out as different by building on the ethos that had developed around the dumplings. Synear sought to focus on low-cost housing. This meant building some distance out from the city. But this then enabled a connection to another of Synear's tenets to come into play. Synear would build on newly developed forestland and would emphasize the green, environmentally sound, and tranquil aspects of their properties to young middle-income house buyers. Thus, Synear developed four principles around which it would focus its property development energies. They are as follows:

1. In Chinese cities most people live in apartments and most are sick of concrete and steel buildings. People want houses – homes with gardens, grass, and flowers. All our buildings are villas.

2. All our buildings are far away from city noise. At least 20 kilometers away from the city so that people can plunge themselves into a paradise after a hard day's work.
3. The backgrounds of our houses are very green and tranquil. Our homes are built in a forest in surroundings that are like rural areas.
4. All our houses are near the "Mother" (or Yellow) River. People have a special emotion for the river and living near her gives them a feeling of harmony and relaxation.

The company that began as a frozen dumpling maker still makes dumplings. But it now makes much more, and each product in its diverse range (dumplings, restaurants, property) reinforces the brand image of the other. The company is now one of China's largest food producers and was an official supplier to the Beijing Olympic Games. Associated with this, Jackie Chan has been recruited as the face of Synear's new Gold Medal Series of quick freeze food products. And, according to *Forbes Magazine*, Li Wei is now the 891st wealthiest person in the world.

1. *Draw an organigraph of Synear. Why do you think this might be a more effective depiction of Synear than an organization chart or a value chain?*
2. *What were the strengths and weaknesses of Synear's initial strategy to copy and replicate Sanquan as the "best practice" model?*
3. *Work through Kim and Mauborgne's five "value innovation" questions to determine the value innovations that Synear's managers have achieved. Can you also identify any examples of "blue ocean" strategies followed by Synear?*

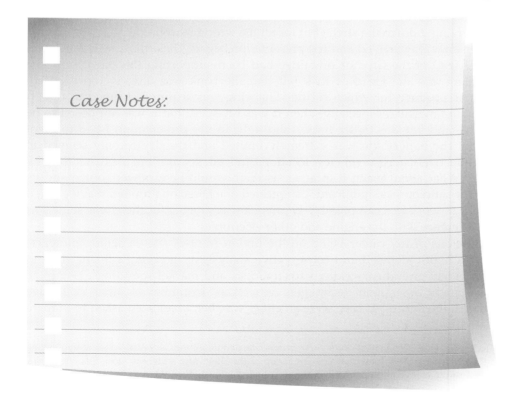

Case Notes:

11-4 Venture Capital*: Gray boxes

With 3 days to go before Christmas, a file landed on my desk with "most urgent" stamped on the cover. Inside was a memo from the Managing Director saying, "In the light of this bank's substantial exposure to this client firm, and the request from this client for further financing, we must review, urgently, the bank's position. A Board meeting has been arranged for Christmas Day to make a decision on this matter. Review all the documentation to date, including the current request, and present your summary recommendations at 10 AM, December 25th, in the Boardroom. Present will be myself, the Chairman and the Heads of Corporate Finance, the Credit Committee, and Risk Finance." Investment banking was living up to its reputation as 24/7.

The client firm had a reputation as an innovator in electronics and was well regarded in the industry. A number of innovations had been patented successfully and the firm continued to grow rapidly. However, the firm was highly indebted and most of this debt was held by our bank. Understandably, the bank was getting very nervous as the amount of outstanding debt continued to grow and there appeared to be no real sign from the firm that any of its products would really be a stellar performer. And now here they were, asking for a substantial increase in funds of £50m for a completely new product.

Shortly after the file landed on my desk, a gray box the size of a small briefcase arrived. It had a few dials and switches and weighed a ton. Attached was a technical note that was hard to follow, but it was clear that the device was supposed to be portable! How would it be carried? It wouldn't fit into anything but the largest of bags and it didn't have its own case. One would certainly be conspicuous carrying it down the street, but for all the wrong reasons.

Christmas Day arrived and my presentation began. The atmosphere was tense, as the Head of the Credit Committee had been supporting this client from the beginning and the Head of Risk felt that the bank was already too exposed. The new product, for which further financing was required, seemed to underwhelm the meeting, especially when it was revealed that it was supposed to be portable and yet was bulky, heavy, and ugly. In my presentation I had to point out that the battery life was extremely limited and the device only seemed to work effectively in relatively few locations. Indeed, it was more likely not to work at all. "What about using it in a car, as there would be a power source and its weight would be less significant?" suggested one Director. I replied that we failed to get it to work in a car, possibly because it was moving, or there was some sort of interference with the engine and other electronics.

Conscious of my career being on the line in front of such a senior audience, I gave a highly detailed and conservative analysis of the client's financials, and drew widely on industry experts for forecasts and market soundings. Using the bank's credit assessment techniques as well as a number of other evaluative methods, the figures, at best, were an either way bet. I had been asked to prepare

---

* This is a real case. The identity of the client firm is revealed under the Case Authors section following the References (pg. 379). Now that you are aware of the client firm's identity, does this affect your answers to the earlier questions? What lessons can be learned about the way in which early-stage finance and entrepreneurial endeavors work alongside each other?

a presentation for a credit committee, and therefore conservative, point of view. I therefore recommended the bank walk away from any further financing of the client as the numbers really did not support further exposure based on the bank's own criteria for loans. I also recommended the bank reduce its exposure to the firm by syndicating some of the debt. For the committee, the fate of the client hung in the balance. To refuse financing would imperil the client's future. There is no doubt that the client would have had a very hard time getting finance from another bank when its own bank had refused it.

The Head of Risk asked: "When should the bank stop lending to a firm that is really not showing results, and just keeps coming up with new products for which there appears to be no demand?" The Head of the Credit Committee responded by remarking that the client had never defaulted on an interest payment and then, to my surprise, said that the numbers were only part of the equation. What he wanted to know was: "What does the client MD think about when he gets up in the morning? What worries him when he is shaving in front of the mirror?" The Managing Director of the bank agreed, saying, "the key to good lending is *really* understanding the entrepreneur – a great idea in the hands of a poor entrepreneur is a disaster, a mediocre idea in the hands of a great entrepreneur is success."

There followed a spirited discussion between the Directors around which they largely agreed that the client MD was passionate about his firm and his products and that he would do anything to get his products to work. After a bruising meeting for all concerned, the Board agreed, late on Christmas Day, that they would support the client and finance the launch of its new product – even though the Head of Risk could not see why anyone would want an oversized, pig-ugly, temperamental gray box!

1. *Would you have supported the decision to lend a further £50m?*
2. *Traditionally, what are the main considerations for banks involved in this form of finance?*
3. *It is clear from the case that it was "touch and go" for the entrepreneur gaining the necessary finance for his product. Why was he successful in eliciting an innovative approach to financing? Could he have improved his approach or "pitch" to the bank?*

Case Notes:

In 2001, the financial services company Egg's call center in Derby (in England's Midlands) was nominated as one of the UK's "most creative and feel-good offices for the digital age." This was a surprising result, given that call centers were supposed to be the 21st-century's sweat-shops – the equivalent of the dreary and mind-numbing factories of earlier times – and that Derby lacks what one might call a "feel-good" reputation. But Egg's call center was designed to be different.

With the opportunity to design and build from the ground up on a green-field site, Egg's vision was to create a vibrant and fun call center that would accommodate over 1,000 people. Its express purpose: to help attract and retain the highest quality personnel. Instead of relying on existing models, Egg's design consultants set about talking to potential staff members aged between 18 and 23 (a typical age for new call-center employees) to find out what sort of work environment would appeal to them.

The result is a huge white aircraft hangar-like building that looks like half an egg, sliced length-wise. It has almost no internal walls, office furniture is configured to enable people to cluster together in teams and to enable employees to reconfigure it as they see fit, and no set seating plan. (Although, it is worth mentioning that Egg employees do admit that despite no set structure, people's patterns did emerge and become ingrained fairly quickly after the Derby center opened.) In each of the four corners of the building are recreational spaces based around different themes (for example, a sports area with room for ball-games, pinball, and so on and a relaxing Mediterranean café) that staff can use depending on their mood.

Egg is not the first company in recent years to attempt to redesign the office or factory, but many consider the company at the forefront of a revolution that is continuing to spread and impact on all of our places of work.

Many trace the beginnings of the workplace revolution to the invention of Apple Computers. Apple made much of not being IBM – the industry standard. It didn't make computers for IBM-type people and the staff didn't work like IBM employees. No corporation uniforms, no strict timetables, no rigid job descriptions, no formal chains of command and time-weary procedures, no sitting alone in an allocated box. This was the story at least, but it was certainly played on in Apple's early advertising for models like the Macintosh and it has become an integral part of the Apple mythology.

Since this time, executives have been empowered to be different in the workplace, to "dress down" on Fridays, or to replace their suits and ties with chinos and soft collars on a more permanent basis. New terms like "open-plan" and "hot-desking" have entered the language, and more and more workspaces contain "chill-out rooms" and fitness centers. But is this revolution in making where we work more comfortable, or more like home, necessarily a good thing? A recently published essay on the trend, called "Game Over! Back to Work," by Jonathan Bell, is not so sure.

Bell claims that the modern office is beginning to resemble a playpen. Not only may all of this just be a ruse to increase productivity – to fool jaded employees into thinking that their company loves them so much that it wants them to have

MAVERICK STRATEGIES

fun, so that these employees, in turn, feel that they owe the company – it may also be a ruse that doesn't actually work. Hence, we may not be too far away from "rediscovering the worth of workspaces that are workspaces rather than romper rooms."

Not that the revolution has been all bad: in many ways it has redressed the imbalance caused by the 20th-century's first workplace mavericks. Ninety years ago, workplace architects, inspired by F.W. Taylor's new doctrine "scientific management," sought to rationalize the workplace and design out all vestiges of individuality. They built so as to maximize sterility and order. Modernism henceforth became the business world's architectural style of choice and offices began to resemble filing cabinets. But, as with most doctrines, this revolution went too far and by the 1980s the backlash that Apple personified was long overdue.

By the end of the 20th century, things had loosened up so much that for many the lines between work and play were becoming increasingly imperceptible. In 2001, a report entitled *Tomorrow's Workplace: Fulfilment or Stress?* envisaged the office of the future as a "recreational center," where the toys and tasks differed little from those found at home. Product designers are already seeing the boundaries blurring. Industrial designer Sam Hecht says that he is not sure if there is much of a difference anymore: "It's very hard [now] to distinguish between objects for the home and for the office."

At the same time, we are witnessing a blurring between work-time and play-time, with employees finding it increasingly difficult to determine whether they are at work or not. Thanks to "advances" in information technology, for many the workday now begins when they start to commute to the office, not when they sit down at their desk. For others, it never really ceases as they are constantly available on the end of a cell phone and most homes now contain a computer and an e-mail connection in a "home office."

Although not specifying exact working hours has become the norm for an increasing class of workers, it is generally understood that most "white-collar jobs" (an increasingly anachronistic term given the relaxation of dress codes) consume more and more of people's time. As Madeline Bunting's book *Willing Slaves: How the Overwork Culture is Ruining Our Lives* explains, in many parts of the labor market "the boundaries between work and play have been eroded: work is play, work is your hobby. Work becomes the organizing principle of your life."

This is fine for some, particularly those creative souls for whom their work is a consuming passion: it is where they find their identity and purpose. But it may be that many of us are not wired that way.

Says Bell: "It may be time to recognize that [the majority] do not find identity and purpose in vintage PacMan machines and bean bags. Innovations like hot-desking fail to recognize that most of us want a permanent workstation that allows us to get our job done. We are starting to realize that long hours spent in the office playing table football are not useful or clever. Many of us love our work [but] don't need side-shows or soft furnishings to keep the relationship alive."

Indeed, Bell believes that a new generation of offices will emerge that acknowledges that good ideas can come from people having the freedom to congregate, but at the same time recognize that a good office is about allowing individuals to focus on doing their jobs quickly and cleanly.

"It's a century since Frank Lloyd Wright's Larkin Building was completed in Buffalo, New York," concludes Bell. "this was perhaps the first modern office building. And here was order and communality, efficiency and common purpose. He may have been on to something." But, in the same year as Bell's essay was published, Egg won another prestigious national award, this time topping the list of call centers in the UK with the most motivated and productive staff.

---

1. *Which of the developments in workplace design described in the case do you think are "value innovations," according to Kim and Mauborgne's definition, and which are just innovations for the sake of innovation? What effects might these "value innovations" have on the development of strategy?*
2. *How might the growing awareness of "diversity management" and the importance of "shaking together" different ideas and perspectives impact on the future shape of workplace design?*
3. *The case describes Apple's maverick approach setting off something of a revolution in workplace design. Do you think IBM and Apple's other competitors should have followed in Apple's footsteps in this regard or should workplace design reflect the particularities of each individual organization?*

Case Notes:

11-6 Danone Argentina: Once a maverick. . .?

One evening in September 2008, Dr. Dirk Van de Put – Groupe Danone's General Manager for Fresh Dairy Products (FDP) and Waters in South and North America – turned off the TV. It had been broadcasting the latest news: financial crisis, recession, perfect storms, credit crunches. . . But the crisis was not only in the news: the first traces that the GFC was affecting his company were already landing on his desk.

Reports from across the Americas were revealing that sales were being affected. The number of people buying Danone products on a monthly basis was declining; and the amount of money spent on those products was also going down. He began to reflect. . .

In 1919 Isaac Carasso produced the first Danone yogurts after being struck by the number of children in his native Barcelona suffering from intestinal disorders. Carasso used lactic ferments from the Pasteur Institute, in Paris. He named his first factory after his son Daniel – Danone in Catalan – and Daniel went on to set up the family business in France in 1929. By the 1990s, through takeovers, partnerships and joint ventures, Groupe Danone had become the third-biggest food group in Europe, symbolized by a little boy gazing at a star.

Since the 1990s, the group has focused upon promoting healthy products, concentrated on four lines: FDP, Waters, Baby Nutrition, and Medical Nutrition. By the end of 2007, a full 100% of sales were generated by food products with a focus on health, up from 39% in 1996. At the same time, the consolidation of the European Union and growth in local competition, led to a decline in industry profits, creating an incentive for more serious investment in other regions, initiating an international expansion into Asia, the Americas, and Africa. By the end of 2007, Groupe Danone employed more than 76,000 people in 159 production sites with no single country representing more than 14% of the company's revenues. Its main brands included Danone, Actimel, and Danonino (FDP), Evian and Volvic (Waters), Nutricia and Cow & Gate (Baby), and Nutricia and FortiCare (Medical).

The GFC was not the first economic crisis that Dr. Van de Put had faced with Danone. As regional manager for Danone Latin America, he had successfully navigated Argentina's economic downfall of 2001. And he had learned much from the experience.

As part of Danone's global expansion, the Argentine market was entered through the acquisition of a controlling stake in Bagley – a local cookies, crackers, and sweets producer. It then added other well-positioned and prestigious brands to its Argentine stable: Villa Alpina, Villa del Sur, and Villavicencio, in bottled water and formed a joint venture partnership with local FDP business Mastellone group. In 2001, Danone generated sales for Ä1,500m in the Latin American region, and was the market leader in all business lines (FDP, Biscuits and Cereal Snacks, and Bottled Water).

Danone Argentina's FDP management team, led by Van de Put, Patrick Sauvageot (CEO of Danone Argentina) and Gustavo Valle (CFO of the FDP business unit and Treasurer Danone Argentina) analyzed the FDP business' situation. Groupe Danone had set a specific goal for Argentina. In Patrick Sauvageot's words: "We had a target: it was to improve the company's profits through an increase in volume and in net sales."

This went against the conventional wisdom that prevailed at the time. Sauvageot stated: "the company already had a share of more than 50% of the Argentine market, and the country's per capita consumption of yogurt was of 6 kg per year per person, a very high volume by the region's standards. The feeling was that the company did not have much room to grow, and that the only way to increase profits would be to reduce costs."

Danone's team had a different view. Sauvageot explained: "France and Spain had per capita consumption levels that were about five times that of Argentina. In those countries, yogurt was sold in smaller pots than in Argentina (125 g against 200 g), and the cost per kilogram was 30% lower. We realized that the market's potential actually depended on us."

So the team pushed for growth. There was a plant working at 30% of its capacity, so there was no need of further investment. The product range in the FDP business consisted of "middle-of-the road" type of products. Applying the European experience regarding price and product size, and using European technology for the new type of packaging, they decided to relaunch "Yogur Entero La Serenisima" with the new name of "Yogurisimo." This yogurt, sold in smaller pots and at a lower price per unit, was introduced as a premium healthy alternative as it had two varieties of lactic ferments.

But soon, the country's economic climate started to be a cause of worry. In the third quarter of 2001, key indicators showed the presence of a recession. The country's currency (the peso) had been subject to a 1-to-1 peg with the US dollar for about 10 years, but the government was finding it increasingly difficult to sustain that monetary equation. The crisis finally broke at the end of 2001, when consumers' incomes were severely restricted – first by the *corralito*[24] and then by the devaluation of the peso. A dilemma arose: could the management team still push ahead with a growth strategy in an economic crisis? And if so how?

Van de Put remembered: "most competitors reacted by applying the 'traditional recipe' used in a case of recession and devaluation: they immediately worked on their costs, raising prices to sustain their margins in US dollars. With raw materials becoming much more expensive, they also began to restructure in order to bring fixed costs down." So his team conceived an innovative strategy: "we knew that, if Danone reacted in the same direction as competitors, it would mean a huge decline in some of our businesses – around 20–30% in volume. We decided to take other measures."

They initially contacted the supermarkets. "It was essential to show consumers a lower – and stable – price. Promising to decrease our own prices and to invest highly in advertising, we asked them to lower their margins by 5%," said Van de Put. Smaller retailers such as traditional convenience stores were also gaining momentum among middle and low income consumers. Valle added: "Because they received deliveries daily and paid in cash – a more than scarce commodity given the economic conditions – it was a priority for us to serve them as well."

"At the same time, the company visited its suppliers and asked them to start selling to Danone 5% cheaper than before. In doing so, Danone guaranteed suppliers that once the crisis was over revenues and volumes would increase. In the meantime, suppliers would accept lower margins but they would survive." Those suppliers with which Danone had no bargaining power were changed, and foreign suppliers (responsible for about 80% of the company's costs in raw materials – excluding milk) were replaced by local ones. In Sauvageot's words, "It was essential for the company to develop and protect its suppliers, many of which were broke or had suffered a drop in their activities. Our suppliers were treated as partners in the crisis. It was like war-time, there was energy, people did things that would seem impossible at other moments."

Then the company focused on consumers. Sauvageot stated: "the downsizing of our products would let consumers perceive that they could buy a yogurt pot for less. The crisis seemed to be an ideal moment to put the idea into practice. At the same time, we printed the price on the packs with the intention of making it clear that we were going to maintain it. That would also keep retailers from applying bigger margins and thus sell the products at higher prices."

Subsequently, foreseeing a general drop in TV advertising, Danone contacted major TV stations in order to make a deal. The company's access to cash earned them a great advantage as Danone used it to get better conditions when hiring advertising air time. Among its advertising, Danone decided to inform the consumer about its decision not to raise prices, and launched commercials that were linked to the crisis. Van de Put recalled the message conveyed by the ads: "We understand that these are very tough times in Argentina, but La Serenisima won't let you down. We have decided that we will not increase our prices and we will offer you some products at a cheaper price."

The need to ride out the crisis was seen to be no reason to delay innovation. Francisco Camacho, who took over Danone Argentina in 2004, stated: "instead of fighting the storm, the company had to accelerate the innovation process compared to previous years. This was achieved through the revalorization of existing products."Besides the launch of Yogurisimo, Serenito and Casancrem were relaunched and underwent a full renovation that included both the upgrade of the value perception and the downsizing of the pot. The company also introduced innovative products with proven international success, such as Danonino. Actimel, which had been imported from Brazil, began to be produced locally. Aiming at the lower income consumer, Danone started offering the sachet packaging for Yogurisimo: through the small gap that this presentation offered against the price of milk, it allowed the consumers to switch to yogurt. In fact, 55% of new yogurt consumers entered the category through the purchase of sachets. Similar innovative approaches were applied in bottled waters too.

"We believed that the best moment to attack was when everybody else was in trouble: while everybody cut their advertising costs, Danone would get much more visibility in the media. We had never advertised heavily, but we made a conscious decision at that time to become one of the most relevant advertisers in Argentina," remembered Valle.

Moreover, the company considered it essential to keep up its trading volumes. In Van de Put's words: "I was convinced that this business was measured in terms of volume. If you lose volume you start to get into big trouble. Critical mass is very important because it pays for your fixed costs, it pays for your distribution system, and it is good for the moral of the company."

The parent company in Paris was understandably nervous. But Van de Put promised: "we will maintain the absolute margin in Pesos in year one, in year two it will increase and in year three we will be back to having the same margin in US dollars that we had before the crisis." Groupe Danone eventually agreed to van de Put's counter-intuitive strategy of growth and innovation in a crisis.

Success did not come quickly, and Van de Put and his team spent a tense few months waiting for positive signs to emerge. It took 4 to 5 months for consumers and media to grasp that Danone was doing things differently and only then did the company start to see a growth in volume. Over the next four years Danone Argentina increased its volume about 20% to 30% each year. And after four years the volume sold doubled the pre-crisis figures. Profits followed a similar path. In 2004, the company had a 69% share in FDP, up from 59% in 2001. And this market, against all odds, had almost doubled its per capita consumption figures. By 2007, Danone's share had risen to 76%.

. . .Back at his desk in September 2008, Dr. Van de Put focused his mind back on the crisis at hand. He looked at the last quarter's global figures. As with most stocks in most markets, Danone's stock prices were plummeting.

He now oversaw operations in nine North and South American countries. Responses to the crisis varied: Brazil was continuing to perform well whereas sales volume in Mexico was softening. Danone US witnessed a marked slowdown in the fourth quarter. The bottled water business continued to be strong, particularly in Mexico and Argentina. But the GFC was going to impact on all the countries for which van de Put was responsible.

Van de Put was confident that his FDP markets still had room to grow, but they were inserted in economies that would soon be shrinking. His experience in Argentina showed him that Danone had been able to ride out adverse conditions through bold action, clever innovations, and strategic partnerships. Could he replicate the strategy in bigger – and different – markets? Would customers, suppliers, and the media react in the same way? Could he (indeed should he), be a maverick once more?

1. *List the strategic innovations employed by Van de Put's team during the Argentine crisis. Why did they work?*
2. *Using frameworks and ideas from earlier Pathfinder chapters (e.g. Chapters 1–5) sketch out how you think the GFC of 2008/9 may impact differently on Dirk's responsibilities from the Argentine crisis eight years earlier.*
3. *Should Van de Put be a maverick once more? What would you recommend he do?*

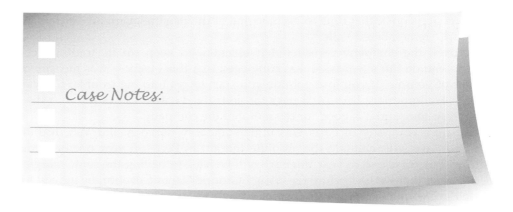

Case Notes:

11-7 Nestlé Russia: Retro future

By the end of the 20th century, according to Hugh Pearman, cultural commentator with *The Sunday Times*, the appearance of cars began to change: "manufacturers ha[d] been driven to take risks. . . to create market niches. Before everyone wanted their products to look the same. Now, they want them to look distinctive. . . Good is bland, bad is good." This was culturally significant, claims Pearman, because "cars dominate our visual surroundings."

Early examples of this distinctiveness included Ford's Scorpio ("bugged eyed and strangely proportioned, but you noticed it," says Pearman), Chrysler's new PT Cruiser is described by its makers as "a love it or hate it car too cool to categorize" (it looks like a 1950s American hotrod) and Chrysler's "yestertech" sports cars like the Prowler and Viper.

Why did such examples start to strike a chord? A decade-long drive, where closing the quality and engineering gap among car manufacturers around the world was the main strategic focus, has left the companies so similar technologically that they are being forced, by the late 1990s to compete increasingly on "different looks." "The globalization of the car industry meant that all cars (and all car ads) came to look much the same everywhere," Pearman explains. "The aim of manufacturers was for the greatest number of people to be unoffended by the look of the product. This avoidance of risk was achieved through focus groups, and meant that national and marque differences were ironed out. Weird French cars ceased to be weird, Japanese cars stopped being ugly, the Americans toned down their once incredible styling in the name of international sales." (Only 41% of focus group members liked the PT while 26% hated it, which used to be more than enough to kill off a prototype). Handling and performance differences also went the way of stylish eccentricity. The car market, says Pearman, "became like architecture's dogmatic modern phase." Homogenization meant it became impossible to express an individual identity through a new car.

Ray Hutton reported that whereas "Not long ago the world car was the thing, car makers having declared that customer tastes had converged and that the latest designs would be as acceptable in Tamworth as they were in Tucson or Tokyo. [But] it didn't turn out that way. Buyer's wanted individuality." Toyota recently claimed that "Our global strategy used to center on 'world cars,' which we would modify slightly to accommodate demand in different markets. Today our focus is shifting to models that we develop and manufacture for selected regional markets." Subsequently, says Hutton, all sorts of niche cars are starting to appear and American cars are once more starting to look "distinctly American."

Citroën, once leaders in quirky French styling, found that its new cars resembled last year's Fords and that consumers were unsure of Citroën's "identity." Renault's head of design, Patrick le Quement describes the change that has happened in the car industry since: "When I joined Renault, my notion of bringing 'Frenchness' to the brand was heresy, we were living through the 'world car' phenomenon. . . but now people recognize that we are so much richer for having, British-ness, Dutch-ness, and German-ness and so on."

And this is where the retro appeared to kick in. As firms had become so good at copying, the most obvious place to look for distinctive styles that could not be copied because they have a long association with a particular brand (and so would obviously be a rip-off), was the back-catalog.

These developments also caused many to question the stock traditionally placed on focus groups. Inventor James Dyson believes that you cannot have customers designing products because individual distinctiveness must be a key part of any successful product. He points out that one of the most boring British cars ever made – the Hillman Avenger – emerged from focus groups, whereas the Mini, one of the most memorable, was one man's local vision.

Pearman was unsure whether the shifts he observed would have enough substance to make them significant for the long term. Consolidation in the car industry and advances in computerized design have made manufacturers adept at making marques appear different, when they are just the same model with a different skin. The new Beetle was just a VW Golf in disguise, he noted. Pearman concluded that the embrace of an individual marque's personality and back catalogue may be "just another passing phase."

However, with a decade of hindsight there is evidence to suggest that strategically plumbing the retro in automobile design may be more than a phase. Since, Pearman wrote of the PT Cruiser and new Beetle, cars like the Mini and the Fiat 500 (modeled on the much loved Bambina) have won numerous Car of the Year Awards and are part of a growing list of "back to the future" designs. And, we can observe similar trends in industries as diverse as sports shoes (all the major brands now have retro ranges), banking (bringing back personal touches like bank managers who know local customers), and children's toys (Mecanno, Transformers, My Little Pony, etc.).

But now an advanced phase of this phenomenon may be taking place. It's not only formerly loved products that are being brought back, but some that people were at best ambivalent about at the time they were first produced. Herpa, a German auto company, is relaunching the Trabant, with the first expected to be shipped to dealers in 2012.

The plastic bodied, smoke-spewing, famously unreliable Trabant became an object of ridicule and a symbol of communism's grim failings in its first incarnation. Even Herpa's General Manager, Daniel Stiegler, calls the original Trabant a "stinky car." But Herpa is betting on the Trabant having developed a cult following, a cult following based partly on the fact that the Trabant was so uniquely bad. Hence, bringing it back is both a retro and an ironic strategy. It's "retronic."

Other retronic examples are emerging. Many in the former Soviet States (interestingly). Two of Russia's best-selling ice creams appeal to memories of the Soviet past. "CCCP," made by a local company, employs the graphic style of soviet posters, often including red as a representative colour of communism and the soviet past; a recognizably constructivist font; and a luminous white – suggesting something miraculous, all-seeing, and powerful. The planet depicted is red, recalling Cold War period propaganda aims and statements that communism would be the entire planet's dominant ideology. And following the success of CCCP, the multinational Nestlé has sought to follow this new "best practice," introducing the "48 kopeks" (the price for ice-cream in the former USSR), which also exploits Soviet and pre-Soviet Russian imagery.

But is such a nostalgia-driven approach to strategic development sustainable, or will the back catalog eventually run dry (indeed, is the re-emergence of products that weren't particularly appreciated first time around evidence that the back catalog of good or missed products is already running dry?). Are strategies that hark back to the past clever, or rather a sign of lazyness or of being bereft of innovative ideas?

Moreover, are there ethical boundaries that firms should consider when engaging in this practice? Are there historical images or products with negative historical associations with regimes that while ironic or funny to some, or which may have a "cult following," that should be off-limits? And might multinational companies like Nestlé need to approach this last issue differently from home-grown ones? It is one thing for a local to have fun with his own history, but a foreigner?

1. *Do you think the trend toward sustaining a company's competitive advantage by mining its back catalogue, described in this case, is a sustainable new form of "best practice"?*
2. *Are there any ethical issues that should limit the types of nostalgia or historical imagery that companies can mine to promote new products or services?*
3. *Might large multinationals be constrained in different ways in this regard than small local companies?*

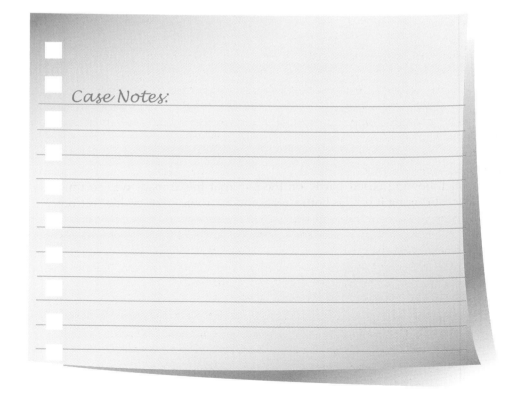

Case Notes:

Strategy problems rarely fit neatly into one or even two analytical categories. Part of the skill of the strategist is being able to discern relevant tools, techniques and concepts from different strategy categories with which to makes sense of complex problems and, critically, to understand how these may interact in order to provide a holistic solution(s). The following integrative cases are designed to test readers' ability to discern different strategic issues within a single case and to attempt to find ways in which multiple analytical techniques may be integrated in order to provide well rounded strategic solutions. These cases might be useful as end of course exams or assignments.

Turkish Delight: Into Africa?

During September the CEO and owner of Turkish Delight, a small travel company based in West London, visited a leading business school in order to get help with the company's Strategy. As an entrepreneur, he has a strong sense of opportunities in the travel industry and he is also a self confessed 'techie' who loves nothing more that to be fiddling around with the technology of his business. The company, Turkish Delight, which he founded five years earlier, resulted from his belief that Turkey would be the next 'big thing' in travel destinations for UK customers, but his employer at the time was not interested in pursuing this idea. Since then there has been a strong and growing interest in Turkey as a holiday destination.

Turkish Delight Ltd offers holidays to the secluded highlands of Turkey. Set in pine forests with a mild climate customers are housed in discrete villas with service available 24/7. The customers are a mix of Yuppies (young upwardly mobile professional persons), Dinkies (double income no kids) from the City of London and the over 50s from around Manchester in the north of England who now have more disposable income as their children have left home and finished further education. The business is very well regarded amongst travel operators and has one of the highest levels of repeat custom in the industry. Its particular strength is customer service with customers being met at departing and arriving airports and personally escorted to their accommodation. Turkish Nationals studying in the UK are recruited to look after customers in Turkey as they are fluent in English and have a deep understanding of Turkish culture and customers. They are retained for 2 seasons only and are not part of the permanent employee base of 20.

Twelve months ago the CEO became aware that another London based travel business was failing due to poor management and over investment in cutting edge technology. In liquidation he was able to procure the technology for very little cost so Turkish Delight can now book customers directly onto specific short and medium haul aircraft having purchased their holiday. This gives customers peace of mind about where they will sit without having to be at the airport many hours in advance and still risk an uncertain outcome. He now realises this side of the business is scalable and can be offered to other travel providers as well. He has begun to do this in order to increase volume rapidly as margins are very low. He also realises that he can book aircraft seats and indeed entire aircraft in advance of anticipated seasonal demand.

The finances of Turkish Delight are quite robust. The company has around £5m cash in the bank with negligible debt and his offices are on a long term lease at attractive rents. For the last financial year ended March 1989 sales were £19m and earnings after tax were £0.4m, which is rather low in relation to other travel companies.

As he stands in the lobby of the business school he is understandably nervous. He has a gut feel that South Africa is the next place to be but he is well aware that now, in 1991, apartheid is a serious issue and no one knows how things will turn out. At the moment businesses are withdrawing from South Africa and those which remain, such as Barclays Bank are receiving a great deal of negative publicity and some bank premises have been vandalised. However he has already visited South Africa to see the situation for himself and has been very impressed. He was shown around a number of excellent, world class hotels who offer accommodation at very competitive rates. The hotels are clearly concerned about the general perception of security and have their own sophisticated forms of secure transport and their facilities are well protected. The main airline has also offered highly competitive airfares for his customers and government officials are clearly going to help with clearing any regulatory hurdles. They have also said that Turkish Delight would only be liable for very low levels of tax for the first two years of operations. The CEO has also carried out a survey of his customers flying to Turkey last month asking whether they would be interested in travelling with his firm to South Africa and 88% said they would. Nevertheless he feels with the growth in his business and the uncertainty around South Africa he should seek your opinion about what his strategy should be?

1. *Consider the data provided and think about what further information you need. (In a classroom setting the professor could provide this information, but the exercise is really about how one thinks about a strategic problem).*
2. *What strategy do you recommend to the CEO?*
3. *What are your justifications for this strategy?*

Natural History New Zealand: Natural Selection?

Natural History New Zealand (NHNZ) has been around for 35 years based at the "end of the earth" in one of the world's southernmost cities: Dunedin. Michael Stedman has been with the company for 21 of those years and CEO over the past decade.

Extinction was a real possibility just a few years ago. NHNZ was a department of Television New Zealand (TVNZ) and dying a slow death. It was making local programs about local wildlife – which it had by this point filmed many times over – to a very small local audience (New Zealand's population is just over 4 million). When the previously state-owned TVNZ was privatized it began to focus more on cost cutting. NHNZ was an obvious target. TVNZ put NHNZ up for sale, and much to their surprise they received 10 offers for NHNZ for all parts of the globe.

In a decision that Stedman attributes to some strange sense of antipodean loyalty, an Australian Company was TVNZ's preferred buyer. "But it was a company that we could have bought. They were too small. They couldn't have given us anything that we couldn't already give ourselves." Stedman told TVNZ executives that he would leave and take the rest of NHNZ's staff with him to set up their own company before he'd watch it be sold to the Australian buyer. TVNZ eventually relented and agreed to sell NHNZ to Stedman's preferred choice: Rupert Murdoch's Fox Corporation.

By combining its particular expertise with Fox's global empire of distributors, partners and buyers, NHNZ has quickly become the world's second largest nature programming production company behind the BBC's Natural History Unit, something that Stedman is very proud of. "The reaction from the BBC when they heard that we were 'going global' was interesting. First they were amused, then, when we didn't go under, they though 'hm'. Then when we started stealing business off them they got annoyed. Now they hate us. We steal a lot of business from them." Stedman is certain that NHNZ will overtake the BBC within the next couple of years.

More staff have been hired in Dunedin (NHNZ is Dunedin's largest employer after the local university and local government authorities). The audience for NHNZ's programs now spans 130 countries and is measured in millions rather than thousands, and, as it has spread its wings, it has picked up an increasing number of awards. Last year a series co-produced with Animal Planet, called Twisted Tales (which traces the strange relationships between particular animals and humans), won an Emmy for 'Outstanding Achievement in a Craft in News and Documentary Programming' for NHNZ writer-zoologists Ian McGee and Quinn Berentson. The next installment of the series has been nominated again this year. Berentson claims that the series was "quite easy to write because we both have twisted minds and we both think along the same lines."

Programs like Twisted Tales indicate a willingness to broaden NHNZ's scope beyond films of animals. This means moving, in Stedman's terms, into a number of "natural extensions." In the word of NHNZ's public relations and marketing people: "We don't just work with wildlife. Our experience extends into genres such as adventure, travel and science, where we venture just as boldly to produce a variety of quality programming . . . We now bring our traditional pioneering spirit to our work in every continent and throughout the world's oceans in pursuit of compelling, often unique stories." Particularly high hopes are held for a series entitled Kill or Cure: The Bizarre and Curious History of Medicine.

Beyond the access to new markets provided by Fox, to what does Stedman attribute NHNZ's global success?

"Being from New Zealand is our biggest asset," Stedman explains. "Whenever we entertain potential clients we really play this up – New Zealand wine, New Zealand food . . . the whole thing." He reasons that people really like the association with New Zealand. It triggers positive associations for those who have had contact with New Zealand before, and a positive curiosity for those who have not.

NHNZ's corporate prospectus also highlights the importance of its 'Kiwi Heritage'. "NHNZ is founded on a passion for telling the stories of New Zealand's unique animals," it explains. Having been one of the first islands to have broken from the earth's primeval land mass, New Zealand's animals are certainly curious – a mix of prehistoric lizards and strange birds, many of whom have 'evolved' to the point of no longer being able to fly, on account of their not having to share the land with mammalian predators not born before New Zealand was set adrift. While not as vibrant or spectacular, in plumage or deed, as their better-known Australian and Asian cousins, they are just as idiosyncratic.

Stedman believe there is a strong link between the nature of a company and the lay of its land: "this is [partly] why we get on so well with the Japanese – having grown up on a rugged isolated island pocketed with communities. They're always saying that we're like them, a bit quiet and introverted, relational, community oriented. They say we have very similar senses of humour." Japan is NHNZ's fastest growing market. "Australians on the other hand are much more extrovert, big and bold. It's a big wide-open land. I think this is why Murdoch gets a bum rap. He's no worse, probably a lot better than, other media moguls, but he's out there being up front and telling it straight. So others, particularly the British, label him a brash upstart Aussie . . . he he he [laughs], the British hate him."

NHNZ's corporate symbol and mascot, New Zealand's indigenous mountain parrot the Kea, also says much about the Company's distinctive spirit. "[Our symbol has] been the Kea for a long time now," Stedman explains, "but we recently revisited it and decided that we were pretty happy with it. I mean the obvious choice would have been a f . . . ing Kiwi, but who wants to be a fat, dozy, dull, nocturnal, flightless bird." Examining the nature of Kea makes it easy to see why NHNZ prefers this association. It is a bird of paradox: "Hooligans, vandals and killers; but superb parents and resourceful providers," says one source. "Endearing and mischievous" says another. The New Zealand Department of Conservation's web-site's entry on the Kea runs as follows:

> To survive in its harsh alpine environment Kea have become inquisitive and nomadic social birds – characteristics which help the Kea to utilize and find new food sources. It is thought to have developed its own special character during the last ice age by using its unusual powers of curiosity in its search for food. Their inquisitive nature often causes Kea to congregate around novel objects and their strong beaks have enormous manipulative power.

One suspects that Stedman may also take a perverse pleasure in stories of Kea tormenting and often killing that other lumbering New Zealand stereotype – the sheep. "You know, a Swiss scientist has determined that on its level of intelligence the Kea should be classified as a primate," he says proudly. This "intelligence" enables the development of sophisticated business relationships. "It is all about relationships," Stedman says, and coming from where NZNH does provides a point of differentiation here as well.

He struggles to put his finger on what it is exactly: "New Zealanders seem to be unusually curious, and it's a genuine curiosity, but they seem to also be quite sensitive to cultural differences, so they don't push too hard. At the same time there's also an inquisitive naivete, but with brains." (I mention a statistic that Air New Zealand use a lot in their marketing – that New Zealanders on average travel more miles in their life time than people from any other nation, "Yes, that makes sense," he says). However, what he is trying to say becomes clearer as he relates one story from his past and two from the NHNZ's present.

"One of my early coups came when I happened to be in LA. I went to a just-released movie called Star Wars and thought it was great. I was in my twenties working on a children's television program for TVNZ and thought it would be great if we could do a feature on it, show a bit of footage, you know. So the next day I rang up the marketing manager of 20th Century Fox and we had a bit of a chat. I asked if he could let me have some stuff. He said 'Sure' and asked where I was staying. The next morning, a huge package arrives, full of film, posters, all sorts of paraphernalia. My US friends asked how I'd managed to pull it off, so I told them that I called the guy up and asked. They would never have thought of doing that. I was too stupid to know that I shouldn't. But the guy didn't seem to mind. New Zealander's often don't feel bound by the 'can'ts' and 'shouldn'ts' that you find in other places."

"It's important to treat people how they like to be treated, but you have to make an effort to find out what this is. A few weeks ago I sent a fax to a Japanese manager and got nothing back. What do you do? Should I fax him again, should I phone him up directly? I mean, you don't want to be pushy. Anyway, I managed to get through to talk to his assistant and asked if I should send another fax. He said, 'Yes, keep sending faxes, he has a big pile of them on his desk, he likes getting them, sooner or later he'll come in and your fax will be on the top and he'll get back to you'. So, I kept sending the faxes and he did, eventually, get back to me."

"A lot of selling supposedly happens at these huge trade conventions. But after days of viewing and being sold to, a lot of people glaze over. You can sense this pretty quickly and if somebody's zombied there's not much point trying to sell to them. It's better to sit back and chat about something completely different, you can always send them an e-mail a couple of days later when they're more relaxed, away from the madness."

All of this seems to give NHNZ a real, albeit intangible, competitive advantage. Stedman relates what he believes to be perhaps the most satisfying thing he has ever been told by a client. "A manager of a Japanese company said 'you are the least arrogant company that we deal with'. You've no idea how much that meant to us." He contrasts the approach of some his competitors. The BBC? "The BBC seems to still walk about with the remains of a colonial outlook, they think they're doing everybody a service by coming in to film other countries with the British approach. Plus they have a huge millstone around their neck – David Attenborough. I mean he's good, but it's hardly ground-breaking." ("I'm more of a David Bellamy fan," he adds, not surprisingly. "I like his passion"). The Americans? "I was at a convention in Japan last week and this group of managers from one of our competitors decides to go out to dinner, on their own . . . for Pizza! I mean how stupid is that."

1. *How would you characterize NHNZ's corporate identity and strategic positioning?*
2. *To what extent is NHNZ's identity a function of its adapting to its strategic environment?*
3. *How would you seek to manage NHNZ's strategy for the future?*

Case Notes:

Universal: Anticipation*

PA: "Mr. John Frobisher of Universal on the line for you, Bob. Will you take the call now?"

John Frobisher was CEO of one of the largest branded foods retailers in the USA. Bob's consultancy in the UK had recently carried out a substantial project for them, investigating a potential acquisition target in Canada.

Bob: "Yes, that's great. Put him straight through."

John: "Hey Bob, how are you doing?"

Bob: "I'm doing fine John – how are you?"

John: "Well, thank you Bob – things are going great. That last presentation you gave to the Board was right on the button. They were very pleased – good clear points, strong conclusion and recommendation; none of this 'sitting on the fence' type analysis we've had before, which leads me to the reason for the call. You know our branded business has been booming here in the US – demand has been strong and consistent for our high-end products. Now we have sorted out our cost structure, so it's the lowest amongst our direct competitors, and beginning to close in on the non-branded producers, we believe we can sustain our profitability in the US for some time to come. However, we must not be complacent. The Board has been wondering why not replicate this success in the UK. There is likely to be demand for products of our quality and our brand may well transfer across border. They wondered who we could ask to look into this for us, as we don't have the resources at Head Office for this task, and I mentioned you and your team. You did a great job on the last project and your credibility here is high. Would you be willing to take this on?"

Bob: "Well John it's great you are pleased with our last project. We'd be delighted to investigate this opportunity for you. As you know, contrary to many big name consulting practices, we do not have templates for projects so we'll have to think over the main issues and get back to you with our thoughts on how we would structure our investigation, the sort of data we would aim to get, and what the deliverables would be."

---

*Note: students are used to getting cases based on historic material with questions that steer them towards certain techniques and tools to be applied to a carefully crafted set of "perfect" data. However, this situation is rare in the real world. More often the questions are about the future, the data need not clear, available data patchy (unreliable, unavailable) at best, and results not clear cut. This case, Anticipation, is much closer to reality – a 15 minute phone call from a client requesting an investigation, with few clues about how such an investigation might be carried out, what data are available (and whether they are available at all), and what deliverables are expected, beyond a definitive recommendation. The exercise then is about shaping research to address a strategic problem. This is a much more open-ended approach than traditional cases and forces readers to create their own structures to shape and address the issue. It shows the value of being able to frame problems, construct analytical enquiry, consider what data might be useful and to think about where they may come from. There is also an important role for being creative in this process.

John: "Sure, Bob – no problem. We like your approach. I have some contacts here at Universal who can help on the data front and when you're ready we can fix up a meeting. Speak soon. Bye."

Bob smiled as he replaced the phone. The best of all worlds, he thought – a large satisfied customer coming back with more assignments. However, as his firm's policy was not to have standard solutions to problems, or a bank of questions, as this led to lazy thinking, his team would have to come up with the key questions for this opportunity and work out what data would be needed as well as how it would be acquired. Somehow they had to decide whether the idea of Universal launching in the UK was sound or fanciful.

1. *Draw up a list of the key questions that are critical to understanding whether Universal should enter the UK market.*
2. *What data would you need to acquire (and how would you get it) to be able to answer your questions?*
3. *How would you seek to manage a strategic entry into the UK and then on into Continental Europe?*

Case Notes:

Exercise Group: Exercising your strategy

The fitness industry in the UK is big business. £3.6bn (2007) are spent every year and the market continues to grow as society becomes increasingly health conscious. It is also very competitive as health clubs compete for the attentions of potential customers and some business models are based upon the ability of clubs to continuously expand membership in order to fund subsequent opening of new buildings. The industry is still fragmented but there are 12 large chains and there is a trend towards consolidation.

The Exercise group is one of the more expensive health clubs with individual fees of some £1500 per year. Its brochures and websites display grand entrances to their facilities with fountains and soft lighting. Inside there are tempting serene pools of light blue water in discretely tiled settings with poolside models in white sauna towels reclining on white sun loungers. The tranquil setting emphasizes space and the diffuse lighting suggests calmness. Other pictures show an individual fit young athletic person in a white leotard in the wide open spaces of a dance studio, contrasting with the wooden strands of the exercise floor.

At the entrance to a typical Exercise group facility are smart receptionists who sometimes welcome you as you slide your membership card through the turnstile card reader. Many facilities are located close to city centres where traffic jams are often a problem. In all facilities, popular music plays in the background to relax you as you enter, perhaps on your journey to or from work, and once admitted one can choose to be active and swim in one of the two swimming pools, head to an exercise class or work out in the large gym zone. Alternatively or afterwards one can go to the bar area for a coffee or snack and sit in the dozen or so comfortable chairs to watch the football on a widescreen television mounted over the sofa. Some regular customers prefer to have a quiet conversation in an adult only area further away from the television, with just the background music muffling other noises. The coffee grinder reminds people in the bar area that the coffee is good quality although it does create some long queues from time to time.

On the walls of the entrance area are a series of very detailed notices about the rules and regulations of the club so members can see that high standards are kept and there is a prominent notice board which lists all the complaints of members in the previous month with colours denoting the extent to which these have been addressed. Some have green colours against the complaints but most are currently being addressed. Also in the lobby area is a market stall of everyday materials and jewellery which are at bargain prices. Next to these is a glass case with pictures of property for sale in the area – most have price tags well in excess of £1m.

If one is aiming to exercise then a thickly carpeted corridor leading from the lobby takes you towards the changing room. You will pass members kitted out in gym, tennis and squash kit as well as damp swimmers just in from the outside pool racing to get into the warm to dry off and change. Once inside the changing rooms there is a television often tuned to news channels although this generally can't be heard clearly over the soothing pop music. There are a large number of wooden lockers although many are already in use, even though the club seems quite empty. Those which are available have a rather strange array of key fobs and it seems that some of the doors are slightly splintered probably due to members losing keys. Many members bring flip flops if they intend to swim as the changing room floors tend to be rather wet and slippery from swimmers coming in from the indoor pool. As one might expect there is a bit of a chlorine smell in the air. There used to be tissues readily available in the changing rooms but these have now been removed as well as the bins in which to dispose of them as the management says they may be a fire hazard.

The indoor pool has subdued lighting and consists of three lanes. One lane is generally taken up with numerous aqua aerobic classes, often for older and less able bodied people and the fast lane is intended for serious swimmers. There is a small pool for young children which can be used at certain times of the day. There is no life guard present at this facility.

Indoor tennis is quite popular with members even though there is no heating in winter and no ventilation in the summer. However as the only indoor facility in the area it attracts those who want year round tennis. From on court one can clearly see the car park outside brightly light with large security lights.

The large gym has some of the latest exercise equipment particularly in terms of weights machines. The running and cycling machines are in good condition and are the ones which always attract the members. All are arranged in a curve so exercisers can see one another and in the centre above them all are pre-programmed televisions which tend to run current affairs programmes with the sound switched off in case members wish to plug into the TV's in their exercise machines, where they have a large number of channels to choose from. Energetic dance music is always playing throughout the gym, to help members get into the 'right' spirit, at various volumes depending on the time of day. Once watching a programme exercisers are not distracted by exercise related data. The temperature is generally well controlled and for those in one half of the gym scents and fragrances from the beauticians' and hairdressers' area next door can be smelled.

Recently the Exercise Group has been experiencing financial difficulty and its membership numbers have been declining. Some have moved to other fitness centres and many have been attracted to the recently refurbished council run facility with its high quality gym, manned swimming pool, squash courts, games hall and annual fee of £400. In order to revitalise its membership, existing members have been promised a series of gifts if they introduce new members, such as bottles of wine, free guest passes, meal vouchers. In addition they have been trying to attract new members with short term membership offers rather than the current annual fee structure.

---

1. *What strategy do you believe the Exercise group thinks it is delivering?*
2. *What strategy do you believe customers of the Exercise Group are experiencing?*
3. *What suggestions might you make to Exercise group management about the implementation of its strategy?*

Delft Belting: MegaFuture?

You are one of a small team of corporate finance executives in the London based investment banking division of one of the largest Japanese banks. Your role is buying and selling companies on behalf of the Bank's clients. Today there is an air of crisis in the department; the Managing Director of the UK and European operation has called a special meeting. The Bank's largest client, 'MegaIndustries', a massive Japanese corporation, has asked the Bank to act as advisor in the purchase of a Dutch Belting company. This is important news as MegaIndustries doesn't appear to be using its normal 'house bank'. Your Bank has been trying to become MegaIndustries's 'house bank' for a long time as this would result in very significant increases in business volume and access to more lucrative projects. The Managing Director is fully aware of the significance of the opportunity.

MegaIndustries is a highly secretive and family controlled company. It is not listed on any stock exchange but its size and power is beyond dispute – just their <u>cash</u> balance at your bank is equal to 5% of your net assets! It is difficult to give a precise figure for the size of MegaIndustries but its total assets are reported to be some US \$335bn! MegaIndustries' business is very broadly based but has a very substantial automotive components division. Their interests are in rubber, plastic and alloy parts used in the automotive sector, such as air ducting, windscreen wipers, timing belts, tyres, alloy trim etc. This MegaIndustries has managed to achieve this position by organic growth in just one country and, apart from a greenfield operation in the US, they have never employed any other methods of corporate expansion. However times change and they now wish to acquire a belting company in Holland, called The Delft Belting Company. Delft Belting came to their attention when they purchased a small sample of their timing belt product to help them fulfil an order. MegaIndustries was very impressed by the quality of the Delft product.

MegaIndustries has never acquired a company before and have therefore put the matter entirely into your hands. They wish you to handle all aspects of the transaction. The only restriction is that they are very reluctant to pay over £90m for the company.

The Delft Belting Company operates out of one factory building in Southern Holland, near Rotterdam, manufacturing rubber belts, which are for use in cars (fan belts, timing belts) and the mining industry (conveyor belts). It supplies belts to the leading automotive companies in Germany, France and to Fiat in Italy. The Chairman, and 100% owner of the business, is Mr van Meerden, who is 30 years old. He founded the business some 7 years earlier with the assistance of Mr Oosterhouse, Director of Sales and Marketing, a 62 year old war hero, well respected in the local Delft community. The business is reported to be growing steadily at around 20% per year. There are no other Belting businesses in Holland. As The Delft Belting Company is a private company there is very little information available. A search on the internet reveals the following figures:

19X1	£m
Sales	120
Cost of Sales	(65)
Gross Profit	**55**
Selling & general admin expenses	(43)
Profit before tax	**12**
Tax	(3)
Net Profit	**9**
	==

Your boss knows that van Meerden is already in talks with other possible bidders for his business and time is of the essence. However he is prepared to talk with you to see if you are a credible bidder. Armed with this information, your boss hands the team air tickets to Rotterdam where you will be met and taken to a neutral venue to meet Mr van Meerden.

In the taxi on the way to Heathrow further information comes in on your Blackberry from your bank in Japan; "MegaIndustries have tried to do this deal before with their house bank. It didn't have a corporate finance capability in Europe so teamed up with an aggressive Wall Street firm that took one look at the figures and said that 'on a PE of 5x, the Delft Belting Company was not worth more than £45m! Mr van Meerden's hoped for £95m was ludicrous.' The Dutch are a very direct people and, when the house bank presented this valuation to Mr van Meerden he told them to 'get lost!' The meeting lasted three minutes!

Rumour has it that a friend of our Bank inside MegaIndustries overheard this story and told MegaIndustries chairman that they hadn't used a very professional firm. He should know that your bank had recently set up a specialist acquisition department to handle M & A transactions in Europe and strongly recommended your team as expert in these deals. This is how our bank has managed to get the mandate!"

In the taxi, the team realise that they need to;

1. *Draw up a list of things they need to know about this deal*
2. *Consider how to negotiate with Mr van Meerden*
3. *Understand rapidly the basis upon which a deal might be negotiated*

The team also know they need to keep a clear record of key decisions made and issues discussed so that if the deal goes wrong they can defend themselves in court. (The team had all seen the morning papers of the ruin of a corporate finance director due to inadequate records, which resulted in his implication in serious fraud). How would you address the three points listed above?

Using *The Strategy Pathfinder* 2nd Edition for Assessments and Examinations

We have had great success in using our approach to micro/live cases in *The Strategy Pathfinder* as end-of-term/course assessments and exam questions. Three approaches for doing this are:

Examinations

1. Pathfinder cases make excellent exam material as they are short (which helps to address the problem of reading speed in English for some students) and thought provoking – this is a major difference with many textbooks where cases are generally just illustrations and lack depth. We tend to use a case as Section B in an exam paper.
2. In our experience students may be adept at using terms and concepts from strategy but when challenged are distinctly hazy as to what they mean in precise terms. In order to ensure that students really do understand core concepts in strategy, we have compulsory questions in Section A of an exam paper, which are of two types. The first requires short definitions of key terms together with an example that may be drawn from a case taught during the course. To this end *The Strategy Pathfinder* 2nd Edition provides a glossary of key terms used in the book. The second set of compulsory questions allows for more discussion around the implications that key theories or concepts have for understanding strategy.

Assessments

We would ask students to select one of the following two options for individual assessment:

1. Students will be asked to select one of the live cases from the book to research further before addressing the case questions. We suggest that they do not use a case that has been covered in the taught course. The advantage of this type of assessment is that the geographic and industrial variety of cases means that there is almost always something with which students identify strongly and this comes through in the effort shown in their assignments.
2. We particularly like students to have the chance to craft their own short live cases as this causes them to (a) think critically about what a strategic issue might look like, (b) consider which strategy framework(s) might be appropriate for analyzing the issue, and (c) recognize that strategy problems rarely fit neatly into one framework.

In our experience executives on short courses find this an appealing option as it allows them to think about a strategic issue close to their interests/experience. At the undergraduate level this generates a great deal of enthusiasm and stimulates excellent work.

An example of how this second approach can be used in a novel form for assessment is produced below.

Term 1 Assessment (100%)

1. The write-up is **2,000 words maximum**. Where scripts exceed the word limit, the **surplus text will not be considered** in awarding marks.
2. Scripts should be 12 point typeface and one and a half lines spaced
3. Marks are given for clarity of layout and overall appearance.
4. The front page must contain
   (a) a declaration of the number of words in the report
   (b) the exam number of the student.
5. The assessment can be handed in at any time to the undergraduate office during the term, but must be handed in before 12 noon, **Friday xth January 20xx**. Late scripts will be penalized.

The assessment is in two parts: (a) a mini-case and (b) a briefing note:

The mini-case

1. The mini-case should be between 800 and 1,200 words in length. The mini-case can be on any **strategic problem** or issue to tackle/resolve/unpack. Organizations that might be focused upon can include commercial, not-for-profit, private, or public firms. Ideally the title of the mini-case will be a provocative question that the student intends to support/expose – for instance, 'Swimming against the tide' (to depict a company that is being overwhelmed by environmental pressures). At the end of the case, there must be one, two, or three questions that could be set for readers of the case.
2. The case should be a real organizational situation (rather than fictitious). Good sources for ideas are the business press (*Financial Times, The Economist, Business Week, Forbes*, etc.). Students should not contact companies. In some instances it is possible to gather primary data (perhaps through observation or survey of fellow students) and secondary data (such as stock prices, etc.). One particularly good assessment last year was a strategic review of the local coffee shop which centred upon student perceptions of its uniqueness.

The key to a good case is setting up a clear issue to be resolved (in the briefing note which follows).

The briefing note

The briefing note can use up the remaining words. It must analyze the case and explain clearly how the material relates to a core concept/technique/tool/theory in strategic management. On balance it is better to demonstrate how this works for just one or two concepts/theories/techniques, rather than many. The value-added is a detailed appreciation of these underpinning frameworks. A suggested structure is an introductory paragraph diagnosing the problem(s) in the mini-case. The note would then focus upon one or two of these problems/issues and show how a technique, concept, or framework may give insight to the problem. There should follow a broader appreciation of how the individual case might relate to broader strategic issues.

Examples of such micro-cases can be found in Angwin, D.N., Cummings, S., and Smith, C. (2011) The Strategy Pathfinder, 2nd edition, Wiley. There are many mini-cases throughout this book and the first case in each chapter also has a briefing note (these notes are rather broader than you need to write).

Good assessments will be those with a tight fit between case material and briefing, i.e., with little unused case material or unfocused briefing note. Those answers that are analytical rather than just descriptive fair best, so be careful that the note does not just list case data without any real analysis and interpretation. As befits the nature of the course, marks are given for critical review. Scripts attracting the highest marks will be able to highlight the implications of the focal issue for other firms, as well as locate it within the wider strategic management field.

<hr>

Marking Guidelines

During the strategy course students are informed that marks are broadly proportioned as follows:

- 30% for the case study
- 50% for the analysis
- 20% for integration between the two sections.

In more detail

Case study

The examiner is looking for a clearly defined strategic problem/issue. This may be more than one issue and recognition of this (should be in the questions they pose) may be rewarded. Marks are for clarity as well as quality of writing: Is the case engaging? Does it raise interesting issues? Are these issues really strategic?

Although the assessment suggests that the case should focus on one firm, it is also acceptable for students to choose an issue that involves several firms, an industry level problem, or a sub-unit within the firm.

Analysis

Although students may raise several questions based upon the case, they should only address one or two, owing to space constraints. Clearly there is a tradeoff here between depth and breadth. The assessment is looking for the skillful use of techniques, frameworks, and concepts from the course, **to add value** to the case study – that is, to reveal something that could not be gained from just a superficial reading of the text. The examiner is not looking for a description of frameworks (in such a short piece, this is not helpful – unless the description reveals value in some way), but skill in their use. It is really a test of whether the student recognizes the strategic issues, understands the frameworks that can be applied to particular problems, and can show how well he or she understands the detail.

Integration

This is about the quality of "fit" between the analysis and the case study. Does the data really fit the analysis? Does the analysis really fit the data? Is there a poor overlap between case material and analysis? Is it necessary for the author to introduce new data in the analysis in order to carry it out? – an item that should have been included in the case study. Is there material in the case study that really should have been in the analysis? Has the student really chosen the "right" or "best" frameworks for the job? For instance, a number of students will tend to view Porter's Five Forces as the ultimate all-purpose strategy framework (in the briefing for the assessment students are strongly advised against using SWOT, as it may be too descriptive, in the wrong hands). If another framework they are expected to know has not been used, then this is a poor fit. It is made very clear that students need to spend time working on the fit between analysis and data, and this will require several iterations – using a highlighter pen is a good tip for spotting redundancy of material.

General Comments

- If SWOT has been used, despite advice during the course, then it really has to be used in a very robust way, or be marked down.
- Remember that, due to space constraints, only one or two issues can be tackled, so although a case may raise other issues that cannot really be addressed at this time, the student should show awareness of those issues in the end-of-case questions.

Marking Grid

For some executive courses a grid is the preferred method for presenting marks. A suggested format is shown in Figure 1.

Candidate no: _____

	< 40	40–49	50–59	60–69	70–79	80 +
CASE 30%						
Originality of case and sources	Little evidence	Partial / descriptive	Good overall grasp	Very good overall grasp	Evidence of conceptual development	Evidence of conceptual originality
Clearly defined strategic problem / issue	Little evidence	Partial / descriptive	Good understanding	Very good level of understanding	Excellent understanding	Outstanding level of understanding
ANALYSIS 50%						
Clarity and quality of writing (inc. sources)	Very confused, lacks structure	Poorly structured	Some structure, tends towards description	Clear and well structured	Excellent clarity and structure	Outstanding clarity and structure
Good balance achieved between breadth and depth	Little evidence	Partial / descriptive	Good understanding	Very good level of understanding	Excellent understanding	Outstanding level of understanding
Skill in using frameworks to add value to the case study	Little evidence	Partial / descriptive	Good understanding	Very good level of understanding	Excellent understanding	Outstanding level of understanding
INTEGRATION 20%						
Quality of fit between analysis and case	Question not answered	Partially integrated	Conscientious; attentive to subject matter	Question addressed and relevant	Excellent synthesis	Outstanding synthesis

Overall mark: ▨

Breakdown and comments:

Section	Mark	Comments
Case (30%)		
Analysis (50%)		
Integration (20%)		

Sample External Examiner Comments

"I have reviewed the corporate strategy scripts sent to me. I believe that this was a great assignment and the course looks like it was well taught."

"The assignment was demanding and stretching. The best assignments showed the level of critical thinking that we should expect. I see the marking as consistent and fair, and good feedback has been given to the students. I also note that the full range of marks has been given."

"What an exciting assignment. Students clearly revelled in the task and the best scripts showed excellent application and understanding. It's refreshing to see a new approach to strategy assessment which enthuses and encourages students to develop their understanding of strategy concepts and techniques."

"This was a challenging assignment that offered students the chance to excel (as demonstrated by the high proportion of first-class marks). Some students found the task very stretching but still managed to produce at minimum a very good descriptive case. The assignment was effective at separating out the 'sheep from the goats'."

Primary Chapter and Case Authors

All of the book's authors worked together on each chapter, but primary authors for each were:

1.	Macro-Shocks	*Duncan Angwin*
2.	Movers and Shakers	*Duncan Angwin*
3.	Industry Dynamics	*Chris Smith*
4.	Corporate Strategy	*Chris Smith*
5.	Strategic Positioning	*Chris Smith*
6.	Corporate Identity	*Stephen Cummings*
7.	Organic Strategy	*Stephen Cummings*
8.	Crossing Borders	*Duncan Angwin*
9.	Navigating Change	*Stephen Cummings*
10.	Sustain Ability	*Chris Smith and Stephen Cummings*
11.	Maverick Strategies	*Stephen Cummings and Duncan Angwin*

Live Case Authors

Introductory case: **Cereality** – Stephen Cummings. The case includes elements from "Snap, Crackle, Cash," *People* (November 22, 2004); "A store for cereal (seriously)," *Business* (October 20, 2004); and "Cereal: It's what's for lunch, dinner," *USA Today* (May 21, 2004).

1.1 **Broadwoods and Steinway** – Duncan Angwin. This case draws on The New Grove Piano (1988); Ehrlich, C. (1990) *The Piano: A History*, Clarendon Paperbacks, Oxford University Press (revised edition).

1.2 **The French and British Armies** – Duncan Angwin. Crecy and Agincourt are not the only examples of heavy French defeat and English victory based on the principles described in the case. The same situation also occurred at Poitiers on September 19, 1356. The case is based on Tuck, A. (1999) *Crown and Nobility: England 1272–1461*, Blackwell Classic Histories of England, 2nd edn, Oxford: Blackwell Publishers; Allmand, S. (1997) *Henry V*, Yale University Press; Luecke, R.A. (1994) *Scuttle Your Ships Before You Advance*, New York: Oxford University Press; Taylor, F. and Roskell, J.S. (eds) (1975) *Gesta Henrici Quinti*, Oxford: Oxford University Press: 76–9, 91.

1.3 **FloraHolland** – Bob Galliers, Sue Newell, and Stephen Cummings. Information is taken from the FloraHolland website (www.floraholland.com).

1.4 **Nike** – Stephen Cummings. This is developed from an earlier case published in the book *Recreating Strategy* by Stephen Cummings (Sage, 2002). The quotation in the postscript is from "Nike to stick with Tiger Woods, but Gatorade quits world No. 1 golfer," from the Fox Sports website (www.foxsports.com.au) downloaded February 27, 2010.

1.5 **Rover** – Duncan Angwin. It contains elements from "The History of Rover P4" (www.roverP4.com) and the BBC documentary *Rover – The Last Chance Saloon*.

1.6 **South Africa** – Stephen Cummings.

1.7 **China Airlines** – Duncan Angwin and Michael Wang.

2.1 **Disney** – Derek Condon. Sources include newspaper, magazine and web based articles.

2.2 **Safeway** – Duncan Angwin. Sources include newspaper, magazine and web based articles.

2.3 **Carlton** – Duncan Angwin. Sources include newspaper, magazine and web based articles.

2.4 **Lafarge and Blue Circle** – Duncan Angwin. Sources include newspaper, magazine and web based articles.

2.5 **Brasilia** – Stephen Cummings. This case draws on two articles from Issue 33, Volume 4 (2010) of the journal *Monocle*: "Rubber soled Tiger – Brazil" by Tyler Brule; and "Ministry of Sun – Brasilia" by Andrew Tuck.

2.6 **The NHS** – Stephen Cummings. It contains elements from "Health Service damned by Virgin Report," *The Scotsman* (July 22, 2000); "Virgin team highlights NHS shambles," *The Guardian* (July 22, 2000); "How Labour has blown £1 billion on consulting outside 'Experts'," *Independent on Sunday* (May 28, 2000); "Britain asks Virgin's Branson for advice on hospitals: Workers sceptical," *Financial Post* (May 8, 2000).

2.7 **Management Gurus** – Stephen Cummings. It contains elements of "Mozart and management: Why companies fall for myths," *Financial Times* (June 15, 2005).

3.1 **Sportswear** – Chris Smith. Adapted from the report "Fair play at the Olympics" by Oxfam GB, available at www.fairolympics.org. See also www.cleanclothes.org.

3.2 **Carrefour** – Duncan Angwin. Sources include newspaper, magazine and web based articles.

3.3 **McDonald's** – Chris Smith. This case is drawn from various newspaper and magazine articles and a number of websites including the McDonald's company website and www.mcspotlight.org .

3.4 **Dell** – Duncan Angwin and Stephen Cummings. It is based on "A struggle over strategy: HP counts the cost of 'playing the other guy's game'," *Financial Times* (February 11, 2005) and "Take two," *The Economist* (May 1, 2008).

3.5 **Ranbaxy** – Stephen Cummings. This contains information from "Ranbaxy revs up", *TMCnews* (TMCnet.com, August 30, 2006); "Ranbaxy deal sparks M&A talk for Indian Pharma," *Business Week* (June 12, 2008); "All together now," *The Economist* (July 26, 2008); and "Patently absurd," *The Economist* (December 6, 2008).

3.6 **BMX** – Stephen Cummings. Quotations are from the film "Joe Kid on a Sting-Ray" by John Swarr and Mark Eaton, *JKOS* (2007).

3.7 **Royal Air Maroc (I)** – Duncan Angwin. Sources include newspaper, magazine and web based articles.

4.1 **Z Enterprises** – Chris Smith. This is a heavily disguised, actual company. "Thank you" to the managers – you know who you are ☺.

4.2 **GE** – Chris Smith. Sources: Reuters, Associated Press and other websites; GE websites and 2009 annual report.

4.3 **Golden Promise** – Chris Smith. This is a heavily disguised, actual company. "Thank you" to the managers – you know who you are ☺.

4.4 **easyGroup** – Duncan Angwin. It is based on easyGroup annual reports for 2001/2002, 2002/2003; easyGroup website; a BBC documentary from "Trouble at the Top" series; BBC news report (March 10, 2005); netimperative.com (January 4, 2005); *Sunday Times* (February 29, 2004).

4.5 **Telco** – Stephen Cummings. Names and places have been disguised. Sources include newspaper, magazine and web based articles.

4.6 **Tata** – Duncan Angwin. Sources include newspaper, magazine and web based articles.

4.7 **Royal Air Maroc** (II) – Stephen Cummings and Duncan Angwin. Sources include newspaper, magazine and web based articles.

5.1 **Tesco** – Chris Smith. This case is drawn from various newspaper and magazine articles and a number of websites.

5.2 **Tele2** – Stephen Cummings. Data is drawn from the websites of the four companies described in the case in addition to the *CEE "Weather report" – Telecoms*, by UniCredit and RolandBerger Strategy Consultants (January 2009); Russia Profile. Org *Telecommunications Report* (downloaded February 4, 2010); and Research and Markets, *4Q09 Russia Mobile Operator Forecast, 2009-2013*.

5.3 **Mother's Preference** – Chris Smith. This is a heavily disguised, actual company.

5.4 **Taytos** – Stephen Cummings. This is developed from an earlier case published in the book *Recreating Strategy* by Stephen Cummings (Sage, 2002).

5.5 **IBB** – Duncan Angwin, Wael Eid, and Ben Knight. This case focuses on the struggles of an Islamic bank to survive in the UK market. It draws on data kindly provided by the Islamic Bank of Britain during 2005, and Al Omar, F. and Abdel-Haq, M. (1996) *Islamic Banking: Theory, Practice and Challenges*, London: Zed; Ariff, M. (1988) Islamic banking, *Asia Pacific Economic Literature*, 2 (2): 46–62; Karbhari, Y., Naser, K., and Shahin, Z. (2004) Problems and challenges facing the Islamic Banking System in the West: The case of the UK, *Thunderbird International Business Review*, 46 (5): 521; Khan, M.S. and Mirakhor, A. (1987) *Theoretical Studies in Islamic Banking and Finance*, Houston, TX: Institute for Research and Islamic Studies; Zaher, T.S. and Hassan, M.K. (2001) A comparative literature survey of Islamic Finance and Banking, *Financial Markets, Institutions and Instruments*, 10 (4): 155–99.

5.6 **World Cities** – Stephen Cummings and Duncan Angwin. Sources include newspaper, magazine and web based articles.

5.7 **InBev** – Stephen Cummings. This is developed from an earlier case published in the book *Recreating Strategy* by Stephen Cummings (Sage, 2002).

6.1 **Pokemon** – Stephen Cummings. It contains elements from "The child is 'father' to the manager: Images of organization," V.H. Ingersoll and G.B. Adams, *Organization Studies*, 1992 (vol. 13, no. 4: 497–520); "Pokemania v. Globophobia," *The Economist* (November 18, 2003); M.E. Porter, "What is strategy?," *Harvard Business Review*, 1996; and "Debunking Japan's model," *The Wall Street Journal* (January 15, 2001).

6.2 **Pharmacia** – David Wilson and Duncan Angwin. Sources include newspaper, magazine and web based articles.

6.3 **Mojo MDA** – Richard Dunford and Duncan Angwin. It is adapted from a case called "Merger in Adland" from the book *Organizational Behaviour: An Organizational Analysis Perspective* (Addison-Wesley, Sydney, 1992: 12–13). © Richard Dunford.

6.4 **John Smith's** – Stephen Cummings. It contains elements from "Lager than life," *Marketing* (April 23, 1998); "John Smith's in £10m sales push," *Marketing* (September 9, 1998); "Media case study: John Smith's," *Marketing* (September 23, 1998); "Cardboard cut-out with cult status," *The Scotsman* (September 24, 1998); "Live update," *Campaign* (September 25, 1998); "Design and advertising brave an uneasy alliance," *Campaign* (May 14, 1999); "John Smith's unveils £20m comedy ads," *The Guardian* (May 8, 2002); and "John Smith's in bitter sweet awards triumph," *The Guardian* (September 19, 2003).

6.5 **Hyundai** – Stephen Cummings. This case refers to the musician analogies outlined in issue 568 of *Car* magazine (2009) and sales data referred to is from publicly available sources.

6.6 **NZ Police** – Stephen Cummings. Sources include newspaper, magazine and web based articles.

6.7 **BBC and Channel 5** – Stephen Cummings. It is based on reporting in *The Times* ("Who's your favourite television channel?" September 9, 1998), *The Guardian* ("'Channel filth' plays the family card," August 12, 2000), *The Independent* ("Channel 5 boss demands explicit sex on television," August 21, 2000), and *The Independent* ("Last night's television," September 19, 2002).

7.1 **Formula 1** – Stephen Cummings. Sources include newspaper, magazine and web based articles.

7.2 **The Band** – David Wilson, Stephen Cummings, and Luisa Acheson. Sources include newspaper, magazine and web based articles.

7.3 **Washington Mutual** – Stephen Cummings. It contains elements of "Rooting for branches" and "Trust me, I'm a banker," both from *The Economist*'s Survey of International Banking (April 17, 2004) and "Bigger usually isn't better in banking," *Atlanta Business Chronicle* (November 21, 2003).

7.4 **The Prudential** – Stephen Cummings. This case contains material from the Prudential's website taken in 2006. With special thanks to Mark Wood.

7.5 **Deutsche Bank** – Stephen Cummings. Sources include newspaper, magazine and web based articles.

7.6 **American Association of Scientists** – Stephen Cummings. Sources include newspaper, magazine and web based articles.

7.7 **The Dalai Lama** – Stephen Cummings. This case includes quotations from "The Dalai Lama on the Global Financial Crisis," *Business Week* (May 18, 2009) and "Dalai Lama – Gier macht Unternehmen krank," *Die Welt Online* (June 20, 2009).

8.1 **Kodak** – Duncan Angwin. This case contains elements from "Kodak's strategy not black and white," *FT Global News Wire, Business Daily Update* (October 5, 2004); "Analysis – Kodak's China moment turns fuzzy, *Reuters News* (July 12, 2001); http://www.factiva.com; Ko, D.C.T.L., Manlu, L., Downing, M., and Tung, A.W.N. (2000) *Kodak in China*, INSEAD/CEIBS. With special thanks to Kalimah A. Priforce, Georgetown University.

8.2 **Korean Airlines** – Stephen Cummings and Duncan Angwin. This case is based on the second author's trip to Korea just before the World Cup, and also contains elements from "Asian culture' link in jet crashes," *The Times* (March 19, 1998).

8.3 **Vodafone/Mannesmann** – Duncan Angwin. Sources include newspaper, magazine and web based articles.

8.4 **Coca-Cola and Toyota** – Stephen Cummings. It contains elements from "Back to classic Coke," *Financial Times* (March 27, 2000); "Ice-cold times for an icon," *The Independent* (January 20, 2000); "Cola: The new political statement," *The New Zealand Herald* (April 19, 2003); "Turkish pop culture," *Time* (September 15, 2003); "Global ads buck local taste trend," *The Australian* (September 11, 2003); and Takeuchi, Hirotaka, Osono, Emi and Shimizu, ihiko (2008) The Contradictions that Drive Toyota's Success, *Harvard Business Review*, June, 96–104.

8.5 **Banque du Sud** – Duncan Angwin. Sources include newspaper, magazine and web based articles.

8.6 **Red Cross/Red Crescent** – Stephen Cummings. Sources include newspaper, magazine and web based articles.

8.7 **HSBC** – Stephen Cummings. It contains elements from www.hsbc.com.

9.1 **Pringle** – Stephen Cummings. It contains elements of "Pringle takes to the catwalk to shed its staid image," *The Independent* (September 16, 2002); "Luxury goods manufacturers face another season of belt tightening," *Sunday Times* (September 22, 2002); "The age of the immortals," *Financial Times* (September 20, 2003); and the BBC video *Pringles – hanging by a thread* (episode 1 of series 5 of the popular "Trouble at the Top" series). It is recommended that this case be used in conjunction with the BBC video, which can be purchased at www.bbcworldwide.com.

9.2 **Reliant** – Duncan Angwin. Sources include newspaper, magazine and web based articles.

9.3 **Baraka** – Stephen Cummings. It draws on reporting from "IMF in need of new faith," *The Guardian* (April 17, 2000); "Eco soundings," *The Guardian* (April 19, 2000); "Bill and Dave show," *Human Resources* (January/February, 1996); "Cook sells Britain's New Look abroad," *The Times* (July 23, 1999). Special thanks to Tony Smith and the staff and students at Baraka College.

9.4 **Church(es)** – Duncan Angwin. Sources include newspaper, magazine and web based articles.

9.5 **The Oakland A's** – Stephen Cummings and Chris Bilton. This case is condensed from the book *Creative Strategy: Reconnecting Business and Innovation* (Wiley, 1010); and it refers to the book *Moneyball: The Art of Winning an Unfair Game* by Michael Lewis (W. W. Norton & Co., 2004).

9.6 **elBulli** – Andres Hatum. Developed from a case in the book *Next Generation Talent Management: Talent Management to Survive Turmoil*, by Andres Hatum (Palgrave Macmillan, 2010). With special thanks to Ferran Adria, Marc Cuspinera, and Juli Soler.

9.7 **Little Chef** – Stephen Cummings. Blumnthal and Pegler quotations are from the television series *Big Chef Takes on Little Chef* produced by Channel 4 (UK), 2009. Additional information from Wikipedia entries on "Heston Blumenthal and Little Chef"; "Why Little Chef hung his hat op," *The Sun* (December 30, 2006); and "Heston Blumenthal – The saviour of Little Chef? That's not quite how the customers see it," *The Guardian* (January 20, 2009).

10.1 **McDonald's** – Chris Smith. Various newspaper and magazine articles and a number of websites including the McDonald's company website and www.mcspotlight.org.

10.2 **Monsanto** – Chris Smith. Figures for the 2003/4 financial year from *Fortune* (May 18, 2005); various sources as indicated in the text, including "Growth though Global Sustainability: An Interview with Monsanto's CEO, Robert B. Shapiro," by Joan Magretta (1997) *Harvard Business Review*, January–February: 79–88.

10.3 **Marcos** – Chris Smith. Sources include newspaper, magazine and web based articles.

10.4 **Handi Ghandi** – Stephen Cummings. It contains elements of "Bapu with beef handi gets great-grandson's goat," by Satish Nandgaonkar, *Calcutta Telegraph* (June 16, 2005); "What's next, Martin Luther Burger King Jr.?" by Constantine von Hoffman, *CMO Magazine* (June 17, 2005); and "Curry boycott," *Lismore Northern Star* (June 25, 2005).

10.5 **Il Ngwesi** – Stephen Cummings. Sources include newspaper, magazine and web based articles.

10.6 **Air New Zealand** – Urs Daellenbach. Sources include newspaper, magazine and web based articles.

10.7 **Post Office** – Stephen Cummings. David Thomas's words are extracted from "Why Pat must be saved for the nation," *The Independent* (November 28, 2000). This case also draws on "Post Office that inspired 'Postman Pat' to close," *The Independent* (June 20, 2003).

11.1 **Apple and Ford** – Stephen Cummings and Chris Bilton. Portions of this case are extracted from the book *Creative Strategy: Reconnecting Business and Innovation*, Chris Bilton and Stephen Cummings (Wiley, 2010). This case also contains source material from Douglas Brinkley's *Wheels for the World* (Penguin, 2003).

11.2 **IRL, Levis and Land Rover** – Stephen Cummings. With special thanks to Glenn A Forster, formerly at Land Rover Australia, and Shaun Coffey, Robert Holt, Melissa Yiannoutsos Paul Benjes, Madhusudan Vasudevamurthy, and Nicholas Long from Industrial Research Limited.

11.3 **Synear** – Shiyong Fan and Stephen Cummings. This case draws on information from "The frozen dumpling economy," *China International Business Magazine*, April 14, 2008.

11.4 **Venture Capital** (a.k.a. Vodafone) – Duncan Angwin. This case is based on an assignment I had early in my investment banking career involving the refinancing of Racal Electronics. The "gray box" in question was the first mobile phone. When it was launched, despite all the problems identified in the case, the product became hugely successful for the company and this business unit was subsequently demerged as Vodafone – now the world's largest mobile phone company.

11.5 **Egg** – Stephen Cummings. It contains elements from "Game over! Back to work," by Jonathan Bell, which appeared in *Wallpaper** (October, 2004); and *Willing Slaves: How the Overwork Culture is Ruining Our Lives* by Madeline Bunting (2004) HarperCollins.

11.6 **Danone Argentina** – Roberto Vassolo. Sources include newspaper, magazine and web based articles.

11.7 **Nestlé Russia** – Stephen Cummings. This case draws on "21st century cars" – Stephen Cummings. It contains elements from "Curiouser and curiouser," H. Pearman, *Sunday Times* (February 7, 1999); "A vintage harvest," R. Hutton, *Sunday Times* (January 7, 2001); "Bigger and bolder," *Sunday Times* (July 15, 2001); "Good car, Bad car," *Sunday Times* (February 10, 2002); "French Revolution," *Sunday Star Times* (November 3, 2002); "Designer cars," *Business Week* (February 16, 2004); "Sign of the Apocalypse: Trabant returns with an EV," by Tony Borroz, *Autopia*, August 14, 2009; and, "Ice cream and 'CCCP': Evoking nostalgia in post-Soviet packaging," *Kseniya Makarenko and Janet Borgerson (2009). Downloaded from* http://blogs.nyu.edu/projects/materialworld/2009/05/ice_cream_and_cccp_evoking_nos.html.

Integrative cases: Turkish Delight – Duncan Angwin. **Natural History New Zealand** – Stephen Cummings. **Universal** – Duncan Angwin. **Exercise Group** – Duncan Angwin. **Delft Belting** – Duncan Angwin.

More live cases relating to this book are available on the companion website www.wiley.com/go/strategypathfinder

Notes

1. Macro-Shocks

1. Stewart, I. (1989) *Does God Play Dice?* 2nd edn. Penguin Books. Stewart traces the origins of chaos to the original formless mass from which the creator molded the ordered universe.
2. Ginter, P. M. and Duncan, W. J. (1990) Macro-environmental Analysis for Strategic Management, *Long Range Planning*, 23 (6): 91–100.
3. Tomlinson, J. (1999) *Globalization and Culture*. Polity: Cambridge.
4. Beck, U. (2002) The Cosmopolitan Society and its Enemies, *Theory, Culture and Society*, 19 (1): 17–44.
5. Volberda, H. W. (1998) *Building the Flexible Firm*. Oxford: Oxford University Press.
6. Courtney, H., Kirkland, J., and Viguerie, P. (1997) Strategy under uncertainty, *Harvard Business Review*, 75 (6): 66–80.
7. Wack, P. (1985) Scenarios: Uncharted waters, *Harvard Business Review*, 63 (6): 139–51.
8. Ansoff, I. and McDonnell, E. (1990) *Implanting Strategic Management*. Upper Saddle River, NJ: Prentice Hall, Inc.
9. Wilson, I. (2000) From Scenario Thinking to Strategic Action, *Technological Forecasting and Social Change*, 65: 23–9.
10. Volberda, H. W. (1998) *Building the Flexible Firm*. Oxford: Oxford University Press.
11. Johnson, G., Scholes, K., and Whittington, R. (2008) *Exploring Corporate Strategy*, 8th edn. FT/Prentice Hall: 179–184.
12. Quinn, J. B. (1978) Strategic Change: Logical Incrementalism, *Sloan Management Review*, 20 (1): 7–21.
13. Romanelli, E. and Tushman, M. L. (1994) Organizational Transformation as Punctuated Equilibrium: an empirical test, *Academy of Management Journal*, 37 (5): 1141–61.
14. Hamel, G. (2000) *Leading the Revolution*. Boston MA: Harvard Business School Press.

2. Movers and Shakers

1. For a more detailed discussion of the separation of ownership and the delegation of authority to the agent, refer to the classic paper by Jensen, M. and Meckling, W. (1976) Theory of the firm: managerial behaviour, agency costs, and ownership structure, *Journal of Financial Economics*, 3: 305–60. The same paper gives details of agency problems but other references building on this include: Amihud, Y. and Lev, B. (1981) Risk reduction as a managerial motive for conglomerate mergers, *Bell Journal of Economics*, 12: 605–16; Jensen, M. (1986) Agency costs of free cash flow, corporate finance, and

takeovers, *American Economic Review*, 76: 323–9; Shleifer, A. and Vishny, R. (1988) Value maximisation and the acquisition process, *Journal of Economic Perspectives*, 2: 7–20. For mechanisms to control agency costs, refer again to the Jensen and Meckling (1976) paper but also look at Fama, E. (1980) Agency problems and the theory of the firm, *Journal of Political Economy*, 88: 288–307; Tosi, H. L. Jr. and Gomez-Mejia, L. R. (1994) CEO compensation monitoring and firm performance, *Academy of Management Journal*, 37: 1002–16; Byrd, J., Parrino, R., and Pritsch, G. (1998) Stockholder–manager conflicts and firm value, *Financial Analysts Journal*, 54: 14–30. An overview of agency in strategic management can be found in Angwin, D. N. (2006) Agency theory perspective, in Jenkins, M. and Ambrosini, V. (2006) *Strategic Management: A multi-perspective approach*, 2nd edn. Palgrave MacMillan.

2. The granting of options also raises accounting questions around how they are to be expensed and what their effect on the profit and loss account may be.

3. For a good discussion of the principal–agent model, read Eisenhardt, K. (1989) Agency theory: an assessment and review, *Academy of Management Review*, 14 (1): 57–74.

4. Cash might not be paid out if it is held for future as yet unidentified investments, or perhaps if the company is in a cyclical business downturn.

5. German banks were restricted in their ability to reduce their share holdings because of tax regulations on disposal. These are now being relaxed.

6. For a critique of the consulting industry, read Micklethwait, J. and Wooldridge, A. (1997) *The Witchdoctors. What the management gurus are saying, why it matters and how to make sense of it*, Mandarin paperbacks; Cummings, S. (2002) *Recreating Strategy*, Sage.

7. Angwin, D. N. and Paroutis, S. (2009) Connecting up Strategy: Are Senior Strategy Directors (SSDs) a missing link? *California Management Review*, Spring.

8. "Toff" is used in English to denote a class divide in general but may have academic overtones.

9. Cummings, S. and Angwin, D. N. (2004) The Future Shape of Strategy: Lemmings or Chimeras? *Academy of Management Executive*, 18 (2): 21–36; Micklethwait, J. and Wooldridge, A. (1997) *The Witchdoctors. What the management gurus are saying, why it matters and how to make sense of it*, Mandarin paperbacks.

10. Porter, M. and Kramer, M. (2002) The competitive advantage of corporate philanthropy, *Harvard Business Review*, 80 (12): 56.

11. For a more detailed discussion of the interaction between agency, agency problem, and stewardship, see Angwin, D. N., Stern, P., and Bradley, S. (2004) The Target CEO in a Hostile Takeover: Agency or Stewardship – can the condemned agent be redeemed? *Long Range Planning*, 37 (3): 239–57.

12. Heracleous, L. and Lan, L. L. (2010) The Myth of Shareholder Capitalism. *Harvard Business Review*, Spring.

13 Rose, J. M. (2007) Corporate Directors and Social Responsibility. Ethics versus Shareholder Value. *Journal of Business Ethics*, 73, 3: 319–331. July.

3. Industry Dynamics

1. We follow Michael Porter (1980) in defining an industry as "the group of firms producing products that are close substitutes for each other." (p. 5). There can be several markets (i.e., groups of customers with similar needs) in an industry and so for example the automotive industry has markets for sports cars, sports utility vehicles, saloon cars, trucks and so on.

2. ROIC expresses Earnings before Interest and Tax (EBIT) as a percentage of Average Invested Capital (i.e. total capital minus cash and current liabilities). It is a measure of

the return on the capital that is invested in the business as a means of creating value (and hence the subtraction of cash assets and current liabilities which are basically interest free loans from suppliers) and correlates significantly with share price over an extended time. The Weighted Average Cost of Capital (WACC) measures how much the overall investment in the company is costing and so ROIC-WACC gives a measure of how much shareholder value is being created or destroyed over any period.

3. Perfectly competitive industries, like "rational" people, are not found in their theoretically pure form in the real world. However many **markets** exist where the final outcome of perfect competition, i.e. a lack of discretion in pricing, is evident e.g. oil, wheat, coffee. A common mistake is the one off confusing commodity **products** where the market is perfectly competitive, with the commodity producing industry wherein large players with large unused capacity face high exit costs. The theoretical perfectly competitive industry earns normal returns, i.e. returns equal to the cost of capital. Sustained losses in capital intensive industries such as the airline industry much of the time, are an indicator of non-perfect competition. Empirical research indicates that if an industry is characterized by any two of 1) overcapacity; 2) many sellers and 3) undifferentiated products then prices tend to be forced down towards marginal cost and returns below the cost of capital. Besanko et al (2009) make this point in the context of discussions on perfect competition and the discussion in the chapter borrows heavily from their insights.

4. Much of the discussion of the life cycle is standard. Grant (2010) offers a detailed treatment in his comprehensive strategy analysis text.

5. Information and communication technology has made imitation faster and more efficient across all domains of human endeavor. Hence comedians find their jokes have a very short life as original material as they whiz around the Internet in nanoseconds and young sports hopefuls can record and imitate the new tricks of the champions in the comfort of their lounge room. It is no surprise to the thinking strategist that efficiency/cost focused methodologies such as Business Process Engineering (BPR) and Activity Based Management (ABM) have significant impacts on managers in mature industries. Similarly it is no surprise that doom-mongering journal articles railing against the perils of such imitation-as-strategy also appear in regular cycles. Unfortunately, impassioned exhortations to "dare to be different!" or "invent the future!" or "innovate or die!" have as much credibility in many mature industries as the directive to "leap to the top of a large building in a single bound" has for most mature adults – no matter how many exclamation marks are used. Make no mistake, one adult may be able to leap to the top but, in the main, those that keep trying to do so lose out to those who use the elevator, just like everyone else. If someone does eventually leap to the top his/her leaping methodology is quickly (and cheaply) copied and everybody goes a-leaping.

6. Kathryn Harrigan (1980 and with Michael Porter in 1983)) has written on decline.

7. Oligopolies are industry structures where the dynamics of game theory most often emerge and, in particular, that part of game theory that deals with zero sum games or, as they are more popularly known, the Prisoners' Dilemma. For example although no one company in the industry might want to reduce prices (as buyers demand) or increase industry capacity, the fear that the others will drop prices (and gain the business) or increase capacity (and hence reduce costs) drives all players to reduce prices and/or increase capacity due to the fear of being left out. After the decision, all competitors make less money because of the price reduction or, in the case of the capacity decision, because the industry is now plagued with chronic over-capacity and the associated increase in costs. Dixit et al (2009) offer a comprehensive treatment of this complex area.

8. Traditionally MES has meant Minimum Efficient **Scale** with the strategic emphasis being on scale based cost reductions (i.e., increasing supply side returns to scale). We

use "size" for two reasons. 1. There are other size based cost dynamics such as scope and experience effects where the former is a version of scale but the latter is driven by cumulative volume (i.e. past "size") rather than current production capacity (scale/scope). 2. On the demand side size is important in those industries that demonstrate network effects, i.e. where the value of the product to the customer is a positive function of the number of other users (increasing demand side returns). Hence in the traditional areas of telephones and in the current industry of web based auction companies (e.g. E-bay) or social networking industries involving such companies as Facebook or Twitter, the value of the product is a positive function of the number of others currently in the "network" and/or the potential customer's expectations of the number of future users. As with many other areas of strategy the potential for network gains has tended to be spectacularly hyped by some. Liebowitz (2002) counters the more extreme claims.

9. Note that size per se does not automatically engender monopoly power; it is the degree of contestability of the market/industry that underpins pricing discretion. If impediments to entry and exit (low exit costs contestability) are low then some "monopolists" are forced to maintain prices at a level that would prevail under competition as the ever-present risk of entry prevents the large firm from engaging in predatory monopoly pricing. This is an argument that some have used in support of Microsoft during that firm's frequent battles with industry regulators in Europe and the US. Microsoft argues (amongst other things) that the nature of the software industry is such that costs of entry and exit are low (the start up of now-monsters such as Google support this view) and innovation such a constant threat to Microsoft's positional power that the firm is forced to continue to innovate and to keep its prices low – neither of which is consistent with monopoly power. Netscape might be forgiven for being somewhat credulous.

10. Brandenburger and Nalebuff (1996: 17)

11. Brandenburger and Nalebuff (1996: 12)

12. Source: Adapted from the report "Fair Play at the Olympics" by Oxfam GB, available at www.fairolympics.org. See also www.cleanclothes.org

13. See Nike in Chapter 1 Macro-Shocks.

14. In the sports apparel and footwear industry the power is concentrated downstream but in others it can be upstream (concentrated) raw material suppliers that have the most power.

15. See the Marcos case (10-3) in the Sustain Ability chapter for more such mechanisms.

4. Corporate Strategy

1. The seminal work on the emergence of the multidivisional structure was carried out by Alfred Chandler, a business historian, whose ground-breaking book *Strategy and Structure, Chapters in the History of American Enterprise* (Cambridge, MA: MIT Press), published in 1962, charted the rise of the M-form in the US and gave rise to the enduring dictum that "structure follows strategy."

2. This may seem a somewhat cynical observation but the basis of "agency theory" lies in the conflict of (self) interests between the owners of firms (shareholders) and their agents, the managers of firms. In this context, Michael Jensen has noted that owner–agent interests clash when it comes to the payout of "free cash flow" (i.e. "cash flow in excess of that required to fund all projects that have positive net present values when discounted at the relevant cost of capital"). While owners might logically expect such cash to be paid out to them, Jensen suggests that "managers of firms with

unused borrowing power and large free cash flows are more likely to undertake low-benefit or even value-destroying mergers" (1986: 328). He strongly advocates high levels of debt as a device to ensure self-discipline on inherently wasteful managers. In a later provocative *Harvard Business Review* article (1989), Jensen argues that the leveraged buyout (LBO), with its high level of debt, is a business form that, due to its debt-enforced focus on efficiency and shareholder value, threatens the "Eclipse of the Public Corporation" (the title of his article).

3. This is an example of a potential "holdup" problem and is normally linked to "relationship-specific assets" (i.e. investments that one party makes that are specific to the needs of another party). It is often impossible to formally specify the nature of the relationship in such a way as to protect the vulnerable party from being exploited once the investment has been made ("incomplete contracting") and hence integration is often the preferred route. There are many specific texts on the complex arena of transaction cost economics but Besanko, D., Dranove, D., Shanley, M., and Schaeffer, S. (2009) *Economics of Strategy*, 5th ed. Boston: Harvard Business School Press, a general text, offers valuable insights in the context of strategy.

4. Rumelt, R. P. (1974) *Strategy, Structure and Economic Performance*, Harvard Business School Press, describes a major study on the relationship between performance and relatedness. He revisited the study in 1986, coming up with essentially the same findings of higher value from related diversification. While some authors were supportive of Rumelt's main contentions, a significant body of research was in disagreement. Overall, using market-based measures of relatedness has produced equivocal evidence on the link between firm performance and the composition of the corporate business portfolio with few strong findings on either side and no consensus. For a summary of the situation and a discussion of possible causes for a lack of a relationship, the interested reader could usefully start with Robins, J. and Wiersema, M. F. (1995) A resource-based view of the multibusiness: empirical analysis of portfolio interrelationships and corporate financial performance, *Strategic Management Journal*, 16 (4): 277–99.

5. Peter McKiernan (1992) *Strategies of Growth*, Routledge, offers a detailed account of the boxes and, in particular, the problems that such classification bring when most businesses fall into the "dog" box, for which the theoretical strategic imperative is "divest."

6. In 1981, there were nine different matrices that managers could choose from, as rival consultancies developed their own frameworks to help beleaguered corporate managers shape their portfolio of business and allocate resources within it (Wind, Y. and Mahajan, V. J. (1981) Designing a product and business portfolio, *Harvard Business Review*, 59 (1): 155).

7. Each factor is given a weight for its importance (adding to a total of 1) and this is multiplied by a ranking (1–5) of how well placed the organization is against others in the industry. For example, if market share (part of competitive position) is deemed to have a weight of 0.3 and the business is well placed as the market leader (5) then the weighted score for market share is 1.5 (0.3 × 5).

8. Risk diversification was always difficult to justify as a benefit to shareholders because, as the capital asset pricing model tells us, it is only unsystematic risk that can be diversified away and shareholders can do this themselves. They can also do so with far lower transaction costs than a corporate entity that generally must buy all of a firm at a takeover premium to normal market price whereas a shareholder can buy a small part of a firm (via shares) at the non-premium market price. Diversifying non-systematic risk at the corporate level is a risk reduction strategy for managers not shareholders.

9. The seminal paper by Prahalad, C. K. and Bettis, R. A. (1986) The dominant logic: a new linkage between diversity and performance, *Strategic Management Journal*, 7 (6): 485–501, brought this cognitive perspective into the mainstream of strategy thinking

and reminded us of the importance for synergy of how senior managers view the businesses (dominant logic) and the interbusiness mechanisms they put in place on the basis of this logic. The authors were responding to the narrowness of traditional product, process, or market measures of diversity/relatedness and stressed instead the importance of the "strategic variety" among the businesses.

10. Within the overall framework of the resource-based view (RBV – see Chapter 5, Strategic Positioning) of the firm, Gary Hamel and C. K. Prahalad have emphasized that core competences are the "central subject of corporate strategy" (1994: 220) but that the organization of the typical multidivisional business into stand-alone business units militates against the development of such competences. Their article, "The Core Competence of the Corporation," in the *Harvard Business Review* (Prahalad and Hamel, 1990: 86) decries the "tyranny of the SBU" as it promotes its own autonomous functioning and fails to facilitate the complex interactions and sharing that are necessary for corporate-wide development and exploitation of core competences.

11. Porter, M. (1987) From Competitive Advantage to Corporate Strategy, *Harvard Business Review* 65 (3): 43–59.

12. Goold, M., Campbell, A., and Alexander, M. have published extensively but most of their major ideas are covered in their book *Corporate-Level Strategy* (1994), John Wiley and Sons.

13. "Cooper Industries' Corporate Strategy," Harvard Business School Case No. 9-391-095.

14. Research into multidivisional businesses routinely reveals the ingenuity of business managers in developing their own specific systems in the face of corporate hegemony.

15. This is a heavily disguised, actual company. "Thank-you" to the managers – you know who you are.

16. The business on which this case is base moved to this kind of structure. It caused mayhem and anguish to start with, but now the MDs would not have it any other way as (a) it has worked (so far!) and (b) it is training them in corporate level thinking/acting ahead of future promotion to corporate level jobs.

5. Strategic Positioning

1. The debate between the impact of industry and the firm on company returns is an ongoing one. Richard Rumelt's (1991) eminently sensible suggestion is that an intermediate position between the two is the most useful with actual balance contingent on the particular industry.

2. Despite what most MBA students believe this insight pre-dates Michael Porter by some time. As far back as 1817 the economist David Ricardo pointed out that industry prices are set by the marginal (highest cost) producer and so other producers with lower costs (competitive advantage) make higher levels of profits. i.e. "The exchangeable value of all commodities, whether they be manufactured or the produce of mines, or the produce of the land, is always regulated, not by the less quantity of labor that will suffice for their production under circumstances very favourable but by the greater quantity of labor necessarily bestowed on their production by those who have no such facilities, by those who continue to produce under the most unfavourable circumstance.'

3. In his earlier version of this matrix Porter (1980:39) used the term "Uniqueness perceived by the customer" instead of "differentiation" advantage and it may have reduced confusion if he had stuck with the idea of uniqueness as an advantage and differentiation as a strategy aimed at building that uniqueness.

4. Mintzberg, H. (1998) Generic Strategies: Toward a Comprehensive Framework, in Lamb, R. B. and Shivastava, P. (eds) *Advances in Strategic Management.* JAI Press.

5. Edith Penrose's (1959) book *The Theory of the Growth of the Firm* is not an easy read but sets out most of the concepts often hailed as new insights by authors in the 1980s/90s.

6. The definitional problems that beset RBV writings are legendary and we have no wish to offer yet another attempted solution. In this chapter we use "competency" and "capability" as interchangeable terms to mean those things that a firm is good at and these, along with tangible assets, people, location etc. are part of the resources a company can make use of in its efforts to survive and thrive. To stay in business a firm needs to be good at many things i.e. have many capabilities, and so a "distinctive" or "core" capability/competency denotes that the firm has a compleitive advantage in that area. The interested reader is recommended to consult Hamel and Heene (Hamel, G. and Heene, A. (1994) *Competence-Based Competition.* New York: John Wiley & Sons.) and Sanchez et al (Sanchez, R., Heene, A. and Thomas, H. (1996) *Dynamics of Competence-Based Competition.* Oxford: Elsevier Science.) for a variety of papers on the RBV including a stroll through the definitional labyrinth. An influential article on core competence is that by Hamel and Prahalad (Hamel, G and Prahalad, C. K (1990) Core Competence of the Corporation, *Harvard Business Review,* May–June: 79–81.) which is the most reprinted *Harvard Business Review* article ever.

7. Luck in strategy is neglected as a dynamic by most theorists but recognized by most managers who would rather be lucky than smart any day. Jay Barney is one academic author who does not discount luck and his (Barney, J. B. (1986a) Strategy Factor Markets: Expectations, Luck and Business Strategy, *Management Science,* 32 (10): 1231–41.) paper brings it into the strategy equation.

8. These points are made by many authors and summarized by Collis and Montgomery (Collis, D. J. and Montgomery, C. A. (1995) Competing on resources: Strategy in the 1990s, *Harvard Business Review,* 73 (4): 118–28.).

9. 2008 Harbour Report on Manufacturing. www.theharbourreport.com

10. A term first used by Rumelt (Rumelt, R. P. (1986) *Strategy, Structure and Economic Performance,* 2nd edn. Boston, MA: Harvard Business School Press.)

11. Sources: various newspaper, websites, television and magazine items.

12. What the case does not reveal is the extent to which Jack Cohen persevered with a no-frills philosophy throughout his tenure firstly as owner, then as chairman/CEO and finally as "honorary life president" but non chairman. He could never resist buying cheap goods or cheap, rundown premises from which to sell these cheap goods. On one occasion a consignment of tins of "Gambos" arrived that he had purchased on holiday in South America. Nobody at Tesco knew what they were, but guessed from the label that they were plums and so stocked them in the canned fruit section. They turned out to be seeded (and hot!) peppers. In 1968 he unilaterally bought the 200 run down stores of former rival Victor Value. It took 18 months for Tesco management to refurbish these premises one at a time. Tesco financed this deal with a rights issue that diluted Cohen's ownership to 16%. In 1973 Cohen again made a deal for a set of run down premises this time offering to buy the "Square Meals" chain from Brooke Bonds. These stores were so dilapidated (some even lacked appropriate planning permission to be in existence) that the Tesco board defied their founder and persuaded Brooke Bonds to buy them back. This, plus being on the losing side of the decision to discontinue Green Shield stamps (the vote was lost by one and was taken several times at the one board meeting), signalled the end of Cohen's unchallenged rule.

NOTES

6. Corporate Identity

1. Rakesh Khurana and Nitin Nohria's call for an 'Oath' for MBA students: "It's Time to Make Management a True Profession." *Harvard Business Review*, October 2008.
2. Porter, M. (1990) *The Competitive Advantage of Nations*. Macmillan.
3. Hofstede, G. (1993) Cultural Constraints in Management Theories, *Academy of Management Executive*, 7 (1): 8–21; Smircich, L. (1983) Concepts of Culture and Organizational Analysis, *Administrative Science Quarterly*, 28 (3): 339–58.
4. Pascale, R. and Athos, A. (1981) *The Art of Japanese Management*. Warner.
5. Hofstede, G. (1993) op. cit.
6. Hankinson, G. and Cowking, P. (1996) *The Reality of Global Brands*. McGraw-Hill: 44.
7. de Mooij, M. (1997) *Global Marketing and Advertising: Understanding Cultural Paradoxes*. Sage: 189.
8. Peters, T. and Waterman, R. (1982) *In Search of Excellence*. Harper & Row.
9. Bilton, C. and Cummings, S. (2010) *Creative Strategy: Reconnecting Business and Innovation*, John Wiley and Sons Ltd.
10. Johnson, G., Scholes, K., Whittington, R. (2008) *Exploring Corporate Strategy*, 8th edn. FT/Prentice Hall.
11. Collins, J. C. and Porras, J. I. (1994) *Built to Last: Successful Habits of Visionary Companies*. HarperBusiness.
12. Cummings, S. (2003) Strategy as Ethos, in Cummings, S. and Wilson, D. (eds) *Images of Strategy*. Blackwell: 41–73.
13. Schultz, M., Hatch, M. J., and Holten Larsen, M. (2000) *The Expressive Organization: Linking Identity, Reputation and the Corporate Brand*. Oxford University Press.
14. Special Report: Designer Cars, *Business Week*, February 16, 2004: 40–8.
15. Davies, G. and Miles, L. (1997) *What Price Reputation?* Haymarket Business Publications.
16. Lewis, D. and Bridger, D. (2001) *The Soul of the New Consumer: Authenticity – What we buy and why in the new economy*. Nicholas Brealey.
17. Roberts, K. (2004) *Lovemarks: the future beyond brands*, Powerhouse.

7. Organic Strategy

1. Heidegger, M. (1962) *Being and Time*. Blackwell.
2. Kunde, J. (2002) *Unique: Now or Never – The Brand Drives the Company in the New Value Economy*. Prentice Hall.
3. Senge, P. (1990) *The Fifth Discipline*. Century Business.
4. de Geus, A. (2000) *The Living Company*. Harvard Business School Press.
5. Collins, J. C. and Porras, J. I. (1994) *Built to Last: Successful Habits of Visionary Companies*. HarperCollins.
6. Nonaka, I. (1991) The Knowledge Creating Company, *Harvard Business Review*, 69 (6): 96–104.
7. Shaw, G., Brown, R., and Bromiley, P. (1998) Strategic Stories: How 3M is Rewriting Business Planning, *Harvard Business Review*, 76 (3): 41–54. See also, Barry, D. and Elms, M. (1997) Strategy Retold: Toward a Narrative View of Strategic Discourse, *Academy of Management Review*, 22: 429–52.
8. Gardner, H. and Laskin, E. (1996) *Leading Minds: An Anatomy of Leadership*. HarperCollins.
9. Brown, J. S. and Duguid, P. (1991) Organizational learning and communities-of-practice: towards a unified view of working, learning and innovation, *Organization*

Science, 2 (1): 40–57; (1998) Organizing knowledge, *California Management Review*, 40 (3): 90–111; (2001) Knowledge and organization: a social practice perspective, *Organization Science*, 12 (2): 198–213; Wenger, E. (1998) *Communities of Practice: Learning, Meaning and Identity*, Cambridge University Press; Wenger, E. and Snyder, W. (2000) Communities of practice: the organizational frontier, *Harvard Business Review*, 78 (1): 138–45.

10. Baker, W. (2000) *Achieving Success Through Social Capital*. Jossey-Bass.

11. Peters, T. and Waterman, R. (1982) *In Search of Excellence*. Harper & Row.

12. Krackhardt, D. and Hanson, J. (1993) Informal Networks: The Company Behind the Chart, *Harvard Business Review*, 71 (4): 104–11; Normann, R. and Ramirez, R. (1993) From Value Chain to Value Constellation: Designing Interactive Strategy, *Harvard Business Review*, 71 (4): 65–77.

13. Evans, P. E. and Wurster, T. S. (1997) Strategy and the New Economics of Information, *Harvard Business Review*, 75 (5): 71–82.

14. Foucault, M. (1977) *Discipline and Punish: The Birth of the Prison*, Allen Lane; (1980) *Power/Knowledge*, Harvester Press.

15. Foote Whyte, W. (1943) *Street Corner Society*. University of Chicago Press.

16. Barney, J. B. (1986b) Organizational culture: Can it be a source of sustained competitive advantage? *Academy of Management Review*, 11 (3): 656–65; Barney, J. B. (1991) Firm resources and sustained competitive advantage, *Journal of Management*, 17 (1): 99–120.

17. Michaels, E., Handfield-Jones, H., and Axelrod, B. (2001) *The War for Talent*. Harvard Business School Press.

18. The origins of the strategy as practice view can be located in the early work of Stewart, R. (1967) *Managers and Their Jobs*, Macmillan, and Mintzberg, H. (1973) *The Nature of Managerial Work*, Harper & Row. More recently it has received conceptual clarification as a domain in Whittington, R. (1996) Strategy as Practice, *Long Range Planning*, 29 (5) Special Issue: 713–36, and a future research agenda has been set out in Johnson, G., Melin, L., and Whittington, R. (2003) Micro Strategy and Strategizing: Towards an Activity-Based View, Guest Editors' Introduction, *Journal of Management Studies*, Blackwell Publishers, 40 (1): 3–22; Whittington, R. (2006) Completing the practice turn, *Organization Studies*, 27 (5) 613–634 and Golsorkhi, D., Rouleau, L., Seidl, D., Vaara, E. (2010) *The Cambridge Handbook of Strategy as Practice*, Cambridge University Press, Cambridge. The strategy as practice movement has an active website: http://www.strategy-as-practice.org and now has a conference track at the Strategic Management Society in the US: http://www.smsweb.org.

19. Cummings, S. (2003) Strategy as Ethos, in Cummings, S. and Wilson, D. (eds) *Images of Strategy*. Blackwell: 41–73.

8. Crossing Borders

1. Smith, A. (1776) *The Wealth of Nations*, Smith, A. (ed.) (1999) Penguin Books/South-Western Publishing.

2. Ricardo, D. (1967) *The Principles of Political Economy and Taxation*. Homewood, IL: Irwin.

3. Vernon, R. (1966) International Investment and International Trade in the Product Life Cycle, *Quarterly Journal of Economics*, 29 (2): 190 –207.

4. Hymer, S. (1970) The multinational corporation and the law of uneven development, in Bhagwati, J. (ed.) *Economics and World Order*. New York: World Law Fund.

5. Brouthers, J. E., Brouthers, K. D., and Werner, S. (1999) Is Dunning's Eclectic Framework description or narrative, *Journal of International Business*, 30 (4): 831– 44.

6. Hall, E. (1960) The silent language in overseas business, *Harvard Business Review*, May 1st: 87–96.

7. Huntingdon, S. P. (1997) *The Clash of Civilisations and the Remaking of World Order.* London: Simon and Schuster.

8. Whiteley, R. D. (1999) *Divergent Capitalisms.* Oxford University Press.

9. Hofstede, G. (1980) *Culture's Consequences: International Differences in Work-Related Values.* Beverly Hills, CA: Sage.

10. Laurent, A. (1986) The cross-cultural puzzle of global human resource management. *Human Resources Management*, 25 (1): 91–102.

11. Trompenaars, F. (1993) *Riding the Waves of Cultural Differences: Understanding Cultural Differences in Business*, London: Nicholas Brealey; Hampden-Turner, C. and Trompenaars, F. (2000) *Building Cross-cultural Competence*, Chichester: John Wiley and Sons Ltd.

12. Kogut, B. and Singh, H. (1988) The effect of national culture on the choice of entry mode, *Journal of International Business Studies*, 19 (3): 411–33; Angwin, D. N. (2001) Mergers and Acquisitions across European borders: National perspectives on pre-acquisition due diligence and the use of professional advisers, *Journal of World Business*, 36 (1): 32–57.

13. Prahalad, C. K. and Doz, Y. L. (1987) *The Multinational Mission: Balancing Local Demands and Global Vision.* New York: Free Press.

14. Porter, M. (1990a) *The Competitive Advantage of Nations*, New York: Free Press; Porter (1990b) The Competitive Advantage of Nations, *Harvard Business Review*, 69 (2): March–April.

15. Porter (1990a), ibid.: 33.

16. c.f. Rugman, A. M. (1990) *Multinationals and Canada–United States Free Trade*, University of South Carolina Press; Crookell, H. (1990) *Canadian–American Trade and Investment under the Free Trade Act Agreement*, Quorum Books.

17. Dunning, J. H. (1993) Internationalizing Porter's Diamond, *Management International Review*, 33 (2) Special Issue: 7–16.

18. Rugman, A. M. and D'Cruz, J. R. (1993) The Double Diamond Model of International Competitiveness: the Canadian experience, *Management International Review*, 33 (2) Special Issue: 17–40.

19. Teece, D. J. (1986) Transaction cost economics and multi-national enterprise, *Journal of Economic Behaviour and Organization*, 7 (1): 21–45.

20. Dussauge, P. and Garrette, B. (1999) *Cooperative Strategy: Competing Successfully Through Strategic Alliances.* John Wiley and Sons Ltd.

21. Hamel, G., Doz, Y. L., and Prahalad, C. K. (1989) Collaborate with your Competitors – and Win, *Harvard Business Review*, 67 (1): 133–9.

22. Angwin, D. N. (2000) *Implementing Successful Post-acquisition Management.* Financial Times/Prentice Hall.

23. Bartlett, C. A. and Ghoshal, S. (1989) *Managing Across Borders: the Transnational Solution.* Boston, MA: Harvard Business School Press.

9. Guiding Change

1. Bartlett, C. A. and Ghoshal, S. (1989) *Managing Across Borders: The Transnational Solution.* Boston, MA: Harvard Business School Press.

2. Kotter, J. P. (1995) Leading Change: Why Transformation Efforts Fail, *Harvard Business Review*, 73 (2): 59–67.

3. Identifying a compelling need for change or creating *a sense of urgency* is seen as crucial by Beer, M. (1987) Revitalizing organizations: Change process and emergent model, *Academy of Management Executive*, 1 (1): 51–6; Johansson, H. J. et al. (1993)

Business Process Reengineering: Breakpoint Strategies for Market Dominance, John Wiley and Sons Ltd; Tichy, N. (1993) *Handbook for Revolutionaries*, New York: Doubleday; Nadler, D. and Tushman, M. (1989) Organizational frame bending: Principles for managing reorientation, *Academy of Management Executive*, 3 (3): 194–204; Stace, D. and Dunphy, D. (1994) *Beyond the Boundaries: Leading and Recreating the Successful Organization*, McGraw-Hill; and a book published by consultants Price Waterhouse Coopers (1995) entitled *Better Change: Best Practices for Transforming your Organization*, Irwin. All of these sources and others, like Beck, R. N. (1987) Visions, values, and strategies: Changing attitudes and culture, *Academy of Management Executive*, 1 (1): 33–40, Chen, M. (1994) Sun Tzu's thinking and contemporary business, *Business Horizons*, 37 (2): 42–8, and Larkin, T. J. and Larkin, S. (1996) Reaching and changing frontline employees, *Harvard Business Review*, 74 (3): 95–104, emphasize the need to develop, effectively *communicate*, and *empower others* to work toward a *vision* of a future organizational state. We are reminded of the particular importance of being aware of the politics at work in an organization, gaining commitment, and *forming a guiding coalition* by Price Waterhouse Coopers (1995), Johansson et al. (1993), Tichy, N. and Sherman, S. (1993) *Control Your Destiny or Someone Else Will*, New York: Doubleday, and Nadler and Tushman (1989), while *emphasizing short-term wins* and *consolidating improvements*, integrating and *institutionalizing* new approaches, and forming a *platform for further change* are highlighted by reengineering exponents and most of the above.

4. Smither, R. D. (1994) *The Psychology of Work and Human Performance*, HarperCollins.

5. Cummings, S. (2002) *Recreating Strategy*, Sage. Original sources: Lewin, K. (1951) *Field Theory in Social Sciences*, Tavistock Publications; Blake, R. R. and Mouton, J. S. (1964) *How to Assess the Strengths and Weaknesses of a Business Enterprise*, Scientific Methods; Lippitt, R., Watson, J., and Westley, B. (1958) *The Dynamics of Planned Change: A Comparative Study of Principles and Techniques*, Harcourt, Brace; Tichy, N. and Devanna, M. A. (1997) *The Transformational Leader*, John Wiley and Sons Inc.

6. Pettigrew, A. and Whipp, R. (1991) *Managing Change for Competitive Success*. Blackwell.

7. Mintzberg, H. and Westley, Y. (1992) Cycles of Organizational Change, *Strategic Management Journal*, 13 Special Issue: 39–59.

8. Wilson, D. (1992) *A Strategy of Change: Concepts and Controversies in the Management of Change*. ITP.

9. Key works on turnarounds include Lovett, D. and Slatter, S. (1999) *Corporate Turnaround*, Penguin Books; Barker, V. L. and Duhaime, I. M. (1997) Strategic change in the turnaround process: theory and empirical evidence, *Strategic Management Journal*, 18 (1): 13–38; Grinyer, P., Mayes, D. G., and McKiernan, P. (1990) The Sharp-benders: achieving a sustained improvement in performance, *Long Range Planning*, 23 (1): 116–25.

10. Dunphy, D. and Stace, D. A. (1990) *Under New Management: Australian Organizations in Transition*. McGraw-Hill.

11. Angwin, D. N. (2000) *Implementing successful post-acquisition management*. Financial Times/Prentice Hall.

12. Hamel, G. (1996) Strategy as revolution, *Harvard Business Review*, 74 (4): 69–82; Hammer, M. and Champy, J. (1993) *Reengineering the Corporation: A Manifesto for Business Revolution*, Nicholas Brealey.

13. Imai, M. (1986) *Kaizen: The Key to Japan's Competitive Success*. McGraw-Hill.

14. Leavy, B. and Wilson, D. (1994) *Strategy and Leadership*. ITP.

15. As Jim March reminds us: "most current leaders seem to be competent and analytical rather than imaginative and visionary . . . they seek to refine the establishment rather than challenge or transform it." March, J. (1999) *The Pursuit of Organizational Intelligence*. Blackwell.

NOTES

16. Bonabeau, E. (2004) The perils of the information age, *Harvard Business Review*, 82 (6): 45–54.

17. Kotter, J. P. and Schlesinger, L. A. (1979) Choosing Strategies for Change, *Harvard Business Review*, 57 (2): 106–14.

18. Lafley, A. G. (2009) What only the CEO can do. *Harvard Business Review*, 87(5):54–62.

10. Sustain Ability

1. World Commission on Economic Development (1987) *Our Common Future*. Oxford: Oxford University Press: 43.

2. Dunphy, D., Griffiths, A., and Benn, S. (2003) *Organizational Change for Corporate Sustainability: A Guide for Leaders and Change Agents of the Future*. New York: Routledge: 83.

3. Elizabet Sahtouris combines evolutionary biology and spirituality to express this interconnectedness. Her writings are available from the website www.ratical .org/LifeWeb.

4. Stuart Hart is an influential writer in this area and several of the terms and ideas in this section are based on Hart, S. (1997) 'Beyond greening: Strategies for a sustainable world, *Harvard Business Review*, 75 (1): 71–91.

5. Wackernagel, M. et al. (1997) Ecological footprints of nations. How much nature do they use? How much nature do they have? Report prepared for the *Rio +5 Forum*.

6. For an insightful review of the CSR literature and its development see McGee, J. (1998) Commentary on corporate strategies and environmental regulations: an organizing framework, in Rugman, A. M. and Verbeke, A. (1998) *Journal of Strategic Management*, Special Edition: Editor's choice, 19 (4): 377–87.

7. Eberstadt, N. (1973) What History Tells Us About Corporate Responsibilities, *Business and Society Review*, 7: 76–81.

8. Friedman, as might be expected, espoused the view that CSR means maximizing shareholders' returns: Friedman, M. (1970) The social responsibility of business is to increase its profits, *Ivey Business Journal*, March/April: 1–5.

9. The good company: a survey of corporate social responsibility, *The Economist*, January 22, 2005: 16.

10. The broader definition quoted from Davis and Blomstrom (1975: 6) suggests that optimizing social good is a more diffuse outcome as a part of which maximizing shareholder value is neither a necessary nor a sufficient component. Davis, K. and Blomstrom, R. L. (1975) *Business and Society: Environment and Responsibility*. New York: McGraw-Hill.

11. Adapted from Hay, R. D., Gray, E. R., and Gates, J. E. (1976) *Business and Society*. Cincinnati, OH: Heath.

12. In book, movie, and television series, "The Corporation" presents the modern corporation as a "psychopath" that is self-serving, lacking empathy with others, and has no sense of remorse or guilt about its negative impacts.

13. Freely adapted from Zenisek, whose model specifically acknowledges a continuum of social responsibility from low (Type I) to high (Type IV): Zenisek, T. J. (1979) Corporate social responsibility: A conceptualization based on organizational literature, *Academy of Management Review*, 4 (3): 359–68.

14. Tim O'Connor of the NikeWatch campaign wrote in his report in 2001: "The Global Alliance's new report on Nike factories in Indonesia found evidence of serious labor abuses, including inadequate wages, forced and illegal overtime, denial of sick leave, menstrual leave, and annual leave, and unacceptable levels of sexual harassment and verbal abuse" (http://www.amnesty.org.uk/business/newslet/spring01/nike

.shtml). In April 2005, Nike published a 108-page report acknowledging the truth of many of these allegations. The report followed 3 years of silence from the company following its payout of nearly £800,000 in settlement of a court case claiming it had made false statements about how employees were treated.

15. In 2004, Shell stated that it had inadvertently fed conflict, poverty, and corruption through its oil activities in Nigeria: http://news.bbc.co.uk/1/hi/business/3796375.stm.

16. Hart, op. cit.: 68 (emphasis in original).

17. Kay, J. (1993) *The Foundations of Corporate Success*. Blackwell.

18. Taken from Salzman, O., Ionescu-Somers, A., and Steger, U. (2005) The business case for corporate sustainability: literature review and research options, *European Management Journal*, 1: 27–36.

19. Waddock, S. A. and Graves, S. B. (1997) The corporate social performance–financial performance link, *Strategic Management Journal*, 18 (4): 303–19.

20. Ibid.

21. Cornell, B. and Shapiro, A. C. (1987) Corporate stakeholders and corporate finance, *Financial Management* 16 (1): 5–14.

22. Reed, D. J. (2001) *Stalking the Elusive Business Case for Corporate Sustainability*. Washington: World Resources Institute.

23. The commonly used "balanced scorecard" (Kaplan and Norton, 1992) reflects this orientation to ensure that all stakeholders and constituencies receive their due consideration *while pursuing the main goal of shareholder value* – i.e. all stakeholders are balanced but some are more balanced than others.

24. Pfeffer, J. (2010) Building Sustainable Organizations: The Human Factor, *Academy of Management Perspectives*, 24(1): 34–45.

25. From 'Growth though Global Sustainability: An Interview with Monsanto's CEO, Robert B. Shapiro' by Joan Magretta, *Harvard Business Review*, 1997, January-February: 79–88.

26. Various sources as indicated in the text.

11. Maverick Strategies

1. Kunde, J. (2002) *Unique: Now or Never – The Brand Drives the Company in the New Value Economy*. Financial Times/Prentice Hall.

2. Nattermann, P. (2000) Best Practice Does Not Equal Best Strategy, *McKinsey Quarterly*, 2; Christensen, C. (2003) *The Innovator's Dilemma*. HarperBusiness.

3. Porter, M. (1996) What is Strategy? *Harvard Business Review*, 74 (6): 61–79.

4. Nordstrom, K. and Ridderstrale, J. (2001) Funky Business, *Financial Times*.

5. Nattermann, ibid.

6. From Tom Peter's very interesting and very popular website www.tompeters.com

7. This chart published by the UK Design Council in 2005 is outlined and discussed Bilton, C. and Cummings, S. (2010) *Creative Strategy: Reconnecting Business and Innovation*, John Wiley and Sons Ltd.

8. Kim, W. and Mauborgne, R. (2003) Think for yourself – stop copying a rival, *New Thinking from INSEAD* and Kim, W. and Mauborgne, R. (2005) *Blue Ocean Strategy: How to Create Uncontested Market Space and Make Competition Irrelevant*. Harvard Business School Press.

9. Foster, R. (1986) *Innovation, the Attacker's Advantage*. Macmillan.

10. Cummings, S. (2002) *Recreating Strategy*. Sage.

11. Calloway, J. (2009) *Becoming a Category of One: How Extraordinary Companies Transcend Commodity and Defy Comparison*. John Wiley & Sons Inc.

12. Godin, S. (2003) *Purple Cow: Transform Your Business by Becoming Remarkable*. Portfolio.
13. Dru, J.-M. (1996) *Disruption: Overturning Conventions and Shaking Up the Marketplace*. John Wiley and Sons Inc.
14. Koestler, A. (1976) *The Act of Creation*. Hutchinson.
15. Sutton, B. (2001) *Weird Ideas That Work: 11½ Practices for Promoting, Managing, and Sustaining Innovation*. Free Press.
16. Schrage, M. (1999) *Serious Play: How the World's Best Companies Simulate to Innovate*, Harvard Business School Press.
17. Kotter, J. P. (2008) *A Sense of Urgency*, Harvard Business School Press.
18. Martin, R. (2009) *The Design of Business: Why Design Thinking is the Next Competitive Advantage*, Harvard Business School Press.
19. Mintzberg, H. (1999) Organigraphs: Drawing How Companies Really Work, *Harvard Business Review*, 77 (5): 87–94.
20. See Cummings, S and Angwin, D. (forthcoming, 2011) Stratography: The Art of Conceptualizing and Communicating Strategy, Business Horizons.
21. Bilton and Cummings, ibid.
22. As cited in Godin, S. (2003) op. cit.
23. Mintzberg, H. (2004) *Managers Not MBAs: A Hard Look at the Soft Practice of Managing and Management Development*. Berrett-Koehler.
24. *Corralito* was the informal name for the economic measures taken in Argentina by Minister of Economy Domingo Cavallo in order to stop a bank run, and which were fully in force for one year. The corralito almost completely froze bank accounts and forbade withdrawals from US dollar-denominated accounts.

Alexander, R. C. (1988) *Fumbling the future*. William Morrow: New York.

Amihud, Y. and Lev, B. (1981) Risk reduction as a managerial motive for conglomerate mergers, *Bell Journal of Economics*, 12 (2): 605–16.

Andrews, K. R. (1971) *The Concept of Corporate Strategy*. Illinois: Dow Jones-Irwin Inc.

Angwin, D. N. (2000) *Implementing successful post-acquisition management*. Financial Times/Prentice Hall.

Angwin, D. N. (2001) Mergers and Acquisitions across European borders: National perspectives on pre-acquisition due diligence and the use of professional advisers, *Journal of World Business*, 36 (1): 32–57.

Angwin, D. N. (2004) Speed in M&A integration: the first 100 days, *European Management Journal*, 22 (4): 418–430.

Angwin, D. N. (2006) Agency theory perspective, in Jenkins, M. and Ambrosini, V. (eds) *Strategic Management: A multi-perspective approach*, 2nd edn. Palgrave MacMillan.

Angwin, D. N. (2007) *Mergers and Acquisitions*, Oxford Blackwell.

Angwin, D. N., Stern, P. and Bradley, S. (2004) The Target CEO in a hostile takeover: Agency or Stewardship – can the condemned agent be redeemed? *Long Range Planning*, 37 (3): 239–57.

Angwin, D. N. and Paroutis, S. (2009) Connecting up Strategy: Are Senior Strategy Directors (SSDs) a missing link? *California Management Review*, Spring, 51 (3): 74–94.

Angwin, D. N. and Vaara, E., Guest Editors (2005) Connectivity in Merging Organizations – beyond traditional cultural perspectives, *Organization Studies*, 26 (10). Special Issue.

Angwin, D. N. and Meadows (2009) The Choice of Insider or Outsider Top Executives in Acquired Companies, *Long Range Planning*, 37: 239–257.

Ansoff, I. and McDonnell, E. (1990) *Implanting Strategic Management*. Upper Saddle River, NJ: Prentice Hall Inc.

Baker, W. (2000) *Achieving Success Through Social Capital*. Jossey-Bass.

Bansal, P. (2005) Evolving Sustainability: A Longitudinal Study of Corporate Sustainable Development, *Strategic Management Journal*, 26 (3): 197–218.

Barkema, H. G., Bell, J. H. and Pennings, J. M. (1996) Foreign entry, cultural barriers, and learning, *Strategic Management Journal*, 17 (2): 151–67.

Barker, V. L. and Duhaime, I. M. (1997) Strategic change in the turnaround process: theory and empirical evidence, *Strategic Management Journal*, 18 (1): 13–38.

Barney, J. B. (1986a) Strategy Factor Markets: Expectations, Luck and Business Strategy, *Management Science*, 32 (10): 1231–41.

Barney, J. B. (1986b) Organizational culture: Can it be a source of sustained competitive advantage? *Academy of Manage-ment Review*, 11 (3): 656–65.

Barney, J. B. (1991) Firm resources and sustained competitive advantage, *Journal of Management*, 17 (1): 99–120.

Barney, J. B. and Hesterly, W. S. (2006) *Strategic Management and Competitive Advantage*. Pearson/Prentice Hall.

Barry, D. and Elms, M. (1997) Strategy Retold: Toward a Narrative View of Strategic Discourse, *Academy of Management Review*, 22 (2): 429–52.

Bartlett, C. A. and Ghoshal, S. (1989) *Managing Across Borders: The Transnational Solution*. Boston, MA: Harvard Business School Press.

Beck, R. N. (1987) Visions, values, and strategies: Changing attitudes and culture, *Academy of Management Executive*, 1 (1): 33–40.

Beck, U. (2002) The Cosmopolitan Society and its Enemies, *Theory, Culture and Society*, 19 (1): 17–44.

Beer, M. (1987) Revitalizing Organizations: Change process and emergent model, *Academy of Management Executive*, 1 (1): 51–6.

Besanko, D., Dranove, D., Shanley, M. and Schaeffer, S. (2004) *Economics of Strategy*. Boston: Harvard Business School Press.

Besanko, D., Dranove, D., Schaeffer, S. and Shanley, M. (2009). *Economics of Strategy* (5th Ed.). NJ: John Wiley & Sons.

Bilton, C. and Cummings, S. (2010) *Creative Strategy: Reconnecting Business and Innovation*, Chichester: John Wiley & Sons.

Blake, R. R. and Mouton, J. S. (1964) *How to Assess the Strengths and Weaknesses of a Business Enterprise*. Scientific Methods.

Bonabeau, E. (2004) The perils of the information age, *Harvard Business Review*, 82 (6): 45–54.

Bowman, C. (1988) *Strategy in Practice*. Harlow: Prentice Hall.

Brandenburger, A. and Nalebuff, B. (1996) *Co-opetition*. New York: Currency Doubleday.

Brouthers, J. E., Brouthers, K. D. and Werner, S. (1999) Is Dunning's Eclectic Framework description or narrative, *Journal of International Business*, 30 (4): 831–44.

Brown, J. S. and Duguid, P. (1991) Organizational learning and communities-of-practice: towards a unified view of working, learning and innovation, *Organization Science*, 2 (1): 40–57.

Brown, J. S. and Duguid, P. (1998) Organizing knowledge, *California Management Review*, 40 (3): 90–111.

Brown, J. S. and Duguid, P. (2001) Knowledge and organization: a social practice perspective, *Organization Science*, 12 (2): 198–213.

Burkan, W. (1996) *Wide-Angle Vision: Beat Your Competition by Focusing on Fringe Competitors, Lost Customers, and Rogue Employees*. NJ: Wiley & Sons.

Businessweek (2004) *Special Report: Designer Cars*. Feb, 16: 40–8.

Byrd, J., Parrino, R. and Pritsch, G. (1998) Stockholder–manager conflicts and firm value, *Financial Analysts Journal*, 54 (3): 14–30.

Calloway, J. (2009) *Becoming a Category of One: How Extraordinary Companies Transcend Commodity and Defy Comparison*. NJ: John Wiley & Sons.

Chandler, A. D. (1962) *Strategy & Structure: Chapters in the History of the American Enterprise*. Cambridge, MA: MIT Press.

Chen, M. (1994) Sun Tzu's thinking and contemporary business, *Business Horizons*, 37 (2): 42–8.

Christensen, C. (2003) *The Innovator's Dilemma*. HarperBusiness.

Coase, R. (1937) The Nature of the Firm, *Economica*, 4: 386–405.

Collins, J. C. and Porras, J. I. (1994) *Built to Last: Successful Habits of Visionary Companies*. HarperCollins.

Collis, D. J. and Montgomery, C. A. (1995) Competing on resources: Strategy in the 1990s, *Harvard Business Review*, 73 (4): 118–28.

Cornell, B. and Shapiro, A. C. (1987) Corporate stakeholders and corporate finance, *Financial Management*, 16 (1): 5–14.

Courtney, H., Kirkland, J. and Viguerie, P. (1997) Strategy under Uncertainty, *Harvard Business Review*, 75 (6): 66–80.

Crookell, H. (1990) *Canadian–American Trade and Investment under the Free Trade Act Agreement*. Quorum Books.

Cummings, S. (2002) *Recreating Strategy*. Sage.

Cummings, S. (2003) Strategy as Ethos, in Cummings, S. and Wilson, D. (eds) *Images of Strategy*. Blackwell: 41–73.

Cummings, S. and Angwin, D. N. (2004) The Future Shape of Strategy: Lemmings or Chimeras? *Academy of Management Executive*, 18 (2): 21–36.

Cummings, S. and Angwin, D. (forthcoming, 2011) Stratography: The Art of Conceptualizing and Communicating Strategy, Business Horizons.

Cummings, S. and Wilson, D. (eds) (2003) *Images of Strategy*. Blackwell.

Davidson, W. (1980) The location of foreign direct investment activity: country characteristics and experience effects, *Journal of International Business Studies*, 11 (2): 9.

Davies, G. and Miles, L. (1997) *What Price Reputation?* Haymarket Business Publications.

Davis, K. and Blomstrom, R. L. (1975) *Business and Society: Environment and Responsibility*. New York: McGraw-Hill.

Davis, K. and Frederick, W. C. (1984) *Business and Society: Management, Public Policy, Ethics*, 5th edn. New York: McGraw-Hill.

de Geus, A. (2000) *The Living Company*. Boston, MA: Harvard Business School Press.

de Mooij, M. (1997) *Global Marketing and Advertising: Understanding Cultural Paradoxes*. Sage.

De Wit, B. and Meyer, R. (1999) *Strategy Synthesis*. ITP.

De Wit, B. and Meyer, R. (2004) *Strategy: Process, Content, Context; An International Perspective*, 3rd edn. Thomson.

Dixit, A., Skeath, S. and Reiley, D. H. Jr. (2009). *Games of Strategy* (3rd ed.). NY: W. W. Norton & Company.

Dru, J.-M. (1996) *Disruption: Overturning Conventions and Shaking Up the Marketplace*. NJ: Wiley & Sons.

Dunning, J. H. (1993) Internationalizing Porter's Diamond, *Management International Review*, 33 (2) Special Issue: 7–16.

Dunphy, D., Griffiths, A. and Benn, S. (2003) *Organizational Change for Corporate Sustainability: A Guide for Leaders and Change Agents of the Future*. New York: Routledge.

Dunphy, D. and Stace, D. A. (1990) *Under New Management: Australian Organizations in Transition*. McGraw-Hill.

Dussauge, P. and Garrette, B. (1999) *Cooperative Strategy: Competing Successfully Through Strategic Alliances*. Chichester: John Wiley & Sons.

Eberstadt, N. (1973) What History Tells Us About Corporate Responsibilities, *Business and Society Review*, 7: 76–81.

Eisenhardt, K. (1989) Agency theory: an assessment and review, *Academy of Management Review*, 14 (1): 57–74.

Evans, P. E. and Wurster, T. S. (1997) Strategy and the New Economics of Information, *Harvard Business Review*, 75 (5): 71–82.

Fama, E. (1980) Agency problems and the theory of the firm, *Journal of Political Economy*, 88 (2): 288–307.

Foote Whyte, W. (1943) *Street Corner Society*. University of Chicago Press.

Foster, R. (1986) *Innovation, the Attacker's Advantage*. Macmillan.

Foucault, M. (1977) *Discipline and Punish: The Birth of the Prison*. Allen Lane.

Foucault, M. (1980) *Power/Knowledge*. Harvester Press.

Friedman, M. (1970) The social responsibility of business is to increase its profits, *Ivey Business Journal*, March/April: 1–5.

Gardner, H. and Laskin, E. (1996) *Leading Minds: An Anatomy of Leadership*. HarperCollins.

Ghemawat, P. (2001) *Strategy and the Business Landscape*. NJ: Pearson Education.

Ghertman, M. and Leontidaes, J. (eds) (1978) *European Research in International Business*. Amsterdam.

Ginter, P. M. and Duncan, W. J. (1990) Macro environmental Analysis for Strategic Management, *Long Range Planning*, 23 (6): 91–100.

Godin, S. (2003) *Purple Cow: Transform Your Business by Becoming Remarkable*. Portfolio.

Goold, M., Campbell, A. and Alexander, M. (1994) *Corporate-Level Strategy: Creating Value in the Multibusiness Company*. New York: John Wiley & Sons.

Golsorkhi, D., Rouleau, L., Seidl, and D. Vaara, E. (2010) *The Cambridge Handbook of Strategy as Practice*, Cambridge University Press, Cambridge.

Grant, R. M. (2005) *Contemporary Strategy Analysis*, 5th edn. Oxford: Blackwell.

Grant, R.M. (2010) *Contemporary Strategy Analysis (7th ed.)*. Chichester: John Wiley & Sons.

Grinyer, P., Mayes, D. G. and McKiernan, P. (1990) The Sharpbenders: achieving a sustained improvement in performance, *Long Range Planning*, 23 (1): 116–25.

Hall, E. (1960) The silent language in overseas business, *Harvard Business Review*, May 1: 87–96.

Hamel, G. (1996) Strategy as revolution, *Harvard Business Review*, 74 (4): 69–82.

Hamel, G. (2000) *Leading the Revolution*. Boston, MA: Harvard Business School Press.

Hamel, G., Doz, Y. L. and Prahalad, C. K. (1989) Collaborate with your Competitors – and Win, *Harvard Business Review*, 67 (1): 133–9.

Hamel, G. and Heene, A. (1994) *Competence-Based Competition*. Chichester: John Wiley & Sons.

Hamel, G and Prahalad, C. K (1990) Core Competence of the Corporation, *Harvard Business Review*, May–June: 79–81.

Hamel, G. and Prahalad, C. K. (1994) *Competing for the Future*. Boston, MA: Harvard Business School Press.

Hammer, M. (1990) Reengineering Work: Don't Automate, Obliterate, *Harvard Business Review*, July–August.

Hammer, M. and Champy, J. (1993) *Reengineering the Corporation: A Manifesto for Business Revolution.* Nicholas Brealey.

Hampden-Turner, C. and Trompenaars, F. (2000) *Building Cross-cultural Competence.* Chichester: John Wiley & Sons.

Hankinson, G. and Cowking, P. (1996) *The Reality of Global Brands.* McGraw-Hill: 44.

Harrigan, K. R. (1980) *Strategies for Declining Businesses.* Lexington, MA: D. C.

Harrigan, K. R. and Porter, M. E. (1983) End-Game Strategies for Declining Industries, *Harvard Business Review,* 61 (4): 111–20.

Hart, S. (1997) Beyond greening: Strategies for a sustainable world, *Harvard Business Review,* 75 (1): 71–91.

Hay, R. D., Gray, E. R. and Gates, J. E. (1976) *Business and Society.* Cincinnati, OH: Heath.

Heidegger, M. (1962) *Being and Time.* Blackwell.

Heracleous, L. and Lan, L.L. (2010) The Myth of Shareholder Capitalism. *Harvard Business Review,* Spring.

Hill, C. W. L. and Jones, G. R. (2004) *Strategic Management Theory: An Integrated Approach,* 6th edn. Boston and New York: Houghton Mifflin Company.

Hitt, M. A., Ireland, R. D. and Hoskisson, R. E. (2001) *Strategic Management: Competitiveness and Globalization,* 4th edn. South-Western.

Hofstede, G. (1980) *Culture's Consequences: International Differences in Work-Related Values.* Beverly Hills, CA: Sage.

Hofstede, G. (1993) Cultural Constraints in Management Theories, *Academy of Management Executive,* 7 (1): 8–21.

Huntingdon, S. P. (1997) *The Clash of Civilisations and the Remaking of World Order.* London: Simon and Schuster.

Hymer, S. (1970) The multinational corporation and the law of uneven development, in Bhagwati, J. (ed.) *Economics and World Order.* New York: World Law Fund Industries.

Imai, M. (1986) *Kaizen: The Key to Japan's Competitive Success.* McGraw-Hill.

Jenkins, M. and Ambrosini, V. (2006) *Strategic Management: A multi-perspective approach,* 2nd edn. Palgrave MacMillan.

Jensen, M. (1986) Agency costs of free cash flow, corporate finance and takeovers, *American Economic Review,* 76 (2): 323–9.

Jensen, M. C. (1989) Eclipse of the Public Corporation, *Harvard Business Review,* 67 (5): 61–75.

Jensen, M. and Meckling, W. (1976) Theory of the firm: managerial behaviour, agency costs, and ownership structure. *Journal of Financial Economics,* 3: 305–60.

Johansen, J. and Vahine, J.-E. (1978) A model for the decision making process affecting pattern and pace of the internationalization of the firm, in Ghertman, M. and Leontidaes, J. (eds) *European Research in International Business.* Amsterdam.

Johansson, H. J., McHugh, P., Pendlebury, A. J. and Wheeler, W. A. III (1993) *Business Process Reengineering: Breakpoint Strategies for Market Dominance.* Chichester: John Wiley and Sons.

Johnson, G., Melin, L. and Whittington, R. (2003) Micro Strategy and Strategizing: Towards an Activity-Based View, Guest Editors' Introduction, *Journal of Management Studies,* Blackwell Publishers, 40 (1): 3–22.

Johnson, G., Scholes, K. and Whittington, R. (2008) *Exploring Corporate Strategy,* 8th edn. FT/Prentice Hall.

Kaplan, R. S. and Norton, D. P. (1992) The Balanced Scorecard: Measures that drive performance, *Harvard Business Review,* 70 (1): 71–80.

Kay, J. (1993) *The Foundations of Corporate Success.* Blackwell.

Kim, W. C. and Mauborgne, R. (2003) Think for yourself – stop copying a rival, *New Thinking from INSEAD.*

Kim, W. C. and Mauborgne, R. (2005) *Blue Ocean Strategy: How to create uncontested market space and make the competition irrelevant.* Harvard Business School Press.

Koestler, A. (1976) *The Act of Creation.* Hutchinson.

Kogut, B. and Singh, H. (1988) The effect of national culture on the choice of entry mode, *Journal of International Business Studies,* 19 (3): 411–33.

Kotter, J. P. (2008) *A Sense of Urgency,* Harvard Business School Press.

Kotter, J. P. (1995) Leading change: why transformation efforts fail, *Harvard Business Review,* 73 (2): 59–67.

Kotter, J. P. and Schlesinger, L. A. (1979) Choosing Strategies for Change, *Harvard Business Review,* 57 (2): 106–14.

Krackhardt, D. and Hanson, J. (1993) Informal Networks: The Company Behind the Chart, *Harvard Business Review,* 71 (4): 104–11.

Kunde, J. (2002) *Unique: Now or Never – The Brand Drives the Company in the New Value Economy.* Financial Times/ Prentice Hall.

Lafley, A. G. (2009) What only the CEO can do. *Harvard Business Review,* 87(5):54–62.

Lamb, R. B. and Shivastava, P. (eds) (1998) *Advances in Strategic Management.* JAI Press.

Larkin, T. J. and Larkin, S. (1996) Reaching and changing frontline employees, *Harvard Business Review,* 74 (3): 95–104.

Laurent, A. (1986) The cross-cultural puzzle of global human resource management, *Human Resources Management,* 25 (1): 91–102.

Leavy, B. and Wilson, D. (1994) *Strategy and Leadership.* ITP.

Lewin, K. (1951) *Field Theory in Social Science.* Tavistock Publications.

Lewis, D. and Bridger, D. (2001) *The Soul of the New Consumer: Authenticity – What we buy and why in the new economy.* Nicholas Brealey.

Liebowitz, S. (2002) *Network Economics: The True Forces that Drive the Digital Marketplace.* New York: Amacon.

Lippitt, R., Watson, J. and Westley, B. (1958) *The Dynamics of Planned Change: A Comparative Study of Principles and Techniques.* Harcourt, Brace.

Lovett, D. and Slatter, S. (1999) *Corporate Turnaround.* Penguin Books.

March, J. (1999) *The Pursuit of Organizational Intelligence.* Blackwell.

Martin, R. (2009) *The Design of Business: Why Design Thinking is the Next Competitive Advantage,* Harvard Business School Press.

McGee, J. (1998) Commentary on 'corporate strategies and environmental regulations: an organizing framework', in Rugman, A. M. and Verbeke, A. (eds) *Journal of Strategic Management,* Special Edition: Editor's choice, 19 (4): 377–87.

McGee, J., Thomas, H. and Wilson, D. (2005) *Strategy. Analysis and Practice.* McGraw-Hill.

McKiernan, P. (1992) *Strategies of Growth.* London: Routledge.

Mendelow, A. (1991) Proceedings of the Second International Conference on Information Systems, Cambridge, MA.

Michaels, E., Handfield-Jones, H. and Axelrod, B. (2001) *The War for Talent.* Harvard Business School Press.

Micklethwait, J. and Wooldridge, A. (1997) *The Witchdoctors. What the* management gurus are saying, why it matters and how to make sense of it. Mandarin paperbacks.

Mintzberg, H. (1973) *The Nature of Managerial Work*. Harper & Row.

Mintzberg, H. (1994) *The Rise and Fall of Strategic Planning*. Free Press.

Mintzberg, H. (1998) Generic Strategies: Toward a Comprehensive Framework, in Lamb, R. B. and Shivastava, P. (eds) *Advances in Strategic Management*. JAI Press.

Mintzberg, H. (1999) Organigraphs: Drawing how Companies Really Work, *Harvard Business Review*, 77 (5): 87–94.

Mintzberg, H. (2004) *Managers Not MBAs: A Hard Look at the Soft Practice of Managing and Management Development*. Berrett-Koehler.

Mintzberg, H., Ahlstrand, B. and Lampel, J. (1998) *Strategy Safari. A guided tour through the wilds of strategic management*. Prentice Hall Europe.

Mintzberg, H., Lampel, J., Quinn, B. and Ghoshal, S. (2003) *The Strategy Process. Concepts, Contexts, Cases*. Global 4th edn. Prentice Hall.

Mintzberg, H. and Westley, Y. (1992) Cycles of Organizational Change, *Strategic Management Journal*, 13, Special Issue: 39–59.

Nadler, D. and Tushman, M. (1989) Organizational frame bending: Principles for managing reorientation, *Academy of Management Executive*, 3 (3): 194–204.

Nattermann, P. (2000) Best Practice Does Not Equal Best Strategy, *McKinsey Quarterly*, 2.

Nonaka, I. (1991) The Knowledge Creating Company, *Harvard Business Review*, 69 (6): 96–104.

Nordtrom, K. and Ridderstrale, J. (2002) *Funky Business*. Pearson Education.

Normann, R. and Ramirez, R. (1993) From Value Chain to Value Constellation: Designing Interactive Strategy, *Harvard Business Review*, 71 (4): 65–77.

Pascale, R. and Athos, A. (1981) *The Art of Japanese Management*. Warner.

Penrose, E. (1959) *The Theory of the Growth of the Firm*. Oxford: Oxford University Press.

Peters, T. and Waterman, R. (1982) *In Search of Excellence*. Harper & Row.

Pettigrew, A. and Whipp, R. (1991) *Managing Change for Competitive Success*. Blackwell.

Pfeffer, J. (2010) Building Sustainable Organizations: The Human Factor, *Academy of Management Perspectives*, 24(1): 34–45.

Porter, M. E. (1980) *Competitive Strategy: Techniques for Analyzing Industries and Competitors*. New York: The Free Press.

Porter, M. E. (1985) *Competitive Advantage: Creating and Sustaining Superior Performance*. New York: The Free Press.

Porter, M. (1987) From Competitive Advantage to Corporate Strategy, *Harvard Business Review*, 65 (3): 43–59.

Porter, M. (1990a) *The Competitive Advantage of Nations*. New York: Free Press.

Porter, M. (1990b) The Competitive Advantage of Nations, *Harvard Business Review*, 69 (2): March–April.

Porter, M. (1996) What is Strategy? *Harvard Business Review*, 74 (6): 61–79.

Porter, M. (1998) *The Competitive Advantage of Nations*. New York: Free Press.

Porter, M. (1999) Philanthropy's new agenda: creating value, *Harvard Business Review*, 77 (6): 121–31.

Porter, M. E. (2008). The five competitive forces that shape strategy, *Harvard Business Review*, January: 78–93.

Porter, M. and Kramer, M. (2002) The competitive advantage of corporate philanthropy, *Harvard Business Review*, 80 (12): 56.

Poundstone, W. (1993) *Prisoner's Dilemma*. Oxford: Oxford University Press.

Prahalad, C. K. and Bettis, R. A. (1986) The dominant logic: a new linkage between diversity and performance, *Strategic Management Journal*, 7 (6): 485–501.

Prahalad, C. K. and Doz, Y. L. (1987) *The Multinational Mission: Balancing Local Demands and Global Vision*. New York: Free Press.

Prahalad, C. K. and Hamel, G. (1990) The Core Competence of the Corporation, *Harvard Business Review*, May–June: 79–81.

PricewaterhouseCoopers (1995) *Better Change: Best Practices for Transforming Your Organization*. Irwin.

Quinn, J. B. (1978) Strategic Change: Logical Incrementalism, *Sloan Management Review*, 20 (1): 7–21.

Reed, D. J. (2001) *Stalking the Elusive Business Case for Corporate Sustainability*. Washington: World Resources Institute.

Ricardo, D. (1817) *Principles of Political Economy and Taxation*. London.

Ricardo, D. (1967) *The Principles of Political Economy and Taxation*. Homewood, IL: Irwin.

Roberts, K. (2004) *Lovemarks: The Future Beyond Brands*. Powerhouse Cultural Entertainment Books.

Robins, J. and Wiersema, M. F. (1995) A resource-based view of the multibusiness: empirical analysis of portfolio interrelationships and corporate financial performance, *Strategic Management Journal*, 16 (4): 277–99.

Romanelli, E. and Tushman, M. L. (1994) Organizational Transformation as Punctuated Equilibrium: an empirical test, *Academy of Management Journal*, 37 (5): 1141–61.

Rose, J. M. (2007) Corporate Directors and Social Responsibility. Ethics versus Shareholder Value. *Journal of Business Ethics*, 73 (3 July): 319–331.

Rugman, A. M. (1990) *Multinationals and Canada–United States Free Trade*. University of South Carolina Press.

Rugman, A. M. and D'Cruz, J. R. (1993) The Double Diamond Model of International Competitiveness: the Canadian experience, *Management International Review*, 33 (2) Special Issue: 17–40.

Rugman, A. M. and Verbeke, A. (1998) *Journal of Strategic Management*, Special Edition: Editor's choice, 19 (4): 377–87.

Rumelt, R. (1984) Towards a strategic theory of then firm in R. Lamb (ed.) *Competitive Strategic Management*. Englewood-Cliffs, NJ: Prentice Hall, 556–570.

Rumelt, R. P. (1974) *Strategy, Structure and Economic Performance*. Boston, MA: Harvard Business School Press.

Rumelt, R. P. (1986) *Strategy, Structure and Economic Performance*, 2nd edn. Boston, MA: Harvard Business School Press.

Rumelt, R. P. (1991) How Much Does Industry Matter? *Strategic Management Journal*, 12 (3): 167–86.

Saloner, G., Shepard, A. and Podolny, J. (2001) *Strategic Management*. NJ: John Wiley and Sons.

Salzman, O., Ionescu-Somers, A. and Steger, U. (2005) The business case for corporate sustainability: literature review and research options, *European Management Journal*, 1: 27–36.

Sanchez, R., Heene, A. and Thomas, H. (1996) *Dynamics of Competence-Based Competition*. Oxford: Elsevier Science.

Schrage, M. (1999) *Serious Play: How the World's Best Companies Simulate to Innovate*. Harvard Business School Press.

Schultz, M., Hatch, M. J. and Holten Larsen, M. (2000) *The Expressive Organization: Linking Identity, Reputation and the Corporate Brand*. Oxford University Press.

Senge, P. (1990) *The Fifth Discipline*. Century Business.

Shaw, G., Brown, R. and Bromiley, P. (1998) Strategic Stories: How 3M is Rewriting Business Planning, *Harvard Business Review*, 76 (3): 41–54.

Shleifer, A. and Vishny, R. (1988) Value maximisation and the acquisition process. *Journal of Economic Perspectives*, 2 (1): 7–20.

Smircich, L. (1983) Concepts of Culture and Organizational Analysis, *Administrative Science Quarterly*, 28 (3): 339–58.

Smith, A. (1776) *The Wealth of Nations*, Smith, A. (ed.) (1999) Penguin Books/South-Western Publishing.

Smither, R. D. (1994) *The Psychology of Work and Human Performance*. HarperCollins.

Sorenson, J. (2005) Why Firms Differ, MBA Thesis, Warwick Business School.

Stace, D. and Dunphy, D. (1994) *Beyond the Boundaries: Leading and Recreating the Successful Organization*. McGraw-Hill.

Stewart, I. (1989) *Does God Play Dice?* 2nd edn. Penguin Books.

Stewart, R. (1967) *Managers and Their Jobs*. Macmillan.

Sutton, B. (2001) *Weird Ideas That Work: 11½ Practices for Promoting, Managing, and Sustaining Innovation*. Free Press.

Teece, D. J. (1986) Transaction cost economics and multi-national enterprise, *Journal of Economic Behaviour and Organization*, 7 (1): 21–45.

Thompson, A. A., Gamble, J. E. and Strickland, A. J. III (2004) *Strategic Management*, 13th edn. McGraw-Hill.

Tichy, N. (1993) *Handbook for Revolutionaries*. New York: Doubleday.

Tichy, N. and Devanna, M. A. (1997) *The Transformational Leader*. NJ: John Wiley & Sons.

Tichy, N. and Sherman, S. (1993) *Control Your Destiny or Someone Else Will*. New York: Doubleday.

Tomlinson, J. (1999) *Globalization and Culture*. Cambridge: Polity.

Tosi, H. L. Jr. and Gomez-Mejia, L. R. (1994) CEO compensation monitoring and firm performance, *Academy of Management Journal*, 37 (4): 1002–16.

Trompenaars, F. (1993) *Riding the Waves of Cultural Differences: Understanding Cultural Differences in Business*. London: Nicholas Brealey.

Trompenaars, F. and Hampden-Turner, C. (1997) *Riding the Waves of Culture: Understanding Cultural Diversity in Business*. Nicholas Brealey.

Van der Heijden, K. (1996) *Scenarios: The Art of Strategic Conversation*. Chichester: John Wiley & Sons.

Vernon, R. (1966) International Investment and International Trade in the Product Life Cycle, *Quarterly Journal of Economics*, 29 (2): 190–207.

Volberda, H. W. (1998) *Building the Flexible Firm*. Oxford: Oxford University Press.

Wack, P. (1985) Scenarios: Uncharted waters, *Harvard Business Review*, 63 (6): 139–51.

Wackernagel, M. et al. (1997) Ecological footprints of nations. How much nature do they use? How much nature do they have? Report prepared for the *Rio +5* Forum.

Waddock, S. A. and Graves, S. B. (1997) The corporate social performance–financial performance link, *Strategic Management Journal*, 18 (4): 303–19.

Wenger, E. (1998) *Communities of Practice: Learning, Meaning and Identity*. Cambridge: Cambridge University Press.

Wenger, E. and Snyder, W. (2000) Communities of practice: the organizational frontier, *Harvard Business Review*, 78 (1): 138–45.

Whitley, R. D. (1999) *Divergent Capitalisms*. Oxford University Press.

Whittington, R. (1996) Strategy as Practice, *Long Range Planning*, 29 (5), Special Issue: 731–6.

Whittington, R. (2000) *What is Strategy? And does it matter?* ITP.

Whittington, R. (2006) Completing the practice turn, *Organization Studies*, 27 (5): 613–634.

Wilson, D. (1992) *A Strategy of Change: Concepts and Controversies in the Management of Change*. ITP.

Wilson, I. (2000) From Scenario Thinking to Strategic Action, *Technological Forecasting and Social Change*, 65: 23–29.

Wilson, M. (2003) Corporate sustainability: What is it and where does it come from? *Ivey Business Journal*, March/April: 1–5.

Wind, Y. and Mahajan, V. J. (1981) Designing a product and business portfolio, *Harvard Business Review*, 59 (1): 155.

World Commission on Economic Development (1987) *Our Common Future*. Oxford: Oxford University Press.

Zenisek, T. J. (1979) Corporate social responsibility: A conceptualization based on organizational literature, *Academy of Management Review*, 4 (3): 359–68.

413

Acknowledgements

We would like to thank the following friends and colleagues for helping create this book.

Rebecca Bednarek, Victoria University of Wellington.

Terry Bowe, Victoria University of Wellington.

Matthew Checkley, Canterbury Christ Church University.

Shaun Coffey, Industrial Research Limited.

Derek Condon, Warwick Business School.

Urs Daellenbach, Victoria University of Wellington.

Richard Dunford, University of Sydney.

Wael Kamel Eid, Islamic Bank of Britain.

Andres Hatum, IAE Business School, Argentina.

Ben Knight, Warwick Business School.

Harminder Singh, Warwick Business School.

Tim Scholes, Senior Partner, IAMCO Ltd.

Tony Smith and the staff and students at Baraka College, Kenya.

Roberto Vassolo, IAE Business School, Argentina.

Michael Wang, Warwick Business School.

Allun Williams, Director of Sales and Marketing, Islamic Bank of Britain.

David Wilson, Warwick Business School.

Mark Wood, MD, Paternoster PLC.

The publishers thank the following for permission to reproduce copyright material:

Figure 1.1: Keith Davis and William C. Frederick, *Business and Society: Management, Public Policy, Ethics*, 5th edition. New York: McGraw-Hill, 1984. Copyright © 1984 by Keith Davis and William C. Frederick. Reprinted by permission of The McGraw-Hill Companies.

Figure 3.6: Adam M. Brandenburger and Barry J. Nalebuff, *Co-opetition*. NY: Currency, 1996. Copyright © 1996 by Adam M. Brandenburger and Barry J. Nalebuff. Reprinted by permission of Doubleday, a division of Random House, Inc.

Figure 5.1: Michael E. Porter, *Competitive Advantage: Creating and Sustaining Superior Performance*, fig 1.3, p. 12. NY: The Free Press, 1998. Copyright © 1985, 1998 by Michael E. Porter. Reprinted by permission of The Free Press, a Division of Simon & Schuster Adult Publishing Group. All rights reserved.

Figure 5.2: Cliff Bowman, *Strategy in Practice*. Harlow: Prentice Hall, 1988. Copyright © 1998 by Prentice-Hall Europe. Reprinted by permission of Pearson Education Ltd.

Figure 5.3 Henry Mintzberg, Generic strategies: toward a comprehensive framework, from R. B. Lamb and P. Shivastava, *Advances in Strategic Management*. JAI Press, 1998. Copyright © 1998 by JAI Press. Reprinted by permission of Elsevier.

Figure 5.4: Michael E. Porter, *Competitive Advantage: Creating and Sustaining Superior Performance*, Fig 2.2, p. 37. NY: Free Press, 1985. Copyright © 1985, 1998 by Michael E. Porter. Reprinted by permission of The Free Press, a Division of Simon & Schuster Adult Publishing Group. All rights reserved.

Figure 6.4: G. Johnson, K. Scholes, and R. Whittington, *Exploring Corporate Strategy*, 7th edition. Harlow: Prentice Hall, 2005. Copyright © 1998 by Prentice-Hall Europe. Reprinted by permission of Pearson Education Ltd.

Figure 8-1.1, US v. China: Geert Hofstede, *Cultures and Organizations: Software of the Mind*, Revised and Expanded 2nd Edition. New York: McGraw-Hill, 2005. Copyright © 2005 by Geert Hofstede BV. Adapted by permission of the author.

Figure 9.2: Henry Mintzberg and Y. Westley, Strategic changes related to organizational changes pp. 39–59, from *Strategic Management Journal* 13, 1992. Copyright © 1992 by John Wiley & Sons Limited. Reprinted by permission of the publisher.

Figure 9.3: David C. Wilson, *A Strategy of Change: Concepts and Controversies in the Management of Change*. Routledge, 1992. Copyright © 1992 by David C. Wilson. Reprinted by permission of Thomson Publishing Services on behalf of Thomson Learning and Routledge.

Figure 9.4: Dexter C. Dunphy and D. A. Stace, *Under New Management: Australian Organizations in Transition*. McGraw Hill, 1990. Copyright © 1990 by Dexter C. Dunphy. Reprinted by permission of McGraw-Hill Education, Australia & New Zealand.

Figure 9.5: Brian Leavy and David C. Wilson, *Strategy and Leadership*. Routledge, 1994. Copyright © 1994 by Brian Leavy and David C. Wilson. Reprinted by permission of Thomson Publishing Services on behalf of Thomson Learning and Routledge.

Figure 9.6: J. P. Kotter and L. A. Schlesinger, pp. 274, *Harvard Business Review*, March/April 1979. Copyright © 1979 by the Harvard Business School Publishing Corporation. Reprinted by permission of Harvard Business Review. All rights reserved.

The publishers apologize for any errors or omissions in the above list and would be grateful to be notified of any corrections that should be incorporated in the next reprint or edition of this book.

Glossary of Core Strategic Management Concepts

80/20 rule   Sometimes called the Pareto distribution, the notion that to be strategic organizations should focus on the 20% of the business/customers/suppliers/stakeholders that make 80% of the difference to the business. The potential weakness of using this logic is that it may not adequately reflect dynamic situations.

Abductive logic   Advocates positing that something might or could be and then reaching out to understand and develop it as a way for spurring substantive innovations. Often used in design thinking in contrast to the conventional inductive or deductive logic.

Absolute advantage   Adam Smith's theory that nations should specialize in production of goods where they have a natural or acquired advantage.

Acquisition   The "A" in M&A. This is where one organization buys a majority stake in another company for control. For the target company shareholders to sell their shares generally requires the payment of a premium. Acquisitions take place when the acquired organization has assets/resources/capabilities that are valuable to the acquirer and are not generally available through other means such as contracting.

Agency problem   When managers (agents) are acting in their own self-interest rather than in the interests of the owner (principal) this is an agency problem. Evidence of this may be seen in decision making which rewards managers rather than shareholders.

Aretaic ethics   An older approach to ethics that emphasizes an organization discovering, promoting and staying true to, its unique virtues and what these provide for the wider community. What we might see today as "ethos" (cf. deontic ethics).

Barriers to entry   A core concept in Porter's 5 forces framework, these are obstacles to be overcome by new entrants if they are to compete successfully in the industry.

Best practice   A "benchmarking" approach where organizations determine who the leader in a particular practice is and then copy that approach. Useful for achieving efficiencies but may diminish differentiation if not used with caution at the strategic level.

Blue Ocean strategy   A strategy that seeks to move an organization away from arenas where competition is fierce (i.e., the red ocean) by doing something that other companies have not considered or cannot compete in.

Boston box   A colloquial name for the first portfolio analytic matrix, developed by the Boston Consulting Group (BCG), that led to the popular use of the terms "cash cow," "star," "dog" and "question mark."

Boundedness   Sometimes referred to as "scarcity of mind," boundedness means: (1) managers always face problems with quality and quantity of information needed to take decisions; (2) even with sufficient information they have limited capacity to process complex information bundles. The result is suboptimal decision making.

Business model   Colloquial term used to express how an organization seeks to turn a profit or created added value. It describes the structure linking intended strategy, its operational and functional requirements and anticipated performance.

Buyer power   A situation where buyers can take advantage of intense competitive rivalry and/or low switching costs and/or their size to seek discounts/better service etc. from a company. Often used in conjunction with the Five Forces of Industry framework.

Californianization   A term to indicate globalization of tastes.

Capabilities   Organizational attributes or combinations of attributes that enable an organization to develop or follow strategies. Because of the systemic nature of capabilities they are often difficult for other organizations to replicate.

CASIS   An acronym (made up of Congruence, non-Appropriable, non-Substitutable, non-Inimitable and Supported organizationally), that provides a useful checklist to question whether a competitive advantage can be sustained.

Change agent   An individual or group that brings about change in an organization.

Comparative advantage   David Ricardo's theory that countries should produce and trade in goods which they are best equipped to produce even though they could produce goods at a lower cost than other countries.

Competencies   Associated with the Resource Based View of strategy, these are the skills and abilities by which resources are deployed effectively throughout an organization.

Competitive advantage   The unique set of assets, capabilities, positions and environmental circumstances that enable an organization to consistently out-perform its competitors in its chosen strategic outcomes.

Competitive scope   The range of markets/customers that the firm addresses in its positioning.

Competitive strategy   How an organizations business units will seek to gain advantage over other players in an industry. Often confused with competitive advantage: while a competitive strategy may lead to and/or protect a competitive advantage this is not necessarily the case.

Complementors   Firms that sell products or services that add value to or "complement" the product/service of the business under consideration as an essential component (e.g., petrol sellers and car companies) or as a valued extra (e.g., wineries and restaurants).

Configuration   This refers to an organization's architecture of structures, processes and relationships through which the organization operates.

Consolidation   Where competitors in a mature or declining industry merge. The effect is to reduce the numbers of organizations and so reduce competitive pressures.

Convergence   Where industries which were previously distinct begin to overlap in terms of customers, products, technologies, activities.

Co-opetition   The idea that it may be better to work with other organizations traditionally seen as competitors.

Core competence   A set of distinctive skills, complementary assets and routines which are fundamental to a firm's competitive capacity and sustainable advantage and which can be deployed across several product markets. The concept is associated with the Resource Based View (RBV) of the firm.

Communities of Practice   Informal social networks bound together by shared expertise, experiences, passion. Can influence thinking and behaviour and be a good source of new ideas and energy that crosses traditional organizational boundaries.

Competitive Strategy   The basis on which a business can understand and manipulate factors which cause inequalities so as to give an organization a sustainable competitive advantage.

Conglomerate   A firm made up of a set of unrelated businesses.

Conglomerate discount   Where the share market devalues the stock value of a conglomerate, often to the point where it becomes lower than the sum of the market capitalization because it believes the conglomerate grouping devalues rather than adds value.

Consortium   A group or association of businesses formed to promote or facilitate a common purpose for mutual benefit. For instance, an organization may be created with multiple owners reflecting a common purpose.

Core values   The shared values that are said to underpin an organization's strategy and way of doing business.

Corporate environmental integrity   Emphasizes an organization's responsibility to manage its processes and products so as to minimize their impact on the physical environment.

Corporate governance   This focuses on who the firm should serve, the distribution of power and relationships among different stakeholders, and the selection and conduct of senior management.

Corporate identity   An increasingly popular notion that organizations, like individuals, have an identity and that understanding and developing this identity may be key to developing a clear and effective strategic position.

Corporate Social Responsibility (CSR)   The concept that the firm, as a corporate "citizen," has ethical responsibilities that go beyond merely obeying the law.

Corporate strategy   Concerns the scope of the product-markets, industries and geographies addressed by the firm as a whole, the boundaries of the firm, and how to manage that scope in a way that adds value.

Corporate Sustainability   The concept that firms should balance the needs of the environment and society with the economic prosperity of the firm.

Cradle-to-grave   The concept that a firm is responsible for its products from conception to final disposal.

Critical Success Factor's (CSFs)   The requirements for strategic success in a particular industry as a particular point in time.

Crowdsourcing   The practice of outsourcing organizational tasks by placing a call on the Internet and inviting all-comers to post submissions often with the lure of a prize or commission for the "best entry."

Cultural distance   A measure of the extent to which cultures vary on key dimensions (see National Culture) – Culture has been variously defined but can be said to be the set of shared beliefs, attitudes, values, goals, and practices that characterizes an institution, organization or group. It is a multi-layered concept drawing upon national, regional, local, industrial and professional contexts. In terms of organizations coming together, through trade or ownership, cultural differences can result in significant friction termed culture clash.

Cultural web   An approach to depicting an organization's culture as a system of inter-related elements.

Deontic ethics   A conventional approach to ethics that encourages organizations to view business ethics in terms of outlining rights, duties and responsibilities to stakeholders, often in the form of codes of conduct (cf. aretaic ethics).

Design thinking   Perhaps the most influential new trend in business thinking in the past few years suggests that managers should be thinking like designers and utilize perspectives such as abductive logic and prototyping.

Determinism   The philosophical view that every event, including human cognition, behaviour, decision, and action is causally determined by previous events.

Differentiation   The offering of services or products which offer benefits to consumers which are i) different from those of competitors and ii) sufficiently valued by consumers that they will pay a premium price sufficient to cover the costs of differentiation.

Diversification   Classically defined in Ansoff's matrix, diversification is when an organization ventures into a new market with new products. Subsequently diversification has also been determined in terms of an organization venturing into new industries requiring new capabilities and competencies. In M&A terms diversification acquisitions are often termed conglomerate acquisitions as differences in industry and capabilities suggests limited scope for managerial synergies. It is generally believed diversification is the riskiest of corporate strategies and results in worse outcomes than less conservative strategic options, although the evidence remains ambivalent.

Divestment   The disposal of an organization's subsidiaries, investments or other holdings by sale, liquidation, listing, employee purchase.

Dynamic capabilities   Higher level processes/capabilities which allow a firm to re-configure its resources in order to adapt to environmental changes. These capabilities can be grown and learned by the organization and its members – often associated with notions of the knowledge society and the learning organization.

Eclectic theory   John Dunning's theory which centres on ownership, location, and internalization (OLI) to determine a firm's motivation for international expansion.

Economies of scale   Economic gains made as the average cost of producing a unit of product or service declines as the volume produced increases.

Economies of scope   Economic gains made when using a resource across multiple activities uses less of that resource than when the activities are carried out independently.

Eight steps of change   John Kotter's framework that suggests that successful strategic change requires eight elements: a sense of urgency; a guiding coalition; articulating a vision; communication that vision; creating short term wins; consolidation; and encouraging more change.

Emergent view   The idea, popularized by Henry Mintzberg, that good strategies are more likely to emerge from interactions between staff, customers, suppliers, etc., at the bottom of the organizational pyramid, rather than being conceived by top senior managers.

ESTEMPLE   An acronym to denote major macro-environmental pressures upon business. Its stands for Economic, Social, Technological, Media, Ecological, Political, Legal, Ethical drivers of environmental change.

Evolutionary transformation   A gradual, organic approach to managing strategic change that encourages new ways to emerge and be developed from within (cf. revolutionary transformation).

Experience curve   The idea that by performing a task many times one becomes more efficient or more expert. In economic terms this means a reduction in unit costs as cumulative output increases. The implications for strategy are that if a firm can expand output faster than competitors it can move down the experience curve more rapidly and open up a widening cost differential.

Exploit versus explore   A dichotomy found in the work of Richard Cyert and James March that organizations can advance strategically by either exploiting existing resources or exploring new opportunities. There is much debate as to what the optimum balance between the two might be.

External dependent stakeholders   These include (1) economic (lenders, customers, suppliers, competitors, distributors) where stakeholders can influence the value creation process; (2) advisory (non-executive directors, consultants, gurus, business schools, lawyers, accountants); and (3) sociopolitical (local authorities, unions) stakeholders.

Fast followers   Organizations which decide to enter into a market place after competitors have already entered and have had time to "test the waters."

First movers   Often used to describe organizations entering an overseas market before competitors, but could also be used to describe entering any new arena. Often termed First Mover Advantage as it may confer benefits for the organization in being able to shape the market in ways advantageous to itself.

Five forces framework   Porter's industry level framework intended to identify the attractiveness of industries on the basis of five major influencing factors.

Flying Geese model   By Kaname Akamatsu to explain Japan's transition from one industry to another and how comparative advantage shifts from one nation to another.

Forecasting   A planning tool to help management to cope with the uncertainty of the future. It is based on certain assumptions based on management's experience, knowledge, and judgment and these estimates are projected into the future using techniques such as Box-Jenkins models, Delphi method, exponential smoothing, moving averages, regression analysis, and trend projection. The technique of sensitivity analysis is also often used which assigns a range of values to uncertain variables in order to reduce potential errors.

Franchising   A contract granted to an organization or individual to operate under a brand often under condition that certain quality practices are followed.

Functional structure   The organization of a firm based upon primary functions including marketing, R&D, human resources, finance.

Game theory   A rigorous theory concerned with the competitive interactions between different organizations. Although appealing, its application can be limited due to real world complexities.

Global sourcing   Purchasing inputs from the most appropriate suppliers from anywhere around the world.

Global strategy   This emphasizes economies of scale through the standardization of products and services.

Good practice   A term first promoted by IBM to try to get around some of the negative effect of thinking in terms of best practice. Whereas best practice can breed complacency once it is achieved or copied, the bringing to the table of different types of good practice can encourage a more open marketplace of ideas.

Greenwashing   Companies "spinning" their products and policies as environmentally friendly to gain a competitive edge.

Growth Vector Components Matrix   Created by Igor Ansoff, this matrix is useful for thinking about strategic development options.

Horizontal integration   The joining of firms at the same competitive level in the industry value chain (i.e., competitors, potential new entrants or substitutes).

Horizontal M&A   Acquisition of an organization in the same industry.

HOS model of factor endowments   By Hecksher and Ohlin, this model argues that, as a country specializes, the main factor of production will become increasingly expensive and rare so encouraging a need to develop other advantages.

Hubris   Overbearing arrogance often used to explain non-rational behavior in top management, such as overpaying for an acquisition.

Hypercompetition   Competition characterized by intense and rapid competitive moves which rapidly erode company advantages and leads to less stable industry structures than before and in which superior profitability is more transitory. The only route to superior performance is through continually recreating and renewing competitive advantage.

Icarus paradox   Based upon the Greek fable of the boy who flew too close to the sun with wings made of wax and subsequently plunged to his death, the paradox is that the greater one's success the more likely one's failure.

Impact matrix   A method for assigning values to expected pressures from the macro-environment in order for an organization to assess the future nature of its context for which it must design an effective strategy.

Industrial organization   That aspect of the theory of strategy theory that focuses on the impact that the environment ("structure") has on the conduct of industry incumbents and hence their performance. The five forces is the most well-known framework from this tradition.

Industry   The group of firms that produce/market products that are direct substitutes in terms of function and features.

Industry forces   The dynamics between rivals, buyers, suppliers, entrants, and potential substitutes in an industry that both emerge from and drive the conduct of firms in pricing, investment, branding, etc.

Industry life cycle   The emergent pattern of growth, maturity and (sometimes) decline that characterizes the outputs, revenues, composition, and characteristics of industries and markets.

Industry structure   The underlying framework of an industry in terms of the relative number and size of firms and the degree to which industry output is concentrated across the spread of firms. The classical "pure" structures are perfect competition, monopolistic competition, oligopoly, and monopoly.

Innovation   The initial commercialization of invention by producing and marketing a new product or service or by using a new method of production.

Institutionalism   This is a view that institutions reflect the deeper and more resilient aspects of social structure. Institutions project authoritative guidelines for social behaviour and are the framework within which organizations must operate.

Intangible resources   Non-physical resources such as reputation, brand, culture, knowledge.

Internal dependent stakeholders   These generally do not have much influence over strategy unless they are a critical resource – i.e., a leading research scientist or control a vital asset – such as a key client relationship.

International product life cycle   Raymond Vernon's theory to explain why the location of different industries changes over time.

International strategy   When an organization begins to expand across borders and is effectively matching its internal strengths with opportunities and challenges in geographically dispersed regions.

Joint venture   An equity joint venture is when two legally distinct organizations invest in a venture which may be a separate entity from the parents.

Knowledge society   The prevalent state of advanced societies toward the end of the 20th century where knowledge becomes a far more valuable resource than land or capital.

Learning organization   Term developed by Arie de Geus in the book *The Living Organization* to describe a company that can "learn" or effectively manage change and improvement by changing itself as perceptions of the environment change.

Licensing   A contract by which an organization may manufacture, sell, distribute products/services of another firm for profit.

Localization   The pressure to be responsive and adapt to local conditions.

Logical incrementalism   A philosophy of management achieving broad organizational goals by making strategic decisions in small steps. It benefits from flexibility but can be time consuming and inefficient.

Long tail economics   The notion that by the beginning of the 21st century advances in information technology and diversifying individual tastes were combining to enable more people to purchase and more organizations to sell minority or tailored products in an ever-broadening range of categories.

M-form   The multidivisional ("M") firm made up of a set of autonomous strategic business units (SBU) responsible for competitive strategy in their own industry/market domain.

Margin The gap between what it costs to produce a product or service and what it can be sold for (or in not-for-profit situations the value that the product or service is perceived to provide). Can also relate returns on investment as the profit between investment and return.

Market imperfections Properties of the market that firms can take advantage of to overcome the price-levelling characteristics of perfect competition (e.g., if economies of scale are significant – an "imperfection" – then big firms can benefit from lower costs than smaller ones).

Market penetration In Ansoff's Growth Vector Components Matrix this is a growth option for an organization and involves expanding in the same market area with existing products. In acquisition terms, this would be termed horizontal M&A.

Matrix structure An organizational design where the line of communication is shared between two or more decision makers with different functional, geographic, and business responsibilities.

MBSA Management By Storying Around, coined by Tom Peters as a play on the idea of Management By Wandering Around. It suggests that good managers should be at the centre of their organizations, picking up on, and spreading, strategic stories.

Merger The "M" in M&A, this is the bringing together of two (or more) organizations as equals. In terms of share price no premium is payable in mergers. In practice mergers are relatively rare as one party generally is, or becomes, dominant in the process.

Middle-class effect An empirical observation that an increase in GDP per capita can have a disproportionately larger positive effect on middle-class disposable income. This can be valuable information for organizations seeking to sell to certain customer segments.

Mission An expression of the types of behaviour that an organization sees as key to achieving its strategy, goals or vision. Generally expressed as a statement.

Multidomestic strategy An organization which emphasizes differentiating products and services through adapting to local market needs.

Multinational Enterprise (MNE) A company that operates in different countries.

National culture There are many definitions for national culture. Geert Hofstede has proposed that differences between national cultures can be recognized along 5 dimensions of: (1) *Power vs. distance*; (2) *Individualism vs. collectivism*; (3) *Masculinity vs. femininity*; (4) *Uncertainty avoidance*; (5) *Long-term vs. short-term orientation.*

Next practice An approach to business improvement that suggest that leap-frogging current best practice to do something new will be more effective than copying current best practice.

Non-dependent stakeholders Stakeholders which influence organizations but are not dependent upon it. These include: (1) governmental bodies, which may be at the industry, regional, national, and supranational levels; (2) technical organizations; and (3) opinion influencers.

Not-for-profit business (NfP) Organizations whose purpose is generally for the betterment of society through charitable, humanitarian, or educational ends. Trustees or owners do not benefit financially.

Open systems view This perspective emphasizes that organizations do not stand in isolation but are interconnected across multiple levels.

Organic development   Growth of the organization through internal development.

Organigraphs   An approach promoted by Henry Minztberg and co-authors that suggests that it is more strategic to think about or draw an organizations structure by depicting what it actually does than through conventional means like organization charts.

Parenting advantage   The ways in which a corporate "parent" (or centre) may add value to the individual businesses that make up a corporation.

Path dependency   Where earlier events and actions influence subsequent decisions and events.

Perfect competition   A theoretical market structure in which a large number of small firms with the same process technology sell undifferentiated products through the same distribution channels to fully knowledgeable customers who have no switching costs.

PEST   An acronym to denote major macro-environmental pressures upon business. It stands for Political, Economic, Social, Technological change. In this book PEST has been subsumed within ESTEMPLE (see above).

Porter's diamond   Common name given the National Diamond Model of International Competitiveness which claims that different nations can draw on different factors and demand conditions, and other factors of industry structure and related and supporting industries (clusters), to develop comparative or absolute advantages.

Positioning   How the firm fits into its market/industry in terms of products, customers, and capabilities in comparison with others in the same market/industry.

Power/interest matrix   A tool for distinguishing the relative importance of different stakeholders in forming a strategy for an organization.

Principal–agent relationship   Ownership of the business (principal) is separated from controller of wealth generation (management).

Process view   A view of strategy that sees examining the process by which strategies are developed as more important or interesting than earlier more static approaches.

Promising practices   Those ideas developed at lower levels of an organization that may have strategic influence if they can be promoted up by middle and senior managers.

Punctuated equilibrium   Popularized by evolutionary scientists Stephen Jay Gould and Niles Eldredge, this is the observation that species remain stable for millions of year, changing very little, followed by a rapid burst of change that results in a new species.

Regional clusters   Geographic concentrations of similar businesses which promotes competition, concentration, and reinforcement. The dynamics of clusters have been used to explain sustained performance/dominance in certain industries.

Related diversification   The joining of firms that have complementary process or market linkages.

Resource Based View   That aspect of strategy theory that focuses on the internal resources/capabilities of a firm and how it best uses these resources to achieve superior performance.

Retrenchment   The disposal of assets and resources in order to improve the strategic/ financial position of the parent organization.

Revolutionary transformation An interventionist approach to strategic change that seeks quick transformation often through the use of external change agents (cf. evolutionary transformation).

Routines The working together of different actors and interdependent actions into a recognizable core pattern. Routines are a primary means by which organizations achieve much of what they do.

S-curve Graphic analogy to show that initial investments in innovation will outweigh returns before the latter pick up. Before returns begin to decline, new innovations in the "pipeline" should be able to replace the previous innovation. The S-curve is not unlike a sequential version of the product life cycle in form.

Scenario thinking A structured process of thinking about and anticipating the unknowable future, without pretense of being able to predict the future or being able to influence the environment in a major way. "*It is a discipline for rediscovering the original entrepreneurial power of creative foresight.*" Pierre Wack.

Sell-offs See divestment.

Six degrees of strategic innovation Framework that utilizes the value chain form to focus creative pursuits toward adding value strategically by providing greater value; reduced costs; greater volume; new ways of relating to markets; the effective crossing of conventional boundaries; or new ways of learning.

SMEs Small and Medium Sized Enterprises. This tier of business has often received significant attention from Government as a potential engine for economic renewal.

Social capital The resources and capabilities that may accrue or be supported by personal and community networks.

Social influencers Stakeholders in organizations who do not have an equity interest but may influence strategy. They include campaigners and activists.

Stakeholders All those who are affected by the actions of the firm whether they are direct participants like employees or shareholders or indirect ones like the local community.

Strategic alliance A general term to describe a range of formal arrangements between businesses which stop short of majority ownership. Strategic alliances can include joint ventures, marketing alliances, co-production arrangements, technology transfers, and other collaborations.

Strategic Business Unit (SBU) Part of an organization for which there is a distinct market different from other SBUs.

Strategic drift A term used to describe an organization which is losing its ability to change sufficiently to remain in fit with its context. This may be due to structural rigidities and boundedness. The implication is loss of performance.

Strategic fit This describes an organization which is well tuned to its context and able to adjust in the face of changing external pressures.

Strategic groups Distinctive sets of competitors adopting similar strategies aimed at similar customer segments where intergroup entry barriers (mobility barriers) prevent easy switching from one group to another.

Strategic leadership keypad   Promotes leaders being at the centre of things in strategic change combining a focus on being the linchpin/communicator between the inside and key stakeholders outside of an organization; distilling a vision; promoting new ideas from within or outside; and mapping a way to a desired future.

Strategic planning   A formalized step-by-step set of procedures for coordinating the strategy process.

Strategic stories   Stories which may seem to be about small things (e.g. an act of kindness toward a customer) that are seen to encapsulate the core values or spirit that underpin an organization's strategy or desired strategy.

Strategy as practice   Similar to the emergent and process views of strategy in shifting the focus away from the content or artefacts of strategy, but looks more at what strategic managers actually do in the present than historical processes.

Stratography   A compound of strategy and geography that promotes drawing or diagramming strategies rather than the conventional approach to communicating strategies just through text.

Structural rigidity   Configurations of assets and resources which may have conferred advantage in the past but become obstacles to change as external environments alter.

Supplier power   A situation where suppliers can use their competitive advantage to secure good contracts and/or premium prices from industry competitors (e.g. Intel in computer hardware). Often used in conjunction with the Five Forces of Industry framework.

Surfing change   An evolutionary transformation analogy that promotes the view that argues to looking for good waves emerging within an organization and then surfing (i.e. promoting) these in order to move toward desires strategies.

Sustainable competitive advantage   A competitive advantage that can be protected and maintained (or grown) over time because they are difficult for competitors to copy or compete with.

Sustainable development   An approach that promotes development that meets the needs of current generations without compromising future generations' ability to meet their needs.

Switching costs   How easy or hard it may be for buyers to shift their allegiance to other competing organizations (e.g. low switching costs tend to lead to lower margins in an industry).

SWOT   An acronym to denote Strengths, Weaknesses, Opportunities, Threats. The main purpose of this analysis is to determine the extent to which an organization "fits" with the demands of its context.

Synergy   A systems perspective whereby 1+1+1 can equal 4. Often used in corporate strategy as a reason why many business units should be grouped together in a corporation.

Systems thinking   Advocates seeing the interconnectedness between things rather than separating out "units of analysis" such as organizations, the environment, customers, etc.

TOWS   A variation on SWOT (see above) whereby external opportunities and threats are considered before categorizing an organization's relative strengths and weaknesses.

Advocates argue that this approach provides more meaningful analysis that the conventional SWOT.

Transnational strategy   This seeks to optimize tradeoffs between global and multidomestic strategies by dispersing the organization's resources according to the most beneficial locations.

Triple bottom line   Reporting environmental and societal performance as well as profitability which has been the traditional and only "bottom line."

Unrelated diversification   The joining of firms that have no common processes or markets.

Value chain   The linked set of activities/functions within a firm that interact to enable the final value-creating offering (product/service) of the firm. At the industry level it can also mean the total set of value-adding links from the first supplier to the final user of a product/service.

Value constellation   A more organic view of value creation that uses more porous and systems thinking analogies to examine the value adding process than the conventional linear and bounded value chain model. Related analogies are value web or value net.

Vertical integration   The joining of firms that are upstream (suppliers) or downstream (customers).

VIRO   Stands for Valuable, Inimitable, Rare and supported Organizationally. Can be used as a checklist to examine whether an organization has a sustainable competitive advantage (i.e. if it's strategy can lead it to "tick" most or all of these attributes). Often related to the RBV.

Virtual organization   Organizations held together through collaboration and networking rather than through formal structures.

Vision   A shared view of where an organization sees its strategy as leading it to in the future. Often expressed in the form of a statement.

Voluntarism   A philosophical term emphasizing the primacy of the will.

WACC   This stands for the Weighted Average Cost of Capital and is the rate a company is expected to pay on average to all its security holders to finance its assets.

Worst practice   Those who suggest that organizations can learn from analyzing their weaknesses or failures, as well as their successes, advocate studying worst practice as much as best practice.

Index